THE WORLD'S HISTORY

Volume I: To 1500

HOWARD SPODEK

Prentice Hall, Upper Saddle River, NJ 07458

Published 2000 by Prentice Hall, Inc.
A Division of Pearson Education
Upper Saddle River, New Jersey 07458

10 9 8 7 6 5 4 3 2

ISBN 0-13-028256-1 (paperback)

This book was designed and produced by
CALMANN & KING LTD., London
www.calmann-king.com

Editorial work by Damian Thompson, Melanie White, Nell Webb, and Gerald Lombardi
Supplementary editorial work by Robert Shore, Lydia Darbyshire, Callie Kendall, Andrew Heritage, Laura Szumanski, and Delia Gaze (glossary)
Design by Ian Hunt Design
Maps by Ailsa Heritage and Andrea Fairbrass
Artworks by Dave Kemp
Picture research by Peter Kent and Callie Kendall
Printed and bound by R.R. Donnelley & Sons Co., USA

Cover picture: Shakyamuni Buddha Preaching on Vulture Peak, Cave 17, Dunhuang Province, China, Silk embroidery. Eighth century C.E. British Museum, London.

Title-page picture: Head of Buddha from Gandhara (Afghanistan). Lime composition. Third century C.E. By courtesy of the Board of Trustees of the Victoria and Albert Museum, London.

BRIEF CONTENTS

CONTENTS

PART 1
Human Origins and Human Cultures

5 million B.C.E.–10,000 B.C.E.

BUILDING AN INTERPRETIVE FRAMEWORK: WHAT DO WE KNOW AND HOW DO WE KNOW IT?

1 THE DRY BONES SPEAK   4

5 million B.C.E.–10,000 B.C.E

WHAT IS PALEOANTHROPOLOGY AND
WHY IS IT IMPORTANT?

PART 2

SettlingDown

10,000 B.C.E.–1000 C.E.

THE FIRST CITIES AND WHY THEY MATTER: DIGS, TEXTS, AND INTERPRETATIONS

2 FROM VILLAGE COMMUNITY TO CITY STATE 38

10,000 B.C.E.–750 B.C.E.

WHAT ARE CITIES AND WHY ARE THEY IMPORTANT?

PART 3
Empire and Imperialism

2300 B.C.E.–1100 C.E.

WHAT ARE EMPIRES AND WHY ARE THEY IMPORTANT?

8 INDIAN EMPIRES   231

1500 B.C.E.–1100 C.E.

**CULTURAL COHESION
IN A DIVIDED SUBCONTINENT**

PART 4
The Rise of World Religions

600 B.C.E.–1500 C.E.

NOT BY BREAD ALONE: HOW DO HISTORIANS UNDERSTAND RELIGION IN WORLD HISTORY?

9 HINDUISM AND BUDDHISM   257

300 B.C.E.–1200 C.E.

THE SACRED SUBCONTINENT: THE SPREAD
OF RELIGION IN INDIA AND BEYOND

PART 5

World Trade

1100–1776 C.E.

CHANNELS OF COMMUNICATION: THE EXCHANGE OF COMMODITIES, DISEASES, AND CULTURE

MAPS

TIMECHARTS

REVIEWERS OF THE TEXT

First Edition Reviewers J. Lee Annis, Jr., Montgomery College; Samuel Brunk, University of Nebraska at Lincoln; Nancy S. Crump, Wayne State College; David L. Ferch, Sierra College; William Jones, Mt. San Antonio College; David L. Longfellow, Baylor University; Mark Mcleod, University of Delaware; Eleanor W. McCluskey, Broward Community College; Joseph Mitchell and Oliver B. Pollock, University of Nebraska at Omaha; John Powell, Penn State University at Erie; David K. Robinson, Northeast Missouri State University; Charles R. Sullivan, University of Dallas.

Second Edition Reviewers Ewa Bacon, Lewis University; Wood Bouldin, Villanova University; James Lindsay, Colorado State University; Frank Nobiletti, San Diego State University; Sandra Norman, Florida Atlantic University; Phyllis Pobst, Arkansas State University; Reniqu Yu, Purchase College, State University of New York.

QUOTED EXTRACTS: ACKNOWLEDGMENTS

For permission to reprint copyright material the publishers gratefully acknowledge the following:

Bantam Doubleday Dell Publishing Group Inc.: *Bhagavad-Gita*, trans. Barbara Stoler Miller, © 1986 Barbara Stoler Miller, by permission of the publisher.

Cambridge University Press: *The New English Bible*, © Oxford University Press and Cambridge University Press 1961, 1970, reprinted by permission; *Cross Cultural Trade in World History* by Philip Curtin (1984).

Columbia University Press: *Poems of Love and War*, trans. A.K. Ramanujan, © 1985 by Columbia University Press; *Introduction to Contemporary Civilization in the West*, © 1954 by Columbia University Press; *Sources of Chinese Tradition* by William Theodore de Bary, © 1960 by Columbia University Press; *Sources of Indian Tradition* by William Theodore de Bary © 1988 by Columbia University Press, all by permission of the publisher.

Harcourt, Brace & Company: *A Brief History of Chinese and Japanese Civilizations*, ed. Conrad Schirokauer; *The City in History* by Lewis Mumford

Houghton Mifflin Company: *The Human Record : Sources of Global History*, eds. A. Andrea and J. Overfield (1990, 1994).

Monthly Review Press: "Woman the Gatherer: Male Bias in Anthropology" by Sally Linton from *Women in Cross-Cultural Perspective: A Preliminary Sourcebook*, ed. Sue-Ellen Jacobs (University of Illinois, 1971).

Oxford University Press, Inc.: *The Republic* by Plato, trans. Francis MacDonald Cornford; *Historical Records*, trans. Raymond Dawson.

Oxford University Press (India): *Asoka and the Decline of the Mauryas* by Romila Thapar, by permission of the publisher.

Penguin UK: *The Travels* by Marco Polo, trans. Ronald Latham; *The Epic of Gilgamesh*, trans. N.K. Sandars; *The Koran*, trans. N.J. Dawood; *History of the Peloponnesian War*, trans. Rex Warner; *Speaking of Siva*, trans. A.K. Ramanujan.

Princeton University Press: *Ancient Near Eastern Texts Relating to the Old Testament*, ed. James Pritchard (1969); *Medieval Cities* by Henri Pirenne (1925).

Random House, Inc.: *The Prince* by N. Machiavelli (Modern Library, 1950); *The Odyssey* by Homer, trans. Robert Fitzgerald.

Simon & Schuster, Inc.: *The Aeneid of Virgil*, trans. Rolfe Humphries, © 1951 by Charles Scribner's Sons, by permission of Scribner; *Popul Vuh*, trans. Dennis Tedlock, by permission of Pocket Books; *The Wonder that was India* by A.L. Basham (Grove/Atlantic Press, 1954); *Chinese Civilization: A Sourcebook*, ed. Patricia Ebrey (1993).

Stanford University Press: *The Pattern of the Chinese Past* by Mark Elvin.

The University of Chicago Press: *The Iliad of Homer*, trans. R. Lattimore (1951), by permission of the publisher.

Yale University Press: *The Moral Economy of the Peasant* by James Scott (1976), by permission of the publisher; poems from *Shang Civilization* by Kwang-chi Chang, trans. Arthur Waley.

Zondervan Publishing House: *Holy Bible: New Revised Standard Version* (1989).

Every effort has been made to obtain permission from all copyright holders, but in some cases this has not proved possible. The publishers therefore wish to thank all authors or copyright holders who are included without acknowledgment. Prentice Hall Inc./Calmann & King apologizes for any errors or omissions in the above list and would be grateful to be notified of any corrections that should be incorporated in the next edition.

PICTURE CREDITS

SUPPLEMENTARY INSTRUCTIONAL MATERIALS

The World's History comes with an extensive package of supplementary print and multimedia materials for both instructors and students.

FOR THE INSTRUCTOR

- The *Instructor's Manual* includes chapter outlines, overviews, key concepts, discussion questions, and suggestions for useful audiovisual resources.
- *Prentice Hall Custom Test* is a commercial-quality computerized test management program for Windows and Macintosh environments. The program allows instructors to select items from the test item file to create tests. It also allows online testing.
- The *Transparency Package* provides instructors with full color transparency acetates of all the maps, charts, and graphs in the text for use in the classroom.

FOR THE STUDENT

- The *Study Guide* (Volumes I and II) provides chapter overviews, objectives, practice tests, essay questions, and map exercises to help reinforce the chapter content.
- The *Documents Set* (Volumes I and II) is a collection of additional primary and secondary source documents organized by chapter. Questions accompanying the documents can be used for discussion or as writing assignments.
- The *Map Workbook* is a collection of map exercises to help students review basic geographical knowledge.
- The *Hammond Historical Atlas of the World* is a collection of maps illustrating the most significant periods and events in the history of civilization. This atlas is available at a discounted price to students when packaged with *The World's History.*
- *World History: An Atlas and Study Guide* is a four-color map workbook that includes over 100 maps with exercises, activities, and questions that help students learn both geography and history. It is available at a discounted price to students when packaged with *The World's History.*
- *Reading Critically About History* is a brief guide to reading effectively that provides students with helpful strategies for reading a history textbook. It is available free to students when packaged with *The World's History.*

- *Understanding and Answering Essay Questions* suggests helpful analytical tools for understanding different types of essay questions, and provides precise guidelines for preparing well-crafted essay answers. It is available free to students when packaged with *The World's History.*
- *Themes of the Times* is a newspaper supplement prepared jointly by Prentice Hall and *The New York Times*, the premier news publication. Issued twice a year, it contains recent articles pertinent to historical study. These articles connect the classroom to the world. For information about a reduced rate subscription to *The New York Times*, call toll-free: 1-800-631-1222.

MEDIA RESOURCES

- *History on the Internet* is a brief guide to navigating the Internet and World Wide Web and using the *Companion Website*™ accompanying *The World's History*. It also includes an introduction to critical thinking skills for effectively evaluating sources found on the World Wide Web, a list of useful sites related to history, and a guide to documenting online sources. This guide is free to students when packaged with *The World's History.*
- The *Companion Website*™ (www.prenhall.com/spodek) works in tandem with the text and features objectives, study questions, web links to related resources on the World Wide Web, document exercises, interactive map activities, message boards and a chat feature, all organized according to the chapters in the text.
- *Powerpoint Images CDROM* for use in Windows or Macintosh environments includes the maps, charts, and graphs in the text on disk for use with Microsoft Powerpoint™, allowing instructors to integrate the graphics into lectures.

For those instructors interested in *online course management and distance learning*, Prentice Hall is pleased to offer a number of options with *The World's History*, including WEBCT and Blackboard online course material to support the text online. For more information, please contact your local Prentice Hall representative.

To my children, Susie, Josh, and Sarah,
who are always in my thoughts;
and to my wife Lisa,
who has made this work possible

PREFACE

WHY HISTORY?

The professional historian and the student of an introductory course often seem to pass each other on different tracks. For the professional, nothing is more fascinating than history. For the student, particularly one in a compulsory course, the whole enterprise often seems a bore. This introductory text is designed to help that student understand and share the fascination of the historian. It will also remind professors of their original attraction to history, before they began the specialization that has almost certainly marked their later careers. Furthermore, it encourages student and professor to explore together the history of the world and the significance of this study.

Professional historians love their field for many reasons. History offers perspective and guidance in forming a personal view of human development. It teaches the necessity of seeing many sides of issues. It explores the complexity and interrelationship of events and makes possible the search for patterns and meaning in human life.

Historians also love to debate. They love the challenge of demonstrating that their interpretations of the pattern and significance of events are the most accurate and the most satisfying in their fit between the available data and theory. Historians also love the detective work of their profession, whether it is researching through old archives, uncovering and using new sources of information, or reinterpreting long-ignored sources. In recent years historians have turned, for example, to oral history, old church records, files of photographs, cave paintings, individual census records, and reinterpretations of mythology.

Historical records are not simply lists of events, however. They are the means by which historians develop their interpretations of those events. Because interpretations differ, there is no single historical record, but various narrations of events each told from a different perspective. Therefore the study of history is intimately linked to the study of *values*.

To construct their interpretations, historians examine the values—the motives, wishes, desires, visions—of people of the past. In interpreting those values, historians must confront and engage their own values, comparing and contrasting these values with those of people in the past. For example, they ask how various people viewed slavery in the slave-holding societies of the past. In the back of their minds they compare and contrast those older values with values held by various people today and especially with their own personal values. They ask: How and why have values changed or remained the same through the passage of time? Why, and in what way, do my values compare and contrast with values of the past? By learning to pose such questions, students will be better equipped to discover and create their own place in the continuing movement of human history. This text, therefore, consistently addresses three fundamental questions: What do we know? How do we know it? What difference does it make? It emphasizes **historiography**, the process of creating historical records. Students will see that these records are neither gospel truth nor fabricated fiction, but a first step in understanding and interpreting the past. They will learn how historians frame questions for study and how the questions that are asked determine the answers that are found. They will learn to frame their own, new questions about both the past and the present.

Professional historians consider history to be the king of disciplines. Synthesizing the concepts of fellow social scientists in economics, politics, **anthropology**, sociology, and geography, historians create a more integrated and comprehensive interpretation of the past. Joining with their colleagues in the humanities, historians delight in hearing and telling exciting stories that recall heroes and villains, the low born and the high, the wisdom and the folly of days gone by. This fusion of all the social sciences and humanities gives the study of history its range, depth, significance, and pleasure. Training in historical thinking provides an excellent introduction to understanding change and continuity in our own day as well as in the past.

WHY WORLD HISTORY?

Why specifically world history? Why should we teach and study world history, and what should be the content of such a course?

First, world history is a good place to begin for it is a new field for professor and student alike. Neither its content nor its pedagogy is yet fixed. Many of the existing textbooks on the market still have their origins in the study of western Europe, with segments added to cover the rest of the world. World history as the study of the inter-relationships of all regions of the world, seen from the many perspectives of the different peoples of the earth, is still virgin territory.

Second, for citizens of multicultural, multi-ethnic nations such as the United States, Canada, South Africa, and India, and for those of the many other countries such as the United Kingdom and Australia which are moving in that direction, a world history course offers the opportunity to gain an appreciation of the national and cultural origins of all their diverse citizens. In this way, the study of world history may help to strengthen the bonds of national citizenship.

Third, as the entire world becomes a single unit for interaction, it becomes an increasingly appropriate subject for historical study. The noted historian E.H. Carr explained that history "is an unending dialogue between the present and the past." The new reality of global interaction in communication, business, politics, religion, culture, and ecology has helped to generate the new academic subject of world history.

THE ORIGINS AND DEVELOPMENT OF THIS TEXT

The inspiration for this text was a ground-breaking four-year program in the School District of Philadelphia, 1988–92. Teachers in the District asked for instruction in world history so that they could better teach their ninth-grade course and, indeed, rewrite its curriculum. In the program established to meet their request, some thirty college professors met with about one hundred Philadelphia teachers. I was the academic coordinator, teaching several of the formal courses offered and responsible for staffing the others. From the courses we designed for teachers came the basic framework for the current text. There is no better, more interactive, more critical, yet more helpful audience for new teaching materials than students who are themselves teachers. Together we learned a great deal about the study and teaching of world history at high school, college, and graduate levels.*

Following this schools-based project, twenty college professors from twelve different colleges and universities and twenty high school teachers from fifteen different schools in the Philadelphia metropolitan region were awarded a substantial grant from the National Endowment for the Humanities to pursue further methods of teaching world history—content and pedagogy—at the college level in ways that would best prepare future teachers. I served as project director. Participation in this two-year collaborative project helped me further to refine the content and the method of the current text.†

Finally, in conjunction with these major projects, I began in 1990 to offer a year-long course in world history at Temple University, Philadelphia. The structure of that course is the structure of this text.

As each chapter was completed, I included it in the reading materials of the course. So the text has had five years of field testing.

ORGANIZATION AND APPROACH

The text, like the year-long course, links *chronology*, *themes*, and *geography* in eight units, or parts of study. The parts move progressively along a time line from the emergence of early humans to the present day. Each part emphasizes a single theme—for example, urbanization or religion or trade—and students learn to use all eight themes to analyze historical events and to develop a grasp of the chronology of human development. Geographically, each part covers the entire globe, although specific topics place greater emphasis on specific regions.

IMPORTANT SPECIAL FEATURES

To provide the students with direct experience of the historian's craft the text includes:

- Primary sources to illuminate the experiences of an age and place directly. Their analysis is an essential part of the study of history.
- Historians' later interpretations to provide perspective on how historical records were produced and fought over. The analysis of these secondary sources is an essential part of the study of historiography.
- Sidebars to provide more detailed discussions of particular issues beyond the narrative. Such supplements appear in every chapter.
- Extensive, clear, and informative charts and maps to represent information graphically and geographically.
- A wide range of illustrations, many in color, to supplement the written word. Some of the illustrations are grouped into "Spotlights" to illuminate specific issues. These include, for example, at the earliest, a Spotlight on the reconstruction of Neanderthals, which explores the ways in which Neanderthals have been represented through time, to, at the latest, a portfolio of the murals of Diego Rivera, indicating how an individual artist interprets and represents the history of his people through his painting.

Collectively, these materials provide a rich, comprehensive, and challenging introduction to the study of world history and the methods and key interpretations of its historians.

REVISIONS IN THE SECOND EDITION

The second edition brings many additions and revisions. Some of the new materials reflect increases in knowledge in the last three years: new material on *Ardipithecus ramidus*, reported in Chapter 1; the oldest known alphabetic writing, a Semitic script discovered in Egypt from 1900 B.C.E., noted in Chapter 2; 9000-year old, still-playable flutes from China, and significant new excavations on the Niger River at Jenne Jeno, reported and discussed in Chapter 4. Others analyze recent events such as the precipitous decline and partial rebound of the economies of several Asian countries; nuclear weapons tests in India and Pakistan; the influence of drug traffic in Latin America; the election of President Mohammed Khatami in Iran and the resignation of President Boris Yeltsin in Russia.

The new materials also respond in part to the author's experience in teaching the text, suggestions made by friends and colleagues, and evaluations gathered by the publisher from professors selected from across the United States. Thus, the discussion of the Roman Empire has been restructured for greater clarity; the coverage of medieval, early modern, and twentieth-century Europe has been expanded; and the history of science has been augmented. The introduction to the twentieth century has been enhanced with new materials on the cold war, decolonization, economic globalization, the internet, the human genome project, and the international drug trade. Greater attention has been given to America's role in the world including its continuing struggles with issues of civil rights at home and abroad.

Chapters now conclude with explicit explorations of the consequences and significance of their subject matter. Comparisons of the institutions of different areas of the world, fundamental to the structure of each part of the text, are now drawn explicitly throughout the book. Several of the "Spotlight" artwork features of the first edition have been replaced by new ones, as have many of the illustrations and several of the maps. Each chapter now includes a "Profile" biography illuminating the significance of an important person from its era. These include emperors and an empress dowager, historians, a film maker, a popular singer, an explorer, religious leaders, a family of archaeologists, warriors, democratically elected political politicians, and some whose careers defy simple categorization. Timecharts in each chapter have been revised and redesigned to improve accessibility and usefulness, and new "Connection" boxes link material between chapters and enhance the chronological framework of the book.

All these changes do not, however, change the essential structure of the text, with its emphasis on chronology, theme, and geography; its integration of text, primary and secondary source materials, maps, and artwork; and its emphasis on the fundamental questions of "What Do We Know?", "How Do We Know It?", and "What Difference Does it Make?"

---

* Carol Parsinnen and Howard Spodek, " 'We're Making History': Philadelphia Educators Tackle a National Issue," *The History Teacher* XXV, No. 3 (May 1992), 321–38.
† Howard Spodek, *et al.*, "World History: Preparing Teachers through High School–College Collaboration, The Philadelphia Story, 1993–1995," *The History Teacher* XXIX, No. 1 (November 1995), 1–41.

ACKNOWLEDGMENTS

After several years of work, at last comes the opportunity to thank publicly the many people who have made this book possible through their encouragement, careful reading of early drafts, comments, and general support. The idea for this text took form in the course of work with many superb teachers in a world history workshop in the School District of Philadelphia. The administrators of that program—Carol Parssinen and Ellen Wylie of the Philadelphia Alliance for Teaching Humanities in the Schools and Jim Culbertson and Joe Jacovino from the School District—set the framework for that program which led to writing this text. I thank them and the many participants who helped make our studies so fruitful. Three of the participants later joined me at Temple University, Philadelphia, in teaching future teachers of history, and I thank Patricia Jiggetts Jones, Gloria Mitchell-Barnes, and Karen Kreider for helping me plan the content and pedagogy of an introductory world history course. Sue Rosenthal reminded me to encourage students to find their own place in history and thus inspired the afterword of this book.

As I prepared a new introductory course in world history at Temple University, I was granted a semester's study leave for which I thank the Temple University Faculty Senate. Throughout this project I received the constant support of Dean Carolyn Adams and department chairs Jim Hilty and Morris Vogel.

Many colleagues have read or discussed parts of this text in manuscript and have made helpful suggestions. Within Temple University's history department these include Barbara Day-Hickman, Ruth Karras, Tim Mixter, Dieu Nguyen, Arthur Schmidt, Teshale Tibebu, and Kathy Walker. Vasiliki Limberis of our religion department and Len Greenfield from anthropology helped with issues outside the immediate discipline. In addition I thank Michael Adas, Al Andrea, Joan Arno, Terry Burke, Tim Burke, Lee Cassanelli, Richard Eaton, Narayani Gupta, Chris Jones, Maghan Keita, Dina Rizk Khoury, Lynn Lees, Alan Mann, David O'Connor, Greg Possehl, Jerry Ruderman, and Gail Vander Heide. Jim Krippner-Martinez' help with Latin America was critical, as was the assistance of Susannah Ruth Spodek on Japan. I trust that all these colleagues and friends will find in the finished book evidence of their contributions, and that they will forgive me for not following their advice even more carefully.

I first used most of the text materials in this book with my students at Temple University. They provided the first indications of what worked well in teaching world history and should be kept in the final product, and what did not and should be scrapped. I thank them both for their patience and for the many suggestions they made.

I owe a great debt to the editors and staff at Calmann & King, London, who saw this book through from its inception to its conclusion. They seemed to know just when to encourage, to support, to understand, and to demand. Rosemary Bradley (now with Prentice Hall) commissioned the book; Melanie White edited and guided the book from beginning to end; Damian Thompson prepared the layout and design and helped select, gather, and caption the illustrations which drive the written text forward; Lee Ripley Greenfield had overall executive charge of the project in its last four years.

The most profound and personal thanks come last. My father and mother, may their memories be a blessing, always encouraged and supported my studies. My father, though a man of business rather than of the academy, always enjoyed historical discussions. Mother, of course, prepared, and presided over, the dinner table at which these discussions took place, often adding her own comments as well.

When I began writing this book, my two older children, Susie and Josh, were already in college. Sarah, the youngest, was still in high school. All three were always in my mind as I wrote. They were my first audience as I asked myself: What should students know about world history? They were usually the first readers of early drafts of each chapter, and their comments were perceptive and helpful. Most gratifying of all: Susie, who spent four years living and working in Japan, graciously provided early drafts of materials on Japan; Sarah, who spent two years with the Peace Corps in Morocco, helped me through issues in the Arab and Berber worlds; and Josh, training as a physicist, reminded me to give proper attention to the importance of science in history. To them I dedicate the first volume of this work.

I met Lisa Hixenbaugh about a year into the writing of this book, and we were married just a few months before its completion. She has enriched and enhanced my life. Graciously and without complaint she gave up time that we might have spent together so that the writing could be completed. She endured interminable monologues on the status of the project. Her support and encouragement helped make the entire task feasible.

ACKNOWLEDGMENTS FOR THE SECOND EDITION

One of the great joys of completing the revisions for a second edition is the opportunity to thank friends and colleagues who helped: Laura Szumanski, Ph.D. candidate in history at Temple University, who drafted several of the biographical "Profiles" with her characteristic fine style and in record time; Jayant Joshi who urged me not to omit Abraham Lincoln and the many struggles for freedom in America, for they belong to the history of the world; Father Jose Heredero who increased the accuracy of coverage and interpretation on Christianity; students in the class of Gail Zlotowitz at Yeshivat Rambam who kept me alert to orthodox Jewish religious sensitivities; the anonymous evaluators of the first edition; sales representatives at Prentice Hall who advised me periodically on the strengths and weaknesses of the text from the viewpoint of the faculty who chose to use it—or not; Nell Webb, whose contributions at Calmann & King added to the enduring support of Melanie White and Damian Thompson; Gerald Lombardi for deft editing.

During the six months of revision, friends and family tolerated my absences from normal socializing; I missed them even more! Students and colleagues tolerated my fragmented attention. My wife put up with even less time together than usual, and more monologues. And special thanks to her parents, Sandra and Al Hixenbaugh, who spent the last couple of days before Lisa and I left for India in 1997 helping to pack up our house, freeing me to sit at the word processor typing the last pages of the first edition in a scene that none of us has forgotten!

HOWARD SPODEK
March 2000

INTRODUCTION

"History will be kind to me, for I intend to write it."

WINSTON CHURCHILL

THE WORLD THROUGH HISTORIANS' EYES

"That's history!" In common usage this phrase diminishes an event as belonging only to the past, implying that it is no longer important and has no further consequence. For the historian, however, history is just the opposite. History records those events that are of greatest importance, of most lasting significance, and of most enduring consequence. History is the assortment of records that humans create, preserve, fight over, revise, and transmit from one generation to the next. It contains the deepest understandings of how we got to where we are now; the struggles fought, won, and lost; the choices made and not made; the roads taken and not taken. We study history to know who we are, who we might have become, and who we might yet become.

HISTORIOGRAPHY

History is not a single, dry record of names, dates, and places. Nor is it a record that somehow, magically, came into being by itself. Historical records are the products of many human choices. From all the events that have occurred, historians choose those they believe worth remembering for inclusion in their accounts and leave out those that seem less relevant. Historians differ, however, in their assessment of the significance of events. They debate which events are most significant and which are less so, which should be included in the records and which may be left out. Differences in historians' assessments lead to the writing and preservation of different histories. These differences are important because they represent different understandings of who we have become, and how, and of who we may become, and how. The debates and discussions of historians in forming and arguing about these assessments form part of the historiographical record. **Historiography** is the study of the making of historical records, of the work historians do and how they do it.

Even when historians are in agreement as to which events are most significant, they may differ in evaluating why the events are significant. One historian's interpretation of events may be diametrically opposed to another's. For example, virtually all historians agree that part of the significance of World War II lay in its new policies and technologies of destruction: nuclear weapons in battle and genocide behind the lines.

In terms of interpretation, pessimists might stress the continuing menace of these legacies of terror, while optimists might argue that the very violence of the war and the Holocaust triggered a search for limits on nuclear arms and greater tolerance for minorities. With each success in nuclear arms limitation and in toleration, the optimists seem more persuasive; with each spread of nuclear weapons and each outbreak of genocide, the pessimists seem to win.

The study of history is thus an interpretation of significance as well as an investigation of facts. The significance of events is determined by their consequences. Sometimes we do not know what the consequences are; or the consequences may not have run their course; or we may differ in our assessments of the consequences. This play between past events and their current consequences is what historian E.H. Carr had in mind in his famous description of history as "an unending dialogue between the present and the past" (Carr, p. 30).

After historians ask the factual questions of Who, Where, When, What, Why, and How, they reach the "So what?" questions. These affect fundamentally the historians' discussion about what to include in their accounts and what to leave out. In world history, where the subject matter is everything that humans have ever done, this problem of selection is fundamental. The problem of interpretation comes with it. These "So what?" questions depend finally on individual interpretation, on the personal values of the historian. Readers, in turn, will evaluate the historians' argument partly by its consistency with the available data, partly by the values implicit or explicit in it, and partly by comparing the author's values with their own. The study of history thus becomes a dialogue between the values of the historian and the values of the student of history. As you read this text, for example, you should become aware of the values held by the author and of your own values as reader.

As historians present their differing interpretations, each tries to mount the most persuasive arguments, marshaling **primary source** materials, that is, materials from contemporary participants in the events; **secondary sources**, that is, later comments on the consequences of the events; and appeals to the sensibilities of the reader. In turn, the reader will be asking: Does the historians' interpretation sound reasonable? Do people really act as the historian suggests they do? Do the motivations suggested by the historian sound reasonable or is some other interpretation more consistent with the primary and secondary sources and with human motivation? When historians differ in their interpretations of events, readers must judge which argument is more persuasive.

HISTORY AND IDENTITY

History is among the most passionate and bitterly contentious of disciplines because most people and groups locate a large part of their identity in their history. Americans may take pride in their nationality, for example, for having created a representative, constitutional democracy that has endured for over 200 years (see Part 7). Yet they may be saddened, shamed, or perhaps incensed by the existence of 250 years of slavery followed by inequalities in race relations continuing to the present (see Part 6). Christians may take pride in two thousand years of missions of compassion toward the poor and downtrodden, yet they may be saddened, shamed, or even incensed by an almost equally long record of religious warfare and persecution of those whose beliefs differed from their own (see Part 4).

As various ethnic, religious, class, and gender groups represent themselves in public political life, they seek not only to understand the history that has made them what they are, but also to attempt to persuade others to understand that history in the same way. Feminist historians, for example, find in their reading of history that **patriarchy**, a system of male-created and male-dominated institutions, has subordinated women. To the extent that they weave a persuasive argument from available data and their interpretation of it, or discover new data and create new interpretations, they win over others to their position.

Meanwhile, other historians may present women's position in the world more as a product of biological differentiation than of human decisions. Some may not even agree that women have been subordinated to men, but argue that both genders have shared in a great deal of suffering (and joy) throughout history (see Parts 1 and 7). The historical debates over the origins and evolution of gender relationships evoke strong emotions because people's self-image, the image of their group, and the perceptions others hold of them are all at stake. And the stakes are high. As historian Gerda Lerner writes in *The Creation of Patriarchy*: "Women's history is indispensable and essential to the emancipation of women" (p. 3)

CONTROL OF HISTORICAL RECORDS

From earliest times, control over the historical records and their interpretation has been fundamental to political rule. The first emperor of China, Qin Shihuang (r. 221–207 B.C.E.), the man who built the concept of a united China that has lasted until today, "discarded the ways of the former kings and burned the writings of the hundred schools in order to make the people ignorant" (deBary, p. 167). So wrote Qia I (201–169 B.C.E.), poet and statesman of the succeeding Han dynasty. Shihuang wished that only his interpretation of China's past, and his place in it, be preserved. Later intellectuals condemned his actions—but the lost records were irretrievable (see Part 3).

Colonial governments seeking to control subject peoples sometimes attempt to interpret their histories by explaining that the conquered people were so backward that they benefited from the conquest.

Later historians may be less kind to the colonizers. Some 1900 years ago the historian Tacitus wrote bitterly of the ancient Romans in their conquest of England: "Robbery, butchery, rapine, the liars call Empire; they create a desolation and call it peace" (*Agricola*, 30).

In our own century, the many nations that have won their freedom from colonialism echo similar resentments against their foreign rulers and set out to revise the historical record in keeping with their newly won political freedom. Jawaharlal Nehru, the first prime minister of independent India (1947–64), wrote in 1944 from the cell in which he had been imprisoned for his leadership of his country's independence movement:

> British accounts of India's history, more especially of what is called the British period, are bitterly resented. History is almost always written by the victors and conquerors and gives their viewpoint; or, at any rate, the victors' version is given prominence and holds the field. (Nehru, p. 289)

Lenin addressing troops in Sverdlov Square, Moscow, May 5, 1920. The leaders of the Russian Communist revolution crudely refashioned the historical record to suit the wishes of the winners. After Lenin's death in 1924, his second-in-command Leon Trotsky (pictured sitting on the podium in the left-hand picture) lost to Josef Stalin the bitter power struggle that ensued. Not only was Trotsky banished from the Soviet Union, but so was his appearance in the official archives (see doctored picture on right).

Philip Curtin, historian of Africa and of slavery, elaborates an equally critical view of European colonial accounts of Africa's history:

> African history was seriously neglected until the 1950s. . . . The colonial period in Africa left an intellectual legacy to be overcome, just as it had in other parts of the world. . . . The colonial imprint on historical knowledge emerged in the nineteenth and early twentieth centuries as a false perspective, a Eurocentric view of world history created at a time of European domination . . . Even where Europeans never ruled, European knowledge was often accepted as *modern* knowledge, including aspects of the Eurocentric historiography. (Curtin, p. 54)

Instead, Curtin continues, a proper historiography must:

> show the African past from an African point of view. . . . For Africans, to know about the past of their own societies is a form of self-knowledge crucial to a sense of identity in a diverse and rapidly changing world. A recovery of African history has been an important part of African development over recent decades. (p. 54)

Even without colonialism, thugs sometimes gain control of national histories. George Orwell's satirical novel *Animal Farm* (published in 1945) presented an allegory in which pigs come to rule a farm. Among their many acts of domination, the pigs seize control of the historical records of the farm animals' failed experiment in equality and impose their own official interpretation, which justifies their own rule. The rewriting of history and suppression of alternative records by the Communist

Party of the former Soviet Union between 1917 and 1989 reveals the bitter truth underlying Orwell's satire (see Part 8).

Although the American experience is much different, in the United States, too, records have been suppressed. Scholars are still trying to use the Freedom of Information Act to pry open sealed diplomatic archives. (Most official archives everywhere have twenty-, thirty-, or forty-year rules governing the waiting period before certain sensitive records are opened to the public. These rules, which are designed to protect living people and contemporary policies from excessive scrutiny, are the rule everywhere.)

Religious and ethnic groups, too, may seek to control historical records. The Roman Catholic Church in 1542 established an Index of Prohibited Books to ban writings it considered heretical. (The Spanish Inquisition, ironically, stored away many records that later scholars used to recreate its history and the history of those it persecuted.) More recently, despite all the evidence of the Holocaust, the murder of 6 million Jews by the Nazi government of Germany during World War II, a few people have claimed that the murders never took place. They deny the existence of such racial and religious hatred, and its consequences, and ignore deep-seated problems in the relationships between majority and minority populations.

HISTORICAL REVISION

Interpretations of events may become highly contested and revised even after several centuries have passed. The significance of the voyages of Columbus was once celebrated uncritically in the United States in tribute both to "the Admiral of the Ocean Sea" himself and to the courage and enterprise of the European explorers and early settlers who brought their civilizations to the Americas. In South America, however, where Native American Indians are more numerous and people of European ancestry often form a smaller proportion of the population, the celebrations have been far more ambivalent, muted, and meditative.

In 1992, on the 500th anniversary of Columbus' first voyage to the Americas, altogether new and more sobering elements entered the commemoration ceremonies, even in the United States. The negative consequences of Columbus' voyages, previously ignored, were now recalled and emphasized: the death of up to 90 percent of the Native American Indian population in the century after the arrival of Europeans; the Atlantic slave trade, initiated by trade in Indian slaves; and the exploitation of the natural resources of a continent until then little touched by humans. The ecological consequences, which are only now beginning to receive more attention, were not all negative, however. They included the fruitful exchange of natural products between the hemispheres. Horses, wheat, and sheep were introduced to the Americas; potatoes, tomatoes, and corn to Afro-Eurasia. Unfortunately, the spread of syphilis was one of the consequences of the exchange; scholars disagree on who transmitted this disease to whom (see Part 5).

WORLD HISTORY VS. WESTERN HISTORY

Because the study of history is so intimately tied to our sense of identity, as individuals, groups, and citizens of the world, the field is emotionally and bitterly contested. For this reason, the place of world history in the American college curriculum has itself been contested. The contest has been primarily between the advocates of European/ Western history and those favoring a global view. Advocates of Western history wish to educate a student to know the central political, cultural, and religious institutions of the Western world, which are the basis of the political life of the United States and the roots of the cultural and religious heritage of most of its citizens. Advocates of world history recognize the validity and importance of these claims, but advance countervailing positions:

- Increasingly dense networks of transportation and communication have brought the world, for many purposes, into a single unit. The growth and consolidation of that global unit deserve its own historical study.

- America is increasingly drawn into a world far wider than Europe alone, with the nations and peoples of the Pacific Rim and of Latin America becoming particularly prominent partners.

- The population of America, always at least 15 percent non-European in ancestry, especially African–American, is now adding large new immigrant streams from Latin America and Asia, increasing the need for knowledge of these

Indians giving Hernán Cortés a headband, from Diego Duran's *Historia de las Indias*, 1547. Bent on conquest and plunder, the bearded Spaniard Cortés arrived on the Atlantic coast of Mexico in 1519. His forces sacked the ancient city of Tenochtitlán, decimated the Aztec people and imprisoned their chief, Montezuma, before proclaiming the Aztec Empire "New Spain." By stark contrast, this bland Spanish watercolor shows local tribesmen respectfully paying homage to the invader as if he were a god; in ignoring the brutality exercised in the colonization of South America, the artist is, in effect, "rewriting" history. (*Biblioteca National, Madrid*)

many cultures and their histories if there is to be a rich, balanced understanding of all the peoples of the United States.

The fierce debate between the advocates of Western history and those favoring world history is thus, in part, a contest for an understanding of the nature of America's population, culture, and place in the world as it has been and may become.

The current text is addressed primarily to American students, and many of its references are to American experience, but as global immigration increases the ethnic diversity of most countries of the world, the same need to understand world history in order to understand national history will increase everywhere.

TOOLS

The study of history requires many tools, and this text includes most of the principal ones:

- The core of historical study is a direct encounter with primary materials, usually documents, but including other artifacts—for example, letters, diaries, newspaper accounts, photographs, and artwork. Every chapter includes representative primary materials.

- Visual images, a strong feature of this book, complement the text, offering non-verbal "texts" of the time.

- "Spotlight" spreads contain brief essays, linked to the main text, that treat pictures as a springboard for discussion.

- Maps place events in space and in geographical relationship to one another.

- Chronological timecharts situate events in time and sequence.

- Brief charts supply summaries as well as contextual information on topics such as religion, science, and trade.

- Biographical sketches of outstanding individuals, and of average ones, provide personal insights and points of identification.

- Various, often conflicting, interpretations demonstrate the existence of multiple perspectives. They help students to challenge their own values and develop their own interpretive criteria.

CHRONOLOGY AND THEME

History is a study of change over time and also of continuities in the face of change. In this text we mark eight turning points in human history, setting each as the focus of a single unit, or part. The choices may seem arbitrary, but they do capture fundamental transformations. They also demonstrate how a historian argues for the significance of one turning point over another. Each turning point is marked by the rise to prominence of a new theme in human history and a new focus in the narrative. For example, we move from an emphasis on early human cultures in Part 1 to agricultural and urban "revolutions" in Part 2, to the establishment of the first empires in Part 3. Within each chronological/thematic part, we stress a single disciplinary or interdisciplinary approach—for example, anthropology in early human cultures, urban studies in the rise of early cities, and political science in the establishment of empires.

We highlight a specific discipline in each chronological part for teaching purposes, in order to demonstrate the usefulness of each discipline in illuminating historical change. We recognize, however, that all the disciplinary approaches and the realities to which they refer, are relevant in each time period. Our method allows readers to understand how various disciplines, alone and together, help us understand the varied aspects of historical narratives.

The eight turning points by which we mark world history and the specific themes and disciplines we pair with them are:

1 The emergence of the first humans and human culture, 4,500,000 B.C.E. to 10,000 B.C.E. Focus on *anthropology* and *historiography*.

2 The emergence of the first cities and urban civilization following the agricultural revolution, 10,000 B.C.E. to 400 C.E. Focus on *interdisciplinary urban studies*.

3 The emergence of early empires, from Sargon of Assyria and Alexander of Macedon through China, Rome, and India, and the trade routes that linked them, 2000 B.C.E. to 200 C.E. Focus on *politics*.

4 The rise and spread of world religions, focusing on Islam, 622–1500 C.E.; reviewing the historical background of Judaism and Christianity and their contemporary systems; and comparing the Asia-centered religions of Hinduism, Buddhism, and the ethical system of Confucianism. Focus on *religion*.

5 World trading systems, 1000–1776, with the linkage of eastern and western hemispheres as the fulcrum, about 1500. By the end of this period, capitalism was defined as a new economic system. Focus on *economics*.

6 Migrations, free and slave, 1000–1750. Focus on *demography*.

7 Revolutions, political and industrial, beginning in Europe and spreading globally, 1750–1914. Focus on *social changes*, especially *changes in family and gender roles*.

8 Technological change and its human control, 1914 to the present. Focus on *the human uses of technological systems*.

COMPARATIVE HISTORY AND HYPOTHESIS TESTING

Because each part is built on comparisons among different regions and civilizations of the world, the reader will become accustomed to posing hypotheses based on general principles, and then testing them against comparative data from around the world. This method of playing back and forth between general theory and specific case study, testing whether the general theory and the specific data fit each other, is at the heart of the social sciences. For example, in Part 2 we will explore the general characteristics of cities, and then check if the generalizations hold up through case studies of various cities around the world. In Part 3, we will seek general theories of the rise and fall of early empires based on comparisons among China, Rome, and India. In Part 4 we will search for commonalities among religious belief systems through a survey of several major religions.

FOCUS
Continuity versus Change in History

Feminist historian Judith Bennett argues that between 1300 and 1700, women's economic and social position did not change much. She also maintains that women's history in Europe is the study of unchanging economic subordination to men at least from 1300 to the present:

In the study of women's work . . . we should take as our central question not transformation . . . but instead continuity. We should ask: why has women's work retained such dismal characteristics over so many centuries? . . . We should ask: why wages for "women's work" remained consistently lower than wages paid for work associated with men? We should ask, in short: why has women's work stood still in the midst of considerable economic change? . . . I think that this emphasis on continuity demands an attention to the mechanisms and operations of patriarchy in the history of women. (p. 164)

Pieter de Hoogh,
A Woman and Her Maid,
c. 1650.
In this Dutch domestic scene, the high walls of the courtyard and the formal business attire of the paterfamilias as he returns home can be read as emphasizing the separation between the male world of public commerce and the female world of private domesticity. (*National Gallery, London*)

FRAMING QUESTIONS FOR MULTIPLE PERSPECTIVES

The text highlights the importance of multiple perspectives in studying and interpreting history. The answers we get—the narrative histories we write—are based on the questions we ask. Each part suggests a variety of questions that can be asked about the historical event being studied, and a variety of interpretations that can emerge in the process of answering them. Often there is more than one "correct" way of understanding change over time and its significance. Different questions will trigger very different research and very different answers. For example, in Part 5 we ask about the stages and processes by which Western commercial power began to surpass that of Asia. This question presupposes the fact that at earlier times Asian power had been superior and asks why it declined and why European power advanced. In Part 7 we ask how the industrial revolution affected and changed relationships between men and women; this question will yield different research and a different narrative from questions about, for example, women's contributions to industrialization, which is a useful question, but a different one.

FINDING ONE'S PLACE IN HISTORY

We want readers to understand world history not as a burden to learn and to live with, but as a legacy within which to find their own place. This text shows people throughout history reckoning with the alternatives available and making choices among them. Their examples should provide some solace, courage, and guidance to readers now making their own choices. History has always been seen as both bondage to the past and liberation from it. We write so that students should understand both potentials, and seek a path of freedom.

BIBLIOGRAPHY

Bennett, Judith M. "Medieval Women, Modern Women: Across the Great Divide," in David Aers, ed., *Culture and History, 1350–1600: Essays on English Communities, Identities, and Writing* (New York: Harvester Wheatsheaf, 1992), 147–75.

Carr, E.H. *What Is History?* (Harmondsworth, Middlesex: Penguin Books, 1964).

Curtin, Philip D. "Recent Trends in African Historiography and Their Contribution to History in General," in Joseph Ki-Zerbo, ed., *General History of Africa*, Vol. I: *Methodology and African Pre-History* (Berkeley: University of California Press, 1981), 54–71.

deBary, William Theodore, *et al.*, comps. *Sources of Chinese Tradition* (New York: Columbia University Press, 1960).

Lerner, Gerda. *The Creation of Patriarchy* (New York: Oxford University Press, 1986).

Nehru, Jawaharlal. *The Discovery of India* (Delhi: Oxford University Press, 1989).

Orwell, George. *Animal Farm* (New York: Harcourt, Brace, 1946).

Tacitus, Cornelius. *Tacitus' Agricola, Germany, and Dialogue on Orators*, trans. Herbert W. Benario (Norman: University of Oklahoma Press, 1991).

Tosh, John. *The Pursuit of History: Aims, Methods, and New Directions in the Study of Modern History*, 2nd ed. (London: Longman, 1991).

THE WORLD'S HISTORY

Volume I: To 1500

Human Origins and Human Cultures

5 million B.C.E.–10,000 B.C.E.

BUILDING AN INTERPRETIVE FRAMEWORK: WHAT DO WE KNOW AND HOW DO WE KNOW IT?

Historians ask some very big questions. Often, of course, the stereotype of the historian searching in dusty archives for concrete, exact bits of data is correct. Detail and accuracy are important. However, profound questions of fundamental importance inspire the historian's rigorous research. In this chapter we address some of the biggest questions of all: Where did humans come from? How did our collective life on earth begin? How are we similar to other living species, and how are we unique?

Many historians would consider such questions to be **pre-history**, for no written records exist to answer them. We choose, however, to include pre-history as part of our search, for we historians are eclectic in our methods; we begin with questions about the past and our relationship to it, and then choose whatever methods help us find answers. In this chapter we find that until the mid-nineteenth century, the answers to our questions about human origins were provided by myths, often religious narratives. Then a re-evaluation of religious and mythical traditions invited a search for new answers and, at about the same time, new techniques of archaeology developed to provide them.

Neanderthal family. A reconstructed scene outside Gorham's Cave, Gibraltar.

What does it mean to be human? This profound question turns most historians and pre-historians to the study of human creativity. Humans are what humans do. We travel and migrate, both out of sheer inquisitiveness as well as to find safe and productive homes. As we shall see, by about 15,000 B.C.E., humans had traveled, mostly over land, and established themselves on all the continents of the earth except Antarctica. We also create and invent tools. Our account will begin with the simplest stone tools dating back millions of years and continue up to the invention of pottery and of sedentary farming some 10,000 years ago. Finally, to be human is to express our feelings and ideas in art, music, dance, ritual, and literature. In this chapter we examine early evidence of this creativity in the forms of sculptures and cave paintings from 20,000 years ago.

1 THE DRY BONES SPEAK

5 million B.C.E.—10,000 B.C.E.

". . . whilst this planet has gone cycling on according to the fixed laws of gravity, from so simple a beginning endless forms most beautiful and most wonderful have been, and are being, evolved."

CHARLES DARWIN

WHAT IS PALEOANTHROPOLOGY AND WHY IS IT IMPORTANT?

HUMAN ORIGINS IN MYTH AND HISTORY

Where did we come from? How did humans come to inhabit the earth? For more than a century, we have sought the answer to these questions in the earth, in the records of the fossils discovered and interpreted by archaeologists and paleoanthropologists (students of the earliest humans). But before the diggers came with their interpretations, we had myths of human origins, stories based on popular beliefs and passed from generation to generation as folk wisdom. To those who believe them, myths of human origins give meaning to human existence. They tell not only *how* humans came to inhabit the earth, they also suggest *why*. Some of these myths, especially those that have been incorporated into religious texts like the Bible, still inspire the imaginations and govern the behavior of hundreds of millions of people around the world.

"Myth and history are close kin inasmuch as both explain how things got to be the way they are by telling some sort of history" (p. 7). So William McNeill opened his presidential address to the American Historical Association in 1985. We usually call "myth" a story we believe untrue, or at least not supported by known facts, yet, McNeill continues, myths have great significance and consequences:

What a particular group of persons understands, believes, and acts upon, even if quite absurd to outsiders, may nonetheless cement social relations and allow the members of the group to act together and accomplish feats otherwise impossible. . . . What a group of people knows and believes about the past channels expectations and affects the decisions on which their lives, their fortunes, and their sacred honor all depend. (p. 22)

EARLY HUMANS AND THEIR ANCESTORS

DATE B.C.E.	PERIOD	HOMINID EVOLUTION	MATERIAL CULTURE
5 million	● PLIOCENE	● Fragments found in northern Kenya; possibly *Australopithecus*	
3.75 million	● PLEISTOCENE	● *Australopithecus* genus, inc. Lucy (east and southern Africa) ● *Homo habilis* (eastern and southern Africa) ● *Homo erectus* (Africa) ● *Homo erectus* thought to have moved from Africa into Eurasia	● Tools ● Stone artifacts ● Use of fire
500,000		● *Homo sapiens* (archaic form) ● Remains of Peking man (*Sinanthropus*) found at Zhoukoudian	
130,000–80,000		● *Homo sapiens* (Africa and western Asia)	● Stone artifacts
100,000–33,000		● Neanderthals (Europe and western Asia)	
40,000	● AURIGNACIAN		● Tools include long blades ● First passage from Siberia to Alaska
30,000	● GRAVETTIAN	● Human remains of the Upper Paleolithic type, *Homo sapiens sapiens* (25,000) found in China	● Venus figures (25,000–12,000)
20,000	● SOLUTREAN		● Chauvet cave, France (18,000)
17,000	● MAGDALENIAN		● Lascaux cave paintings (*c.* 15,000) ● Altamira cave paintings (*c.* 13,550)

EARLY MYTHS

Akkad

What, then, have been some of the more powerful and widely accepted myths of the origin of human life? One of the earliest known myths is the *Enuma Elish* epic of the people of Akkad in Mesopotamia, discovered in King Ashurbanipal's library at Nineveh, 669–626 B.C.E., but probably dating back to almost 2000 B.C.E. The goddess Tiamat and her consort Kingu revolt against the existing gods of Mesopotamia. These gods call on Marduk, a young, strong god, who defends the old order by defeating, killing, and dismembering the rebellious deities.

According to the *Enuma Elish*, the victorious gods created humans out of the blood of the defeated and slain leader of the rebels. The humans were to devote themselves to the service of the victors. In the context of the violent city-states of Mesopotamia at the time the epic was written down, this myth gave meaning and direction to human life and affirmed the authority of the powerful priestly class.

India

India, vast and diverse, has many different myths of the origin of humans. Two of the most widespread and powerful illustrate two principal dimensions of the thought and practice of Hindu religious traditions (see Chapter 9). The ancient epic *Rigveda*, which dates from about 1000 B.C.E., emphasizes the mystical, unknowable qualities of life and its origins:

> Who verily knows and who can here declare it,
> whence it was born and whence comes this creation?
> The Gods are later than this world's production.
> Who knows then whence it first came into being?
> He, the first origin of this creation, whether he
> formed it all or did not form it, whose eye controls
> this world in highest heaven, he verily knows it …
> or perhaps he knows not.

In contrast to this reverent but puzzled view of creation, another of the most famous hymns of the *Rigveda*, the Purusha-sakta, describes the creation of the world by the gods' sacrifice and dismemberment of a giant man, Purusha:

> His mouth became the Brahmin; his arms were
> made into the Warrior, his thighs the People, and
> from his feet the Servants were born.
> The moon was born from his mind; from his eye
> the sun was born. Indra and Agni came from his
> mouth, and from his vital breath the Wind was born.
> (Ch. 10; v. 129)

In this account, humans are part of nature, subject to the laws of the universe, but they are not born equal among themselves. They are created with different qualities, in different castes. This myth of creation supports the hierarchical organization of India's historic caste system (see pp. 263–4).

West Asia

Perhaps the most widely known creation myth is told in the book of Genesis in the Hebrew Bible. Beginning from nothing, in five days God created heaven and earth; created light and separated it from darkness; created water and separated it from dry land; and created flora, birds, and fishes, and the sun, moon, and stars. God began the sixth day by creating larger land animals and reptiles, and then humans "in his own image."

Genesis assigns humans a unique and privileged place as the final crown and master of creation. Humans are specially created in God's own image, with dominion over all other living creatures. When the creation of humans and the charge to them are complete, God proclaims the whole process and product of creation as "good." Here humans hold an exalted position within, but also above, the rest of creation.

Vishnu represented as the whole world, Indian painting from Jaipur, nineteenth century. In the Hindu trinity Brahma is the creator of the world, Vishnu is its preserver, and Shiva its destroyer. The earth and all living beings—Brahma's creation—are often referred to as figments in the dream of Vishnu. He is the energy underlying all forms of life (see picture, p. 268). (*Victoria & Albert Museum, London*)

THE FUNCTION OF CREATION MYTHS

For thousands of years various creation myths have presented people with explanations of their place in the world, their relationship to the gods, to the rest of creation, and to one another. The narratives have similarities, but also sharp differences. Some portray humans as the exalted crown of creation, others as reconfigured parasites; some depict humans as partners with the gods, others as their servants; some suggest the equality of all humans, others stress a variety of caste, race, and gender hierarchies. To some degree, surely, people transmitted the myths as quaint tales told for enjoyment only, but the myths were also seen as providing guidance on how people should understand and live their lives.

Until the late eighteenth century, the myths were the only accounts we had of the origins of humans. No other explanations seemed necessary. In any case, no one expected to find actual physical evidence for the processes by which humans came to be.

EVOLUTIONARY EXPLANATIONS OF HUMAN ORIGINS

By the mid-1700s some philosophers and natural scientists in Europe challenged the Bible's story of individual, special creation of each life form. They saw so many similarities among different species that they could not believe that each had been created separately. But they could not demonstrate the processes through which these similarities and differences had developed. They saw some creatures changing forms even during their life cycle, like the metamorphosis of the caterpillar into the moth, or the tadpole into the frog, but they could not establish the processes by which one species metamorphosed into another. They knew the processes of breeding by which farmers encouraged the development of particular strains in their farm animals and plants, but they lacked the conception of a time frame of millions of years that would allow for the natural evolution of a new species from an existing one.

Challenging the biblical account required a new method of inquiry, a new system for organizing knowledge. In the mid-eighteenth century

these new forms began to emerge (see Chapter 15). In this new intellectual environment, Denis Diderot (1713–84), compiler of the first modern encyclopedia, suggested that as animals experience new needs in their environment they produce new organs to adapt and transmit them to their descendants. The physician Erasmus Darwin published a similar argument in 1794. Jean-Baptiste de Lamarck, a student of natural history, published additional similar views in 1809 after he classified the collections of plants and animals in the Paris Museum of Natural History. We now know that these men were on the right track, but that they had missed a key point.

Finally, Erasmus' grandson, Charles Darwin (1809–82), and Alfred Russel Wallace (1823–1913), separately, formulated the modern theory of the biological evolution of species. With the earlier theorists, they also saw the mounting evidence of biological similarities among related species, they understood that these similar species were, in fact, related to one another, not separate creations, and they allowed a time frame adequate for major

"That Troubles Our Monkey Again," cartoon of Charles Darwin from *Fun*, November 16, 1872. As scientists and theologians struggled to come to terms with the implications of evolutionary theory, popular reaction was often hostile and derisive. In this cartoon from a contemporary British weekly, Darwin is caricatured as an ape checking the pulse of a woman—or, as the cartoonist ironically refers to her, a "female descendant of marine ascidian" (a tiny invertebrate).

transformation of species to take place. They then pushed on to demonstrate the method by which small differences within a species were transmitted from generation to generation, increasing the differentiation until new forms were produced.

Both Darwin and Wallace reached their conclusions as a result of extensive travel overseas. Darwin carried out his observations on a scientific voyage around the world in 1831–6 aboard the British warship *Beagle*, and especially during his stay in the Galapagos Islands off the equatorial west coast of South America. Wallace traveled for many years in the islands of southeast Asia. In 1855 he published a paper "On the Habits of the Orang-Utan of Borneo," suggesting a common ancestor for primates and man. In 1858 Wallace and Darwin published a joint paper on the basic concepts of evolution. In 1859 Darwin published his findings and conclusions in *On the Origin of Species by Means of Natural Selection*, a book that forever altered humankind's conception of itself.

Darwin explained that the pressure for each organism to compete, survive, and reproduce created a kind of natural selection. The population of each species increased until its ecological niche was filled to capacity. In the face of this population pressure, the species that were better adapted to the niche survived; the rest were crowded out and tended toward extinction. Small differences always appeared within a species: some members were taller, some shorter; some brighter colored, others less radiant; some with more flexible hands and feet, others less manipulable. Those members with differences that aided survival in any given ecological setting tended to live on and to transmit their differences to their descendants. Others died out. A kind of breeding process was taking place within nature. Darwin called this process "natural selection" or "survival of the fittest."

Darwin's argument challenged two prevailing mythological views of creation, especially the biblical views. First, the process of natural selection had no goal beyond survival and reproduction. Unlike many existing creation myths, especially biblical myths, evolutionary theory postulated no **teleology**, no ethical or moral goals and purposes of life. Second, the theory of natural selection described the evolution of ever more "fit" organisms, better adapted to their ecological environment, evolving from existing ones. The special, separate creation of each species was not necessary.

To support his argument, Darwin compared natural selection to the selection process practiced by humans in breeding animals. Farmers know that specific traits among their animals can be exaggerated through breeding. Horses, for example, can be bred either for speed or for power by selecting those horses in which the desired trait appears. In nature the act of selection occurs spontaneously, if more slowly, as plants and animals that have traits more appropriate to an environment survive and reproduce while others do not.

In the isolated Galapagos Islands, Darwin found various kinds of finches, all of which were similar to each other except in their beaks. He rejected the idea that each kind of finch had been separately created. Rather, there must have been an ancestor common to them all throughout the islands. Because each island offered slightly different food sources, different beaks were better suited to each separate island. The different ecological niches on each separate island to which the birds had immigrated had evoked slightly different evolutionary development. So from a single, common ancestor, new species evolved over time, on the different islands.

For Darwin, the process of natural selection of more complex, better adapted forms also explained the evolution of humans from simpler, less well-adapted organisms. Perhaps this was "the Creator's" method. Darwin concluded *On the Origin of Species*:

> Thus, from the war of nature, from famine and death, the most exalted object which we are capable of conceiving, namely, the production of the higher animals, directly follows. There is grandeur in this view of life, with its several powers, having been originally breathed *by the Creator* [my italics] into a few forms or into one; and that, whilst this planet has gone cycling on according to the fixed law of gravity, from so simple a beginning endless forms most beautiful and most wonderful have been, and are being, evolved. (*On the Origin of Species*, reproduced in Appleman, ed., *Darwin*, p. 131)

Note, however, that the words "by the Creator" did not appear in the first edition. Darwin added them later, perhaps in response to criticisms raised by more conventional Christian religious thinkers.

Within a decade, Darwin's work, and the parallel work of Alfred Russel Wallace, had won over the scientific community. In 1871, Darwin published *The Descent of Man*, which extended his argument to the evolution of humans, concluding explicitly that "man is descended from some lowly organized form" (Appleman, ed., p. 208).

The search now began for evidence of the "missing link" between humans and apes, for some creature, alive or dead, that stood at an intermediate point in the evolutionary process. In this search archaeology flourished, and the adjunct field of paleoanthropology, which explores the nature of early humans in their environment, was born. We shall now investigate the findings, and disputes, of these disciplines.

THE EVOLUTIONARY RECORD: HOW DO WE KNOW?

THE ARCHAEOLOGICAL RECORD

We begin the discussion of the archaeological search for the missing link with an account of the major discoveries in the order they were uncovered, addressing the question "How do we know?" At the conclusion, in the chart on page 18 and the representation of skulls on page 19 we see how the pieces of the puzzle fit together in a chronology of evolutions representing "What we know."

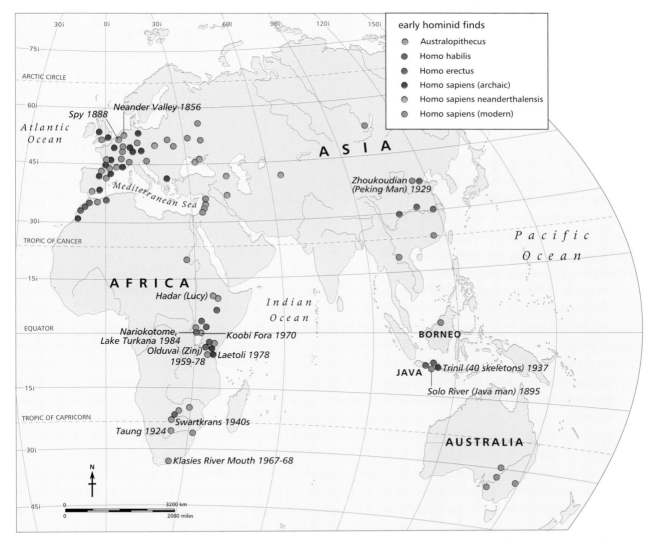

Human ancestors Fossil remains of the earliest direct human ancestors, *Australopithecus* and *Homo habilis*, dating from 1 million to 5 million years ago, have been found only in tropical Africa. The unique soil and climatic conditions there have preserved the fossils. *Homo erectus* remains, from 1.5 million years ago, are the earliest to be found outside Africa. They, along with *Homo sapiens*, have been found throughout Eurasia.

SPOTLIGHT
Reconstructing Neanderthals

Marcellin Boule, a paleoanthropologist at the French National Museum of Natural History, published his (mis)understanding of the anatomy of the Neanderthals between 1911 and 1913. Boule

Figure 1 Diorama of "bovine" Neanderthals.

described the Neanderthal as walking like an ape, with a spine that had no curves, and hunchbacked, with its head pushed forward on top of its spine. He believed that the Neanderthal's long, low skull allowed little space for the segments of the brain that carry higher intelligence. Boule wrote of the "brutish appearance of this muscular and clumsy body, and of the heavy-jawed skull that declares the predominance of a purely vegetative or bestial kind over the functions of the mind" (cited in Time-Life, *The Neanderthals*, p. 19). Later paleoanthropologists found numerous errors in Boule's reading of the fossil record, but for many years his interpretation, and others similar to it, carried great weight. Museum representations carried the erroneous message to the general public. Consider, for example, **figure 1** from a diorama displayed for decades by the world-famous Field Museum of Natural History in Chicago.

How much freedom does an anthropologist, or an artist, have in reconstructing images of the Neanderthals from skeletal

remains? In representing Neanderthals as clumsy and unintelligent, Boule was misreading the fossil bones. Then, his imagination carried him further as he reconstructed the soft tissue that does not survive as fossils: the hair, flesh, and cartilage. **Figure 2** represents

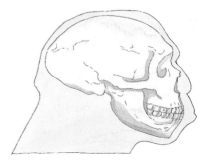

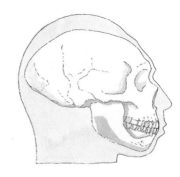

Figure 2 Alternate reconstructions from Neanderthal skull.

two different reconstructions of a Neanderthal man based on a single skull found in La Chapelle-aux-Saints, France, the same skull from which Boule reconstructed his images. The lower diagram is much more human looking, the one on the top far more ape-like. Both are justifiable interpretations based on the evidence available.

Moving beyond the individual skeleton in isolation, teams of experts from disciplines such as biology, geology, and climatology cooperate to reconstruct the natural setting of human and hominid development. As Neanderthal skeletons have been found from northern Europe to Africa, from Gibraltar to Iran, these natural settings vary greatly. In **figure 3**, the Natural History Museum in London represents Neanderthals living in a nuclear family, based on remains discovered at various caves at Gibraltar. Many Neanderthals also lived in larger bands of up to twenty to thirty individuals.

Scholarship on Neanderthals takes new turns with new research technologies. Researchers at the University of Illinois at Chicago, for example, have applied computer technology for reconstructing faces from the skeletal remains of unidentified children to creating images of Neanderthal faces with greater accuracy than ever before. In **figure 4**, Paul Neumann prepares to graft images of living humans on to Neanderthal skulls, bringing new life to the "dead" past.

Figure 3 Reconstructed scene of Neanderthal family outside Gorham's Cave, Gibraltar.

BIBLIOGRAPHY
Bahn, Paul G. ed. *Archaeology* (Cambridge; Cambridge University Press, 1996).

Constable, George and the Editors of Time-Life Books. *The Neanderthals* (New York: Time-Life Books, 1973).

Figure 4 Computer manipulation of Neanderthal facial profiles.

Neanderthals

In August 1856, workers quarrying for limestone in a cave in the Neander Valley near Düsseldorf, Germany, found a thick skullcap with a sloping forehead and several skeletal bones of limbs. Some speculated that it was a deformed human. Others thought it was a soldier lost in a previous war. Other, similar, skeletal remains had been found, but without any clearer understanding of their meaning.

In 1863, Thomas Henry Huxley (1829–95), a leading advocate of Darwin's theory of evolution, argued that the skull was part of a primitive human being who stood between non-human primates and *Homo sapiens*, our own species. He claimed that it was the "missing link." Against those who thought in terms of biblical time spans, Huxley argued that "Evolution will extend by long epochs the most liberal estimate that has yet been made of the Antiquity of Man" (cited in Fagan, *Journey*, p. 10). In 1864, the English anthropologist William King gave a name to the find that signified this intermediate position: *Homo neanderthalensis*. When similar bones and skulls were discovered in Belgium in 1888, scholars began to see that Neanderthal man, far from being a single random accident, was part of a distinct species. Research on Neanderthals continues even now (see Spotlight, pp. 10–11), and in October 1999 palaeoanthropologists Alban Defleur of the University of the Mediterranean at Marseilles, France, and Tim White from the University of California at Berkeley reported in an article in the journal *Science* that at least some Neanderthals were cannibals. The evidence comes from a cave in southern France. A total of seventy-eight bones from at least two adults, two teenagers, and two children of about seven show that the flesh from all parts of the bodies was carefully removed. Bones were smashed with rocks to get at the inside marrow and skulls were broken open. The Neanderthal bones and the bones of deer were tossed together into a heap and show similar marks from the same stone tools. As Defleur notes, "If we conclude that the animal remains are the leftovers from a meal, we are obliged to expand that conclusion to include humans." On the other hand, there are many other examples of Neanderthals burying their dead carefully, suggesting that their cultural behavior differed from group to group.

LANDMARKS IN EARLY LIFE

Years ago (millions)	Geological period	Life form
2500	Archaean	earliest living things
590	Cambrian	first fossils
505	Ordovician	first fish
438	Silurian	first land plants
408	Devonian	first amphibians
360	Carboniferous	first reptiles
286	Permian	reptiles expanded
248	Triassic	first mammals and dinosaurs
213	Jurassic	first birds
144	Cretaceous	heyday of dinosaurs
65	Cretaceous	mammals flourished; dinosaurs extinct
25	Tertiary	first hominoid (ancestor of apes and humans)
5	Tertiary	first hominid (human ancestor)
0.01	Quaternary	modern humans appeared

Homo erectus

In 1891, Eugène Dubois (1858–1940), a surgeon in the Dutch army in Java, Indonesia, inspired by the earlier findings of Alfred Russel Wallace, was exploring for fossils. Employing the labor of convicts in Dutch prisons, along the bank of the Solo River, he discovered a cranium with a brain capacity of 900 cubic centimeters (compared to the modern human average of 1400 cc), a molar, and a femur. Dubois claimed to have discovered "pithecanthropus," ape-man. This find, widely referred to as Java Man, was the first early hominid discovered outside Europe. (Hominids are the human family, from our earliest ancestors and relatives emerging as the human line branched off from apes, up to and including ourselves at present.) Dubois' Java Man forced scholars to consider the theories of the evolution of humans more seriously and to understand the process in a global context.

In 1929, in the vast Zhoukoudian cave 30 miles (48 kilometers) from Beijing, the Chinese archaeologist Bei Qen-Xung and his colleagues discovered a skullcap of *Homo erectus* from about 500,000 years B.P. (Before the Present, a time frame used by archaeologists). In the next few years, in this fossil-rich cave, they discovered fourteen more fossil skulls and the remains of some forty individuals, whom they dated from 600,000 to 200,000 years ago. The cave seems to have been the home of a band of hunters living in a forested, grassy, riverine area, and eating plants as well as animals such as bison and deer. With a brain capacity ranging from 775 to 1300 cubic centimeters and a height up to 5 feet 6 inches (1.7 meters), anatomically Peking (Beijing) Man was almost identical to Java Man.

Beginning in 1937, G.H.R. van Koenigswald, who had followed Dubois' discoveries by returning to Java, excavated a nearly complete skull of *Homo erectus*. This led directly to the discovery of some forty individuals who had lived in Java in 900,000–100,000 B.P. These forty skeletons represent one-third of all the *Homo erectus* skeletons uncovered to this day in the entire world. Another third were in the Zhoukoudian cave. The most complete skeleton we have of *Homo erectus* was discovered, however, in 1984 on the shores of Lake Turkana, Kenya, by Richard Leakey.

Australopithecus africanus

In 1924, in South Africa, a student of professor of medicine Raymond Dart, at the University of Witwatersrand, called to his attention some fossils in a quarry near Taung. After investigation, Dart proclaimed the Taung skull to be *Australopithecus africanus*, "southern apelike creature of Africa," a 2-million-year-old ancestor of humans. Setting out to substantiate Dart's claims, another medical doctor in South Africa, Robert Broom, searched for more fossils. In 1938, he discovered and named *Paranthropus robustus*, or "robust creature parallel to man." Continuing his searches, in the 1940s, in Swartkrans, South Africa, Broom discovered yet another species, which turned out to be *Homo erectus*, the same as had been discovered in China and Java.

Between 1945 and 1955, Dart and his colleagues began to discover bone tools among the hominid

fossils. Dart claimed that he had found the first known hominid culture, dating back 3 million years. Dart also claimed that these hominids had discovered and used fire, a hypothesis based on brown coloration on the bones. Later evaluation suggested that the coloration had come from the dark mineral manganese of the ground in which they lay, but evidence of the use of fire from 1 million years ago, the earliest known control of fire, was subsequently found at Swartkrans. Although some of their claims concerning human control of fire and creation of tools were exaggerated, Dart and his colleagues were extending their concerns beyond the archaeology of the individual hominid skeletons themselves to paleoanthropology, the study of the entire environment in which these hominids had lived. They included in their ecological analyses the animals whose fossils they discovered by the hundreds.

Homo habilis

In the 1930s, Louis Leakey (1903–72) was also excavating in Africa. His most important excavations, however, which were carried out with his wife Mary (1913–96), came between 1959 and 1978 in the Olduvai Gorge, where the Great Rift Valley cuts through northern Tanzania (see Profile, p.14). The Great Rift Valley runs from the Jordan River valley and the Dead Sea southward through the Red Sea through Ethiopia, Kenya, Tanzania, and Mozambique. The Rift is a fossil-hunter's delight. From at least 7 million years ago until perhaps 100,000 years ago, it was a fertile, populated region; it is geologically still shifting and, therefore, has covered and uncovered its deposits over time. Rivers that run through the Rift Valley further the process of uncovering the fossils, and it is volcanic, generating lava and ash that preserve the fossils caught within it and provide the material for relatively accurate dating.

At Olduvai in 1959, the Leakeys discovered *Zinjanthropus boisei*, soon nicknamed Zinj. At first they thought, and hoped, that Zinj might be an early specimen of *Homo*, but its skull was too small, its teeth too large, its arms too long, and its face too much like an ape's. Zinj, who was 1,750,000 years old, was an *Australopithecus*, a hominid closer to apes than to modern humans.

Continued excavations at Olduvai turned up skull fragments of creatures with brain capacities of 650 cubic centimeters, between the 400–500 cc of australopithecines and the 1400 cc of modern

PROFILE
Louis and Mary Leakey
ARCHAEOLOGISTS

With his brilliant finds in the Olduvai Gorge in East Africa, and his tireless efforts at publicizing them, Louis Leakey (1903–72) took paleoanthropology to the public and revolutionized how we think about early humans and their evolution. Before him, most scientists had believed that the earliest human evolution had taken place in Asia; he demonstrated that Africa was the most likely location. His most important finds included the first Proconsul skull complete with face, an early link between monkey and ape; *Zinjanthropus boisei*, a member of the *Australopithecus* genus, at the time the only ape fossil known; and *Homo habilis*, "handy person," who had lived at about the same time as Zinj, demonstrating that *Homo* and *Australopithecus* had lived side by side about 2 million years ago.

Born in Kenya to missionary parents, Louis grew up among the Kikuyu, and was initiated as a member of the tribe. He was most comfortable in the Kikuyu language and published a three-volume anthropological study entitled *Southern Kikuyu*. He had a brilliant academic career at Cambridge University in England, although he suffered rugby injuries that afflicted him with headaches and epilepsy for the rest of his life. The legendary energy that inspired his field work, and the academic fund-raising to support it, also led him to seek the limelight and to exaggerate the significance of many of his discoveries. He was scorned as well as praised by his colleages. Throughout his adult life, he also turned his charismatic charms to attracting young women, another part of his legend. He left his first wife, Frida, just after she delivered their second child, to live with and later marry Mary Douglas Nicol (1913–96). The scandal devastated not only his parents but also his professors and colleagues, putting his early academic career at risk.

Mary, however, was perhaps the perfect academic colleague for the young man. Her father, Erskine Nicol, brought his family from London to southern France where the cave paintings at Dordogne inspired Mary's interest in prehistory and where she began to draw prehistoric artifacts. When they met, Leakey hired her to illustrate his book *Adam's Ancestors*. Soon he invited her to Olduvai Gorge. On site, it was actually Mary who found the skull of the 16-million-year-old Proconsul africanus and the skull of Zinj. Then she painstakingly reconstructed both of these finds from hundreds of fragments. Within the profession, Louis was described as "flamboyant," Mary as meticulous and "scientific." Their son Richard, himself a distinguished archaeologist, talked about the mesh of their styles: "Her commitment to detail and perfection made my father's career. He would not have been famous without her. She was much more organized and structured and much more of a technician. He was much more excitable, a magician." The difference in styles, combined with Louis' attraction to many younger women, finally led to their estrangement, both personal and professional. After Louis' death, Mary's talents became even more clear when she discovered perhaps the most famous of all the Leakey discoveries, the 3.5-million-year-old hominid footprints at Laetoli (see picture opposite). Mary retired from active excavation in 1984 and died in Nairobi in 1996.

Louis and Mary Leakey examining the palate of the Zinj skull, 1959.

humans, and the Leakeys named them *Homo habilis*, "handy person," because of the stone tools they made and used in scavenging, hunting, and butchering food. The Leakeys' discoveries at Olduvai furthered the search for the ancestors of modern humans in several directions: they pushed back the date of the earliest known representative of the genus *Homo* to 1.5–2 million years ago; they indicated the extent of the tool-using capacity of these early *Homo* representatives; and they reconstructed the ecology of the region 2.5–1.5 million years ago, placing *Homo habilis* within it as hunter and scavenger. Along with the earlier discoveries of Dart and Broom, they identified Africa as the home of the earliest hominids and the earliest representatives of the genus *Homo*.

In the 1970s, Richard Leakey (1944–), the son of Louis and Mary, was excavating at Koobi Fora on the east side of Lake Turkana in Kenya, and he discovered additional bones of the species *Homo habilis*. The finds confirmed the size of its brain at about 650 cc; its opposable thumb, which allowed it to grip objects powerfully and manipulate them precisely, and thus to make tools; and its upright, bipedal (two-legged) walk, evident from the form of its thigh and leg bones.

Australopithecus afarensis

In 1974, at Hadar, Ethiopia, near the Awash River, Donald Johanson (1943–) discovered "Lucy," the first known representative of *Australopithecus afarensis*, named for the local Afar people. (Lucy herself was named for the popular Beatles song "Lucy in the Sky with Diamonds.") This important discovery pushed back the date of the earliest known hominid to about 3.2 million years B.P. Lucy's overall height was between 3 feet 6 inches and 4 feet (91–120 centimeters). Her weight was an estimated 60 pounds (27 kilograms). The archaeologists were able to uncover about 40 percent of her total skeleton. In later excavations at Hadar, numerous additional skeletons were found, including the first complete skull of an *Australopithecus afarensis*, discovered by Johanson in 1992.

The cranial capacity of Lucy and her fellow *Australopithecus afarensis* was only 400 cubic centimeters, too small for her to be a *Homo*. Her pelvis was too small to allow the birth of offspring with a larger skull, but the form of that pelvis, and the fit of her knee joints, characterized Lucy as a two-legged hominid. Lucy had walked upright. She was a kind of bipedal ape, and, in her

Hominid footprints, Laetoli, Northern Tanzania. These footprints in ash at Laetoli confirmed that hominids were walking upright 3.5 million years ago. The tracks suggest that *Australopithecus afarensis* had a slower, more rolling gait than modern man, although the prints reveal well-defined feet. Mary Leakey (pictured), who discovered the prints, saw in them a slight sideward turn, a hesitation in direction, which she interpreted as the first evidence of human doubt.

bipedalism, an ancestor of modern humans. Further evidence of the bipedalism of these apelike creatures came from Laetoli, Tanzania, where, in 1978, Mary Leakey discovered the footprints of two *Australopithecus afarensis* walking side by side. In volcanic ash, she found seventy footprints walking a distance of 80 feet (24 meters). The ash provided material for dating the prints; they were 3.5 million years old.

Ardipithecus ramidus

In 1994, seventeen fossils of a new genus, *Ardipithecus ramidus*, "ground ape," were discovered at Aramis in the bed of the Awash River not far from the Lucy find. They were analyzed by an international team of Tim White from the University of California at Berkeley, Gen Suwa from the University of Tokyo, and Berhane Asfaw from the Paleoanthropology laboratory of the Ethiopian Ministry of Culture and Sports Affairs. Ten of the fossils were teeth, two were from the cranium, the remainder were bones from the left arm. Later, the team recovered about 80

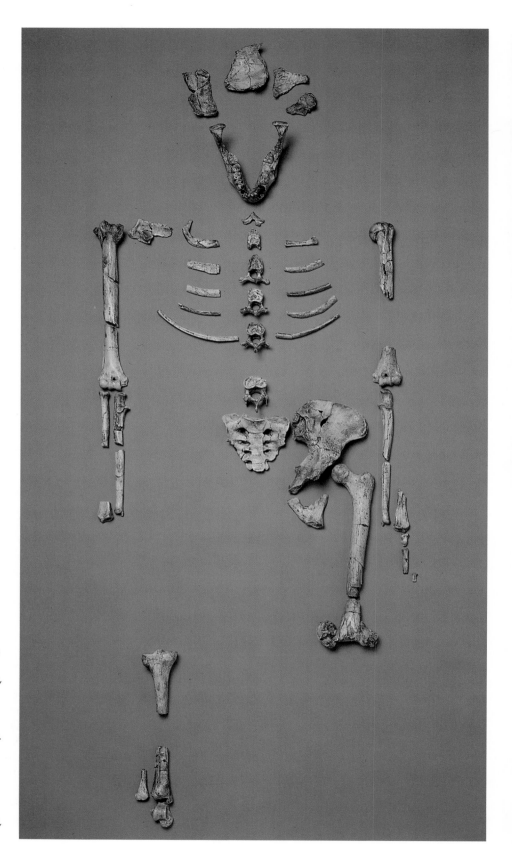

**"Lucy" skeleton,
Australopithecus afarensis,
found at Hadar, Ethiopia.**
"Lucy" is thought to have
lived about 3.2 million years
ago and was at the time of
her discovery in 1974 the
earliest known hominid
ancestor of modern man. She
had humanlike hands and
could walk upright; however,
there is no evidence that she
made or used tools, and her
sturdy, curved arms are still
consistent with tree-climbing.
Until the discovery of
Ardipithecus in 1994, Lucy
was the most complete
hominid skeleton from the
period before 2 million years
ago. (*Natural History Museum,
London*)

percent of an *Ardipithecus ramidus* skeleton. It dated to 4.4 million years, pushing back the date of the earliest ape-like hominid by a half million years.

Because evolution is a process of change over time, there is no more discussion of *the* missing link between apes and humans, but *Ardipithecus ramidus* was *a* missing link in the evolutionary process.

> They [the fossils] represent the remains of a species that lies so close to the divergence between the lineages leading to the African apes and modern humans that its attribution to the human line is metaphorically—and literally—by the skin of its teeth. . . . The metaphor of a "missing link" has often been misused, but it is a suitable epithet for the hominid from Aramis. (Wood, pp. 280–1)

Homo sapiens

The earliest known anatomically modern *Homo sapiens* (Human, wise) fossil was discovered in 1967–8 by the anatomist Ronald Singer and the archaeologist John Wymer in caves at the Klasies River Mouth on the coast of South Africa. These fossil remains of the oldest known example of the species *Homo sapiens* date to 75,000 to 115,000 B.P. They include lower and upper jaws, skull fragments, teeth, and bones of limbs. With them were found thousands of stone quartzite tools, an abundance of bones from numerous land mammals, and the remains of hundreds of thousands of shellfish, suggesting a diet rich in meat and seafood. The Klasies River Mouth discovery raised most provocatively the question of where the first *Homo sapiens* emerged and how they spread.

Before turning to these questions relating to modern humans, let us summarize our current knowledge of the process of hominid evolution.

PUTTING IT ALL TOGETHER

A SUMMARY OF HOMINID EVOLUTION:
WHAT DO WE KNOW?

Our account so far has emphasized How We Know. It has examined some of the major archaeological excavations that have shaped our current understanding of hominid evolution. Now we put those various discoveries into a framework that shows their relationship to one another. We begin to see how each discovery is a building block in our structure of understanding. The chart on page 18 represents that structure. Harvard biologist Stephen Jay Gould has called it the "luxuriant bush" of hominid evolution for we no longer see evolution as a straight-line process moving from apes to humans, but rather as a process resulting in many different species. The arrangement of skulls on page 19 is another representation of the chronology of evolution.

AFRICAN ORIGIN

Almost all paleoanthropologists and archaeologists believe that *Homo erectus* appeared first in Africa and spread from there to Asia and, perhaps, to Europe between 1 and 2 million years ago. But then the scholars split into two camps: the "multi-regionalists" argue that *Homo erectus* evolved into *Homo sapiens* in each region of migration; the "out-of-Africa" camp argues that *Homo erectus* evolved into *Homo sapiens* only in Africa and that about 100,000 years ago the new humans emigrated to the rest of the world in another wave of emigration from Africa. The former thesis is often called the candelabra theory, since it sees the evolutionary branches beginning far back in history in many different locations; the other is often designated the "Noah's Ark" theory, since it proposes a much more recent common ancestry in Africa (see diagram, p. 20).

The two groups of scholars therefore disagree on the origin of racial differentiation among humans. All agree that the varieties of racial development are responses to different ecological niches. If the evolution to *Homo sapiens* began in several different locations based on the *Homo erectus* species already having lived there for up to 2 million years, racial differentiation is very old. If all modern *Homo sapiens* share a common origin until just 100,000 years ago and began to differentiate by race only after emigrating from Africa to new locations, these differences are much more recent. At present, the "out-of-Africa" camp are in the majority. They point out that it is common for just one branch of any particular species to evolve into another and ultimately to displace all the other branches. Indeed, that process is more common than the mutual evolution of all the branches. They therefore tend to minimize the significance of race as a relatively recent, and only "skin-deep," difference among the peoples of the earth.

THE DOMINANT CURRENT VIEW OF THE EVOLUTIONARY PROCESS

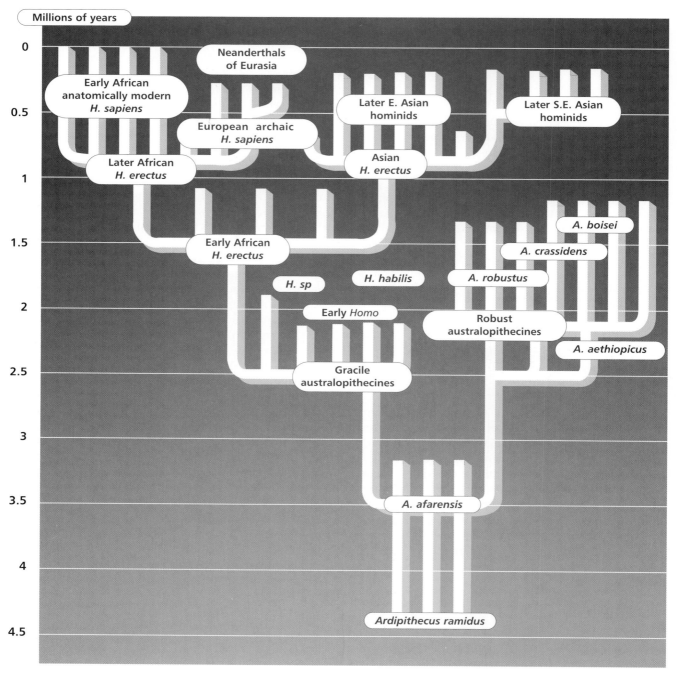

Millions of years

Neanderthals of Eurasia

Early African anatomically modern *H. sapiens*

Later E. Asian hominids

Later S.E. Asian hominids

European archaic *H. sapiens*

Later African *H. erectus*

Asian *H. erectus*

Early African *H. erectus*

A. boisei

A. crassidens

H. sp

H. habilis

A. robustus

Early *Homo*

Robust australopithecines

A. aethiopicus

Gracile australopithecines

A. afarensis

Ardipithecus ramidus

Popular thought usually imagines a straight-line development from apes to humans, but anthropologists speak of a human "bush," a variety of interacting and inter-breeding species that finally produced *Homo sapiens*. Most anthropological models see *Ardipithecus ramidus* and *Australopithecus afarensis* as the first steps in the branching-apart of humans from apes about 5 million years ago. One line of further evolution led toward modern *Homo sapiens*. All the other hominid forms, those in our own line and those in other lines, subsequently became extinct. The model above suggests that the final stages of evolution took place in Europe and Asia as well as Africa, thereby siding with the Candelabra thesis (see p. 20).

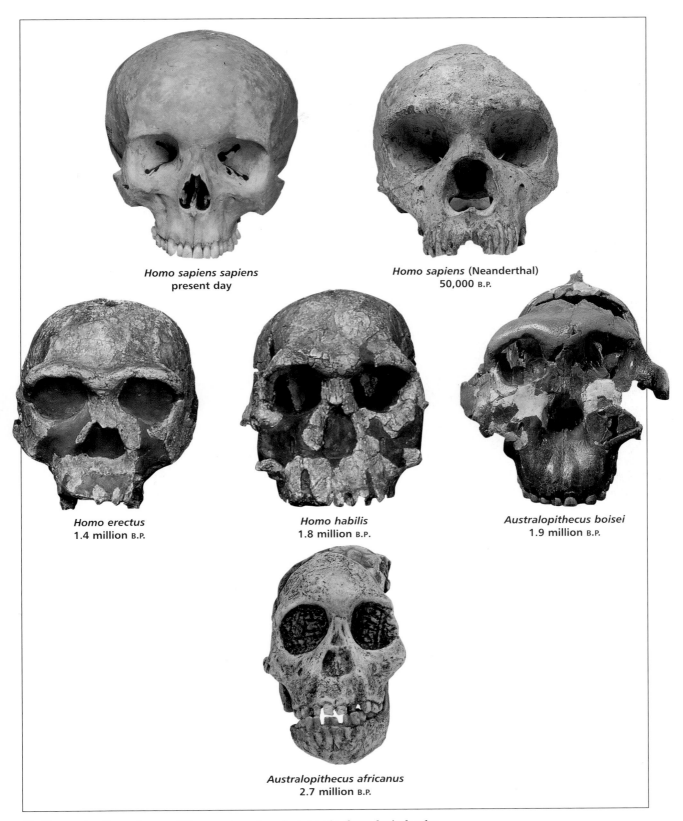

Homo sapiens sapiens
present day

Homo sapiens (Neanderthal)
50,000 B.P.

Homo erectus
1.4 million B.P.

Homo habilis
1.8 million B.P.

Australopithecus boisei
1.9 million B.P.

Australopithecus africanus
2.7 million B.P.

Skull reconstructions of some of the ancestors of modern man in chronological order.

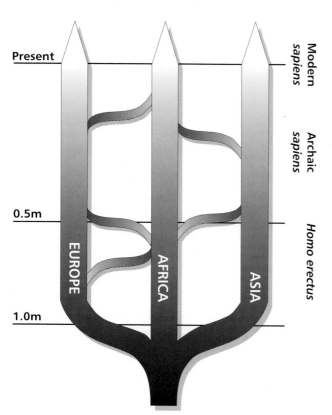

CANDELABRA
No migration, no replacement

Present

0.5m

1.0m

Modern *sapiens*

Archaic *sapiens*

Homo erectus

EUROPE   AFRICA   ASIA

The candelabra, or multiregional, model suggests that *Homo erectus* emigrated from Africa throughout Europe and Asia and developed into *Homo sapiens* separately in all three regions. Some interbreeding did take place.

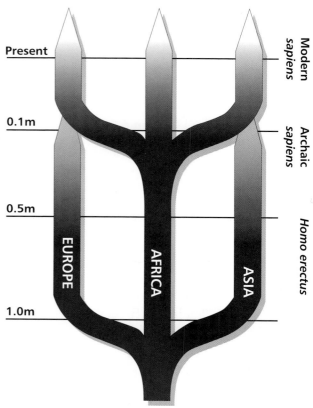

NOAH'S ARK
Migration, replacement

Present

0.1m

0.5m

1.0m

Modern *sapiens*

Archaic *sapiens*

Homo erectus

EUROPE   AFRICA   ASIA

The Noah's Ark model suggests that *Homo erectus* did emigrate from Africa, but then died out everywhere else. The evolution to *Homo sapiens* took place only among those that remained in Africa—who later emigrated to Europe and Asia.

READING THE GENETIC RECORD

In the search for the time and place of the origins of *Homo sapiens*, a different kind of discovery, based on genetics rather than fossils, on laboratory research rather than field excavations, emerged about thirty years ago. At the University of California at Berkeley and at Emory University in Atlanta, scientists began to study the DNA record of human and animal genes. DNA is each cell's chemical code of instructions for building proteins. The DNA research reveals the degrees of similarity and difference among the creatures studied.

Differences and similarities in the proteins and DNA of animals (including humans) living today suggest the date up to which they might have shared common ancestors before separating into different streams of evolution. In 1970, for example, biochemists Vincent Sarich and Allan Wilson first analyzed the protein albumin and the DNA of apes and humans and found that, genetically, modern humans are 97 percent the same as chimpanzees and 96 percent the same as gorillas. They argue that chimpanzees, gorillas, and humans must have shared common ancestors until about 5 million years ago when evolutionary separation must have occurred. This genetic dating matches and reinforces the fossil record.

Both Wilson and Emory scientist Douglas Wallace, extending the method further, have used mitochondrial DNA (genetic material found outside the cell nucleus) to hypothesize that *Homo sapiens* emerged solely from Africa around 100,000 years ago. This confirmation of the "out-of-Africa" theory is, however, controversial—and debate continues to rage. The journal *Nature* frequently carries the reports.

CULTURAL CHANGE AND BIOLOGICAL CHANGE

In addition to the physiological changes favored by natural selection, hominids began actively to shape their environment through cultural activities. *Homo habilis* sculpted stone tools of increasing sophistication. They apparently hunted, scavenged, and gathered in groups and shared their booty. Increasing facility in tool-making would mark all future stages of the evolution of the genus *Homo*.

As the *Homo* brain continued to develop and get bigger, it became impossible for the genus *Homo* to give birth through a relatively narrow birth canal to a child with a fully formed brain in a fully formed cranium. The brain capacity of the young must continue to develop for some time after birth. (The brain of a newborn human weighs about 14 ounces (400 grams), doubles to 35 ounces (990 grams) in about one year, and reaches 45 ounces (1.27 kilograms), adult size, only by about age six or seven.) Within the genus *Homo*, therefore, parents must devote significant time to nurturing and teaching their young children. In addition, in female *Homo sapiens* the oestrus cycle, the alternating period of fertility and infertility, occurs each month rather than seasonally, allowing them to bear children more frequently than other primates. Increased childbearing further increases the time and energy devoted to nurturing the young. Because of the increased attention to nurturing, cultural life could flourish.

Homo sapiens, like *Homo erectus* before them, migrated and spread over the entire earth, except the polar regions. Unlike their predecessors, however, they developed forms of symbolic expression, apparently spiritual and cultural in nature, including burial rituals and artwork that is sometimes stunningly beautiful and creative. These cultural forms suggest that about 35,000 years ago the human brain, but not the rest of human anatomy, went through some further evolutionary development. *Homo sapiens* (wise human) evolved into *Homo sapiens sapiens* (wise, wise human).

KEY STAGES IN HUMAN DEVELOPMENT

4.5 m B.C.E.	First appearance of bipedalism.
2 m B.C.E.	Change in structure of forelimbs—bipedalism is perfected. Gradual expansion and reorganization of the brain. Hunting, scavenging, and gathering cultures stimulate production of stone tools.
500,000 B.C.E.	Rapid brain growth.
200,000 B.C.E.	First forms of *Homo sapiens*. Early speech development. Fire now in use.
40,000 B.C.E.	Interglacial period. Existence of modern humans, with fully developed brain and speech. Tools constructed from component parts.
c. 25,000 B.C.E.	Cave art and portable art in Europe. Human migration begins from Asia into America.
10,000 B.C.E.	Invention of bow and arrows. Domestication of reindeer and dog (N. Eurasia). Settled food production.
8000–4000 B.C.E.	Increase of human population by 1500 percent. Domestication of sheep and goats (Near East). Earliest pottery (Japan). Farming spreads to W. Europe. Rice cultivation starts in Asia.
3000 B.C.E.	Writing, metals.

KEY QUESTIONS REMAINING

The study of early hominids and their evolution into *Homo sapiens sapiens* is filled with questions. Every new excavation and laboratory method of analysis presents new data but often raises questions as well. Sometimes a new discovery can be easily assimilated into existing models: *Ardipithecus ramidus*, for example, had a place ready for it in the evolutionary charts. "The presence of a hominid much like it had been predicted" (Wood, p. 281). Sometimes, however, discoveries are unexpected and create new problems. The analysis of mtDNA, at first viewed as a breakthrough in our understanding of an "African Eve," later posed challenges of method, interpretation, and reliability that remain unresolved.

At present, archaeologists and paleoanthropologists are asking these major questions:

FOCUS
Gender Issues and Cultural Evolution

In 1971 anthropologist Sally Slocum, writing under the pseudonym of Sally Linton, published one of the first feminist critiques of the current understanding of the evolution of hominids. Slocum was responding to a conference and set of papers published from it in 1968 entitled *Man the Hunter*. One of the papers, by Sherwood Washburn and C. Lancaster, asserted: "The biology, psychology, and customs that separate us from the apes—all these we owe to the hunters of time past." This argument, Slocum replied, put excessive emphasis on aggressive behavior, the tools and organized planning required for hunting, the importance of fresh meat in the hominid diet, and male activities generally.

In "Woman the Gatherer: Male Bias in Anthropology," Slocum asserts that gathering was more important than hunting:

> We know that gathering was important long before much animal protein was added to the diet, and continued to be important. Bones, sticks, and hand-axes could be used for digging up tubers or roots, or to pulverize tough vegetable matter for easier eating. If, however, instead of thinking in terms of tools and weapons, we think in terms of *cultural inventions*, a new aspect is presented. I suggest that two of the *earliest and most important* cultural inventions were containers to hold the products of gathering, and some sort of sling or net to carry babies. (p. 46)

Further, she argues, the skills of raising and nurturing young children, usually women's tasks, evoked more innovation and perhaps more development of the brain than did hunting:

> I suggest that longer periods of infant dependency, more difficult births, and longer gestation periods also demanded more skills in social organization and communication—creating selective pressure for increased brain size without looking to hunting as an explanation. The need to organize for feeding after weaning, learning to handle the more complex social–emotional bonds that were developing, the new skills and cultural inventions surrounding more extensive gathering—all would demand larger brains. Too much attention has been given to the skills required by hunting, and too little to the skills required for gathering and the raising of dependent young. The techniques required for efficient gathering include location and identification of plant varieties, seasonal and geographical knowledge, containers for carrying the food, and tools for its preparation. (pp. 46–7)

Slocum concluded that she could reach her new interpretations only after confronting assumptions of male dominance. As she puts it, "The basis of any discipline is not the answers it gets, but the questions it asks."

---

1 Did *Homo sapiens* evolve in a more or less straight line, family tree development from *Ardipithecus ramidus* and *Australopithecus afarensis* through *Homo habilis* and *Homo erectus*, or was there a "bush" of clades, related species, and subspecies at every level? Was the development through that "bush" different from evolution supported by the majority of paleoanthropologists?

2 In what ecological environment did the australopithecines live? *Australopithecus afarensis*, according to Johanson and the Leakeys, seemed to inhabit a savanna region in which bipedalism was an advantage in crossing open land quickly and efficiently. Paleoecological studies surrounding *Ardipithecus ramidus*, however, suggest a wooded habitat.

3 What were the group living conditions of australopithecines and of the genus *Homo*? Were they monogamous, as some researchers have claimed? Did they live in groups, and if so, of what size? Clearly they came together to hunt, scavenge, and share the preparation and eating of food, but did they also live more permanently at home bases?

4 To what extent did early members of the genus *Homo* hunt and to what extent did they forage and scavenge? Apparently they did both, hunting small game and scavenging the remains of big game left over from the kills of predatory animals. Further studies of regional ecology and of fossils of human prey will reveal more about the diet of our early ancestors and their method of food procurement.

5 Fire was first used and then controlled by *Homo erectus*, perhaps 1 million years ago, as discovered in the Swartkrans cave in South Africa, more certainly in China 500,000 years ago. Fire gave warmth, light, protection from predators, a means of cooking food, a hearth around which a feeling of community could develop, and thus the capacity of turning a cave into a home. Can we know more about when and how this mastery occurred?

6 Why did each of the evolutionary lines die out, the various *Australopithecus robustus* and *boisei* species of 1–2 million years ago, the later hominids of east and southeast Asia, and the "archaic" *Homo* species of approximately 100,000 years ago, such as *Homo sapiens neanderthalensis*?

7 When did the genus *Homo* become capable of speech? What is the relationship between the biological evolution of *Homo* and the mastery of new cultural skills, such as control of fire, group planning, tool-making, speech, and the use of symbols? To what extent do biological changes enable cultural change? Conversely, to what extent do cultural advances enable species to survive biologically, perpetuating themselves and their offspring?

8 What was the division of labor between males and females in the various hominid species? Were males more likely to hunt and scavenge abroad, and females more likely to raise children and gather food near to home? (see Focus opposite). What was the significance of the large difference in size between males and females among the australopithecines?

THE THEORY OF SCIENTIFIC REVOLUTION

We have given a lengthy introduction on the emergence of the first humans. Many historians would choose to move more quickly toward the present, although, of course, in covering 4.5 million years in one chapter we *are* moving swiftly! Some historians would be more comfortable covering "historic" times and places—that is, working with written records—but we have chosen to elaborate this account not only for its intrinsic interest but also because it helps demonstrate most clearly our concern with "how we know" as well as with "what we know," a concern that continues throughout this text.

Paleoanthropologists maintain a lively debate about each of their findings and interpretations. They not only present their views but situate them within the ongoing debates in their field. This admirable procedure should inform all historical research and presentation, showing the historical record as an ongoing search and argument. Existing data may be reevaluated; new data may be added; interpretations may be revised; new questions may arise. The historical record is never complete.

Amendments to the historical record, however, are usually minor additions to, or revisions of, a pattern already well known. Thomas Kuhn, in his pathbreaking study of the history of science, *The Structure of Scientific Revolutions*, wrote of his own field that

> normal science . . . is a highly cumulative enterprise, eminently successful in its aim, the steady extension of the scope and precision of scientific knowledge. Normal science does not aim at novelties of fact or theory and, when successful, finds none. (Kuhn, p. 52)

The history of the evolution of hominids, for example, usually follows this pattern of "normal science." Thus when *Ardipithecus ramidus* was discovered in 1994, paleoanthropologists were not surprised. "There was . . . enough 'morphological space' between the hypothetical common ancestor of African apes and hominids, on the one hand, and *A. afarensis* on the other, to predict that a hominid, as yet undiscovered, would occupy it" (Wood in *Nature*, p. 281). This was normal science filling in an existing model, or paradigm, with new detail.

Sometimes, however, new discoveries challenge existing paradigms. At first the new discoveries are discounted as exceptions to the rule. But when the anomalies increase, scientists seek new explanatory paradigms. Darwin's breakthrough followed this second pattern of scientific revolution. His discoveries on the voyage of the *Beagle* and his subsequent analyses of his findings challenged the existing concepts of creation that were based on biblical narratives. Darwin provided a radically different scientific explanation of the mechanisms of evolution that displaced the biblical paradigm. Both Darwin's scientific analysis and Genesis' mythological narrative, however, postulate the creation of an entire cosmos and world, replete with flora and fauna, before humans achieve their place in the universe and begin to name the other species.

Major revisions of the historical record often follow a similar trajectory. A general pattern of explanation is followed until new research raises new questions and new theoretical paradigms provide more fitting explanations for all the available data and information. Throughout this text we shall continue to see changes in historical explanation over time. A "paradigm shift" may occur not only as a result of the discovery of new data, or of new interpretations better fitting the available data, but also in response to new questions being raised that may not have been asked before. The historical record, like the scientific record on evolution, is always subject to reevaluation.

HUMANS CREATE CULTURE

The first appearance of *Homo sapiens* in the archaeological record dates to about 120,000 years ago in South Africa at the Klasies River Mouth excavation, although the DNA record suggests that their first appearance might have been as early as 250,000 B.C.E. Since that time the species

Two Aurignacian implements, France, Mesolithic era (c. 30,000 B.C.E.). Stone Age cultures first appeared in western Europe in 33,000 B.C.E. and underwent constant changes in technology—implying a gradual evolution in human behavior. By the Aurignacian era, flint-end scrapers (right) were employed in processing skins, woodworking, and carving artifacts like this bone spearpoint (left). (*Natural History Museum, London*)

Homo sapiens has not changed anatomically. The skeletons unearthed at the Klasies River Mouth are no different from our own. About 100,000–50,000 years B.C.E., however, a new creativity appeared in the cultural and social life of *Homo sapiens*, perhaps the result of a modification in the internal structure of the brain. The people who lived before this development are called "archaic" *Homo sapiens*; those with the new cultural capabilities are considered a new subspecies, *Homo sapiens sapiens* (Human wise, wise). They are us.

The remainder of this chapter presents seven creative behaviors that mark the arrival of *Homo sapiens sapiens*. First, we persisted. We are the lone survivor from among all the hominids of the last 5 million years. Second, we continued to spread to all parts of the globe in waves of migration that had begun even earlier. Third, we built small, temporary settlements to serve as base camps for hunting and gathering. Fourth, we continued to craft more sophisticated tools from stone. The steady improvements in tool technology give this period its archaeological names. The entire period is called the old stone age, **Paleolithic**, and exhibits slow progression from the Lower Paleolithic, older old stone age, the remains of which are found lower in the ground, ending about 150,000 B.C.E., to the newer old stone age or Upper Paleolithic, which continued to about 10,000 B.C.E. (The Mesolithic and Neolithic, middle and new stone ages, 8000–6000 B.C.E. and 6000 B.C.E. to about 3000 B.C.E., respectively, will be explored in Chapter 2.) Fifth, by about 25,000 B.C.E., on cave walls and in stone, we began to paint and sculpt magnificent works of art and symbolism. Sixth, we elaborated more sophisticated use of language. Seventh, by 10,000–15,000 B.C.E., we began to domesticate plants and animals, introducing the art and science of agriculture.

HOW DID WE SURVIVE?
HOW DO WE KNOW?

From about 120,000 B.C.E., when we first appear in the archaeological record, until about 35,000 B.C.E., anatomically modern *Homo sapiens sapiens* seems to have coexisted alongside archaic *Homo sapiens* in several sites. The best studied are caves in the area of Mount Carmel near Haifa, Israel. First excavated in 1929 by Dorothy Garrod of Cambridge University, these caves have revealed skel-

etons and tools of both Neanderthals and modern humans. The fossils from the Tabun, Amud, and Kebara caves seem to be Neanderthals; those from Skhul and Qafzeh appear more modern.

DATING ARCHAEOLOGICAL FINDS

Continuous improvements in dating techniques have changed our understanding of the relationships among the *Homo* residents who inhabited these caves. The most common technique, since its discovery in 1949, is **radiocarbon dating**, sometimes called the carbon 14 (C14) method. Living organisms contain the same percentage of atoms of radioactive carbon as the atmosphere in which they live. When they die, the radiocarbon atoms disintegrate at a steady, known rate. By measuring the amount of radiocarbon remaining in a fossil skeleton, scientists can calculate backward to the date of death. Because the total amount of radiocarbon in any organism is small, little is left after 40,000 years, and the method does not work at all beyond 70,000 years. Until 1987, paleoanthropologists using carbon 14 dating believed that Neanderthals dated to approximately 60,000–50,000 years B.C.E., and *Homo sapiens sapiens* to 50,000–45,000.

After 1987, the method of **thermoluminescence** was applied to burned flints discovered in the caves. Radioactivity occurring in nature releases electrons in flint and clay, but they can finally escape only when the substance is heated. When the flints were first burned by the people of the caves, the electrons freed up to that time were released. Reheating the flints in the laboratory today releases the electrons stored up since the first burning. Scientists calculate the date of the first burning by measuring the light of those electrons. This technique works not only for burnt flint from 50,000–300,000 years of age, but also for burnt clay, enabling scientists to date pottery from the last 10,000 years.

The measurement of age through thermoluminescence gave new and astounding dates to the skeletons in the caves. The oldest Neanderthal, from Tabun, dated to 120,000–100,000 B.C.E.; the two *Homo sapiens sapiens* at Qafzeh and Skhul were almost equally old, at 92,000 B.C.E.; the two Neanderthal specimens at Kebara and Amud dated to 60,000–50,000 B.C.E. One can only conclude, therefore, that Neanderthals and modern humans had coexisted in the area of modern Israel for tens of thousands of years. Moreover, they had shared similar types of tools. The simpler, smaller Mousterian stone tools (named for the village of Le Moustier in southwestern France where they have been most clearly documented) of the Neanderthals were used alongside the thinner, longer, more precisely crafted Aurignacian tools (named for another hunter-gatherer site in southern France) of the moderns.

How, then, did modern *Homo sapiens sapiens* eventually displace all other hominids? Three principal interpretations, in various combinations, have been suggested. The first is that modern humans defeated all the other hominids through aggression, warfare, and murder. This theory suggests a violent streak in the earliest humans. The second theory suggests that processes of mating and reproduction among the species bred the new human. This suggests that our immediate ancestors made love not war, and that we contain a Neanderthal heritage. Finally, it has been proposed that modern humans successfully filled up the ecological niche available, outcompeting archaic *Homo sapiens* for the available resources. According to this final theory, modern humans did not directly confront the archaic forms but displaced them—in a sense, we ate them out of house and home.

GLOBAL MIGRATION

Homo sapiens sapiens appeared in Africa not later than 120,000 B.C.E., evolving from *Homo erectus*. Within 30,000 years the species began to appear throughout Europe and Asia. Harvard anthropologist Clive Gamble asserts that it was not

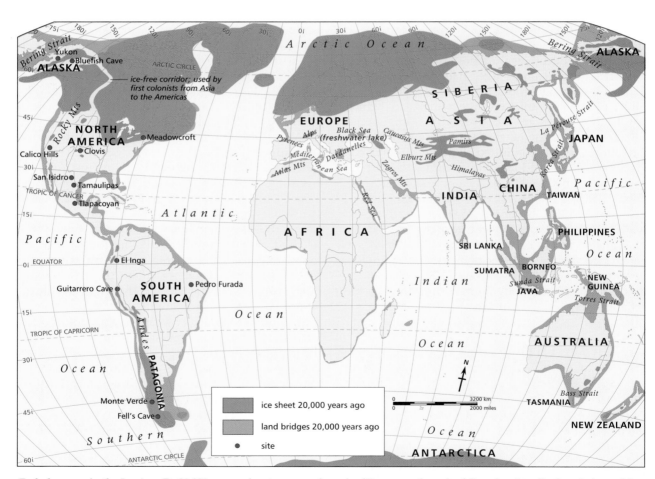

Early humans in the Ice Age By 20,000 B.C.E., when ice covered much of Europe and much of Canada, virtually the whole world (except Polynesia) had been colonized. Early humans were able to spread north because water frozen into ice sheets reduced sea levels so much that land bridges appeared, linking most major areas. The cold was intense, and the migrants' survival depended on their ability to stitch together animal hides into primitive clothing, control fire, and hunt large mammals.

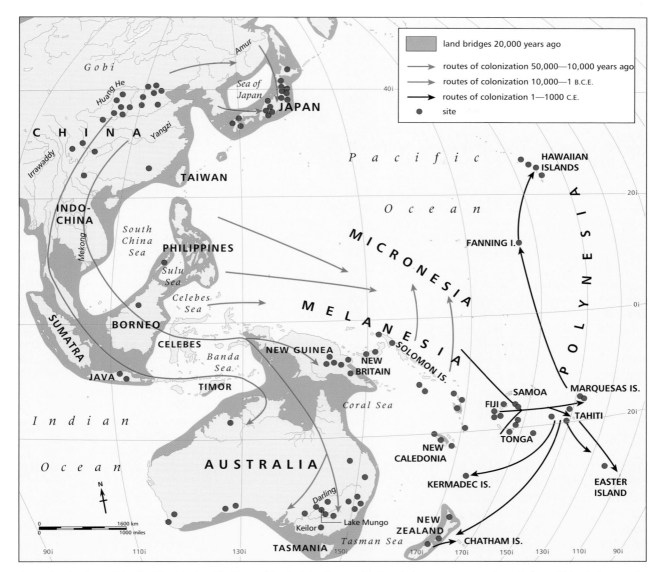

The colonization of the Pacific The land bridges of the last Ice Age enabled early humans to spread south from China to Java and Borneo. There some knowledge of navigation was required to cross the Banda Sea to New Guinea and Australia. The most spectacular voyages were undertaken by the Polynesians, who journeyed hundreds and thousands of miles by canoe into the uncharted Pacific waters.

simply a part of human nature to migrate around the globe. Rather, each migration was purposeful and specific. From earliest prehistory, people weighed their choices and opportunities, and chose appropriate actions. Global migration was the ultimate outcome.

Brian Fagan's analysis of the "Saharan pump" provides an example of such migration. Up to about 90,000 B.C.E., when the earth was in a warm, wet stage, the Sahara region was fertile and attractive to human settlement, and people and animals from southern Africa migrated there. But

then began an "ice age," one of the periods of global cooling that have affected the earth's climate over millions of years. When the ice age of about 90,000 B.C.E. began, much of the earth's water was frozen. The Sahara dried up, turning the land to desert, and people and animals emigrated. Some may have turned back to southern Africa; some may have journeyed toward the North African coast (a few archaeologists believe that they may have crossed the Straits of Gibraltar into western Europe); still others may have followed the Nile valley corridor into western Asia. So began what Fagan calls *The Journey from Eden*, the first step in a global process of migration.

To reach the most distant areas, such as Australia, the islands of the Pacific, and the Americas, took tens of thousands of years. These migrations required changes in climate as well as in the skills of *Homo sapiens sapiens*. The successive ice ages of 90,000–10,000 years ago froze much of the water of the seas, reducing sea levels, extending the coasts of the continents, and creating land bridges linking modern China with Japan, southeast Asia with the Philippines and Indonesia, and Siberia with Alaska. As long as the ice ages continued and the waters of seas and oceans were in frozen retreat, people could migrate across land passages. There were exceptions. The Pacific islands known as Polynesia were not connected by land bridges to anywhere. This helps explain why they were peopled so much later in history than most other regions. Only in 1000 B.C.E. was Polynesia colonized by native New Guineans, performing extraordinary feats of navigation in simple canoes.

INCREASED POPULATION AND NEW SETTLEMENTS

Gradually, as human population expanded, so, too, did the number of human groups and the closeness or "density" of their relationships to one another. Such increasing density and population pressure became a staple of human history. Some groups chose to stand and fight for their territory, others reached accommodation with newcomers, and yet others emigrated, either by choice or by force, following losses in battle. These patterns, too, have repeated themselves for tens of thousands of years, and today there are some 20 million refugees in the world.

How large were these groups? They had to include enough members to provide security in defense and cooperation in work, yet be small enough to resolve the interpersonal frictions that threatened the cohesion of the group and the safety of its members. Calculated from the experience of modern hunter-gatherers, such as the Khoisan of the African Kalahari Desert, and theoretical mathematical models of group process, a five-family group of twenty-five persons seems the ideal balance. Mating and marriage rules

might well have required, as they often do today, choosing a mate from outside the immediate band. For such an **exogamous** marriage pattern to function, "a tribe would require at least 475 people to provide an adequate mating pool or a mating network of nineteen twenty-five-member bands, a theoretical figure reasonably close to the real life 500" found in modern hunter-gatherer societies, concludes anthropologist John Pfeiffer in *The Creative Explosion* (p. 192).

How much territory did such bands require to support themselves? Anthropologist H. Martin Wobst calculated that an individual using the technology of Upper Paleolithic times (150,000–10,000 B.C.E.) would have required 77 square miles (200 square kilometers) of relatively unproductive land or 7–8 square miles (20 square kilometers) of fertile land to meet survival needs. At such densities, the area of the United States (excluding Alaska and Hawaii) might have supported a maximum of 600,000 people; the entire world, 10 million at most, although actual populations were less. Bands began to stake out their own territories, and to mark out boundaries.

> There is increasing evidence that Upper Paleolithic groups may have occupied certain key locations on a more stable, semi-permanent basis, which would almost inevitably act as a further incentive to the definition of more sharply defined social territories, and to a more formalized pattern of reciprocal relationships between the occupants of adjacent territories. (Mellars, p. 356)

The groups began to establish small settlements. The Neanderthals had occupied upland sites, but the later Cro-Magnon *Homo sapiens sapiens* (named for the region in France where this subspecies was originally discovered) moved down into the more valuable valleys and riverbeds. About half of their sites are within 1100 yards (1000 meters) of a river, and all of them are near fords or shallows. These sites not only allow for easy crossing, but they are also at the points of animal crossings and therefore good for hunting.

Tools took on regional patterns both in processes of manufacture and in styles of aesthetic appearance. These local patterns marked off each group from its neighbors. Mellars argues that this regional, tribal differentiation, marking the production of increasingly sophisticated tools, suggests also the development of "relatively complex, structured language" (Mellars, p. 359) (see p. 34).

CHANGES IN THE TOOLKIT

STONE TOOLS

Even as the pace of exploration, migration, and trade increased, the clearest changes in human development appeared in our stone toolkits. From about 2.5 million years ago until about 150,000 years ago, the dominant technology of *Homo erectus* had been Acheulian hand-held axes and cleavers made of stone (named for St. Acheul in northern France, but actually developed first in Africa and only later throughout Europe and Asia).

About 250,000 B.C.E. the European sites, and some elsewhere, reveal a more sophisticated technique, the Levallois (named for a suburb in Paris where the first examples were discovered). This Levallois technique produced more precise tools, including side scrapers and backed knives, fashioned by more consistent patterns of preparing flakes from the stone, and a more standardized final shape and size. This technique marked the emergence of archaic *Homo sapiens*.

The technology of *Homo sapiens sapiens* developed much more rapidly. By about 40,000 B.C.E., Aurignacian tools were being produced in or near a cave near the present-day village of Aurignac in the Pyrenees. This technology included narrow blades of stone as well as tools crafted from bone, ivory, and antler. Gravettian styles followed, about 30,000 to about 20,000 B.C.E; then came Solutrean styles, 20,000–17,000 B.C.E., which included the production of the first known needles; Magdalenian, about 17,000–12,000 B.C.E., which included barbed harpoons carved from antlers; and finally Azilian, 12,000–8000 B.C.E. Each location and time period had its own aesthetic style, and each produced an increasing variety of tools. Tool patterns began to differ increasingly from one region to another, suggesting the formation of new communities among small hunter-gatherer bands, and a greater sense of separation and distinction between groups.

Not all tools were directly related to food production, nor even to work. Flutes from as early as 35,000 B.C.E., made from the bones of birds, reindeer, and bears, suggest that creating and performing instrumental music had already become part of the human repertoire. Aesthetics and play already had their roles.

THE EARLIEST TOOL KITS

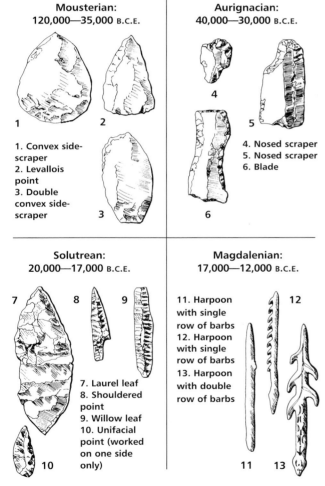

Mousterian:
120,000—35,000 B.C.E.

1. Convex side-scraper
2. Levallois point
3. Double convex side-scraper

Aurignacian:
40,000—30,000 B.C.E.

4. Nosed scraper
5. Nosed scraper
6. Blade

Solutrean:
20,000—17,000 B.C.E.

7. Laurel leaf
8. Shouldered point
9. Willow leaf
10. Unifacial point (worked on one side only)

Magdalenian:
17,000—12,000 B.C.E.

11. Harpoon with single row of barbs
12. Harpoon with single row of barbs
13. Harpoon with double row of barbs

Many of the earliest human tools were crafted from stone and show increasing sophistication. The "tool kits" shown here are named for the four different locations in which they were found. At first, humans simply chipped away at stone until edges and points were exposed. Later they began to carve the stone to meet more specific needs. The development took 100,000 years.

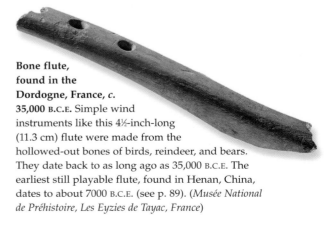

Bone flute, found in the Dordogne, France, c. 35,000 B.C.E. Simple wind instruments like this 4½-inch-long (11.3 cm) flute were made from the hollowed-out bones of birds, reindeer, and bears. They date back to as long ago as 35,000 B.C.E. The earliest still playable flute, found in Henan, China, dates to about 7000 B.C.E. (see p. 89). (*Musée National de Préhistoire, Les Eyzies de Tayac, France*)

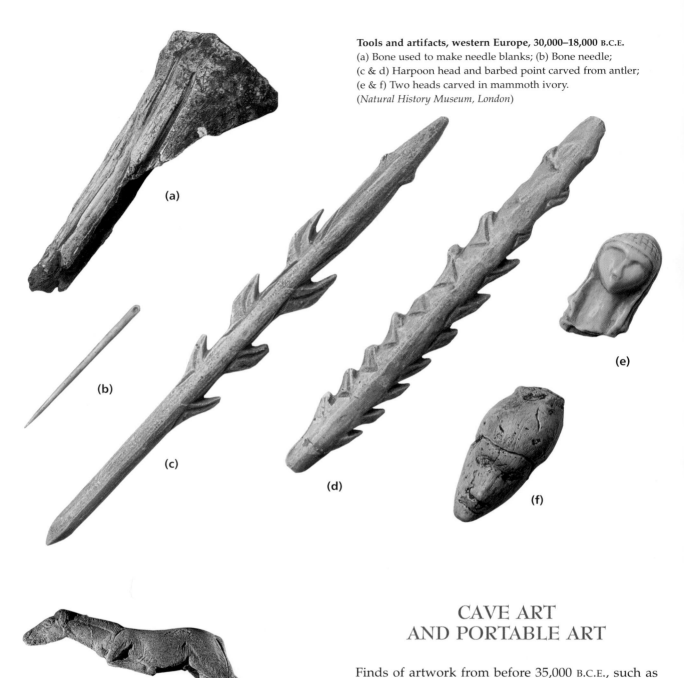

Tools and artifacts, western Europe, 30,000–18,000 B.C.E.
(a) Bone used to make needle blanks; (b) Bone needle;
(c & d) Harpoon head and barbed point carved from antler;
(e & f) Two heads carved in mammoth ivory.
(*Natural History Museum, London*)

(a)

(b)

(c)

(d)

(e)

(f)

CAVE ART AND PORTABLE ART

Finds of artwork from before 35,000 B.C.E., such as beads, pendants, and incised animal bones, are rare and disputed. Cave paintings and the statuettes came later, and they appeared in numerous sites around the world. At Kundusi, Tanzania, Mary Leakey discovered stylized ocher paintings of human beings dating back perhaps 25,000 years. On the southern coast of Australia, in the Koonalda Cave, a flint mine at least 20,000 years old, a crisscross of abstract finger patterns was engraved into the soft limestone. In

Spearthrower, Montastruc, France, 12,000 B.C.E. More than 14,000 years ago, beauty played an integral part in purely functional objects. Spearthrowers allowed hunters to propel their missiles with a surer aim and added leverage, as is symbolized by the streamlined and powerful figure of this leaping horse. Did the shape of the bone suggest the animal, or did the artist search for a bone to match his (or her) preconceived idea?

eastern Australia at about the same time, people were stenciling images of a hand and a pipe and stem onto the walls of Kenniff Cave. And at Kakadu, in northern Australia, a series of rock paintings begin about 20,000 B.C.E. Local peoples continued to paint new ones almost to the present.

In Europe, the artwork begins with some figurines and some wall painting as early as 30,000 B.C.E. and climaxes about 17,000–12,000 B.C.E. More than 200 decorated caves and more than 10,000 decorated objects (portable art) have been discovered in Europe, 85 percent of them in southern France and northern Spain. Many of the tools from the Magdalenian period, as noted above, were fashioned to be beautiful as well as practical. Many of the figurines include delicately

carved features, such as the face and hair on the figurine from about 22,000 B.C.E. discovered at Brassempouy, France, and only about 1½ inches (4 centimeters) high (see picture (e), opposite). Many others pay scant attention to face and personal features, but accentuate and exaggerate sexual organs and buttocks, such as the 25,000-year-old figurine discovered at Dolní Vestonice, Moravia. On some cave walls, people have created bas reliefs, shallow sculptures still attached to the rock, of similarly exaggerated female forms. The portable art represents a desire to create and enjoy beautiful objects. The exaggerated forms of the female, "Venus" objects that appear throughout Europe and on into northwestern Asia suggest also a desire for human fertility.

FOCUS
Women's Tools, Women's Work

Not all tools have survived. Those made from natural fibers have, of course, disintegrated, which precludes exploring the preparation of food and clothing. A fascinating book by Elizabeth Wayland Barber, *Women's Work: The First 20,000 Years: Women, Cloth, and Society in Early Times*, explains why these functions usually belonged to women. Barber cites an article by anthropologist Judith Brown that argues that most societies have decided, overtly or tacitly, that women's work must be compatible with the demands of child care. Women can and do undertake all kinds of work, but the only work on which the community relies on a regular basis is work compatible with child care, including pregnancy, breast feeding, and child watching.

> Such activities have the following characteristics: they do not require rapt concentration and are relatively dull and repetitive; they are easily interruptable and easily resumed once interrupted; they do not place the child in potential danger; and they do not require the participant to range very far from home. (Brown, cited in Barber, pp. 29–30)

What tasks fit this description? Spinning, weaving, sewing, and food preparation. "Food and clothing:

These are what societies worldwide have come to see as the core of women's work (although other tasks may be added to the load, depending upon the circumstances of the particular society)" (Barber, p. 30). For historians of the stone age, the problem of presenting this aspect of the human record is in finding evidence, because food substances and textiles decay with hardly a trace.

What can we speculate about the first clothing? Some "Venus" figures (see p. 32) had sculpted on them skirts made of twisted strings suspended from a hip band. The sculpture itself indicates that woven strings of fiber rather than a single piece of leather were worn. Speculating on the use of these early string skirts, Barber notes that they would not have provided much warmth or protection, and she suggests that they were symbolic of the sexually attractive see-through adornments that women must have worn to attract men or to invoke spirits to increase their fertility. The further representation of loosely woven, transparent, short skirts on later sculptures supports these theories. Combining artifacts from the past and examples from the present, historians begin to reconstruct a whole area of technological development, most likely in the hands of women, that had been overlooked through the focus on stone tools.

The first of the cave art was rediscovered only in 1868, although the 14,000-year-old art of this cave, at Altamira near Santander, Spain, was not recognized as prehistoric until 1902. By now, 200 caves decorated with artworks have been discovered in Europe, most of them in the river valleys of southwest France and the adjacent Pyrenees and the Cantabrian Mountains of northern Spain. The latest discoveries, stunning in the variety of animal life depicted and the artistry employed, have been the Cosquer Cave in 1991 and the Chauvet Cave in December 1994. The painters used natural pigments like ocher that produced reds, browns, and yellows, and manganese oxides that made black and violet. Blues and greens have not been found. Human figures are rare in the European caves, the usual representations being of large animals, such as bison, deer, wild oxen, and horses. Occasionally there are mammoths, lions, and even fish. Fantasy figures, such as unicorns, also appear. At caves such as Le Tuc d'Audoubert, France, sculptures of clay bison have been found. In many caves, human hands have been stenciled onto cave walls by projecting pigment around the hands. No one knows how the pigments were applied, but the most common guess is that they were chewed and then either spat directly or blown through a pipe onto the walls.

Some of the cave art was abstract, some representational, some painted, some in relief, but it was not continued past the Magdalenian age, about 12,000 B.C.E, when the traditions and their meanings were abandoned. Many of the techniques of the cave paintings, such as perspective and the feeling of movement, did not reappear in Western art until the Renaissance, about 1400 C.E. (see p. 404). When the cave art was rediscovered in the nineteenth century, its antiquity was not understood. Ever since its rediscovery, however, people have wondered about its function and meaning.

The first interpretation to gain widespread acceptance argued that the paintings represented a kind of magic designed to bring good fortune to the hunters of the animals represented on the cave walls. The seemingly abstract geometrical patterns, argued the Abbé Henri Breuil, represented hunting equipment such as traps, snares, and

Clay bison, from Tuc d'Audoubert, Ariège, France, after 15,000 B.C.E. Most cave art owes its survival to the very particular atmospheric conditions formed in the limestone caves in which they were sealed thousands of years ago. Only a very small number of sculptures have survived. The one reproduced here—in high relief—shows a female being pursued by a male bison.

weapons. The mural paintings of animals may represent a hope for their fertility so that the hunters might find abundant prey. Other interpretations of the functions of the cave art followed. Margaret Conkey, author of *Art and Design in the Old Stone Age*, argued that the caves were meeting grounds to which neighboring bands of people returned each year to arrange marriages and to cement political and social alliances. The different styles of paintings in each cave represent the artistic production of many different groups.

The art is often located not at the mouth of the cave, where it would have been on daily view of the campsites, but deep in the inner recesses. Why were so many images—about one-third of the total—painted so deep in the caves? It has been suggested that they were not just decorative, but

"Venus" figurine, found at Dolní Vestonice, Moravia, c. 23,000 B.C.E. Several hundred early female figures have been recovered, but no male figures. This seems to support the thesis that these statuettes were created, not so much as representations of ideal feminine beauty, but as fertility charms—notice how the breasts, buttocks, and thighs are emphasized to the exclusion of any individualizing facial traits.

Chauvet Cave, Rhône-Alpes region, France, 18,000 B.C.E. On Christmas Day 1994, a team of archaeologists led by Jean-Marie Chauvet discovered a cave 1640 feet (500 m) deep in the Ardèche River Canyon. The cave's 300-plus Paleolithic wall paintings of horses, buffalo, and lions are the earliest examples anywhere in the world.

were links to ancient spirits, which were re-membered and invoked in the dark depths of the cave. David Lewis-Williams, a South African arch-aeologist trying to puzzle through the origins of the cave art not only in western Europe but also in Namibia, southern Africa, where cave art goes back more than 25,000 years, observed the sham-anistic rituals of the San people of the Kalahari desert. Shamans self-induce trances through the use of drugs, breathing exercises, singing, dancing, and rhythmic clapping. They enter into trance states of increasing intensity in which they "see" first geometric patterns, then images from nature, and finally creatures not found in nature at all. Sometimes they see these various images as projections on the wall. Lewis-Williams suggests that the Upper Paleolithic cave paintings represent such shamanistic hallucinations or visions from trance states.

The cave art and the portable art of 25,000–10,000 B.C.E. begin the known record of human aesthetic creation. For the first time we have examples of what humans felt to be beautiful and therefore worth creating and preserving. From this time onward, the desire to create and appreciate beauty is part of the human story. The cave creations also give us insight into their creators' search for meaning and purpose in life. Our art gives outward expression to our understanding of and our deepest feelings about our place in the world. In our art we express our fears and our hopes for ourselves, our loved ones, our communities, our world. Through our art we attempt to connect with larger forces in the world and to communicate with one another. By studying the form and meaning of art, historians attempt to understand the external aesthetics and the inner world of the people who produced it.

LANGUAGE AND COMMUNICATION

Language is an intangible innovation, invisible in the archaeological record. It must be inferred from more solid evidence: global migration, fixed settlement sites, new tools and new materials, regional differences in production, trade across long distances, social hierarchies often marked by personal adornment and ritual burials, and the creation of art and instrumental music. Lewis Binford concludes:

> If you ask "what makes this possible," you'd say intelligence, yes. But more important is language, and, specifically, symboling, which makes abstraction possible. I don't see any medium through which such a rapid change could occur other than a fundamentally good, biologically based communication system. (cited in Lewin, p. 163)

Exactly when the system of spoken language emerged is much debated, especially because we can only infer the answer from circumstantial evidence. The craniums of archaic *Homo sapiens*, such as Neanderthals, were as large as, or even larger than our own, and they seem to have indentations indicating the presence of areas in the brain that influence speech capacity. Archaic *Homo sapiens* probably possessed a larynx that had descended sufficiently low in the throat to produce the sounds of modern human language.

The dispute enters here. Some anthropologists believe that with this biological equipment, humans began slowly to develop modern language and speech through cultural evolution. Others, notably linguist Noam Chomsky, believe that a change took place within the organization of the brain that gave humans a new capacity for language. Chomsky draws his conclusion from analyzing similarities in the "deep structure" of languages around the world. These universal similarities suggest that the rules of syntax of human language are embedded in the brain. Chomsky argues that just as humans are born to walk so they are born to talk. Just as bipedalism is not a learned cultural capacity, but has evolved biologically, in the same way talking is not culturally learned but has biologically evolved. The use of individual languages is, of course, culturally specific.

Modern language provided the ability to communicate with others on an individual basis. It also allowed for increasingly elaborate social structures and greater complexity in human relationships. It facilitated deliberation over ethical principles of conduct for guiding and regulating those relationships. Moreover, it allowed for increasingly sophisticated internal thought and reflection. We could become more introspective as well as more communicative with others. The sophisticated psychological and social relationships that make us human became possible only with the development of language.

AGRICULTURE: FROM HUNTER-GATHERER TO FARMER

Some hunter-gatherers began to stay for longer periods at their temporary campsites. They noted the patterns of growth of the grains they gathered and the migration habits of the animals they hunted. They began to experiment in planting some of the seeds of the largest, most nutritious cereals in the Middle East and Europe; maize in the Americas; root crops in southeast Asia. In addition to pursuing animals as prey, men may have tried to restrict their movements to particular locations, or to have built their own campsites at points frequented by the animals, adjusting human movements to those of the animals. They learned to domesticate dogs, and domesticated dogs may have accompanied the first Americans on their travels across Beringia. In the Middle East the sheep was the first species to be domesticated, perhaps 10,000 years ago.

By 15,000–10,000 B.C.E., humans had the biological and cultural capacity to farm and raise animals. But first they had to want to do so. Otherwise why give up hunting and gathering? Why settle down? Perhaps the transformation took place at sites of especially valuable and accessible natural resources, such as the fishing sites of the Jomon people of Japan, or the quarries of obsidian stone, used for making sharp cutting tools, around Çatal Hüyük in modern Turkey. A permanent source of food to eat or materials to trade might have outweighed the desire to shift with the seasons and travel with the herds.

Perhaps rising population pressures left humans no alternative. The press of neighbors restricted scope for travel. On limited land, hunter-gatherers found that planting their own crops and domesticating their own animals could provide them with more food than hunting and gathering. Despite the risks of weather and of plant and animal diseases that left agricultural settlements vulnerable, some groups began to settle. Ten thousand years ago, almost all humans lived by hunting and gathering. Two thousand years ago, most were farmers or herders. Moreover, in the midst of this transformation, which created the first agricultural villages, cities, too, grew up as the central administrative, economic, and religious centers of their regions. A new era was beginning. It is the subject of the next chapter and Part 2.

BIBLIOGRAPHY

Barber, Elizabeth Wayland. *Women's Work: The First 20,000 Years: Women, Cloth, and Society in Early Times* (New York: W.W. Norton & Co., 1994).

Brown, Judith. "Note on the Division of Labor by Sex," *American Anthropologist* LXXII (1970), 1075–6.

Chauvet, Jean-Marie, Eliette Brunel Deschamps, and Christian Hillaire. *Dawn of Art: The Chauvet Cave, the Oldest Known Paintings in the World* (New York: Abrams, 1996).

Clottes, Jean and Jean Courtin. *The Cave Beneath the Sea: Paleolithic Images at Cosquer* (New York: Abrams, 1996).

Conkey, Margaret W. *Art and Design in the Old Stone Age* (San Francisco: Freeman, 1982).

Darwin, Charles. *The Origin of Species by Means of Natural Selection or the Preservation of Favored Races in the Struggle for Life*, reprinted from the Sixth Edition, ed. Edmund B. Wilson (New York: Macmillan Company, 1927).

Darwin, Charles. *The Works of Charles Darwin*, ed. Paul H. Barrett and R.B. Freeman, Vol. XV *On the Origin of Species* 1859 (New York: New York University Press, 1988).

Darwin, Charles. *Darwin*, ed. Philip Appleman (New York: W.W. Norton and Co., 2nd ed., 1979).

Defleur, Alban, Tim White *et al.* "Neanderthal Cannibalism at Moula-Guercy, Ardèche, France," *Science* (October 1, 1999), 286:128–131.

Fagan, Brian M. *The Journey from Eden* (London: Thames and Hudson, 1990).

Fagan, Brian M. *People of the Earth* (New York: HarperCollins Foresman and Co., 8th ed., 1995).

Fedigan, Linda. "The Changing Role of Women in Models of Human Evolution," *Annual Review of Anthropology* XV (1986), 22–66.

Gamble, Clive. *Timewalkers: The Prehistory of Global Colonization* (Harvard University Press, 1994).

Gould, Stephen Jay. *Ever Since Darwin: Reflections in Natural History* (New York: Norton & Company, 1977).

Holm, Jean, with John Bowker, eds. *Myth and History* (London: Pinter Publishers, 1994).

Johanson, Donald, Lenora Johanson, and Blake Edgar. *Ancestors: In Search of Human Origins* (New York: Villard Books, 1994).

Leakey, Richard and Roger Lewin. *Origins Reconsidered* (New York: Doubleday, 1992).

Lee, Richard B. and Irven DeVore, eds. *Man the Hunter* (New York: Aldine, 1968).

Lewin, Roger. *The Origin of Modern Humans* (New York: Scientific American Library, 1993).

Linton, Sally (pseud. for Sally Slocum). "Woman the Gatherer: Male Bias in Anthropology," in Sue-Ellen Jacobs, ed. *Women in Perspective: A Guide for Cross-Cultural Studies* (Urbana: University of Illinois Press, 1971).

McNeill, William H. *Mythistory and Other Essays* (Chicago: University of Chicago Press, 1986).

Mellars, Paul and Chris Stringer, eds. *The Human Revolution: Behavioural and Biological Perspectives on the Origins of Modern Humans* (Princeton: Princeton University Press, 1989).

Morell, Virginia. *Ancestral Passions: The Leakey Family and the Quest for Humankind's Beginnings* (New York: Simon & Schuster, 1995).

The New English Bible (New York: Oxford University Press, 1976).

Past Worlds: The (London) Times Atlas of Archaeology (London: Times Books Ltd., 1988).

Pfeiffer, John. *The Creative Explosion* (Ithaca: Cornell University Press, 1982).

Scott, Joan W. "Gender: A Useful Category of Historical Analysis," *American Historical Review* XCI (1986), 1053–76.

White, Tim D., Berhane Asfaw, and Gen Suwa. "Ardipithecus ramidus, A Root Species for Australopithecus," in F. Facchini ed. *The First Humans and Their Cultural Manifestations* (Forli, Italy: A.B.A.C.O., 1996), 15–23.

Wood, Bernard. "The Oldest Hominid Yet," *Nature* Vol. 371 (Sept. 22, 1994), 280–81.

2 *Settling Down*

THE FIRST CITIES AND WHY THEY MATTER: DIGS, TEXTS, AND INTERPRETATIONS

The establishment of urban settlements marked a new era in many parts of the world. Although the physical existence of the new cities, with their thousands of inhabitants, is the most obvious transformation, many equally significant, though less tangible changes, accompanied it. Cities were nodes in the regional networks of exchange of goods and culture, and they encouraged the production of sophisticated arts, the specialization of labor, and the elaboration of a social hierarchy. Most significantly, however, cities signaled the emergence of a state organization. The new state, hand-in-glove with the new city, provided leadership, organization, control of official armed power, an inegalitarian stratification of population, and power over the people, sometimes with their consent, sometimes without. In all these functions, the ancient city reminds us of our own.

Unlike modern cities, however, almost all early cities were relatively small. The largest contained perhaps 100,000 people in 8 square miles (20 square kilometers); most had only a few thousand inhabitants. Until the industrial revolution in the late nineteenth century, a few thousand people concentrated in 100 acres (40 hectares) might have constituted a city, for cities held only a tiny percentage of the total population of any region. Most of the world's population were farmers or hunter-gatherers when the first cities were invented. The multiplication of cities and urban residents that we see today took place only after the industrial revolution created new urban factories, transportation hubs, and mass labor

Teotihuacán, Mexico. The Pyramid of the Moon (foreground) is linked to the Pyramid of the Sun by the Avenue of the Dead.

forces. Moreover, many of the early cities, although small, were centers of independent city-states; most cities today are single points in much larger national and even international networks.

Finally, the earliest cities emerged in each of seven regions around the world. They developed as cosmo-magical shrines. Paul Wheatley traced this concern for the supernatural in the Chinese city especially, but it is a phenomenon we will see from Mesopotamia to the Nile, from the Indus to the Niger, and perhaps most of all in the Valley of Mexico and in the high Andes Mountains. Many of the early cities were dedicated to gods and were built on existing shrine centers. As the cities grew, the shrines grew with them, providing a more profound meaning to the lives of their inhabitants by linking their mundane existence to transcendent and powerful supernatural forces.

2 FROM VILLAGE COMMUNITY TO CITY STATE

10,000 B.C.E.—750 B.C.E.

"Man is by nature a zoon politikon, a creature of the city-state."

ARISTOTLE

WHAT ARE CITIES AND WHY ARE THEY IMPORTANT?

FOOD FIRST: THE AGRICULTURAL VILLAGE

Until about 12,000 years ago humans hunted and gathered their food, following the migrations of animals and the seasonal cycles of the crops. They established temporary base camps for their activities, and caves served them for homes and meeting-places, but they had not established permanent settlements. They had begun to domesticate some animals, especially the dog and the sheep, but they had not yet begun the systematic practice of agriculture. Then, about 10,000 B.C.E., people began to settle down, constructing the first agricultural villages. Why did they do it? Is food production through agriculture easier than hunting and gathering? Surprisingly the answer seems to be "no." Research by Cohen and Reed suggests that, with the technology available at that time, adult farmers had to work an equivalent of 1000–1300 hours a year for their food, while hunter-gatherers needed only 800–1000 hours. Moreover, agricultural work was more difficult.

Why did they change? An appealing, although unproved, answer is that increasing population pressure, perhaps accompanied by worsening climatic conditions, forced people to take on the more productive methods of agriculture. Scientists estimate that even in a lush tropical environment, 0.4 square miles (1 square kilometer) of land could support only nine persons through hunting and gathering; under organized, sedentary agricultural techniques, the same area could support 200–400 people. In the less fertile sub-tropical and temperate climates into which the expanding populations were moving at the end of the last ice age, after about 13,000 B.C.E., hunting and gathering were even less productive. To survive, sedentary agriculture was a necessity. The myth of Shen Nung, the Chinese inventor of agriculture and its wooden tools (and of poetry), captures the transformation:

> The people of old ate the meat of animals and birds. But in the time of Shen Nung, there were so many people that there were no longer enough animals and birds to supply their needs. So it was that Shen Nung

		EARLY WEST ASIA	
DATE	POLITICAL	RELIGION AND CULTURE	SOCIAL DEVELOPMENT
4500 B.C.E.	• Ubaid people in Mesopotamia		
3500 B.C.E.	• Sumerians (3300–2350)	• Cuneiform writing • Sumerian pantheon • Ziggurats built	• Urbanization in Mesopotamia
3000 B.C.E.	• Hereditary kings emerge		• Mycenaean traders in Aegean • Invention of the wheel • Bronze casting • Sumerian city–states (2800–1850)
2500 B.C.E.	• Ur, First Dynasty (2500–2350) • Akkadian kingdoms (2350–2150); Sargon of Akkad (2334–2279) • 3rd Dynasty of Ur (c. 2113–1991)	• Akkadian language used in Sumer • *Epic of Gilgamesh* (c. 2113–1991)	
2000 B.C.E.	• Semitic rulers gain control of Mesopotamia • 1st dynasty of Babylon (c. 1894–1595) • Hammurabi (1792–1750) • Hittites in Asia Minor		
1500 B.C.E.	• Hittite Empire (c. 1460–1200)	• "Golden age" of Ugarit	• Code of Law
1000 B.C.E.	• Assyrian Empire (900–612)	• Hebrew Scriptures recorded	
750 B.C.E.	• Sargon II (d. 705) • Sennacherib (c. 705–681) • Ashurbanipal (d. 626) • Fall of Nineveh (imperial capital) (612) • Nebuchadnezzar (605–562)	• *Gilgamesh* (complete version) • Homer (*fl.* 8th century) • Hesiod (*fl.* 700)	
600 B.C.E.	• Neo–Babylonian Empire	• Library at Nineveh	
500 B.C.E.	• Persian Empire in control of Mesopotamia		

taught the people how to cultivate the earth. (Bairoch, p. 6)

In addition to increasing agricultural productivity, villages facilitated an increase in creativity of all kinds. It may have taken longer to raise food than to hunt and gather it, but the sedentary farmers did not stop work when they had secured their food supply. In their villages they went on to produce textiles, pottery, metallurgy, architecture, tools, and objects of great beauty, especially in sculpture and painting. Did the agriculturists work comparatively harder than the hunter-gatherers simply to survive under greater population pressure, or because they craved the added rewards of their extra labor, or both? We can never know for sure, but the agricultural village opened new possibilities for economic, social, political, and artistic creativity—while closing others. It changed forever humanity's concepts of life's necessities and potentials.

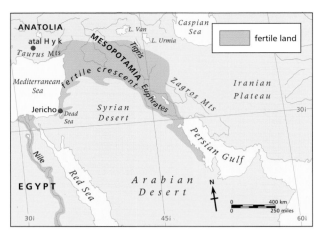

The Fertile Crescent The Tigris and Euphrates rivers gave life to the first known agricultural villages, about 10,000 years ago, and the first known cities in human history, about 5000 years ago. Fertile land extended to the Mediterranean and some contact apparently continued on to the Nile Valley. Its parameters were defined to the north and east by mountains and semi-arid plateaux and to the south by arid regions receiving less than 10 inches (250 mm) of rainfall per year.

Basic Crops and Livestock

The first agricultural villages that archaeologists have discovered date to about 10,000 B.C.E. They are located in the "fertile crescent," which curves from the Persian Gulf and the Zagros Mountains in the east and south, on the border of today's Iraq and Iran, northwest into Anatolia, present-day Turkey, and then turns south and west through present-day Syria, Lebanon, and Israel on the Mediterranean Sea. Here, wild grasses, the ancestors of modern wheat and barley, provided the basic grains, first for gathering, and later for cultivation. By 8000 B.C.E. the Natufians, named for their valley in northern Israel, and the peoples immediately to the south, in the Jordan River valley near Jericho, were growing fully domesticated cereals. Peas and lentils and other pulses and legumes followed. The peoples of the fertile crescent hunted gazelles and goats. Later, they domesticated the goat and the sheep. In Turkey they added pigs; around the Mediterranean, cattle.

In other parts of the world, agriculture and animal domestication focused on other varieties. In the western hemisphere, these included maize, especially in Mesoamerica, and root crops such as manioc and sweet potatoes in South America. Amerindians domesticated the llama, the guinea pig, and the turkey. Domesticated dogs probably accompanied their migrant masters across the

Bering Straits about 15,000 years ago. Perhaps the process of domestication was then repeated with the dogs found in the Americas.

In southeast Asia and in tropical Africa, wild roots and tubers, including yams, were the staple crops. In the Vindhya Mountain areas of central India, rice was among the first crops to be cultivated, about 5000 B.C.E. Anthropologists are uncertain when rice was first cultivated, rather than just being harvested from the wild, in southeast and east Asia, but a date similar to India's seems likely. From earliest times, as today, China's agriculture seems to have favored rice in the south and millets in the north. Some crops, including cotton and gourds, were brought under cultivation in many locations around the globe.

Our knowledge of early agriculture continues to grow as the archaeological record is expanded and revised. European sedentary agriculture, for example, which was once thought to have been borrowed from the Near East, may have been a local response to changing climate conditions.

Neolithic Tools, Products, and Trade

The era in which villages took form is usually called **Neolithic**, or New Stone Age, named for its tools rather than its crops. In the fertile crescent, where the process first began, this corresponds to about 8000–4000 B.C.E. For cutting, grinding, chopping, scraping, piercing, and digging, village artisans fashioned new tools from stone. Archaeological digs from Neolithic villages abound with blades, knives, sickles, adzes, arrows, daggers, spears, fish hooks and harpoons, mortars and pestles, and rudimentary plows and hoes.

As villages expanded their economic base these stone tools were often valued as items of trade. Obsidian—a kind of volcanic glass—was traded from Anatolia and is found in hundreds of digs from central Turkey to Syria and the Jordan valley. Among other items of trade, recognized by their appearance in digs a long distance away from their point of origin, are seashells, jade, turquoise, and ceramics.

Although ceramics occasionally appear among non-sedentary populations, the weight and fragility of clay make pottery essentially a creation of the more established Neolithic village. As a vessel for storage, pottery further reflected the sedentary character of the new village life. The fine designs and colors decorating its pottery became the most distinctive identifying mark of the Neolithic

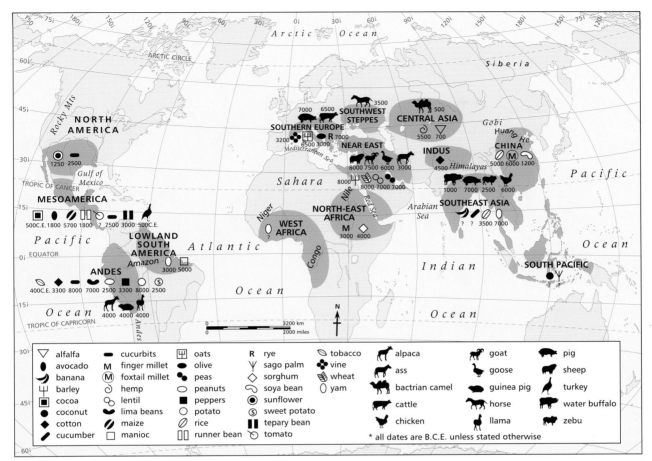

The origins of agriculture and domestic animals. The development of agriculture and the domestication of animals took place independently in different parts of the world, but the Near East, Mesoamerica, southeast Asia, and China were among the first and most significant regions. Cereal grasses such as wheat, barley, rice, and maize, and tubers such as potatoes, yams, and cassava, became staple crops in the major centers. This cultivation of plants was complemented by the domestication of wild animals, beginning with dogs, cattle, goats, sheep, pigs, and, in the western hemisphere, llamas.

village, and archaeologists often designate eras, locations, and groups of people by descriptions of their pottery—the "grayware," the "red glazed," or the "cord-marked," for example. Simple pottery is easy to make and accessible to anyone, but specialized craftspeople developed ceramics into a medium of artistic creativity. Fine ceramic jewelry, statuary, and figurines attained great beauty and were frequently used in religious rituals.

Historical change, however, does not proceed in a uniform, straight line. Historians must be alert not only to general patterns, but also to exceptions. Some villages did form on an economic base of hunting-and-gathering. In southern Japan, for example a non-agricultural village society appeared among the Jomon people along with some of the earliest and most beautiful of pottery. Jomon pottery, which is marked by distinctive cord lines,

dates back to 10,500 B.C.E. and spread from the southern island of Kyushu, northward through Honshu, reaching Hokkaido by 6500 B.C.E. The Jomon villagers supported themselves from fishing, hunting deer and wild boar, and gathering and storing nuts. They created stone tools and lived in caves and in pit-houses in settled villages with central, communal buildings. Yet the Japanese did not develop agricultural cultivation for another several thousand years.

THE FIRST CITIES

The first cities were constructed on the economic base of sedentary village agricultural communities. In excavating these earliest cities around the globe, archaeologists ask which city forms were invented

SPOTLIGHT
Ban Po, China

INTERPRETING AN EARLY NEOLITHIC VILLAGE

While digging the foundation for a factory ten miles (16 kilometers) west of X'ian, China, in 1953 workers uncovered one of the world's oldest and best-preserved Neolithic villages dating back to 6000 B.C.E. Archaeological investigation revealed that the residents cultivated millet and domesticated pigs and dogs. They practiced slash-and-burn (swidden) agriculture; pollen samples show distinct alternating periods of cultivation and fallow.

The Ban Po Excavation, preserved today under an enormous hangar-like structure, provides insights not only into the life of the villagers, but also into the interpretive frameworks of the modern archaeologists and government officials responsible for the site. **Figure 1** presents a model of the original village displayed on-site. It represents Ban Po's three housing styles: square, round, and an oblong split-level, with part underground and part above. Underground pits used for storage are visible throughout the village. A moat surrounds the entire settlement.

A large square building dominates the village center. What function did it serve? In many regions such a structure might have housed a political or religious official. Here, the official posting on the excavation identifies the central structure as "a place for the Ban Po inhabitants to discuss public affairs." This emphasis on shared community planning is consistent with understandings of many early villagers, before the establishment of states. It is also consistent with the ideology of the current Chinese communist government: Before the creation of states, village communities were egalitarian and self-governing.

Figure 2 represents one of the three forms of housing. Its perimeter is identified by the holes in the ground, still recognizable today, that were made by the wooden posts supporting the walls. Building materials were all natural to the area, from the plaster of the floor

Figure 1 Model reconstruction of Ban Po.

Figure 3 Burial urn from Ban Po, 4500 B.C.E.

Farming in China Evidence of the earliest established agriculture in east Asia is found in the arid but fertile regions of north central China, along the central reaches of the Huang He (Yellow River). Villages such as Ban Po grew up on the floodplain, rich in alluvial and loess deposits, where drought-resistant plants such as millet could be cultivated.

and walls to the straw of the thatched roof and the brushwood covering the external walls.

Burial urns, **figure 3**, held the remains of children who died young. Seventy-six such burial urns have been discovered within the residential area. Adults were buried in a public graveyard to the north of the village, adjacent to a pottery production center with six kilns. Some 250 graves were excavated there. It is unclear why children and adults were buried separately.

Ban Po villages stored their grain in some 200 pits that were dug throughout the village. An interpretive sign on-site explains "This reflects *public ownership* in the clan community" (my emphasis). Could the scattering of the storage pits suggest instead *private ownership*, in which each family had its own nearby pit? How deeply does the official ideology of a nation affect its interpretation of archaeological remains? How deeply does each reader's value system affect his or her interpretation?

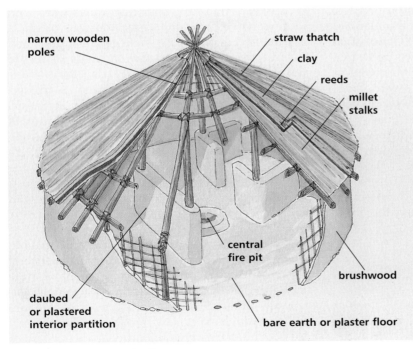

Figure 2 Typical Ban Po dwelling.

THE EARLIEST URBAN SETTLEMENTS

3500 B.C.E.	Rise of Sumer, southern Mesopotamia.
3100	Emergence of Egyptian state; new capital at Memphis.
2500	Development of Mohenjo-Daro, urban civilization on the Indus plain.
2500	City-states in northern Mesopotamia and the Levant, dominated by palace complexes.
1800	Urban growth after Shang dynasty established in northeast China.
1200	Formative period in Mesoamerica, marked by first shrine centers, especially the Olmec.
c. **400** B.C.E.	City states in Mesoamerica and South America.
400 C.E.	Urbanization of Jenne-Jeno, Nigeria, sub-Saharan Africa.

indigenously, by their own inhabitants, and which were borrowed from earlier examples or, perhaps, imposed from outside on local rural populations. Technically, the question is one of **innovation** versus **diffusion**. Thus far, most experts agree that innovative primary urbanization, not borrowed or imposed from outside, took place in seven places: five river valleys in the eastern hemisphere—Mesopotamia, the Nile, the Indus, the Huang He, and the Niger—and, in the western hemisphere, along the Gulf of Mexico and in the interior valleys of Mexico, and in the Andes Mountains. The birth of primary urbanization took place in these seven locations at very different times, with Mesopotamia the oldest at about 3300 B.C.E. and the Niger the most recent at about 400 C.E.

THE MEANING OF CITIES

Cities transform human life. The physical form of the early cities tells the story vividly. Even today we can trace on the surface of the earth the 5500-year-old designs of the first cities and the irrigation systems that supported them. Remnants of walls and fragments of monuments of these first cities still rise from their sites. From under the surface archaeologists salvage artifacts: bricks; pottery; tools of wood, bone, stone, and metal; jewelry; and skeletons of citizens and slaves. The technology of the early cities included new means of transportation; we find the remains of wheeled vehicles and of sailboats. The earliest city dwellers advanced their skills in metallurgy, and products of their craftsmanship in copper, tin, and their alloys abound in the archaeological excavations. In recognition of these technological breakthroughs we often call the era of the first cities the "bronze age."

But cities are more than bricks and mortar, metal and artifacts. They require institutions for their larger scale of organization and administration. As society and economy became more complex, new class hierarchies emerged. Professional administrators, skilled artisans, long-distance traders, local merchants, and priests and kings enriched the diversity and sophistication of the growing cities. External relations with other cities required skilled negotiations, and a diplomatic corps emerged. Armies mobilized for defense and attack. In short, with the growth of the city the early state was also born, with its specialized organization, centralized rule, and powerful armies.

To keep track of business transactions and administrative orders, the proclamations of rulers and the rituals of priests, the legends of gods and the histories of the city, new methods of record keeping were developed. At first these were tokens, pictures, seals, personalized markings, and, in the Andes, *quipu*, knots made in special lengths of string (see picture, p. 379). By about 3300 B.C.E., in Sumer, which is geographically equivalent to today's southern Iraq, the world's first system of writing had evolved, one of the most revolutionary inventions in human history. The prestigious occupation of scribe was born, and schoolteachers soon followed. (College professors took much longer.)

From earliest times, city dwellers and analysts understood and commented on the significance of the first urban revolution. Today, we have more reason than ever to value and to evaluate its 5000-year-old heritage, for in modern times we are living through two new urban revolutions. By 1800 the industrial revolution opened a new era of urban development that re-invented the cities of western Europe and North America (see Chapter 16). In the twentieth century peasants streamed by

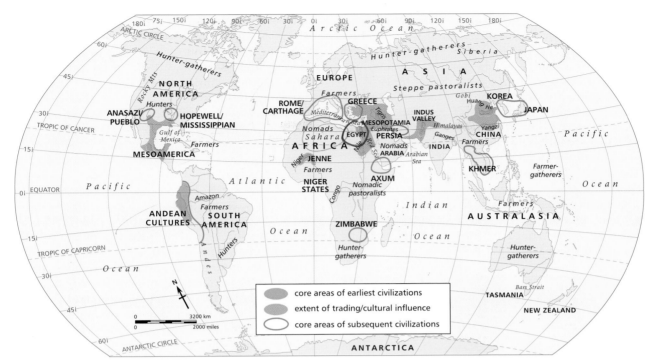

The spread of civilizations The first civilizations developed where unique local climatic and soil conditions, favorable to settled agriculture, occurred, mostly in major river basins. With the development of an agricultural surplus came the growth of urban centers, trade, and population. Secondary civilizations tended to develop in regions adjacent to these heartlands, or along trade routes between them.

the millions and tens of millions from rural villages to mammoth cities, creating massive, unprecedented urban environments around the globe (see Part 6). So we search humanity's earliest experiences with cities not only to understand our ancestors but also to understand ourselves.

SUMER

SUMER: WHAT DO WE KNOW?

The Birth of the City

The Sumerians pioneered the world's first urban revolution in Mesopotamia. They migrated into southern Mesopotamia about 3500 B.C.E., perhaps from around the Caspian Sea, but no one knows for sure. Archaeological excavations of pottery show the earlier presence in Mesopotamia of the Ubaid peoples, beginning about 4500 B.C.E. The use of Semitic word forms and names by the Sumerians suggest that Semites, too, had preceded them in the area. But for a millennium, from 3300

B.C.E. until 2350 B.C.E., the Sumerians lived in warring city-states and dominated the region. In 2350 B.C.E., Sargon, the Semitic ruler of Akkad, just to the north, conquered Mesopotamia and ruled it as a consolidated empire.

After some 200 years under Akkadian rule, the Mesopotamian city-states regained independence and resumed their inter-urban warfare until about 1750 B.C.E., when Hammurabi of Babylon dealt them a final defeat and the Sumerian peoples began to vanish from history. The cities they had built—Kish, Uruk, Ur, Nippur, Lagash, Umma, and dozens of smaller ones—died out, having fought each other to exhaustion. Mesopotamia was conquered successively by Hittites, Assyrians, Babylonians once again, Achaeminid Persians, and Greeks under Alexander the Great. The Sumerian cultural legacy lived on, however, absorbed into the literature, philosophy, religion, law, and new patterns of urbanization of their conquerors.

Size

What are the characteristics of the urban revolution in Mesopotamia? How do its cities differ from the earlier villages? The most obvious feature is that urban scale in physical size, population, and territorial control is much greater. The Neolithic village housed a few dozens or a few hundreds of residents on a few acres. Jericho, the oldest known sedentary agricultural village, was founded about 8500 B.C.E. and grew to about 10 acres (4 hectares) by 7000 B.C.E. It was surrounded by a stone wall 10 feet (3 meters) thick, capped at one point by a stone tower 30 feet (9 meters) high. The largest Neolithic site in the Near East, Çatal Hüyük in Anatolia, grew by 5500 B.C.E. to occupy slightly more than 30 acres (12 hectares). It became a town. By comparison, the first cities of Mesopotamia were ten times larger, accommodating about 5000 people.

Stone tower and wall, Jericho, *c.* **8000 B.C.E.** Before Sumer, a Neolithic community based at Jericho in the Jordan valley, Palestine, was the first to develop cereals of a fully domesticated type. In 8000 B.C.E these farmers, keen to secure their settlement in the arid environment, constructed a stone perimeter wall 10 feet (3 m) thick that was strengthened at one point by a circular stone tower over 30 feet (9 m) high. This wall is one of the earliest such defenses known.

Over time, the larger ones reached populations of 35,000–40,000 and covered more than 1000 acres, 1½ square miles (3.88 square kilometers). The major cities were walled and the ramparts of Uruk (modern Warka, biblical Erech), the city of the king-god-hero Gilgamesh, stretched to a circumference of 6 miles (9.7 kilometers), engirdling a population of 50,000 by 2700 B.C.E. By 2500 B.C.E. Sumer held 500,000 people, four-fifths of them in its cities and villages! Urbanism in Sumer became a way of life.

Control of the Countryside

To support these growing urban populations, the range of control of the Sumerian cities over the surrounding countryside, and its agricultural and raw material resources, continued to expand. The Russian scholar I.M. Diakanoff estimated that the total sway of Lagash, one of the major cities, extended over 1200 square miles (3100 square kilometers). The king, priests, and private citizens controlled the fields of this area (cited in Kramer, *The Sumerians*, p. 76).

Civic Loyalty

Networks of irrigation canals supported agriculture in this arid region and expanded Sumerian control over the land and its productivity. Irrigation permitted settlement to extend southward to central Mesopotamia, where the first cities would later emerge about 3300 B.C.E. The construction and maintenance of the canals required larger gangs of workers than the work teams that were based on family and clan alone. Loyalties that had been limited to blood relatives now extended beyond kinship to civic identity. In organizing these public works projects, a sense of citizenship, based on a shared space rather than on blood kinship, was born. As Numa Fustel de Coulanges, writing about a similar phenomenon in pre-Classical Greece, pointed out, the concept of legal identity and loyalty based on geography is the real beginning of city life.

Leadership and the State

Organizing the canal systems required more powerful leaders than villages had known. At first, this leadership appears to have been exercised by councils of aristocratic elders, who worked closely with religious leaders of the temple-

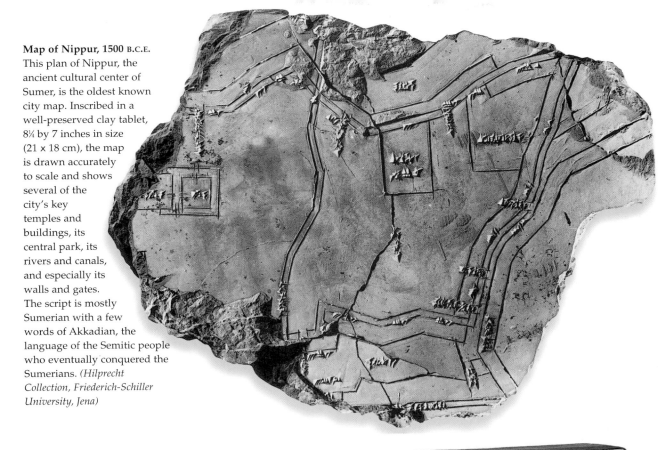

Map of Nippur, 1500 B.C.E. This plan of Nippur, the ancient cultural center of Sumer, is the oldest known city map. Inscribed in a well-preserved clay tablet, 8¼ by 7 inches in size (21 × 18 cm), the map is drawn accurately to scale and shows several of the city's key temples and buildings, its central park, its rivers and canals, and especially its walls and gates. The script is mostly Sumerian with a few words of Akkadian, the language of the Semitic people who eventually conquered the Sumerians. *(Hilprecht Collection, Friederich-Schiller University, Jena)*

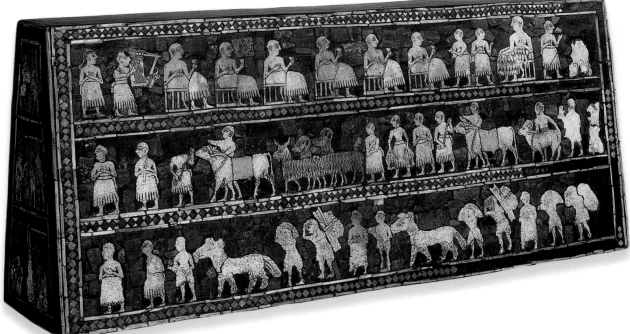

Standard of Ur, from Iraq. Sumerian, Early Dynastic II. *c.* **2800–2400** B.C.E. In Sumer the city-state was created as strong kings came to rule over walled cities and the surrounding countryside. This banqueting scene, found in a tomb in the royal cemetery at Ur, shows the court drinking to the health of the king. The boxlike "standard" is thought to have rested on top of a long pole during festive processions. *(British Museum, London)*

ziggurats. In times of crisis, especially during warfare with other cities, the council appointed a temporary single leader, but after about 2800 B.C.E., these men began to assume the position of hereditary kings and to rule in conjunction with temple priests. Political power and organization were both centralized and sanctified. Thus was the state born and consolidated.

Religion: The Priesthood and the Cosmo-magical City

Considerable power rested with the priests of the many deities of Sumer. In contrast to modern patterns, in which the countryside is often considered more religious than the secular city, the authority of the ancient temple community gave the religious establishment enormous prestige and power in the city, and urban ritual practice was more

FOCUS
The City as Ceremonial Center

The geographer Paul Wheatley summarized a great deal of his own research and that of many other scholars in stressing the religious and ceremonial significance of the ancient city, a significance not so apparent in our own cities of today:

> Whenever, in any of the seven regions of primary urban generation we trace back the characteristic urban form to its beginnings we arrive not at a settlement that is dominated by commercial relations, a primordial market, or at one that is focused on a citadel, an archetypal fortress, but rather at a ceremonial complex. . . . The

predominantly religious focus to the schedule of social activities associated with them leaves no room to doubt that we are dealing primarily with centers of ritual and ceremonial. Naturally this does not imply that the ceremonial centers did not exercise secular functions as well, but rather that these were subsumed into an all-pervading religious context. . . . Above all, they embodied the aspirations of brittle, pyramidal societies in which, typically, a sacerdotal [priestly] elite, controlling a corps of officials and perhaps a praetorian [elite] guard, ruled over a broad understratum of peasantry.
(Wheatley, pp. 225–6)

Ziggurat at Ur, Iraq, 2300 B.C.E. For the plain-dwelling Sumerians, mountains represented the mysterious sources of the waters that brought vegetation to the valleys. It is not surprising, then, that the buildings they conceived for sacred rituals—ziggurats, a form of stepped pyramids—were made in the form of holy mountains.

fully elaborated than was the rural counterpart (see Focus, opposite).

To consolidate their temporal and supernatural influences, the priests built in the cities great temples, called **ziggurats**, a form of stepped fortress. (Ziggurats are probably the model for the Bible's Tower of Babel, which was depicted as a threat to the God Jehovah.) The ziggurats dominated the fields that the priests controlled and farmed, rented out, or turned over to their servants and favorites. As their power increased, the priests built the ziggurats taller and more massive. From within these vast temple complexes, they controlled huge retinues, including artisans and administrators, and retained gangs of field workers to farm the temple's estates. Temples employed and fed multitudes. The chief temple in the city of Lagash, for example, provided daily food and drink (ale) to some 1200 people by about 3000 B.C.E. The leading temples became virtual cities within cities.

Rituals, especially those of the priests and kings, suggest further the significance of religious thought in the minds of Sumerians. On New Year's day the king of Ur proceeded to the top of the city's major ziggurat where he was symbolically married to the goddess of fertility, Inanna. The entire population witnessed this affirmation of his divinity. Royal burials also asserted the divinity and authority of the king. Sir Leonard Wooley described the death pit adjacent to the royal burial place in Ur, which he excavated in the 1920s:

> Six men servants carrying knives or axes lay near the entrance lined up against the wall; in front of them stood a great copper basin, and by it were the bodies of four women harpists, one with her hands still on the strings of her instrument. Over the rest of the pit's area there lay in ordered rows the bodies of sixty four ladies of the court. All of them wore some sort of ceremonial dress . . . Clearly these people were not wretched slaves killed as oxen might be killed, but persons held in honor, wearing their robes of office, and coming, one hopes, voluntarily to a rite which would in their belief be but a passing from one world to another, from the service of a god on earth to that of the same god in another place. (pp. 70–72)

The royal graves required specialized artisans. While most common people were buried in small brick vaults in basement chambers of their own houses, and some were interred in cemeteries out-side the city walls, the royal tombs were elegant. Their arches, vaults, and domes, suggesting new levels of architectural skill, were built of brick and stone, and many of the funeral objects interred with the dead were of gold and silver. As in other ancient civilizations we shall encounter in later chapters, some of the royal dead were accompanied by attendants who were sacrificed for the purpose and were buried nearby. They, too, were adorned with jewelry of gold and silver.

Occupational Specialization and Class Structure

The priests and the political-military rulers were only the most powerful of the new classes of specialists that emerged in the complex, large cities. Managers, surveyors, artisans, astronomers, brewers, warriors, traders, and scribes—all in addition to the farmers working their own fields and those of the temples and landowners—gave the cities a far more sophisticated hierarchical class structure than villages possessed.

Arts and Invention

Creativity flourished. Artisans crafted works of art in terra cotta, copper, clay, and colors surpassing village standards in their beauty and technical skill. Cylinder seals (small cylinders of stone engraved with designs for stamping clay tablets and sealing jars) became a common form of practical art in Sumer and spread as far as Anatolia and Greece. Astronomers established an accurate calendar based on lunar months that enabled them to predict the onset of seasons and to prepare properly for each year's planting and harvesting. Musicians created, designed, and played the lyre and composed and chanted songs, often dedicated to gods. Designers and architects, supervising armies of workers, built the canals of the countryside and the monuments of the cities.

Sumerians apparently invented the first wheels, the potter's wheel for ceramics and wagon wheels for transportation. They dramatically improved the plow, harnessing it for oxen. Metallurgists, smelting their new alloy of copper and tin, ushered in the bronze age, and from the new metal fashioned tips for the plow as well as "tools such as hoes, axes, chisels, knives, and saws; arms such as lance points and arrowheads, swords, daggers, and harpoons; vessels and containers; nails, pins, rings, and mirrors" (Kramer, *The Sumerians*, p. 103).

Trade and Markets; Wheeled Cart and Sailboat

Traders carried merchandise by land, river, and sea, in the world's first wheeled carts and sailboats, as well as by donkey caravan. Rich in agricultural commodities and artisan production but poor in raw materials, Sumerians traded with the inhabitants of hilly areas to the north for wood, stone, and metal. They sailed into the Persian Gulf to find copper and tin and then continued along the Arabian Sea coast as far east as the Indus valley for ivory and ceramics. They traveled east overland through the passes of the Zagros Mountains to bring back carnelian beads from Elam. Shells from the Mediterranean coast that have been found in Sumer indicate trade westward, probably overland, as well.

In the city marketplace, merchants sold locally produced foodstuffs, including vegetables, onions, lentils and beans, more than fifty varieties of fish taken from the Tigris and Euphrates rivers, milk, cheese, butter, yoghurt, dates, meat—mostly mutton—and ale. In vats in their homes, women, especially, brewed up to 40 percent of the barley and wheat harvest into ale for home use and for sale. For taste, effect, and storage purposes the Sumerians preferred ale to grain. (Hops had not yet been introduced to enable the processing of ale into beer.)

Monumental Architecture and Adornment

For the Sumerians, the size and elegance of their cities and monuments were a source of great pride. The earliest introduction to Gilgamesh, hero of the greatest surviving Sumerian epic, proclaims his excellence as city builder:

Soundbox of royal harp, from the tomb of Queen Puabi at Ur. Sumerian, *c.* **2600 B.C.E.** Many sumptuous artworks were discovered buried in the royal cemetery at Ur in the tombs of Sumerian kings and queens. Though the meaning is often obscure, the motifs and poses used in the decorations are often also found in west Asian and Egyptian art of about the same period, suggesting the possibility of cultural transmission. (*University Museum, Philadelphia*)

Engraved cylinder seal (left) and impression (right). Seals were first used as signatures before the invention of writing. The cylinders produce continuous patterns that are repetitive, but the figures themselves are remarkably naturalistic.

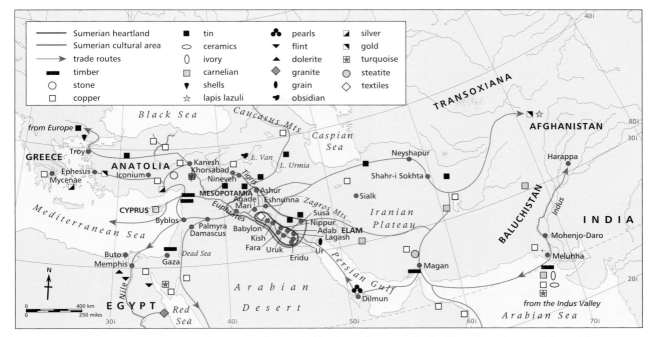

Mesopotamian trade The Sumerian trading network, revealed by the wide range of valuable and exotic materials used by Mesopotamian craftsmen, was both extensive and sophisticated, drawing on resources often well over 2000 miles distant. Egyptian tomb paintings show Semitic merchants with donkey caravans, while some of the earliest writing is found on Sumerian clay tablets recording commercial transactions.

In Uruk he built walls, a great rampart, and the temple of blessed Eanna for the god of the firmament Anu, and for Ishtar the goddess of love. Look at it still today: the outer wall where the cornice runs, it shines with the brilliance of copper; and the inner wall, it has no equal. Touch the threshold, it is ancient. Approach Eanna the dwelling of Ishtar, our lady of love and war, the like of which no latter-day king, no man alive can equal. Climb upon the wall of Uruk; walk along it, I say; regard the foundation terrace and examine the masonry: is it not burnt brick and good? The seven sages laid the foundations. (*The Epic of Gilgamesh*, p.61)

Gilgamesh is discussed more fully on page 54.

Art work adorned the city, especially the temple precincts. Sculptures, murals, mosaics, and especially stone **bas reliefs** provided not only beauty and elegance, but represented pictorially key scenes in the history of the cities and their rulers.

Thus, from king and priest through professionals, artisans, craftsmen, farmers, and laborers, specialization and division of labor and a hierarchical class structure marked the city's social and economic life as far more complex than that of the smaller, simpler village.

Writing and Literature

The Sumerians invented writing, thereby altering human history. Although some of the earliest town dwellers in other parts of the world—the settlers of the Niger valley of West Africa, the Olmec and Teotihuacanos of Mesoamerica, and the Chavin and Inca of the Andes Mountains of South America—achieved urban forms without writing, most of the earliest cities did invent some system of recording. As in Sumer, these systems moved "from token to tablet"—that is, from a simple recording of business transactions and registration of ownership through designated tokens, often marked with individual notations, through picture writing, to **ideograms**, and finally to phonetic, alphabetical writing.

As we shall see in Chapters 3 to 5, not all civilizations followed this sequence. In China, for example, the first writing seems to have been symbolic inscriptions on oracle bones, and they seem to have represented an attempt to divine the future. Chinese as a written language has only recently been transliterated into a phonetic alphabet; its basic script is still ideographic. The Chavin and Inca developed a form of recording transactions and chronology through knots made

Pictographic c. 3000 B.C.E.										
Early cuneiform representation c. 2400 B.C.E.										
Late Assyrian c. 650 B.C.E.										
Sumerian phonetic equivalent and meaning	k / eat	mušen / bird	sag / head	gu^4 / ox	še / barley	ud / day	šu / hand	ku^6 / fish	a / water	b / cow

Writing was invented in west Asia in the fourth millennium B.C.E. and developed from the need to keep a record of business transactions. From the wedge-shaped marks formed by a hollow-shaped reed, or stylus, cuneiform script evolved gradually. In this pictographic script, stylized drawings are used to represent words; each pictograph stands for a syllable, and abstract concepts are conveyed by using concrete notions that are close in meaning (e.g. "open mouth" for "eat"). See Spotlight, pp. 66–7.

in strings called *quipu* (see picture, p. 379), but they did not develop an independent system of writing. Nor did the people of the Niger valley.

Writing facilitated communication, commerce, administration, religious ritual, and, later, the recording and transmission of literature. It enabled society to enlarge to a scale never seen before. It encouraged a self-consciousness and historical analysis previously unknown. It created a "knowledge industry," transmitted through systems of formal education and headed by scribes. Samuel Noah Kramer, the great expositor of ancient Sumerian texts, pointed out: "as early as 3000 B.C., some scribes were already thinking in terms of teaching and learning. . . . by the middle of the third millennium B.C., there must have been a number of schools throughout Sumer where writing was taught formally." In a sense this textbook had its origins in Sumer some 5000 years ago.

Writing not only enriched the lives of the Sumerians, it has enabled our own historical study to recapture crucial information about their society. The discovery of that writing, and its deciphering, is barely a century old.

SUMER:
HOW DO WE KNOW?

The Sumerians wrote no historical interpretive accounts of their accomplishments, but at least five kinds of written materials help us to reconstruct their past. King lists give us not only the names and dates of many of the principal kings of the major cities but also some chronology of their continuing warfare. Royal correspondence with officials illuminates relations with neighbors. Epics transmit Sumerian values and their sense of the heroic, while lamentations recount the continuing devastation wrought by their inter-city religious warfare. Finally, legal codes suggest the principles and hierarchies of their everyday life.

Despite their accomplishments, the Sumerians and their literature were lost to history for at least 2000 years. Indeed, even the history of their Semitic neighbors in the region was little known except through tangential references in the Bible. The locations of even the greatest of the historic sites passed from memory until they were recovered in the late nineteenth century.

Early modern investigations of the lost civilizations of Mesopotamia and its literature were driven by interest in biblical history. In the twelfth century, Rabbi Benjamin of Tudela, who was visiting Mosul (in northern Iraq), correctly identified the nearby ruins of ancient Nineveh, but his find was not published until the sixteenth century. The identification of Babylon had to wait until 1616. During the seventeenth and eighteenth centuries, travelers through Mesopotamia continued to identify ruins in Mesopotamia with biblical sites. They also began, unsystematically, to send stones and tablets with inscriptions back to Europe. In 1811, James Rich, a resident for the British East India Company in Baghdad, began to examine and map the ruins of Babylon and even to excavate

He-Goat and Flowering Tree. Offering stand for fertility god. Sumerian, from Ur, *c.* **2500** B.C.E. This offering stand was created with a magical as well as a functional purpose in mind, being intended to work as a fertility charm too. The goat, an ancient symbol of male sexuality, is shown rearing up against a flowering tree, emblem of nature's fecundity. (*British Museum, London*)

parts of it. He sketched and investigated the mounds of ancient Nineveh. He collected tablets, bricks, boundary stones, and cylinders, which began the nucleus of the Mesopotamian antiquities collection of the British Museum, London. But no one could decipher their cuneiform script (see Spotlight, pp. 66–7).

The Sumerians had invented cuneiform writing, using reed styluses to make wedge-like forms (*cuneus* means wedge in Latin), part pictographic, part alphabetic, on clay tablets. Later conquerors had adapted this script for writing Akkadian, Assyrian, and Babylonian. The conquest of Alexander the Great in the fourth century B.C.E., however, helped to introduce the more functional Aramaic alphabet and cuneiform died out. The last known cuneiform text had been written in 75 C.E.

In the 1830s and 1840s, near Kermanshah, Persia, H.C. Rawlinson, a British army officer, began to copy the inscriptions from a cliff at Behistun. The stone was 300 feet (90 meters) above

SOURCE
The Epic of Gilgamesh

Much of what we know about the ancient Sumerian imagination and world vision comes from its greatest literary work, a series of tales about the hero Gilgamesh that were woven together into *The Epic of Gilgamesh*. Its most complete version comes from various shorter stories found in the library at Nineveh from about 750 B.C.E., but earlier fragments in the Sumerian excavations corroborate the antiquity of the core legends going back to the time Gilgamesh ruled Uruk, about 2600 B.C.E.

Gilgamesh introduces the first hero in written literature:

> I will proclaim to the world the deeds of Gilgamesh. This was the man to whom all things were known; this was the king who knew the countries of the world. He was wise, he saw mysteries and knew secret things. . . . When the gods created Gilgamesh they gave him a perfect body. Shamash the glorious sun endowed him with beauty, Adad the god of the storm endowed him with courage, the great gods made his beauty perfect, surpassing all others, terrifying like a great wild bull. Two-thirds they made him god and one-third man.

The first depiction of the hero as a city builder, as noted above:

> In Uruk he built walls, a great rampart, and the temple of blessed Eanna for the god of the firmament Anu, and for Ishtar the goddess of love.

The first male bonding, forged through a test of physical strength in an epic wrestling match:

> They broke the doorposts and the walls shook, they snorted like bulls locked together. They shattered the doorposts and the walls shook. Gilgamesh bent his knee with his foot planted on the ground and with a turn Enkidu was thrown. Then immediately his fury died. [Enkidu praises Gilgamesh's strength.] So Enkidu and Gilgamesh embraced and their friendship was sealed.

Enkidu had been created by Aruru, the goddess of Uruk, who had also created Gilgamesh. He lived in the forest. *Gilgamesh* highlights the suggestive myth of Enkidu's seduction by an urban harlot, who then lures him from the wilderness to the pleasures of the city as well as to his wrestling match with Gilgamesh:

> . . . the harlot and the trapper sat facing one another and waited for the game to come . . . on the third day the herds came; they came down to drink and Enkidu was with them. . . . The trapper spoke to her: "There he is. Now, woman, make your breasts bare, have no shame, do not delay but welcome his love. Let him see you naked, let him possess your body. When he comes near

uncover yourself and lie with him; teach him, the savage man, your woman's art, for when he murmurs love to you the wild beasts that shared his life in the hills will reject him." She was not afraid to take him, she made herself naked and welcomed his eagerness; as he lay on her murmuring love she taught him the woman's art.

For six days and seven nights they lay together, for Enkidu had forgotten his home in the hills; but when he was satisfied he went back to the wild beasts. Then, when the gazelle saw him, they fled. Enkidu would have followed, but his body was bound as though with a cord, his knees gave way when he started to run, his swiftness was gone. And now the wild creatures had all fled away; Enkidu was grown weak, for wisdom was in him, and the thoughts of a man were in his heart. So he returned and sat down at the woman's feet, and listened intently to what she said. "You are wise, Enkidu, and now you have become like a god. Why do you want to run wild with the beasts in the hills? Come with me. I will take you to the strong-walled Uruk, to the blessed temple of Ishtar and of Anu, of love and of heaven: there Gilgamesh lives, who is very strong, and like a wild bull he lords it over men." When she had spoken Enkidu was pleased; he longed for a comrade, for one who would understand his heart. "Come, woman, and take me to that holy temple, to the house of Anu and of Ishtar, and to the place where Gilgamesh lords it over the people. I will challenge him boldly . . ."

The epic unveils a driving ambition for fame and glory, both for himself and for his city, as Gilgamesh courageously chooses to enter the strongholds of Humbaba, guardian of the forest, and, with Enkidu, to fight him.

I will go to the country where the cedar is cut. I will set up my name where the names of famous men are written; and where no man's name is written I will raise a monument to the gods . . . I, Gilgamesh, go to see that creature of whom such things are spoken, the rumour of whose name fills the world. I will conquer him in his cedar wood and show the strength of the sons of Uruk, all the world shall know of it.

The importance of metallurgy and metals, especially for weapons, is revealed:

He went to the forge and said, "I will give orders to the armourers: they shall cast us our weapons while we watch them." So they gave orders to the armourers and the craftsmen sat down in conference. They went into the groves of the plain and cut willow and box-wood; they cast for them axes of nine score pounds, and great swords they cast with blades of six score pounds each one, with pommels and hilts of thirty pounds. They cast for Gilgamesh the axe "Might of Heroes" and the bow of Anshan; and Gilgamesh was armed and Enkidu; and the weight of the arms they carried was thirty score pounds.

The victory of Gilgamesh and Enkidu over Humbaba parallels the massive assault by urbanites on the natural resources of the world, turning the products of nature into objects of trade and commerce, and using them to build cities.

Now the mountains were moved and all the hills, for the guardian of the forest was killed. They attacked the cedars, the seven splendours of Humbaba were extinguished. So they pressed on into the forest . . . and while Gilgamesh felled the first of the trees of the forest Enkidu cleared their roots as far as the banks of Euphrates.

Lower Mesopotamia has no stone, wood, or metal. To get these raw materials, Sumerians had to send parties over long distances to quarry, cut, and dig; to trade; and to conquer. The mixed responses of the gods to the murder of Humbaba suggest the deep ambivalence of the Sumerians to their own increasing power:

[Gilgamesh and Enkidu] set [the corpse of] Humbaba before the gods, before Enlil; they kissed the ground and dropped the shroud and set the head before him. When he saw the head of Humbaba, Enlil raged at them, "Why did you do this thing? From henceforth may the fire be on your faces, may it eat the bread that you eat, may it drink where you drink."

SOURCE
The Code of Hammurabi

Hammurabi legislated in the name of the gods for the benefit of his people:

Anum and Enlil named me
　　to promote the welfare of the people,
　　me, Hammurabi, the devout god-fearing prince,
　　to cause justice to prevail in the land,
　　to destroy the wicked and the evil,
　　that the strong might not oppress the weak
　　. . . that justice might be dealt the
　　orphan and the widow.

The legislation was wide ranging and included:
• Laws governing slavery, including a prohibition on concealing a fugitive slave.
• Laws for maintaining the irrigation canals, and penalizing a landlord who allows his dikes to break causing damage to his neighbor's crop.
• Numerous laws governing marriage, bride price, dowry, adultery, and incest. Although women do own the dowries given them, their rights of ownership are limited. Marriage is presented in large part as a commercial transaction, in which the groom's family pays a bride-price to the bride's father while the bride's father gives her a dowry. Childlessness is grounds for divorce but the husband must return his wife's dowry. Behavioral restraints in marriage are unequal: if the husband "has been going out and disparaging her greatly," the wife may leave, taking her dowry; if the wife is "a gadabout, thus neglecting her house (and) humiliating her husband," he may have her drowned.
• Laws of adoption that recognize the parental rights of the adoptive parents over those of the biological parents.

If a seignior has destroyed the eye of a member of the aristocracy, they shall destroy his eye.

If he has broken another seignior's bone, they shall break his bone.

If he has destroyed the eye of a commoner or broken the bone of a commoner, he shall pay one mina of silver.

If he has destroyed the eye of a seignior's slave or broken the bone of a seignior's slave, he shall pay one half his value.

• Laws specifying payments to physicians as well as punishments for medical malpractice. Both vary in accord with the class of the patient.
• Laws of consumer protection for house buyers, boat renters, contractors for services. In one case, a brutal punishment for faulty workmanship indicates that common people, too, were viewed as commodities:

"If [the collapse of a building] has caused the death of a son of the owner of the house, they shall put the son of that builder to death."

• Laws fixing payments for services, rental rates, and daily wages for various occupational categories, suggesting powerful state control of the economy.

Stele of Hammurabi, from Susa, Iran, *c*. 1760 B.C.E. Hammurabi, the great king of Babylon, is the first known ruler to have created a detailed legal code. On this commemorative stone slab, he is shown receiving the Babylonian laws from the sun-god Shamash (compare Moses receiving the Torah from God, p. 299). The laws themselves are inscribed below on the stele. (*Louvre, Paris*)

the ground, and Rawlinson had a scaffolding constructed so that he could reach it, sometimes hanging suspended from a rope. Rawlinson and other scholars found that the three scripts represented different, but related languages. Two were in Old Persian—one in an alphabetic script, the other in cuneiform—and the third was in a cuneiform version of Elamite. Now the key to deciphering cuneiform, and thus rediscovering Sumerian, was at hand.

In the 1840s, extensive archaeological digs in Mesopotamia uncovered thousands of tablets and fragments, especially at Khorsabad in the palace of Sargon II (r. 721–705 B.C.E.), ruler of Assyria in the eighth century B.C.E., and at Nineveh, in the library of King Ashurbanipal, his great-grandson (r. 669–626 B.C.E.). Beginning in 1877, excavations of Sumerian sites began, first at Lagash, then at Nippur, where 30,000 tablets and fragments were excavated, most in Sumerian. Later excavations were carried on at Fara, Adab, Kish, Warka (the modern Arabic name for the city called Uruk by the ancient Sumerians, and Erech in the Hebrew Bible), Ur, and Eridu. Through texts and digs the Sumerians—their economy, belief systems, and culture—were resurrected.

Most of the texts deal with practical, everyday business transactions and administration. One contains the first known recipe for the ale that Sumerians enjoyed so much. Others recorded the world's first written literature.

Gilgamesh (see Source, pp. 54–5) presents a world of many gods before whom humans are passive and frightened subjects. Gilgamesh, however, defers neither to human nor to god. Devastated by the death of his closest friend Enkidu, he sets off to the underworld in search of eternal life. Along the way he encounters the Sumerian prototype of Noah. Utnapishtim tells him of a flood that destroyed all human life except his family. They had been saved by a god who counseled him to build a boat. In the bleak underworld of the dead, Gilgamesh obtains a plant that will give eternal youth, but on his return voyage a snake rises from the water and snatches it from him. Gilgamesh recognizes a fundamental truth: "Misery comes at last to the healthy man, the end of life is sorrow" (p. 93) and "There is no permanence" (p. 106). Resigned to death, Gilgamesh returns to Uruk. Finally, he dies at a ripe old age, honored and mourned by his fellow citizens.

A second form of written document that marks the evolution to a more complex society is the legal code. Archaeologists discovered at Ur fragments of a legal code that dates to the twenty-first century B.C.E., and legal systems must have already existed even before this. Legal systems remained crucial for all Mesopotamian urban societies. The post-Sumerian code of the Babylonian King Hammurabi (see Source opposite), formulated about 1750 B.C.E. (but rediscovered to the modern world only in 1901–02), seems to have been built on the earlier concepts.

EARLY URBANIZATION: SOME MODERN CRITIQUES

Politically, each of the major cities of Sumer was also a state, ruling over the contiguous agricultural areas and often in conflict with neighboring city-states. The bas relief pictorial records of the city-states often depict royal armies, military expeditions, conquests, and a general appreciation, even an exaltation, of warfare. The armies included the personal palace guards of the king, professional soldiers, and additional forces conscripted in times of war. The fighting seems to have been frequent, and the main combatants were the largest of the city-states: Kish, Uruk, Ur, and, later, Lagash and Umma. Battles were fought hand-to-hand and also from donkey-drawn chariots.

The warfare was especially destructive because the kings and soldiers believed themselves to be upholding the honor not only of their cities but also of their gods. A Hymn to the Ekur, "Mountain House," the famous temple of the god Enlil in the city of Nippur, fixes the link between the city, its chief temple, and its principal god:

> The great house, it is a mountain great,
> The house of Enlil, it is a mountain great,
> The house of Ninlil, it is a mountain great,
>
> (Pritchard, p. 582)

When cities are sacred, conflicts between them mean holy war, fights to the finish.

The "Lamentation over the Destruction of Ur," which was addressed to Ningal, goddess of the Ekushnugal Temple, describes that city's utter destruction after the Elamites sacked it, exiled its ruler, and destroyed the temple, about 1950 B.C.E.:

After your city had been destroyed, how now can you exist!

After your house had been destroyed, how has your heart led you on!

Your city has become a strange city; how now can you exist!

Your house has become a house of tears, how has your heart led you on!

Your city which has been made into ruins—you are no longer its mistress!

Your righteous house which has been given over to the pickax—you no longer inhabit it,

Your people have been led to slaughter—you are no longer their queen . . .

(Kramer, The Sumerians, p. 142)

Lewis Mumford, one of the most respected modern commentators on the history of cities, regarded this early union of power, religion, and continuous warfare as a permanent curse of urban life:

Once the city came into existence, with its collective increase in power in every department . . . mass extermination and mass destruction came to prevail. . . . war, even when it is disguised by seemingly hardheaded economic demands, uniformly turns into a religious performance; nothing less than a wholesale ritual sacrifice. (p. 42)

The socialist philosopher Karl Marx further blamed the first cities for establishing two fundamental antagonisms in human society—the conflict between city and countryside and class conflict. In *Capital* he wrote: "The foundation of every division of labor that is well developed, and brought about by a change in commodities, is the separation between town and country. It may be said that the whole economic history of the society is summed up in the movement of this antithesis." In *The German Ideology*, he wrote: "Here first became manifest the division of the population into two great classes, which is directly based on the division of labor and on the instruments of production."

The first Sumerian cities did, indeed, foster division of labor into occupational categories, but the hierarchies seem to have been more differentiated than Marx suggests. We have noted the roles of kings, priests, landowners, architects, scribes, long-distance traders, local merchants, artisans, cooks, farmers, soldiers, laborers—the whole panoply of occupational categories absent in villages but forming the backbone of a sophisticated urban economy and society. Priests and kings did hold great wealth and power, and much control of the means of production, but it is not clear that they formed an exclusive category of "haves" versus "have nots." The spectrum seems to have been more varied, including a substantial group of middle classes. But there is, nevertheless, much evidence of the enormous power of the aristocracy. The death pits of kings and their servants suggest that the Sumerians may have acquiesced in enormous royal and priestly power.

At the bottom of the hierarchy were slaves. People entered slavery in four ways: some were captured in battle; some were sentenced to slavery as punishment for crimes; some sold themselves (or their family members) into slavery to cope with poverty and debt; and some were born into slavery. We have no record of the number or proportion of slaves in the general population of Sumer and its cities. The law codes' extensive regulations of slaves and slavery suggest, however, their widespread existence.

Finally, the transformation of society from a rural, egalitarian, kin base to an urban, hierarchical, territorial, and class base may have provided the entering wedge for the subordination of women. Some women in Sumer had great power. Several seem to have held independent high administrative posts in major temples controlling large land holdings. Some like Shagshag, wife of King Uruinimgina (also known as Urukagina), c. 2300 B.C.E., held similar powers in the name of their husband. Lady Pu-abi (c. 2500 B.C.E.) was discovered in death-pit 800, adorned with gold and buried with several other bodies, presumably servants, suggesting a woman of high rank, perhaps a queen. Women in Sumer generally had certain basic rights, including the rights to hold property, engage in business, and serve as legal witness. Nevertheless, argues the feminist historian Gerda Lerner, women, even queens, were often only pawns in the power struggles of men. Before the evolution of city-states, with their warfare and hierarchical class structures, Lerner argues, the status of women and men had been more equal.

Lerner enlists the historical record to demonstrate that inequalities between men and women are not products of unchanging and unchangeable biological differences, but rather cultural patterns emerging at specific times, created by humans, that can be altered to restore a previous equality. She cites the anthropologist Rayna Rapp:

In pre-state societies, total social production was organized through kinship. As states gradually arose, kinship structures got stripped and transformed to underwrite the existence and legitimacy of more powerful politicized domains. In this process . . . women were subordinated with (and in relation to) kinship. (Lerner, p. 55)

Patriarchy and gender hierarchy, Lerner and Rapp both argue, were not natural to human society; they were introduced for the first time in human history in the cities of Sumer. Our own historical era, they imply, should reject them.

The evidence from both pre-state societies and early Sumer concerning gender relations is fragmentary, and many eminent scholars suggest that Lerner's interpretations go beyond the available data. However, the new questions addressed by contemporary feminist historians to the ancient data will continue to motivate new research into neglected aspects of the past.

MYTHISTORY

The modern critiques of Mumford, Marx, and Lerner remind us how seriously the past, and our preconceptions—or myths—about it, have influenced our thinking. They urge us to rethink in order to redirect our future from repeating some terrible mistake of the distant urban past: making warfare into a religious obligation, isolating city from countryside, establishing oppressive class distinctions, and institutionalizing patriarchal suppression of women.

Underlying these warnings, however, is yet another myth. The pre-urban agricultural village, it is widely believed, was more egalitarian, less warlike, more integrated into nature. We do not know if this was so. Pre-urban villagers produced no written records, and their artifactual remains are thin, inconclusive, and subject to widely divergent interpretation. Scholars draw many of their conclusions concerning pre-urban life from observing isolated groups in today's world, such as the !Kung people of the African Kalahari desert of a generation ago. But here, too, both observations and interpretations differ.

We do know, however, that early cities facilitated accomplishments that people then and now considered vitally important: increases in human population (a questionable asset under today's conditions, but not then); economic growth; effective organization for common tasks; creative breakthroughs in technology, art, and, perhaps most significantly, in writing and literature; the inauguration of a rule of law (see Source, p. 56); and the formation of a non-kin-based community with a sense of purpose and humanity.

They did not always succeed. In addition to the critiques cited above, the city-states could not work out a system of government and regulation that would enable them to live in peace. Both powerful and vulnerable, oscillating between psalms of victory and lamentations of defeat, they seemed to fall into one of two painful alternatives: inter-state warfare or conquest by imperial rulers. Their shortcomings cost them dearly. As long as each political entity was a law unto itself, as were the city-states of Sumer, and of classical Greece, and of pre-Han China, and of India during much of its history, and of medieval Europe, war was the likely result. This problem of warfare among competitive states persists to our own day, although the scale has escalated from the city-state to the independent nation-state.

SUMER: KEY EVENTS AND PEOPLE

c. **3300** (B.C.E.)	Sumerians invent writing.
c. **3000** (B.C.E.)	Sumerians become dominant power in southern Mesopotamia.
c. **2800– 2340**	Sumerian city-states: early dynastic period sees spread of Mesopotamian culture to the north.
c. **2350**	Sargon captures Sumer and establishes Semitic dynasty at Akkad, the new capital.
c. **2125– 2027**	Third dynasty of Ur.
c. **1900**	Ammorites at Babylon.
1792– 1750	Reign of Hammurabi; Babylon is the new capital of Mesopotamia.
c. **1600**	Invasion by Hittites and Kassites, destroying Hammurabi's dynasty.

The evolution of the large, complex city implies the evolution of a state capable of organizing and administering it. In aristocratic and monarchical Sumer, much depended on the disposition of the king. Even Gilgamesh, who ended his royal career devoted to, and honored by, his people, had begun differently. In Gilgamesh's youth, "the men of Uruk muttered in their houses":

> his arrogance has no bounds by day or night. No son is left with his father, for Gilgamesh takes them all, even the children . . . his lust leaves no virgin to her lover, neither the warrior's daughter nor the wife of the noble.

They realized that it should have been different— "The king should be a shepherd to his people"— but they apparently had to submit. The only recourse they saw was muttering in their houses and praying to their gods.

This question of the proper organization of the state became the key question of urbanization since the time of Gilgamesh and the Sumerian city-states. Two thousand years afterward—and two thousand years before our own day—in the city-states of ancient Greece, Aristotle summed up the issue:

> When several villages are united in a single complete community, large enough to be nearly or quite self-sufficing, the state comes into existence, originating in the bare needs of life, and continuing in existence for the sake of a good life . . . man is by nature a political animal [*zoon politikon*, a creature of the polis or city-state] . . . the association of living beings who have this sense makes a family and a state . . . justice is the bond of men in states, for the administration of justice, which is the determination of what is just, is the principle of order in political society.

From the time of Sumer, the political questions, the questions of how to organize and administer the **polis** or city-state to achieve a good life, have been central to the process of urbanization. In Sumer the answers depended on the edicts of the king and the priests. In the next two chapters, we shall see how these questions and answers evolved in other primary cities and city-states around the world.

CONNECTION: *The reign of Sargon I and Mesopotamia's first empires, pp. 123–4*

BIBLIOGRAPHY

Aristotle. *Basic Works*, trans. and ed. Richard McKeon. (New York: Random House, 1941).

Bairoch, Paul. *Cities and Economic Development: From the Dawn of History to the Present*, trans. Christopher Braider. (Chicago: University of Chicago Press, 1988).

Cohen, Mark. *The Food Crisis in Prehistory* (New Haven: Yale University Press, 1977).

Fagan, Brian M. *People of the Earth: An Introduction to World Prehistory* (New York: HarperCollins, 8th ed., 1995).

Gilgamesh, The Epic of, trans. and ed. N.K. Sandars. (Harmondsworth, Middlesex: Penguin Books, 1972).

Kramer, Samuel Noah. *History Begins at Sumer* (New York: Doubleday and Co., Inc., 1959).

Kramer, Samuel Noah. *The Sumerians: Their History, Culture, and Character* (Chicago: University of Chicago Press, 1963).

Lerner, Gerda. *The Creation of Patriarchy* (New York: Oxford University Press, 1986).

Marx, Karl. *Capital: A Critique of Political Economy*, trans. Ben Fowkes (New York: Vintage Books, 1977).

Marx, Karl and Friedrich Engels. *The German Ideology* (New York: International Publishers, 1939).

Moore, Andrew M.T. "The Development of Neolithic Societies in the Near East," *Advances in World Archaeology*. Vol. 4., ed. Fred Wendorf and Angela E. Close (Orlando: Academic Press, Inc., 1985).

Mumford, Lewis. *The City in History* (New York: Harcourt, Brace and World, Inc., 1961).

Oppenheim, A. Leo. *Ancient Mesopotamia. Portrait of a Dead Civilization* (Chicago: University of Chicago Press, 1964).

Past Worlds: The Times Atlas of Archaeology (Maplewood, NJ: Hammond Inc., 1988).

Postgate, Nicholas. *The First Empires* (Oxford: Elsevier Phaidon, 1977).

Pritchard, James B., ed. *Ancient Near Eastern Texts Relating to the Old Testament* (Princeton: Princeton University Press, 3rd ed. with supplement, 1969).

Redman, Charles L. *The Rise of Civilization: From Early Farmers to Urban Society in the Ancient Near East* (San Francisco: W.H. Freeman and Co., 1978).

Sjoberg, Gideon. "The Origin and Evolution of Cities," *Scientific American*. (September 1965), 19–27.

Wheatley, Paul. *The Pivot of the Four Quarters* (Chicago: Aldine Publishing Company, 1971).

Wooley, C. Leonard. *Excavations at Ur* (London: Ernest Benn, Ltd., 1954).

3 RIVER VALLEY CIVILIZATIONS

7000 B.C.E.—750 B.C.E.

"[Cities exhibit] marked individuality, so strong, so full of 'character' from the beginning that they have many of the attributes of human personalities."

LEWIS MUMFORD

THE RISE OF CITIES AND STATES ALONG THE NILE AND INDUS

Two urban civilizations flanked Mesopotamia: the Nile valley to the southwest and the Indus valley to the southeast. Scholarly opinion is divided as to whether these two city systems learned to build cities and states from the Mesopotamian example or invented them independently. Whatever the truth, peoples of these three river valleys created separate and distinct patterns of urbanization and political life.

In the Tigris–Euphrates valley, development of the physical city and the institutional state went hand-in-hand. In the Nile valley, the creation of the Egyptian state had greater significance than the growth of individual cities. In the Indus valley we have extensive archaeological information on the cities, but know next to nothing about the formation of the state. Until scholars learn to decipher the script and language of the Indus civilization, our knowledge of their institutional development will remain limited.

EGYPT: THE GIFT OF THE NILE

The pyramids and Sphinx at Giza near modern Cairo in the north of Egypt, the temples at Karnak and Thebes in the south, and the pharaohs' tombs nearby in the Valley of the Kings proclaim the wealth, skills, and organizational capacity of ancient Egypt. Despite these monumental structures, we know less about Egypt's ancient cities than about those of Mesopotamia, for the Nile, the ribbon of water that is Egypt's life, has washed away many ancient structures and eroded their foundations. On the other hand, we know much more about the Egyptian state, and for ancient Egypt, the written record provides more information than the physical artifacts.

EARLIEST EGYPT: HOW DO WE KNOW?

During its 5000 years of recorded history, Egypt was conquered and ruled by several civilizations. Rule by indigenous dynasties

ANCIENT EGYPT

DATE	POLITICAL	RELIGION AND CULTURE	SOCIAL DEVELOPMENT
3500 B.C.E.		• Hieroglyphics in use	• Villages in Nile valley
3000 B.C.E.	• Archaic Period (c. 3000–2700)	• Ruler of Egypt becoming godlike	• First use of stone in building
2500 B.C.E.	• Old Kingdom (c. 2700–2200)	• Step pyramid at Saqqara • Pyramids at Giza, including Great Pyramid (of Khufu)	• Irrigation programs along Nile
2000 B.C.E.	• First Intermediate Period (c. 2200–2050) • Middle Kingdom (c. 2050–1750) Second Intermediate Period (c. 1750–1550)	• Golden age of art and craftwork (1991–1786)	• Social order upset; few monuments built (2181–1991) • Country divided into principalities (1786–1567)
1500 B.C.E.	• New Kingdom (c. 1550–1050)	• Akhenaten (d.1335) rejected pantheon for worship of Aten • Temple complexes at Karnak/Luxor	• Began with colonial expansion; ended with divided rule
1000 B.C.E.	• Third Intermediate Period (c. 1050–650); three Libyan dynasties (from 945) give way to a Nubian one (from 751)	• Book of the Dead (c. 1000)	• Revival of prosperity and restoration of cults
650 B.C.E.	• Late Period (650–332)		• Completion of Nile–Red Sea canal
500 B.C.E.	• Alexander the Great founds Alexandria (332)		
100 B.C.E.		• Rosetta Stone	
30 B.C.E.	• Romans conquer Egypt		

began about 3100 B.C.E. and continued with few exceptions for 2600 years. For the next 2500 years, foreign rulers dominated Egypt: Persia conquered in 525 B.C.E., followed by Alexander the Great in 332 B.C.E., and Rome in 30 B.C.E. As the Roman Empire divided in 395 C.E. (see p. 188), Egypt came under the rule of Byzantine Christians until they, in turn, were conquered by Arabs in 641 C.E. Islam then gradually became the dominant religious culture, and remained so even after Europeans came to dominate Egypt in the late nineteenth century. Egypt has undergone so many transformations over such a long time that its earliest indigenous roots are hard to uncover. Even the language of ancient Egypt has been lost; today Arabic is Egypt's main language. Many cities in Egypt carry several names, imposed by successive conquerors. For example, the city called Nekhen by the Egyptians was renamed Hierakonpolis by the Greeks.

The modern attempt to reconstruct the past of ancient Egypt began with Napoleon's invasion in 1798. His military expedition failed to establish French rule in Egypt, but the historical and linguistic research it encouraged led to the recovery of much of Egypt's past. In 1799 an officer in Napoleon's engineering corps discovered a large stone near the western, or Rosetta, mouth of the Nile. The Rosetta Stone (see p. 67) carried an inscription from the year 196 B.C.E. by the Greek ruler of Egypt in three languages: the most ancient Egyptian script, hieroglyphics; demotic Egyptian, a simplified script based on the hieroglyphs; and Greek. By comparing the ancient Egyptian forms with the Greek, which he knew, Jean François Champollion le Jeune began to decipher the hieroglyphs, as well as their simplifications into later scripts. In 1822 he published the results of his work. Modern Egyptology was born.

Writing began early in Egypt, almost simultaneously with ancient Mesopotamia, about 3500–3000 B.C.E. Egyptians may have learned the concept of writing from Mesopotamia, but in place of cuneiform, they developed their own hieroglyphic script (see Spotlight, pp. 66–7). In fact some scholars believe that the invention of writing in Egypt was completely independent of the Mesopotamian invention, and possibly preceded it. Scribes, an important and highly regarded occupational group in ancient Egypt, later invented two shorthand transcriptions of hieroglyphs—first, hieratic script, later, the even more abbreviated form, demotic script. They wrote on stone tablets, like the Rosetta Stone; on limestone flakes; on pottery; and on papyrus, a durable paper-parchment, made by laying crossways the inner piths of the stalk of papyrus plants and pressing them until they formed into sheets.

As in Mesopotamia, some of the earliest Egyptian writing is notation for business and administration. Over the millennia it grew into a rich literature, including chronological lists of kings, religious inscriptions, spells to protect the dead (see Source, p. 75), autobiographies (see Source, p. 76), stories, wisdom texts of moral instruction, love poems, hymns to gods, prayers, and mathematical, astronomical, and medical texts. From this literature, scholars have reconstructed a substantial picture of the history of Egypt. But for the earliest 500 to 1000 years, until about 2400 B.C.E., the written records are thin. They do, however, provide a list of *nomes*, or administrative districts, suggesting the structure of the Egyptian state as early as 2900 B.C.E. They also provide lists of the earliest kings of Egypt.

King lists written on stone about 2400 B.C.E., and on papyrus about 1200 B.C.E., combined with lists compiled by the Greek historian Manetho in the third century B.C.E., give the names of the entire sequence of kings from Zekhen and Narmer,

The Great Sphinx and the Pyramid of Khefren, Giza. The greatest of all the pyramids, the burial tombs of the pharaohs, are at Giza, near modern Cairo, and date to around 2600–2500 B.C.E. The face of the sphinx—a mythological creature with a lion's body and a human head—is thought to be a likeness of King Khafre, who ruled Egypt some time after 2600 B.C.E.

about 3100 B.C.E, all the way through the Persian conquest in 525 B.C.E. and Alexander the Great's victory in 332 B.C.E. After that event we know the basic chronology of Egypt's political history from many sources.

Archaeological excavations, primarily for monumental objects, began in 1858, although tomb robbing and the theft of ancient artifacts had been continuous from earliest times. The annual expeditions of British Egyptologist W.M. Flinders Petrie, beginning in 1880, introduced more scientific archaeological studies of Egypt and of Nubia, immediately to the south. By about 1900 scholars had identified the basic outlines of Egypt's history from, perhaps, 3600 B.C.E. to their own time.

EARLIEST EGYPT: WHAT DO WE KNOW?

By 12,000 B.C.E., residents of Nubia and Upper Egypt were using stones to grind local wild grasses into food, and by 8000 B.C.E., flour was prepared from their seeds. By 6000 B.C.E. the first traces appear of the cultivation of wheat and barley, grasses and cereals, and of the domestication of sheep and goats. To the west, the Sahara was becoming drier and some of its inhabitants may have moved to the Nile valley bringing with them more advanced methods of cultivation. Between 4000 and 3000 B.C.E. the bronze age began in Egypt as the new metal was used in tools and weapons. Population increased, as did the size of villages, and by 3300 B.C.E. the first walled towns appeared in the upper Nile, at Nagada and Hierakonpolis. Tombs for their rulers and elites were built nearby.

King lists, records of the *nomes* of Upper Egypt, and inscriptions and designs on pottery suggest strongly that Egyptian national life and history began with the unification of the kingdom about the year 3000 B.C.E. A single king, perhaps Narmer, succeeded in bringing all Egypt under his rule. The king was becoming a god, responsible for maintaining *ma'at*, justice and order, throughout the kingdom. The increase in monumental tombs and funerary objects suggests an increasing hierarchy and an uneven distribution of wealth, two common characteristics of state building. A more or less unified artistic style in both pottery and architecture after that time mirrors the unification of Egyptian politics.

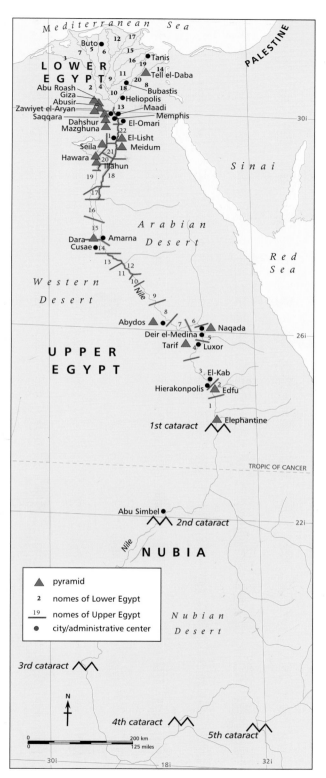

Land of the Nile Stretching over 1000 miles along the Nile River, ancient Egyptian civilization depended on a strong government. The kingdom was divided into Lower and Upper Egypt, and further subdivided into *nomes* (tax districts).

SPOTLIGHT

Writing

INVENTING IT, DECIPHERING IT

The contents of commercial packages, the names of their owners, lists of all kinds—these were the subject matter of the world's first writing, invented in Sumer about 3300 B.C.E. The earliest Sumerian scribes employed styluses made of bone or of hollow reed stems to incise **pictograms,** picture representations of the objects of their writing, onto clay tablets. By 3000 B.C.E. they were representing the key features of the pictures in wedge-shaped

signs that we call **cuneiform**, (*cuneus* means wedge in Latin). Some cuneiform signs represent whole words, but others represent individual phonetic sounds based on the words. **Figure 1**, a clay tablet from about 3000 B.C.E., represents the transitional period, combining some picture representation with some cuneiform. Read from right to left, it lists various rations to be distributed over a five-day period, including the name and location of the recipient.

As the cuneiform became more sophisticated, so too did the subject matter, and by about 2400 B.C.E. Sumerian writing began to transmit stories, proclaim political and military victories, sing the poetry of lovers, praise the glories of gods, and lament the fall of cities. Written literature had begun. Many later peoples in the region, Elamites, Babylonians, Assyrians, and Akkadians, adopted cuneiform to write their own languages. Tens of thousands of Sumerian clay tablets have been excavated and transferred to research institutions around the world.

How did scholars learn to read the cuneiform? At Behistun, twenty miles from Kermanshah, Iran, a huge rock inscribed with 414 lines in Old Persian and 263 in Elamite came to the attention of British army officers in the mid-nineteenth century. The two inscriptions were translations of one another, enabling linguists who could already read the Persian to decipher the cuneiform script.

A similar process of decipherment yielded the secrets of the ancient Egyptian **hieroglyphs** (Greek for "sacred carvings"). The earliest of these pictographs

Figure 1 Clay tablet with cuneiform, Jemdet Nasr, Iraq, 3000 B.C.E.

Figure 2 The "Rosetta Stone," ancient Egyptian, 196 C.E. (*British Museum, London*)

date to about 3300 B.C.E., the concept probably deriving from Sumer although the forms of the writing are different. A stone inscription in three scripts—hieroglyphic, a later Egyptian shorthand called demotic, and Greek— was discovered at Rosetta in the Nile Delta by an officer in the French army in 1799. This "Rosetta stone" (**figure 2**) enabled scholars to decipher the hieroglyphs by comparing them with the Greek that they did know. Coincidentally, the earliest hieroglyphs had also been written on stone, but after about 2600 B.C.E. Egyptian scribes usually wrote on papyrus, "paper" produced from pressing a weave of flattened reeds together. The dry desert air of the Nile valley preserved multitudes of these papyrus manuscripts.

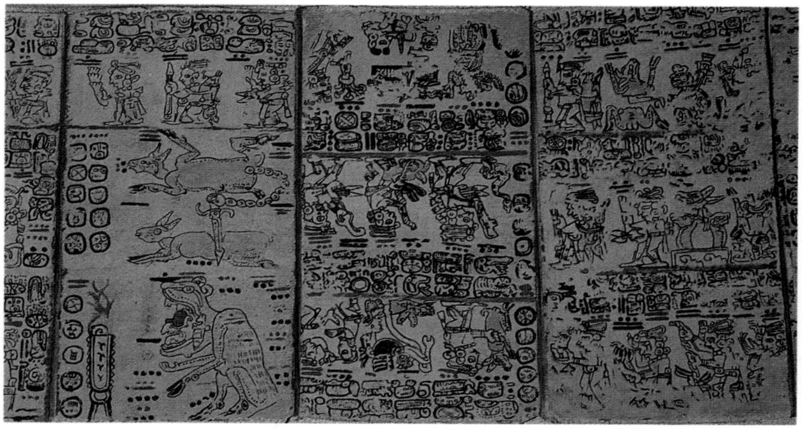

Climaxing a century and a half of research, scholars in the 1980s scored new breakthroughs in the decipherment of the hieroglyphic writing of the Central American Maya peoples, which dates back as far as 100 B.C.E. The "Madrid Codex" (**figure 3**), named for the city where it is now stored and dating to 800–1200 C.E., is one of the four books remaining from the Maya. Written on beaten-bark paper, folded like an accordion, it is read from left to right to the bottom of the page, then turned over for the next page. Its hieroglyphs and pictures, developed independently of any contact with the eastern hemisphere, provide an almanac of calendrical, astronomical, religious, ritual, and sacrificial information. The 1980s scholarship has also deciphered the accounts of the wars and conquests of the Maya kings, adding a new dimension to our understanding of their life and culture.

The oldest known alphabetic writing, a Semitic script with influences dating to about 1900 B.C.E., was discovered on limestone in the Egyptian desert near Thebes in 1999. The *New York Times* described this alphabetic writing as "an invention by workaday people that simplified and democratized writing, freeing it from the hands of official scribes. [It] was revolutionary in a sense comparable to the invention of the printing press much later" (November 14, 1999, p. A–1).

Figure 3 The "Madrid Codex," Mayan, 800–1200 C.E.

The Palette of King Narmer, *c.* **3200** B.C.E. This slate palette, used for ritual purposes, shows the power of King Narmer, who had just united Upper and Lower Egypt. In the top register, Narmer (left) inspects the bodies of dead enemies (right); at the bottom, the strength of the pharaoh is symbolized by the bull shown destroying the walls of a city. (*Egyptian Museum, Cairo*)

By 2700 B.C.E. Egypt exhibited the cultural complexity associated with early civilizations, including a national religious ideology and the centralized control of political administration and even of artistic productivity. Nevertheless, thousands of small, largely self-sufficient communities seem to have persisted within a largely decentralized economy for the local production and consumption of food and basic commodities.

In ancient Egyptian records the creation of a centralized kingdom was more valued than the construction of individual cities. Unlike Mesopotamia, Egypt has almost no existing record of independent city-states. The Nile River, the passage of time, overbuilding, and re-cycling have exacted their toll:

Few pharaonic towns have survived in anything like their original form. Some have disappeared beneath the rising alluvium, others have been destroyed by the overbuilding of later generations, while those which remained reasonably intact have suffered severely from the depredations of the peasantry looking for *sebakh* (a fertilizer made from sediment) among the ruins. (Walters, cited in Cotterell, p. 38)

Written records for the earliest years do not provide much help:

The Early Dynastic period is calculated as having lasted for nearly 500 years [3100–2613 B.C.E.], but the almost total absence of written evidence makes it a dark age for historians, illuminated only infrequently. (Walters, cited in Cotterell, p. 23)

The Cities

We do have some information, however. Flinders Petrie, who established the foundations of modern, systematic archaeology in Egypt about a century ago, argued that by 3600 B.C.E. a string of villages lined the Nile River, at intervals of every 20 miles (30 kilometers) or so. The village economies were based on cereal agriculture, and they were linked by trade along the river, although, since they mostly produced the same basic foodstuffs, these villages traded only a little among themselves. They give little evidence of social stratification. These settlements characterized the "Nagada I" period (*c.* 3500 B.C.E.).

Among the villages, however, somewhat larger market towns must have grown up. Geographers have developed "central place theory" to describe the growth of villages into towns, and it suggests that where ecological factors are approximately equal, as they would have been along the Nile, equally spaced, small settlements will grow up. Then, because the functions of administration, business, and transportation require some centralization, some of the villages will begin to house those functions. These selected villages, spaced strategically at larger intervals in the landscape, will grow into larger settlements, and perhaps even into full-fledged cities.

In early dynastic Egypt, the siting of the administrative headquarters of the *nomes*, regional administrative units, would have given just such a boost to the towns in which they were located. Some settlements also hosted additional functions, including irrigation control and religious observance. Urban consolidation marks the beginning of "Nagada II" culture (*c.* 3300 B.C.E.). The development of Hierakonpolis along the Nile in Upper Egypt illustrates the process.

Excavations under a team led by Michael Hoffman in about 1980 found that the population of Hierakonpolis grew from a few hundred in 3800 B.C.E. to 10,500 by 3500 B.C.E. At least two cemeteries served the city, one for common people, another for the wealthier traders and more powerful administrators. What precipitated the population growth, occupational specialization, and social hierarchy? Hoffman argues that the ecological balance between desert and grassland collapsed, perhaps because of droughts that occurred periodically along the Nile, or perhaps because of overgrazing. Local leaders introduced and implemented irrigation systems that saved agriculture and even enriched it. These changes enhanced the economy of the region and created the subsequent growth and change. Indeed, Hierakonpolis seems to have been the capital from which Pharaoh Narmer, the mythical Menes, unified Egypt.

Political/administrative leaders continued to create irrigation systems along the Nile. Anthropologist Karl Butzer has noted the introduction of irrigation programs in Old Kingdom Egypt, *c.* 2700–2200 B.C.E., the development of the Fayyum Lake region and the transfer of population to it during the Middle Kingdom, *c.* 2050–1750 B.C.E.; and the development of "shaduf" irrigation during the New Kingdom, *c.* 1550–1050 B.C.E. Egypt, the gift of the Nile, had different, and much less frequent problems with its water supply than did Mesopotamia, but here, too, the control of water resources influenced the formation of cities and the state.

Hierakonpolis housed a palace, a temple, and prominent tombs. Perhaps the city flourished because its temple community and worship became especially attractive to surrounding villages. The combination of irrigation, administration, and worship built the city.

Earlier archaeological reports seemed to suggest that after unification under a single pharaoh, Egyptian cities were not usually walled. The central government may have taken action against the kind of inter-city warfare that characterized Mesopotamia, rendering defensive walls unnecessary. Also, although invasions occurred from time to time and required defensive precautions, the desert to the east and west of the Nile valley provided an adequate natural shield. More recent excavations, however, question this view of open cities. The walls of some cities have been uncovered, and archaeologists are beginning to suspect that other walls may have been removed and the materials used for other purposes. Robert Wenke, Professor of Anthropology at the University of Washington, endorses this revised view:

> Most of the major Old Kingdom Upper Egyptian settlements seem to have been walled complexes of tightly packed mudbrick houses. . . . Few of the Old Kingdom sites in the Delta seem to have been enclosed in walls, but it is entirely possible that these Old Kingdom Delta settlements in fact had walls that have long since been destroyed by the action of *sebakhiin*—farmers who dig out old occupations and use the sediments for fertilizing and raising agricultural fields. (Wenke, p. 312)

Excavations at El-Kab, across the Nile from Hierankopolis, revealed a city enclosed in a wall, 1600 feet square, dating to 1788–1580 B.C.E. This wall, in turn, seems to have

Figurine of bone and ivory, "Nagada I" period, *c.* 4000–3600 B.C.E. Egypt's rise to a mighty empire had modest roots: a string of loosely affiliated villages lining the Nile. This attractive figurine, whose eyes are inlaid with lapis lazuli, was unearthed from a tomb of this early, predynastic age. (*British Museum, London*)

PROFILE
Akhenaten
AND HIS CITY AKHETATEN

Modern excavations at Amarna on the east bank of the Nile unearthed the ruins of an ancient Egyptian capital that owed its entire existence to the idiosyncratic vision of one ruler—King Amenhotep IV, better known as Akhenaten.

Within a few years of coming to the throne, King Amenhotep IV (r. 1353–35 B.C.E.) challenged the order of ancient Egypt by adopting a new monotheistic religion. Instead of worshiping a whole pantheon of gods, he offered his devotion to a single deity—Aten, god of the solar disk (or sun). Amenhotep appointed himself mediator between his people and the god and abandoned his official dynastic name in favor of Akhenaten ("he who serves Aten"). The name of Ammon, principal god of the old religion, was swiftly erased from inscriptions throughout Egypt, as were the words "all gods" in certain texts.

To bolster the new order and escape the power of the hostile priesthood, Akhenaten moved his capital 200 miles (300 kilometers) north from the established center of Thebes to an untouched site in the desert. The city that he built was named Akhetaten ("horizon of Aten"; present-day Amarna) and it was here that Akhenaten, the Great Royal Wife Queen Nefertiti, and their six daughters practiced the new religion. The eccentricity of Akhetaten's ruler was reflected in the city's architecture, sculpture, and wall painting. Solid statements of eternity gave way to a freedom of expression that emphasized the here-and-now. Aten was worshiped in an open temple that ushered in the sun's rays rather than in the dark, austere sanctuary usually designated for worship. Residential buildings included spacious villas with large gardens and pools to house wealthy officials. In artistic expression, solemnity gave way to an unprecedented liveliness and invention. Curious depictions of Akhenaten's drooping jaw and misshapen body capture his individuality, marking a departure from the highly stylized representations of previous pharaohs. (Perhaps they were sculpted by his opponents who took pleasure in representing his deformities.)

In the late nineteenth century, over 300 clay cuneiform tablets were discovered by Egyptian farmers in the ruins of Akhetaten. These tablets, known as the Amarna Letters, formed part of an archive of royal correspondence between Asian princes and the courts of Amenhotep III and Akhenaten. It appears that Akhenaten ignored repeated pleas for assistance from countries facing foreign invasion. Moreover, his isolated position, both geographically and intellectually, threatened the stability of Egypt's empire. When he died, Akhenaten's successors abandoned Akhetaten and later razed it to the ground. The capital returned to Thebes where the old religious and political order could resume.

Sandstone statue of Akhenaten, Amarna period. (*Egyptian Museum, Cairo*)

Wooden model of a sailing boat from Meir, Egypt, *c.* 2000 B.C.E. The presence of a mummy on board this Twelfth-dynasty model boat indicates that it was intended as a funerary artifact, used to symbolize the journey of the dead into the afterlife. We can glean important details about early Egyptian vessels—from the large central sail to the figures on deck, representing the pilot, the owner, and sailors working the halyards. (*British Museum, London*)

intersected a more primitive town, of circular or oval shape surrounded by a double wall.

Largest of all the Nile towns, presumably, were the political capitals—first in the north at Memphis, later in the south at Thebes, occasionally at other locations. Most of the spectacular temples and monuments at Thebes today, for example, date only to the eighteenth and nineteenth dynasties, 1550–1196 B.C.E. Archaeologists cannot excavate below these monuments to reach older urban levels, and the residential buildings of that older city are probably below the current water table. They are irrecoverable.

The best known capital city archaeologically is Akhetaten (sometimes referred to as Amarna, the name of the village at the site today), which was built by the Pharaoh Akhenaten (r. 1353–35; see Profile opposite), as the capital of his own religious philosophy, the worship of the sun, Aten, as the only god (except for the pharaoh himself). Akhetaten, however, is unrepresentative of other Egyptian cities. It was built comparatively late, as a capital, and was in use during only one reign. Subsequent pharaohs so hated Akhenaten's religion that they dismantled the city and used its building materials on other sites.

Other types of cities completed the urban network. Trade cities, especially in the Nile delta, linked Egypt internally and to the outside world. As early as 3650 B.C.E.,

the city of Buto in the Nile delta near the Mediterranean, served as the port of landing for shipping from the Levant and Mesopotamia. At El-Omari, further south in the delta, many imports of goods from the Mediterranean coast have been found. Goods off-loaded in these ports must have

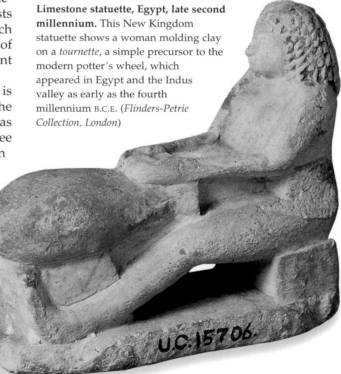

Limestone statuette, Egypt, late second millennium. This New Kingdom statuette shows a woman molding clay on a *tournette*, a simple precursor to the modern potter's wheel, which appeared in Egypt and the Indus valley as early as the fourth millennium B.C.E. (*Flinders-Petrie Collection, London*)

been trans-shipped in smaller boats or carried by donkey caravan to Maadi, near Memphis. Maadi was the trade link between the delta and Upper Egypt.

Finally, there were the burial sites. Lewis Mumford, the great architect/planner/historian of the city, and Paul Wheatley, the geographer/ anthropologist, maintained that shrine locations preceded cities. Egypt may be their best example. At least from the first dynasty, 2920 B.C.E., large

cemeteries with rich burial goods have been found throughout the Nile valley and delta. Kings and members of the court were buried at Abydos in southern Egypt in tombs of modest size but excellent craftsmanship (see Focus below). A group of high officials was buried in the north, near Saqqara, in mudbrick tombs, and their funerary goods included copper objects and stone vessels. At the beginning of the second dynasty, 2770 B.C.E., the royal necropolis, the city of tombs,

FOCUS
The Legend of Isis, Osiris, and Horus

The legend of Isis, Osiris, and their son Horus triumphing over disorder and evil represents in mythic terms the importance of the unification of Egypt. Osiris represented order (ma'at) and virtue; his brother, Seth, disorder and evil. Seth tricked Osiris into lying down inside a box and then set the box on the Nile. Isis, Osiris' wife and sister, found the box and brought Osiris back home. Seth, however, seized the body and cut it into fourteen pieces. Once again Isis found the body and brought it back to Egypt. From the dead body, she conceived a son, Horus. Horus defeated Seth in battle and gave Osiris new life, this time as king and principal god of the underworld.

Horus became a patron god of the pharaohs. He was the first Egyptian god worshiped nationally. In painting and sculpture he is often depicted in the form of a falcon, either representing the king, perched on his head or shoulder, or atop the double crown, which symbolized the unity of Upper and Lower Egypt. The pharaohs believed that if they lived proper, ordered lives they would be united with Osiris after they died.

In some representations Horus and Seth are seen in reconciliation, binding Egypt into a single state. Seth represents southern areas around Nagada and Thebes; Horus, less specifically, represents the north.

Stele from the tomb of Djet (the "Serpent King"), Abydos, c. 3000 B.C.E. Horus, in the form of a falcon, is pictured above a serpent representing Djet, the "Serpent King," and the façade of a palace (*pharaoh* literally meant "great house" or "palace"). (*Louvre, Paris*)

was sited at Saqqara itself. Adjacent to the burial sites were the towns of the workers. Several of these workers' towns have been excavated, most notably Deir el Medina, near the Valley of the Queens, opposite Thebes, although it dates to a later period.

The State and its Architecture

Who first unified the upper and lower Nile into the single kingdom of Egypt? Most king lists mention Menes, but some name Narmer. Some scholars believe that these were two different names for the same person. The event took place about 3100 B.C.E., but tombs of kings excavated at Abydos predate this by about 200 years. Perhaps these were kings of local regions, or perhaps unification was actually accomplished under a "pre-dynastic" king before Menes. Or unification may have been a long process and "Menes" simply symbolizes the whole process. As noted, scholarly knowledge of this early period up to the fourth dynasty, which begins the Old Kingdom, c. 2700–2200 B.C.E., is especially fragmentary.

In the third dynasty, 2649–2575, King Djoser had a *mastaba* built to hold his remains at death. This forerunner of the pyramids shows an astonishing royal control over labor, finances, and architectural and building techniques. The administrative organization and economic productivity of government continued to increase, until, by the end of this dynasty, Egypt had extended its control of the Nile valley as far south as the first cataract (river rapids), its classical southern frontier. At the same time, Egypt's artistic genius continued to develop in the sculpture of its tombs and the sophistication of its script.

Within a half century, architects realized the beauty of filling in the steps of the *mastaba* to create the simple triangular form of the true pyramid. Kings of the fourth dynasty, 2575–2465, supervised the construction of the greatest pyramids in history. The 450 foot (137 meter) high pyramids of Khufu (Cheops; r. 2551–2528) and of Khefren (r. 2520–2494), and the smaller pyramid of Menkaure (r. 2490–2472), all arranged in a cluster with the Sphinx, proclaim aspiration to immortality, creative vision, and organizational power. The sculpture, reliefs, paintings, and inscriptions in the pyramids and in the many tombs of court officials and other powerful men of the time express the highest artistic achievements of the era. Tombs of queens and officials are situated in

GODS OF THE EGYPTIANS

Belief in one god (Aten, represented by the sun) was promoted during the reign of Akhenaten (r. 1353–1335), when the capital of Egypt was moved from Thebes to Amarna. At other times, the Egyptians worshiped a pantheon, whose main gods and goddesses are listed below:

Amon-Re The universal god, depicted as ram-headed

Anubis Jackal-headed god of funerals, son of Nephthus and Osiris. He supervised the weighing of souls at judgment

Hathor The goddess of love, represented either as a woman with a cow's horns or as a cow with a solar disk

Horus The falcon-headed god of light

Isis Goddess of magic and fertility; sister and wife of Osiris; as mother of Horus, she was mother goddess of all Egypt

Nephthus Sister of Isis, this funerary goddess befriended dead mortals at judgment

Osiris Ruler of the underworld and chief judge of the dead, Osiris is normally depicted mummified or as a bearded man wearing the crown of Upper Egypt and with a flail and crook in his hands

Ptah Magician and patron of the arts and crafts, Ptah later became judge of the dead. Normally represented as a mummy or holding an ankh (looped cross)

Seth The god of evil and the murderer of Osiris

Thoth The supreme scribe, depicted either with the head of an ibis or as a dog-headed baboon

Step pyramid of King Djoser, Saqqara, Egypt, *c.* **2700** B.C.E. This step pyramid, forerunner to the ancient architectural masterpieces at Giza (see picture, p. 64), developed from the *mastaba*, a low rectangular benchlike structure that covered a grave. The purpose of this early pyramid, effectively a 200-foot-high (61 m) ziggurat without a temple on top, was to mark and protect the underground tomb chamber 90 feet (27 m) below.

Cutaway of Great Pyramid of Khufu, Giza. The rectangular plan and stepped form of Djoser's pyramid were gradually modified to become the colossal, smooth-faced monuments with which we are familiar. This pyramid is some 450 feet (137 m) high on a square base occupying 13 acres and was built using forced labor.

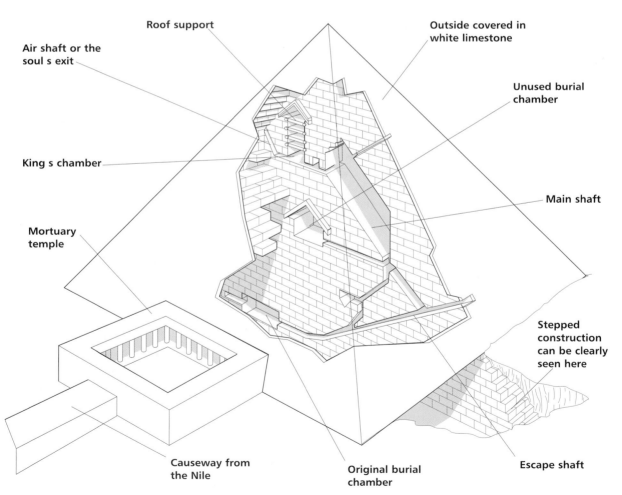

Roof support

Outside covered in white limestone

Air shaft or the soul s exit

Unused burial chamber

King s chamber

Main shaft

Mortuary temple

Stepped construction can be clearly seen here

Causeway from the Nile

Original burial chamber

Escape shaft

proximity to the kings' pyramids to reflect their power and rank. (Tomb robbing was, however, so common that we have no idea how long any of them lay undisturbed in their tombs.)

Following Menkaure, whose pyramid was already smaller than those of Khufu and Khefren, the building of such enormous monuments diminished, which may reflect a lessening of Egyptian power generally.

Egyptian trading, raiding, and mining initiatives began to extend southward into Nubia, above the first cataract of the Nile. These expeditions were protected and consolidated through the construction of the Buhen fortress at the second

---

SOURCE

The Egyptian Book of the Dead and the "Negative Confession"

Many ancient Egypt texts concern the attempt to secure eternal happiness after death. A selection from these mortuary texts has been collected by modern scholars and titled *The Book of the Dead*. A segment of these texts presents the "negative confession" of a deceased person in the court of judgment of the dead protesting his innocence of evil and crime:

I have not committed evil against men.
I have not mistreated cattle.
I have not committed sin in the place of truth.
I have not tried to learn that which is not meant for mortals.
I have not blasphemed a god.
I have not done violence to a poor man.
I have not done that which the gods abominate.
I have not defamed a slave to his superiors.
I have not made anyone sick.
I have not made anyone weep.
I have not killed.
I have given no order to a killer.
I have not caused anyone suffering.
I have not cut down on the food or income in the temples.
I have not damaged the bread of the gods.
I have not taken the loaves of the blessed dead.
I have not had sexual relations with a boy.
I have not defiled myself.
I have neither increased or diminished the grain measure.
I have not diminished the measure of land.
I have not falsified the land records.

I have not added to the weight of the balance.
I have not weakened the plummet of the scales.
I have not taken milk from the mouths of children.
I have not driven cattle away from their pasturage.
I have not snared the birds of the gods.
I have not caught fish in their marshes.
I have not held up the water in its season.
I have not built a dam against running water.
I have not quenched a fire at its proper time.
I have not neglected the appointed times and their meat-offerings.
I have not driven away the cattle of the god's property.
I have not stopped a god on his procession.
I am pure: I am pure: I am pure: I am pure. . . .

Behold me—I have come to you without sin, without guilt, without evil, without a witness against me, without one against whom I have taken action. I live on truth, and I eat of truth. I have done that which men said and that with which gods are content. I have satisfied a god with that which he desires. I have given bread to the hungry, water to the thirsty, clothing to the naked, and a ferry-boat to him who was marooned. I have provided divine offerings for the gods and mortuary offerings for the dead. So rescue me, you; protect me, you.

(Pritchard, pp. 34–6)

SOURCE
The Autobiography of Si-nuhe and the Glorification of Court and Capital

Si-nuhe, a high-ranking official and royal attendant, fled from the Egyptian court when a new king came to the throne. Apparently he feared that his loyalty to the new ruler was suspect and his safety endangered. A skilled warrior and administrator, even in self-imposed exile he earned high positions in several Asian kingdoms. In Si-nuhe's old age, however, the king of Egypt and his family invited him back to the court so that he could spend his last years "at home" in comfort and be buried with appropriate rites.

This personal tale of reconciliation is almost certainly based on reality. Its glorification of Egypt over other countries, of the city over the countryside, and especially of the royal capital and the royal court represented the beliefs of the Egyptian elite. This account of the career and the moral personality of a court official, and of the excellence of the reigning pharaoh, is an outstanding example of the autobiographies inscribed in ancient Egyptian tombs.

Si-nuhe's story became one of the most popular classics of Egyptian literature, and manuscripts that include it began to appear about 1800 B.C.E. and continued to about 1000 B.C.E. One modern scholar refers to it as "the crown jewel of Middle Egyptian literature" (Lichtheim, I, 11).

Si-nuhe returned to the capital, then in the city of Lisht, near the Faiyum Lake.

So I went forth from the midst of the inner chambers, with the royal children giving me their hands. Thereafter we went to the Great Double Door. I was put into the house of a royal son, in which were splendid things. A cool room was in it, and images of the horizon. Costly things of the Treasury were in it. Clothing of royal linen, myrrh, and prime oil of the king and of the nobles whom he loves were in every room. Every butler was busy at his duties. Years were made to pass away from my body. I was plucked, and my hair was combed. A load of dirt was given to the desert, and my clothes to the Sand-Crossers. I was clad in fine linen and anointed with prime oil. I slept on a bed. I gave up the sand to them who are in it, and wood oil to him who is anointed with it. I was given a house which had a garden, which had been in the possession of a courtier. Many craftsmen built it, and all its woodwork was newly restored. Meals were brought to me from the palace three or four times a day, apart from that which the royal children gave, without ceasing a moment.

There was constructed for me a pyramid-tomb of stone in the midst of the pyramid-tombs. The stone-masons who hew a pyramid-tomb took over its ground-area. The outline-draftsmen designed in it; the chief sculptors carved in it; and the overseers of works who are in the necropolis made it their concern. Its necessary materials were made from all the outfittings which are placed at a tomb-shaft. Mortuary priests were given to me. There was made for me a necropolis garden, with fields in it formerly extending as far as the town, like that which is done for a chief courtier. My statue was overlaid with gold, and its skirt was of fine gold. It was his majesty who had it made. There is no poor man for whom like has been done. (Pritchard, pp. 18–22)

cataract, probably at about the time of the building of the great pyramids. That fortress, too, seems to have declined after about 2400 B.C.E., although trading and raiding expeditions continued.

The ninety-four-year-long reign of Pepy II (r. 2246–2152 B.C.E.) brought the Old Kingdom almost to its end. Perhaps this pharaoh continued to rule beyond his capabilities. The later years of his reign have not produced historical records, and they may, indeed, be mythical. Several kings succeeded Pepy, but their reigns were short, and none seems to have exercised national control. As central authority weakened, provincial officials in each *nome*, called nomarchs, asserted their powers. They collected and kept the taxes, and their private armies ruled locally. Based on the size and records of cemeteries, the death rates seem to have increased at this time. Famine was prevalent. Apparently the Nile did not reach optimal flood heights for agriculture, and weak rulers could not create adequate irrigation works to make up for it.

From State to Empire

In 2134 B.C.E. the Old Kingdom fell. At first, several nomarchs held independent local power. Then two separate centers began to stand out in the contest for power: Herakleopolis to the north and Thebes in the south. Finally, about 2040 B.C.E., King Mentuhotpe of Thebes defeated his rivals in the north and re-united the kingdom, initiating the Middle Kingdom, *c.* 2050–1750 B.C.E. The Middle Kingdom saw the state develop more organization and power than ever before. It administered Egypt efficiently and spread its power into Nubia and into the Middle East more aggressively than before, as Egypt began to rule over more distant, foreign peoples. It became an **empire**. That story is told in Part 3, in Chapter 5. At the same time, both the fine arts and literature flourished.

The Middle Kingdom was overthrown by foreign invaders. They were called "Hyksos" or "ruler of foreign lands," and little is known of their origins or their rule. When Egyptian kings expelled the Hyksos about 1550 B.C.E., Egypt began its New Kingdom. The New Kingdom, perhaps the most powerful in Egypt's ancient history, was probably the strongest in terms of internal control and external conquest. It, too, became an empire and lasted until about 1050.

CONNECTION: *Egypt and empire, pp. 125–30*

THE INDUS VALLEY CIVILIZATION AND ITS MYSTERIES

The civilization of the Indus valley was redis-covered only in the 1920s. Archaeologists have now identified over 1000 settlement sites of this civilization distributed over more than 400,000 square miles (1 million square kilometers), making it the most widespread civilization of its time. Archaeologists have pushed back the origins of settlement history in the region to 7000 B.C.E., fixed the apex of its material and cultural creativity at about 2500–2000 B.C.E., and identified its forward connections as far as the Ganges civilization, which developed into urban form in 700 B.C.E. The three largest cities of the Indus valley—Harappa (for which the civilization is often named), Mohenjo-Daro, and Kalibangan—may have housed 35,000–40,000 inhabitants each. It is not known which of the three, if any, served as the capital.

We see the urban formations in the excavations, but we do not know if the Harappan civilization developed urban institutions for governance, trade, religion, or worship, much less the quality of any such institutions. While Egypt had a state but, perhaps, few cities, Harappa had cities but no clearly delineated state. Indeed, some scholars argue that the Indus valley did not create state structures at all. Until the Harappan language is deciphered, its civilization will remain mysterious: How was it organized? Why did it disperse? How did it move eastward? In what ways did it enrich its successor, the Aryan civilization of the Ganges River valley?

THE INDUS VALLEY: HOW DO WE KNOW?

In 1856 Britain ruled India. Builders of the section of the East Indian Railway connecting Lahore and Karachi found hundreds of thousands of old fire-baked bricks in the semi-desert area and used them to lay the road bed. Among the old bricks, workers discovered steatite stone seals marked with artistic designs. They gave some of the seals to Major General Alexander Cunningham, a British officer who was visiting in the area. In 1861, Cunningham retired from the army and was appointed first Surveyor General of the

THE INDUS VALLEY

DATE	POLITICAL	CULTURE AND RELIGION	SOCIAL DEVELOPMENT
7000 B.C.E.			• Traces of settlements; trade with Mesopotamia
3000 B.C.E.			• Cotton cultivated
2500 B.C.E.	• Height of Harappan civilization in northern India (2500–2000)		• Cities of Harappa and Mohenjo–Jaro
2000 B.C.E.	• Collapse of Harappan civilization (2000–1900)	• Evidence of decline in standards of architecture	
1500 B.C.E.	• Immigration of Aryans into India (*c.* 1250)		
1000 B.C.E.	• Aryan immigrants reach west Ganges valley (*c.* 1000) and build first cities (*c.* 750)		• Iron tools used to clear Ganges valley for agriculture (*c.* 1000)

Archaeological Survey of Northern India. He alerted archaeologists to the Indus find, but formal, systematic excavations did not begin until 1920, under John Marshall, Director General of Archaeology in India. Marshall commissioned Daya Ram Sahni to survey a huge mound that rose above the desert floor where the seals had been found. Sahni's excavations soon revealed a 4500-year-old city, Harappa. Two years later, R.D. Banerji, an Indian officer of the Survey, recognized and began to excavate a twin site 200 miles (500 kilometers) to the southwest, later named Mohenjo-Daro, "Hill of the Dead." The two cities had many urban design and architectural features in common. Both were about 3 miles (5 kilometers) in circumference, large enough to hold populations of 40,000.

With these two excavations, an urban civilization that had been lost for thousands of years was uncovered. Before these excavations, scholars had believed that the civilization of India had begun in the Ganges valley with the arrival of Aryan invaders from Persia or central Asia about 1250 B.C.E. and the construction of their first cities about 700 B.C.E. The discovery of the Harappan cities pushed the origin of Indian civilization back an additional 1500 years and located it in an entirely different ecological zone.

The revelations multiplied. In the late 1930s, Ernest Mackay discovered and excavated Chanhu-Daro, a smaller town of the Harappan civilization. At the same time, Sir Aurel Stein, known for his archaeological discoveries in Persia and Mesopotamia, found further Harappan settlements in Baluchistan, Sind, and Rajputana. As Director of the Archaeological Survey, Mortimer Wheeler continued the excavations in both Mohenjo-Daro and Harappa in the late 1940s and early 1950s. In the early 1950s, extensive excavations began in Gujarat, especially at Lothal near Cambay. Although these sites were more recent than the Indus valley excavations, they were similar in design and architecture. Their discovery extended the time-frame of the Indus civilization forward by several centuries and its geographical frame southeastward by hundreds of miles.

Excavating in these relatively recent and peripheral sites, archaeologists like Gregory Possehl of the University of Pennsylvania Museum, and Jim Shaffer of Case Western Reserve University, have explored the relationship of the Indus civilization to that of the Ganges a thousand years later. Unlike John Marshall, who felt that the two civilizations were discontinuous and that the Aryan invaders had thoroughly destroyed the earlier Harappan civilization, both Possehl and Shaffer argued that Harappan civilization had not been destroyed, but had become de-urbanized and more rural. The cities may have come to an end, but Harappan culture and influence persisted. They could be found in the agricultural practices and religious symbolism of the Aryans.

As the end date of Harappan civilization was pushed forward, so its origin was pushed backward. In the 1980s an archaeological team from France, working under Jean-François Jarrige, and with the cooperation of the Department of Archaeology of Pakistan, excavated the settlement of Mehrgarh in the foothills of the Bolan Pass, but still on the Indus valley side. The Mehrgarh site has yielded early settlement artifacts going back to 7000 B.C.E. and, with ever-increasing sophistication, coming forward to 2500–2000 B.C.E. Jarrige explained:

> One and one-half millennia before the emergence of the Indus civilization, large settlements with elaborate architectural features and a vast network of communication already existed in the greater Indus valley. (p. 29)

Harappa, with its antecedents going back to Mehrgarh, Jarrige asserted, was not a derivative of Mesopotamia but had grown up indigenously. It is conceivable that the later civilizations of both Mesopotamia and the Indus had a common ancestor in the settlements of the hills and mountains between them.

Excavation of the two largest cities has now reached severe limits. The city of Harappa was vandalized for thousands of years before, as well as during, the railroad construction, and few artifacts remain to be discovered. Mohenjo-Daro sits on a high water table, and any deeper excavation threatens to flood the site. It is impossible to dig down to the foundation level of the city.

Further exploration of Mohenjo-Daro's surface, however, continues to yield fascinating results. An expedition from the University of Aachen, Germany, began its survey of the surface of Mohenjo-Daro in 1979. Michael Janson and his team discovered an outlying segment of Mohenjo-Daro about a mile away from the known city.

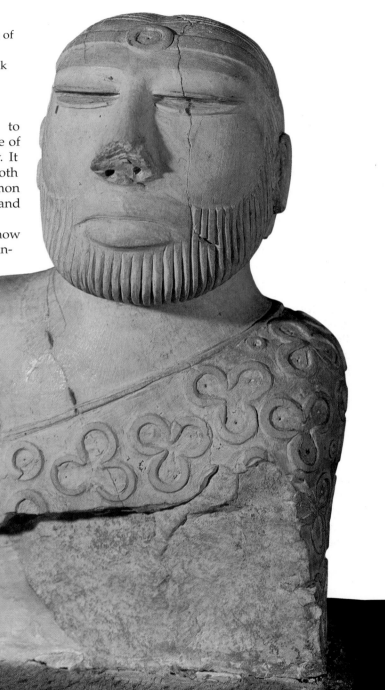

Limestone bust from Mohenjo-Daro, *c.* **2300–1750** B.C.E. This half-figure with horizontal slits for eyes, flat thick lips, and fringes of beard is thought to have represented a priest or shaman because of the way the robe is hung over its left shoulder. Despite its monumental appearance, the figure is only 7 inches (17.8 cm) high. (*National Museum of Pakistan, Karachi*)

Was it part of an industrial area or a residential suburb? It is impossible to determine. The discovery, however, identifies Mohenjo-Daro as a larger city than Harappa. Perhaps it was the capital city of the civilization.

Written records, the key that re-opened the civilizations of ancient Mesopotamia and Egypt, are lacking in the Indus valley. The only written materials so far discovered are seal inscriptions that give only limited information, and thus far, even they have not been interpreted satisfactorily. Scholars such as Akso Pranpola seem to have identified some specific names and dates on the seals, but other academics dispute these interpretations.

Without written records our understanding of Indus civilization is limited. Artifactual remains give a good representation of the physical cities and settlements, but not of their institutions. Moreover, while we can make educated guesses about the function and meaning of the remaining artifacts and physical structures from our own perspective, we do not have the words of the Harappans themselves to explain their own understanding of their civilization.

THE INDUS VALLEY: WHAT DO WE KNOW?

Archaeological evidence to date reveals an urban civilization with its roots beginning as early as 7000 B.C.E. in simple settlements like Mehrgarh in the foothills of the Bolan Pass. Over the millennia, people moved down into the plains and river valley. At first, they may have moved into the forested river valley only in the colder months, herding their flocks of sheep and cattle, including the humped zebu, back to the hills for the summer. Over time they may have decided to farm the river-watered alluvial lands of the valley. They began to trade by boat along the Indus and even down the Indus into the Arabian Sea and, further, into the Persian Gulf and up the Tigris and Euphrates into Mesopotamia. Goods from the Indus have been found in Mesopotamia and vice versa (see map, p. 51).

By about 2500 B.C.E., a thriving civilization reached its apex, maintaining it for about 500 years. One thousand sites of the Indus civilization have been located. Each of the two largest settlements, Harappa and Mohenjo-Daro, has a core area of about 3 miles (5 kilometers) in circumference, while Mohenjo-Daro also had a suburb— residential or industrial—about a mile away. Both cities accommodated about 40,000 people.

Both cities share similar features of design. To the north is a citadel, or raised area; to the south is a lower town. In Mohenjo-Daro, the citadel is built on an architectural platform about 45 feet (14 meters) above the plain, and it measures 1400 feet (430 meters) by 450 feet (140 meters). On the summit was a bath 8 feet (2.4 meters) deep and 23 feet (7 meters) by 29 feet (8.8 meters) in area. Numerous cubicles—perhaps small, individual baths—flanked it. Adjacent to the large bath was a huge open space, identified as a granary, where food was stored safe from possible flood. Other spaces may have been used for public meetings. Fortified walls mark the southeast corner, and it appears that the entire citadel was walled.

In the nearby lower city were private residences. The lower city was layed out in a gridiron, with the main streets about 45 feet (14 meters) wide. Almost every house had its own well, bathing space, and toilet, consisting of a brick seat over a drainage area. Brick-lined drains flushed by water carried liquid and solid waste to sumps, where it would be collected and carted away, probably to fertilize the nearby fields. The town plan was orderly and regular. Even the prefabricated, fire-baked bricks were uniform in size and shape. A uniform system of weights and measures was also employed throughout.

The regularity of plan and construction suggest a government with great organizational and bureaucratic capacity, but no truly monumental architecture clearly marks the presence of a palace or temple, and there is little sign of social stratification in the plan or buildings. Those burials that have been discovered are regular, with the heads pointing to the north, and with some grave goods, such as pots of food and water, small amounts of jewelry, simple mirrors, and some cosmetics. These were not the extravagant burials of Egypt or even of Mesopotamia.

Interpretations of these artifacts stress the apparent classlessness of the society, its equality, efficiency, and public conveniences. Some interpreters view these qualities negatively, equating them with oppressively rigid governments and drab lives. Archaeologist Walter Fairservis argues that the cities changed little over long periods of time and, unlike the cities of Mesopotamia and the Nile, "lacked dynamism." With no contemporary literature to guide us, interpretation of what is found is in the eyes, and the value system, of the beholder.

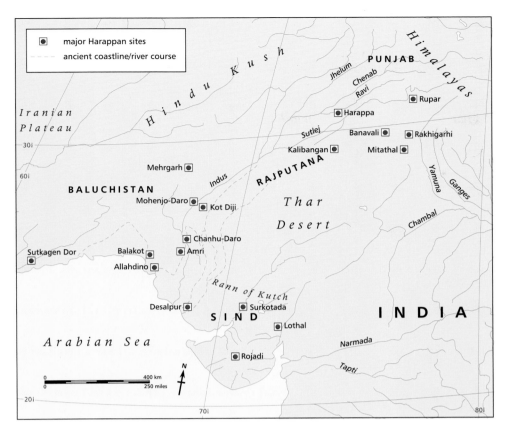

Hindu Kush

Iranian Plateau

PUNJAB

Himalayas

Jhelum

Chenab

Ravi

● Rupar

● Harappa

Sutlej

Banavali ● ● Rakhigarhi

Kalibangan ● Mitathal ●

Mehrgarh ●

BALUCHISTAN

Indus

RAJPUTANA

Thar Desert

Yamuna

Ganges

Chambal

Mohenjo-Daro ● ● Kot Diji

● Chanhu-Daro

Sutkagen Dor ● Balakot ● ● Amri

Allahdino ●

Rann of Kutch

Desalpur ● ● Surkotada

SIND

INDIA

● Lothal

Arabian Sea

Narmada

● Rojadi

Tapti

0 ____ 400 km
0 ____ 250 miles

N

Cities of the Indus
Confined to the north and west by mountains, and to the east by desert, the Indus valley had, by 2500 B.C.E., developed a sophisticated urban culture based on individual walled cities, sharing common patterns of urban design. In terms of geographical extent this civilization was the largest in the world in its time.

We also do not know if this uniform, planned civilization had a single capital city, or several regional capitals, or no centralized political system at all. Was it like Egypt before unification or after unification? Was it like Mesopotamia, with numerous city-states all participating in a single general culture? All three suggestions have been made.

Crafts in the Indus included pottery making, dyeing, metal working in bronze, and bead making. Bead materials included jade from the Himalayas, lapis lazuli from Afghanistan, turquoise from Persia, amethyst from Mewar in India, and steatite, which was found locally. Small sculptures in stone, terra cotta, and bronze presumably represent members of the society, and guesses as to the identity of some include a priestly or

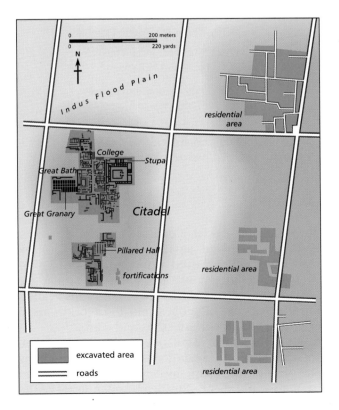

Indus Flood Plain

residential area

College

Stupa

Great Bath

Great Granary

Citadel

Pillared Hall

fortifications

residential area

excavated area

roads

residential area

Planned Cities With an area of 150 acres, and about 40,000 inhabitants, Mohenjo-Daro was a thriving Indus city. Excavations reveal a raised citadel area, containing ceremonial and administrative buildings, and a residential quarter centered on boulevards about 45 feet (14 m) wide, with grid-patterned streets, an underground sewerage and drainage system, and a range of brick-built dwellings.

Limestone dancing figure from Harappa, *c.* 2300–1750 B.C.E.
This dancing figure displays a grasp of three-dimensional movement and vitality rare in the arts until much later periods. Human sculptures in contemporary Mesopotamia and Egypt are by contrast symbols of pure power, either immutable ideals of divinity or semidivine kingship. Indeed, this Harappan accomplishment is so extraordinary that some scholars have cast doubt on its early date. (*National Museum of India, New Delhi*)

EARLY SCIENCE AND TECHNOLOGY (7000–1000 B.C.E.

7000–6000	Pottery made in Middle East
c. **5500**	Copper, gold, and silver worked in Mesopotamia and Egypt
c. **4000–3500**	In Asia and Africa, potter's wheel and kiln invented; mud bricks used; spindle developed for spinning; basket-making begins
c. **3500–3000**	Plow and cart invented; bronze cast and cuneiform writing developed in Sumer
3100	Reed boats in Egypt and Assyria; appearance of hieroglyphs in Egypt
3000	Cotton cultivated in the Indus valley
c. **2500**	Wooden boats used in Egypt; ink and papyrus writing material used
2050	First glass in Mesopotamia
1790	Mathematics and medicine practiced in Babylon
1740	War chariots introduced from Persia to Mesopotamia (and later Egypt)
1370	Alphabetic script used in western Syria
1000	Industrial use of iron in Egypt and Mesopotamia

governmental official, a dancing girl, and a mother goddess. Dice and small sculptures of bullock carts were probably used as toys and games.

The first known use of cotton as a fiber for weaving textiles occurred in the Indus valley, introducing one of India's and the world's most enduring and important crops and crafts.

By about 2000 B.C.E. the architecture of the Indus civilization began to decline. New buildings and repairs to existing structures lacked attention to quality and detail. Residents began to leave the

The citadel of Mohenjo-Daro, *c.* **2300 B.C.E. and later.** The citadel at Mohenjo-Daro, a massive, mud-filled embankment that rises 43 feet (13 m) above the lower city, was discovered by archaeologist Daya Ram Sahni while investigating the second-century C.E. Buddhist stupa (burial mound) that can be seen in the distance. The citadel's summit houses the remains of several impressive structures, of which the most prominent is the so-called Great Bath (foreground).

towns along the Indus and to relocate northeastward into the Punjab, to towns like Kalibangan, and southeastward, to towns like Lothal in Gujarat. Meanwhile, newcomers—squatters—seem to have moved into the old cities. Again a variety of arguments suggests the reasons for the decline in the cities and the geographical redistribution of their populations. Perhaps the river changed course or became erratic; perhaps the soil became too saline; perhaps the forests were cut down and topsoil eroded.

An older opinion—that the Indus civilization was destroyed by the invasion of Aryan peoples from somewhere northwest of India—is now less widely held. It rested on Harappan archaeological evidence and Aryan literature. Several sets of skeletal remains in Mohenjo-Daro indicate violent deaths, while Aryan religious texts suggest that the invaders burned and destroyed existing settlements. The *Rigveda*, one of the earliest and most important of these texts, tells of the destructive power of the god Indra:

> With all-outstripping chariot-wheel, O Indra, thou far-famed, hast overthrown the twice ten kings of men
>
> With sixty thousand nine and ninety followers . . .
> Thou goest on from fight to fight intrepidly,
> destroying castle after castle here with strength.
>
> (i, 53)
>
> . . . in kindled fire he burnt up all their weapons,
> And made him rich with kine and carts and horses.
>
> (ii, 15)

The Aryan god of fire, Agni, is still more fearsome:

> Through fear of you the dark people went away, not giving battle, leaving behind their possessions, when, O Vaisvanara, burning brightly for Puru, and destroying the cities, you did shine. (7.5.3)

Newer archaeological evidence, however, suggests that the decline, de-urbanization, and dispersal of the Indus civilization seem to have preceded the

Aryan invasion. Further evidence suggests that the Aryans may not have swept into the region in a single all-conquering expedition, but in a series of smaller waves. The arrival of the Aryans may have only completed the Harappan decay.

LEGACIES OF THE INDUS

Interchange between the resident Harappans and the invading Aryans produced new, hybrid cultural forms that we know primarily from the Aryan records. Ironically, these records are almost entirely literary and artistic. Reversing the Harappan pattern, the early Aryans have left a treasure of literature, but virtually no architectural or design artifacts.

Four legacies of Harappa stand out. First, the Aryan invaders were a nomadic group, who must have adopted at least some of the arts of settlement and civilization from the already settled residents. Second, as newcomers to the ecological zones of India, the Aryans must also have learned methods of farming and animal husbandry from the Harappans. Later, however, as they swept eastward into the Ganges valley, they confronted a new ecology based on rice cultivation and the use of iron. Here Harappan skills were useless. Third, a three-headed figure frequently appearing in Harappan

Steatite seal of seated "yogi," Mohenjo-Daro, *c.* **2300–1700** B.C.E. This famous seal is important for several reasons, chief among them being that it may show the first representation in Indian history of a deity in human form. Sir John Marshall suggested that it appears to delineate a prototype for the later Hindu god Shiva. (*National Museum of Pakistan, Karachi*)

seals resembles later representations of the Aryan god Shiva. Perhaps an earlier Harappan god may have been adopted and adapted by the Aryans.

Finally, the Aryan caste system, which ranks people at birth according to occupation, color, and ritual purity, and prescribes the people with whom they may enter into social intercourse and marry, may reflect the need of the Aryans to regulate relationships between themselves and the Harappans. To claim and maintain their own supremacy, the Aryans may have elaborated the social structures of the caste system and relegated the native inhabitants to permanent low status within it.

The Aryan groups grew increasingly skilled and powerful as they moved east. The first known archaeological evidence of their urban structures dates to about 700 B.C.E. and is found in the Ganges valley. We will read more about it when we analyze the first Indian empire, in Chapter 8.

CONNECTION: *Settlement in South Asia after 1500 B.C.E.,* pp. 232–5

BIBLIOGRAPHY

Aldred, Cyril. *The Egyptians* (New York: Thames and Hudson, 1986).

Allchin, Bridget and Raymond. *The Birth of Indian Civilization: India and Pakistan before 500 B.C.* (Baltimore, MD: Penguin Books, 1968).

Baines, John and Jaromir Malek. *Atlas of Ancient Egypt* (New York: Facts on File Publications, 1980).

Cotterell, Arthur, ed. *The Penguin Encyclopedia of Ancient Civilizations* (London: Penguin Books, 1980).

Fagan, Brian. *People of the Earth: An Introduction to World Prehistory* (New York: HarperCollins, 8th ed., 1995).

Fairservis, Walter. *The Roots of Ancient India* (Chicago: University of Chicago Press, 2nd ed., 1975).

Hassan, Fekri A. "The Predynastic of Egypt," *Journal of World Prehistory* II, No. 2 (June 1988), 135–85.

Janson, Michael R.N. "Mohenjo-daro: Type Site of the Earliest Urbanization Process in South Asia," Spodek and Srinivasan, 35–51.

Jarrige, Jean-François. "The Early Architectural Traditions of Greater Indus as Seen from Mehrgarh, Baluchistan," Spodek and Srinivasan, 25–33.

Kemp, Barry J. *Ancient Egypt: Anatomy of a Civilization* (London: Routledge, 1989).

Lichtheim, Miriam. *Ancient Egyptian Literature: A Book of Readings* (Berkeley: University of California Press, 3 vols., 1973).

Mumford, Lewis. *The City in History* (New York: Harcourt Brace, and World, 1961).

Noble Wilford, John. "Egypt Carvings Set Earlier Date for Alphabet," *New York Times* (November 14, 1999), A–1, 16.

Past Worlds: The (London) Times Atlas of Archaeology (Maplewood, NJ: Hammond, Inc., 1988).

Piggott, Stuart. *Prehistoric India* (Baltimore, MD: Penguin Books, 1952).

Possehl, Gregory L., ed. *Ancient Cities of the Indus* (New Delhi: Vikas Publishing, 1979).

—— ed. *Harappan Civilization: A Recent Perspective* (New Delhi: Oxford University Press and IBH Publishing, 2nd ed., 1993).

Pritchard, James B., ed. *Ancient Near Eastern Texts Relating to the Old Testament* (Princeton: Princeton University Press, 3rd ed. 1969).

Shaffer, Jim G. "Reurbanization: The Eastern Punjab and Beyond," Spodek and Srinivasan, 53–67.

Spodek, Howard and Doris Meth Srinivasan, eds. *Urban Form and Meaning in South Asia: The Shaping of Cities from Prehistoric to Precolonial Times* (Washington: National Gallery of Art, 1993).

Time-Life Books. *Time Frame 3000–1500: The Age of God-Kings* (Alexandria, VA: Time-Life Books, 1987).

—— *Time Frame 1500–600 BC: Barbarian Tides* (Alexandria, VA: Time-Life Books, 1987).

Wenke, Robert J. "The Evolution of Early Egyptian Civilization: Issues and Evidence," *Journal of World Prehistory* V, No. 1 (September 1991), 279–329.

Wheatley, Paul. *Pivot of the Four Quarters* (Chicago: Aldine Publishing Company, 1971).

Wheeler, Mortimer. *Civilizations of the Indus Valley and Beyond* (London: Thames and Hudson, 1966).

4 A POLYCENTRIC WORLD

1700 B.C.E–1000 C.E

"Only by accepting a major role for ideology as a direct source of power can one understand the institutions of these civilizations, their history, and the elaborate cultural concepts that sustained them."

ARTHUR DEMARE

CITIES AND STATES IN EAST ASIA, THE AMERICAS, AND WEST AFRICA

This chapter completes the survey of the seven areas of primary urbanization. It covers the four areas which developed primary urbanization somewhat more recently: Yellow River valley of China; two regions of the western hemisphere—Mesoamerica and the South American Pacific coastal plain with the adjacent Andes Mountains that tower above it; and the Niger River valley of West Africa. The first cities in these regions date from as early as 1700 B.C.E. in China to as late as 400 C.E. in the Niger valley. They include cities that were not in major river valleys as well as some that were. They all show evidence of state formation, but they include settlements that did not have written languages and records, and therefore require us to base our understanding entirely on the archaeological record and to stretch our definition of urbanization.

CHINA: THE XIA, SHANG, AND ZHOU DYNASTIES

Chinese historical texts tell of three early dynasties—the Xia, the Shang, and the Zhou—that ruled over large regions of China. In its time, each ruled over the most powerful single kingdom among the embattled states of northern China. All were based primarily around the Huang He (Yellow River) valley in north China. State formation may have begun under the Xia, *c.* 2205–1766 B.C.E., although records are too sparse to recreate its cities and institutions. The archaeological record on urbanization under the Shang, *c.* 1766–1122 B.C.E., is far more revealing and reliable. The Zhou, *c.* 1100–256 B.C.E., consolidated both city and state, and left extensive archaeological remains and written records. None of the

EARLY CHINA

DATE	POLITICAL	RELIGION AND CULTURE	SOCIAL DEVELOPMENT
8000 B.C.E.		• Neolithic decorated pottery	• Simple Neolithic society established
5000 B.C.E.	• Yangshao culture in China (5000–2700)	• Marks on Yangshao pottery possibly writing	• Penal code; defensive structures round villages
3500 B.C.E.	• Longshan late Neolithic culture	• Delicate Longshan ceramics	• Farming, with domesticated animals
2000 B.C.E.	• Xia dynasty (2205–1766) • Shang dynasty (1766–1122)	• The "sage kings" in China known from legend; first known use of writing in this area • City of Zhengzhou (c. 1700) • Under Shang, bronze vases found in ceremonial burials	• Agricultural progress • Cities (by 1700) under control of Shang kings
1100 B.C.E.	• Zhou dynasty (1100–256)	• Poetry extant from Zhou period	• Under Zhou, iron, money, and written laws in use
500 B.C.E.	• Warring States period (481–222)	• Confucius (d. 479) • Great Wall of China begun (214) to keep out Xiongnu	• Crossbow invented (c. 350)
100 B.C.E.		• Sima Qian (d. 85)	

three dynasties succeeded in annexing all its enemies and building a single unified empire. That process would come later.

The traditional chronological dating suggests that the states succeeded one another, but recent evidence indicates that there may, in fact, have been considerable overlap. For centuries, they may have coexisted in neighboring regions, with first one, then another, having comparatively greater power and prestige. One of the leading archaeologists of China today, K.C. Chang, describes

> the political interrelationship of Hsia [Xia], Shang, and Chou [Zhou], as three parallel, or at least overlapping, polities. . . . Hsia, Shang, and Chou were subcultures of a common—ancient Chinese—culture, but more particularly they were political groups in opposition to one another. (*Shang Civilization*, p. 348)

By the time of the Shang Dynasty, if not already in the Xia, cities had been founded in north China as centers of administration and ritual. State formation was well under way, and cities served as capitals and administrative centers. The entire dynastic state was ruled through its urban network. Capitals were frequently shifted, suggesting that new rulers wanted to make their mark through new construction, or that confrontations with neighboring, enemy states required strategic redeployments for improving offensive or defensive positions. The regional cities and their administrations were frequently entrusted to blood relatives of the king. It appears that rulers performed productive economic functions for their subjects, especially in water control. In exchange the lineages on top lived lives of considerable wealth while those on the lower levels had little as sharp class differences emerged in the early dynastic states. The cemeteries of different classes were geographically segregated into different neighborhoods within the city and its suburbs, and were of different quality.

Like primary cities in other parts of the world, the Chinese cities were also, as we shall see, cosmo-magical centers (see Focus pp. 92–3), with the kings presiding over rituals as well as administration and warfare. Indeed, the warfare was necessary to supply the human and animal sacrifices that were central to the rituals.

EARLIEST TIMES: HOW DO WE KNOW?

Texts

Texts ascribed to the Chinese teacher Confucius (551–479 B.C.E.) refer to the Xia and Shang dynasties but give little detail. Confucius lamented "the insufficiency of their records and wise men" (Chang, p. 2).

Later, Sima Qian (Ssu-ma Ch'ien; c. 145–85 B.C.E.), court historian of the Han dynasty, wrote the first of China's official historical annals. Sima, who had access to many texts that have not survived to today, devoted a chapter to the Shang royal house beginning with its legendary founder Xie, who located his capital in a town called Shang, now believed to have been in eastern Henan. Successive rulers moved this capital eight times. Xie's fourteenth successor, Tang, established the hereditary dynasty of Shang. Once in power, the Shang dynasty established a series of successive capital cities, all of which are in north China. Seven are recorded. Sima's sources of information were limited, however, and his chapter mostly outlined the genealogy of the rulers, recounted moralistic tales of their rule, and briefly noted their capital cities.

Oracle Bones

A new source of information came to light in the 1890s and early 1900s. Numerous oracle bones—some apparently hidden away for many years, others recently uncovered—appeared in antique markets in China. Over the decades, more than 100,000 were discovered. These bones of birds, animals, and especially the shells of turtles, had been inscribed with markings and writings for use in predicting the future. Inscribed and marked lightly, they were placed in a fire and tapped lightly with a rod until they began to crack. The cracks were then "read" by specialists in predicting the future. A poem from the later Zhou dynasty noted the use of oracle bones in deciding the location of a new city:

> The plain of Chou was very fertile,
> Its celery and sowthistle sweet as rice-cakes.
> "Here we will make a start; here take counsel,
> Here notch our [turtle]."
> It says, "Stop," it says, "Halt.
> Build houses here."
>
> (Chang, *Shang Civilization*, pp. 31–2)

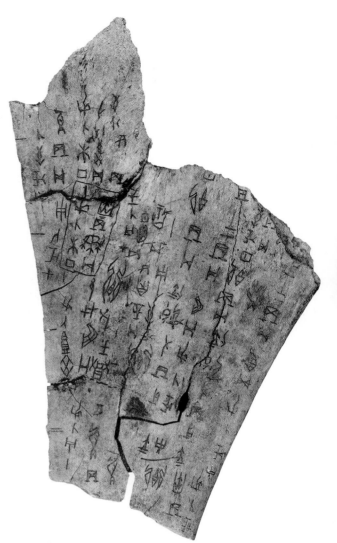

Inscribed oracle bone, China. Shang Kings communicated with their ancestors through both sacrificial rituals and divination. Diviners would pose questions—about health, harvest, or politics—by applying a red-hot poker to animal bones or turtle shells and then analyze the resulting heat-induced cracks. *(East Asian Library, Columbia University)*

Some of the oracle bone inscriptions confirmed the names and approximate dates of the Shang rulers whom Sima Qian had listed. The location of the bones and the content of their inscriptions encouraged archaeologists to search further in the north central Chinese plains, near the point where the Yellow River flows out of the mountains. They concentrated on Anyang.

Archaeology

Archaeology was in fashion in China in the 1920s. Peking man had been discovered at Zhoukoudian (see p. 13) and, in the process, a new generation of Chinese archaeologists had received on-the-job training. Meanwhile, the new "doubting antiquity" school of Chinese historiography began to question the dating and to challenge the authenticity of many ancient Chinese historical events. In response, the newly established National Research Institute of History and Philology dispatched the young archaeologist Dong Zobin to explore the Anyang region. Dong recommended excavating for oracle bones. These excavations, mostly under the direction of Li Ji, uncovered not only bones but also sites from the Shang dynasty. These led to the discovery of artifacts from earlier eras as well. Ancient texts, bronzes, oracle bones, and excavations reinforced one another in recounting parts of ancient China's urbanization and state formation. Civil war in China, beginning in 1927, and war with Japan, beginning in 1937, interrupted excavations until 1950, but since then, continuous archaeological research has yielded new understandings.

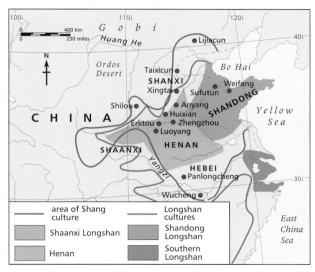

Shang China Centered where the Huang He (Yellow River) enters its floodplain from the mountains of northeast China, the Longshan farming communities of about 2500 B.C.E. benefited from rich alluvial soils and extensive metal ore deposits. By 1800 B.C.E. a powerful, highly organized, urban, metal-working culture, the Shang, had developed.

EARLIEST TIMES: WHAT DO WE KNOW?

The Earliest Villages

Thousands of years before the Xia dynasty, as early as the eighth millennium B.C.E., Neolithic pottery decorations marked the transition from hunting and gathering into the culture of farming and village life. This Yangshao culture, first excavated in 1921, was named for the location in which it was first discovered in western Henan province. Excavations continue in Henan and in late 1999 archaeologists in China and at the Brookhaven National Laboratory in the United States reported uncovering a set of tiny flutes carved some 9000 years ago from the wing bones of a large bird. Three thousand years older than the next known playable instruments, from Sumer, one of them is still playable. (The "Neanderthal" flutes discovered in southern France [see picture, p. 29] are no longer playable.) The sounds of this flute playing a Chinese folk song are available at the Brookhaven web site, http://www.bnl.gov/bnl.web/flutes.html.

The Yangshao lasted to c. 2700 B.C.E. Farmers of this era grew millet, wheat, and rice, and domesticated pigs, dogs, goats, and perhaps horses. They lived mostly in river valleys, and the villages were often surrounded with earthen walls for defense. Ban Po, discussed in the Spotlight on pages 42–3, is the best excavated village of the Yangshao culture.

Slightly later and slightly to the northeast, a more sophisticated Neolithic culture, the Longshan, grew up. The people of the Longshan made their pottery on wheels, whereas the Yangshao had coiled or molded their pots by hand. The Longshan people domesticated sheep and cattle, which were not seen in Yangshao sites. Longshan graves were dug under their own homes, while the Yangshao had buried their dead in graveyards far from their villages. Sometimes Longshan funeral urns were cemented into foundation walls, suggesting ancestor worship.

Several hundred miles to the east, somewhat further down the Yellow River in Shandong, and one or two centuries later, yet another branch of Longshan culture developed, with yet another distinct type of pottery, often distinctively reddish-brown and gray in color, quite different from the black of the Longshan of Henan. Although the high points of Yangshao and the western and eastern Longshan cultures appeared at successively later times, they overlapped each other to a considerable extent.

The Henan Longshan culture was characterized in later historical accounts as harsh, having "a penal code internally and armed forces externally"

EARLY CHINESE CULTURE

5000 (B.C.E.)	Rice cultivation, basketry, weaving, use of wooden tools, primitive writing
3000	Domestication of sheep, cattle, water buffalo
2000	Human grave sacrifices
1900	Metal working, class system, domestication of horse
1200	Chariots in warfare

(cited in Chang, p. 339). Excavations reveal the burials of victims of killing, some decapitated and showing signs of struggle, suggesting warfare between villages. The defensive walls of pounded earth that encircle some of the villages support this hypothesis, as does the presence of bronze knives.

Historical Evidence of the Xia Dynasty

At Erlitou, east of Luoyang, in western Henan, a culture was discovered in precisely the areas described by ancient texts as the site of the legendary Xia dynasty. The pottery at Erlitou seemed intermediate in style and quality between the earlier Longshan and the later Shang. Although the link is not certain, many archaeologists took Erlitou to be representative of the Xia dynasty.

The Xia, like the later Shang and Zhou, seems to have been ruled by specific internal clans, each with its own king. As the historian Mark Elvin puts it, kingship and kinship were interrelated. As head of both his biological clan and his geographical realm, the king performed rituals, divinations, and sacrifices; waged war; constructed irrigation and flood control works; and administered his government. The king mediated between the world of the spirits and the world of humans. He was thought to be descended from the god of the spirits who controlled human health, wealth, agriculture, and warfare. The king's assertion of his right to perform sacrifice in any particular place was, in effect, his assertion of his right to rule over that place. Rights over ritual implied rights over land and people (Blunden and Elvin, p. 73).

Even before the Xia dynasty, control over water had been vital. The first settlements had avoided the immediate flood plain of the Yellow River, one of the most hazardous in the world. Its bed filled with the silt from the mountains, the Yellow River has jumped its course twenty-six times in recorded history, wreaking untold devastation. As early as the Longshan culture, people built great levees and canals for flood control, drainage, and irrigation. Chinese legend credits the first success in taming the Yellow River to one of the culture heroes of ancient history, Yu the Great of the twenty-third century B.C.E. The legend reflects the reality of a royal house's gaining power in part through its ability to organize great gangs of laborers to construct a system of water control.

The Xia dynasty went further with human organization. It assembled armies, built cities, carved jade, cast and worked bronze into both weapons and ritual vessels, created the pictograms that would evolve into Chinese script, and may have designed China's first calendar.

Similarities among the Three Dynasties

All three of these earliest dynasties, the Xia, Shang, and Zhou, built walled towns. Indeed, in written Chinese the same character, *cheng*, represents both city and city wall. At times these towns were loosely connected to one another, forming a network of rule and trade. At other times, when a single powerful king headed the dynasty, a single capital city predominated. Archaeologists see many similarities among the towns and the political structures of all three dynasties. In the absence of earlier written records, they cite literary evidence from later dynasties as evidence for patterns in the earlier dynasties. For example, in arguing for the supremacy of royal rule during the Shang Dynasty, K.C. Chang takes his supporting proof from "Pei shan," a poem of the Zhou dynasty:

> Everywhere under Heaven
> Is no land that is not the king's
> To the borders of all those lands
> None but is the king's slave.
>
> (trans. Arthur Waley; cited in Chang, *Shang Civilization*, p. 158)

Another well-known poem from the western Zhou rulers uses blunt imagery to suggest royal oppression and a parasitic relationship between ruler and ruled. Chang suggests that it may also be applied to Shang and Xia times:

Big rat, big rat,
Do not gobble our millet.
Three years we have slaved for you,
Yet you take no notice of us.
At last we are going to leave you
And go to that happy land;
Happy land, happy land,
Where we shall have our place.

(trans. Arthur Waley; cited in Chang,
Shang Civilization, p. 238)

CITY AND STATE UNDER THE SHANG

"The Shang state can be characterized, simply, as the network of such towns that was under the Shang king's direct control" (Chang, p. 210). The king ruled from his capital city. Regional cities were apportioned to his designated representatives, who were usually blood relatives. These relatives were granted title to land, shares in the harvests, and rights to build and control the regional capital cities. In exchange, they represented and served the king and his interests in the provinces.

Territorially, the Shang dynasty was always based in northern and central Henan and southwestern Shandong. At its most powerful it extended as far south as Wucheng, south of the Yangzi River; east to the Pacific, incorporating the Shandong Peninsula; north into Hebei and southern Manchuria; and west through Shanxi into the mountains of Shaanxi. At its greatest extent it may have controlled 40,000 square miles (100,000 square kilometers). On the fringes, Shang territories were interspersed with those of other rulers, and warfare between them was apparently frequent.

The capital was shifted often, but always remained within the core area of Shang urbanization. One of the earliest capitals was located at Luoyang; later, and for many decades, it was at Zhengzhou; and, finally, *c.* 1384 B.C.E., at Anyang. Luoyang has been difficult to excavate because it lies directly under a modern city. Zhengzhou, however, has been excavated extensively. Founded *c.* 1700 B.C.E., its core covered about 1¼ square miles (3 square kilometers), enclosed by a wall 4½ miles (7 kilometers) long and, in places, still surviving to a height of 30 feet (9 meters).

Inside the walled area lived the royal family, the nobility, and their retainers. Outside this palace/ritual center was a network of residential areas; workshops making bone, pottery, and bronze artifacts; and cemeteries. The class divisions written into this spatial pattern were reinforced by the geography of the suburbs: to the north were the dwellings and graves of the wealthy and powerful, marked by ritual bronze vessels and sacrificial victims; to the south were the dwellings of the commoners and their burial places in trash pits. Occupations tended to be inherited within specific family units (compare the caste system of India discussed in Chapters 8 and 9). Many *zu*, or lineage groups, corresponded to occupational groups. K.C. Chang argues that the emblems of the Shang family lineages also suggest their occupations.

Anyang, the Last Shang Capital

The final, most powerful, and most elaborate capital of the Shang dynasty was at Anyang. Shang texts report that the nineteenth king, Pan Gieng,

Shang dynasty bronze wine vessel, fourteenth to eleventh century B.C.E. The thousands of Shang bronze vessels that survive today continue to astonish us with their technical mastery and elegance. They testify to the elite's willingness to devote huge quantities of a precious resource to ritual purposes. During times of war, such bronzes were often melted down to produce weapons but once peace resumed, they were recast into ritual objects. *(Historical Museum, Beijing)*

FOCUS
The Cosmo-Magical City

In his classic and convincing *Pivot of the Four Quarters*, Paul Wheatley argues that ancient Chinese cities, like most ancient cities, began as ritual centers. He calls these cities "cosmo-magical." Archaeological and textual records support this interpretation for China. Consider, for example, this Zhou poem illustrating the siting of a royal capital. The process begins with reading the oracle shell of a tortoise to determine its location and ends with sacrifices to mark the completion of construction:

> Of old Tan-fu the duke
> At coming of day galloped his horses,
> Going west along the river bank
> Till he came to the foot of Mount Ch'i.
> Where with the lady Chiang
> He came to look for a home.
>
> The plain of Chou was very fertile,
> Its celery and sowthistle sweet as rice-cakes.
> "Here we will make a start; here take counsel,
> Here notch our tortoise."
> It says, "Stop," it says, "Halt.
> Build houses here."
>
> So he halted, so he stopped,
> And left and right
> He drew the boundaries of big plots and little,

> He opened up the ground, he counted the acres
> From west to east;
> Everywhere he took his task in hand.
>
> Then he summoned his Master of Works,
> Then he summoned his Master of Lands
> And made them build houses
> Dead straight was the plumb-line,
> The planks were lashed to hold the earth;
> They made the Hall of Ancestors, very venerable.
>
> They tilted in the earth with a rattling,
> They pounded it with a dull thud,
> They beat the walls with a loud clang,
> They pared and chiselled them with a faint *p'ing, p'ing*;
> The hundred cubits all rose;
> The drummers could not hold out.
>
> They raised the outer gate;
> The outer gate soared high.
> They raised the inner gate;
> The inner gate was very strong.
> They raised the great earth-mound,
> Whence excursions of war might start.

The rituals seem to have conferred worldly benefits. Potential enemies fled. The poem continues:

Headless skeletons of human sacrificial victims, tomb 1001, Anyang, China. The royal tombs discovered at Anyang testify to the wealth and power of the Shang rulers. Numerous servants and prisoners-of-war gave their lives willingly or unwillingly to accompany their masters to the grave. The heads of the decapitated figures shown here were located elsewhere in the tomb.

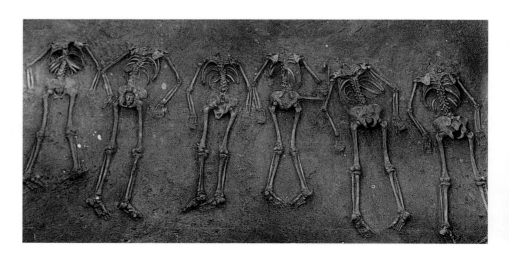

And in the time that followed they did not abate their sacrifices

Did not let fall their high renown;

The oak forests were laid low,

Roads were opened up.

The K'un tribes scampered away;

Oh, how they panted!

> (trans. Arthur Waley; cited in Chang, *Shang Civilization*, pp. 159–60)

Oracle records recognize more than twenty titles of officials grouped into three categories: ministers, generals, and archivists,

> but the most important categories of officials insofar as our available data are concerned are the diviners . . . and the inquirers. . . . Jao Tsung-yi enumerated the activities of as many as 117 diviners and inquirers in the oracle records. Ch'en Meng-chia counted 120. (Chang, p. 192)

Besides the diviners, a cadre of priests performed religious rituals, including human sacrifices.

Military force was needed to sustain these rituals, by providing the prisoners-of-war to be sacrificed when rituals demanded. Oracle records speak of Shang military campaigns of 3000, 5000, and even 13,000 troops. As many as 30,000 prisoners-of-war were claimed in one large battle, and 300 prisoners were sacrificed in a ritual of ancestor worship. Archaeological finds show that 600 humans were sacrificed at the completion of a single house; 164 for a single tomb.

Burial pit, unearthed at Liulihe, Hebei province, Western Zhou period. Evidence for the centrality of ritual in ancient Chinese culture can be found in this tomb, which contains the remains of horses and chariots. These important instruments of rule would have been regarded as valuable offerings to the gods and were thus buried along with their owner.

moved his capital to Yin and that the dynasty remained there until its fall 273 years later. Archaeologists identify that site as Anyang. This capital was the center of a network of sites stretching about 200 miles (320 kilometers) from northwest to southeast. The core area around Anyang is difficult to excavate fruitfully. The city burned to the ground, and farmers have been plowing the area, and robbers pillaging it, for 3000 years. Remains of royal graves and of buildings that appear to be royal palaces hint at the greatness of the ancient city, but they do not yield many secrets.

The Shang dynasty fell to the Zhou around 1122 B.C.E., but it did not disappear, just as the Xia had not disappeared when it had fallen to the Shang c. 1766 B.C.E. Instead, in defeat, these kingdoms continued to exist, albeit with diminished territories and powers. Until the Qin dynasty unified China in 221 B.C.E., the defeat of a dynasty did not mean that it completely disappeared. Rather, it became one of the many smaller kingdoms competing for power in continuous warfare in north China.

CONNECTION: *China and empire, 200 B.C.E.–910 C.E., pp. 195–230*

THE WESTERN HEMISPHERE: MESOAMERICA AND SOUTH AMERICA

The first cities of the Americas share several characteristics with those of east Asia. They began as cosmo-magical shrine centers, linked by **shaman** priest-rulers to otherworldly realms. They developed into city-states with important functions in rule and trade as well as in religion, and some even incorporated whole empires under their sway. Specific individual cities, most notably Teotihuacán, had enormous cultural influence over other settlements that were spread across great distances.

There were also great differences between the hemispheres. Geographically, the cities of the western hemisphere were built at water's edge, usually near lakes or small rivers, but not on major

THE EARLY AMERICAS			
DATE	**POLITICAL**	**RELIGION AND CULTURE**	**SOCIAL DEVELOPMENT**
6000 B.C.E		● Stone tools in Mexico (6700)	
5000 B.C.E			● Plants (including maize) cultivated in Mesoamerica
3000 B.C.E			● Villages established in Mesoamerica; gourds and beans grown
2500 B.C.E	● Maya culture originated	● Pottery from Mesoamerica (2300)	
1500 B.C.E	● Olmecs, Gulf of Mexico (1500 B.C.E.–400 B.C.E.) ● Zapotecs, S. Mexico (1400 B.C.E –900 C.E.)	● Olmec center of San Lorenzo; pottery, mirrors, ceramics	
1000 B.C.E	● Chavin, N. Peru (c. 900–200 B.C.E) ● Tiwanaku, Bolivia (c. 800 B.C.E–1200 B.C.E.)		
200 B.C.E	● First Teotihuacán buildings, Valley of Mexico ● Moche, N. coast of Peru (200 B.C.E.–600 C.E.)		
100 B.C.E	● Nazca, Peru (1–600 C.E.)		
500 C.E	● Maya culture (S. Mexico, Guatemala, Belize) at peak (325–900) ● Teotihuacán culture at peak (450–600) ● Huari, Peru (c. 650–800)		● Teotihuacán population 100,000 ● First fully developed towns in the Mississippi valley (c. 700)
1000 C.E	● Toltecs (900–1170) ● Chimu, N.W. Peruvian coast (c. 1000–1470)		
1200 C.E	● Aztecs (c. 1100–1521) ● Inca, Andean S. America (c. 1200–1535)	● Aztec pictographs and hieroglyphs ● Aztec gold, jade, and turquoise jewels, textiles, and sculptures	● Aztec tribute empire over over surrounding lands from capital of Cuzco

river systems. Technologically, the people of the Americas did not use metals in their tools. In fact, they hardly used metal at all except for ornaments, jewelry, and artwork. They used neither wheels nor draft animals in transportation. Llamas served as pack animals for small loads, but otherwise goods were carried by hand, dragged, or shipped by canoe. Construction and transportation were thus far more labor intensive than in most of Afro-Eurasia. Finally, except for the Maya, the cities of the Americas did not create writing systems. Some, like the Zapotecs and Toltecs, used limited hiero-glyphic symbols and calendar formats, but these did not develop into full, written languages. In Afro-Eurasia, only in the Niger River area did settlements grow into cities without developing writing systems.

In many respects, the cities of the western hemisphere had one foot in the stone age. The archaeologist Richard MacNeish has underlined the comparatively slow evolution of urban society in the western hemisphere. Stone tools ground by hand first appeared in central Mexico about 6700 B.C.E.; the domestication of plants began about 5000 B.C.E.; villages were established about 3000 B.C.E.; pottery appeared about 2300 B.C.E.; and population suddenly increased in about 500 B.C.E. These processes were much slower than in the river-valley civilizations of Eurasia.

ORIGINS: MIGRATION AND AGRICULTURE

Humans arrived in the western hemisphere from across the Beringia land bridge (connecting Alaska and Siberia) between 15,000 and 40,000 years ago and then spread throughout both North and South America (see map, p. 26). By 5000 B.C.E., they were cultivating maize, at least in small quantities, as well as gathering wild crops and hunting animals. By around 3000 B.C.E. they also grew beans and gourds.

Working with botanists, Richard MacNeish documented the beginnings of domestication of maize in the valley of Tehuacan, 200 miles (320 kilometers) southeast of Mexico City. He traced the development from wild corn cobs about 5000 B.C.E. to an early variety of modern corn 5000 years later. In subsequent excavations in Peru, MacNeish found that the cultivation of maize began there by 4000 B.C.E., perhaps introduced from Mesoamerica. In both regions, at about the same time, the other two staples of the American diet, beans and

squashes, also appear. Further, in the Andes mountains, potatoes and root crops were also grown. The valley of Mexico and the high Andes of Peru thus became incubators of much of the civilization of the Americas from an early date. Agricultural innovation, urbanization, and the foundation of empires originated in these regions and spread outward.

MESOAMERICAN URBANIZATION

By 2000 B.C.E., the agricultural foundations for an urban civilization were in place in Mesoamerica. Farmers throughout present-day Mexico and central America were cultivating maize, gourds, beans, and other food crops. In addition to farming dry fields, their methods included "slash-and-burn," which kept them moving from place to place in search of new land; "pot irrigation," dipping pots into wells and simply pouring the water onto the fields; canal irrigation; and, in low-lying swamplands, the creation of *chinampas*, raised fields or so-called "hanging gardens." Chinampas were created by piling up the mud and the natural vegetation of the swamps into grids of raised land crisscrossed by natural irrigation channels. When the Spanish arrived in 1519, they estimated that the chinampas could feed four persons per acre; more recent archaeological estimates of their productivity suggest eight.

Olmec Civilization along the Gulf Coast

On the basis of these agricultural systems, localized permanent settlements that centered on religious shrines and were led by local chiefs began to emerge. Trade and shared cultural and ceremonial practices gave a common character to specific geographical regions within Mesoamerica. Along the Gulf coast of Mexico, the earliest of these civilizations, the Olmec, took shape from about 1200 B.C.E.

The Olmec built raised platforms, settlements, and shrines above the low-lying woodlands. The first that we know of was built at San Lorenzo about 1150 B.C.E. Labor brigades constructed *chinampas*, and the population of the settlement may have reached 2500. Olmec artwork—representations of animals and mythological creatures in sculpture and bas relief—suggests a shared religious and "cosmo-magical" basis to the society. About 900 B.C.E. the San Lorenzo site was

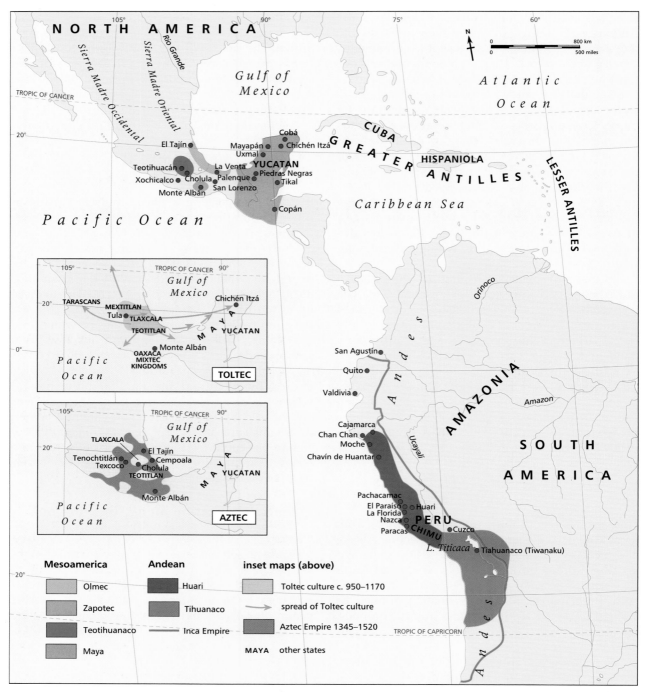

Classic cultures of the Americas Sophisticated urban cultures developed in two tropical regions of the Americas: humid southern Mexico and the more temperate valleys of the central Andes. Both regions witnessed a succession of distinctive cultural and political centers. The Maya civilization of the Yucatán emerged, by 250 C.E., as the outstanding power in Mesoamerica, while the Huari empire of the Andes prefigured that of the Inca. In South America, urban civilizations appeared both near sea level along the Pacific coast and in the Andes Mountains, at altitudes from 6,500 to 12,000 feet (2000 to 3700 meters).

Colossal head from San Lorenzo, Veracruz, Mexico, before 400 B.C.E. Weighing around ten tons, this massive sculpted head is one of nine that were found at San Lorenzo. Made from basalt and carved with stone tools, the heads originally stood in rows on the site and are most probably portraits of Olmec rulers. All display the same full, resolute lips and broad, flat noses. Similar sculptures were also found at La Venta. *(Museo Regional de Veracruz, Jalapa, Mexico)*

destroyed, its artwork defaced. No one today knows why.

About one hundred years later, some 100 miles (160 kilometers) to the northeast and closer to the Gulf, Olmec peoples at La Venta built a small island in the middle of a swamp, and constructed on it an earth mound, half again as large as a football field and 100 feet (30 meters) high. Buildings atop the mound were probably used as temples. Monumental stone sculptures, including some of the giant stone heads typical of Olmec art, also mark the space. Some of them probably served also as altars. The stone building materials were transported here from at least 60 miles (97 kilometers) away, the jade from much further. La Venta flourished for four centuries until about 400 B.C.E. it, too, was destroyed and its monuments defaced. Again, no one today knows why.

Zapotec Civilization in the Oaxaca Valley

Olmec products—pottery, ritual objects, mirrors, and ceramics—appeared in the highlands around modern Oaxaca as early as 1150 B.C.E., along with natural products, such as obsidian and seashells from around the Gulf of Mexico. At first, therefore, scholars believed that the Zapotec culture of the Oaxaca valley was an offshoot of the Olmec. More recent finds in the village of San Jose Mogote, dating to 1400–1150 B.C.E., demonstrate, however, that the Zapotecs had begun settlements no later than the Olmecs. The imported products reflected trading between the two groups.

Zapotec civilization peaked on the slopes of Monte Albán. By 400 B.C.E. ceremonial and public buildings dotted the summits of the hills. The settlement grew over the centuries, reaching its peak in the centuries after 200 C.E., when up to 50,000 people lived there. The settlement was not entirely concentrated into a single city, but extended over 15 square miles (39 square kilometres), with some 2000 terraces built into the hills, each with a house or two and its own water supply. Temples, pyramids, tombs, and an array of religious images suggest the importance of cosmo-magical symbolism among the Zapotecs, too. Monte Albán peaked in population and creativity about 700 C.E. and then declined.

Teotihuacán in the Valley of Mexico

Meanwhile, in the valley of Mexico, another civilization was coalescing, dominating the lands near it, and finally creating a substantial empire. At its core, about 40 miles (65 kilometers) to the northeast of present day Mexico City, stood Teotihuacán, one of the great cities of the ancient world. René Millon, an archaeologist at the University of Rochester who supervised an immense project mapping all the thousands of structures in the city, wrote of "how radically different Teotihuacán was from all other settlements of its time in Middle America. It was here that the New World's urban revolution exploded into being" (Millon, p. 83). At its peak, about 550 C.E., Teotihuacán accommodated about 100,000 inhabitants on some 8 square miles (20 square kilometers). Teotihuacán civilization had no system of writing so, again, our knowledge is limited to the excavation and interpretation of physical artifacts.

The city sat astride the major communication line between the valley of Mexico and the passes eastward to the Gulf of Mexico. Life in the city was a gift of the low-lying lake system of the valley of Mexico, especially of nearby Lake Texcoco. The lakes provided irrigation waters for the fields of the Teotihuacán valley and salt, fish, and waterfowl. Basalt, limestone, and chert stone for building and clay for pottery were readily available in the valley, but other raw materials were imported, notably obsidian for tools and weapons from Pachuca and Otumba in the surrounding mountains. Marine shells and copal (a tree resin used as incense) were imported from the Gulf region, and feathers of the quetzal bird came from the Mayan regions of the southeast. Trading outposts of Teotihuacán appeared 700 miles (1100 kilometers) south in Maya areas, and Teotihuacán ceramics have been found as far south as Tikal (see the discussion of Maya civilization on page 100). More than 400 workshops in the city produced pottery, obsidian manufactures, ornaments fashioned from seashells, and art and jewelry from jade and onyx.

A huge pyramid, at its base as broad as the great pyramid of Khufu in Egypt, though only half as high, dominated the Teotihuacán cityscape. The pyramid sits above a natural cave that early inhabitants enlarged into a clover-leaf-shaped chamber. The combination of natural cave and pyramid suggests that local people may have believed that this cave was the "navel of the universe." As Mircea Eliade, the historian of religions, has demonstrated, the belief that all human life, or at least the lives of the local people, had emerged upward onto earth from a "navel," a single specific geographical point, was widely held in many civilizations of the ancient world. (The Garden of Eden story is a later variant of this belief.) Two additional massive shrines—the adjacent, smaller Pyramid of the Moon, and a central temple dedicated to the god Quetzalcoatl—enhance the religious dimensions of the city. Throughout its lifetime, and indeed even afterward until the Spanish conquest, Teotihuacán attracted multitudes of pilgrims from as far away as Guatemala.

The first buildings of Teotihuacán appeared about 200 B.C.E. One hundred years later, there were still only about 600 inhabitants. By 150 C.E., however, the population had grown to 20,000 and the area to 5 square miles (13 square kilometers). At about this time the Pyramids of the Sun and the Moon were constructed. Then the population multiplied as the city exploded with religious, trade, artisanal, and administrative functions and personnel.

The city was laid out on a monumental, geometric grid that centered on the 150 feet (45 meter) wide Avenue of the Dead, the north–south axis of the city. More than seventy-five temples line this road, including the Pyramid of the Sun. The Pyramid of the Moon demarcated its northern terminal. The regularity of the city plan suggests a powerful government and, indeed, a large administrative headquarters, the Ciudadela, dominates the southeastern terminus of the

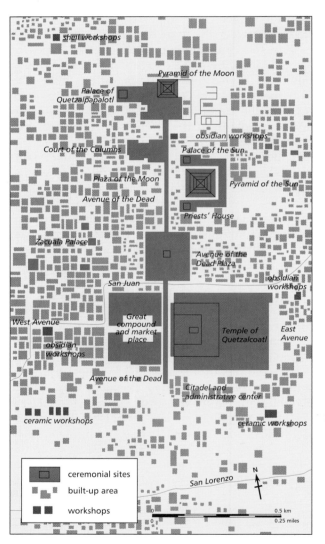

Teotihuacán Between 400 and 750 C.E., high in the Valley of Mexico, Teotihuacán was the dominant power in Mesoamerica. Covering over 7.5 square miles, with a population of 100,000, the city was laid out on a regular grid plan connecting the elements of a massive ceremonial complex. The residents thrived on agriculture, craftwork, and trade in ceramics and locally quarried obsidian.

Avenue. The placement of the central Temple of Quetzalcoatl within the Ciudadela implies a close relationship between religion and administration.

At its peak, about 500–650 C.E., Teotihuacán exercised a powerful imperial force over its immediate surrounding area and exerted spiritual, religious, cultural, economic, and military influence for hundreds of miles, especially to the south, into Maya areas. In 650, however, the city was deliberately burned down. Teotihuacán began to decline in significance. By 750 its power was broken, its population scattered to smaller towns and rural areas. Several reasons have been suggested: the region may have become increasingly arid, incapable of supporting so large a population; increasing density of population, augmented by government programs for moving rural populations into the city, might have led to conflict and revolt from within; neighboring city-states, pressured by the increasing militarization in Teotihuacán, may have attacked the city. These are,

however, only educated guesses. In the absence of written records, no one knows for sure.

Cities interact with one another in networks of exchange, so advances or declines in one usually echo in the others. Teotihuacán and Monte Albán both declined simultaneously about 750 C.E., but smaller, nonurban centers kept the political, cultural, and religious legacies of Teotihuacán alive in the region. (Compare this with the experience of western Europe after the decline of Rome, discussed in Chapter 6.) Three subsequent civilizations—the Toltec, the Aztec, and the Maya—absorbed and perpetuated its influence.

Toltec Civilization in the Valley of Mexico

When the Toltecs arrived in the valley of Mexico from the north and came to dominate the region from a new capital at Tula, about 900 C.E., they apparently ruled on Teotihuacán foundations and built their chief ceremonial center in honor of

Teotihuacán, Mexico, with the Pyramid of the Moon (foreground) linked to the Pyramid of the Sun by the Avenue of the Dead.
By 200 B.C.E. in the valley of Mexico, the combined effects of intensified trading, growing religious activity, and huge surpluses of food led to the founding of this major city, which for centuries enjoyed religious, political, and economic dominance in the region. Teotihuacán reached an enormous size (8 square miles; 2072 hectares) and population (100,000) before eventually being deliberately, and mysteriously, burned down in 650 C.E.

Quetzalcoatl. Their rule, however, was shortlived. About 1170 C.E. still newer immigrants destroyed the Toltec temples and government.

Aztec Civilization in the Valley of Mexico

After Tula fell, the Aztecs entered the valley. They established settlements on the southeastern shores of Lake Texcoco and built Tenochtitlán as their capital only 40 miles (65 kilometers) from the earlier site of Teotihuacán. As the Aztecs built their large, militaristic empire, the population of Tenochtitlán grew to 200,000. Militarism and the demand of their gods for human sacrifice led the Aztecs into a constant quest for captives to sacrifice and, therefore, into constant warfare with their neighbors. When the Spanish conquistadores arrived in 1519, the neighboring peoples helped them overthrow the Aztecs and their empire. The Spanish then razed Tenochtitlán to the ground and established their own capital, Mexico City, atop its ruins (see Chapter 12).

Teotihuacán's third legacy was to the Maya.

Maya Civilization: How Do We Know?

The Maya live today in the Yucatán peninsula of Mexico, in Guatemala, and in Belize. For centuries the connection between their current, often impoverished, existence and the glories of their civilization in the third through the tenth centuries C.E. had been lost. Then, in 1839–41, a New York lawyer, John Lloyd Stephens, and a Scottish artist, Frederick Catherwood, discovered the remnants of the cities of Copán and Palenque in the rainforests of Mesoamerica, and Uxmal and Chichén Itzá in the Yucatán. Stephens and Catherwood wrote and painted what they saw and made rubbings of the designs they found on Maya **stelae,** stone marker tablets. They brought to Europe and the United States information about this civilization that had long been lost to the outside world and demonstrated the lost link between the modern Maya and the earlier, destroyed cities of Mesoamerica. Their book, *Incidents of Travels in Central America, Chiapas, and Yucatan*, published in 1841, opened the modern academic study of the Maya. This was almost exactly the same time as H.C. Rawlinson and others were rediscovering the great archaeological sites of Mesopotamia and deciphering its language.

Stelae and other inscriptions revealed the Maya language, but no one could read it. Even the Maya themselves, prevented by the Spanish from keeping their language alive (see Chapter 13), had forgotten the script. Scholars could read parts of the elaborate and sophisticated Maya calendar system, but they could not discern whether the events recorded were historical, mythical, or some combination of the two. In the 1950s and 1960s, at Harvard University, Tatiana Proskouriakoff began to demonstrate that the Maya stelae recorded the reigns and victories of real kings who had ruled real states. Adding to Proskouriakoff's interpretation of the glyphs, the Russian scholar Yuri Knorozov demonstrated, against fierce opposition, that the Maya script included representations of phonetic sound as well as of full words. In the 1970s a new generation of linguistic scholars began to decode the syntactical structure of the writing. They learned to distinguish which signs represented nouns and which verbs, and where they fell in the structure of the narrative. They were well on their way to discovering Maya history.

The archaeologists Linda Schele and David Freidel finally mastered the hieroglyphs and scripts of the people of the city of Palenque. They found records of their copious warfare, the exact lineage of the Palenque kings, and the picture of a tree used to symbolize the king—the Maya represented their royal families as forests of trees and forests of kings. Schele and Freidel found a record of constant warfare among the local shaman kings and their profoundly religious local city-states. The wars were fought in search of captives to serve as slaves and as human sacrifices to the demanding gods (see Profile, pp. 106–7).

The Maya calendar recorded three related chronologies: dates and events in cosmic time periods of thousands of years; historic events in the lives of specific rulers and their states; and the yearly cycle of agricultural activity. Maya rituals were permeated by the sense of living at once in the world of here-and-now and in a spiritual realm connected with other worlds and gods (see Source opposite). Their kings were **shamans,** bridges between the two worlds (see picture, p. 103).

The Maya shared a single, general culture and two closely related languages, one from the southern, lowland region, another from the northern highlands.

Although fiercely competitive, the Maya, like the ancient Greek city-states, presented a unified ethnic

SOURCE
The Popul Vuh

The *Popul Vuh* is the most complete existing collection of creation myths to survive the Spanish conquistadores. Originally written in Maya hieroglyphs, it was transcribed into Latin in the sixteenth century and then translated into Spanish by a Dominican priest in the eighteenth century. The selection cited here is reminiscent of the biblical story of the tree in the garden of Eden whose fruits were forbidden. But the tale in *Popul Vuh* has even more significant differences. The tree, a calabash, is forbidden because the skull of a god, named One Hunahpu, was placed in a fork in it. As a young woman reached out to take the fruit of the tree, the skull spat out saliva on her, making her pregnant and thus preserving the god's lineage among humans.

And this is when a maiden heard of it, the daughter of a lord. Blood Gatherer is the name of her father, and Blood Woman is the name of the maiden.

And when he heard the account of the fruit of the tree, her father retold it. And she was amazed at the account:

"I'm not acquainted with that tree they talk about. 'Its fruit is truly sweet!' they say." "I hear," she said.

Next she went all alone and arrived where the tree stood. It stood at the Place of Ball Game Sacrifice:

"What? Well! What's the fruit of this tree? Shouldn't this tree bear something sweet? They shouldn't die, they shouldn't be wasted. Should I pick one?" said the maiden.

And then the bone spoke; it was here in the fork of the tree:

"Why do you want a mere bone, a round thing in the branches of a tree?" said the head of One Hunahpu when it spoke to the maiden. "You don't want it," she was told.

"I do want it," said the maiden.

"Very well. Stretch out your right hand here, so I can see it," said the bone.

"Yes," said the maiden. She stretched out her right hand, up there in front of the bone.

And then the bone spat out its saliva, which landed squarely in the hand of the maiden.

And then she looked in her hand, she inspected it right away, but the bone's saliva wasn't in her hand.

"It is just a sign I have given you, my saliva, my spittle. This, my head, has nothing on it—just the bone, nothing of meat. It's just the same with the head of a great lord: it's just the flesh that makes his face look good. And when he dies, people get frightened by his bones. After that, his son is like his saliva, his spittle, in his being, whether it be the son of a lord or the son of a craftsman, an orator. The father does not disappear, but goes on being fulfilled. Neither dimmed nor destroyed is the face of a lord, a warrior, craftsman, orator. Rather, he will leave his daughters and sons. So it is that I have done likewise through you. Now go up there on the face of the earth; you will not die. Keep the word. So be it," said the head of One and Seven Hunahpu—they were of one mind when they did it.

This was the word Hurricane, Newborn Thunderbolt, Raw Thunderbolt had given them. In the same way, by the time the maiden returned to her home, she had been given many instructions. Right away something was generated in her belly, from the saliva alone, and this was the generation of Hunahpu and Xbalanque.

And when the maiden got home and six months had passed, she was found out by her father. Blood Gatherer is the name of her father.

Agricultural Towns of North America

Agricultural settlements took root in many locations in continental North America in the first few hundred years C.E. Several grew into small towns, reaching their maximum size about 1000–1400 C.E., and some scholars see the signs of early urbanization. Nevertheless, these towns are not included among the seven sites of primary urbanization because few of them reached a population size that might be considered urban; nor do they demonstrate clearly a non-agricultural base to their economies. They may also be derivative of earlier settlements to the south. For example, those in the southwestern United States, like the Hohokam, Mogollon, and Anasazi peoples, show evidence in their art work and building patterns of influences from Mexico and even South America.

The first fully developed towns in the Mississippi valley appeared about 700 C.E. Their inhabitants built temple mounds and left evidence of elaborate, ritual funerals, suggesting a hierarchical social and political organization. The largest of the temple mound towns, Cahokia, occupied land along the Mississippi, across the river and a few miles east of present-day Saint Louis. Cahokia held a population of 10,000 in the city and 38,000 in the region in the twelfth and thirteenth centuries. Around the town were sited some 100 mounds that served as burial tombs or as platforms for homes of the elite. The mounds resemble those of Mexican cities and suggest interchange between the two regions. Archaeologist Brian Fagan concludes, "There is every reason to believe that Cahokia was planned and controlled by a powerful central authority and that there were many craft specialists" (Fagan, p. 336). Cahokia, like almost all the towns of North America, was in decline, or even deserted, before the arrival of European invaders after 1500 for reasons that are not entirely clear. Archaeologists continue active research in the towns of North America, their cultures, and their links to one another and to other regions.

Earthen jar in the form of a human face, Fortune Mound, Arkansas, Mississippian, 1000–1700 C.E. French explorers, who reached the towns of the Mississippi valley in the sixteenth century, discovered a ranked matrilineal society, headed by a chief and divided into four well-defined classes. This effigy vessel may represent either a dead ancestor or a trophy head taken in war. The arrival of Europeans, who brought contagious diseases with them, triggered the gradual decline of early urban centers in North America. (*Peabody Museum, Cambridge, Mass.*)

identity to outsiders—especially those who spoke other languages (Schele and Freidel, p. 51).

The number of kingdoms ruled by kings grew from perhaps a dozen in the first century B.C. to as many as sixty at the height of the lowland civilization in the eighth century.

Maya Civilization: What Do We Know?

The Maya built on Olmec and Teotihuacano foundations as well as on their own practices. Arriving in the Yucatán and central America, they began to construct ceremonial centers by 2000 B.C.E. Between 300 B.C.E. and 300 C.E., they expanded their centers to plazas surrounded by stone pyramids and crowned with temples and palaces. The classic phase, 300–600 C.E., followed with full-fledged cities and monumental architecture, temples, extensive sacrifices, and elaborate burials, and the Olmec and Teotihuacán cultural influences are evident. Maya culture flourished in the southern lowlands, and major construction took place at Palenque, Piedras Negras, Copán, Coba, and elsewhere.

Tikal, in today's Guatemala, is one of the largest, most elaborate, and most completely excavated of these cities. In its center, Tikal holds five temple

A blood-letting rite, limestone lintel from Yaxchilán, Mexico (Maya), *c.* **725** C.E. The king, Lord Shield Jaguar, in his role of shaman, brandishes a flaming torch to illuminate the drama about to unfold. His principal wife, Lady Xoc, kneeling, pulls through her tongue thorn-lined rope that falls into a woven basket holding blood-soaked strips of paper cloth. These will be burned and thereby transmitted to the gods. Few works of art made by the Maya capture so completely the link between their political and religious ideas in an appropriately sacramental style. (Having deciphered the hieroglyphics of the Mayan calendar, scholars know that this event took place on October 28, 709 C.E.) (*British Museum, London*)

pyramids, up to 200 feet (60 meters) high and built from 300 to 800 C.E. (One appeared so massive, powerful, and exotic that film-maker George Lucas used it as a setting for *Star Wars*.) As the first modern archaeologists hacked away the tropical rainforest and uncovered this temple core, they concluded that Tikal was a spiritual and religious center. Later they uncovered housing and water cisterns that accommodated up to 50,000 people outside the temple precincts. This find led them to change their assessment of Tikal. Instead of viewing it as a purely religious shrine, they began to see it as a large city of considerable regional political and economic significance as well. Still later, as the hieroglyphic script was deciphered, the extent of expansionism, warfare, and human sacrifice was also uncovered. At the height of its powers, Tikal's authority covered almost 1000 square miles (2500 square kilometers) containing 360,000 people. Most Maya states held only 30,000–50,000 subjects.

By 900 C.E., the great classical period of the Maya in the southern lowlands ended. No one knows why. The most frequent hypotheses include: excessive population pressure on natural resources, especially agriculture; climatic changes beyond the

Temple I at Tikal, Guatemala (Mayan), before 800 C.E. At its height the city-state of Tikal covered almost 1000 square miles (2500 square km) and was home to 360,000 inhabitants. Its symbols of authority were centralized in its monumental shrines. This unusually steep stepped pyramid—230 feet (70 m) high—would have been the backdrop for self-inflicted blood-letting and the sacrifice of prisoners of war as offerings to the gods.

CIVILIZATIONS FLOURISHING IN CENTRAL AMERICA BEFORE COLUMBUS

Olmec   *c.* 1500–400 B.C.E. Gulf of Mexico. First complex society in region, with centralized authority. Known for carvings of giant stone heads and jade animals.

Maya   *c.* 2000 B.C.E.–900 C.E. S. Mexico, Guatemala, Belize. Most enduring of the Middle American civilizations, the Mayans had by 325 C.E. become superb astronomers who built stepped pyramids, smelted metal tools, and developed hieroglyphs.

Zapotec   *c.* 1400 B.C.E.–900 C.E. S. Mexico. Built ceremonial center of Monte Albán and peaked as a civilization around 300 C.E.

Teotihuacán   *c.* 300 B.C.E.–750 C.E. Valley of Mexico. Major trading and cultural center. At its peak populated by 100,000 inhabitants in an area (8 square miles) larger than Rome. Contains huge Pyramid of the Sun, Mexico's largest pre-Columbian edifice.

Toltec   *c.* 900–1170 C.E. Central Mexico. Toltecs ruled much of the country from Tula (northeast of Mexico City), where symbols of blood and war predominate, and the similar city of Chichén Itzá in Yucatán.

Aztec   *c.* 1100–1521 C.E. Central Mexico. Sophisticated culture run by priestly aristocracy that built capital of Tenochtitlán. Known for their architecture, textiles, and a complex sacred calendar, the Aztecs were conquered by the Spanish in 1519–21.

ability of the Maya to adjust to; excessive warfare that wore out the people and destroyed their states. No one knows for sure.

No one knows, either, why at the time of the Maya decline in the lowlands, new Maya cities and states grew up in the northern highlands of the Yucatán peninsula, notably at Uxmal and Chichén Itzá. These cities, in turn, declined by 1200, and the last Maya capital, Mayapán, was constructed between 1263 and 1283. It adapted many of the cultural monuments of Chichén Itzá, but grew only to some 10,000 to 20,000 inhabitants. Mayapán seemed militaristic, beleaguered, and possessed of tough sensibilities as evidenced by wholesale human sacrifices. The city was later destroyed in civil wars in the mid-1400s.

By the time the Spanish conquistadores reached Mesoamerica in 1517, only a few small Maya towns remained. The period of Maya power and splendor had ended. The Toltecs, too, had fallen by then. The Aztecs had become the reigning power, and they were destroyed by the Spanish.

URBANIZATION IN SOUTH AMERICA

South America had few established trade links with Mesoamerica, but the two regions share many similarities. Both regions constructed religious shrine centers that seem to have dominated their general cultural foundations by about 1500 B.C.E.; they developed small city-states that defined local cultural variations from about 300–200 B.C.E.; created proto-empires throughout significant regions about 500–600 C.E.; and generated large, urban empires—the Aztecs in the valley of Mexico, the Inca in the Andes—that were destroyed by the Spanish. Both developed trading relationships between their coastal regions and their mountainous inland cores. But the contrast between coast and inland mountains is far more striking in South America. The Pacific coast of Ecuador, Peru, and Chile is a desert in most places. The prevailing winds come not from the Pacific, but from the Amazon basin to the east. The Andes Mountains thus have little rainfall from the Pacific Ocean to trap on their western slopes, but they do intercept the precipitation from the Atlantic, making the eastern slopes fertile while leaving the west coast dry. The most spectacular urban civilizations of South America took root in the 10,000 foot (3000 meter) high plains and passes of the Andes rather than in the arid Pacific coast

PROFILE
Great-Jaguar-Paw
MAYAN KING OF TIKAL

By deciphering, translating, and interpreting the stelae at Tikal, Linda Schele and David Freidel recreate an heroic moment of military victory in the life of the king Great-Jaguar-Paw and in the history of his kingdom. Their interpretation is based primarily on the stela illustrated here and on comparison with later stelae representing the same event:

> Despite the fact that he was such an important king, we know relatively little about Great-Jaguar-Paw's life outside of the spectacular campaign he waged against Uaxactun. His reign must have been long, but the dates we have on him come only from his last three years. On one of these historical dates, October 21, A.D. 376, we see Great-Jaguar-Paw ending the seventeenth katun [a ritual cycle of twenty years]. . . .This fragmentary monument shows him only from the waist down, but he is dressed in the same regalia as his royal

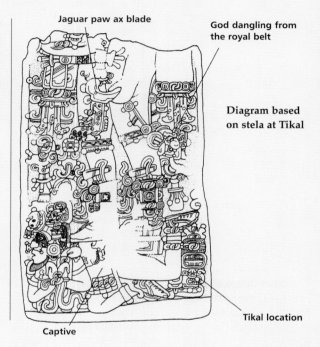

Jaguar paw ax blade

God dangling from the royal belt

Diagram based on stela at Tikal

Tikal location

Captive

below. The contrast with the river-basin civilizations of Afro-Eurasia could not be more vivid.

Coastal Settlements and Networks

The Pacific coast is not, however, uninhabitable. It yields abundant quantities of fish, seaweed, and salt. Even today these ocean products are traded to the mountain cities in exchange for their food crops. In some areas the cultivation of cotton is also possible, and coastal Peru rivals the Indus valley as the home of the first production of cotton textiles, about 4500 B.C.E. The quality of the textiles and the colorful designs dyed into the cotton show up most clearly in the burial cloths of semi-mummified bodies in the Paracas peninsula near Pisco, Peru.

In addition, although climatically a desert, the coast does have some small mountain-fed rivers running through it. People who could organize labor brigades to channel the rivers for irrigation created ceremonial centers along the coast,

beginning perhaps by 2000 B.C.E. The oldest of these shrine centers, and the one closest to the Pacific, is El Paraiso, near modern Lima, at the mouth of the Chillon River. Built in a typically U-shaped complex of buildings, El Paraiso appears to have been constructed by people from many separate villages and kin groups. Few lived at El Paraiso, but apparently the shrine served them all, and many used the location as a burial place.

The largest of the shrine centers is Sechin Alto, a 130 foot (40 meter) high mound, 1000 feet (300 meters) by 800 feet (270 meters), on which was built a U-shaped ceremonial complex surrounded by houses and platforms. The oldest building dates to 1300 B.C.E. It continued to expand until 400 B.C.E.

The Moche In the Moche valley of coastal northern Peru, settlements of up to 2000 separate structures had grown up by 200 B.C.E. From about 200 B.C.E. to 600 C.E., in this and neighboring valleys, the Moche state established itself. The Moche created irrigation

ancestors, with the god Chac-Xib-Chac dangling from his belt. His ankle cuffs display the sign of day on one leg and night on the other. . . . He holds an executioner's ax, its flint blade knapped into the image of a jaguar paw. In this guise of warrior and giver of sacrifices, he stands atop a captive he has taken in battle. The unfortunate victim, a bearded noble still wearing part of the regalia that marks his noble station, struggles under the victor's feet, his wrists bound together in front of his chest. He will die to sanctify the katun ending at Tikal.

Warfare was not new to the Maya. Raiding for captives from one kingdom to another had been going on for centuries, for allusions to decapitation are present in even the earliest architectural decorations celebrating kingship. The hunt for sacrificial gifts to give to the gods and the testing of personal prowess in battle was part of the accepted social order and captive sacrifice was something expected of nobles and kings in the performance of their ritual duties. Just as the gods were sustained by the bloodletting ceremonies of the kings, so they were nourished as well by the blood of noble captives. Sacrificial victims like these had been buried as

offerings in building terminations and dedications from late Preclassic times on, and possibly even earlier. . . .

The war waged by Great-Jaguar-Paw of Tikal against Uaxactun, however, was not the traditional hand-to-hand combat of proud nobles striving for personal glory and for captives to give to the gods. This was war on an entirely different scale, played by rules never before heard of and for stakes far higher than the reputations or lives of individuals. In this new warfare of death and conquest, the winner would gain the kingdom of the loser. Tikal won the prize on January 16, A.D. 378. . . .

The subjugation of Uaxactun by Great-Jaguar-Paw and Smoking Fog [his commander-in-chief], which precipitated this new kind of war and rituals, survives in the inscriptional record almost entirely in the retrospective histories carved by later rulers at Tikal. The fact that these rulers kept commemorating this event shows both its historical importance and its propaganda value for the descendants of these conquerors. (Schele and Freidel, pp. 144–8)

systems, spectacular monuments, and important tombs. In the late 1980s, at nearby Sipan, Peruvian archaeologist Walter Alva discovered three royal tombs that demonstrate the social and political stratification of the society. Each tomb housed a lord, sometimes made of gold, and surrounded by servants, who had been buried with him. Paintings and ceramic designs within the tombs show the sacrifice of prisoners-of-war (see Spotlight, pp. 108–9). The Moche built provincial centers in nearby river valleys from which they apparently ruled, traded, and introduced irrigation systems.

The Chimu By about 600 C.E. the Moche left the region, for reasons not entirely clear, and were succeeded by the Chimu kingdom that controlled twelve coastal river valleys. The Chimu built irrigation and water storage facilities, trade networks, and a powerful state that stretched some 1000 miles (1600 kilometers) along the Peruvian coast. Their monumental capital, Chan Chan, built

near the earlier Moche, was surrounded by a 35 foot (11 meters) high mud wall, and it covered nearly 4 square miles (12 square kilometers), with palaces, temples, administrative offices, and housing for the common people. Chan Chan contained ten royal compounds. Apparently each king in turn built his own center, ruled from it during his life, and was buried in it after his death.

In each area they dominated, the Chimu built subsidiary administrative centers that formed a network reaching as far south as modern Lima. The Chimu empire reigned until it was conquered by the Inca in 1470. Ironically, thanks to the Inca transportation and communication network, Chimu artwork influenced western South America even more after the Inca conquest than it had before.

Urbanization in the Andes Mountains

The Chavin Despite these coastal settlements and networks, most scholars believe that the core areas

SPOTLIGHT
The Royal Tombs at Sipan

"The richest treasure ever excavated archaeologically in the Western hemisphere," proclaimed archaeologist Walter Alva when he discovered the Moche Royal Tombs at Sipan, a village on the Pacific coast of Peru.

The Moche kingdom had flourished from about the first to the sixth century C.E., but it appeared that the best of its art, especially the art of precious metals, had been looted by centuries of grave robbers. In late 1986, however, police nabbed a group of robbers who had just uncovered some new treasures. They informed Walter Alva of the nearby Museo Nacional Bruning de Lambayeque and he began digging professionally, unearthing materials that dated from the first to the third century C.E. Hollow beads, many of them fashioned from gold "into a wondrous variety of shapes and sizes," were the first discoveries. A banner, 19.5 inches (48.5 centimeters) high **(figure 1)**, covered in sheets of gilded copper, had perhaps been carried in royal processions. Personal adornments included an ear ornament **(figure 2)**, 9.4

centimeters (4.2 inches) in diameter, representing a warrior fashioned from hammered gold and clad in a tunic of turquoise. Alva's team named him "The Lord of Sipan."

The central burial figure in the first tomb was "the skeleton of a man wrapped in a cotton shroud . . . . In his left hand and mouth

were lumps of copper. He wore a gilded copper helmet, and resting on his right forearm was a round copper shield" (Alva and Donnan, p. 55). Red textiles, now decomposed, must have been his burial shroud. Several skeletons of humans and animals accompanied his. A second tomb held skeletons of an adult male,

Figure 1 Banner, cleaned and reconstructed (tomb 1).

Figure 2 Warrior ear ornament, cleaned and reconstructed (tomb 1).

two twenty-year-old females, a teenage male, an eight to ten-year-old child, llamas, a dog, and a snake. A third tomb, from a somewhat earlier period, yielded a single adult male buried with a teenage girl, a llama, ornaments, ceramics, two elaborately carved spear throwers, a gold scepter, burial masks, and necklaces of gold beads, some in the shape of spiders **(figure 3)**, 8.3 centimeters (4.1 inches) in diameter. They named this male "The Old Lord of Sipan." Nearby, the archaeologists found decomposed rooms containing ceramic vessels, miniature ornaments, and the dismembered bones of humans and llamas.

The discoveries were breathtaking, but what did they mean? In the Fowler Museum of the University of California, Los Angeles, Christopher Donnan had charge of some 125,000 photographs of Moche objects in museums and collections around the world. They provided context. Many Moche fine line drawings illustrate various priests engaged in warfare and performing human sacrifices. Sipan confirmed these realities: in tomb one a Warrior Priest; in tomb two a Bird Priest; in the third tomb a Warrior Priest of an earlier era. The dismembered bones suggested that the sacrifices and dismemberment of victims had been performed nearby. Moche drawings also depict a "Decapitator," a supernatural figure resembling a spider, for "Spiders capture their prey, tie them with ropes of web, and later extract their vital fluids – just as Moche warriors [did]" (p. 139). Collectively, the treasures of "one of the most remarkable civilizations of the ancient world" (p. 227) had been resurrected from the royal tombs at Sipan.

Figure 3 Spider bead, cleaned and reconstructed (tomb 3).

Mummy wrapped in textiles, Pisco, Paracas Peninsula, Peru, *c.* 500 B.C.E. The weaving artistry of the Pacific Coast Indians was virtually unrivaled among prehistoric cultures. Cotton and wool materials have survived remarkably well in the dry coastal environment, especially in huge underground cemeteries where the dead were wrapped in fabric burial shrouds.

1200–200 B.C.E. The civilization is named for its best known and largest ceremonial center at Chavin de Huantar, which flourished in central Peru from about 900 to about 200 B.C.E. Chavin temples include a pantheon of gods preserved in paintings

CIVILIZATIONS OF SOUTH AMERICA

Chavin   *c.* 1200–200 B.C.E. N. Peru. Farming society, comprising different regional groups, whose main town may have been a pilgrimage site.

Moche   200 B.C.E.–600 C.E. N. coast of Peru. Modeled ceramics of animals in a realistic style. Religious and political life focused on the Huaca de la Luna (artificial platform) and Huaca del Sol (stepped pyramid).

Nazca   ?1–600 C.E. Peru. Known principally for its series of enormous figures drawn with lines of pebbles. Best seen from the air, the largest (a hummingbird) is 900 feet (275 m) long.

Tiwanaku   *c.* 200 C.E.–1200 C.E. Bolivia. Named for the ancient city, near Lake Titicaca, that was occupied by a series of five different cultures, then abandoned.

Huari   *c.* 650–800 C.E. Peru. Empire whose style of architecture and artifacts, similar to Tiwanaku's, was dispersed throughout the region.

Chimu   *c.* 700–1470 C.E. Northwest Peruvian coast. Large urban civilization (capital: Chan Chan) responsible for fine gold work, record-keeping, and aqueducts. Conquered by the Aztecs.

Inca   *c.* 1200–1535 C.E. Andean South America. Last and largest pre-Columbian civilization (capital: Cuzco) that was destroyed by Spanish conquistadores in the 1530s.

of South American urbanization were in the Andes, the 20,000 foot (6000 meter) high mountain chain that parallels the Pacific coast for the entire length of South America. From earliest times to today, there has been considerable "vertical trade," linking coastal lowlands with high mountain areas in an exchange of the different products of their different ecologies. With the trade came networks of cultural, religious, and political communication, and some archaeologists have argued that the civilization of the Andes Mountains was developed from "maritime foundations" (Moseley).

The first known civilization of the Andes, the Chavin, flourished for about a millennium,

and carvings, including jaguar-like humans with serpents for hair, eagles, caymans, and many mixed figures, part human, part animal, reminiscent of similar figures in China. Like El Paraiso and the coastal shrines, Chavin seems to have been built by the joint efforts of many nearby kin and village groups. At its height, it held only 2000 inhabitants, but its culture and its gods inspired common religious forms in the vicinity, and carried them throughout the high Andes.

Tiwanaku, Huari, and Nazca Some 600 miles (1000 kilometers) to the south, south of Lake Titicaca, on today's border between Peru and Bolivia, at an elevation of 12,000 feet (3700 meters), lay the largest open, flat plain available for agriculture in the Andes. By 200 C.E., Tiwanaku (Tihuanaco) at the southern end of the lake, near the modern La Paz, became the capital of the region. Its rulers irrigated their high plains, *altiplano*, region to support perhaps 20,000 people and to create a ritual center of monumental structures and religious and spiritual practices that suffused the Andes and the coast. When Tiwanaku collapsed, for reasons now lost to history, successor states in the region, notably at Huari and Nazca, kept alive many of their administrative and religious practices.

The Inca These five states—Chimu, Chavin, Tiwanaku, Huari, and Nazca—established found-ations on which the Inca built their powerful but shortlived empire, which stretched for 2000 miles (3200 kilometers) from north to south and as far as 200 miles (320 kilometers) inland, during the years 1476–1534. The Inca adapted many of the gods and religious symbols, artwork, ceramics, and textiles of these earlier states. They built a new capital, Cuzco, at 10,000 feet (3000 meters), and connected it to all the mountain and coastal regions of their empire by an astonishing 25,000 mile (40,000 kilometer) system of roads, with tunnels, causeways, suspension bridges, travel lodges, and storage places. The roads were sometimes broad and paved, but often narrow and unpaved, especially because the Inca had no wheeled vehicles. Enforced, *mit'a* labor was exacted from local populations for the construction.

In 1438, Cusi Yupanqui was crowned "Inca," or king-emperor, after he won a victory over a neighboring tribe, and forged his quarreling peoples into a conquering nation. Thereafter, the whole nation was called Inca. Cusi Yupanqui established an hereditary monarchy, and his descendants built a great empire from his early conquests. They employed the *mit'a* system of enforced labor, demanding unpaid labor for part of each year from all adults in the empire for public construction. The Inca did not develop writing, but they did create an abacus-like system of numerical recording through the use of knots tied on strings. These *quipu* held the administrative records of the empire (see picture, p. 379).

Nazca lines, San Jose pampa, Peru desert, *c.* **500** C.E. Another of the successor states of Tiwanaku, the Nazca, created great patterns of lines drawn with pebbles on the desert surface. The designs, like this 900-foot-long (275 m) hummingbird figure, are visible only from the air, and their function and meaning are as elusive as the culture that fashioned them.

In each conquered region, the Inca established administrative centers, from which tax collectors gathered two-thirds of the crops and the manufactured products, like beer and textiles, half of it for the state, half for the gods and their priests. They established state workshops to produce official and consumer goods, and they seem to have encouraged significant standardization of production, for Inca arts and crafts show little variation over time and place. Inca religion apparently encouraged different gods and worship for different people. The sun god was the chief deity, and the emperor was considered his descendant; the nobility worshiped the military god Viracocha; while the common people continued to worship their own indigenous spirits, along with the newer sun god. The organization and the study of empire, however, take us to Part 3.

WEST AFRICA: THE NIGER RIVER VALLEY

Until 1977, all the cities in sub-Saharan Africa that were known to archaeologists had developed along patterns introduced from outside the region. Meroe and Kush on the upper Nile had adapted urban patterns from Egypt; Aksum in modern Ethiopia had followed examples of urbanization from both the Nile valley and from the trading powers of the Indian Ocean, including the Roman Empire; port cities along the East African coast, such as Malindi, Kilwa, and Sofala, had been founded by traders from across the Indian Ocean; the walled stone enclosures, called **zimbabwes**, built in the region of

modern Zimbabwe and Mozambique to house local royal rulers, had been initiated through contact with Swahili traders from the coast (see p. 381).

In west Africa, the first known cities, such as Timbuktu, Jenne, and Mopti along the Niger River, and Ife and Igbo Ukwu deeper south in the Yoruba lands near the tropical forests, had been built as centers of exchange. They were thought to be responses to the arrival of Muslim traders from north Africa who crossed the Sahara southward after the seventh century C.E. Archaeologists believed that Africans, like Europeans, had learned of city building from outsiders.

WEST AFRICA BEFORE URBANIZATION

The most important developments of pre-urban west Africa were iron smelting, apparently initiated by contact with north Africa; the development of new artistic traditions, especially by the Nok peoples; and the spread of agricultural civilization by the Bantu people. Iron smelting entered the archaeological record in west Africa suddenly about 500 B.C.E. In most places the technology jumped from stone to iron directly, with only a few examples of copper-work in between. Most archaeologists interpret this technological jump to indicate that iron working was introduced from outside, probably from the Phoenician colonies along the north African coast, and they find evidence for this idea in the rock art of the Sahara desert. Along the routes crossing the desert, rock engravings and paintings dating from between 1200 B.C.E. and 400 B.C.E. depict two-wheeled chariots that suggest trans-Saharan traffic.

THE EARLY AFRICAS			
DATE	POLITICAL	RELIGION AND CULTURE	SOCIAL DEVELOPMENT
500 B.C.E.		● Nok terra cotta sculptures	● Iron smelting ● Bantu adopting settled agricultural lives
250 B.C.E.	● Jenne–jeno founded	● Copper and semi–precious stone ornaments from Niger	
500 C.E.	● Ancient Ghana recorded by Arab visitors		● Cities in Niger valley (400)
1000 C.E.	● Foundation of Benin (c. 1000)		
1200 C.E.	● Ghana falls; Kingdom of Mali founded		

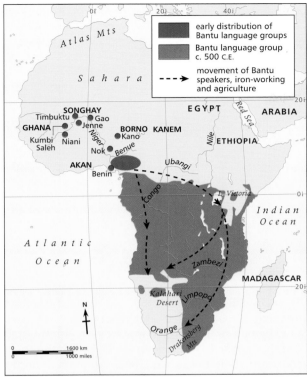

The spread of Bantu About 1500 B.C.E. an extraordinary cultural migration began to transform sub-Saharan Africa. From their homeland near the Niger delta, groups of Bantu-speaking farmers began to move east and south, spreading cattle domestication, crop cultivation, and iron-working. By about 500 C.E. southern Africa had been reached, the original hunter-gatherers having been marginalized to remote regions such as the Kalahari Desert.

In northern Nigeria, the Nok peoples were producing terra cotta sculptures, especially of human heads, from about 500 B.C.E. Living in settlements along the Niger, near its confluence with the Benue in modern Nigeria, the Nok also built iron-smelting furnaces, dating to 500–450 B.C.E.

Meanwhile, also in the lower Niger, some Bantu peoples were giving up nomadic pastoralism for settled agriculture, although many remained nomadic for a long time. They began great migrations southward and eastward over thousands of miles, introducing their languages, their knowledge of iron production, and their experience with settled agriculture. In one thousand years, 500 B.C.E. to 500 C.E., the Bantu carried their languages, their new, settled way of life, and their metallurgical skills almost to the southern tip of Africa.

JENNE-JENO: HOW DO WE KNOW?

Neither the Nok nor the Bantu built cities. Other people of the Niger River, however, did. In excavations that began in 1977 and continue today, Susan and Roderick McIntosh, archaeologists at Rice University in Houston, Texas, uncovered Jenne-jeno, "Ancient Jenne," the first known indigenous city in sub-Saharan Africa. The Jenne-jeno settlement began about 250 B.C.E. as a small group of round mud huts. Its herding and fishing inhabitants were already using iron implements, and the village grew to urban size by 400 C.E., reaching its peak of settlement by about 900 C.E.

The physical form of the city was different from that of the other six centers we have studied. A central inhabited area of some 80 acres (32 hectares) was surrounded by a city wall 10 feet (3 meters) wide and 13 feet (4 meters) high with a perimeter of 1¼ miles (2 kilometers). Near this central area were some forty smaller, but still substantial additional settlements. They extended to a radius of 2½ miles (4 kilometers). "Conservative estimates of between 7,000 and 13,000 persons for Jenne-jeno and between 15,000 and 27,000 for that site plus the 25 satellites within a one-kilometer radius just begin to tell the true story of mid-to-late first millennium population density"

Head from Jemaa, Nigeria, c. 400 B.C.E. The Nok were a nonliterate farming people that occupied the Jos Plateau in northern Nigeria during the first millennium B.C.E. Their distinctive sculptures—of elephants, snakes, monkeys, people, and even a giant tick—are boldly modeled and skillfully fired in terra cotta. This powerful lifesize head would probably have formed part of a full-length statue. (*National Museum, Lagos, Nigeria*)

4: A POLYCENTRIC WORLD (1700 B.C.E.–1000 C.E.)   113

Pirogues, Niger River. For hundreds and even thousands of years fleets of graceful pirogues, like these photographed near Jenne, have carried the cargoes of the 2600 mile long Niger River valley — gold, ivory, textiles, grains, fish, and slaves — as well as the goods imported from the Sahara and beyond — salt, ceramics, glass, and copper — to waiting customers and merchants.

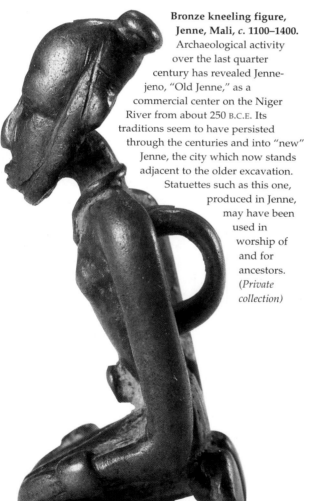

Bronze kneeling figure, Jenne, Mali, *c.* 1100–1400. Archaeological activity over the last quarter century has revealed Jenne-jeno, "Old Jenne," as a commercial center on the Niger River from about 250 B.C.E. Its traditions seem to have persisted through the centuries and into "new" Jenne, the city which now stands adjacent to the older excavation. Statuettes such as this one, produced in Jenne, may have been used in worship of and for ancestors. (*Private collection*)

(R. McIntosh, p. 200). By the year 1000, the settled area may have included 50,000 persons.

Excavations through numerous levels revealed that the people of Jenne-jeno ate fish from the river, rice from their fields, and beef from their herds. They probably drank the cows' milk as well. At least some wore jewelry and ornaments of imported copper and semi-precious stones. Dozens of burial urns, each up to 3 feet (1 meter) high, yielded human skeletons arranged in fetal position. The urns date from 300 to 1400 C.E., and their burial inside and adjacent to the houses suggests a reverence for ancestors. Statuettes in a kneeling position set into walls and under floors further suggest the probability of ancestor worship.

This part of the religious and cultural heritage of Jenne-jeno seems to have endured. The McIntoshes believe that these statuettes were the forerunners of similar sculptures used in Jenne as late as 1900 in sacrifices and prayers to and for ancestors. Although not built primarily as a shrine center, Jenne-jeno included religious functions as an important part of its activities, as its modern counterpart does today. The McIntoshes also found similarities between the arrangement of the huts of Jenne-jeno 1000 years ago and the grouping of family huts today. In ancient times as in modern, they argue, the husband-father lived in one large central hut while one of his wives occupied each of the surrounding huts.

Jenne-jeno must have engaged in trade because even in 250 B.C.E. its inhabitants were using iron and stone that had to be brought from at least 30 miles (48 kilometers) away. Sandstone for their

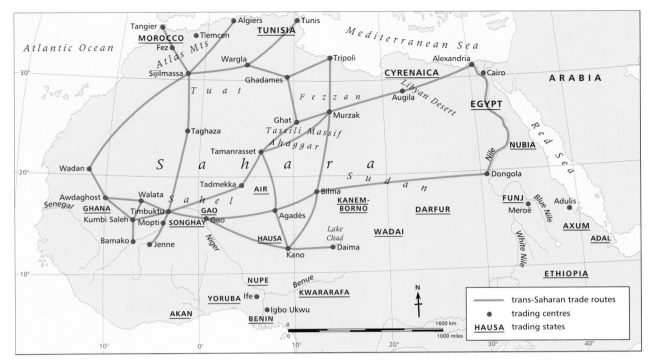

Trade across the Sahara Ivory, gold, hardwoods, and slaves were the magnets which drew trading caravans south across the arid Saharan wastes, often following routes established before the desert had formed. These routes linked the classical cultures of the Mediterranean and southwest Asia with an array of rich trading states strung along the Sahel/Sudan axis.

grinding stones had to have been imported from at least 60 miles (97 kilometers) away, while copper and salt came from hundreds of miles away. The McIntoshes discovered one gold earring, dating to about 750 C.E. The nearest site of gold mining was 500 miles (800 kilometers) away. Perhaps the people of Jenne-jeno traded the fish of the Niger and the rice of their fields for these imports. Some Jenne-jenoites may have become professional merchants.

Innovation in architectural concepts may also have come to Jenne from external contacts. By about 900 C.E. some rectangular houses began to appear among the circular ones, perhaps introduced through contact with northern peoples.

Outside contacts increased with the introduction of camel transportation across the Sahara about 300 C.E. and with the Muslim Arab conquest of north Africa about 700 C.E. (see p. 347). Especially after 1200 C.E., Muslim traders crossing the Sahara linked the savanna and forest lands of the south to the cities of the Mediterranean coast. Most scholars have argued that these external contacts and trade possibilities encouraged the growing importance of new cities like Timbuktu, Jenne, Niani, Gao, Kano, and, further south, Benin. The McIntoshes suggest an opposite perspective: These cities pre-date the

northern connections, and, indeed, their prosperity and control of the trade routes and the gold further to the south encouraged the northerners to dispatch their camel caravans across the Sahara.

By 1100, the settlements peripheral to Jenne-jeno began to lose population. Some of their inhabitants apparently moved to the central settlement. In another century the rural population also began to decline. By 1400, Jenne-jeno and its satellites were no more. Why? Roderick McIntosh cites several possible, but not certain, causes: "growing warfare and slave raiding…, changes to family structure and land rights…, migrations…, and … new forms of social stratification" (R. McIntosh, p. 203).

STATE FORMATION?

Could the settlements of the Middle Niger at Jenne-jeno be an example of early urbanism without a strong centralized government? Without a state? The McIntoshes certainly think so. They suggest that the population at Jenne-jeno lived in neighboring clusters that were functionally interdependent rather than in a single urban center with a prominent core marked by large scale, monumental architecture as was found in most of the other centers of primary urbanization. They see this settlement pattern as "a precocious, indigenous, and highly individual form of urbanism" (R. McIntosh, p. 203). They suggest that Jenne-jeno rose on the basis of trade and expanded into geographically neighboring, interactive settlements, but without a hierarchical social structure, without "overt signs of chiefly power" (S. McIntosh, p. 396), without a government. In contrast to primary urbanization in all the other regions of the world we have examined, Jenne-jeno may have experienced relative equality and cooperation among its citizens rather than competition, dominance, and coercion.

On the other hand, a comparative assessment might suggest that Jenne had developed only to about the stage of the Olmec settlements, and had not yet created the kind of centralized authority that emerged clearly and powerfully among the later Maya. Had Jenne-jeno persisted longer and grown larger, perhaps centralization and stratification would have developed. Indeed the presence of a central settlement surrounded by smaller adjacent settlements suggests that some hierarchy was already emerging. Did Jenne-jeno represent an alternative kind of urbanization, as the McIntoshes argue, or was it a settlement that was on its way to full-scale conventional urbanization? These are the kinds of questions of comparison that archaeologists—and historians—love to debate.

CONNECTION: Later cities and states in sub-Saharan Africa, pp. 347–8

THE FIRST CITIES: WHAT DIFFERENCE DOES IT MAKE?

With the creation of cities, humanity entered into many new forms of living. The first of these cities, in the river valleys of Mesopotamia and the Nile almost 5500 years ago, introduced not only new scale and density in human settlement patterns but also new technology in the metallurgy of copper, tin, and bronze; monumental scale in architecture; and specialization and hierarchy in social, political, and economic life. These cities flourished also as nodes in networks for the exchange of goods and ideas. The invention of writing in these cities not only gave new life to cultural creativity, but also provided new means of record keeping for the

bureaucrat, businessperson, and scholar. These new cities allowed and demanded complex and hierarchical government to keep them functioning. Although we sometimes see cities today as homes of secularism and heterogeneity, these early cities were "cosmo-magical" in their dedication to specific gods and in their physical and ritual organization. Differences in climate and culture separate Egyptian from Mesopotamian urbanization, but they also shared many similarities. We know somewhat less about Egyptian urbanization because the Nile itself washed away many of its foundations, but more recent archaeology has uncovered Egyptian as well as Sumerian city walls and residential structures.

Sumer and Egypt provide what scholars sometimes refer to as a "master narrative," a conventional, widely accepted view of historical transformation, suggesting that historical process at other times and places will follow similar patterns. Each of our subsequent case studies has reinforced some dimensions of the "master narrative" while challenging others.

• Indus valley urbanization suggested that a generally consistent civilization could extend over an immense geographical space, over thousands of years. A few of its cities stood out as capitals, but even after they were evacuated other cities of the far-flung network kept the civilization alive. Moreover, Indus agricultural practices were adopted and adapted by invaders who transplanted some of them from the Indus valley to the Ganges valley.

• Early Chinese urbanization, represented in the historical record through oracle bones and through the geometrical design of city plans, placed added emphasis on the cosmo-magical dimension of cities, although the rulers did not neglect to mobilize large and powerful armed forces.

• In the Americas, cities like Teotihuacán and the later cities of the Maya demonstrated again the importance of monumental, religious architecture, although each additional excavation reveals the extent of both long-distance trade and of everyday, mundane activities as well. Urbanization in the Andes mountains indicates that not all early cities needed river beds. Urban rulers could construct fabulous networks for trade, communication, and troop movement at forbidding altitudes. From their capital cities they could launch empires. They could also administer cities, and even empires, without having invented writing.

• In the Niger River valley of West Africa, the single urban settlement that has been excavated challenges the "master narrative," suggesting that cities may develop through the inter-relationship of adjacent smaller settlements without the need for hierarchy, centralization, government structure, and written language. The data presented thus far may be, however, subject to different interpretations. Perhaps the central mound in Jenne-jeno does, in fact, represent some hierarchical structure. Or perhaps it is a collection of contiguous villages rather than an urban center. The interpretation depends in part on how far the definition of a city and its functions may be—and ought to be—stretched. Continuing excavation and interpretation will help decide the degree to which the "master narrative" concerning early urbanization will hold up, and to what degree new ideas of the role of urbanization in human history are yet be formulated.

BIBLIOGRAPHY

Alva, Walter and Christopher Donnan. *The Royal Tombs of Sipan* (Los Angeles: Fowler Museum of Cultural History, University of California, Los Angeles, 1993).

Blunden, Caroline and Mark Elvin. *Cultural Atlas of China* (New Haven: Facts on File, 1983).

Chang, Kwang-chih. *The Archaeology of Ancient China* (New Haven: Yale University Press, 3rd ed., 1977).

Chang, Kwang-chih. *Shang Civilization* (New Haven: Yale University Press, 1980).

Coe, Michael, Dean Snow, and Elizabeth Benson. *Atlas of Ancient America* (New York: Facts on File, 1986).

Connah, Graham. *African Civilizations* (Cambridge: Cambridge University Press, 1987).

Cotterell, Arthur, ed., *The Penguin Encyclopedia of Ancient Civilizations* (London: Penguin Books, 1980).

Curtin, Philip, Steven Feierman, Leonard Thompson, and Jan Vansina. *African History from Earliest Times to Independence* (New York: Longman, 2nd ed., 1995).

deBary, William Theodore, *et al.*, comp., *Sources of Chinese Tradition* (New York: Columbia University Press, 1998).

Demarest, Arthur and Geoffrey Conrad, eds, *Ideology and Pre-Columbian Civilizations* (Santa Fe, NM: School of American Research Press, 1992).

Eliade, Mircea. *The Sacred and the Profane* (New York: Harper and Row, 1959).

Fagan, Brian. *People of the Earth: An Introduction to World Prehistory* (New York: HarperCollins, 8th ed., 1995).

Keightly, David N., ed. *The Origins of Chinese Civilization* (Berkeley: University of California Press, 1983).

MacNeish, Richard S. "The Origins of New World Civilization," *Scientific American* (November 1964). Reprinted in *Scientific American, Cities: Their Origin, Growth, and Human Impact* (San Francisco: W.H. Freeman and Company, 1973), 63–71.

McIntosh, Susan and Roderick McIntosh. "Finding West Africa's Oldest City," *National Geographic* CLXII No. 3 (September 1982), 396–418.

McIntosh, Roderick James. *The Peoples of the Middle Niger: the Island of Gold* (Oxford: Blackwell, 1998).

McIntosh, Susan Keech, ed. *Excavations at Jenné-Jeno, Hambarketolo, and Kaniana (Inland Niger Delta, Mali), the 1981 Season* (Berkeley: University of California Press, 1995).

Millon, René. "Teotihuacan," *Scientific American* (June 1967). Reprinted in *Scientific American, Cities: Their Origin, Growth, and Human Impact*, 82–91.

Moseley, Michael E. *The Maritime Foundations of Andean Civilization* (Menlo Park, CA: Cummings, 1975).

Murray, Jocelyn, ed. *Cultural Atlas of Africa* (New York: Facts on File, 1982).

Schele, Linda and David Freidel. *A Forest of Kings: The Untold Story of the Ancient Maya* (New York: William Morrow, 1990).

Scientific American, ed. *Cities: Their Origin, Growth, and Human Impact* (San Francisco: W.H. Freeman and Company, 1973).

Time-Life Books. *Time Frame 3000–1500 BC: The Age of God-Kings* (Alexandria, VA: Time-Life Books, 1987).

—— *Time Frame 1500–600 BC: Barbarian Tides* (Alexandria, VA: Time-Life Books, 1987).

—— *Time Frame AD 200–600: Empires Besieged* (Alexandria, VA: Time-Life Books, 1988).

Times (London). *Past Worlds* (Maplewood, NJ: Hammond Inc., 1988).

Zhang, Juzhong, *et al.* "Oldest Playable Instruments Found at Jiahu Early Neolithic Site in China," *Nature*, Vol. 40 (September 23, 1999), 366–68.

Empire and Imperialism

2300 B.C.E.–1100 C.E.

WHAT ARE EMPIRES AND WHY ARE THEY IMPORTANT?

The first empires grew up in the areas of the first civilizations we studied in Part 2—that is, Mesopotamia, the Nile valley, and the Yellow River valley. The Akkadian Empire of Sargon, about 2350 B.C.E., is the first for which we have documentary evidence, and it was followed in the same Mesopotamian region by the Babylonians and, later, by the Assyrians. In their successions we see a pattern that will become familiar in this part: the building of a large, powerful military force in the hands of a strong ruler, followed by a decline, a challenge by an outsider, the overthrow of the old empire, and the rise of a new one.

Chapter 5 begins with Akkad as the earliest example of empire building. Egypt provides the second example, and then we turn to the Persian Empire. In Persia's struggle against Greece in the fifth century B.C.E., we see a fundamental clash between monarchy and democracy, and between empire and city-state. A confederation of small, local city-states stopped the conquering force of the world's most powerful empire. Ultimately, however, in the subsequent dissolution of the Greek system into civil war and the succession of Alexander the Great, we see one of the great ironies of history. Those cities that had earlier prided themselves on their independence and their victory over the largest empire of the time, lost their independence and became integrated into Alexander's empire.

Chapter 6 will explore in greater depth the empire of Rome, while Chapter 7 examines those of China and, briefly, its daughter civilization in Japan. Chapter 8 explores India and

Hall of the Hundred Columns, Persepolis, Iran, 550–330 B.C.E. The remains of these audience halls still inspire a sense of imperial grandeur.

touches on southeast Asia. These three systems controlled vast areas, had enormous impact on tens of millions of people, and have continued to make their influence felt to our own time. They represent turning points in the history of most of humankind.

Rome, China, and India were so successful that their ideologies of empire—their explanations of why they should rule—prevailed for centuries. Indeed, the Roman Empire endured for almost a thousand years, from about 500 B.C.E. to almost 500 C.E., and if we include the Eastern Empire, based in Constantinople, Rome's duration is some 2000 years. Moreover, Rome inspired an imperial image that was expressed throughout later Europe in the so-called Holy Roman Empire. The Chinese Empire, founded in 221 B.C.E., lasted more or less continuously until 1911 C.E., and some would argue that it persists even today in new, Communist garb. The first emperor to rule almost all of the Indian subcontinent, Ashok (Aśoka) Maurya (r. 273–232 B.C.E.), is still commemorated today on every rupee currency note printed in India. Throughout these chapters, we also consider the trade routes that kept these three great empires in communication with each other.

5 DAWN OF THE EMPIRES

2300 B.C.E.–300 B.C.E.

"Our opinion of the gods and our knowledge of men lead us to conclude that it is a general and necessary law of nature to rule whatever one can."

THUCYDIDES

"To the size of states there is a limit."

ARISTOTLE

EMPIRE-BUILDING IN NORTH AFRICA, WEST ASIA, AND THE MEDITERRANEAN

THE MEANING OF EMPIRE

New York proudly calls itself the Empire State; Daimler Chrysler advertises its Chrysler Imperial luxury automobile; until recently, Britain maintained the "Imperial Gallon" as a measure of volume. Yet today the word "imperialism" has a generally negative connotation. The demise within the past generation of many empires, most recently that of the Soviet Union, has met with general approval around the world. Why does the concept of empire evoke such conflicting attitudes? What is an empire?

Empires grow from the conquest of one people by another—in fact, a definition of empire is the extension of political rule by one people over other, different peoples. Empires have been as natural in human history as the desire of people for power and control over other people and their resources, and they have been as frequent as

the ability of rulers to build military organizations capable of attaining those goals.

The word "empire" stirs in most of us conflicting images and feelings. We think of the monumental structures of palaces and the ruling establishments of the emperor and the leadership core. In our imaginations we see majestic buildings, adorned with the finest artworks. The emperor and the imperial administrators, we imagine, wear the finest clothes, eat the choicest foods, enjoy the most select luxuries, and support and command the most powerful technologies. Often they encourage great creativity in the arts and in learning. Sometimes, however, we see them using their power over others in acts of cruelty, arrogance, irresponsibility, and decadence.

We see, too, vast marketplaces and, perhaps, ports and dockyards processing goods from the far corners of the empire, since one of the purposes of empire building is to bring natural riches to the imperial power. Leading into the capital city, connecting it with the remotest areas of empire, are lines of communication and transportation, sea lanes, and, most important of all, roads. Specific examples stand out. Notable are the grand canals linking the rich agricultural lands of south China to the capital in the north and dating back as early as the Sui dynasty, in the seventh century C.E. Similarly, the phrase "All roads lead to Rome," the capital of an equally powerful empire, may have been an exaggeration, but its central idea was correct. Empires bring exotic goods and diverse peoples together under a common ruler. People of different languages, religions, ethnic origins, and cultural and technological levels are brought under a single, centralized rule.

ANCIENT GREECE AND ITS NEIGHBORS

DATE	POLITICAL	RELIGION AND CULTURE	SOCIAL DEVELOPMENT
600 B.C.E.	• Cyaxares of Media (r. 625–585) • Age of Greek tyrants (657–570)	• Zoroaster (630–553)	• City–states in Greece
550 B.C.E.	• Cyrus II (559–530); defeat of Medes, Lydia, Babylon • Peisistratus (d. 527) controlled Athens • Cambyses II (530–522) conquered Egypt	• Pasargadae and Susa developed	• Nile–Red Sea canal
500 B.C.E.	• Darius I (522–486); Persian Empire extended to Indus River; war against Greek city states • Ionian revolt (499) • Battle of Marathon (490) • Xerxes I (486–465) • War between Athens and Sparta: 1st Peloponnesian War (461–451)	• Pythagoras (d. *c.* 500) • Piraeus established as port of Athens • Persepolis built	• Athens at the height of its power. Acropolis built (*c.* 460); architecture, city-state democracy, political philosophy flourish
450 B.C.E.	• Pericles (d. 429) and Delian League • 2nd Peloponnesian War (431–404) and end of Athenian power	• Persian script written down • "Golden Age" of Athens • Aeschylus (d. 456) • Herodotus (d. *c.* 420) • Sophocles (d. 406) • Euripides (d. 406) • Thucydides (d. *c.* 401)	• Persian Empire: regional laws codified; roads built; centralized administration; irrigation systems extended
400 B.C.E.		• Socrates (d. 399)	
350 B.C.E.	• Philip II (359–336) and Alexander the Great (336–323) extend Macedonian Empire • Athens and Thebes defeated (338), ending Greek independence • Alexander conquers Asia Minor (334) and Egypt (332), and reaches Indus (326)	• Aristophanes (d. *c.* 388) • Plato (d. 347) • Aristotle (d. 322) • Demosthenes (d. 322) • Alexandria (Egypt) founded (331) • Persepolis burned (331)	• Spread of Hellenistic culture
300 B.C.E.	• Ptolemies in Egypt • Seleucids in Asia		

Vast systems of administration are needed to hold the imperial structure together. In order to organize and maintain communication and exchange among all parts of the empire, a system of administration must be established. The administrators and rulers must also regulate the fate of conquered peoples in accordance with the needs of the empire. Some are granted full citizenship, most of the remainder receive fewer rights and privileges, while those at the bottom, especially war captives, might be enslaved. A few—those who proved particularly dangerous or costly to the imperial rulers—might be executed, with a warning to potential rebels.

The administration must ensure either that different kinds of monies from various parts of the empire are consolidated into a single system of coinage or that means of exchanging them are readily available. It must communicate across the many languages of the empire, and it may adopt and impose a single administrative language so that the writ of empire is universally understood. It must establish a legal system with at least some degree of uniformity. Indeed, the administration must provide sufficient uniformity in language, currency, weights, measures, and legal systems to enable it to function as a single political structure. Perhaps the most significant administrative task of all is the collection of taxes from its subjects and tribute from those it conquers. Such revenues represent the continuing financial profits to the rulers.

Twentieth-century scholars emphasize two forms of imperial rule: **hegemony** and **dominance**. For the imperial power, hegemony is to be preferred, for this is rule that the subjects accept willingly. They may admire the empire's power or justice; they may benefit from the stability and peace it imposes, from the technological improvements it introduces, from the more extensive networks it develops and opens to their trade and profit, from the cultural sophistication it exhibits and shares with them, or from the opportunities for new kinds of advancement that membership in the empire may offer. If imperial membership is perceived to have such benefits, the subject peoples may welcome it peacefully, even eagerly. They may accept the ideology of the imperial power and its explanation for the legitimacy and benefit of its foreign rule. In short, hegemony can be defined as foreign rule that governs with the substantial consent of the governed.

Should the imperial ideology not be acceptable, however, rulers will impose their government through dominance, the exercise of sheer power. In these circumstances, military force, and the threat to exercise it, are central to the empire's existence, so the state expends vast sums on recruiting, training, and equipping its armies. The troops mobilize across the vast spaces of empire, using the same roads that carry the imperial commerce. The military is often supplemented by offensive and defensive architecture; perhaps the most famous example is the Great Wall of China, built about 220 B.C.E. to keep the Mongols and the Huns (Xiongnu) from invading China. Imperial rulers may try to win the allegiance of conquered peoples by conferring benefits—legal, economic, social, educational, and political—but ultimately, the final recourse is coercion.

No wonder we feel ambivalent about great empires. They control enormous resources and may use them to create productive, beautiful, inspiring civilizations, but the benefits of empire are not shared evenly. We are often appalled at the subjection of conquered peoples. The glory of empire rests on the control of the many by the few; slaves and war captives are among those who pay the heaviest price. So, while we may be awed by the glory and majesty of empire, we may also be inspired by the anti-imperial revolts of conquered peoples eager for self-rule.

Resistance to imperial rule is as normal as empires themselves. Rulers of empires usually dominate because they are able to mobilize more power than the peoples they control. Often, intentionally or unintentionally, the secrets of their power spread among the conquered, thereby enriching their lives. The subject populations learn from the technology introduced by their conquerors, whether it is the use of weapons, materials, military formations, agricultural methods, administrative organizations, or techniques of production. Empires that begin by using their superiority to rule, eventually produce change among the peoples they conquer. Subject peoples, who may originally have felt some gratitude toward their imperial benefactors, may later grow resentful, restive, and finally rebellious. Goths, for example, no longer wished to be subordinate to Romans, nor Mongols to Chinese, as we shall see in Chapters 6 and 7. Empires are not static. They rise and they fall. Ironically, the imperial masters are often forced to trade places with those they had subjugated.

The causes of the decline and fall of empires include:

- Failure of leadership—the inability of the empire to produce or select rulers capable of maintaining the imperial structures;

- Overextension of the administration—the inability of the imperial rulers to sustain the costs of a far-flung empire while coping simultaneously with critical domestic problems;

- Collapse of the economy—the overextension of empire to territories so remote or so difficult to subdue and to govern that costs outrun benefits;

- Doubts over the ideology—the end of belief in the justice or benefit of empire, which may occur either when cynical colonizers abandon the colonial enterprise, or when frustrated colonized peoples revolt, or both;

- Military defeat of the empire by the combined forces of external enemies and of colonized people in revolt.

THE EARLIEST EMPIRES

MESOPOTAMIA AND THE FERTILE CRESCENT

Mesopotamia's earliest power centers were independent city-states that could not reach political accommodation among themselves. They fought constantly for land, irrigation rights, and prestige, as we can see from the scenes of warfare that fill the bas relief artwork from third-millennium Sumer. From this artwork and from cuneiform records, archaeologists have reconstructed two main antagonists, the cities of Lagash and Umma, which, with their allied forces, dominated the warfare of the time. Victory by either one, however, or by any of the city-states over any of the others, was frequently avenged in the next generation.

Geographically, the city-states of Mesopotamia were also vulnerable to immigrant groups crossing their territory and challenging their powers. About 2350 B.C.E., Sargon (r. c. 2334–2279 B.C.E.), leading an immigrant group of Semitic peoples from the Arabian peninsula, entered Sumer. The new

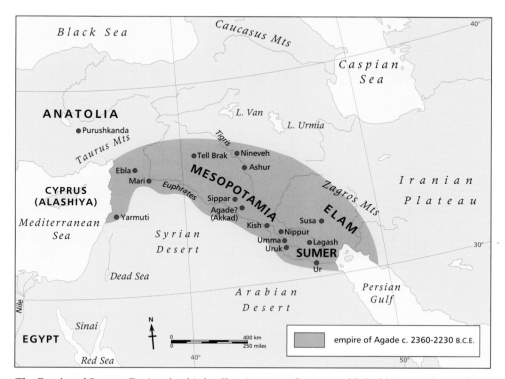

The Empire of Sargon During the third millennium B.C.E. Sargon established his control over the city-states of southern Mesopotamia, creating the world's first empire. Building a capital at Agade, he founded the Akkadian dynasty, which for a century ruled the Fertile Crescent, from the Persian Gulf to the Mediterranean Sea.

Bronze head of an Akkadian ruler (Sargon I?), *c.* 2250 B.C.E.
Exuding royal self-confidence, this near-lifesized bronze
head probably depicts Sargon I, founder of the Akkadian
dynasty. For over half a century, Sargon dominated one city-
state after another until he had conquered most of
Mesopotamia. After his death, his successors worshiped him
as a god.

measurements throughout the empire were
standardized: "The measures of length, area, dry
and liquid capacity, and probably also weight were
integrated into a single logical system which
remained the standard for a thousand years and
more" (Postgate, p. 41). Finally, Sargon imposed his
own imagery and ideology of empire. Documents
were dated from the founding of the Akkadian
kingdom, legal oaths were taken in the name of
the Akkadian king, and Sargon installed his own
daughter as high-priestess of the moon-god
Nanna at Ur.

Sargon's empire lasted for about a century, and
was followed by other outsiders, the Gutians, and
then by a revival of internal Sumerian power under
Ur-Nammu. Culturally, Sumer was so advanced
that it influenced even its conquerors, the Akkadians, the Gutians, and later arrivals. The Akkadian
language, however, did supplant Sumerian by
about 2000 B.C.E.

Politically, Sumer's system of independent city-
states did not endure. The next conquerors were
again Semitic nomads, the Amorites, who founded
a new dynasty at Babylon about 1900 B.C.E. They,
too, were absorbed culturally by Sumer. Their sixth
ruler, Hammurabi, is most famous for his law codes
(see p. 56), but he was also a skilled military leader
who defeated the Sumerian city-states and created
the Babylonian Empire which stretched from the
Persian Gulf to Syria and endured for 250 years,
until its defeat about 1500 B.C.E. by the Hittites.

For a thousand years rival empires in the
region—Hittites, Assyrians, Mitannis, and Babylonians—competed for power. The Israelites under
their kings, David and Solomon, *c.* 1000–922 B.C.E.,
also had a period of expansion within the region, as
did the Phoenician trading cities along the coast.
The Egyptians entered actively into local warfare
for some centuries, 1600–1200 B.C.E., and were
always a force in the political balance of the region.

The city-state organizational structure of Mesopotamia, and its geographical openness, had left
the region very vulnerable. As the city-states fought
destructively among themselves, they were repeatedly attacked by, and absorbed into, powerful
empires. Some of these empires were based outside
the region, others grew up, or transplanted themselves, within the region. The Mesopotamians had
to expend their resources on military technology
and organization as their local units of government
faced increasing challenges from ever-greater
powers that sought to consolidate them into ever-
larger empires.

arrivals settled in and around northern Sumer and
called their land Akkad. Sargon led the Akkadians
to victories over the leading cities of Sumer, over
the Elamites to the east, over northern Mesopotamia, and over a swath of land connecting
Mesopotamia to the Mediterranean. He founded
the Akkadian capital at Agade, a city whose exact
location is now unknown.

Historical records are skimpy, but those that do
exist correspond to our assessment of the key
characteristics of empire. First, the Akkadians
conquered widely. Administrative tablets of the
Akkad dynasty have been found as far away as
Susa, several hundred miles to the east in Persia,
suggesting a far-flung governmental administration. Second, after razing the walls of the major
cities of Ur, Lagash, and Umma, Sargon displaced
the traditional local civilian hierarchies with his
own administrators, designated the "sons of
Akkad." Third, the Akkadian language was used in
administrative documents in Sumer. Fourth,

EGYPT AND INTERNATIONAL CONQUEST

Egypt's background to empire was very different from Mesopotamia's. First, the region was protected from outside invasion by the deserts to the west and east, and by cataracts (steep rapids) on the Nile River toward the south. Second, from very early times Egypt was governed as a unified state.

Statues and pictures usually depict Egyptian pharaohs wearing crowns. Until about 3000 B.C.E., the most important of these was a tall white crown with a vulture symbolizing dominance over the upper Nile valley of southern Egypt. Later pharaohs often wore an additional crown, a squat red one with a cobra, to symbolize their conquest of Lower Egypt, the northern lands of the Nile delta. From about 3000 B.C.E., when the legendary god-king Menes united Upper and Lower Egypt, until about 2134 B.C.E. the kingdom remained united. The subsequent breakup of Egypt into warring segments, especially the division between the delta and the upper Nile valley, suggests that through the centuries the original split may never have been completely healed. On the other hand, as Egyptologist John Baines of Oxford University suggests, the kingdom may have been forged from many geographical parts. Scholars need to be alert to the evidence and not be swayed by presuppositions:

> The idea of two Predynastic kingdoms may be a projection of the pervasive dualism of Egyptian ideology, not a record of a true historical situation. More probably there was a gradual unification of a previously uncentralized society. (*Baines and Malek*, p. 31)

Geography encouraged Egyptian unity. With vast deserts separating the Nile valley from the outside world to the east and west, and cataracts on the

Five-string painted wooden harp, tomb of Ani, Thebes, c. 1200 B.C.E. This harp from the Nineteenth Dynasty, inlaid with ivory, terminates in a head wearing the royal double crown, a symbol of the conquest and unification of Upper and Lower Egypt. (*British Museum, London*)

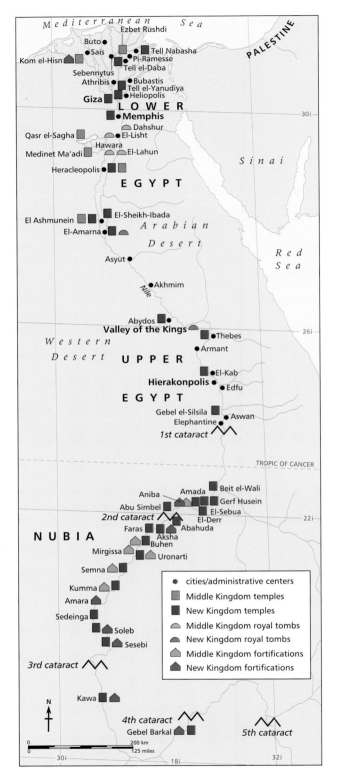

Middle and New Kingdom Egypt By 2040 B.C.E. the unification of Egypt into a centralized, militaristic state was under way. Its hierarchic society focused on the priesthood and the dynastic succession of semi-god rulers, the Pharaohs. The consolidation of power was reflected in the size and scale of royal building projects, including fortifications, new cities, temples, and grandiose tombs, and by conquests in Nubia.

Nile making southward sailing difficult, Egypt tended naturally to become a single administrative unit incorporating the entire Nile valley from the first cataract northward to the Mediterranean Sea. Situating the capital city at Memphis (near today's Cairo), where the Nile River disgorged into the delta, centralized and unified the government. The centrality of the pharaohs' palaces and the awesome ceremonial pyramids nearby further proclaimed national unity.

The kingdoms sometimes did fracture, as in the period c. 2200–2000 B.C.E., when north and south split apart. But from 3000 B.C.E. to the present, Egypt has usually remained a single political unit. So we think of it as a kingdom with a single government ruling a single civilization rather than as an empire of one people ruling over others.

This unity was forged from the diversity of peoples who came to inhabit Egypt. Semites from the desert to the east, Phoenicians from the sea coast, Blacks from Nubia and the heart of Africa, and Europeans from across the Mediterranean immigrated and amalgamated into a common national stock, which intermarried and recognized each other without apparent reference to race or ethnicity. Martin Bernal's *Black Athena* discusses this mixture of peoples in linguistic and cultural terms. Paintings of ancient Egyptians show them sometimes pale in color, sometimes black, very often red.

Egyptian forces did not always stay within their own borders, however. During the Middle Kingdom, c. 2000–1750 B.C.E., Egyptians moved into Nubia, the territory stretching southward some 900 miles (1400 kilometers) from just above the first cataract in the Nile, at present-day Aswan in Egypt, to present-day Khartoum, capital of the Sudan. At first, the move was only into lower Nubia. During the New Kingdom, c. 1550–1050 B.C.E., however, Egypt conquered the heartland of central Nubia, the core of the sophisticated, independent state and a source of gold, minerals, wood, and recruits for Egypt's army and police.

Separated from Egypt by the cataracts of the Nile, Nubia's black, African people represented just

Relief from the temple of Beit el-Wali (detail), Lower Nubia, c. 2000–1850 B.C.E. The rich variety of produce here presented to Ramses II after his conquest of Lower Nubia—bags of gold, incense, tusks, ebony logs, ostrich eggs, bows, shields, fans, and wild animals—seems to mirror the ethnic diversity on display. Pale-, brown-, and black-skinned peoples coexisted in Egypt and Nubia. (*British Museum, London*)

one of the strands that made up the cosmopolitan mix of people in Egypt, and historical records indicate continuing political and military rivalry between the two kingdoms. Egypt's conquest of Nubia was an imperial expansion. Nubia later expelled the Egyptian conquerors and even marched northward to capture Egypt itself. For half a century, 712–657 B.C.E., Nubia ruled over an empire of its own, which included all of Egypt. Thereafter Nubia remained strong, with its capital

first at Napata and later at Meroe, while Egypt fell into decline.

Egypt also pursued imperial ventures along the trade routes into the Levant, occupying Syria and Palestine at the height of the New Kingdom, 1530–1200 B.C.E. Here, frequent conflict with the powerful Hittites culminated in perhaps the first major battle in history, fought at Qadesh, Syria, in 1285 B.C.E. Although the Egyptian pharaoh Ramses II claimed a crushing victory, the Hittites continued to

Royal pyramids and adjacent iron slag heaps at Meroe, Sudan, c. 600 B.C.E. The rulers of Meroe and Egypt shared many artistic traditions, but often gave them a distinctive local interpretation, as can be seen in the forms of their pyramids and palaces.

maintain a hold along the eastern Mediterranean. Thutmosis I (r. 1504–1492 B.C.E) not only extended Egypt's control southward to the fourth cataract of the Nile, but also northwest as far as the Euphrates River, creating Egypt's greatest historical empire. The small states of Syria and Palestine managed to remain self-governing, but Egypt stationed army units and administrative officials in the region and collected taxes. Here in western Asia, Egypt seemed more interested in access to raw materials than in governance.

Egypt's imperial control over remote and div-erse peoples met resistance from local powers within the Fertile Crescent. The Hittites, the Babylonians, and, especially, the Mitannis mounted frequent revolts. They developed a new weapons system: two-wheeled, horse-drawn chariots carrying archers in bronze armor, shooting bronze-tipped arrows. Egypt's military technology lagged, and Egyptian control was ended by about 1200 B.C.E., although its political and economic influence in the region continued for centuries.

Suffering defeats in the Levant and Nubia, Egypt was pushed back within its river and desert

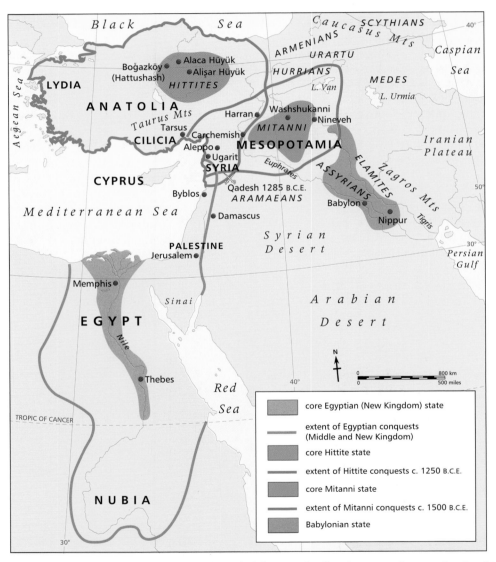

The empires of southwest Asia Toward the end of the second millennium B.C.E. three empires fought for control of the Fertile Crescent. Egyptians, Mitannians of northern Mesopotamia, and Hittites of Anatolia came into direct conflict. Building on strong political control over their core regions, each dispatched powerful armies with the most up-to-date weapons to seize more territory from the others.

niche as a powerful and independent nation-state—the world's oldest and most deeply rooted—but no longer an empire. Indeed, Egypt itself came under attack and even occupation. In 671 B.C.E., while Nubians ruled southern Egypt, Assyrians conquered and occupied the north.

THE ASSYRIANS

Assyrians, descendants of the Akkadians, had thrice emerged triumphant from the continuous warfare in Mesopotamia among the Hittites, the Mitannians, the Babylonians, and themselves. In the twentieth century B.C.E. they had gained their independence, and some prosperity through the trade of their private businessmen. Then, subjugated by the Mitannians, they regained their independence in the thirteenth century to lose it again to the Arameans about 1000 B.C.E. Around 900 B.C.E. a Neo-Assyrian (New Assyrian) kingdom began a series of conquests, sweeping westward to the Mediterranean coast, northward to Syria and Palestine, and southeastward into Babylon. Infantry provided the Assyrian main force, while archers riding in chariots led the attacks, and battering rams and siege towers assaulted fixed positions.

More than most ancient empires, the Assyrians controlled conquered peoples through policies of forced migration. They deported some nations into exile from their homelands, including ten of the tribes of Israel who were subsequently "lost," that is they lost their sense of ethnic and religious identity and presumably ceased their opposition to the Assyrians, just as the conquerors had hoped. In other regions, the Assyrians imported their own people to settle among the defeated peoples and keep them under control.

Only the last of the Neo-Assyrian kings, Ashurbanipal (669–626 B.C.E.), is known to have been literate, and he constructed a great library in his capital at Nineveh. 20,000 tablets are still preserved from that library, including the earliest complete version of *The Epic of Gilgamesh* (see pp. 54–5).

King Esarhaddon conquered Egypt in 671 B.C.E., making Assyria the greatest power of its day. His successors held the entire province, driving the Nubians from the southern regions and suppressing rebellions. Assyria finally withdrew from Egypt, defeated not primarily by the Egyptians, but by internal dynastic struggles, and by the combined forces of Babylonians, Arameans, the Medes of Iran, and Scythian invaders who attacked Assyria's Mesopotamian heartland. The Assyrian capital, Nineveh, fell in 612 B.C.E.

EGYPT UNDER OCCUPATION

Egypt had become one of the contestants in the many wars for control over the eastern Mediterranean and, like many of the other powers, Egypt employed Greek mercenary soldiers. Trade and cultural exchange also increased between Egypt and Greece, and many of the historical

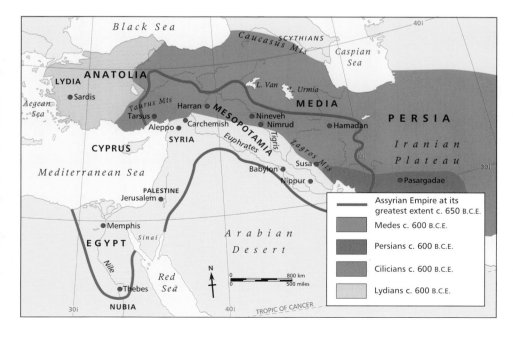

Assyria and its rivals The shifting political map of southwest Asia was dominated between 850 and 650 B.C.E. by the powerful and martial Assyrians, who even occupied Egypt. Anatolia was fragmented into smaller states. To the north a powerful federation of Median tribes was a growing threat. In 614, in alliance with the Babylonians, they crushed Assyria.

records of this time and region derive from the work of Greek historians.

Egypt continued to fall into the empires of others. It was conquered by the Persians in 525 B.C.E. Two centuries later, in 332 B.C.E., Alexander the Great captured Egypt from Persia, and in 30 B.C.E., Egypt passed to the next great Mediterranean empire, that of Rome. Some of these conquests are noted in later sections of this part.

PERSIA

Medes and Persians began to appear in the region east of Mesopotamia about 1300 B.C.E., bringing with them the use of iron. By the mid-ninth century B.C.E., written cuneiform records confirm the archaeological evidence of their arrival. At first the Medes were more numerous and powerful, but later the Persians came to predominate. Both groups were **Indo-Europeans**—that is, in language and cultural heritage they were related to some of the same major groups who came to inhabit Europe and northern India. Cyaxares of Media (r. 625–585 B.C.E.) established an army; conquered the Scyth-

ians, another immigrant group in the region; sealed an alliance with the Babylonians by marrying his granddaughter to the son of their ruler; and, together with them, captured Nineveh, the capital of Assyria. Assyria was destroyed as a major military force. A new **balance of power** among the Egyptians, Medes, Babylonians, and Lydians resulted in western Asia.

The balance was broken, however, when Cyrus II, the Great, of Persia (r. c. 559–530 B.C.E.) defeated the other three kingdoms and incorporated them into his own empire. He conquered, first, the Medes in 550; then, in 546, the Lydians with their king, the fabulously wealthy Croesus; and finally, in 539, the Babylonians. Under Cyrus, the Achaeminids (named in honor of their legendary ancestor Achaemenes) dominated the entire region from Persia to the Mediterranean. Cyrus died in 529 B.C.E., defending this empire against attacks from the east.

His eldest son, Cambyses II (r. 530–522 B.C.E.), expanded Cyrus' conquests. Crossing the Sinai Desert, he captured Memphis, the capital of Egypt, and carried its pharaoh back to Susa in captivity, thus completing the conquest of all of the major powers that had influenced the Middle East.

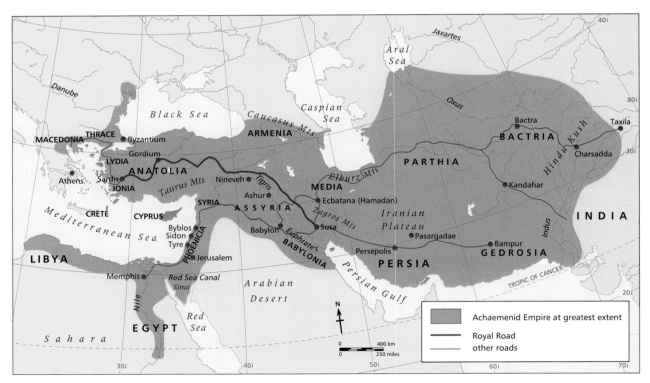

Achaemenid Persia The Medes and the Persians were united under Cyrus the Great in 550 B.C.E. to form the Achaemenid or Persian Empire. Cyrus and his successors, notably Darius and Xerxes, extended the empire to the Indus in the east and to Egypt and Libya in the west, and twice invaded Greece.

Egypt frequently revolted and large garrisons were required to keep it under control, so the Achaeminids under Darius I (r. 522–486 B.C.E.) completed a canal across the desert, connecting the Nile River and the Red Sea. This early "Suez Canal," first envisioned by the Egyptians as a trade route, became a troop supply line for Persian control over Egypt.

Darius also extended the Persian empire more deeply into the Indian subcontinent, as far as the Indus River. The Achaeminids now controlled some of the most valuable trade routes in Asia; the **satrapy**, or colony, of "India" submitted one-third of the annual cash receipts of the Achaeminids, and Indian troops served in the Achaeminid armies. From this time forward, Indian- and Persian-based powers would regularly confront one another across the borders of what is today Afghanistan and Pakistan. Meanwhile, in the west, Darius expanded onto the fringes of Europe, capturing Thrace and Macedonia, and bringing the Persian Empire to its greatest extent.

Attempts to move further were stymied. The Scythians to the north and west fought a kind of guerrilla warfare that the massed forces of the Persians could not overcome. To the south and west, Darius' armies of invasion into Greece were defeated at Marathon in 490 B.C.E. Under Darius' eldest son, Xerxes I (r. 486–465 B.C.E.), wars continued between the Persian Empire and the Greek city-states. The Greeks were hard pressed and lost many important battles, and in 480 B.C.E. Xerxes' troops captured and burned the Acropolis at Athens. But overall, the Greeks held off the invading Persians until 465 B.C.E., when Xerxes was assassinated. Thereafter the Persians lost the will and the power to fight. Persia continued to intervene in the politics of the Greek city-states, contributing financial aid to its allies among them but no longer dispatching military forces. A confederation of small, democratic, Greek city-states had managed to repulse the mighty Persian Empire. *The Persian Wars*, written by Herodotus in the late fifth century B.C.E. and presenting the story from a Greek perspective, is the first great book of secular history still preserved (see Source, p. 141).

IMPERIAL POLICIES

The Persian imperial form of rule and administration changed in the three generations from Cyrus II its chief architect, through his son and successor Cambyses II, to Darius I, its most powerful emperor. The differences among the three emperors became especially clear in their policies for achieving a balance between the power of the central government and the desire of local, conquered peoples for some degree of autonomy. Under Cyrus and Darius, Persia respected local customs and institutions even as the empire expanded. Cambyses was more dictatorial, and met an early end.

Cyrus II

When Cyrus (r. *c.* 559–530 B.C.E.) conquered the Medes, he allowed their king to escape with his life. He administered his newly acquired lands through the existing Median bureaucracy and army, allowing Median officials to keep their positions, though under Persian control. When Cyrus conquered Lydia, he spared Croesus and even enlisted his advice as a consultant. In conquered Ionian cities he retained local rulers who were willing to work under Persian direction. On defeating Babylon, his most powerful rival, Cyrus chose to rule in the name of the Babylonian god Marduk and to worship daily in his temple, thus maintaining the support of the priests. He continued to employ local bureaucrats and to protect and secure the trade routes that brought wealth to the empire and secured the loyalty of the merchant classes.

Perhaps most strikingly, Cyrus allowed the peoples that Babylonia had captured and deported to return to their homes. For example, he permitted the Jewish community of exiles in Babylon to return home to Judaea and to rebuild their temple in Jerusalem. He also returned to them the gold and silver that had been taken from the temple. The 40,000 exiles who returned over 1000 miles (1600 kilometers) to Judaea hailed Cyrus as their political savior and kept their renewed state loyal to the Persian Empire.

Cambyses II

Unlike his father, Cambyses (r. 530–522 B.C.E.) seems to have lost sight of the need for restraint in both the expansion and the administration of his empire. His conquest of Egypt and his use of Egyptians in his own administration of that land followed Cyrus' model, but then he overextended his reach. His attempted campaign against the Phoenician city of Carthage in distant north Africa failed when Phoenician sailors in his own navy refused to fight. An army sent south from Egypt to Nubia, attempting to capture its fabled gold supplies, failed to reach its destination and retreated from the desert in tatters. Cambyses may not have been emotionally stable, and it was rumored that he kicked to death his pregnant wife/sister. When he died, as he was returning to Persia to put down an insurrection, it was further rumored that he had committed suicide. His seven-year rule had been costly to Persia.

Darius I

Darius (r. 522–486 B.C.E.), a general in the Persian army and prince of the Achaeminid dynasty, succeeded to the throne by murdering the previous incumbent Bardiya (r. 522) and ruled for thirty-five years. He was more deliberate, more balanced, and more capable as an administrator than Cambyses, and he became much richer as emperor than either of his predecessors. Like Cyrus, he used local administrators to staff local governments. He sought to create smaller, more efficient units of government by increasing the number of administrative units, or **satrapies,** even faster than he expanded the empire. Some of the regional administrators, or satraps, were local elites; some were Persian. In each satrapy, loyalty to the empire was assured by the presence of Persian army units, which reported directly back to the king, and by a secretary, who monitored the actions of the satrap and also reported back to Persia.

Darius commissioned the design of the first written Persian script. He established the tradition that royal inscriptions were to be trilingual—in Persian, Babylonian, and Elamite. In the midst of the multitude of languages used across the empire, these were to be the official written languages of administration. The most widely spoken public language was Aramaic, however, and this language of the common people throughout much of the eastern Mediterranean greatly influenced the development of formal Persian.

Legal codes varied among the satrapies to reflect local usage, and the Persian rulers frequently codified and recorded these laws. Tax codes were rationalized. The size and productivity of agricultural fields were measured, evaluated, and recorded, with their tax rate fixed at about 20 percent. In each satrapy the various taxes—on industry, mining, ports, water, commerce, and sales—were gathered by a Persian collector. Most of the revenues were

Lion killing a bull, bas relief, Persepolis, Iran, 550–330 B.C.E. The great palace complex of Persepolis, encompassing many smaller palaces within it, was designed as the central symbol of Darius' empire. Construction began in 518 B.C.E. and took some seventy years to complete. Scenes such as this bas relief of a lion killing a bull seem to emerge from Achaeminid mythology, which read the signs of the zodiac, Leo following Taurus, as representing the end of the old year and the coming of the new.

Homage rendered to Darius, bas relief, Persepolis, Iran, 550–330 B.C.E. On New Year's Day, ambassadors of each of Persia's twenty and more satrapies presented themselves to the emperor in his audience hall at Persepolis. Darius, bejeweled and arrayed in royal robes of purple and gold, received them.

remitted to Persia, but some were retained locally for administrative and development expenses.

Darius built, maintained, and guarded an imperial system of roads, the most famous of which was a 1700-mile (2735-kilometer) royal road, stretching from his capital at Susa to Sardis across Anatolia (but not quite reaching the Mediterranean). Along these roads he established a series of inns for travelers and a royal courier service with stations at about every 15 miles (24 kilometers). He completed the construction of the Nile–Red Sea canal, which the Egytians had abandoned.

To increase agricultural production, Darius renewed the irrigation systems of Mesopotamia, and encouraged the introduction of new crops from one part of the empire to another. He standardized the gold coinage of the empire, and permitted only his own imperial mints to strike the official coinage, the gold daric, in his name. Agriculture and commerce flourished, and not only for the benefit of the wealthy. Goods for everyday use—leather sandals, cheap cloth, iron implements and utensils, and pottery—were produced in increasing quantities.

Substantial sums of the enormous wealth of the flourishing empire went to the construction of four capital cities. Cyrus had built up Pasargadae and its great gardens as a retreat and capital. He had also begun to rebuild Susa, the old Elamite capital, which continued to serve as the principal administrative center under the Persians. Darius added here an impressive palace for himself. In the summer, Susa was too hot, so Darius moved the court to Ecbatana, the former capital of the Medes, in the northern hills. But as his most sumptuous and lavish capital, and the one in the most Persian style, Darius built Persepolis.

EMPERORS OF PERSIA

The heart of the Persian Empire came together from two separate kingdoms: the original homeland of the Persians, known as Fars or Parsa (now in southwest Iran); and Media (now in northwest Iran). When Cyrus the Great conquered his Median overlord in the sixth century B.C.E., the two realms were united. Persians and Medes in any case shared ethnic origins—they were both Aryans, the word from which Persia gets its modern name, Iran.

Cyrus II, the Great	**559–530** (B.C.E.)
Cambyses II	**530–522**
Bardiya	**522**
Darius I	**522–486**
Xerxes I	**486–465**
Ataxerxes I	**465–424**
Xerxes II	**424–423**
Sogdianus	**424–423**
Darius II	**423–404**
Ataxerxes II	**404–359**
Ataxerxes III	**359–338**
Arses	**338–336**
Darius III	**336–330**

In accordance with the political theory that had evolved in imperial Persia, the emperor legally possessed all the property of the realm as well as the power of life and death over his subjects. Darius had not, however, elected to become a god. He was probably a follower of the religion of the teacher Zarathustra, or Zoroaster as the Greeks called him, believing in one god of goodness and light, represented by fire and engaged in continuing warfare with the forces of evil, darkness, and falsehood. Moreover, like his predecessor Cyrus, Darius had not tried to impose his religious beliefs on the peoples he conquered. He tried to soften the imposition of imperial administration and tax collection by maintaining local traditions and by enlisting local elites to serve in his administration. Like Cyrus, Darius managed to balance imperial majesty with local autonomy.

GREEK CITY-STATES: REALITY AND IMAGE

As Darius expanded his empire into western Anatolia (present-day Turkey) and began to conquer the Greek city-states of that region, he encountered a different form of political organization to that of the Persian imperial structure. The Greek city-state, or **polis**, was an intentionally small, locally organized government based on a single central city with enough surrounding land to support its agricultural needs. Most of the city-states had populations of a few thousand, with only the very largest of them exceeding 40,000 people.

Geography and topography played a large part in limiting the size of the Greek city-state. In and around the Greek peninsula, mountains, rivers, and seas had kept the units of settlement rather small and isolated. When a region could no longer support an expanding population, it hived off colonies to new locations. Most of the Greek city-states in Anatolia seem to have originated as colonial settlements of older cities on the Greek mainland, part of an array of Greek city-states that spread throughout the Mediterranean coast, extending as far west as present-day Marseille in France and Catalonia in Spain. Although separate and usually independent politically, the city-states were united culturally by the use of the Greek language, a mythistory centered on the *Iliad* and *Odyssey* of the poet Homer (see Source below), and such

SOURCE

Homer and the Value System of Early Greece

The historical folk tales from which Homer (8th century B.C.E.) wove his two great epic poems, the *Iliad* and the *Odyssey*, had probably circulated orally since the 12th century B.C.E. This was the time of the Trojan War, the fulcrum on which both epics turn. The *Iliad* tells of this war, which, Homer writes, was launched by a coalition of Greek city-states against the Trojans in response to the seduction of Helen, the wife of the king of Sparta, by Paris, the son of the king of Troy. Just as the war begins in a personal vendetta, so, too, individual feuds during the war break out among the Greeks themselves, for personal more than for political reasons. The bitter personal quarrel between Agamemnon, brother of the king of Sparta and himself king of Mycenae, and Achilles, the mightiest of the Greek warriors, cripples the effectiveness of the Greek coalition and dominates the storyline of the *Iliad*. The *Odyssey* tells the still more personal post-war story of Odysseus' ten-year struggle to reach his home in Ithaca and of his ultimate reunion with his wife and son in that kingdom.

Although many literary critics believe that "Homer" was really more than one author, most today believe that just one person wrote, or dictated, the epics. The stories on which Homer bases his poetic accounts were probably well known among the Greeks of his time. Homer's lasting reputation and fame rest on his skill in crafting these stories into coherent narratives told in poetry of great power. Further, by focusing on personal stories within the national epics, Homer created images of human excellence (*arete* in ancient Greek) at levels of heroism which inspire readers to this day. He writes with equal power of excellence in war and in love.

Bravery in warfare is a cardinal virtue, and, in the *Iliad*, Homer portrays Hektor, the mightiest of the Trojans, praying that his son might inherit his own strength in battle, and even surpass it. The child's mother would apparently share this vision of her son as warrior:

> Zeus, and you other immortals, grant that this boy, who is my son,
> may be as I am, pre-eminent among the Trojans,
> great in strength, as am I, and rule strongly over Ilion;
> and some day let them say of him: "He is better by far than his father",
> as he comes in from the fighting; and let him kill his enemy
> and bring home the blooded spoils, and delight the heart of his mother.

> (*Iliad*, VI:476–481)

Praising excellence in warfare and combat, Homer portrays Odysseus, Telemachus, and their followers in the *Odyssey* as fierce raptors swooping down upon their prey:

> After them the attackers wheeled, as terrible as falcons
> from eyries in the mountains veering over and diving down
> with talons wide unsheathed on flights of birds,
> who cower down the sky in chutes and bursts along the valley—
> but the pouncing falcons grip their prey, no frantic wing avails,
> and farmers love to watch those beaked hunters.
> So these now fell upon the suitors in that hall,
> turning, turning to strike and strike again,
> while torn men moaned at death, and blood ran smoking
> over the whole floor.

> (XXII:310–319)

Homer sang equally vividly, and far more sweetly and poignantly, of excellence in love. As the *Odyssey* moves toward its conclusion, hero and heroine, Odysseus and Penelope, make love after a wartime separation of twenty years:

> Now from his breast into his eyes the ache
> of longing mounted, and he wept at last,
> his dear wife, clear and faithful, in his arms,
> longed for as the sunwarmed earth is longed for by a swimmer
> spent in rough water where his ship went down
> under Poseidon's blows, gale winds and tons of sea.
> Few men can keep alive through a big surf
> to crawl, clotted with brine, on kindly beaches
> in joy, in joy, knowing the abyss behind:
> and so she too rejoiced, her gaze upon her husband,
> her white arms round him pressed as though forever.
> . . . .   (XXIII:234–244)

> So they came
> into that bed so steadfast, loved of old,
> opening glad arms to one another,
> Telemachus by now had hushed the dancing,
> hushed the women. In the darkened hall
> he and the cowherd and the swineherd slept.
> The royal pair mingled in love again
> and afterward lay revelling in stories:
> hers of the siege her beauty stood at home
> from arrogant suitors, crowding on her sight,
> and how they fed their courtship on his cattle,
> oxen and fat sheep, and drank up rivers
> of wine out of the vats.
> Odysseus told
> of what hard blows he had dealt out to others
> and of what blows he had taken—all that story.
> She could not close her eyes till all was told.

> (*Odyssey* XXIII:298–313)

War and love, the bloody heroism of the battlefield and the warm intimacy of family life—Homer addressed both in imagery which has inspired readers, and listeners, to this day.

SPOTLIGHT

Everyday Life in Ancient Greece

Much of the literature and art of ancient and classical Greece represented a search for personal excellence and aesthetic perfection: Homer's epic heroes, Plato's ideal forms, Aristotle's celestial spheres, the architecture and sculpture of the Acropolis in Athens. But some observers regarded the search for artistic perfection as financially wasteful and politically misguided. Opponents criticized Pericles for endangering the defense of

Athens through wasteful extravagance in gussying up the city "like a harlot with precious stones, statues, and temples costing a world of money" (Plutarch, p. 191). And while Athens' public architecture remains a model of beauty until today, private housing in the city was quite dingy.

An alternative aesthetics devoted to representing everyday life appeared, although it left no formal artistic canon. In the late sixth century, in Boeotia, bordering Athens to the west, small terra cotta figurines representing people at work in

quite ordinary jobs were produced in large numbers, frequently to be placed in tombs. These included barbers cutting hair, porters carrying baskets, and, in **figure 1** here, one of the most common tasks of all, a farmer behind his plow guiding two oxen through the fields. A statuette of an equally common daily activity is represented in

Figure 1 Terra cotta statuette of man with plow and oxen, Boeotia, sixth century B.C.E. (*Louvre, Paris*)

Figure 2 Terra cotta figurine of woman kneading dough, Tanagra, Boeotia, fifth century B.C.E. (*American School of Classical Studies, Athens*)

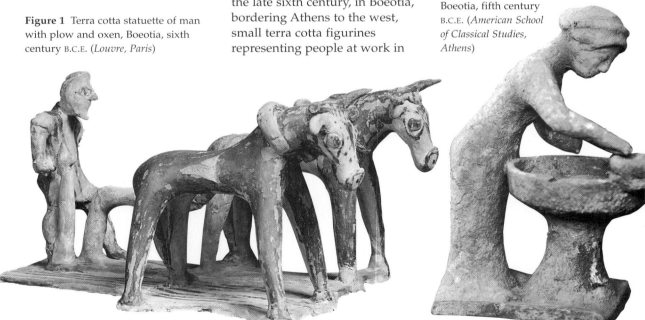

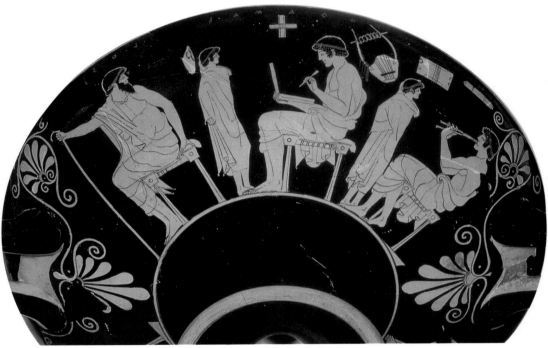

figure 2, a woman kneading dough in a stone basin. This terra cotta dates to the fifth century, contemporary with classical Athens. **Figures 3** and **4**, painted on a single red-figure cup, also of the fifth century, depict four scenes from the education of a young man—learning to play the lyre and the flute, and learning to read and write, all under the watchful eye of a pedagogue. These vase paintings, in their subject matter and their style, represent a mid-point between everyday activities (for the upper classes) and classical forms.

Figure 3 and 4 Two halves of a red-figure cup by the sculptor Douris, fifth century B.C.E. (*Staatliche Museen, Berlin*)

FOCUS

Minoans and Myceneans: The Earliest City-States of the Aegean

How Do We Know?

Until the 1870s scholars of classical Greece believed that the Greek city-states had begun their slow evolution about the ninth century B.C.E. after hundreds of years of political and military turmoil. Naturally they knew of Homer's great epic poems of the Trojan War, the *Iliad* and the *Odyssey* (see Source, pp. 134–5), in which the king of Mycenae led the Greek city-states in war against Troy around 1400 B.C.E., but they understood these tales of earlier times to be myths without foundation in fact.

Then, in the 1870s, Heinrich Schliemann, a classicist and amateur archaeologist, discovered evidence of the existence of city-kingdoms at both Troy and Mycenae, dating to about 1600 to 1450 B.C.E., while in 1900 Arthur Evans discovered a massive palace complex at Knossos, north-central Crete, that confirmed the possible reality of the mythical king Minos. Thus archaeologists discovered two ancient kingdoms, with trade links, confirming popular folk legends and locating some of the roots of Greek civilization a thousand years further back in time.

What Do We Know?

Immigrants began to settle Crete about 6000 B.C.E. By 3000 B.C.E., they had built villages, and by 2000 B.C.E. at Knossos they erected the first and largest of at least four major palace complexes on the island. The palaces combined three functions: elaborately furnished royal residences, religious and ritual centers, and headquarters for administering the Cretan economy. The craftspeople of Crete produced bronze tools, gems, and extraordinarily fine pottery, eggshell-thin vessels which they exported throughout the eastern Mediterranean. As an island kingdom located at the crossroads of multiple trade routes, Crete excelled in commerce.

Pictographic writing existed from at least 2000 B.C.E. and about 1700 B.C.E. syllabic writing was introduced. Known as Linear A, this script has not yet been deciphered. About 1450 B.C.E., some, now unknown, disaster led to the destruction of three of the major palaces. (For a time scholars believed that eruptions of the volcano Thera might have caused the destruction, but deep-sea excavations show that the eruption was too early, *c.* 1625 B.C.E., and too far distant to have caused such devastation.) Crete seems to have become more deeply enmeshed in the affairs of Mycenae at this time. A new script, called Linear B, was created for transcribing Greek, suggesting that this had now become the language of Crete. In 1370 B.C.E. the palace at Knossos was also destroyed, and Crete came under the sway of Mycenae. Finally the glories of Knossos were lost, preserved for thousands of years only in legend.

Homer portrays Mycenaeans as brave and heroic

---

festivals as the Olympic games, held every four years after 776 B.C.E.

Some of the Greek cities in Anatolia had earlier fallen under the kingdom of Lydia. These and more were now captured by Darius' empire. Although Persian rule rested rather lightly, and the Greek city-states of Anatolia were permitted to retain their own form of local government as long as they paid their taxes to Persia, some of them revolted and called on the Greek cities of the peninsula to aid the resistance. Athens, joined by Eretria, tried, halfheartedly and unsuccessfully, to assist its overseas

relatives with ships and soldiers. According to Herodotus, Darius

> asked who the Athenians were and, being informed, called for his bow, and placing an arrow on the string, shot upward into the sky, saying as he let fly the shaft, "Grant me, Zeus, to revenge myself on the Athenians!" After this speech, he bade one of his servants every day, when his dinner was spread, three times repeat these words to him, "Master, remember the Athenians."
>
> (*The Persian Wars*, V:105)

warriors as well as active sailors and traders. They carried on extensive trade and cultural exchange with Crete, including sharing the use of Linear B script. After 1450, when several of Crete's important towns were destroyed, Mycenae came to dominate the relationship. Mycenae was home to several small kingdoms, each with its own palace or citadel and accompanying cemetery of beehive-shaped tombs. The greatest of the cities was Mycenae itself, the administrative center of the entire region, surrounded by a colossal wall up to 25 feet (7 meters) thick and entered through a massive gate topped with huge stone lions looking down on all who entered and left. The site is rich in the evidence of warfare: weapons, armor, paintings of warriors, and, at the seashore a few miles distant, ships of war. Some of the kings, at least, were quite wealthy: one was buried with 11 pounds (5 kilograms) of gold, and the funeral "mask of Agamemnon" was a work of consummate craftsmanship in gold. Scholars have been unable to discover the reason for the fall of Mycenaean civilization; perhaps it was invaded, perhaps it imploded in internal warfare. By the end of the twelfth century B.C.E., all the palaces and towns of Mycenae were destroyed or abandoned.

The archaeological excavations of Schliemann and others who followed him, however, demonstrated that for some five hundred years in Mycenae, and for a thousand in Crete, local, brilliant, urban civilizations had flourished. Their fall ushered in the Greek "Dark Ages," a period of general upheaval throughout much of the eastern Mediterranean. The Greeks even lost their knowledge of how to write. Apparently additional waves of nomadic immigrants entered Greece from the north. By about 850 B.C.E. the peoples of Greece began to emerge from an age of darkness and once again to settle, to build towns, to trade overseas, to receive new waves of immigrants that increased their population, and to restore their written culture.

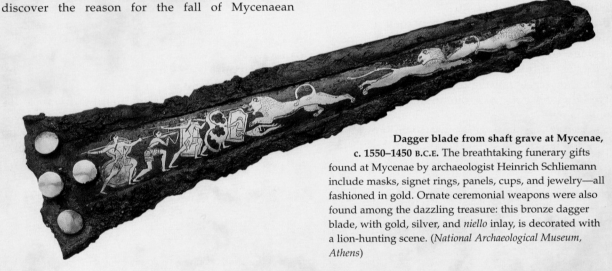

Dagger blade from shaft grave at Mycenae, c. 1550–1450 B.C.E. The breathtaking funerary gifts found at Mycenae by archaeologist Heinrich Schliemann include masks, signet rings, panels, cups, and jewelry—all fashioned in gold. Ornate ceremonial weapons were also found among the dazzling treasure: this bronze dagger blade, with gold, silver, and *niello* inlay, is decorated with a lion-hunting scene. (*National Archaeological Museum, Athens*)

By the turn of the fifth century B.C.E. the cultural, geo-political, and military struggle between the Greek city-states and the Persian Empire had begun. In 512 and again in 492, Persia under Darius had crossed the Hellespont into Europe, and invaded and taken parts of Thrace. In 490, Darius dispatched a naval expedition directly across the Aegean in order to punish Athens for its part in the revolt in Anatolia.

War with the Persians tested the Greeks' fundamental mode of political organization. Persia was a huge, centrally governed empire; each Greek city-state was individually independent, although many had joined into regional confederations and leagues for mutual assistance and trade. Persia was headed by a single emperor who set policies for the entire empire; each individual Greek city-state, for the most part, was governed by an assembly of all its adult, free, male citizens. These assemblies passed laws, judged criminal and civil cases, provided for administration and implementation of legislation, and arranged for military defense as the need arose. The Greek city-states were moving toward democracy; they understood their legal systems to be their own creation and responsibility, neither ordained by the gods nor imposed by a powerful external emperor.

Moreover, the city assemblies had organized themselves by **deme,** or neighborhood. Political identity was thus based on geographical residence in the city, not on heredity and kinship, nor on class and wealth. This new concept of civic identity allowed the city to welcome new residents and the ideas they brought with them, regardless of their place of origin. It allowed people of different ethnic origins, even of enemy ethnic stocks, to enter the city, although they were not eligible for full citizenship. The human interaction in the small Greek city-state nurtured the intellect of its citizens. Life in the *polis* meant constant participation in a kind of ongoing public seminar. As Socrates (*c.* 470–399 B.C.E.), the leading philosopher of fifth-century Athens, said: "I'm a lover of learning, and trees and open country won't teach me anything, whereas men in the town do" (Plato, *Phaedrus*, 230:d).

How could the tiny Greek city-states hold off Darius' imperial armies and keep their incipient democracies alive? First, they had the enormous advantage of being close to home, with a good knowledge of local geography and conditions. Second, the largest among them, especially Athens and Sparta, chose to cooperate in defense against a common enemy. When the Persian fleet of 600 ships landed 20,000 Persian soldiers at Marathon in 490 B.C.E., a force of some 10,000 Greek **hoplite** soldiers

(see picture below), mostly Athenian, confronted them. The hoplite forces were solid phalanxes of soldiers arrayed in tight lines, the right arm and shield of one man pressed against the left shoulder of the other, in row on row, so that if a soldier in the front row fell, one from the next line took his place. (In these hoplite formations, each individual soldier is crucial to the welfare of all. Many analysts have seen in this egalitarian military formation the rationale for Athenian political democracy.)

The discipline of the Athenians, plus their strategy of letting their center fall back and then outflanking and surrounding the ensuing Persian charges, defeated their enemy. At the Battle of Marathon in 490 B.C.E. Persia lost 6400 men, Athens 192. The remaining Persians reboarded their ships, however, and sailed for Athens and a second round of fighting. The Athenian general at Marathon, Miltiades, sent his fastest runner, Pheidippides, racing back to Athens to tell of the victory at Marathon to strengthen the resolve of the Athenians at home and to hasten their preparations for battle. Pheidippides delivered the message, and died of exhaustion on the spot. (The marathon race of today is named for his 26-mile/41.8-kilometer run.) Darius planned to attack Greece again, then, but rebellion in Egypt and a struggle for succession within his own family diverted his attention until his death in 486 B.C.E. He was succeeded by his son Xerxes (r. 486–465 B.C.E.), who mounted a renewed attack on the Greek mainland

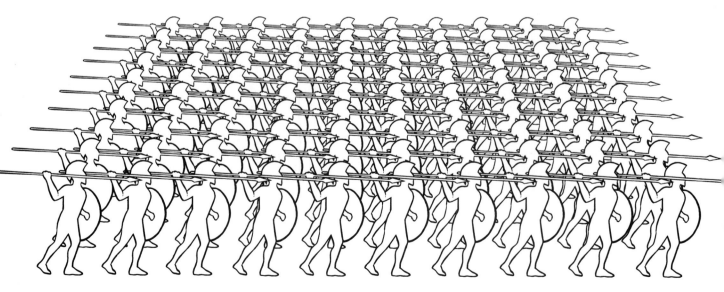

Formation of Greek hoplites. The soldiers of the Greek armies, called hoplites, fought in especially tight formations, row upon row of soldiers pressed closely together, so that they were completely dependent on one another and upon the entire formation. Some historians argue that this interdependency encouraged them to seek a democratic voice in formulating Greek political policies.

Greek trireme. The Greeks developed triremes (with three banks of oars) as warships and had them specially strengthened so that they could ram other ships. The triremes were slower and less maneuverable than the Persian ships. To compensate, the Greeks put soldiers aboard and, at Salamis, relied mostly on hand-to-hand combat.

SOURCE

Herodotus Describes Darius' Preparations for War Against Greece

Herodotus (c. 485–420 B.C.E.), the "father of history," took the whole known world as his subject matter, although his reports on lands distant from the Mediterranean, such as India, are more myths and legends than accurate accounts. *The Persian Wars*, his greatest work, portrays the great war of 499–479 B.C.E. as a moral as well as a military conflict between two continents, two polities, and two ideologies. For Herodotus the Greeks represent Europe, the city-state, and democracy, the land, the form of government, and the values to which he is committed; the Persians represent Asia, empire, and despotism, the enemy. Herodotus seeks explanations for the war in chains of events rooted deeply in the past as well as in the personalities of contemporary leaders making immediate decisions. Herodotus believed that the gods abhorred human arrogance, so his depiction of Darius' furious preparation for retaliation against the Greeks prepares the reader for the irony of Darius' death before he could mount his invasion.

Now when tidings of the battle that had been fought at Marathon reached the ears of King Darius, the son of Hystaspes, his anger against the Athenians, which had been already roused by their attack upon Sardis, waxed still fiercer, and he became more than ever eager to lead an army against Greece. Instantly he sent off messengers to make proclamation through the several states, that fresh levies were to be raised, and these at an increased rate; while ships, horses, provisions, and transports were likewise to be furnished. So the men published his commands; and now all Asia was in commotion for three years, while everywhere, as Greece was to be attacked, the best and bravest were enrolled for service and had to make their preparations accordingly. (*The Persian Wars*, VII:1)

THE GREAT PELOPONNESIAN WAR

435 (B.C.E.)	Civil war at Epidamnus
432	Sparta declares war on Athens
431	Peloponnesian invasion of Athens
421	Peace of Nicias
415–413	Athenian invasion of Sicily
405	Battle of Aegospotami
404	Athens surrenders

by land and sea in 480 B.C.E. Xerxes himself marched southward from Macedonia to Thessaly, in the direction of Athens and the Peloponnese. Courageous resistance by the Spartan general Leonidas and his troops at Thermopylae cost the lives of all the defenders, but won time for the Athenians to evacuate their city and regroup their forces. Xerxes continued to push onward to Athens, capturing, burning, and plundering the city and its Acropolis, but the Athenian warriors had withdrawn to the nearby port of Piraeus and the Bay of Salamis. A force of some 1000 Persian ships was bearing down on the same location. Fortunately for the Athenians, the city had devoted the silver of its mines at Laurion to constructing a fleet of 200 triremes, named for the three levels in which its approximately 170 rowers were arranged, and to fortifying Piraeus. When the opposing fleets engaged, between the island of Salamis and the mainland of Attica, the Athenians bottled up the more massive Persian fleet in the Salamis Channel. The Greeks lost 40 ships; the Persians lost 200. Xerxes sailed for home, and Persia never again attacked Greece by sea.

The Persians did, however, continue to fight by land. In the next year, 479 B.C.E., in alliance with their subjects in Macedonia and some northern Greeks, they prepared an army of some 100,000 men at Plataea, on the edge of the plains opening southward to Athens and the Peloponnese. Sparta and Athens formed an alliance with some other

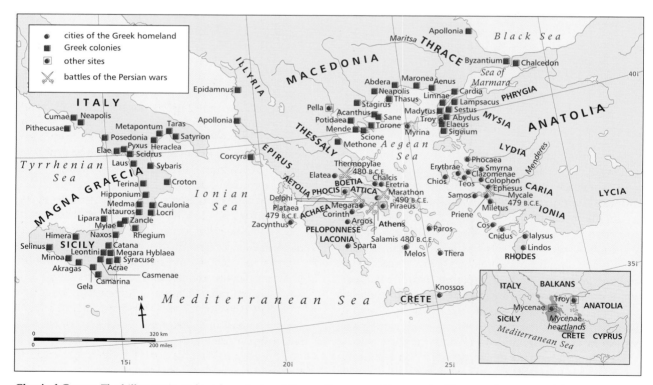

Classical Greece The hilly terrain and sea-boundaries of Greece discouraged the growth of large settlements, and Greek philosophers also stressed the importance of local community. When population grew too great the citizens encouraged their younger cohort to establish new city-states of their own. The resulting spread of settlements established Greek influence all the way from Sicily to Anatolia.

city-states to field an opposing army of about 40,000. Despite initial confusion in the ranks, the allied Spartan and Athenian forces destroyed the Persian armies and their camp, annihilated the elite guard, and killed Mardonius, the Persian general. At about the same time, the Greek fleet defeated the surviving Persian fleet at Mycale, on the Ionian coast of Anatolia.

In the face of these losses, and with weaker leadership at home, Persia left Europe, never to return in such force. (Still powerful, however, the Persians did continue to exert influence in Greek affairs from a distance, by subsidizing allies. Its later contributions to Sparta in the Peloponnesian War helped to fund its victory.) The small Greek city-states, led by arch-rivals Athens and Sparta, had shown an ability to combine in the face of a common enemy. They had demonstrated the virtues of small-scale, local units of society and the resilience of popular, democratic forms of government. Conversely, the Persians had exhibited one of the great flaws of empire: the tendency to overextend its powers.

ATHENS: FROM CITY-STATE TO MINI-EMPIRE

With the Persian threat removed, the Greek city-states turned at first to rebuilding their losses. The historical records that remain tell us most about Athens, the largest, most illustrious, and most provocative of the city-states.

Athenian Democracy: Historical Background and Historians

In the year 600 B.C.E., Solon (*c.* 630–*c.* 560 B.C.E.), who had risen to high office as a general and a poet, ended the monopoly over public office held by the Athenian hereditary aristocracy. He opened to all free men participation and voting in the decision-making public assembly, although only those meeting certain income levels could be elected to high public office. The Council of Four Hundred, which Solon also created, represented the interests of the wealthy and noble factions, while the assembly balanced them with the voices of more common men.

Perhaps more importantly, Solon cancelled all public and private debts, and abolished the practice of enslaving people to pay off their debts. Solon's reforms crumbled when he left office, and decades of struggle between rich and poor and between men of different hereditary clans ensued until

about 550 B.C.E. when Peisistratus seized control of the government. Peisistratus (d. 527 B.C.E.) fostered economic growth through loans to small farmers; export promotion programs; road construction; and public works, including major building programs for the beautification of Athens and its Acropolis. On Peisistratus' death, the city-state again fell into disarray and even civil war. In 510 B.C.E., at the invitation of a faction of Athens' noblemen, the king of Sparta, already Athens' greatest rival, invaded Athens, besieged the Acropolis, and deposed the descendants of Peisistratus.

Through all the warfare and strife, the ideals of Solon survived. A new ruler, Cleisthenes (*c.* 570–*c.* 500 B.C.E.), came to power and dramatically reorganized the city and its surrounding countryside. He did away with the aristocratic family centers of power by registering each Athenian as a citizen according to his geographical residence, or *deme*, in the city. Similarly, he reorganized the electoral districts of Attica, the region around Athens, into ten electoral units, creating new political identities and allegiances. The assembly resumed meeting about every ten days, and all male citizens were expected to participate; 6000 were necessary for a quorum. Above the assembly, and setting its agenda, was a Council of Five Hundred, even more open than Solon's Council of Four Hundred had been, since members were selected from each *deme* for one-year terms by lottery, and members were not allowed to serve for more than two terms. When Darius' Persian Empire challenged Athens, and the Greek city-states generally, the contrast between the combatants was stark: city-state versus empire; local administration versus imperial power; evolving, decentralized democracy versus established, centralized imperial control.

Following the victory over the Persians in the fifth century B.C.E., Athens was at the height of its power and prestige under the military and civic leadership of Pericles (*c.* 495–429 B.C.E.). Historians began to reflect on its origins, accomplishments, and the challenges it had faced. Indeed, the modern profession of history as a systematic attempt to understand the influence of past experience on the present began in Athens. Two of the most outstanding historians of the fifth century B.C.E. have given us the history of the city and its relationships with its neighbors. Herodotus (d. *c.* 420 B.C.E.) wrote *The Persian Wars*, and in the narrative recaptured a general, but anecdotal, history of the whole eastern Mediterranean and eastward as far as Persia and India. Thucydides (d.

c. 401 B.C.E.), far more systematically and carefully, recounted the subsequent *History of the Peloponnesian War*, and the events surrounding those three decades of anarchy and warfare among the city-states of Greece. Collectively, native historians narrated the evolution of Athens from city-state to mini-empire.

Architecture, Design, the Arts, Philosophy, and Drama

Greek victory, led by Athens, triggered immense pride in the city-state, its democratic philosophy (see Source pp. 148–9), and its artistic creativity. The physical design of the city itself tells much of its origins, functions, and ideals, as R.E. Wycherley's *How the Greeks Built Cities* points out. Athens rose from a plain, and with each level upward its functions and the architecture became more exalted. At the bottom were the houses of commoners, built simply from local materials of stone and mud, with little concern for architectural merit. Further up the hill was the **agora**, or civic and market center, with clusters of buildings for trade in goods, ideas, and political decision-making. These public buildings were more elegant, designed for greater comfort and show. Nearby were gymnasia for exercise and competition. In the splendor of the *agora* Athenians demonstrated the value they placed on public life and on physical prowess and discipline. Further to the side, built into the side of the hill, was an amphitheater where plays were regularly performed, often representing in dramatic form scenes from Greek mythological history and suggesting their significance in understanding the moral issues of the day. At the

Parthenon, Athens, 447–432 B.C.E. The Parthenon on the Athenian Acropolis was a temple dedicated to the goddess Athena, the city's patron-deity. It was built at the instigation of Pericles as a symbol of Athens' growing importance and represents, in architectural terms, the summit of classical Greek achievement.

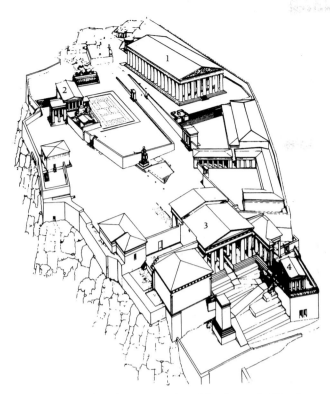

Plan of Acropolis. The construction of the Acropolis (Greek for "high city") beginning in *c.* 460 B.C.E. under the leadership of Pericles, signified the beginning of a Golden Age for Athens. The plan above indicates some of its most celebrated buildings—the Parthenon (1), the Erectheum (2), the Propylaea (3), and the Temple of Athena Nike (4).

philosophy explored the working of the city-state itself and the relationship of the individual to it. Plato's own teacher, the philosopher Socrates (*c.* 470–399 B.C.E.), had argued for the supremacy of the city-state over the individual. The citizen had obligations to the state for all the benefits he

A marble, second-century-C.E. copy of the statue of Athena Parthenos, dedicated in 438 B.C.E. Phidias' 40-foot (12 m) Athena, the divine guardian of the city, dominated the central chamber of the Parthenon on the Acropolis. This miniature Roman copy of the destroyed statue hardly suggests the glittering magnificence of the enormous gold-and-ivory original, a powerful symbol of the might of the goddess and her city, Athens. (*Acropolis Museum, Athens*)

top of the hill, on the Acropolis ("city on high"), surrounded by a wall, were the chief temples of the city, especially the shrine of the goddess Athena, the divine guardian of the city.

During the war years, the Persians had destroyed and burned much of Athens. When victory was secure, the Athenians not only rebuilt and improved their city, they now crowned its Acropolis with stunning new architecture and art. Architects and urban designers Ictimus and Callicrates planned the new Acropolis and built the Parthenon while the sculptor Phidias carved the friezes on the Parthenon and created a 40-foot (12-meter) high statue of Athena, the city's patron goddess, to reside within it.

Philosophers such as Socrates and Plato introduced questions, methods of analysis and of teaching, and examinations of the purpose of life, which continue to command attention for their range and depth. Plato's prize student, Aristotle (384–322 B.C.E.), later wrote that man is a *zoon politikon*, a "political animal," a creature of the city-state, and many of the key works in Greek history, drama, and

received from it, but had no rights to claim against the power of the state.

For Socrates the Athenian state was father and mother; he derived his sense of self and purpose from the education the state gave him and from his continual debates with fellow citizens both in public and private. He opposed and satirized the **sophist** philosophers who earned their salaries by training future statesmen how to argue any side of any question without necessarily staking any personal commitment. Through his incessant questions, he taught *his* students to be thoughtful but critical about the truths of others and about their own truths, and, after having reached their own conclusions, to live their own truths fully even if it meant their death, as it did for Socrates himself.

Plato, Socrates' leading pupil and the founder of the Academy, which endured for centuries as Athens' leading school of philosophy, chose the state as his subject in his search for justice. Early in one of his greatest works, *The Republic*, he proposes, in the name of Socrates:

> There is a justice of one man, we say, and, I suppose, also of an entire city? . . . Is not the city larger than the man? . . . Then, perhaps, there would be more justice in the larger object, and more easy to apprehend. If it please you, then, let us first look for its quality in states, and then only examine it also in the individual, looking for the likeness of the greater in the form of the less.
>
> (*The Republic*, II:368:e.)

The ideal state, according to Plato, would be administered by a philosopher-king who by virtue of innate good character and intensive training would know and do what was best for all citizens in the state.

Aristotle, Plato's greatest pupil, addressed an astonishing array of subjects: logic, physics, astronomy, metaphysics, religion, rhetoric, literary criticism, and natural science; but he, too, devoted some of his most important writing to ethics and politics. His analysis of the principal forms of constitutional government in his *Politics* remains a useful introduction to the field even today. Aristotle later was engaged as a tutor to Alexander the Great of Macedon, although how much influence he had over the future world-conqueror is a matter for conjecture.

In the theaters of Athens, drama was born and flourished. The pursuit of justice, morality, and equity was a core theme. Athenian playwrights invented the dramatic forms of tragedy and comedy, and their most important plays all include themes related to the evolution of their city and its institutions. Aeschylus' (524?–456 B.C.E.) *Oresteia* trilogy follows three generations of murders within the royal family of Atreus, as one act of revenge provokes the next, until finally, in a trial at Athens, Athena, patron goddess of the city, acquits Orestes, suggesting that divinely ordained vengeance will be replaced by human justice and the cycle of murder will be ended. *Oedipus Rex* of Sophocles (496–406 B.C.E.), perhaps the most famous single play of ancient Athens, centers on the family tragedy of Oedipus' murder of his own father, the King of Thebes, and his subsequent marriage to his own mother. (Oedipus did not know that the man he killed was his father and that he had married his own mother. Oedipus had been abandoned as an infant and raised by shepherds.) The play opens with the people of Thebes gathered round King Oedipus, before his tragedy is revealed, crying out for his help in arresting a plague that is afflicting the city. Oedipus' own moral corruption has brought the plague on the city, although that is revealed only later. Sophocles' *Antigone* confronts the conflict in loyalty to family versus loyalty to the city-state, as Antigone chooses to bury her brother Polynices despite the royal decree to leave his corpse unattended as an enemy of the state. Euripides (480–406 B.C.E.) saw more clearly Athens' move toward imperialism, and criticized it in *The Trojan Women*. Aristophanes' (450?–385? B.C.E.) hilarious, sexually explicit comedy, *Lysistrata*, portrays the women of Athens and Sparta agreeing to go on strike sexually until their men stop fighting the Peloponnesian wars. So long as the men make war the women will not make love! The best of the Athenian dramatists addressed directly the political and social issues that confronted their city.

THE LIMITS OF CITY-STATE DEMOCRACY

HOW DO WE KNOW?

WHAT DO WE KNOW?

The very art and literature through which citizens praise their city-states contain within themselves the core of a critique against the legacy of the city-state. Socrates' justification of the state demonstrates that even in the most democratic Greek city-state, government could exact respect and service from the citizen, but the citizen had few rights vis-à-vis the state. The citizen had the right, and indeed the obligation, to participate in the activities of the state and to serve the state, but not to have the state serve him.

For women, even the right of participation was absent. Participatory democracy was reserved for men. *The Reign of the Phallus: Sexual Politics in Ancient Athens* by art historian Eva Keuls rages against Athens as both cruelly misogynist and aggressively militaristic, and suggests that these two characteristics were interrelated. Classical Athens, Keuls argues, was a **phallocracy**,

a society dominated by men who sequester their wives and daughters, denigrate the female role in reproduction, erect monuments to the male genitalia, have sex with the sons of their peers, sponsor public whorehouses, create a mythology of rape, and engage in rampant saber-rattling. (p. 1)

Psykter (wine cooler) painted by Douris with cavorting satyrs, 500–490 B.C.E. Feminist historian Eva Keuls argues that, contrary to the cradle-of-civilization clichés, Athenian society was excessively warlike and women-hating. She finds much of her evidence on Greek vases of the type used in male drinking parties. (*British Museum, London*)

Two Views of Athenian Democracy

PERICLES' FUNERAL ORATION

As political and military leader of Athens, 460–429 B.C.E., Pericles delivered this eulogy at a mass-funeral of troops who had died of plague in the early years of the Peloponnesian War. As reported by Thucydides, it is one of the great proclamations of the civic, aesthetic, moral, and personal virtues of the Athenian city-state:

> Our system of government does not copy the institutions of our neighbors. It is more the case of our being a model to others, than of our imitating anyone else. Our constitution is called a democracy because power is in the hands not of a minority but of the whole people. When it is a question of settling private disputes, everyone is equal before the law; when it is a question of putting one person before another in positions of public responsibility, what counts is not membership of a particular class, but the actual ability which the man possesses. No one, so long

as he has it in him to be of service to the state, is kept in political obscurity because of poverty. . . .

> We [obey] those whom we put in positions of authority, and we obey the laws themselves, especially those which are for the protection of the oppressed, and those unwritten laws which it is an acknowledged shame to break. . . .

> When our work is over, we are in a position to enjoy all kinds of recreation for our spirits . . . all the good things from all over the world flow in to us, so that to us it seems just as natural to enjoy foreign goods as our own local products. . . .

> Our love of what is beautiful does not lead to extravagance; our love of the things of the mind does not make us soft. We regard wealth as something to be properly used, rather than as something to boast about. As for poverty, no one need be ashamed to admit it: the real shame is in not taking practical measures to escape from it. Here each individual is interested not only in his own affairs but in the affairs of the state as well: even those who are mostly occupied with their

Keuls finds most of her evidence in the painting on Greek vases, specifically of a type used in male drinking parties, but she asserts that additional support for her claims is widespread and easily accessible. She then asks, and answers, the historiographical question: Why have we not heard more of these phallocratic elements previously?

> The story of phallic rule at the root of Western civilization has been suppressed as a result of the near-monopoly that men have held in the field of Classics, by neglect of rich pictorial evidence, by prudery and censorship, and by a misguided desire to protect an idealized image of Athens. (p. 1)

Plato (c. 429–347 B.C.E.) recognized the prejudices against women in his society. When he suggested in his visionary *Republic* that women should be treated equally with men in their access to the highest professional and civic responsibilities, and in the education needed to achieve them, he knew

that his ideas were revolutionary for Athens in his time and that they would be greeted with derision. Plato himself believed that men were generally more talented than women, but he argues here that both should be offered equal access to political opportunity. On the issue of gender equality, he seemed to remain consistent with his general philosophy: the state should encourage each citizen to reach his or her educational potential, and should direct the most talented into governmental affairs.

> There is no occupation concerned with the management of social affairs which belongs either to women or to men, as such. Natural gifts are to be found here and there in both creatures alike; and every occupation is open to both, so far as their natures are concerned, though woman is for all purposes the weaker. . . . Women of this type must be selected to share the life and duties of Guardians with men of the same type, since they are competent

own business are extremely well informed on general politics—this is a peculiarity of ours: we do not say that a man who takes no interest in politics is a man who minds his own business; we say that he has no business here at all. We Athenians, in our own persons, take our decisions on policy or submit them to proper discussions: for we do not think that there is an incompatibility between words and deeds; the worst thing is to rush into action before the consequences have been properly debated. . . .

I declare that our city is an education to Greece, and I declare that in my opinion each single one of our citizens, in all the manifold aspects of life, is able to show himself the rightful lord and owner of his own person, and do this, moreover, with exceptional grace and exceptional versatility. (Book II:37–41; pp. 145–8)

SOCRATES ON THE RIGHTS OF THE STATE OVER THE INDIVIDUAL

Condemned to death on trumped-up charges of corrupting the political morals of youth and blaspheming against the gods of Athens, Socrates is offered the opportunity to escape and live out his life in another city-state. He refuses. He notes that the state has acted through formal legal process and has the right to execute him. He, in turn, has the obligation to accept the sentence. In Plato's *Crito*, Socrates explains his rationale.

Are you too wise to see that your country is worthier, more to be revered, more sacred, and held in higher honor both by the gods and by all men of understanding, than your father and your mother and all your other ancestors; and that you ought to reverence it, and to submit to it, and to approach it more humbly when it is angry with you than you would approach your father; and either to do whatever it tells you to do or to persuade it to excuse you; and to obey in silence if it orders you to endure flogging or imprisonment, or if it sends you to battle to be wounded or to die? That is just. You must not give way, nor retreat, nor desert your station. In war, and in the court of justice, and everywhere, you must do whatever your state and your country tell you to do, or you must persuade them that their commands are unjust. But it is impious to use violence against your father or your mother; and much more impious to use violence against your country. (Plato, *Crito* XII:51:b)

and of a like nature, and the same natures must be allowed the same pursuits. . . . Now, for the purpose of producing a woman fit to be a Guardian, we shall not have one education for men and another for women, precisely because the nature to be taken in hand is the same. . . . If we are to set women to the same tasks as men, we must teach them the same things. They must have the same two branches of training for mind and body and also be taught the art of war, and they must receive the same treatment. . . .

Now that we have started on this subject, we must not be frightened of the many witticisms that might be aimed at such a revolution, not only in the matter of bodily exercise but in the training of women's minds, and not least when it comes to their bearing arms and riding on horseback. (*Republic*, V:452–6; pp. 149–54)

Aristotle confirmed Plato's apprehensions, but not his optimism nor his sense of potential equality.

Aristotle wrote of women: "The temperance of a man and of a woman, or the courage and justice of a man and of a woman, are not, as Socrates maintained, the same; the courage of a man is shown in commanding, of a woman in obeying" (*Politics*, I:13; 20–25; p. 1144). Aristotle quotes with approval the general view that "Silence is a woman's glory" (I:13; 30; p. 1145). In practice, Athens followed Aristotelian rather than Platonic views on the role of women in public life.

Even among males, only the sons of native-born Athenian mothers and fathers were eligible for citizenship. Slaves captured in war, and even allies, could not gain citizenship. The Roman emperor Claudius reflected, "What proved fatal to Sparta and Athens, for all their military strength, was their segregation of conquered subjects as aliens" (Tacitus, p. 237). When Classical Athens reached its maximum population, 250,000, only about one adult Athenian in six qualified for citizenship. These limits on Athenian democracy increased domestic social strains.

ATHENS BECOMES AN IMPERIAL POWER

Most ironically, the city-state of Athens, having led the Greek city-states in the struggle against the Persian Empire, subsequently set out to construct an empire of its own. Following major victories in the Persian wars, Athens assembled its principal allies into the Delian League, with its council and treasury situated in Delos. At first, membership was voluntary, but soon Athens forbade withdrawal. Thucydides reports the consequences:

> Naxos left the league [c. 470 B.C.E.] and the Athenians made war on the place. After a siege Naxos was forced back to allegiance. This was the first case when the original constitution of the League was broken and an allied city lost its independence, and the process was continued in the cases of the other allies as various circumstances arose. The chief reasons for these revolts were failures to produce the right amount of tribute or the right number of ships, and sometimes a refusal to produce any ships at all. For the Athenians insisted on obligations being exactly met, and made themselves unpopular by bringing the severest pressure to bear on allies who were not used to making sacrifices and did not want to make them. In other ways, too, the Athenians as rulers were no longer popular as they used to be. (I:98; p. 93)

In 454 B.C.E. Pericles moved the treasury of the Delian League to Athens and appropriated its funds in order to create at Athens a spectacular center of power and authority, particularly by building the Parthenon and expanding the fleet. Then:

> the Athenians began to encroach upon Sparta's allies. It was at this point that Sparta felt the position to be no longer tolerable and decided by starting this present war to employ all her energies in attacking and, if possible, destroying the power of Athens. (I:118; p. 103)

In 432 B.C.E. Sparta declared war. The struggle was for power, not for higher ideals. Thucydides, historian of the conflict, portrays Athens setting forth its claims increasingly bluntly in statements of **realpolitik** (power politics). He reports the Athenian ultimatum bullying the people of the island of Melos and calling on them to submit to Athenian authority:

> Our opinion of the gods and our knowledge of men lead us to conclude that it is a general and necessary law of nature to rule whatever one can. (V:105; p. 404)

Melos nevertheless chose to resist. When the Athenians finally conquered the Melians, they "put to death all the men of military age whom they took, and sold the women and children as slaves" (V:116; p. 408).

By 404 Sparta, supported by Persian funding, defeated Athens and captured the city. Both sides were exhausted. Nevertheless, warfare soon resumed among the Greeks with Thebes and Corinth now entering the lists as major contenders. The balance of power among city-states had no further stability. Each major city-state sought advantage over the others and the stronger continued to force the weaker into subordinate alliances. Greece fell into the intermittent warfare of its city-states.

THE EMPIRE OF ALEXANDER THE GREAT

To the north of the major Greek city-states lay the rougher, less urbanized Macedonia, a borderland between Greece and the Slavic regions to the north and east. The principal language and culture of Macedonia were Greek, but other languages and less cultivated manners were also present. Here in 359 B.C.E., in the Macedonian capital of Pella, Philip II (r. 359–336 B.C.E.) persuaded the Macedonian army to declare him king, in succession to his brother, who had died in warfare.

After consolidating his power in Macedonia, Philip declared two goals. The first of these was to unify and bring peace to Greece; the second, to liberate the Greek city-states in Asia Minor from Persian control. Skillful as a diplomat and careful to introduce economic improvements in the lands he conquered, Philip nevertheless realized that his army was the real key to achieving his goals. He built up its phalanxes, armed the soldiers with spears up to 15 feet (4.6 meters) long, and augmented the foot soldiers with powerful and swift cavalry. Philip led the troops himself, suffering numerous, serious wounds in battle.

Between 354 and 339 Philip conquered the Balkans from the Danube to the Aegean coast and from the Adriatic to the Black Sea. To pacify and administer the area, he established new towns, which were populated by both Macedonians and local peoples. Similarly, he employed many local people in his administration. Within Greece proper his accomplishments were more mixed. He won some allies, like Thessaly; defeated the armies of several city-states; and mediated the end of a war between two coalitions of Greek city-states. He was honored with election as president of the Pythian Games at Delphi in 346, but his overtures for greater power in Greece were bitterly opposed by Athens and Thebes.

The orator Demosthenes (384–322 B.C.E.) delivered three "Philippics," public addresses calling Athens to battle against the Macedonian king and predicting the end of Athenian democracy if Philip defeated the city-state. In the face of this opposition, Philip declared war on Athens and its allies, defeating them at Chaeronea in 338 B.C.E. Philip now sought to create a self-governing league of Greek city-states, to accomplish his first goal, and to forge an alliance between Macedonia and the league to fight Persia, his second goal. But he was assassinated in 336. His twenty-year-old son, Alexander, continued his father's mission.

Like his father Philip and like the Persian emperors Cyrus II and Darius I, Alexander (356–323 B.C.E.) followed a policy of benevolent despotism much of the time. But, also like them, he implemented this policy only after his power had been amply demonstrated. Unfortunate Thebes provided an early site for this demonstration. Soon after assuming the throne, Alexander had marched north to the Danube River to suppress revolts in Thrace. Mistakenly informed that Alexander had been killed in battle, Thebes revolted against his local forces. Alexander quickly marched his troops back to Thebes, captured and sacked the rebel city, killed 6000 of its inhabitants, and sold into slavery 20,000 of those who survived.

In 334 Alexander was ready to cross into Asia, where his first major victory came at Granicus. From there he continued southward, forcing the Persians out of the Greek cities that lined the Ionian coast. To make sure that the Persians would not return, Alexander marched eastward through Anatolia with 35,000 Greek troops, routing the 300,000-man army of the Persian Emperor Darius III at Issus in 333 B.C.E., and forcing Darius himself into flight.

Alexander continued southward down the coast of the eastern Mediterranean. At Tyre, which held out in siege against him for seven months, he again demonstrated power and brutality, killing 7000 men and selling 30,000, mostly women and children, into slavery. Elsewhere, however,

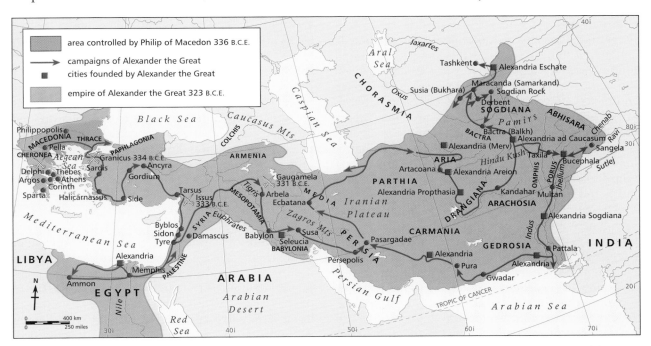

The Empire of Alexander In 338 the Greek city-states were defeated by Philip of Macedon. His son, Alexander, extended the imprint of Greek culture far beyond its Mediterranean homeland. In a series of whirlwind campaigns between 334 and 323 B.C.E., Alexander gained control of Syria and Egypt and then destroyed the might of Persia. He took his armies east to the Indus and north to central Asia, but died at age 33 in Babylon.

Alexander showed the velvet glove, respecting local religions, ruling through local hierarchies, and maintaining local tax rates. To drive Persia from the Mediterranean basin and to establish his own control, Alexander continued south and then west, conquering Egypt. He was welcomed as Egypt's liberator from Persian rule and treated as a god by the Egyptian priests of the god Amon, whose shrine he visited. At the western end of the Nile delta, Alexander laid the foundation of what would be for several centuries the most attractive and cultured city of the Mediterranean coast, Alexandria.

His appetite whetted, again a common experience with empire builders once they begin their careers, Alexander moved onward to conquests previously unplanned. He set out to conquer the Persian Empire and make it his own. He marched northeastward across the Fertile Crescent and through Mesopotamia. At Gaugamela in 331 B.C.E. he again faced the Persian emperor, Darius III, and again routed him. The historical capital cities of Babylon, Susa, Persepolis, and Pasargadae lay open to Alexander. He destroyed Persepolis, Darius' own capital, almost totally, then, having captured the heartland of the Persian Empire, he set off to conquer the eastern half as well, finally reaching and capturing the Indus River valley in the east, and Sogdiana, across the Oxus River, in the northeast. Although he had wanted to continue into India as far as the Ganges, his troops mutinied. They would go no farther. As he was returning from his new frontiers, Alexander contracted a fever and died in 323 B.C.E. in Babylon at the age of thirty-three. Several accounts report that he was poisoned. Some said that the instigator was his own former teacher Aristotle. In the battle for succession among his generals, Alexander's wife Roxane and their thirteen-year old son were murdered.

The empire Alexander created did not survive two generations. In the east, local rulers regained power in India and Afghanistan. In the west, the Greeks returned to their internal warfare, finally breaking up once more into individual city-states, kingdoms, and leagues. Macedonia remained a separate kingdom and meddled in Greek affairs. Two major kingdoms emerged: Egypt under the dynasty of Ptolemy, which ruled through a Greek and Macedonian elite until the Roman conquest; and the empire established by Seleucus I Nicator (d. 281 B.C.E.), who was governor of Babylon when the empire split apart, and who added to his own

domain Iran, Afghanistan, and Anatolia. But the Seleucid Empire, too, fragmented. Parthians reclaimed Persia in the east, and Anatolia divided into numerous local governments. By 200 B.C.E. the Seleucid Empire was limited primarily to the area around Syria.

THE LEGACY OF ALEXANDER: THE HELLENISTIC ECUMENE

What were the legacies of the empire Alexander built? He made the language and culture of Greece dominant among the ruling intellectual and commercial elites from the Mediterranean, east to India, Afghanistan, and the borders of Russia, and south as far as Egypt. A common dialect of Greek, known as Koine, spread as the language of educated people throughout the ancient western world. Waves of Greek administrators, businessmen, and soldiers followed Alexander's conquests and helped to transmit Greek culture. At the same time, their

The "Alexander Mosaic," first century B.C.E. mosaic copy from Pompeii (see Spotlight, pp. 170–1) of a painting by Philoxenos, c. 300 B.C.E. This mosaic portrays the Battle of Issus (333 B.C.E.) in terms of a personal duel between Alexander the Great and Darius, Emperor of Persia. Darius (right) is shown about to turn and flee in his chariot as the youthful Alexander (left), wild-haired and helmetless, charges toward him. (*Museo Archeologico Nazionale, Naples*)

expression of Hellenic culture was often infiltrated by local customs, especially the imperial ceremonial forms of Persia. The simplicity of the earlier Hellenic culture was transformed into the more complex, elaborate, and cosmopolitan Hellenistic culture of Alexander. One striking example of its spread and mix can be seen in some of the first representations of the Buddha in sculpture from the area of India/Pakistan after it was conquered by Alexander. These sculptures represent the Buddha wearing a toga (see Spotlight, p. 288).

To make travel and commerce, as well as conquest and administration, more feasible, Alexander built roads, canals, and whole new cities, including at least sixteen Alexandrias across the length and breadth of his conquests, using the gold and silver captured from Persia to finance

many of these constructions. The most famous and illustrious Alexandria was the metropolis in Egypt, which became the leading city of its day. Egyptian Alexandria housed palaces, administrative centers, theaters, stadia, the greatest library of Greek knowledge, containing 700,000 manuscripts, and the final resting place of Alexander himself.

At the eastern end of the empire, on the Oxus River in today's Uzbekistan, the Greeks constructed, on Persian foundations, Ai Khanoum, a small, well-defended city centered on a palace. Ai Khanoum was rediscovered and excavated only in the 1960s, and archaeologists believe it may prove to be Alexandria Oxiana, a lost city from the age of Alexander the Great.

Between Alexandria in Egypt and Ai Khanoum in central Asia were dozens of cities and small

PROFILE

Alexander the Great

HISTORICAL REINTERPRETATIONS

The twenty-year-old Alexander succeeded to the throne of Macedonia in 336 B.C.E. after the assassination of his father, Philip II. No stranger to warfare, Alexander had fought by his father's side just two years beforehand as he defeated Athens at the Battle of Chaeronea. Applauded by the army, Alexander succeeded to the throne without opposition and continued his father's career of conquest. Over the next twelve years, his disciplined army traversed some 22,000 miles (35,400 kilometers), conquering lands that stretched from Egypt in the west to the Indus River in the east. Alexander's empire was the largest ever known and in 324 B.C.E. he declared himself a god. A year later, at the age of thirty-three, Alexander died in Babylon from an illness induced by heavy drinking. On his deathbed he reputedly declared, "Let the job go to the strongest."

By the end of his life, however,

> there were few men, and *a fortiori* fewer women, who lamented Alexander's passing. In Greece and Asia alike, during his lifetime and for several centuries after his death, he was regarded as a tyrannous aggressor, a foreign autocrat who had imposed his will by violence alone. When the news of his death in Babylon reached Athens, it was the orator Demades who crystallized public reaction. "Alexander dead?" he exclaimed. "Impossible; the whole world would stink of his corpse." (Green, p. 477)

In these words historian Peter Green introduces a brief historiographical sketch of Alexander's reputation through the ages.

The earliest remaining accounts of Alexander's life date from the first century B.C.E., at least 200 years after his death, while the most reliable and fullest of the earliest biographies still extant, that written by Arrian Flavius Arrianus, dates to the second century C.E. For the most part, all historians work from these same basic records, but their assessments reflect the issues and conditions of their own day.

Arrian, who lived at the height of the Roman empire, and approved of it, praises Alexander for his conquests. Alexander was the prototype of Rome's own Caesars. Closer to our own times, in the late eighteenth and nineteenth centuries, during the democratic era of the American and French

towns, which served as seeds of Greek culture throughout the empire. The Alexandrian Empire and its successors built a Hellenistic **ecumene**— that is, a unified urban culture, encompassing vast lands and diverse peoples. Some of its cities, which had long, independent Greek heritages, retained strong elements of their pre-Alexandrian culture and even their autonomy. These were the cities of the Greek heartland, such as Athens, Sparta, Thebes, Corinth, and Delphi. Others were cities of empire, built later by Alexander and his successors either from the ground up or on existing but relatively minor urban bases. These cities served as new regional capitals, to administer the new empire, to extend its economy, and to broadcast its culture. Alexandria in Egypt and some fifteen other Alexandrias as well as Seleucia-on-the-Tigris were principal examples.

Alexander and his successors also administered their empire through the already existing indigenous urban framework, but added to it the principal institutions and monuments of Hellenistic culture: temples to Greek gods frequently located on a walled acropolis; theaters; an *agora*; civic buildings such as a *bouleuterion* (council chamber) and *prytaneion* (town hall); gymnasia; and stadia. Examples of this style of urban Hellenization in newly conquered lands included Susa, Damascus, Tyre, Kandahar, and Merv. Residents of these varied cities might feel themselves to be both citizens of the locality and participants in a semi-universal ecumene, although the balance of these

revolutions, and of the Greek War for Independence (see Chapter 15), historical opinion turned against Alexander. George Grote's *History of Greece* (1888) represented both Philip and Alexander as "brutalized adventurers simply out for power, wealth, and territorial expansion, both of them inflamed by the pure lust for conquest" (Green, p. 482).

On the other hand, Johann Gustav Droysen, an ardent advocate of a reunified, powerful Germany (see Chapter 17), saw Alexander as a model. Droysen's scholarly biography, *Alexander der Grosse* (1833), praised Alexander for introducing Greek culture into large parts of Asia. As their empire expanded in the nineteenth and early twentieth centuries many British scholars also adopted a favorable view of Alexander. William Tarn's two-volume biography saw his conquests as instrumental in spreading a social philosophy of the Brotherhood of Man, bringing together Greeks and Persians, the conquerers with the conquered. Even in our post-imperial day, Cambridge University scholar N.G.L. Hammond agrees, citing the essay by the biographer Plutarch (*c.* 46–126 C.E.):

He harnessed all resources to one and the same end, mixing as it were in a loving-cup the lives, manners, marriages and customs of men. He ordered them all to regard the inhabited earth as their fatherland and his armed forces as their stronghold and defense.

Nonetheless, Green remains critical, arguing that his own assessment is closest to that at the time of Alexander's death:

his all-absorbing obsession through a short but crowded life, was war and conquest. It is idle to palliate this central truth, to pretend that he dreamed. . . of wading through rivers of blood and violence to achieve the Brotherhood of Man by raping an entire continent. He spent his whole life, with legendary success, in the pursuit of personal glory, Achillean *kleos*; and until very recent times this was regarded as a wholly laudable aim. The empire he built collapsed the moment he was gone; he came as a conqueror and the work he wrought was destruction (p. 488).

Head of Alexander, from Pergamon, western Turkey, *c.* **200** B.C.E. (*Archaeological Museum, Istanbul*)

feelings might vary from city to city and from time to time. A sharp division intensified between urban high culture, now very much Hellenized throughout the empire, and the rural areas, which continued their traditional patterns of life without much change.

The empire allowed trade and culture to flow in all directions. Greek ships have been found as far west as the British Isles as well as in the Indian Ocean in the east. At Taxila, Ai Khanoum, Begram, and Merv, European, African, and Asian trade routes intersected. The Persians had begun to create an Asian–African–European ecumene, but Alexander carried the process further and deeper. Rome, already beginning to rise by the time of Alexander, would later extend a similar imperial mission throughout much of Europe to the west and north, although Rome would not control the east, as we shall see in Chapter 6.

EMPIRE-BUILDING:

WHAT DIFFERENCE DOES IT MAKE?

Mesopotamians, Egyptians, Persians, Greeks, and Macedonians launched their imperial ambitions from very different backgrounds. Mesopotamians and Greeks began as city-states, while Egyptians and Persians started as consolidated nations. Out of the fractious chaos of the Greek city-states

Macedon built its small state to imperial dimensions under a father and son who ruled as ambitious and skillful kings. Although our coverage was necessarily sketchy, we have seen that each empire erected a central capital; administered a government based in that center that could control the provinces; provided a uniform language, coinage, and legal system across the empire; constructed a road and communication network; articulated an ideology of empire that won the loyalty of many of its citizens and subjects; and created art and architecture to impress on friend and foe alike the power of the empire. Each assembled military forces to apply coercion where necessary.

A time finally came for each empire to rein in its ambitions and limit further expansion. Sometimes it reached the limit of its capacity to conquer and administer profitably; sometimes it was defeated in warfare; often it encountered a combination of both these humbling experiences.

The imperial armies of Alexander the Great refused to proceed to newer, more distant conquests beyond the Indus River. So he turned back toward home. Ironically, Alexander's school tutor had been the philosopher Aristotle, who had written: "To the size of states there is a limit" (*Politics*, VII:4; p. 1325). Aristotle's ideal political unit was the Greek city-state because it promoted the maximum personal participation in democratic government through intense social and political interaction among the citizens:

> If the citizens of a state are to judge and to distribute offices according to merit, then they must know each other's characters; where they do not possess this

Dying Gaul, Roman copy in marble of a bronze original of c. 230–220 B.C.E. When Attalus I of Pergamum defeated an enemy force of Gauls, a series of statues showing dead or dying invaders was cast. This poignant example illustrates the many artistic developments in sculpture that epitomize Hellenistic Greece: a special emphasis on the portrayal of suffering and pain, dramatically conveyed through facial expression; a widening subject-matter (not merely male and female nudes); a twisting pose for the body; and a design that allows the composition to be viewed from all sides. (*Museo Capitolino, Rome*)

knowledge, both the election to offices and the decision of lawsuits will go wrong. When the population is very large they are manifestly settled at haphazard, which clearly ought not to be. (VII:4; p. 326)

In choosing to build an empire rather than a city-state, Alexander was neither the first nor the last student to disregard his teacher's advice. (Alexander wanted the Greek city-states to be self-governing, but he did not want other areas to have such powers.) Nor was Aristotle the first or last to weigh the relative merits of small, local democratic government units against those of large, centralized bureaucracies. Similar debates still go on in our own day. Debates over the usefulness, limits, and legitimacy of empire were also central to the political thought of ancient Rome, China, and India, the three huge empires that are the focus of Chapters 6, 7, and 8.

BIBLIOGRAPHY

Aristotle. *Basic Works*, ed and trans. Richard McKeon (New York: Random House, 1941).

Baines, John and Jaromir Malek. *Atlas of Ancient Egypt* (New York: Facts on File, 1980).

Bernal, Martin. *Black Athena: The Afroasiatic Roots of Classical Civilization* (New Brunswick, NJ: Rutgers University Press, 1987).

Green, Peter. *Alexander of Macedon* (Berkeley: University of California Press, 1991).

Hamilton, J.R. *Alexander the Great* (London: Hutchison University Library, 1973).

Hammond, Mason. *The City in the Ancient World* (Cambridge: Harvard University Press, 1972).

Hammond, N.G.L. *The Genius of Alexander the Great* (Chapel Hill: The University of North Carolina Press, 1997).

Herodotus. *The Persian Wars*, trans. George Rawlinson (New York: Modern Library, 1942).

Homer. *Iliad*, trans. Richmond Lattimore (Chicago: University of Chicago Press, 1951).

Homer. *Odyssey*, trans. Robert Fitzgerald (New York: Doubleday & Co., 1961).

Hornblower, Simon. *The Greek World 479–323 BC* (London: Methuen, 1983).

Keuls, Eva C. *The Reign of the Phallus: Sexual Politics in Ancient Athens* (New York: Harper and Row, 1985).

Levi, Peter. *Atlas of the Greek World* (New York: Facts on File Publications, 1982).

Mumford, Lewis. *The City in History* (New York: Harcourt, Brace and World, 1961).

O'Brien, John Maxwell. *Alexander the Great: The Invisible Enemy* (London: Routledge, 1992).

Past Worlds: The (London) Times Atlas of Archaeology (Maplewood, NJ: Hammond, Inc., 1988).

Plato. *Apology*, trans. F.J. Church (Indianapolis: Library of Liberal Arts, 1956).

—— *The Collected Dialogues of Plato*, ed. Edith Hamilton and Huntington Cairns (New York: Bollingen Foundation [distributed by Pantheon Books], 1961).

—— *The Republic of Plato*, trans. Francis MacDonald Cornford (New York: Oxford University Press, 1945).

Plutarch. *The Lives of the Noble Grecians and Romans*, trans. John Dryden, revised by Arthur Hugh Clough (New York: Modern Library, n.d.).

Postgate, J.N. *Early Mesopotamia* (London: Routledge, 1992).

Saggs, H.W.F. *The Might that Was Assyria* (London: Sidgwick & Jackson, 1984).

Sophocles. *Oedipus Rex and Oedipus at Collonus*, trans. Robert Fitzgerald in *The Oedipus Cycle* (San Diego: Harcourt Brace Jovanovich, 1969).

Tacitus. *The Annals of Imperial Rome*, trans. Michael Grant (Baltimore: Penguin Books, 1959).

Tarn, W.W. *Alexander the Great*. 2 Vols. (Cambridge: Cambridge University Press, 1948).

Thucydides. *History of the Peloponnesian War*, trans. Rex Warner (Harmondsworth: Penguin Books, 1972).

Time-Life Books. *Time Frame 3000–1500 BC: The Age of God-Kings* (Alexandria, VA: Time-Life Books, 1987).

—— *Time Frame 1500–600 BC: Barbarian Tides* (Alexandria, VA: Time-Life Books, 1987).

—— *Time Frame 600–400 BC: A Soaring Spirit* (Alexandria, VA: Time-Life Books, 1987).

—— *Time Frame 400 BC–AD 200: Empires Ascendant* (Alexandria, VA: Time-Life Books, 1987).

Wycherley, R.E. *How the Greeks Built Cities* (Garden City, NY: Anchor Books, 1969).

CHAPTER 6

ROME AND THE BARBARIANS

750 B.C.E.–480 C.E.

". . . remember Romans, To rule the people under law, to establish the way of peace"

VIRGIL

"They create a desert and call it 'Peace.'"

TACITUS

FROM CONQUEST, COLONIZATION, AND ALLIANCE TO REVOLT, BANKRUPTCY, AND DISMEMBERMENT

THE EXTENT OF THE ROMAN EMPIRE

All roads, by land and sea, led to Rome. Situated on the Tiber River, not far from the sea and the river's intersection with Italy's north–south mountain chains, Rome served as a center of communication and trade for the Italian peninsula. To the sea that surrounds the peninsula, the Romans gave the name "Mediterranean," the middle of the earth, for the Mediterranean is surrounded by the three continents that were known to them: southern Europe, northern Africa, and western Asia. In time, Roman armies conquered and ruled an empire that radiated outward to encompass the Italian peninsula, the lands surrounding the Mediterranean, and many territories still more distant. They began to call the Mediterranean *Mare Nostrum* ("Our Sea").

At its greatest extent in the second century C.E., the Roman Empire sprawled over

2700 miles (4400 kilometers) east to west and 2500 miles (4000 kilometers) north to south, extending from Scotland to the Persian Gulf. It ruled between 70 and 100 million people of vastly diverse ethnic, racial, religious, and cultural roots. At its most powerful, between 27 B.C.E. and 180 C.E., Rome enforced the **Pax Romana**, the Roman peace, a reign of stability and relative tranquillity throughout all these vast regions.

FOUNDING THE REPUBLIC

The legendary date for the founding of the city of Rome is 753 B.C.E., and although this is probably not exact, it is approximately correct. For two and a half centuries the city was ruled by kings of neighboring Etruria, the land to Rome's north. The Romans learned much from these Etruscans about city building, art, religion, mythology, and even language. As Rome entered the Mediterranean trade networks of the Etruscans, merchants and craft workers immigrated to the city. The Etruscan king Servius Tullius (579–534 B.C.E.) reformed the military, creating the *Comitia centuriata*, a deliberative ruling council composed of representatives of the soldiers of Rome. This assembly of Roman citizens persisted for centuries after Etruscan rule had ended, reinforcing the connection between the armies of Rome and its government.

About 509 B.C.E., the wealthy, powerful, veteran citizens of Rome expelled the Etruscan kings. They declared Rome a **republic**, from the Latin **res publica**, public property, in contrast to its earlier status as the private property of the Etruscan kings. Although they overthrew the monarchy, the new oligarchs—the small, elite group of rulers— retained many other political institutions. Their armies remained the center of power. Because soldiers were expected to provide their own arms, only men with some wealth and property could command and rise in the ranks. They in turn were ordered by class, according to the quality and cost of the weapons they provided, and divided into military units called **centuries**, or groups of one hundred, as they had been under the Etruscans. The leaders of the centuries continued to meet together in assembly to elect magistrates and decide questions of peace and war.

THE ROMAN EMPIRE

DATE	POLITICAL	RELIGION AND CULTURE	SOCIAL DEVELOPMENT
500 B.C.E.	• Rome independent of Etruscan rule (509); republic founded		
450 B.C.E.	• Rome sacked by Gauls (390)		• Laws of Twelve Tables promulgated
350 B.C.E.	• Roman expansion into Italy south of Po (327–304)		
300 B.C.E.	• 1st Punic War (264–241)		• Earliest Roman coinage (280–75)
250 B.C.E.	• 2nd Punic War (218–201) • Hannibal invaded Italy • Roman conquest of Cisalpine Gaul (202–191)	• Stoicism – Zeno	
200 B.C.E.	• Rome annexed Spain (197) • Conquest of Macedon (167)	• Polybius (200–118)	
150 B.C.E.	• 3rd Punic War (149–146) • T. Gracchus tribune (133) • G. Gracchus tribune (123 and 122) • Gallia Narbonensis a Roman province	• Carthage destroyed • Corinth destroyed	• Pax Romana led to widespread trade throughout Empire; roads built
100 B.C.E.	• Sulla conquers Greece • Civil war in Rome (83–2) • Conquest of Syria (66) • 1st Triumvirate (60)		• Spartacus slave revolt (73–71)
50 B.C.E.	• Civil war (49) • Caesar dictator (47–44) • 2nd Triumvirate (43) • Annexation of Egypt (30) • Augustus Caesar (d. 14 C.E.)	• Cicero (d. 43) • Virgil (d. 19) • Augustus deified on his death • Forum in Rome • Livy (d. 17 C.E.)	

The magistrates, administrative and judicial officials, administered the Roman government. At the lowest level of **quaestor** they had limited financial authority. At the highest level, **consuls** held power that extended over all the lands Rome ruled. At each level, two officials were paired, so that they would have to consult with one another, and neither could seize excessive power. The power of the former kings, for example, was now shared between the two consuls in this new system of checks and balances. (In extraordinary emergencies, one man could be named as dictator for the limited term of six months.) As magistrates ended their one-year (renewable) term of office, they automatically entered the Senate of Rome, the highest legislative and consultative body of the government.

EXPANSION TO EMPIRE

The Conquest of Italy

The Roman Republic established alliances with other nearby city-states in Latium and began to challenge the Etruscans. In 405 B.C.E., the Romans besieged Veii, a principal city of the Etruscans only 12 miles (20 kilometers) from Rome, and captured it in 396 B.C.E. Although Rome itself was sacked by Celtic invaders (see p. 185) in 390 B.C.E., the setback was brief, and Rome's expansion continued. By 264 B.C.E., it controlled all of Italy south of the Po valley. In its expansion, Rome often offered its opponents a choice between alliance and conquest. Subsequently it bestowed various levels of

THE ROMAN EMPIRE

DATE	POLITICAL	RELIGION AND CULTURE	SOCIAL DEVELOPMENT
25 C.E.	• Christianity reaches Rome • Invasion of Britain (43)		
50 C.E.	• Trajan (98–117)	• Seneca (d. 65) • Destruction of Temple in Jerusalem (70) • Pompeii and Herculaneum buried by eruption of Vesuvius (79)	• Jewish revolt (66–73) • Roman women gain new rights
100 C.E.	• Dacia conquered by Trajan • Hadrian (117–38)	• Tacitus (d. 120) • Trajan's column and forum (112–113) • Pantheon in Rome • Hadrian's Wall	
150 C.E.	• Marcus Aurelius (161–180)	• Apuleius (d. c. 170) • Galen (d. 199)	
200 C.E.	• Caracalla (212–217) • Decius (249–51)	• Baths of Caracalla	• Roman citizenship for all males
250 C.E.	• Gallienus (253–268)	• Persecution of Christians	
300 C.E.	• Constantine (r. 306–337)	• Edict of Milan (313) • Constantinople inaugurated (330)	
350 C.E.		• St. Augustine (354–430) • End of state support for paganism (394)	
400 C.E.	• Sack of Rome (410)		
450 C.E.	• End of Roman Empire in West (476)		
550 C.E.			• Justinian codifies Roman law

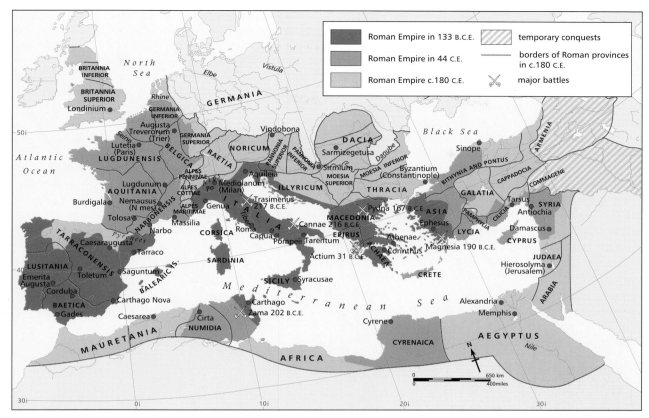

The Roman Empire Rome built its empire on military expansion, first within Italy by overthrowing its neighbors, then across the Mediterranean by defeating the Carthaginians, then northwest to Gaul and Britain and north to the Danube. Rome offered many benefits to the peoples it conquered, but finally its power rested in its armies.

Roman citizenship throughout Italy to induce its residents to support Rome and join its armies.

Roman armies, and a new navy designed to dominate the Mediterranean, continued to expand Roman rule. In the next 140 years Rome conquered Carthage, its arch-rival across the Mediterranean in north Africa; Cisalpine Gaul, the Celtic region of Italy between the Alps and the Po River; Macedonia and the city-states of Greece; most of Spain; and southern France (Gaul). Of these wars, the most bitter and the most decisive, were the three Punic Wars against Carthage, in 264–241, 218–201, and 149–146 B.C.E.

The Conquest of Carthage and the Western Mediterranean

Carthage, only 130 miles (210 kilometers) across the narrow waist of the Mediterranean from Italy, had developed as a trade outpost of Phoenician seafarers. Just as Rome had dominated Italy, the Carthaginians had dominated the north central coast of

Africa and the western Mediterranean. One of their trade networks had focused on the mineral wealth of Spain, especially its silver mines, and to protect that route, Carthage had developed ports and cities in Sicily and Sardinia. It controlled trade outposts even on the Italian mainland in Etruria. Carthage (in Latin Punicum—that is, "of the Phoenicians") and Rome were set on a collision course.

The fighting opened in Sicily in 264 B.C.E. By 241 B.C.E. when the first Punic War ended, Rome was victorious both on land and at sea. Four years later, Rome took advantage of a mutiny among Carthaginian troops in Sardinia to occupy both Sardinia and Corsica. In 227 B.C.E., it annexed them. For the first time, Rome had provinces outside the Italian peninsula. Carthage, however, rebuilt its forces, especially in Spain. When the Spanish city of Saguntum asked for Roman help, the Romans intervened and threatened Carthage's Spanish colonies. The brilliant, twenty-seven-year-old Carthaginan commander Hannibal (247–183 B.C.E.) defeated Rome's troops in 219 B.C.E., and the second

Punic War had begun. It continued for almost twenty years.

Hannibal unexpectedly took the offensive by land, marching tens of thousands of troops and thirty-seven elephants 1000 miles (1600 kilometers) along the French coast, over the Alps, into the Po valley and toward Rome. In two months he overran most of north Italy and destroyed the armies sent against him. But Hannibal could not break the power of Rome. Most of Rome's allies remained loyal and Rome raised new armies. Those cities that went over to Hannibal, like Capua, Syracuse, and Tarentum, were recaptured. Hannibal did annihilate a Roman army at Cannae in south Italy, but ultimately he was isolated there. Meanwhile, Rome won victories in Spain (211–206 B.C.E.), especially under the general Scipio Africanus. In 204 B.C.E.

Scipio invaded Africa. Hannibal returned to defend his homeland, but was defeated by Scipio at the Battle of Zama (202 B.C.E.) 75 miles (120 kilometers) southwest of Carthage. The war was over. Carthage became a dependency of Rome. In the Third Punic War (149–146 B.C.E.), Rome utterly destroyed Carthage (see Focus opposite).

Expansion into Spain and France

With the Carthaginian threat ended, Rome conquered the Gauls in Italy north of the Po and south of the Alps, 202–191 B.C.E., and annexed the territory. It annexed Spain in 197 B.C.E., but treated that province so harshly that constant revolts simmered until Rome finally crushed them in 133 B.C.E. In southern Gaul (France), Rome's ally Massilia

Capitoline Wolf, *c.* **500 B.C.E.** According to legend, Rome was founded by Romulus and Remus, twin sons of Mars, at the spot where they were rescued from the River Tiber and suckled by a she-wolf. The group of she-wolf with twins was adopted as the symbol of Rome, although the children in this particular statue were added almost two thousand years later, in the Renaissance. (*Museo Capitolino, Rome*)

FOCUS

"New Wisdom"—Rome's Policy of Brute Force

When, in 148 B.C.E., the Greek city-state of Corinth and its allies flouted Roman wishes, and even attacked Roman envoys, Rome razed Corinth to the ground, sold all its surviving inhabitants into slavery, and carried its artistic works to Rome. Similar brutality met Carthage's attempts to defend itself against Rome's treacherous African ally King Masinissa of Numidia. Disregarding Carthage's claims that its land was being encroached upon, Rome sided with its ally, provoked the third Punic War (149–146 B.C.E.), conquered Carthage, sold its survivors into slavery, and sowed salt into the soil so that it would never again flourish. As they had done in Macedonia and Greece, the Romans annexed their conquests, incorporating all of Carthage into the Roman province of Africa. Rome had become mistress of the Mediterranean, which the Romans began to call *Mare Nostrum*, "Our Sea."

Named the "New Wisdom," Rome's brutal use of military power served as a warning to potential foes. Roman generals were not pressed to win quick, brilliant victories, but to defeat the enemy through patient, deliberate preparation, and decisive force. Ideally, the enemy would be so awed by Roman forces that it would never dare oppose them. Indeed, the next addition to Rome's holdings came by inheritance when, in 133 B.C.E., the king of Pergamum in Asia Minor bequeathed his kingdom to Rome at his death.

(Marseille) asked for help against Gallic tribes and by 121 B.C.E. Rome had annexed most of southern France (modern Provence).

The Conquest of the Greeks: The Eastern Mediterranean

In the eastern Mediterranean, the Romans encountered Macedonians and Greeks, the proud heirs of Alexander the Great who still ruled the lands that he had conquered and Hellenized. Rome's first battle on Greek soil came in 200 B.C.E., and it began the complete restructuring of political power in the eastern Mediterranean. At the death of Alexander the Great in 323 B.C.E. his empire had divided into three regional kingdoms. In 203–202 B.C.E. two of these kingdoms, Macedonia and Syria, where the Seleucid dynasty ruled, combined to threaten the third, Egypt, where the Ptolemaic family ruled. Neighboring Greek city-states encouraged Rome to use these divisions to establish its own balance of power in the region. Rome accepted the invitation, warning Macedonia not to interfere in Greek affairs. Philip V of Macedon rejected this warning, but was defeated. In victory, the Romans declared the Greek city-states of the eastern Mediterranean "free," granting them nominal independence, but, in fact, placing them under Roman control.

Rome had similarly warned Antiochus III, the Great, of Syria to stay out of Europe and Egypt. When Antiochus ignored the warning, he was crushed, pushed back to Syria, and forced to pay a huge indemnity.

In the next generation, Philip V's son Perseus (r. 179–168 B.C.E.) was defeated decisively at Pydna in 168 B.C.E. ending the Macedonian monarchy. Also in 168 B.C.E. Rome again protected Egypt from the Seleucids, asserting its own control of the eastern Mediterranean. Rome was now the dominant power throughout the Mediterranean.

The Conquest of Northwestern Europe

During the entire period of the Roman Empire, numerous ethnic and tribal groups were on the move throughout Europe, especially northern Europe. These included a variety of Germanic groups—Ostrogoths, Visigoths, Franks, Vandals, and Lombards—as well as Celts and Huns. By the third century B.C.E. some of the German groups were settling into village life and beginning to establish small tribal states in central and northern

Europe, but as more groups continued to push in from Central Asia, including the ferocious Huns, northern and central Europe remained in constant flux. Tribes migrated, fought each other, and constantly pressed on the Roman frontiers. Dealing with all these Barbarian groups was one of Rome's greatest challenges.

Northern Gaul (modern France) seemed stably divided among various Gallic and Celtic peoples until the Helvetii, Celts driven out of Switzerland, began to invade. In response, Julius Caesar (100–44 B.C.E.), the Roman commander in north Italy and southern Gaul, moved with his army into central and northern Gaul. Caesar's *Gallic Wars* tells of his conquests in 58–52 B.C.E. By the time his campaigns ended in 49 B.C.E., all Gaul belonged to Rome.

Completing the Conquests: The Empire at its Zenith

In the east, the general Pompey (106–48 B.C.E.) added Syria and most of Asia Minor to the empire in 66 B.C.E. In 63 B.C.E. he captured Jerusalem, the capital of Judaea, although he allowed a Jewish king to rule as a client-monarch. Pompey favored such indirect rule through local potentates throughout the east, where sophisticated governmental structures had existed for centuries. He also founded some forty cities as centers of Roman political influence.

The richest state in the east, Egypt, remained quasi-independent. As he fought in the civil war after the assassination of Julius Caesar in 44 B.C.E.,

PROFILE
Augustus Caesar
EMPEROR

Julius Caesar (c. 100–44 B.C.E.) seized control of the Senate of Rome and became dictator in 47 b.c.e., but three years later he was assassinated. His adopted son and heir was his grandnephew Octavian, who took the new name of Gaius [son of] Julius Caesar. By 30 B.C.E., he had defeated his rivals and enemies—Brutus, Mark Anthony, Cleopatra—to become master of a re-unified Roman world. A grateful Senate heaped him with honors, including in 27 B.C.E. the title "Augustus," meaning "sacred" or "venerable." His achievements were immense and after his death, the Romans made Augustus a god.

Under one name or another, Augustus ruled Rome for fifty-six years until his death in 14 B.C.E. He fought wars that stabilized the borders of the empire while ensuring peace and facilitating trade, commerce, and economic growth throughout the Mediterranean. He restructured imperial administration into a form that lasted for almost two centuries. He inaugurated public projects that beautified Rome and kept its workers employed. He pacified the Roman masses and won over the aristocracy. He patronized the arts and literature, which flourished in Rome's Golden Age. He built

new roads and cities throughout the length and breadth of the empire.

Augustus instituted conservative policies affecting religion and family life. He introduced incentives for producing children and enforced laws against adultery. He believed in the authority of men over women and forced his daughter Julia into three devastatingly unhappy marriages. In the face of the general religious skepticism and indifference of the Roman upper classes, Augustus rebuilt temples and encouraged the worship of ancestral gods.

Our primary sources on Augustus' life are limited, and almost all of his own autobiography has been lost. Therefore, the "Res Gestae Divi Augusti," or account of the accomplishments of Augustus, has become a crucial text. Written for the people of Rome by Augustus himself shortly before he died and inscribed on several temples throughout the empire, it records the emperor's own statement of how he wanted to be remembered. Its thirty-five paragraphs fall into three sections: the offices and honors bestowed on him; his personal donations for public purposes; and his accomplishments in war and peace:

the Roman general Mark Antony (*c.* 82–30 B.C.E.) established his headquarters in Egypt. Antony betrayed Rome by sharing local rule with Cleopatra, queen of Egypt (r. 51–30 B.C.E.). Octavian (63 B.C.E.–14 C.E.), Julius Caesar's adopted son and designated heir, defeated Antony and Cleopatra at the Battle of Actium in 31 B.C.E., formally annexed Egypt, and won the title of Emperor Augustus Caesar (see Profile below).

As the empire continued to expand through military conquests, Rome's generals demanded, and were granted, increasing powers until, with Augustus, they supplanted republican, civilian government with an administration headed by the commander-in-chief. Before we analyze the significance of this political transformation, however, let us complete our account of the continuing geographical expansion of the empire.

Augustus annexed Switzerland, Austria, and Bavaria in 16–15 B.C.E. and established Rome's historical frontier in central Europe at the Danube River. After an attempt to conquer central Germany failed in 9 C.E., the Rhine became the normal border in the northeast.

England and Wales were conquered in the 40s C.E. and became the Roman province of Britain. Some 2000 miles (3200 kilometres) to the east, the Emperor Trajan (r. 98–117 C.E.) conquered Dacia, modern Romania, and briefly annexed Armenia and Parthia (Mesopotamia).

Trajan's successor, Hadrian (117–138 C.E.), consolidated Roman gains. He permanently withdrew

1. At the age of nineteen, on my own initiative and at my own expense, I raised an army by means of which I liberated the Republic. . . . the people elected me consul and a triumvir for the settlement of the commonwealth . . . .

3. I waged many wars throughout the whole world by land and by sea, ... and when victorious I spared all citizens who sought pardon. . . . About 500,000 Roman citizens were under military oath to me.

15. To the Roman plebs I paid 300 sesterces apiece in accordance with the will of my father [Julius Caesar]; and in my fifth consulship [29 B.C.E.] I gave each 400 sesterces in my own name out of the spoil of war, reaching never less than 250,000 persons . . . . In the eighteenth year of my tribunician power and my twelfth consulship [29 B.C.E.] I gave out of the spoils of war 1,000 sesterces apiece to my soldiers settled in colonies . . . . received by about 120,000 persons. . . . In my thirteenth consulship [2 B.C.E.] I gave sixty denar-ii apiece to those of the plebs who at that time were receiving public grain. . . . a little more than 200,000 persons.

19. I built. . . the senate house and. . . the temple of Apollo. . . .

22. I gave a gladiatorial show three times in my own name, and five times in the names of my sons or grandsons; at these shows about 10,000 fought. . . . Twenty-six times I provided for the people . . . hunting spectacles of African wild beasts in the circus or in the Forum or in the amphitheaters. . . .

23. I turned over to their masters for punishment nearly 30,000 slaves who had run away from their owners and taken up arms against the state.

28. I established colonies of soldiers in Africa, Sicily, Macedonia, in both Spanish provinces, in Achaea, Asia, Syria, Narbonese Gaul, and Pisidia. Italy, moreover, has twenty-eight colonies established by me which grew large and prosperous in my lifetime. . . .

31. Royal embassies from India, never previously seen before any Roman general, were often sent to me. . . .

(Lewis and Reinhold, Vol. I, pp. 561-572)

Augustus of Prima Porta, **early 1st century** C.E. (*Musei Vaticani, Rome*)

the Roman forces from Mesopotamia back to the Euphrates and he built a wall west to east across the narrow neck of England in the northern part of Britain. Twenty-five years later, his successor, Antoninus Pius, built another wall some 50 miles (80 kilometers) further north. The limits of the Roman Empire had been reached.

IMPERIAL ROME: HOW DO WE KNOW?

Multiple Perspectives

Thus far we have studied the expansion of Rome from city-state to imperial power. On pages 172–94 we will analyze the institutions of the empire, its decline and fall, and its significance. Here we pause to examine the sources of information on which this history is based.

The earliest years of Rome's history are shrouded in legends. The most famous of these sets the founding of the city in 753 B.C.E. From that time Rome was ruled by Etruscan kings from the neighboring northern area of Etruria until they were expelled in 509 B.C.E. and a self-governing republic was established in Rome, its government elected by the citizens. The city was sacked by invading Celts in 390 B.C.E., and most of the records preserved until that time were lost. The only surviving traces are segments incorporated into accounts recorded by historians following the invasion. Most of what has been preserved are lists of rulers, at first the kings but later the chief elected officials: consuls, **praetors**, and **tribunes**.

During the later republic historians began consciously to write the history of the city. The most famous of the early historians was Polybius (*c.* 200–*c.* 118 B.C.E.), a Greek brought to Rome as a political captive. Polybius narrated the overwhelming event of his own time, Rome's conquest of an empire through its victories over Carthage, Macedonia, and Spain:

> There can surely be no one so petty or so apathetic in his outlook that he has no desire to discover by what means and under what system of government the Romans succeeded in less than fifty-three years [220–167 B.C.E.] in bringing under their rule almost the whole of the inhabited world, an achievement which is without parallel in human history. (*The Histories* I:1; p. 443, cited in Finley)

Column of Trajan, Rome. Dedicated 113 C.E. The Romans built tall commemorative columns in order to celebrate the power and military might of the empire. The Column of Trajan is covered by a continuous strip of carving that tells the story of the Emperor Trajan's victories over the barbarian tribes along the Danube.

The Roman aqueduct at Segovia, Spain, early first or second century C.E. Unlike the Greeks, the Romans are remembered less for their art than for their great engineering feats. The need to improve the water supply to Roman settlements increased along with urban population growth. The popularity of the public bathing houses heightened the demand even more. The Romans developed a massive network of aqueducts to channel water into cities across uneven terrain.

Livy (59 B.C.E.–17 C.E.) praised the glories of Rome's later expansion to imperial dimensions, but he decried the class conflict between Rome's aristocrats and its common people that was ripping apart Rome's self-governing, elected, republican form of government.

Tacitus (*c.* 55–120 C.E.) continued the story to the height of imperial power. He praised the heroism of the Roman conquerors, but he also understood the anguish and bitterness of the conquered peoples. In *Agricola*, Tacitus attributes to the Celtic chieftain Calgacus one of the most devastating critiques of imperialism ever articulated. In Tacitus' account, Calgacus condemns

the Romans, whose tyranny cannot be escaped by any act of reasonable submission. These brigands of the world have exhausted the land by their rapacity,

Arch of Trajan, Benevento, 114–117 C.E. Triumphal arches are another peculiarly Roman means of celebrating the power of the ruler and his empire. This particular arch, dedicated to Trajan, stands at the point where the road to Brindisi, a port on the east coast, branches off the Appian Way, the first major road in the Romans' strategic network.

so they now ransack the sea. When their enemy is rich, they lust after wealth; when the enemy is poor, they lust after power. Neither East nor West has satisfied their hunger. They are unique among humanity insofar as they equally covet the rich and the poor. Robbery, butchery, and rapine they call "Empire." They create a desert and call it "Peace."

(I:129, cited in Andrea and Overfield)

Other historians also illuminated the empire from its fringes rather than from its center, and they, too, were often critical of the effects of empire on its subjects. For Jewish historians, such as Philo of Alexandria (*c.* 13 B.C.E.–*c.* 45 C.E.) and Josephus (*c.* 37–*c.* 100 C.E.), as for Christian theologians, such as Tertullian (*c.* 155–*c.* 225 C.E.) and Augustine, bishop of Hippo in north Africa (354–430 C.E.), the Roman Empire was not the central concern, but it was an inescapable presence. They had to take account of Rome in their own teaching, writing, and actions (see p. 321), and although they were not prepared to praise the empire, they counseled accommodation rather than direct military opposition. They wrote of coping with Rome's power from their own marginal positions.

As the empire began to decay, more mainstream historians became critical. Dio Cassius (*c.* 150–*c.* 235 C.E.) nostalgically recalled the rule of Augustus as Rome's golden age and lamented the empire's subsequent decline "from a monarchy of gold to one of iron and rust."

In addition to these formal histories, leading men of the empire often left important documents that shed light on their times. The great orator and political leader Cicero (106–43 B.C.E.) left dozens of letters, fifty-seven public speeches, and extensive writings on public affairs. Julius Caesar's account of the *Gallic Wars* describes his military organization and strategy, the Roman virtues that characterized his troops, and the land and the peoples against which he fought. In part, this was a propaganda piece, preparing the path for Caesar's assertion of personal power in Rome.

Rome has also bequeathed rich material artifacts. Much of the infrastructure of the empire—its roads, aqueducts, stadiums, public baths, forums, temples, triumphal arches—as well as substantial parts of many of the military camps and cities it constructed still stand. Roman coinage and statuary are everywhere. The cities of Pompeii (see Spotlight, pp. 170-1) and Herculaneum, comprising a total population of about 20,000, were buried in dust and cinders in the volcanic eruption of Mount Vesuvius in 79 C.E., giving, when they began to be uncovered in the eighteenth century, an unparalleled view of the city's structure and furnishings. Off-shore, archaeologists have uncovered sunken ships in the Italian Mediterranean that shed light on Roman trade missions and their cargoes. They have also been able to reconstruct *latifundia*, rural estates that were controlled by rich owners who bought up family farms and ran them as plantations.

Archaeological digs also uncover the history of the many Gothic, Celtic, and other groups of migrating peoples who lived on the fringes of the empire, later settled within its territories, and finally established their own states on those lands as the empire was dismembered. Their settlements, burial grounds, tools, and artwork yield significant information about their lives,

ROMAN EMPERORS

Augustus (27 B.C.E.–14 C.E.)

Julio-Claudian dynasty	Tiberius (14–37) Caligula (37–41) Claudius (41–54) Nero (54–68)
Flavian dynasty	Vespasian (69–79) Titus (79–81) Domitian (81–96)
Age of the Antonines	Nerva (96–98) Trajan (98–117) Hadrian (117–138) Antoninus Pius (138–161) Marcus Aurelius (161–180) Commodus (180–193)
Severan dynasty	Septimius Severus (193–211) Caracalla (212–217) Elagabalus (218–222) Severus Alexander (222–235)
The late empire	Philip the Arabian (244–249) Decius (249–251) Gallus (251–253) Valerian (253–260) Gallienus (253–268) Claudius (268–270) Aurelian (270–275) Tacitus (275–276) Florian (276) Probus (276–282) Carus (282–283) Numerianus (283–284) and Carinus (283–285) Diocletian (284–305)

SPOTLIGHT
Pompeii

A ROMAN TOWN

The volcano Vesuvius erupted on August 24, 79 C.E., burying the town of Pompeii, and its smaller neighbor Herculaneum, under 13 feet (4 meters) of pumice stone, ash, and gravel. Some of the town's 10,000 inhabitants fled on the first day of the eruption, escaping with their lives. Those who did not were trapped in the next two days' rain of volcanic ash. The ash cooled and solidified around them, so archaeologists have been able to recover their forms by pouring concrete into the molds left where their bodies decayed. **Figure 2** indicates that dogs as well as human beings suffered.

Although covered over, the fate of Pompeii was known through the eyewitness account of Pliny the Younger:

> They debated whether to stay indoors or take their chance in the open, for the buildings were now shaking with violent shocks, and seemed to be swaying to and fro as if they were torn from their foundations. Outside, on the other hand, there was the danger of falling pumice-stones, even though they were light and porous; however, after

Figure 1 Temple of Apollo, Pompeii, with Vesuvius in the background.

comparing the risks, they chose the latter.*

Archaeologists began to excavate Herculaneum in 1783, Pompeii in 1765. Preserved like time capsules, these cities revealed their urban design, buildings, furniture, and household objects. Pompeii was walled, with seven gates, and housed a forum, council chamber, offices of magistrates, temples dedicated to Apollo and Jupiter, market buildings, a stock exchange, law court, theater, auditoria, an amphitheater for gladiatorial contests and wild beast hunts, three Turkish-style baths, workshops, shops, brothels, and homes. **Figure 1** resurrects the Temple of Apollo and shows Vesuvius, still active to this day, in the background. Carbonized food, preserved and sealed in hot volcanic mud, suggests the everyday menus of the inhabitants. Walls, surviving to their full

Figure 3 The young Hercules wrestling with a snake, fresco, House of the Vettii, Pompeii.

Figure 2
Cast of the body of a watch dog, Pompeii.

height, have preserved vivid murals from the residences and businesses, the best of them since carried off to the National Museum in Naples. We have already seen, on pp. 152–3, one of the most valuable and beautiful of the Pompeii mosaics, depicting the victory of Alexander the Great over Darius at the Battle of Issus. Since this mosaic itself copies an earlier, lost painting from about 300 B.C.E. its preservation is especially fortunate.

The murals on the walls of many homes reflect both opulence and cultured taste. Those in the house of the Vettii **(figure 3)** present scenes from Greek mythology. Specific elements also allude to contemporary Roman interests and power; for example, the eagle at the top center position in the painting symbolizes the might of the Roman army.

* Cited in Paul G. Bahn, *The Cambridge Illustrated History of Archaeology*, p.59.

even though they had no writing systems until they learned from the Romans.

With such extensive artifacts complementing the rich documentary record, scholars can reconstruct the rise and fall of the Roman Empire and its relationships with neighboring peoples. As new topics are explored, such as the extent of slavery, the treatment of women, and the patron–client relationship, relatively abundant materials provide the raw materials to answer new questions.

THE INSTITUTIONS OF EMPIRE: FROM REPUBLICAN ROME TO IMPERIAL ROME

MILITARY POWER

From its beginning, Rome was a military state. According to one legend, its founders, Romulus and Remus, were sons of Mars, the god of war. An alternative legend, described in Virgil's *Aeneid*, which was written during the age of Augustus, depicted Rome as founded by Aeneas, one of the heroes of Troy.

Rome's armies were central to its life and it excelled in military organization and technology. Its professional armed legions proved superior even to the Greek phalanxes. Although it had never possessed a navy, Rome built one that conquered Carthage, the greatest seapower of the day. Coming against great walled towns in the east, it developed unprecedented machinery to besiege the walls, catapult firepower into them, and batter them down. Confronting groups of migrating Goths, it created new, mobile cavalry units to supplement its more conventional legions.

To be a free man was to serve as an officer in the army. Within Italy, captured city-states were required to supply not gold and taxes but men for the armies. At the time of Julius Caesar, the average Italian male served seven years in the army. Under Augustus, soldiering became more professional: men enlisted for between sixteen and twenty-five years. Conquered peoples outside of Italy also contributed troops to Rome's armies. The Barbarians who invaded the empire were often encouraged to settle in Roman territories and to enlist in Roman armies. A spiral of imperial expansion resulted. As Rome expanded, so did its armed forces; it then expanded further in part to capture the wealth to pay its larger armies; this expansion, in turn, enlarged its armies once more.

In the field, the soldiers built their support systems: strings of fortress watch-towers along all the borders, military camps, administrative towns, roads, and aqueducts. Roman engineering feats astonished the world in their day, and many of them remain to astonish us as well. Many of the walled military camps were kernels from which sprouted later towns and cities, one of Rome's most distinctive contributions. These urban outposts established Rome's military and administrative rule in the midst of rural, even nomadic, regions. In the reign of Augustus, these nodes were linked by 50,000 miles (80,000 kilometers) of first-class roads and 200,000 miles (320,000 kilometers) of lesser roads.

Rome's military leaders were at first constrained by the aristocratic senate and the general assembly of Rome. Later, the generals began giving the orders. General Gaius Marius campaigned to have himself elected consul in 107 B.C.E. He broke with the normal practice of recruiting only troops who owned property, and accepted soldiers who were indebted to him personally for their maintenance. Elected consul six times between 107 and 100 B.C.E., Marius restructured the armies into more efficient organizations. He arranged large allotments of land for veteran soldiers in north Africa, Gaul, Sicily, Greece, and Macedonia. The armies now depended for their welfare on him rather than on the state.

The generals began to compete among themselves for power, instigating civil war in Rome. To fight against Mithridates IV, king of Pontus, the Roman Senate called on a new general, Sulla. Marius, however, arranged to have the command transferred to himself. In response, Sulla rallied soldiers loyal to him and invaded Rome, initiating the first civil war. He declared Marius an outlaw and left with his troops for Greece, where he defeated Mithridates. Meanwhile Marius, joined by another general, Cinna, seized Rome and banned Sulla. Sulla returned with his army, invaded Italy and Rome, and had himself declared dictator, a position he held for two years, and then abdicated.

Twenty years later, in 60 B.C.E., two great generals, Julius Caesar and Pompey, and Crassus, a wealthy businessman who aspired to generalship, formed a "**triumvirate**" to rule. The three competed among themselves until Caesar won out. Caesar ruled as dictator from 47 until 44 B.C.E., when he was assassinated by rivals who felt he had usurped too much power. Caesar's successor, Augustus (63 B.C.E.–14 C.E.), was also a military hero who triumphed in civil wars. He, too, was part of a "triumvirate," until he defeated his rival Mark Antony, ending another civil war.

With Augustus Rome became an imperial monarchy, a government ruled by a single military commander, the imperator, or Emperor and his armies. For years generals had wanted this centralized power. Now, in gratitude, the Senate was willing to turn it over to Augustus. Augustus rejected the title of monarch, preferring to be called "princeps," or "first citizen." This gesture of humility fooled no one. With Augustus' reign, the imperial form of government begins even though the Senate and the consuls and other magistrates survived. From Augustus on, all real power in the Roman state lay in the hands of the Emperor.

As the size and wealth of the empire grew, many Romans felt that they had conquered the world but lost their souls. They spoke not of victory, but of loss. The historian Livy, writing at the height of the age of Augustus, lamented the end of innocence:

> with the gradual relaxation of discipline, morals first gave way, as it were, then sank lower and lower, and finally began the downward plunge which has brought us to the present time, when we can endure neither our vices nor the cure.
>
> (Lewis and Reinhold, Vol. I, p. 8)

Livy proclaimed the widely held myth of an older, golden age of simplicity which had been lost:

> No state was ever greater, none more righteous or richer in good examples, nor ever was where avarice and luxury came into the social order so late, or where humble means and thrift were so highly esteemed and so long held in honor. For true it is that the less men's wealth was, the less was their greed. Of late, riches have brought in avarice, and excessive pleasures the longing to carry wantonness and license to the point of personal ruin and universal destruction.
>
> (Lewis and Reinhold, Vol. I, p. 8)

This nostalgia for the past had two related, but different versions. One drew on examples from the days of simple, rustic equality before the advent of the Etruscan kings. It condemned the maltreatment of the plebeians and the slaves at the hands of the patricians that had begun under Etruscan rule and intensified under the Republic. The other regretted the later transfer of power from the Senate to the generals. It wished to recreate the days of the oligarchic, patrician republic.

CLASS AND CLASS CONFLICT

Class and class conflict, however, were a staple of Rome's history. The system of government under the early Republic had included only about 7 to 10 percent of the population: the wealthy, the powerful, and some with hereditary ties to Rome. The overwhelming majority, those without property or long-standing ties, and, of course, slaves and women, could not serve as officers in the military and were thus excluded from government. The two classes, patricians, (from the Latin "pater," father) and "plebeians," commoners without hereditary ties to the state, had become increasingly polarized under Etruscan rule, as the patricians forbade intermarriage with the plebeians and monopolized the magistracies, the Senate, and even the religious offices of the state. In response the plebeians had looked to the Etruscan king as their protector. The fall of the monarchy reduced the status of the plebeians still further.

The Struggle of the Orders, the conflict between patricians and plebeians, marked more than a half century—494 to 440 B.C.E.—of the early republic. The plebeians relied on their ultimate strengths: their bodies and their numbers. They were the foot soldiers of Rome, and their periodic boycotts of the patricians, by withdrawing to the Aventine Hill, threatened the city of Rome itself. In 451 B.C.E., in an attempt to resolve the conflict, a commission of ten patricians codified Rome's laws into Twelve Tables. The patricians were pleased with their apparent liberality, but the plebeians were horrified when they recognized the force of all the laws that were imposed upon them. Slowly, under pressure, the patricians yielded power, and the first plebeian consul was elected in 360 B.C.E. A series of measures to relieve debt was also passed, although indebtedness continued to be a problem throughout Roman history.

Patriarchs, Patrons, and Clients

Asymmetrical power relationships characterized all of Roman life under the Republic. The earliest enduring social structure in Rome was the patron–client relationship. Strong men acted as protectors of the weak; the weak, in turn, provided services for the strong as requested. The same relationship structured the family. The father of the family, the paterfamilias, had the right of life and death over his children as long as he lived. In reality, fathers were not tyrants, and in exercising the

FOCUS
Gender Relationships

According to Roman custom and practice, a woman's role was subordinate to man's. Subject to her father throughout his life, a woman was, after his death, required to obey the advice of her husband or a legally appointed guardian in any kind of legal or business transactions. (In practice, if she had reached adulthood, she usually gained her independence at the death of her father, as did her brothers.) Marriages were arranged by the families of the bride and groom. Motherhood was considered the most significant rite of passage for women, and free-born women were exempted from having a guardian after giving birth to three children, freed women after four.

Women were respected if they lived chastely and more or less contentedly within these guidelines of family, motherhood, and domesticity. The feminine ideal was the faithful and loyal *univira*, the "one-man woman." A woman caught in adultery was banished from her home and might well be executed; men apprehended in adultery were not punished. Women found drinking wine could also be punished; again, men could not. These principles of behavior were, of course, fully applicable only to the upper classes. The masses of lower-class free women entered the working world outside the home, and slaves had little control over their lives. The prevalence of prostitution further indicated the

Mosaic of Neptune and Amphitrite (detail), Herculaneum, before 79 C.E. Art sometimes seems to contradict the legal evidence concerning gender relationships in the Roman Empire. The artist responsible for this mosaic of the sea-god Neptune and his wife Amphitrite has accorded the couple an apparent equality.

limited applicability of the Roman female ideal. The excavation of Pompeii has uncovered seven brothels.

At times even upper-class women escaped the constraints. The growth of urban life, especially in the capital at Rome in the first century B.C.E., offered new opportunities to a few upper-class Roman women to gain education and even to participate in public life, although sometimes behind the scenes. New marriage laws enabled them to live as equals of their husbands and gave them the right to divorce and to act without reference to a legal guardian. Women did not, however, have access to the professions or to public political office.

Augustus sought to restore the earlier family order. He made adultery a criminal offense, punishable by exile, confiscation of property, and even execution. Indeed, he exiled his own daughter and only child, Julia, for sexual profligacy. He encouraged marriage and childbearing and punished celibacy. These laws were widely disobeyed and opposed, but they reveal to us the link in Augustus' mind between a well-ordered family and a well-ordered empire, a link that was repeated in the official policies of many empires throughout history. (Compare China and India in Chapters 7 and 8, Britain in Chapter 16, Japan in Chapter 17, and Germany in Chapter 18.)

right to choose their children's occupations and spouses, and to control their economic possessions, they would normally try to consider their needs and desires. Nevertheless, fathers had the legal power to act as they wished: they continued to have control over their daughters' economic lives even after their marriages, for these rights did not pass to the husbands (see Focus, opposite). These rights were enshrined in the law of patria potestas, the right of the head of the household. Similar patron–client relationships later characterized imperial control over conquered provinces. They were the Roman way.

Imperial expansion exacerbated class conflicts within Rome. The benefits of the conquests went mostly to the rich, while the yeoman farmers, who supplied the troops, were often bankrupted by the wars. After serving in the army for years, they would return home to find that in their absence their wives and children had not been able to maintain the family farms and might even have sold them to owners of large estates, *latifundia*, and left for the city, impoverished.

Urban Splendor and Squalor

Class divisions were most glaring in the capital. The city of Rome itself grew seemingly without limit and without adequate planning. As it came to control Italy and then the Mediterranean, Rome's population multiplied, reaching 1 million by about the first century C.E. Some of the newcomers were wealthy and powerful, and they adorned the city, adding new examples of Greek architecture and urban design to the earlier Etruscan forms. They replaced wood, mud, and local volcanic rock with concrete and finer stone. Augustus himself boasted that he had found Rome a city of brick and left it one of marble. The poor also came streaming into the city, but from bankrupt family farms. For them, Rome was a nightmare. Lewis Mumford, the historian of urbanization, highlighted the contrast:

> The houses of the patricians, spacious, airy, sanitary, equipped with bathrooms and water closets, heated in winter by hypocausts, which carried hot air through chambers in the floors, were perhaps the most commodious and comfortable houses built for a temperate climate anywhere until the twentieth century; a triumph of domestic architecture. But the tenements of Rome easily take the prize for being the most crowded and insanitary buildings produced in Western Europe until the sixteenth

century. . . . Not only were these buildings unheated, unprovided with waste pipes or water closets, unadapted to cooking; not merely did they contain an undue number of airless rooms, indecently over-crowded: though poor in all the facilities that make for decent daily living, they were in addition so badly built and so high that they offered no means of safe exit from the frequent fires that occurred. And if their tenants escaped typhoid, typhus, fire, they might easily meet their death in the collapse of the whole structure. Such accidents were all too frequent.

> These buildings and their people constituted the core of imperial Rome, and that core was rotten. As Rome grew and its system of exploitation turned more and more parasitic, the rot ate into ever larger masses of urban tissue. The main population of the city that boasted its world conquests lived in cramped, noisy, airless, foul-smelling, infected quarters, paying extortionate rents to merciless landlords, undergoing daily indignities and terrors that coarsened and brutalized them, and in turn demanded compensatory outlets. These outlets carried the brutalization even further, in a continuous carnival of sadism and death. (pp. 220–21)

Attempts at Reform

Mumford refers to the "bread and circuses" that characterized Rome from the time of the reforming Gracchi brothers, Tiberius Sempronius (163–133 B.C.E.) and Gaius Sempronius (153–121 B.C.E.). As tribune of the people in 133 B.C.E., Tiberius proposed distributing some public lands among the poor, especially among poor soldiers. Opposed to this liberal proposal and fearing that Gracchus was attempting to gain too much political power for himself, a number of senators, supported by their clients, clubbed Tiberius and 300 of his supporters to death. This was the first political murder over a public policy issue in Rome in nearly 400 years. Despite the murder, the redistribution of public land did take place.

In 123 B.C.E., Gaius Gracchus was elected tribune. He extended his brother's plan for land redistribution by establishing colonies for the resettlement of some of the poor people of Rome, as well as for their commercial advancement, in the regions conquered in the Punic Wars, including Carthage itself. He also introduced subsidized grain sales to the poor people of Rome. Gaius' measure was later expanded into a dole of free bread for the poor people of Rome. Gaius argued that citizenship should be granted to all Latins and to the local civic officials in all other communities.

He was not equally sensitive to the problems of non-Italians, however, for his legislation exploited the provinces by enabling Roman knights to serve as "publicans" or tax farmers. These tax farmers struck an agreement with the state to turn over a fixed amount of net taxes while retaining the right to collect from their region as much as they were able and to keep the balance for themselves. Tax farming enabled the state to collect taxes without monitoring the process; it enabled the tax farmers to become wealthy; and it exploited the people

---

SOURCE
Romes's Code of Laws: Two Contrasting Perspectives

Rome's incipient international law has been described by modern historians from two very different perspectives. Michael Grant, Fellow of Trinity College, Cambridge, describes the written law in glowing terms as:

> one of the most potent and effective ideas that the Romans ever originated. . . . It demonstrated that a body of law could be established upon a foundation acceptable to the members of different peoples and races at any and every phase of social, economic, and political evolution; and so it brought the laws of the Romans nearer to universal applicability than any others that have ever been devised, and it uniquely displayed their genius for social organization. (Grant, pp. 104–5)

Nicholas Purcell, on the other hand, writing in the *Oxford History of the Classical World*, acknowledges the majesty of Roman law in theory, but emphasizes the perversion of the law in practical application.

> The law was not always sufficiently universal, and the underprivileged might well not reap its benefits. Jewish nationalist writers, for example, compare the hypocrisy of Rome to the ambiguous associations of the unclean pig: "Just as a pig lies down and sticks out its trotters as though to say `I am clean' [because they are cloven], so the evil empire robs and oppresses while pretending to execute justice." (Boardman *et al.*, p. 582)

Purcell cites Juvenal, the satirist, on the inability of law to curb the arbitrary violence of Roman soldiers:

> Your teeth are shattered? Face hectically inflamed, with great black welts? You know the doctor wasn't too optimistic about the eye that was left. But it's not a bit of good your running to the courts about it. If you've been beaten up by a soldier, better keep it to yourself. (Cited in Boardman *et al.*, 575)

Legal theory and practice did not always coincide in ancient Rome (just as they do not always coincide today). The poor did not receive the same protection and benefits as the rich, soldiers abused their authority, and laws were not always applied consistently. Even Grant concedes the persistent class bias of Roman law:

> Roman law, despite all its concern for equity, had always favored the upper echelon of society, from which its own practitioners originated; and now, from the time of Trajan or Hadrian onwards, such preferential treatment became crystallized in legal forms. This greater explicitness was ominous, for . . . it confirmed the depressed status of the underprivileged and thus deepened the basic rift that in the following centuries would help bring the empire down. (Grant, p. 325)

Roman power reinforced Roman hegemony. Revolt often simmered in the conquered territories, especially among the most exploited. Augustus' own account of his actions noted: "I pacified the sea by suppressing piracy. In that struggle I turned over to their masters for punishment nearly 30,000 fugitive slaves who had taken up arms against the state" (Lewis and Reinhold, I: 569). Three great slave revolts wracked the empire, two of them before Augustus, one after: 70,000 slaves resorted to armed resistance in the Great Slave War in Sicily, 134–131 B.C.E.; a second revolt in Sicily, 104–100 B.C.E., broke out when it seemed that Germanic tribes would invade Italy and keep the imperial troops occupied in the north; the revolt among the gladiators led by Spartacus in 73–71 B.C.E. was eventually crushed, and 6000 slaves were crucified on the roads leading into Rome.

Revolts in the conquered provinces were also brutally crushed. When Rome believed that Corinth might be planning a revolt in 146 B.C.E., the city was razed to the ground. Jews revolted three times— 66–73 C.E., 115–117 C.E., and 132–135 C.E.—resulting in the destruction of Judaea as a Jewish state, the physical destruction of Jerusalem and its principal Temple, and the establishment of a Roman colony, Aelia Capitolina, on its site.

being taxed. Gaius auctioned off the collection of taxes in Asia. While this profited the elite and helped to secure their loyalty to him personally, it impoverished the residents of the Roman province of Asia. Many senators became increasingly hostile to Gaius Gracchus, and in 121 B.C.E. he too was assassinated along with his fellow tribune, Flaccus. Some 3000 of his supporters were executed.

The reforms of the Gracchi brothers seemed blocked, but in fact they set the framework for the end of the republic a century later. They challenged the power of the senate and exposed the problems of the poor and the war veterans, while their enemies employed violence, murder, and thuggery as tools for making public policy. Julius Caesar and Augustus Caesar, the two men most responsible for finally turning the republic into a militaristic empire headed by a single person, learned from the experiences of the Gracchi brothers to play on Rome's class divisions and to garner the support of the lower classes.

A new method of coping with class conflict was developing: "bread and circuses." Rome bribed the poor, many of them former soldiers from its conquering armies, with a dole of free bread. Up to 200,000 people a day were served. The dole encouraged them to while away their time in public religious festivities, races, the theater, and gladiatorial contests of great cruelty, which pitted man against man and man against beast in spectacles witnessed by tens of thousands. Between them, the arenas of Rome, including Rome's largest race-track, and the Colosseum, parts of which exist even today, could accommodate one half of Rome's adult population. On days of gladiatorial contests, as many as 5000 animals, including elephants and water buffalo, were slaughtered. Hundreds of humans, too, were slain in a single day. The combination of spectacle and free food was offered to sedate the unemployed urban masses.

Augustus and his successors continued these policies designed to keep the plebeians quiet without actually solving the problems of unemployment and lack of dignity. Until its final collapse, the empire was threatened by unrest and revolt and one of the reasons for the popularity of Christianity in Rome was its message of compassion and salvation for the poor and downtrodden (Chapter 10).

EXTENDING CITIZENSHIP AND INTERNATIONAL LAW

Empires are ultimately sustained by military force, but successful empires must also win at least some degree of support from among the conquered peoples, some measure of hegemony. Rome won such support through several of its political, cultural, economic, and ideological policies. First, politically, it bestowed benefits on conquered peoples, especially the benefits of citizenship.

All free Roman males were citizens automatically; the rest of the men of Italy, however, were not. In 381 B.C.E., the town of Tusculum, some 15 miles (24 kilometers) from Rome and surrounded by Roman territory, seemed poised to oppose Rome. The Romans won the Tusculuns over, however, by offering incorporation into Rome and full citizenship. In 338 B.C.E. full citizenship was bestowed on four additional Latin cities; others received partial citizenship with no voting rights but with rights of property, contracts, and the right to marry Roman citizens. They were also freed of property taxes. Roman citizenship also protected its beneficiary from arbitrary arrest and violence.

In 91 B.C.E. Marcus Livius Drusus the Younger, was elected tribune, the office established to protect the interest of the plebeians. Drusus proposed extending citizenship and the vote to all the Italian allies, but the Roman Senate rejected the proposal. Drusus was later assassinated, leaving the Italians frustrated and furious. So began the "Social War" or "War of the Allies." After two years, however, Rome did offer full citizenship to all Italians who had remained loyal and even to those who agreed to put down their arms. It extended full citizenship north as far as the Po River, and partial citizenship up to the Alps Mountains. So, grudgingly, citizenship was offered as an inducement to loyalty. In newly annexed lands, the aristocrats, the group to whom Rome usually granted these rights and obligations, regarded even partial citizenship as attractive.

The policy continued on a limited basis as Rome expanded. Augustus Caesar announced in 14 C.E. that there were 4,937,000 citizens in the empire, about 2 million of them in the provinces. At that time, the total population of the empire was between 70 and 100 million. In 212 C.E., the Emperor Caracalla officially proclaimed citizenship for all free males in the empire, although ambiguous legal restrictions limited the effect. Provincials could occupy the highest offices in the empire: senator, consul, and even emperor. The Emperor Trajan (r. 98–117) was from Spain; Septimius Severus (r. 193–211) from north Africa; Diocletian (r. 284–305) from Dalmatia (modern Croatia).

The development of international law, the *jus gentium* (law of nations; see Source, p. 176), also helped to unite and pacify the empire. After its victory in the first Punic War, 241 B.C.E., Rome interacted more than ever with foreigners and with subjects of Rome who did not have citizenship. To deal with legal cases between Romans and these others, a new official, the *praetor peregrinus* (literally, foreign magistrate), was appointed. The law developed from his judgments was the *jus gentium*. Over time, this law was codified, first by Hadrian, and later, in the east, by the Emperor Justinian (r. 527–565 C.E.).

ECONOMIC POLICIES FOR THE EMPIRE

The empire brought extraordinary benefits to the rulers, but the costs could also be heavy and eventually became oppressive. The Romans levied tribute, taxes, and rents, and recruited soldiers from the peoples they conquered. They settled their own soldiers in captured lands, turning those lands into Roman estates and enslaving millions of people to work on them. They exploited their political power for the economic advantage of their own traders and military and administrative elites. Imperial rule and the opening of imperial markets brought opportunities for economic development and profit in the conquered provinces, although most of these went to the local wealthy elites who possessed the capital and skills to take advantage of them. In general, Roman rulers were solicitous of the upper classes in the provinces, both because of a shared class position and because they believed that the loyalty of these elites was crucial to maintaining Roman hegemony.

The requirements of feeding and provisioning the city of Rome, which had a population of about a million by the time of Augustus, called on vast resources throughout the empire. The most important requirement was grain. Supplies were drawn from Sicily, Egypt and the north African coast, Spain, and the lands surrounding the Black Sea. More specialized products were imported from all parts of the empire: olive oil and wine came from within Italy, Spain, and the Mediterranean shores; pottery and glass from the Rhineland; leather from southern France; marble from Asia Minor; woolen textiles from Britain and northern France, Belgium, and the Netherlands; slaves from many lands. For gladiatorial contests in the Colosseum and for general display in Rome, lions were brought from Africa and Asia, bears from Scotland, horses from Spain, crocodiles and camels from Egypt, and leopards and rhinoceroses from northwest Africa. The transportation of bulk commodities, especially within the empire, was most often by sea.

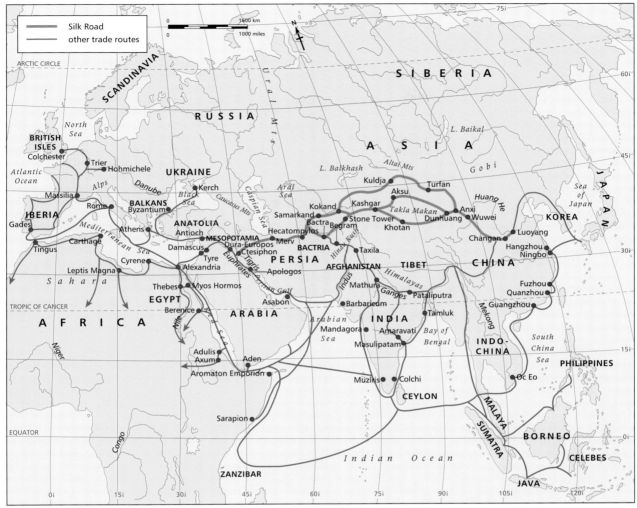

Eurasian trade The commercial links that bound the ancient world were both extensive and sophisticated. Self-sustaining individual networks—the Saharan caravans, the Arab dhows plying the Indian Ocean, the fleets of Chinese junks coasting east Asia, and most famously the Silk Routes traversing central Asia—linked at key entrepots such as Alexandria and Oc Eo by sea, and Ctesiphon and Kashgar by land, to form a truly intercontinental trading system.

A few other extremely large cities, like Alexandria, also needed to import extensively to provide for their hundreds of thousands of inhabitants, but most of the empire was locally self-sufficient. In this pre-industrial age, most people worked on the land, most production was agricultural, and most produce was consumed near the place of production, especially in the newly conquered and settled regions of western Europe. To incorporate these regions into the empire, the Romans constructed and promoted new cities as administrative, military, and financial centers. These included the cores of modern London, Paris, Lyon, Trier, Nimes, Bruges, Barcelona, Cologne, Budapest, and many other European cities. In the midst of nomadic and migrating peoples, in an empire that rested on agriculture, Rome laid the foundations of a small but potent ruling urban civilization.

At the height of its power, the empire contained more than 5000 civic bodies. The orator Cicero referred to Narbonne, Rome's administrative capital in southern Gaul (from about 118 B.C.E.), as "a colony of Roman citizens, a watch tower of the Roman people, a bulwark against the wild tribes of Gaul" (cited in Mumford, p. 209). Roman rule especially attracted and benefited the urban upper classes in the conquered regions, and helped to urbanize some leaders of the newly arriving immigrant German settlers.

Timgad, North Africa. Timgad, in Algeria, was founded as a military and administrative fortress around 100 C.E. and designed as a perfect square with a grid plan for the streets. The Romans tended to adhere to standard templates of town construction, despite variations in local topography, and Timgad is one of the clearest surviving models of what a provincial headquarters looked like.

People of wealth and power could command specialty goods and generate small but significant streams of intercontinental, long-distance, luxury trade. For such commerce to flourish, trade routes had to be kept safe. The Pax Romana secured the Red Sea routes, which allowed the import of frankincense, myrrh, and other spices from the Arabian peninsula and the Horn of Africa and spices and textiles from India, some of them transshipped from China. By the first century C.E., sailors had discovered that by sailing with the summer monsoon winds they could reach India from Egypt in about four months. They could then return with the winter monsoon, completing the round trip within a year.

Rome's repayment in this exchange was mostly precious metals. Hoards of gold coins from Rome have been discovered in south India, with smaller treasuries in China, southeast Asia, and east Africa. The historian Pliny complained that the trade drained Italy's precious metals, but the profits to be made back home were extraordinary: "In no year does India absorb less than 50,000,000 sesterces of our Empire's wealth, sending back merchandise to be sold with us at a hundred times its original cost" (cited in Lewis and Reinhold, vol. II, p. 120).

For the luxury trades to flourish, the roads had to be maintained and kept safe, so the Pax Romana was essential. The need for safety was most evident in the silk trade, which prospered when Augustan Rome, Parthian Mesopotamia and Iran, Kushan India, and Han China (see pp. 206–15)—the four empires that spanned the silk routes—were at their peaks. Goods traveled from Luoyang and Xian in China, across the mountains of central Asia, connecting finally at one of the great trading emporia of Begram, Bactra, or Merv. From there, they would continue to the Mediterranean. Silk, light and valuable, was the principal export westward, but lacquerware and bronzes were also carried. A storehouse discovered in 1938 in Begram, which stood at the crossroads of China, India, Persia, and the Mediterranean, revealed some of the principal luxury goods of this intercontinental trade: lacquerwork from China; ivory statues and carvings from India; alabaster, bronze, and glass works from the Mediterranean. Astonishingly, many of the carriers of these treasures seem to have been the steppe nomads of central Asia, the Huns and other "barbarians," who at other times attacked and plundered the empires across which they now traded (see p. 246).

Officially, the Roman upper classes scorned trade as beneath their status. Unofficially, they often entered into contracts with freedmen, their own ex-slaves, to front for their commercial enterprises. Trade was lucrative, and they did not wish to lose the profits. The preferred methods of earning a livelihood were from land ownership, tax collecting for the state, or military conquest, but even generals, like Julius Caesar, profited from the sale of slaves captured in war. Roman traders could be very exploitative. Especially when working in Rome's provinces, they could inspire great hatred. When Mithridates VI, king of Pontus in northern Anatolia, invaded the Roman province of Asia in 88 B.C.E. he encouraged Asian debtors to kill their Roman creditors. Eighty thousand Italian and Italian-Greek businessmen were reported murdered (Grant, p. 184).

In the late second century C.E. internal revolts and external attacks by Gothic peoples brought an end to the Pax Romana and introduced major obstacles to this trade. Roads and markets were no longer secure, and only items that could be consumed locally were worth producing. The production of glass, metals, and textiles in northern Europe, for example, was cut back sharply. Provisioning the city of Rome became more difficult. The population of cities fell, and the cities became less coercive of their suppliers, but as their levels of consumption and the protection they offered declined they also provided less profit and incentive to producers. Trade and productivity faltered. As the Pax Romana began to break down down politically and militarily, trade declined and became more localized.

CULTURAL POLICIES FOR THE EMPIRE

To win and secure allies, Rome not only granted citizenship, codified international law, and built a remarkable physical infrastructure of towns and roads for unifying the empire, it also developed a culture that it brought to the people it conquered. Roman cultural achievements had lagged far behind those of Greece, but as Rome conquered the Greek city-states, it began to absorb the culture of those it conquered. The first prose history of Rome was written in Greek by Fabius Pictor in 202 B.C.E. and the first great historian of Rome was the Greek Polybius (see p. 166). Greek language and literature were adopted by many of the Roman aristocratic classes, as were the architectural, sculptural, and painting traditions of the Greeks. The Romans borrowed from the Greeks as they had earlier borrowed from the Etruscans.

Rome carried this polyglot culture outward in its conquests in Europe and Asia. Its schools in the provinces spread Greek as well as Latin among the tribal Goths and Gauls. Greek was the language of high culture. Latin, however, became the language

The Colosseum, Rome, *c.* 72–80 C.E. Built to house spectacular entertainments, such as mock sea-battles and gladiatorial combats, for audiences of up to 50,000 people, the Colosseum combined Greek decorative traditions with Roman engineering ingenuity, epitomized in the advanced use of concrete as a building material.

Canopus, Hadrian's Villa, Tivoli, *c.* **135** C.E. Rome's wealthy and powerful elites commanded private luxuries beyond the imagination of the average Roman. The Villa of the Emperor Hadrian comprised a series of buildings, gardens, and pools—this one representing a well-known Egyptian canal—laid out on the side of a hill in Tivoli. The complex was designed to bring the more sophisticated pleasures of city life to the country.

of administration. Roman troops constructed amphitheaters, stadiums, and baths wherever they went, the Roman invention of concrete making such constructions feasible. In these settings Roman rulers provided theaters and spectacles modeled on those in Rome.

Rome's sense of superior and inferior, its class consciousness, doubtless encouraged its conquest of other peoples, deemed inferior, and was encouraged, in turn, by the success of those conquests. Rome's greatest epic poem, the *Aeneid*, written by Virgil at the time of the emperor Augustus and singing his praise, exults in this belief in Rome's superiority. At the same time, it upholds the concept of *noblesse oblige*, the duty of the superior to help the inferior:

> . . . Behold the Romans,
> Your very own. These are Iulus' children,
> The race to come. One promise you have heard
> Over and over: here is its fulfillment,
> The son of a god, Augustus Caesar, founder
> Of a new age of gold, in lands where Saturn
> Ruled long ago; he will extend his empire
> Beyond the Indies, beyond the normal measure
> Of years and constellations, where high Atlas
> Turns on his shoulders the star-studded world.
> . . . remember Romans,

> To rule the people under law, to establish
> The way of peace, to battle down the haughty,
> To spare the meek. Our fine arts, these, forever.
> (*Aeneid*, Book VI, 822–31, 893–6; trans. Rolphe Humphries)

Coin showing profiles of the Emperor Nero and the Empress Agrippina, 55 C.E. Successive emperors tried to scapegoat the Christians. Nero blamed them for the fire that struck Rome in 64 C.E., and by the end of the first century membership of the Christian community had been made a crime. However, persecution provided the religion with martyrs and increased group unity. (*British Museum, London*)

Religion in The Empire

Officially, Rome celebrated a religion centralized on the person of the emperor-god. After the deification of Augustus at his death, the official priesthood offered animal sacrifices to him and later to his successors, adding these to the traditional sacrifices to the major pagan gods, especially Jupiter, Juno, and Minerva. Birthdays and death anniversaries of the emperors were celebrated as holidays.

Beyond these rituals, however, Roman religious policies allowed a great deal of flexibility. For the most part, as long as the emperor was venerated and the legitimacy of the state was not questioned, diverse religious practices were allowed to flourish. Mithraism, a religion in which Mithras, a Persian

GREEK AND ROMAN GODS

In the second century B.C.E., Greece was absorbed by the Roman Empire. In the process the Romans adopted and adapted many Greek myths, linking their own gallery of gods to Greek legends and deities.

Greek	Roman	
Aphrodite	Venus	Goddess of love and beauty
Apollo, Phoebus	Apollo, Phoebus	Greek god of sun, god of music, poetry, and prophecy
Ares	Mars	God of war
Artemis	Diana	Virgin huntress, goddess of the moon
Asclepius	Aesculapius	God of medicine
Athena (Pallas)	Minerva	Goddess of wisdom and art
Cronus	Saturn	Father of the supreme god: Zeus or Jupiter
Demeter	Ceres	Goddess of the harvest
Dionysus	Bacchus	God of wine and fertility
Eros	Cupid	God of love
Hades, Pluto	Dis	God of the underworld
Hephaestus	Vulcan	God of fire
Hera	Juno	Queen of heaven, wife of Zeus/Jupiter, goddess of women and marriage
Hermes	Mercury	Messenger of the gods, god of roads, cunning, commerce, wealth, and luck
Hestia	Vesta	Goddess of the hearth
Hymen	Hymen	God of marriage
Irene	Pax	Goddess of peace
Pan	Faunus	God of flocks and shepherds
Persephone	Proserpina	Goddess of corn and the spring, goddess of the dead
Poseidon	Neptune	God of the sea
Zeus	Jupiter, Jove	Supreme ruler of gods and men, king of heaven, and overseer of justice and destiny

sun god, was worshiped, emphasized discipline and loyalty. It was especially popular within the military. Sects that challenged the authority of the empire or the emperor, however, were not tolerated. Rome cracked down on worship of the god Bacchus in 186 B.C.E., fearing that lower class members of this cult might turn against the state. The Roman government also clashed with Judaism and with early Christianity, both of which refused to recognize the emperor as divine and generally believed that state power was inferior to God's laws. Indeed, for the first three centuries of the existence of Christianity, many Romans viewed the new religion as atheistic because Christians did not accept the traditional gods, and as treasonable because it spoke of a kingdom of heaven that was distinct from the Roman earthly empire.

Stoicism

Many thoughtful Romans were attracted to Stoicism, a philosophy founded by the Greek Zeno about 300 B.C.E. Stoicism, named for the *stoa* (covered walkway) in Athens where Zeno taught, began with a cosmic theory of the world as a rational, well-ordered, and coherent system, and argued from it to the moral theory that humans should therefore accept, without joy or grief, free from passion, everything that takes place in this world. A corollary of this view stated that people should treat one another with decency because we are all brothers and sisters.

Cicero (106–43 B.C.E.), one of the most important of Roman orators, commentators, and statesmen, was much influenced by Stoic beliefs, and he wrote: "The private individual ought first, in private relations, to live on fair and equal terms with his fellow citizens, with a spirit neither servile and groveling nor yet domineering" (Cicero, *On Duties*, cited in Lewis and Reinhold, vol. I, p. 273). Almost a century later, Seneca (*c.* 4 B.C.E.–65 C.E.), a disciple of Cicero's philosophy, elaborated: "What is the principal thing? A heart . . . which can go forth to face ill or good dauntless and unembarrassed, paralyzed neither by the tumult of the one nor the glamor of the other" (Seneca, *Natural Questions*, cited in Lewis and Reinhold, vol. II, pp. 165–6). Although Stoics did not advocate the end of slavery, they did propose more humane treatment. Writing on the treatment of slaves, Seneca proposed a kind of Golden Rule: "Treat those below you as you would be treated by those above you" (Seneca, *Moral Epistles*, cited in Lewis and Reinhold, vol. II, p. 180).

Stoicism reached the height of its influence a century later with the selection of Marcus Aurelius Antoninus as emperor (r. 161–180 C.E.). He ruled through two decades of almost continuous warfare, economic upheaval, internal revolts, and plague. Through it all, Marcus Aurelius remained courageous and Stoic. He recorded his thoughts in his *Meditations*, one of the most philosophically reflective works ever written by a man in a position of such power:

> Keep thyself then simple, good, pure, serious, free from affectation, a friend of justice, a worshipper of the gods, and help men. Short is life. The universe is either a confusion, and a mutual involution of things, and a dispersion; or it is unity and order and providence . . . If the [latter], I venerate, and I am firm, and I trust in him who governs. (VI:30, 10)

CHRISTIANITY TRIUMPHANT

By the time of Marcus Aurelius, Christianity was making serious inroads into Roman thought. The Stoic philosophy was not far removed from the Christian concept of an orderly world and concern for social welfare. To these beliefs, Christianity added faith in a god actively intervening in human affairs and, specifically, the doctrines of the birth, life, and miracles of Jesus. This combination of beliefs was very attractive to increasing numbers of Romans, and despite severe persecution of Christians under several emperors—Nero (r. 54–68), Marcus Aurelius (r. 161–180), Maximinus I (r. 235–238), Decius (r. 249–251), Valerian (r. 253–260), and Diocletian (r. 284–305)—over the course of three centuries Christianity became acceptable in Rome and flourished. At first it attracted the poor, who were moved by Jesus' concern for the downtrodden, but later, more powerful classes also joined, attracted by both the organization and message of the Church. The Church promoted greater freedom for women, with a few reaching positions of prominence as deaconesses and abbesses, and it began to incorporate some of the sophistication of Greek philosophy, attracting a new intellectual leadership. (For a fuller discussion of early Christianity and its relationship to the Roman Empire, see p. 317.) By the time of Constantine, one out of five inhabitants of the Roman empire was a Christian.

In 313 C.E. the joint emperors, Constantine and Licinius, issued the Edict of Milan, which recognized Christianity as a valid faith, along with paganism. After 324 C.E., when Constantine ruled alone, he favored Christianity as a religion that had brought miraculous benefits to himself personally and to his empire, and he made it the official state religion. Thereafter Christianity spread freely throughout the conquered lands and peoples of northwestern Europe. The network of roads and towns created to facilitate administration also served to transmit the message of Christianity, and members of the Roman Catholic clergy frequently became the bridge between the practices of Christian Rome and those of the "barbarians." After emerging as the official state religion, Christianity succeeded in having government support for pagan cults terminated in 394 C.E. and even the most widespread of them, Mithraism, with its message of loyalty to the emperor, died out. Christianity emerged triumphant.

CONNECTION: *The rise of Christianity, pp. 308–30*

THE BARBARIANS AND THE FALL OF THE ROMAN EMPIRE

For the Romans, as for the Greeks before them who coined the term, "Barbarian" referred to peoples who spoke unknown foreign languages, were alien, and were usually considered inferior. (It was only later that the word took on connotations of "savage" and "violent.") Rome labeled many of its neighbors on its far-flung borders Barbarians, including the Celts of central Europe, the various Germanic groups of northern and eastern Europe, and the steppe nomads of central Asia. These peoples did not have cities, written languages, formal government structures, established geographical boundaries, codified laws, or specialization of labor. Some, like the Celts and Germans, lived in villages and carried on settled farming. The steppe peoples were nomadic, spending their lives in their saddles riding, herding, and often fighting among themselves in far-off central Asia. Such peoples, the Romans must have thought, could benefit from the civilizing influences of the empire. Perhaps Virgil had this in mind when he was writing the *Aeneid*.

CELTS

The Celts had arrived in central Europe as early as 2000 B.C.E. Burials indicate their respect for horse-riding warriors and the slow development among them of iron technology in weapons and tools. The Hallstatt cemetery in Austria reveals a greater use of iron by the eighth century B.C.E. and shows trade with Greek civilization. A cemetery at La Tène in Switzerland shows continuing Greek and then Roman influences from the fifth century B.C.E. to the first century C.E. In 390 B.C.E. the Celts sacked Rome, and by 200 B.C.E. Celtic groups had covered central Europe and were pushing outward toward Spain, the British Isles, the Balkans, and Anatolia. Learning from Greek and Roman examples, they built **oppida**, fortified towns, throughout their territories. The largest of these covered more than a half square mile (130 hectares). Ultimately, however,

Funerary bronze couch from the Hallstatt prince's tomb at Eberdingen-Hochdorf, near Stuttgart, Germany, *c.* 530 B.C.E. This couch demonstrates the remarkable sophistication of some early Celtic art. It was buried in the tomb of a sixth-century B.C.E. Celtic chieftain in Germany, along with other possessions reflecting the wealth and importance of the dead man. (*Württembergisches Landesmuseum, Stuttgart*)

Maiden Castle, Dorset, England. This Iron Age hillfort was the capital of the Durotriges, a Celtic tribe. Despite its massive bank-and-ditch defenses, Maiden Castle, like many other Celtic strongholds, eventually succumbed to Roman assault in the mid-first century C.E.

the Celtic peoples were conquered by Roman armies. They were killed, or assimilated, or fled to Ireland, Scotland, and Wales, where, to some degree, they continue today to preserve the Celtic language and culture.

GOTHS (GERMANIC PEOPLES)

The Goths—Germanic peoples—settled at first in northern Europe outside the Celtic and Roman strongholds. By 600 B.C.E. they had established small villages, and by about 500 B.C.E. they had begun working with iron. With the discovery of richer iron deposits and contact with Greek and Roman technology, the Goths developed more sophisticated tools and weapons. Much of what we know of this early period comes from burials in bogs in northern Germany and Denmark.

Romans and Germans had faced each other along the Rhine since Julius Caesar had conquered Gaul, and along the Danube from the time Augustus had secured that border. They had skirmished, traded, and at times penetrated each other's territories. In 370 C.E., steppe nomads began

to invade across thousands of miles from central Asia, bringing pressure to bear on the whole of Europe, and in response to this pressure, the Goths began to migrate westward, pushing more vigorously into Roman territories. These massive Germanic invasions upset the rough balance of power that existed between Rome and the Goths, threatening the stability of the empire. Ultimately, the Goths formed their own states within the imperial territories. (A second Germanic emigration occurred about 500 C.E. as a response to floods in the areas of north Germany and Denmark. Among the emigrant Germanic groups, the Saxons sailed across the North Sea and the English Channel to Britain, where they came to form a substantial part of the population.)

HUNS

The Romans called all the steppe peoples who invaded Europe in 370 C.E. "Huns," but the Huns were, specifically, only one of the principal groups of warrior-nomads who inhabited the flat grasslands from European Russia to Manchuria. They virtually lived on their horses, herding cattle, sheep, and horses as well as hunting. They lived in tents and used wagons to transport their goods as they moved from place to place, especially in their annual shift between summer and winter locations.

THE "BARBARIANS": HOW DO WE KNOW?

The steppe peoples had no written language, and their nomadic life style has left few archaeological remains. We know about them in part from burials, especially of the Scythians, a group living in southern Russia and in the Altai Mountains of Mongolia. Mostly we know of them from the accounts of the peoples whose lands they invaded: Romans, Greeks, Chinese, and Indians. All these accounts report them as fierce, mobile, swift, and terrifying warriors on horseback, armed with powerful bows, swords, and lances. In more peaceful times, the Huns carried the goods of the overland silk routes through central Asia.

The Huns were not mentioned in Latin histories until Ammianus Marcellinus (330–395 C.E.) described them, but the Chinese historian Sima

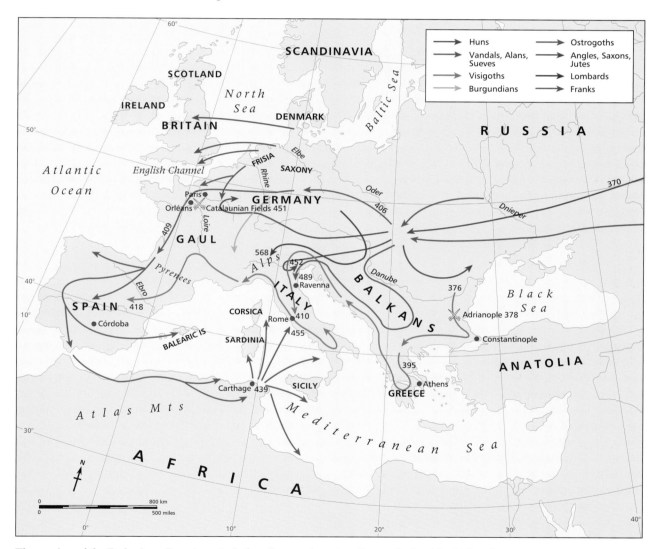

The coming of the Barbarians Rome's control of northern and western Europe declined in the fourth century C.E. as successive waves of Germanic peoples began to migrate and colonize the outer reaches of the empire. When the Huns began to advance westward from central Asia they pushed before them additional Gothic peoples who increased the pressures on Rome. Other Huns were meanwhile pushing south into India and east into China. (For Barbarian invasions into China, see map on p. 208. For invasions into India, see map on p. 244.)

Qian had already depicted them as coarse warriors 500 years earlier:

> During the Ch'ien-yuan reign [140–134 B.C.E.] . . . the Son of Heaven made inquiries among those of the Hsiung-nu [Huns] who had surrendered and been made prisoners, and they all reported that the Hsiung-nu had overcome the king of the Yueh-chih and made a drinking vessel out of his skull. The Yueh-chih had decamped and were hiding somewhere, constantly scheming how to revenge themselves on the Hsiung-nu. (Sima Qian, p. 274)

Further elaboration by Sima delineates several groups of steppe nomads who frequently fought among themselves and sometimes invaded China itself. The Hsiung-nu may not actually have been Huns, but even if not, they were a related group of steppe nomads.

Although they lived in **ordo**, tent encampments, the Huns' living arrangements and political structures were by no means random. Many groups had chiefs and even governments, and their leaders lived in the most elaborate of the tents. When the Huns invaded Europe, Romans observed emissaries of various peoples enter the tent of Attila, their leader, to conduct political negotiations.

At the time Augustus ruled Rome, groups of steppe nomads were engaged in battles that would ultimately help to topple the Han dynasty in China (see p. 214). They were also beginning the attacks on India that would make two of the groups the rulers of north India: the Kushanas, 150–300 C.E., and the Hunas, 500–550 C.E. (see p. 246). The Huns arrived in Europe in 370 C.E., defeating and displacing the Germanic Alans, Ostrogoths, and Visigoths and pushing them in the direction of Rome.

THE DECLINE AND DISMEMBERMENT OF THE ROMAN EMPIRE

Rome proved vulnerable to the invaders, especially because of a plague that wiped out up to a quarter of the population of some areas in 165–180 C.E. During the reign of Marcus Aurelius (r. 161–180 C.E.), the Goths began to invade the Danube basin. Some penetrated into Greece, and across the Alps and into Italy. "Barbarian" invasions continued for hundreds of years, ultimately leading to the break-up of the Roman Empire.

For seven years, 168–175 C.E., Marcus Aurelius fought against the invaders, but he also recognized that they could be assimilated into the empire for mutual benefit. The Germans wanted to establish settlements, so he offered them land within the borders of the empire that they could develop; they were soldiers, so he offered them positions in Rome's armies. Some of the Gothic groups accepted assimilation into the empire. Others wished simply to plunder and withdraw. Still others wished to seize portions of the empire for themselves and settle. Invaders repeatedly penetrated the borders represented by the Danube and the Rhine. In 248 C.E. the Emperor Decius (r. 249–251) defeated an invasion of Goths in the Balkans, but he was himself killed by another Gothic group. The Goths continued into the Balkans and beyond into Asia Minor. They took to ships and attacked Black Sea commerce, in the process cutting off large parts of Rome's grain supplies. Meanwhile, further west, other nomadic groups, Franks and Vandals, swept across the Rhine into Gaul, Spain, and as far south as north Africa.

The empire struck back. The Emperor Gallienus (r. 253–268 C.E.) created a mobile cavalry, and he moved the imperial military headquarters from Rome to Milan in the north, better to confront invaders into Italy. In a series of battles, Roman armies preserved Italy for the empire. Gallienus died in a plague and was succeeded as emperor by Aurelian (r. 270–275), an even more brilliant and energetic general. In a series of battles, Aurelian protected Rome's western and northern borders, although he abandoned Dacia and pulled back to the Danube.

In the east, too, Rome defeated revolts. The greatest challenge came as the new, expansive Sassanian dynasty in Persia confronted Rome in Armenia and Syria. In 260 C.E. the Roman Emperor Valerian (r. 253–260 C.E.) was captured and held prisoner for the rest of his life. Nevertheless, Rome recaptured its eastern areas, partly because the Sassanians treated the inhabitants of these lands so badly that they revolted. Zenobia, the widow of the leader of semi-independent Palmyra, declared the independence of Syria and Mesopotamia, and annexed Egypt. Her revolt lasted only a few years, and in 273 C.E. Aurelian defeated her and brought her back to Rome in chains.

Continuing warfare forced the decentralization of Rome's power from the capital to distant provincial battlefields, and from civilian control by the Senate in Rome to generals in the field. Soldiers in Gaul, Britain, and Spain declared their general Postumus (r. 259–268 C.E.) the independent emper-

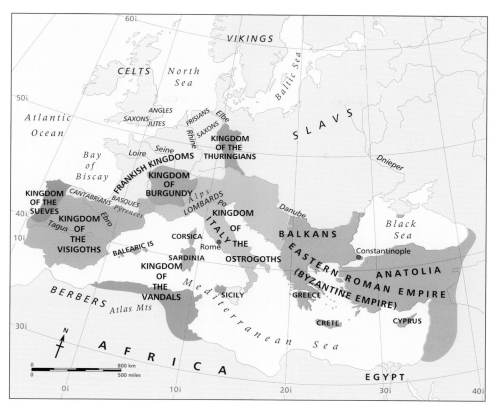

Rome's successors Following the sack of Rome by the Ostrogoths in 455 C.E., a new map of Europe emerged. The Roman power base had shifted east to Constantinople, forming the Byzantine Empire. The steppe invaders, keen to emulate the Romans, had created new kingdoms in Italy, Africa, and Iberia, while Germanic peoples were struggling to create a new power balance in the north.

or of those regions, although their mutiny was defeated by Aurelian in 274 C.E. Militarily, the empire had staged an extraordinary comeback. Thinking that an aura of pomp and majesty would be helpful, the Emperor Diocletian (r. 284–305 C.E.) claimed for himself a sanctity and splendor never before seen in Rome. The expense of his battles and the splendor of his court bankrupted the empire and brought misery to its inhabitants. To cope with the attacks on far distant borders, emperors established subsidiary capitals, and in 330 C.E. Constantine established Constantinople as a secondary capital for ruling the east. After 395 C.E., one emperor in Rome and another in Constantinople formally divided the empire, West and East.

"Barbarian" tribes continued to breach the imperial borders and defenses. Valentinian I (r. 364–375) was the last emperor capable of driving them back effectively. From this time on, driven forward by the invasion of the Huns, the Germans pushed against Roman defenses in increasing numbers. In 378 C.E. Valentinian's brother, the eastern Emperor Valens (r. 364–378), lost two-thirds of the

eastern armies—and his life—in battle against the Visigoths at Adrianople. Valens' successor, Theodosius I (r. 379–395 C.E.), who ruled from Constantinople, settled Visigoths within the empire, requiring them to provide soldiers and farmers for the imperial armies and lands. This "federate" status for Goths and other "barbarians" became a common pattern, with Goths, Franks, Alans, and Vandals settling within the imperial borders in increasing numbers. The empire was Roman in name, but was mixed in terms of population, armies, and leadership.

Alaric, the Visigoth (c. 370–410 C.E.), invaded Italy in 401, and in response the Roman Emperor Honorius (r. 395–423 C.E.) removed the capital to Ravenna, a more defensible city on the east coast of Italy. Alaric invaded Italy again in 407, and in 410 he sacked Rome. At the end of 406, combined armies of Goths, Vandals, Suevi, Alans, and Burgundians crossed the Rhine into Gaul and moved into Spain. At first they sacked, looted, and burned, but within a few years they were establishing their own settlements and local kingdoms, displacing or merging with Roman landlords. The Vandal King Geiseric (r. 428–477 C.E.) crossed into north Africa, seizing Carthage and its agriculturally rich hinterlands. Gaining control of a fleet, he challenged Roman control of the Mediterranean. The Romans could not defeat him.

The Huns were building up their own imperial confederacy in central Europe. Their most powerful leader, Attila, who commanded them from 434 to 453 C.E., ruled from the Baltic to the Danube. He invaded Italy in 451 C.E., threatening Rome and withdrawing only on the intervention of Pope Leo I. After Attila's death in 453 C.E., his armies dissolved and never again regained their power.

In 476 C.E., the German general Odoacer deposed the last Roman Emperor in the West, Romulus Augustulus, who was never replaced. Odoacer became the first barbarian king of Italy (r. 476–493), and thus the five-centuries-old Roman Empire came to an end. Some historians argue that the empire lived on in Constantinople, the eastern capital, but the Greek culture of this city, its rule over only the eastern Mediterranean region, and its separation from Rome and the Western Empire made it a very different cultural and political center. By about 600 C.E. the Byzantine Empire, with a political system based on Constantinople, is usually seen as an independent entity rather than merely the continuation of Rome in the east.

In the west, the Roman imperial system continued to function for at least a further two more centuries, although its leadership and its legions were in the hands of Germans and other invading groups. But it is hard to call it either an "empire" when there was no emperor and no allegiance to a central government, or "Roman" when it was led by Germans and Goths and when its capital was no longer in Rome.

CAUSES OF THE DECLINE AND FALL

Structural problems had been visible in the Roman Empire even at the height of its power. Internally, the conflict between the elite and the masses continued, under different names, throughout the history of the Republic and the empire. The cost of sustaining the empire by military force overtaxed the imperial economy, impoverishing the middle classes and the remaining agricultural classes. The yeoman-farmer class, the class that had first built up the Roman republic, was ruined, and although the rich continued to live off their estates in Italy and elsewhere, and the senatorial classes continued to do well, popular support for the imperial ideal had disappeared. In earlier times, an ever-expanding frontier had brought new economic resources to support the empire, but expansion had come to an end in the second century. The empire was overextended.

In addition, the quality of the empire depended on the quality of its emperors, but Rome had no viable system of succession. In the century between Marcus Aurelius and Diocletian, more than eighty men assumed command as emperor, and many of these were assassinated. In the third century C.E., as fighting in the border regions decentralized the empire, competing armies fought to have their generals selected as emperor. The results were devastating to the economy, administration, and morale of the empire.

Rome could no longer win its frontier battles against invaders, but neither could it continue to assimilate Goths and others into its armies and settlements as subordinates. The Roman armies and vast territories of the empire had become heavily Germanic, and when whole tribes of Goths began to serve together in single units under Gothic commanders, questions of the army's loyalty to the empire arose. Romans and Germans saw each other as "other," alien, and the Romans even forbade intermarriage. As Germanic peoples began to take over leading positions, the empire effectively ceased to be Roman.

The rise of Christianity as the principal religion and philosophy of the empire (see pp. 317–18) also suggested that the Roman desire for earthly political power was evaporating. At first, Christianity was accepted by the poor, who used it as a means of expressing their disaffection from the power of the Caesars. Later, however, when Constantine declared Christianity to be a legal state religion in 313 and *the* official state religion in 324, more mainstream Romans converted. Christianity offered an alternative focus for human energy. The eighteenth-century English historian Edward Gibbon argued in *The History of the Decline and Fall of the Roman Empire* that Christianity turned people against this-worldly attractions and power. Later historians regard this as an overstatement, but Christianity did preach that one's eternal salvation was more important than fighting for the empire. It siphoned energy toward more spiritual and humanitarian goals, and toward competition with other religious groups.

More recently, scholars have suggested that

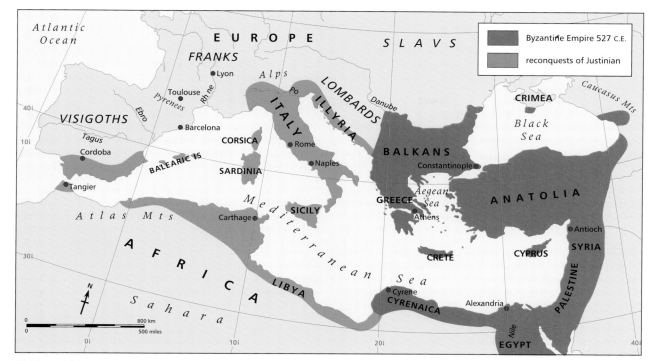

The Byzantine Empire Despite the erosion of Roman power in western Europe by 457 C.E., the East Roman or Byzantine Empire survived with varying fortunes for another thousand years—albeit Greek-speaking and Orthodox Christian—until 1453. Centered on Constantinople, its heartland straddled the crossroads between Europe and Asia. Only briefly, under Justinian (483–565), did it recover control of the western Mediterranean.

climatic change reduced agricultural productivity and the economy. Still others have noted that severe epidemics killed up to a quarter of the population in some imperial centers between 165 and 180 C.E. and again between 251 and 266 C.E. These diseases sapped the empire of manpower and production and left it more open to attack. These biological and ecological arguments complement the more traditional explanations of Rome's fall: overextension; financial and military exhaustion; a failure of leadership; the rise of new, alternative value systems; and the infiltration of Germanic peoples, which fragmented the empire into new, separate, independent states that no longer wished to be subordinated to Rome.

CONNECTION: *The reign of Charlemagne (771–814), pp. 329–30*

THE PERSISTENCE OF EMPIRE IN THE EAST

On May 11, 330, the Emperor Constantine inaugurated the "New Rome which is Constantinople," to share with Rome, as co-capital, the administration of his huge empire. From its inception three elements characterized the new city: Greek language and culture; Roman law and administration; and Christian faith and organization. While the western half of the empire survived only another century and a half, the east continued on its own for another thousand years until 1453 C.E., becoming an empire of its own, called Byzantium after the name of the Greek city around which Constantinople was built.

Like the west, the east had to withstand military attack. Germanic tribes crossed the Danube, but found Constantinople impregnable, defended behind huge walls built by the emperor Theodosius II (r. 408–450). The Byzantine emperor Justinian (r. 527–565) even recaptured many of the western regions including north Africa, southern Spain, Sicily, Italy, and even Rome itself, but the costs in wealth and manpower crippled his empire. After his death most of these western conquests were lost while the Persians constantly warred with the Byzantines in the east.

In religious issues, too, Justinian seemed to over-reach. When many Syrian and Egyptian Christians declared themselves **Monophysites**, believers that Jesus' nature was only divine, not human, Justinian oppressed them in the name of religious conformity and imperial authority. In doing so, he created antagonisms that smoldered for centuries and contributed to the loss of these provinces to the Muslims in the seventh century C.E.

Justinian's legal, administrative, and architectural initiatives produced more lasting results. He had the Roman system of Civil Law codified in four great works known collectively as the Justinian Code, thus helping to perpetuate an administration of great competence. In time, the Code became the basis for much of modern European law. He adorned Constantinople with numerous new buildings, crowned by the Church of Hagia Sophia, the Church of Holy Wisdom. Other churches, forts, and public works were built throughout the empire.

The emperor Heraclius (r. 610–641) defeated the Persian empire, but he and his successors could not hold back the troops which burst out of Arabia after 632 inspired with the religious zeal of newborn Islam (Chapter 11). The Arabs captured much of the land of the Byzantine empire, including Syria and Egypt with their disaffected Monophysites (see p. 339). For centuries, the Christian Byzantine empire based in the Balkans and Asia Minor would confront Islam religiously and militarily. The Byzantine empire organized its armies into **themes**, administrative districts and army units in which peasants were given farms in payment for their military service. These themes and the impregnable fortifications of Constantinople were the empire's bulwark in confronting Arab armies.

The **iconoclastic** controversy, the bitter battle over the use of images, or **icons**, in Christian worship (see Spotlight, pp. 324–5), beginning in 726, further demonstrated the importance of Christian doctrine in the life of the Byzantine empire, and the continuing strain in its political-religious relationship with the Roman church. Indeed the great leaders of the Byzantine empire were known for both their military prowess and their religious leadership. Basil I (r. 867–886) not only kept control of the

Hagia Sophia, Constantinople, 532–7. The Hagia Sophia (Church of the Holy Wisdom), built under the Emperor Justinian, is an imposing visual symbol of the power of the Eastern Empire. The minarets, or pointed towers at the four corners, were added in the fifteenth century when the Ottomans captured Constantinople and the church was converted into a mosque.

Balkans and crushed the Bulgar invaders, and initiated a dynasty which reconquered Crete, Syria, southern Italy, and much of Palestine from the Arabs, but he also healed the religious rift with Rome for a time.

Ultimately, beginning in the late eleventh century C.E., the Byzantine empire was brought down by a combination of religious and political antagonisms. Battered from the north by invading Normans and Slavs, the Byzantines turned to the pope in Rome for help against the Islamic Seljuq Turks from the east who had overrun Asia Minor (Chapters 11 and 14). In response, the pope preached the crusades, but in 1204 crusaders—against the Pope's orders—conquered and sacked Constantinople. The Byzantines recovered the city in 1261 but their empire was irreparably weakened, and in 1453 finally succumbed to the Turks.

How had the Byzantine empire managed to survive for 1000 years after Rome had fallen? The administrative system of the Byzantines deserved much of the credit, as Yale University Professor Deno John Geanakoplos has explained:

> Consisting of a group of highly educated officials trained primarily at the university or, rather "higher school" of Constantinople, the civil service was organized into a hierarchical system of considerable complexity even by today's standards. Taxes were collected regularly, justice was administered, armies were raised and put into the field, and the functions of the state in general were very adequately carried out. It may be said that in its period of greatest power (330–c. 1050) the Byzantine government, despite all its faults (excessive love of pomp and protocol, bureaucratic tendencies, and frequent venality), functioned more effectively, and for a longer period, than virtually any other political organism in history. (Geanakoplos, p. 3.)

The ruling classes were never as isolated and alienated from the common people as in the west. The eastern empire was also less geographically overextended. Even when its more distant territories were lost, it could defend its heartland. Its sources of wealth and military manpower were in Thrace and Anatolia, geographically close to its center of political power in Constantinople, which remained an impregnable fortress for almost 1000 years. In these settled lands, the Byzantine empire had an older and stronger urban tradition than the west, and its cities remained viable centers of commerce long after most cities in the west had all but disappeared. The fiercest of the invading Gothic tribes turned away from these more settled regions and marched westward toward the more open agricultural lands of the Roman empire. In all these ways, the east was different from the west and was able to survive as an imperial state for another thousand years.

THE ROMAN EMPIRE: WHAT DIFFERENCE DOES IT MAKE?

The Roman Empire laid foundations that have lasted until today in language, law, urban and regional development, and religious organization. Rome's language, Latin, was the official language of the empire, and it persisted as one of the two languages (with Greek) known by all educated Europeans until the seventeenth century, continuing as the language of ritual prayer for the Roman Catholic Church until the mid-twentieth century. Latin formed the base of the Romance languages (Italian, Spanish, Catalan, Portuguese, French, and Romanian) and contributed substantially to English.

Roman law, which developed and was codified over several centuries, inspired the transition to modern, codified law in much of Europe, including the Napoleonic Codes, which the French general and emperor institutionalized wherever he ruled in early nineteenth-century Europe (see Chapter 15). The hundreds of towns that Rome founded and developed as administrative and military centers throughout the empire provided the nuclei around which the urban structure of much of modern Europe and northern Africa developed. The 50,000 miles (80,000 kilometers) of well-paved roads, which connected the cities of the empire, laid the foundation for much of modern Europe's land transportation patterns.

Even after its decline and fall c. 476 C.E. the Roman Empire continued to shape the vision and the administration of hundreds of millions of people. In 330 C.E. the Emperor Constantine inaugurated Constantinople as an eastern, sister capital of the Roman Empire, and that city continued to rule much of the eastern Mediterranean for another thousand years, until 1453 C.E. (see p. 317). Meanwhile in western Europe, during that millennium, the Roman Catholic Church adapted the

Roman imperial administrative organization for its own uses. Much of this organization persists to the present. When the emperor Constantine gave Christianity legal status throughout the empire, and chose it as his own religion, he opened the gates for its unprecedented growth (see p. 305). The Holy Roman Empire, which ruled much of central Europe for some 900 years from 800 C.E., also styled itself a successor to Rome, although the comparison was somewhat remote (see pp. 328–30).

Images of the Roman Empire remain powerful even to our own times. The British Empire, which girdled the globe from the eighteenth to the mid-twentieth centuries, proudly described itself as recreating and extending the imperial military power, administration, legal system, and technological superiority that had characterized Rome. Like the early Romans, the British claimed to have stumbled into their imperial possessions rather than to have actively pursued them (see Chapter 16).

BIBLIOGRAPHY

Andrea, Alfred and James H. Overfield. *The Human Record* (Boston: Houghton Mifflin Co., 3rd ed., 1998).

Antoninus, Marcus Aurelius. *Meditations*, trans. H. G. Long in Whitney J. Oates, ed., *The Stoic and Epicurean Philosophers* (New York: Modern Library, 1940).

Aries, Philippe and Georges Duby, eds. *A History of Private Life: I: From Pagan Rome to Byzantium* (Cambridge: Harvard University Press, 1987).

Boardman, John, Jasper Griffin, and Oswyn Murray, eds. *The Oxford History of the Classical World* (New York: Oxford University Press, 1986).

Brown, Peter. *The Rise of Western Christendom* (Malden, MA: Blackwell, 1996).

Carcopino, Jerome. *Daily Life in Ancient Rome* (New Haven: Yale University Press, 1940).

Clark, Gillian. *Women in Late Antiquity: Pagan and Christian Life Styles* (Oxford: Oxford University Press, 1993).

Cornell, Tim and John Matthews. *Atlas of the Roman World* (New York: Facts on File, 1983).

Cotterell, Arthur, ed. *The Penguin Encyclopedia of Ancient Civilizations* (London: Penguin Books, 1980).

Fantham, Elaine, *et al. Women in the Classical World* (New York: Oxford University Press, 1994).

Finley, M.I., ed. *The Portable Greek Historians* (New York: Viking Press, 1959).

Frank, Andre Gunder and Barry K. Gillis, eds. *The World System: Five Hundred Years or Five Thousand* (New York: Routledge, 1993).

Geanakoplos, Deno John. *Byzantium: Church, Society, and Civilization Seen Through Contemporary Eyes* (Chicago: University of Chicago Press, 1984).

Gibbon, Edward. *The History of the Decline and Fall of the Roman Empire*, abridged by D.M. Low in 3 vols. (New York: Washington Square Press, 1962).

Grant, Michael. *History of Rome* (New York: Scribner's, 1978).

Hunt, Lynn, *et al. The Challenge of the West* (Lexington, MA: D.C. Heath, 1995).

Jones, A.H.M. *Augustus* (New York: W.W. Norton & Co., 1970).

Lewis, Naphtali and Meyer Reinhold. eds. *Roman Civilization: Selected Readings:* Vol I: *The Republic and the Augustan Age*; Vol II: *The Empire* (New York: Columbia University Press, 1990).

Luttwak, Edward N. *The Grand Strategy of the Roman Empire* (Baltimore: Johns Hopkins University Press, 1976).

McNeill, William. *Plagues and Peoples* (Garden City, NY: Anchor Books, 1976).

Mirsky, Jeannette, ed. *The Great Chinese Travellers* (Chicago: University of Chicago Press, 1964).

Mumford, Lewis. *The City in History* (New York: Harcourt, Brace, and World, 1961).

Pantel, Pauline Schmitt, ed. *A History of Women:* Vol I: *From Ancient Goddesses to Christian Saints* (Cambridge: Harvard University Press, 1992).

Parker, Geoffrey, ed. *The (London) Times Atlas of World History* (London: Times Books, 4th ed. 1993).

Past Worlds: The (London) Times Atlas of Archaeology (Maplewood, NJ: Hammond, 1988).

Periplus of the Erythraean Sea, trans. and ed. G.W.B. Huntingford (London: Hakluyt Society, 1980).

Ramage, Nancy and Andrew Ramage. *Roman Art: Romulus to Constantine* (Englewood Cliffs: Prentice Hall, 1991).

Runciman, Steven. *Byzantine Civilization* (Cleveland: World Publishing Co., 1933).

Sima Qian. *Records of the Historian: Chapters from the Shih Chi of Ssu-ma Ch'ien*, trans. Burton Watson (New York: Columbia University Press, 1969).

Time-Life Books. *Time Frame 400 BC–AD 200: Empires Ascendant* (Alexandria, VA: Time-Life Books, 1988).

Time-Life Books. *Time Frame AD 200–600: Empires Besieged* (Alexandria, VA: Time-Life Books, 1988).

Virgil. *Aeneid*, trans. Rolphe Humphries (New York: Charles Scribner's Sons, 1951).

CHINA

"The August Emperor gave a vigorous display of his authority, and his virtue brought together all the states, and for the first time brought unity and supreme peace."

QIN SHI HUANGDI

FRACTURE AND UNIFICATION: THE QIN, HAN, SUI, AND TANG DYNASTIES

When we last discussed the north China plain in Chapter 4, the Zhou dynasty, 1100–256 B.C.E., was in decline. As the dynasty began to weaken, the powerful, independent states of the region fought among themselves so constantly that China's historians have named the years between 481 and 221 B.C.E. the Warring States period. In 221 B.C.E., after hundreds of years of warfare, the Qin dynasty defeated the others, unifying north China and creating the first Chinese Empire.

This chapter will consider the Chinese Empire during its first 1100 years, from 221 B.C.E. to 907 C.E. The Qin dynasty ended in 206 B.C.E., only four years after the death of its founder. Then the Han dynasty ruled for four centuries, from 202 B.C.E. to 2 C.E. and from 26 to 220 C.E., with a brief twenty-four-year **interregnum** (2–26 C.E.), during which an outsider reigned. For the next three and a half centuries, 220–589 C.E., authority was divided and fractured. Finally China was reunified under another shortlived dynasty, the Sui (581–618), and was ruled for three centuries by the illustrious, expansive Tang dynasty (618–907). During this time China created political and cultural forms that would last for another thousand years, and, as we shall see in Chapter 20, perhaps even to the present.

We begin with a consideration of the sources—How Do We Know? We then examine the key accomplishments under China's imperial rulers—the conquest, consolidation, and confirmation of the empire—and the expansion of China to include "outer China," the distant, conquered provinces inhabited by people not ethnically Chinese. In addition, we outline relationships with peoples to the south and southwest, who were ultimately incorporated into China, and with Korea and Japan, whose cultures were influenced profoundly by China. We close by comparing and contrasting the Chinese Empire with that of Rome.

THE CHINESE EMPIRE: HOW DO WE KNOW?

Our main historical sources for the Shang period are artifacts—such as oracle bones used for divination—uncovered by archaeological excavations. For the succeeding Zhou period, a series of written texts is available. Five of these were later canonized by China's most central political and moral philosopher, Confucius (551–479 B.C.E.), and by his disciples, as especially fine examples of the philosopher's own thought and his concern for history, music, the arts, and rituals:

- the *Book of Documents*, a collection of various statements of early kings and their ministers;

- the *Book of Changes*, the *I Ching*, which details methods of predicting the future through casting sticks;

- the *Book of Songs*, which contains 305 poems, about half of which relate to the everyday lives of ordinary people, half to issues of court politics and rituals;

- the *Spring and Autumn Annals*, which contains brief chronologies from Lu, Confucius' home state;

- *Rites and Rituals* (three texts, grouped together as one), which combines both philosophies and rituals of the court.

In addition to these five, Confucius' own teachings were recorded by his disciples in *The Analects*. A large body of interpretation and commentary grew up around each of these texts.

Other philosophers are also represented in collections from the late Zhou period. **Daoism**, a philosophy of spontaneity in the face of nature and the cosmos, produced two major works: the *Classic of the Way and Its Power*, ascribed to Laozi (Lao-tzu), a sixth-century mystical philosopher, but more probably composed in the third century B.C.E.; and the *Zhuangzi*, written by the philosopher Zhuang Zhou at about the same time. **Legalism**, a philosophy of government characterized by strict laws and strict enforcement, was taught in treatises by Han Feizi (Han-Fei-tzu; d. 233 B.C.E.). There were also several historical texts, often exaggerated and even fabricated, such as the *Intrigues of the Warring States*, from the third century B.C.E. Books of etiquette and ritual reveal the hierarchical and mannered style of proceedings of the state governments. Many of these texts not only cast light on earlier periods but also illuminate the thought and action of the Han dynasty and beyond.

Recording the past was valued both for itself and for the moral principles it was believed to teach. China therefore prepared and transmitted

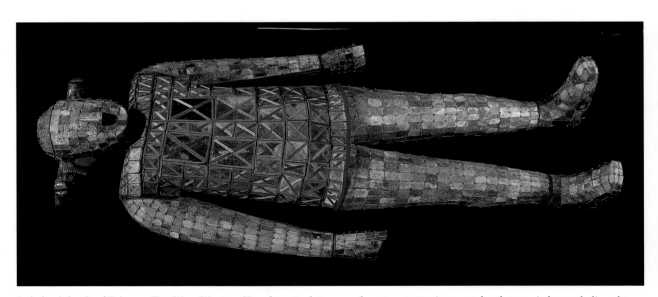

Jade burial suit of Princess Tou Wan, Western Han dynasty, late second century B.C.E. As a very hard stone, jade was believed to be an effective preservative. When the Princess Tou Wan, daughter-in-law of the Emperor Jingdi, died, a burial suit was created for her using 2160 pieces of jade tied together with gold wire.

the most fully and continuously documented history of any ancient empire. Building on this legacy of historical literature, the Han emperor Wudi (r. 141–87 B.C.E.), created a new official position, the Grand Historian of the Han court, with the responsibility of preparing a comprehensive history of the entire Chinese past. The first to hold the post was Sima Tan (d. 110 B.C.E.). He was succeeded by his son Sima Qian (145–85 B.C.E.), one of the greatest historians in world history (see Profile, p. 198). The father began and the son completed the *Shi Qi* or *Records of the Historian*. In 130 chapters it recounted the history of the people of China from mythological times to the first century B.C.E. Sima Qian divided the materials into five sections, which became the pattern for future historians as well. The sections were: "Basic Annals" of the court; "Chronologies" of important events; "Treatises" on such diverse special topics as rites, music, calendar, astronomy, major canals, and economics; "Hereditary Houses" or accounts of major feudal families; and "Memoirs," primarily biographical accounts of famous people in China, including a number of foreigners. In 98 B.C.E., Sima Qian

CHINA–FROM QIN TO TANG

DATE	POLITICAL	RELIGION AND CULTURE	SOCIAL DEVELOPMENT
250 B.C.E.	• Zhou dynasty ends (256) • Qin Shi Huangdi initiates Qin dynasty (221–206) • Revolts against Qin (207)	• Han Feizi (d. 233) • Daoism • Legalism • Great Wall	
200 B.C.E.	• Liu Bang (202–195) first emperor of Han dynasty		
150 B.C.E.	• Han Wudi (141–87)	• Confucian Academy established (124)	• Travels of Zhang Qian
100 B.C.E.	• Reign of usurper Wang Mang (9–23 C.E.)	• Sima Qian (145–85) • Invention of paper	
50 C.E.		• First mention of Buddhism in China	
200 C.E.	• Han dynasty ends (220) • Age of Disunity (221–331) • Three Kingdoms (220–280)		
300 C.E.	• Jin dynasty (265–316) • Northern Wei dynasty (386–534)	• Buddhism expands • Gu Kaizhi (334–406)	
600 C.E.	• Sui dynasty (581–618) • Tang dynasty (618–907)	• Invention of block printing • Grand canal completed (610) • Buddhist cave art	• Boundaries of empire extended to Mongolia, Turkestan, Afghanistan, Pakistan, and Iran • Tang briefly held North Korea and Vietnam
650 C.E.	• Empress Wu (684–705)		• First pharmacopoeia
700 C.E.	• Battle of Talas River (751) • An Lushan rebellion (755–63)	• Wang Wei (701–62) • Li Bai (701–61) • Du Fu (712–70) • Porcelain produced	
800 C.E.		• Repression of Buddhism	
900 C.E.	• Collapse of Tang, leading to disunity (907–960) • Song dynasty (960–1279)		

PROFILE
Sima Qian
COURT HISTORIAN

Sima Tan (d. 110 B.C.E.) and his son Sima Qian (145-85 B.C.E.) both earned the title of Grand Historian to the Han Emperor Wudi. The position was hereditary. Sima Tan reported to his son "Our forbears were Grand Historians of the Zhou house," but in those days they were "in charge of astronomical matters" and dynastic chronologies. Now father and son transformed the task to one of evaluating the quality of governments and rulers. They created the art of Chinese history as a commentary on politics and ethics.

At the very end of his great work, *Shi Qi*, 130 chapters recounting the history of China from mythological times almost to his own, Sima Qian includes an autobiographical sketch:

> Qian was born at Longmen. He ploughed and kept flocks on the sunny slopes of the mountains near the Yellow River. By the age of ten he was reading aloud the ancient writings. At twenty he journeyed south to the Yangtze and Huai rivers, ascended Kuaiji to search for the cave of Yu, espied Jiuyi, went by water down to Yun and Xiang, journeyed north and crossed the Wen and Si to investigate the traditions in the cities of Qi and Lu, and observed the customs handed down by Master Kong [Confucius], and took part in the archery competition held at Mount Yi in Cou. He suffered distress in Po, Xie, and Pengcheng, and returned home via Liang and Chu. Afterwards Qian served as a palace gentleman, and received orders to be sent on the western expedition to the south of Ba and Shu. Having gone south and captured Qiong, Ze, and Kunming, they returned and made their report on the mission. (Dawson translation, p. xix.)

So his training included farming, literature, travel, adventure, anthropological research, archery, court service, and warfare. If historians improve with their own experience of life, since it enables them to understand more fully the lives of the people they study, then Sima Qian was off to a good start. His father charged him with the historian's task, to be performed at extraordinary standards of excellence:

> When I die, you are bound to become the Grand Historian; and having become Grand Historian, do not forget what I intended to argue and put down in writing. Moreover, filial piety starts in the service of parents, is next to be found in the service of rulers, and finally in the establishment of one's own character. For the most important aspect of filial piety is for your name to be spread abroad in later generations in order to bring glory to your father and mother. (Dawson translation, xix-xx.)

The highlight of Sima Qian's historical writing is its emphasis on biography, a traditional Chinese literary form that he developed into a vehicle for commenting on the political and ethical policies of the state not only in the past but also in his own time. His judgments could be fierce and they sometimes got him into trouble. Personally, his support for his friend General Li Ling at a time when the general was in great disfavor in court led to Sima Qian's castration (see opposite). Later the Han Emperor Wudi was so angered by Sima Qian's account of his father, the Emperor Jingdi, that he had this chapter removed. Sima Qian included in the *Shi Qi* speeches from the Warring States period advocating strategies for one state to gain power over another. The Han government chose to suppress this information as well and "for over a century access to the copy in the imperial library was extremely difficult, as the work and its author were considered unorthodox if not dangerous" (Nienhauser, p. xii). Later, however, imperial feelings apparently mellowed and Sima Qian won the reputation of greatest master of the early Chinese historical tradition.

defended a military leader out of favor with the emperor and the court. As a punishment, he had to choose between execution and castration. He chose castration in order to complete his work:

> It is because I regretted that it had not been completed that I submitted to the extreme penalty without rancor. When I have truly completed this work, I shall deposit it in some safe place. If it may be handed down to men who will appreciate it and penetrate to the villages and great cities, then though I should suffer a thousand mutilations, what regret would I have? (deBary (1999), p. 372)

Sima Qian completed his accounts up to *c.* 100 B.C.E. Ban Biao (3–54 C.E.) added tens of chapters of "Supplementary Chronicles," and his son, Ban Gu (32–92 C.E.), wrote the *Han Shu*, or "History of the Han Dynasty," to 22 C.E. Ban Gu established the tradition of compiling a history of each dynasty, a form continued in the *Hou-Han shu* or "History of the Later Han," and enduring into the twentieth century. In addition, essays, stories, and documents preserved on wood or carved in stone give further evidence of the history of the Han. Similar official dynastic histories and private materials provide our sources for the Era of Division and the Sui and Tang dynasties. For these periods also, there are far more remains of poetry, literature, and art, as well. Later, Sima Guang (1019–86 C.E.) wrote a monumental general history of China from earliest times to his own day, based largely on all these earlier documents and including many that have subsequently been lost.

Because the official histories carry their own biases and focus almost entirely on issues of the central government and its court, unofficial materials from the provinces are especially useful in giving additional viewpoints. Grave sites and tombs yield documents, inscriptions, and engravings, and these often include relief sculptures of the activities of the deceased during his or her life. The burial goods represent in miniature the deceased's house, tools, carriages, boats, farms, and equipment. They often included terra cotta figures or painted frescoes of colleagues from life: entertainers, musicians, servants, and maids.

Archaeologists have uncovered important additional written sources. A cache of documents sealed in a cave in Dunhuang, on the northwest edge of China proper, was discovered by the British archaeologist Aurel Stein in his expeditions in central Asia in 1900–15. They included private and official business documents, contracts, textbooks for students in various fields, instruction in moral education, stories and poems. The cave housed a Buddhist monastery, and many of the documents highlight the Buddhist influence on China at the time. Subsequent Sino-Swedish expeditions in 1927–34 uncovered additional fragments, covering the period 100 B.C.E.–100 C.E. Since the 1960s archaeological sites in central China have continued to yield additional materials.

THE QIN DYNASTY: WHAT DO WE KNOW?

The map on page 208 charts the expansion of the Qin dynasty from its geopolitical base around the confluence of the Yellow and Wei rivers to its control of the whole of north China and a segment of the south. The Qin conquest ended centuries of fighting among the warring dynasties of north China that began with the decline of the Zhou dynasty and lasted through the period of the Warring States, 481–221 B.C.E. The Qin defeated other regional states over the course of perhaps a century, until by 221 B.C.E. they could rightfully claim to have established an empire, the first in China's history and one that has lasted (almost) to the present.

MILITARY POWER AND MOBILIZATION

Armed force was fundamental in the Qin's conquest. Poems from the *Book of Songs*, dating from the early years of the Zhou dynasty, suggest the ubiquity of warfare in early China:

> Which plant is not yellow?
> Which day don't we march?
> Which man does not go
> To bring peace to the four quarters?
>
> Which plant is not brown?
> Which man is not sad?
> Have pity on us soldiers,
> Treated as though we were not men!
>
> We are neither rhinos nor tigers,
> Yet are led through the wilds.
> Have pity on us soldiers,
> Never resting morn or night.

Terra cotta army from the tomb of Qin Shi Huangdi, Qin dynasty, 210 B.C.E. The vastness of the terra cotta army—it comprised 7000 "soldiers"—buried near the tomb of the First Emperor of Qin and the care with which each life-sized figure was molded suggest at once the enormous power of the Qin army and the emperor's concern with the afterlife.

A thick-furred fox
Scurries though the dark grass.
Our loaded carts
Proceed along the Zhou road.   (Ebrey, p. 13)

The Qin not only conquered north China, they also defeated the Xiongnu, or border tribes to the north and west of China proper. They gained authority over northern Korea, and defeated some of the Yue tribes in the south. The first Qin emperor was Qin Shi Huangdi, "the first august emperor of the Qin." (Compare the title of "Caesar Augustus" of Rome.) In 1974 archaeologists digging near his mausoleum discovered a ceramic army of 7000 life-sized soldiers and horses, arranged in military formation and armed with bronze weapons, spears, longbows, and crossbows (a Chinese invention). In 1976, a second excavation uncovered an additional 1400 chariots and cavalrymen in four military units. The next year a much smaller pit was discovered, holding what appeared to be a terra cotta officer corps. These thousands of figures were not mass produced. Each figure was modeled and painted separately, even down to its elaborate hairstyle, which symbolized its specific military office. The figures apparently represented the elite of the imperial troops, and were fashioned to accompany the emperor to his own tomb and afterlife.

The Qin mobilized tens of thousands of men also for enormous public works projects. After conquering the other states of north China they completed the remaining gaps in the 1500-mile (2400-kilometer) Great Wall of China in seven years with a work force of one million laborers. This Wall was to keep the Xiongnu "barbarians" of the north out of China proper and, with its 40-foot (15-meter) high watch towers constructed every few hundred yards, to serve as a first warning in case of attempted invasion. The first emperor conscripted 700,000 laborers to construct his palace, a complex large enough to hold 40,000 people.

ECONOMIC POWER

Some of the enormous public works projects of the Qin were undertaken to increase the economic productivity of the empire. During the centuries of their rise to power, they had built canals and river transport systems in both the Wei River system in the north and the Min River system in Sichuan. In Sichuan they irrigated the region around Chengdu, turning it into a granary for the nation. The transportation and irrigation systems they built in the northern state of Shanxi transformed it into an area so rich in agricultural productivity and the means of transporting it that they could control all of north China from this base. The Qin also captured the richest sources of iron ore and two of China's best ironworking facilities, crucial resources for fashioning both tools and weapons.

Great Wall of China. Begun 214 B.C.E., rebuilt repeatedly. "The seven wonders of the world are not comparable to this work," wrote one awestruck seventeenth-century observer of this most imposing relic of China's past. Faced with brick and stone and averaging 25 feet (7.6 m) high and wide, the wall is studded with towers that serve as signaling stations, warning of the approach of mobile enemies.

EARLY ADVANCES IN WEAPONRY

3000 (B.C.E.)	War chariot invented. In Mesopotamia and southeastern Europe first metal swords and shields made (bronze).
2000	First armor made, from bronze scales, in Mesopotamia.
c. **700**	The Phoenicians and Egyptians invent galleys—warships powered by oars.
500	Giant crossbows and catapults used by the Greeks and Carthaginians.
200	Hand-held crossbow now being used in China.
300 (C.E.)	Stirrups used in China.
950	Gunpowder used by Chinese for signaling devices and fireworks.
1250–1300	Bronze and iron cannon probably used by the Chinese; in Europe, first recorded use of cannon is 1326.

ADMINISTRATIVE POWER

Administratively, Qin Shi Huangdi ruled through a bureaucracy. He did away with the **feudal** system, by which officials had been appointed on the basis of their personal, often family, ties to the court and therefore owed allegiance to the emperor personally rather than to the empire in the abstract. Now people were chosen for office on the basis of ability; their tasks were fixed and governed by systematic, formalized, written rules; and their work was rewarded or punished according to the degree of their efficiency and fidelity. The empire was divided into some forty administrative units called "commanderies." Each commandery was staffed with three leading officials: a civil authority, a military authority, and an inspector representing the emperor. The three officials served as checks and balances to the others' authority: no one individual could assert too much power and threaten the control of the emperor at the center.

The Qin standardized as they centralized. They fixed weights and measures, values of coinage, the size of cart axles and of the roads they traveled. They standardized the legal code. Perhaps most important of all, the Qin standardized the written form of the Chinese language, possibly the most important single act of political and cultural unification in China's history. To this day, despite great variation in the local forms of spoken Chinese, written Chinese is uniform throughout the country, just as the Qin established it.

THE FALL OF THE QIN DYNASTY

Qin Shi Huangdi died in 210 B.C.E. and was buried in the enormous mausoleum he had created, accompanied by the vast ceramic army he had ordered (see p. 200). Within four years his apparently powerful, centralized, productive, well-organized dynasty had collapsed. Despite the apparent strengths, the Qin had oppressed to the breaking point the nation and its peasantry, the 90 percent of the population who paid the taxes, served in the armies, built the public works projects, and the women who quietly supported all these projects through their work at home. Several hundreds of thousands of these peasants were dispatched to fight the Xiongnu in the far north and northwest on both sides of the Great Wall. As the *Han History* later reported:

> The first emperor of Qin sent forth the men of the empire to guard the northern loop of the Yellow River. For more than ten years they were exposed to the rigors of military life, and countless numbers died. . . . He also made the empire transport fodder and grain, beginning with the coastal commanderies of Huang, Qu and Langye, whose inhabitants had to take these commodities to the northern loop of the Yellow River. . . . Although the men toiled at farming, there was not enough grain for rations; and the women could not spin enough yarn for the tents. The common people were ruined. (Cited in Elvin, p. 27)

In addition to these systemic problems, the fight over the succession to Qin Shi Huangdi's throne destroyed the dynasty. A contest for power broke out between a minister, Li Si; another court official, the eunuch Zhao Gao; and the emperor's own son. In the struggle, many supporters of the former emperor were murdered by the son on advice from his minister. Fear and disloyalty flourished. Each person seemed concerned only for his own survival and aggrandizement. Qin Shi Huangdi had instituted bureaucracy in place of personal rule throughout the empire, but personal politics still dominated the imperial court. Finally, Zhao forced the emperor's son to commit suicide, but then he himself was assassinated. While the court was convulsed in these internal struggles, rebels broke into the capital at Xianyang and captured power. Warfare continued until, in 202 B.C.E., the rebel leader Liu Bang emerged victorious and established the Han dynasty.

IDEOLOGIES OF EMPIRE

China's historical record was written and preserved by an official elite trained in philosophy. Perhaps this is the reason for China's profound concern with the philosophy and ideology of empire. Emperors in their public proclamations and writers in their records stress the importance of their philosophy to the actual process of building, sustaining, and guiding the empire.

LEGALISM

During his reign Qin Shi Huangdi set up various inscriptions on stone in various parts of his empire. These proclaimed his values and policies—for example, after he put down a rebellion in the far northeast he inscribed on the city walls:

> Then he mobilized armies, and punished the
>   unprincipled, and those who perpetrated
>   rebellion were wiped out.
> Armed force exterminates the violent and rebellious,
>   but civil power relieves the guiltless of their
>   labors, and the masses all submit in their hearts.
> Achievements and toil are generously assessed, and
>   the rewards even extend to cattle and horses, and
>   his bounty enriches the land.
> The August Emperor gave a vigorous display of his
>   authority, and his virtue brought together all the
>   states, and for the first time brought unity and
>   supreme peace.
> City walls were demolished [suggesting that they
>   were no longer necessary for defense],
>   waterways were opened up, and obstacles were
>   flattened.
> When the physical features of the land had been
>   determined, there was no conscript labor for the
>   masses, and all under heaven was pacified.

> Men take pleasure in their farmland, and women
>   cultivate their tasks, and all matters have their
>   proper arrangement.
> His kindness protects all production, and for long
>   they have been coming together in the fields,
>   and everyone is content with his place.
> (Sima Qian, p. 74)

In another inscription he wrote:

> When the sage of Qin took charge of his state,
>   he first determined punishments and names,
>   and clearly set forth the ancient regulations.
> He was the first to standardize the system of
>   laws, examine and demarcate duties and
>   responsibilities, so as to establish unchanging
>   practices. (Sima Qian, p. 82)

He proclaimed a code of sexual conduct:

> If a man commits adultery, to kill him is no
>   crime, so men hang on to the standards of
>   righteousness.
> If a wife elopes to remarry, then the son will not
>   have a mother, and so everyone is converted
>   into chastity and purity. (Sima Qian, p. 83)

In his rulings Qin Shi Huangdi followed many of the policies of the political philosopher Han Feizi (d. 233 B.C.E.). Han Feizi called himself a Legalist because he believed that strict laws, strictly enforced, were the best assurance of good and stable government. Han Feizi's statements quoted here are quite consistent with the policies actually adopted by Qin Shi Huangdi:

> The intelligent sovereign makes the law select
> men and makes no arbitrary promotion himself.
> He makes the law measure merits and makes no
> arbitrary regulation himself. . . . To govern the
> state by law is to praise the right and blame the
> wrong. . . . To correct the faults of the high, to
> rebuke the vices of the low, to suppress disorders,
> to decide against mistakes, to subdue the arrogant,
> to straighten the crooked, and to unify the
> folkways of the masses, nothing could match the
> law. . . . If law is definite, the superiors are
> esteemed and not violated. If the superiors are not
> violated, the sovereign will become strong and able
> to maintain the proper course of government.
> Such was the reason why the early kings esteemed
> Legalism and handed it down to posterity.

The means whereby the intelligent ruler controls his ministers are two handles only. The two handles are chastisement and commendation. (Han Fei Tzu, I:40,45–7)

DAOISM

This concern for law and order, reward and punishment, recommended by Han Feizi and his school of Legalism, characterizes the regime of Qin Shi Huangdi. There were, however, at least two other major schools of political and ethical thought prominent in China by this time, Daoism and Confucianism. Daoism was a more mystical school, not usually directly applicable to government, but often a solace to public men in their private lives. Daoism is often seen as an inspiration to artists, and, because it advocates a high regard for nature, it is often seen as an inspiration to natural scientists as well. The legendary founder of Daoism and author of its key text, the *Daodejing*, is Laozi (*c.* 604–*c.* 517 B.C.E.), but the school and the book more likely date to the third or fourth centuries B.C.E. Its teachings are cloaked in paradox and mystery:

The Way that can be spoken of is not the constant Way;
The name that can be named is not the constant name.
The nameless is the beginning of Heaven and Earth;
The named is the mother of all things.

Do away with sageliness, discard knowledge,
And the people will benefit a hundredfold.
Do away with humaneness, discard righteousness,
And the people will once more be filial and loving,
Dispense with cleverness, discard profit,
And there will be no more bandits and thieves.
These three, to be regarded as ornaments, are insufficient.
Therefore let the people have something to cling to:
Manifest plainness,
Embrace uncarved wood,
Diminish selfishness,
Reduce desires.

What is softest in the world
Overcomes what is hardest in the world.
No-thing penetrates where there is no space.
Thus I know that in doing nothing there is advantage.
The worldless teaching and the advantage of doing nothing—there are few in the world who understand them.

The more prohibitions there are in the world,
The poorer are the people.
The more sharp weapons the people have,
The more disorder is fomented in the family and state,
The more adroit and clever men are,
The more deceptive things are brought forth.
The more laws and ordnances are promulgated,
The more thieves and robbers there are.
Therefore the sage says:
I do nothing (*wuwei*),
And the people are transformed by themselves.

(deBary, 1999, pp. 79–90)

Finally, the Daoist view of simplicity seems to have little need for government:

Let the state be small and the people be few.
There may be ten or even a hundred times as many implements,
But they should not be used.
Let the people, regarding death as a weighty matter, not travel far.
Though they have boats and carriages, none shall ride in them.
Though they have armor and weapons, none shall display them.
Let the people return once more to the use of knotted ropes [instead of writing; compare the *quipu* of the Incas]
Let them savor their food and find beauty in their clothing, peace in their dwellings, and joy in their customs.
Though neighboring states are within sight of one another,
And the sound of cocks and dogs is audible from one to the other,
People will reach old age and yet not visit one another. (deBary, 1999, p. 94)

CONFUCIANISM

More central to Chinese political as well as ethical thought were the teachings of Confucius (551–479 B.C.E.), a philosopher and political adviser from the small state of Lu in modern Shandong. Confucius began his career as a scholar from a young age. He mastered the six arts of ritual, music, artery, chariot driving, calligraphy, and arithmetic, and then began his career as a teacher. At a time when China was divided into many states, often in conflict, he formulated principles that he thought would bring peace, contentment, dignity, and personal cultural

Rubbing of an engraved stone slab depicting Laizi, from the Wu Liang shrine, erected in 151 C.E. at Jiaxiang in Shandong province. Under the Han dynasty, the celebration of filial piety advocated by Confucius took a more exaggerated form, so that men were sometimes appointed to official posts on the basis of their reputation as good sons. Even when he was over seventy years old, Laizi is said to have tried to convince his parents that they were still young by continuing to play with his toys like a boy.

development at least to the elites of his time. Although Confucius was unsuccessful in finding employment as an adviser in any single state, his disciples kept his vision alive, and it has permeated Chinese thought and, often, government policy.

Confucius felt that good government depended on good officials, men of *jen*, or humanity, benevolence, virtue, and culture. Little concerned with the supernatural, he believed that a moral order pervaded the universe and that it could be understood. In contrast to the tumult of his own day, Confucius believed that in the early days of the Zhou dynasty there had been a golden age of peace and order, wisdom and virtue. In those days, political leaders had understood the importance of feudal hierarchy, rituals, music, and art, but the neglect of these elements of humanism and rationalism, and the absence of schools that taught them to new leaders, had reduced China to chaos.

Confucius believed in the essential goodness and educability of each individual, and believed that the virtues of the past could be regained. He believed in the centrality of the "gentleman" (*junzi*), the morally based leader who had the vision to move the society toward peace and virtue. Such a gentleman would and should be concerned about political leadership and the proper ordering of the state. For Confucius, however, gentlemen were not born but made, fashioned through proper education. Believing that character, not birth, was important, he taught whoever would come to him. Confucius' own era was too violent for his teachings to find immediate acceptance.

As we have seen, the Qin dynasty did not welcome his teachings either, but eventually the next dynasty, the Han, did. Under the Han, Confucius' ethical and political values came to dominate the culture and thought of China's scholars and intellectuals. They continued powerful for most of the following 2000 years, also influencing the political thought of Korea, Japan, and southeast Asia. Confucian scholars kept alive the five literary classics of the Zhou dynasty and added to them Confucius' own teachings, *The Analects* (see Source, p. 206).

QIN SHI HUANGDI, THE LEGALISTS, AND THE CONFUCIANISTS

The philosophies of Legalism and Confucianism collided during the Qin dynasty. In direct contrast to the Confucianists' reverence for the past, Li Si, the prime minister, argued that the administration of the Qin was far superior to the government of any earlier time. Li Si argued that "In antiquity all under Heaven was divided and in chaos, and nobody was capable of bringing unity to the rest" (Sima Qian, p. 30). The Qin success was the result of its decision to replace feudal administration with an orderly system of laws and appointment to office on the basis of efficiency in accordance with Legalist principles. Li Si recommended that the Confucian classics be collected and burned so that the past could no longer be held up as an alternative to present policies. In 213 B.C.E. the burning of the books took place. Subsequently, as Confucian scholars continued to oppose Qin Shi Huangdi, he had 460 scholars buried alive. These acts of anti-intellectualism and brutality are reported by Sima Qian, as official historian of the Han government. They leave the Legalist Qin with a dismal reputation. The cruel intrigues and struggles for succession that helped end the Qin confirm that view.

One of the enduring philosophical concepts of Chinese imperial politics was the Mandate of Heaven. Heaven, not a personal god but the cosmic forces of the universe, underpinned rulers of high moral stature and undercut those who lacked it. Heaven conferred its mandate on the moral and revoked it from the immoral. Dynasties were thus held accountable for their actions, and they could not expect to rule forever. The evidence of their loss of cosmic connection would be made manifest, not only in the usual political and economic strife of a weak administration, but also through nature itself going awry in the form of floods, droughts, or other natural disasters. Throughout Chinese history, rebels against an emperor would cite evidence of his having lost the "Mandate," while those supporting new rulers would proclaim their possession of it. Han historians made clear their belief that the Qin dynasty had lost the Mandate of Heaven.

Nevertheless, the Qin had brought China to a new stage of political development: the empire had been founded; an effective bureaucratic administration had been established; and careers had been opened to new men of talent. All these innovations were to last, in changing measures, for 2000 years.

SOURCE
Confucius and The Analects

We have no record of Confucius' writing down his own teachings. *The Analects*, a collection of thoughtful perceptions attributed to him, were apparently recorded and compiled by disciples of his disciples. Because these aphorisms—497 verses in twenty chapters—are brief, unelaborated, unorganized, and written in ideographic form, their exact meaning is not always clear, but these same qualities promote the reader's engagement with and interpretation of the text. *The Analects* have been a part of the education of every Chinese school student for centuries, at least until the Communist revolution in 1949. The selections here represent typical issues for Confucius: the importance of formal, humanistic education in forming proper character; teaching and learning by example; focus on the world of here-and-now; and respect for others, especially for parents and elders.

A young man is to be filial within his family and respectful outside it. He is to be earnest and faithful, overflowing in his love for living beings and intimate with those who are humane. If after such practice he has strength to spare, he may use it in the study of culture.

Lead them by means of regulations and keep order among them through punishments, and the people will evade them and will lack any sense of shame.

Lead them through moral force (*de*) and keep order among them through rites (*li*), and they will have a sense of shame and will also correct themselves.

In education there should be no class distinctions.

Shall I teach you what knowledge is? When you know something, to know that you know it. When you do not know, to know that you do not know it. That is knowledge.

The noble person is concerned with rightness; the small person is concerned with profit.

I am not one who was born with knowledge; I am one who loves the past and is diligent in seeking it.

The Three Armies can be deprived of their commander, but even a common person cannot be deprived of his will.

The wise have no doubts; the humane have no sorrows; the courageous have no fears.

Before you have learned to serve human beings, how can you serve spirits. . . .

When you do not yet know life, how can you know about death?

Look at nothing contrary to ritual; listen to nothing contrary to ritual; say nothing contrary to ritual; do nothing contrary to ritual.

What you would not want for yourself, do not do to others.

Zigong asked about government. The Master said, "sufficient food, sufficient military force, the confidence of the people." Zigong said, "If one had, unavoidably, to dispense with one of these three, which of them should go first?" The Master said, "Get rid of the military." Zigong said, "If one had, unavoidably, to dispense with one of the remaining two, which should go first?" The Master said, "Dispense with the food. Since ancient times there has always been death, but without confidence a people cannot stand."

(deBary, 1999, pp. 45–60)

Throughout Chinese history, some groups rebelled against Confucius' ethical principles. Peasant rebels, a frequent presence throughout the centuries, condemned Confucius' emphasis on order and harmony. In the late nineteenth and twentieth centuries, as China saw itself fall behind the technological and military achievements of the Western world, Confucian traditions were challenged with renewed vigor (see Chapters 17 and 20). Critics argued that Confucianism was incompatible with equality, scientific education, rebellious youth movements, dignity of physical labor, peasant equity, and equal rights for women. The Communist government which ruled China after 1949 attacked Confucius especially bitterly in 1973 and 1974 during the Cultural Revolution, asserting that in his own day Confucius had served as a representative of the slave-owning aristocracy.

THE HAN DYNASTY

When Liu Bang (r. 202–195 B.C.E.) prevailed in the warfare that ended the Qin dynasty, the empire remained intact. One ruling family fell and another took its place and asserted its own control, but the empire itself continued united under a single emperor. The principal Legalist ministers who had guided the Qin were replaced, but the administrative bureaucracy continued to function.

Change came in the leadership style of the new dynasty. Liu Bang was himself a commoner and a soldier, perhaps illiterate, with many years of warfare still ahead of him—he died in battle in 195 B.C.E.—but as his ministers he chose educated men with Confucian principles. Slowly, a new social and political hierarchy emerged, with scholars at the top, followed by farmers, artisans, and merchants. Legalism still influenced the administrative systems, and Daoism's emphasis on nature and emotion continued to be attractive, but Confucius' ethical teachings captured the imagination of the court.

The influence of Confucianism appeared in four other areas. First, history became more important than ever. The appointment of Sima Tan and then of his son Sima Qian as court historians established the tradition of imperial record keeping. The Confucian notion of the importance of tradition and continuity prevailed over the Legalist idea of discounting the past.

Second, in 124 B.C.E. the most powerful and long lived of the Han rulers, Wudi or Emperor Wu (r. 141–87 B.C.E.), established an elite imperial academy to teach specially selected scholar-bureaucrats the wisdom of Confucius and its applicability to problems of governance. The emperor also declared that knowledge of the Confucian classics would be a basis for promotion in the imperial civil service. Although the academy could at first educate only fifty men, it grew in size until in the later Han period it could accommodate 30,000 men. In Han times, the landed aristocracy still gained most of the places in the bureaucracy, but the principle of appointment and promotion based not on birth but on success in an examination in the Confucian classics was finally established during the Tang dynasty (618–907 C.E.).

Third, an imperial conference of Confucian legal scholars was convened in the imperial palace in 51 B.C.E. to codify and establish the principles for applying case law. This established and consolidated the Chinese legal system for centuries to come.

Finally, Confucian scholars, both male and female, began to establish principles of conduct for women. Confucius had spoken of the importance of five relationships in human society: ruler-subject; father-son; husband-wife; older brother-younger brother; and friend-friend. The first four were hierarchical relationships of superior-inferior. Little, however, had been written about the role of women.

ADMONITIONS FOR WOMEN

During the Han dynasty, several authors decided to address this subject (see Spotlight, pp. 212–3). Ban Zhao (45–116 C.E.), sister of the famous court historian Ban Gu, wrote *Admonitions for Women*, a text of advice on the virtues appropriate for aristocratic women, which was divided into seven sections on humility, resignation, subservience, self-abasement, obedience, cleanliness, and industry.

In ancient times, on the third day after a girl was born, people placed her at the base of the bed, gave her a pot shard to play with, and made a sacrifice to announce her birth. She was put below the bed to show that she was lowly and weak and should concentrate on humbling herself before others. Playing with a shard showed that she should get accustomed to hard work and concentrate on being diligent. Announcing her birth to the ancestors showed that she should focus on continuing the sacrifices. These three customs convey the unchanging path for women and the ritual traditions.

Humility means yielding and acting respectful, putting others first and oneself last, never mentioning one's own good deeds or denying one's own faults, enduring insults and bearing with mistreatment, all with due trepidation. Industriousness means going to bed late, getting up early, never shirking work morning or night, never refusing to take on domestic work, and completing

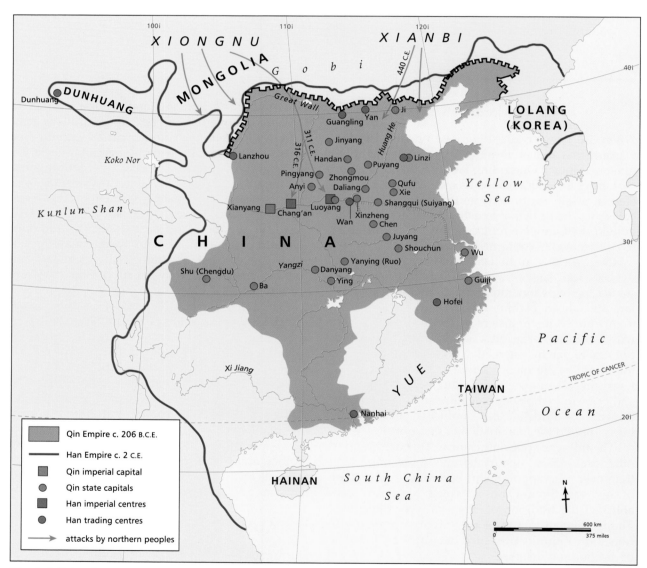

Classical China In 221 B.C.E. two centuries of internecine rivalry—the "Warring States" period—ended with the rise to centralized power of the Qin dynasty, but internal revolt and external pressures on the borders precipitated further civil war. The Han dynasty emerged as the new rulers in 202 B.C.E. They refortified the northern walls, and extended imperial control far to the south and west, deep into central Asia along the silk route, defining a Chinese territorial extent that has been asserted down to the present day.

everything that needs to be done neatly and carefully. Continuing the sacrifices means serving one's husband-master with appropriate demeanor, keeping oneself clean and pure, never joking or laughing, and preparing pure wine and food to offer to the ancestors. (Ebrey, p. 75) (see Spotlight, pp. 212–13)

Placing a similar stress on the virtues of self-sacrificing service, Liu Xiang (79–8 B.C.E.) wrote the *Biographies of Heroic Women*, which recounted the virtues of 125 women. He especially praised the mother of the philosopher Mencius, the greatest of the Confucian scholars. Liu Xiang quotes Mencius' mother telling her son of her concept of women's obligations:

> A woman's duties are to cook the five grains, heat the wine, look after her parents-in-law, make clothes, and that is all! Therefore she cultivates the skills required in the women's quarters and has no ambition to manage affairs outside of the house. The *Book of Changes* says, "In her central place, she attends to the preparation of the food." The *Book of Songs* says, "It will be theirs neither to do wrong nor to do good,/Only about the spirits and the food will they have to think." This means that a woman's duty is not to control or to take charge. Instead she must follow the "three submissions." When she is young, she must submit to her parents. After her marriage, she must submit to her husband. When she is widowed, she must submit to her son. These are the rules of propriety. (Ebrey, p. 73)

(Compare and contrast contemporary Indian perspectives on women's obligations as cited briefly on pp. 237 and 239, and Roman policies on p. 174.)

The pervasive Confucian stress on hierarchy and deference permeates these prescriptions for women's conduct. However, throughout Han times—but not after—women could inherit property, divorce, and remarry after divorce or widowhood. And (see p. 215) even the most highly placed women sometimes rebelled against Confucian ideals.

MILITARY POWER

The Han emperors were no less militaristic than the Qin. Confucian principles of moral rectitude held sway among the educated elites, but the government did not dispense with formal legal systems nor did it forsake offensive or defensive warfare. The standing army numbered between 300,000 and 1,000,000, and all able-bodied men between the ages of twenty or twenty-three and fifty-six were conscripted, serving for one year of training and one year of duty in the capital or in battle on the frontiers. They could be recalled in case of warfare. Throughout the Han dynasty, China was engaged in incessant battles with the Xiongnu and other tribes around the Great Wall (see map opposite). Indeed, as we shall see shortly, the Han forced open a corridor through Gansu in the direction of Xinjiang (Turkestan). One of the reasons for this expansion was to open markets for silk in the west. Parthian traders carried goods on this trade route

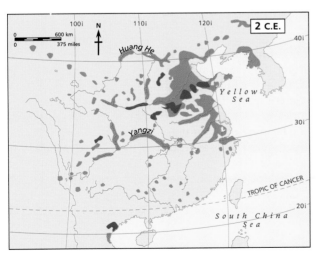

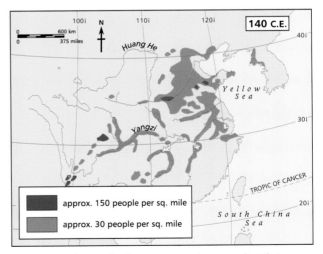

Chinese expansion A substantial shift in Chinese population distribution began during the first two centuries C.E., a fact that can be traced from Han census records. As land-hunger and pressure from the Xiongnu and the Tibetans on the northern border forced migration from the densely populated northeast, and as techniques for rice cultivation in the humid basin of the Yangzi improved, the lands to the south were mastered, and population clusters developed along the river valleys.

as far as Rome (see p. 249). China also wanted to secure a supply of horses from distant Bactria for the military. On the northern borders, where Chinese, Mongol, Tibetan, and Barbarian forces fought, each learned the strengths and weaknesses of the other. A Chinese strength was the crossbow. A very significant Mongol and Tibetan strength was cavalry, mounted on strong, fast horses. To achieve military parity, the Han emperors sought and found a supply of equivalent horses in central Asia. The Gansu corridor served as an access route, and Emperor Wu garrisoned it with 700,000 soldiers. Administrative records written on wooden strips have survived to tell of the lives of these immigrant soldier-colonizers in some detail.

POPULATION AND MIGRATION

The Han dynasty also consolidated its holdings in the comparatively unpopulated south. A population map of China from the year 2 C.E., based on the earliest preserved census in the world, shows the disparity of population distribution. The Chinese heartland was clearly the north; in the south population was sparse, mostly settled along the rivers. In both the south and the border regions, military-agricultural colonies were established to provide military defense and economic development. The Chinese attempted to win the local populations over to Chinese culture, and often succeeded, but

not always. On the borders and in the southeast they met opposition, and rebellions against the Chinese settlers erupted in 86, 83, and 28–25 B.C.E.

In the south, in general, there was little indigenous population and little hostility or resistance to the coming of northerners. The regional Yue or Viet tribes were more often involved in fighting one another, although in 40 C.E. there was a revolt, and violence broke out on at least seven occasions between 100–184 C.E. Perhaps the increased resistance was evoked by the vast increase in the flow of population to the south. Compare the distribution of population in the year 140 C.E., when the second preserved census was taken, with the map showing the population in 2 C.E. The total population had declined from about 58 million to about 48 million, but the regional distribution had shifted from 76 percent in the north and 24 percent in the south, to 54 and 46 percent respectively. The population of the northwest decreased by 6.5 million; of the northeast, by 11.5 million. The likely causes of the population losses on the border were continuing pressure from the Xiongnu and the Tibetans, while in the northeast plain, the great floods caused by the Yellow River breaking its banks and twice changing its course, in c. 4 C.E. and again in 11 C.E., may have affected the population distribution. The military and natural turbulence also impoverished China's civilian population, as the empire allocated more and more resources to support the army, expansionism, and the court in the capital of Chang'an.

ECONOMIC POWER

The economy of Han China grew with the exploitation of new sources of wealth from along the Yangzi River, Sichuan, and the south. New inventions in mining (including salt mining), paper production, the compass, the breast-strap harness for horses, a redesigned plowshare, hydraulic engineering, and the tapping of natural gas increased wealth and productivity. The road through the Gansu corridor to Xinjiang (Turkestan) brought increased knowledge of distant lands and new trade possibilities. In 138 B.C.E. Emperor Wudi dispatched Zhang Qian to inner

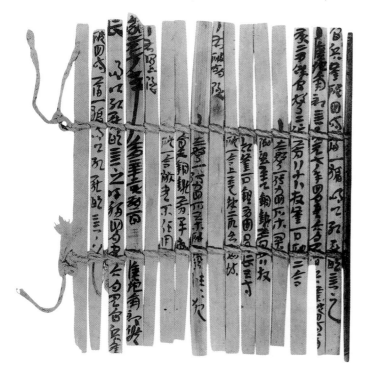

Inventory written on bamboo, 95 C.E. Government bureaucracy expanded with military and economic power under the Han dynasty, producing an enormous number of documents on wooden and bamboo strips. This inventory lists the equipment of two infantry units. (*British Library, London*)

Asia to seek enemies of the Xiongnu who might serve as allies of the Chinese. Zhang returned twelve years later without new alliances, but with precious new information on lands as far west as Bactria, in modern northern Afghanistan. New trade possibilities opened not only in horses, but also in silk. Parthian traders served as intermediaries between the Chinese and Roman Empires. By 57 B.C.E. Chinese silk had reached Rome. The first silk route had been opened. Geography and cartography flourished, and gazetteers began to be published.

The cost of military expeditions and garrisons, and the expenses of the self-aggrandizing court ate up the gains, however. Having dramatically lowered the land revenues when they first took office, the Han emperors began once again to raise them. They also began to nationalize private enterprise, by bringing it under state control, not in order to promote efficiency or honesty but to gain the profits for the state. Although commerce and business were theoretically held in low regard by Confucianists, businessmen flourished under the Han, and Sima Qian praised their enterprise:

> There is no fixed road to wealth, and money has
> no permanent master. It finds its way to the man of
> ability like the spokes of a wheel converging upon
> the hub, and from the hands of the worthless it
> falls like shattered tiles. A family with a thousand
> catties of gold may stand side by side with the lord
> of a city; the man with a hundred million cash may
> enjoy the pleasures of a king. Rich men such as
> these deserve to be called the "untitled nobility,"
> do they not? (Sima Qian, p. 356)

Emperor Wu sought to expropriate some of this wealth to pay for his military ventures and his imperial court. He altered coinage, confiscated the land of the nobility, sold offices and titles, and increased taxes. He established government monopolies in the production of iron, salt, and liquor, and he took over part of the grain trade, arguing that this was a means of stabilizing prices, but actually so that he could secure profits for his government. On his death, his successor, the Emperor Zhao, arranged a debate between his chief minister, who advocated continuing the state monopolies on salt and iron, and a number of Confucian scholars, who opposed them. The minister argued the need:

> We cherish the goal of raising a great army and
> driving the Xiongnu back north. I again assert that

Stone relief of harnessed cattle found at Mizhi, Shaanxi province. Technological advancements, such as the development of the animal-drawn plow, went hand in hand with the increase in the area of cultivated land under the Han dynasty.

> to do away with the salt and iron monopolies and
> equable marketing system would bring havoc to our
> frontier military policies and would be heartless
> toward those on the frontier. (Ebrey, p. 61)

The Confucians opposed the policy of costly military expansion and the government plan to take over businesses in order to finance this expansion. Their argument sounds almost Daoist in its statement that a benevolent king has no enemies:

> The master conqueror need not fight, the expert
> warrior needs no soldiers, and the great commander
> need not array his troops. If you foster high
> standards in the temple and courtroom, you need
> only make a bold show and bring home your troops,
> for the king who practices benevolent government
> has no enemies anywhere. What need can he then
> have for expense funds? (Ebrey, p. 61)

The Confucians distrusted businessmen as self-seeking and corrupt, and they feared that government-run business would multiply that corruption:

SPOTLIGHT
A Han Dynasty Code of Conduct

The poet Zhang Hua (*c.* 232– 300 C.E.) observed his ruler's court with its ministers and courtiers, wives and concubines, and concluded that the traditional Confucian rules of conduct were being violated, especially after the fall of the centralized Han dynasty. To provide a code of conduct, Zhang composed *Admonitions of the Instructress of the Ladies in the Palace.* They define the position of a privileged but highly regulated upper class of women within the rigid, hierarchical Chinese court.

About a century later Gu Kaizhi (*c.* 334–406), painter at the court of Nanjing, transcribed segments of the *Admonitions* and illustrated them in nine scenes in an elegant scroll painting. Although the original has been lost, a tenth-century copy survives in the British Museum, painted on fine silk weave 137 inches long and 9¾ inches wide (3.48 m by 25 cm).

In **figure 1**, Gu Kaizhi depicts one imperial concubine combing the hair of another in front of a mirror with cosmetic materials arrayed in finely lacquered boxes kept near at hand.

Opposite her another lady of the court gazes intently into her mirror as she paints her eyebrows. Zhang Hua's text, which inspired the painting, reads:

> Men and women know how to adorn their faces, but there is none who knows how to adorn his character. Yet if the character be not adorned, there is a danger that the rules of conduct may be transgressed. Correct your character as with an axe, embellish it as with a chisel; strive to create holiness in your own nature.

In **figure 2**, Gu has painted a woman in her chamber in conversation with a visiting gentleman who sits on the bench at her bedside. Gu, who was noted for his ability to represent psychological insights through his portraits, has created this scene to illustrate Zhang's Admonition:

> If the words that you utter are good, all men for a thousand leagues around will make response to you. But if you

Figure 1 Gu Kaizhi, two concubines in front of a mirror, *Admonitions …*, fourth century C.E.

depart from this principle, even your bedfellow will distrust you.

Gu was also praised for his use of landscape to represent philosophical concepts. His treatment of another of Zhang's Admonitions demonstrates this talent. Zhang wrote:

In nature there is [nothing] that is exalted which is not soon brought low. Among living things there is nothing which having attained its apogee does not henceforth decline. When the sun has reached its mid-course, it begins to sink; when the moon is full it begins to wane. To rise to glory is as hard as to build a mountain out of dust; to fall into calamity is as easy as the rebound of a tense spring.

To illustrate Zhang's perception of the fragility of human accomplishment, and of all of nature as well, Gu has painted a glorious scene of nature in its richness (**figure 3**), a mountain peak alive with wild animals, under a radiant sun and moon, and at the side—a hunter aiming his crossbow.

Artistically, the Admonitions unify the arts of poetry, philosophy, calligraphy, and painting. In the wake of the fall of the Han dynasty they reaffirm the moral, ethical, and aesthetic teachings of Confucius, emphasizing dignity in personal behavior and sensitivity in human relationships. Finally,

Figure 2 Gu Kaizhi, a woman and a gentleman in conversation, *Admonitions …*, fourth century C.E.

although the Admonitions are to be delivered to the ladies of the palace by an "Instructress," in fact Zhang, the poet-philosopher, and Gu, the painter-calligrapher, are both males.

Figure 3 Gu Kaizhi, mountain scene, *Admonitions …*, fourth century C.E

The government officers busy themselves with gaining control of the market and cornering commodities. With the commodities cornered, prices soar and merchants make private deals and speculate. The officers connive with the cunning merchants who are hoarding commodities against future need. Quick traders and unscrupulous officials buy when goods are cheap in order to make high profits. Where is the balance in this standard? (Ebrey, p. 63)

The emperor came to accept the Confucian argument and relinquished at least some government-run monopolies.

ADMINISTRATIVE POWER

The bureaucracy of the early Han seemed to run well, and the adoption of Confucian principles tempered some of the harshness of the Legalist codes. In addition, the wars that the Qin had pursued to establish China's borders made fighting somewhat less necessary for the Han. For two hundred years even the problems of succession, problems that had ultimately helped destroy the Qin dynasty, were negotiated effectively, if sometimes quite cruelly. Nevertheless, the absence of clear principles of imperial succession continued, and in 9 C.E. the Han temporarily fell from power because there was no clear successor.

In 1 B.C.E., the Emperor Ping inherited the throne at the age of eight. A regent, Wang Mang, was appointed to run the government during the boy's minority, and when Ping died, Wang Mang became *de facto* ruler, in 9 C.E., declaring himself founder of a new dynasty. His policies, however, alienated virtually everyone. Fighting against the Xiongnu, breaking up large estates, reinstating the prohibition on the sale of land, fixing commodity prices, terminating Han noble status and reducing them to commoners, cutting bureaucratic salaries, confiscating villagers' gold in exchange for bronze—these policies inflamed both rich and poor, nobility and commoners, urban and rural folk. To add to his problems, just at the beginning of Wang Mang's regency, the Yellow River jumped its banks and changed course twice in five years, wreaking immense devastation to property and loss of life. (The Yellow River carries great quantities of silt and has a very shallow bed. It has jumped its banks, and carved out new channels for itself numerous times in China's recorded history.) In 23 C.E., a combination of Xiongnu invasions in the north, the rebellion of Han nobles near the capital, and, after 18 C.E., the revolt of the Red Turbans, a mass movement centered in the Shandong peninsula, which had been most devastated by the river's flooding, brought down Wang Mang and led to the reinstatement of the Han dynasty.

The later Han dynasty, 23–220 C.E., did not have the same strength as the former Han. To cope with continuing incursions, the later Han made alliances with the barbarians, inviting them to settle within the Wall, to provide soldiers for Chinese armies, and even to intermarry with the Chinese. (These policies are similar to Rome's actions in its border regions; see p. 188.) Although this pattern demonstrated the weakness of the Chinese central government, it also contributed to the **sinicization** of the tribal barbarians; they learned the language, culture, and administrative patterns of the Chinese. Reversing the pattern of tribute of the years of strong government, the later Han gave silk cloth to the border tribes so that they would not invade. Later Han emperors also removed the capital from Chang'an eastward to the less exposed Luoyang.

The movement of population to the south increased the wealth of the empire generally, but the increase went largely to merchants and landlords. Peasants continued to be exploited and oppressed by the exactions of these landlords and of the imperial government. As government taxes increased, peasants sold off their private holdings and went to live and farm under the jurisdictions of local landlords. Here, they sought to evade government taxes and military conscription. The landlords themselves faced a dilemma. As members of the governing elites, they were to collect and remit taxes to the central government and to turn over their tenants for conscription, but as landlords and local potentates, it was to their advantage to retain the taxes and the tenants' labor for themselves. Strong central governments were capable of demanding loyalty and collection; the later Han, however, frequently failed. Peasants absconded, the government's tax and labor bases diminished, and provincial notables developed independent power bases.

The beginning of the end of the Han is usually dated to 184 C.E. when a revolt of hundreds of thousands of peasants broke out. The rebellion, called the Yellow Turban revolt for the headgear worn by the rebels, was incited by Zhang Jue, a Daoist healer who proclaimed that a new era would begin with the fall of the Han. It broke out simultaneously in sixteen commanderies throughout the south, east, and northeast of China. Although this specific revolt was suppressed, it triggered a continuous string of additional outbreaks.

At least four factions struggled for power within the palace—the emperor who, after the death of Emperor Ling in 189, was a young child; the bureaucrats, advisers, palace guards, and regent to the young emperor; the eunuchs in the court, about 2000 castrated men chosen primarily for their direct loyalty to the emperor and the women of the court; and the women of the court and their families. Since each emperor had several wives and consorts, competition among them was fierce, both for their own recognition and for recognition of their sons at court, even as heir to the emperor. After the death of an emperor, his widows and his mother often remained embroiled in court politics to defend their own positions and those of their family.

In the last decades of Han rule, 189–220 C.E., the court was buffeted from the outside and divided on the inside. For example, on September 25, 189 C.E., generals in the court murdered some 2000 eunuchs, destroying their influence on the Han court. By the year 220, when the last Han emperor, Xian, abdicated, the court had no center and the lands of the empire had already been divided among numerous, competing warlords.

THE "THREE KINGDOMS AND SIX DYNASTIES" PERIOD

On the fall of the Han dynasty, China divided into three states: the Wei in the north, ruling over some 29 million people; the Wu in the south, ruling over 11 million; and the Shu in the west, ruling over 7 million. From 265 to 316 C.E. a single dynasty, the Jin, reunited China briefly. Then, for 273 years, 316–589 C.E., China was divided. The most prominent division fell along a north–south axis, with the dividing line approximately following the basin of the Huai River, halfway between the Yellow River to the north and the Yangzi River to the south.

This division was characterized by a number of geographical features. To the north, the top soil is a fine yellow dust called loess. Borne by winds from the west it is 250 feet (75 meters) deep to the north of Chang'an, a region with little irrigation. The agriculture in this area has been dry-field and mostly carried on by owner-operators, and its principal crops are wheat, millet, beans, and turnips. The region is intensely cold in winter. The south, by contrast, has many waterways, which are useful for both irrigation and navigation. The warmer weather, even subtropical in the far south, makes it possible to grow rice and tea, which were introduced from southeast Asia probably toward the end of the Han dynasty. The area is typically organized into landlord-tenant estates, better able to promote irrigated rice cultivation. During the centuries of imperial division, six successive dynasties governed the south, while a series of non-Chinese barbarian dynasties ruled the north. Warfare and ecological disaster in the north steadily pushed people southward, shifting the balance of population to a southern majority by this period (see map, p. 209). It appeared that the Chinese Empire, like that of Rome, had divided forever.

While China was rent politically, however, its culture and ethical ideologies remained alive and served to maintain its traditions of unity. In the south, especially, the arts, painting, calligraphy, and poetry flourished, frequently with the themes of spiritual survival amid political disarray. The Chinese language, too, continued to unite all literate Chinese as their means of communication. A poem by Tao Yuanming (365–427), who retired from a government post to take up the life of a country gentleman, captured all these elements:

> I built my cottage among the habitations of men,
> And yet there is no clamor of carriages and horses.
> You ask: "Sir, how can this be done?"
> "A heart that is distant creates its own solitude."
> I pluck chrysanthemums under the eastern hedge,
> Then gaze afar toward the southern hills.
> The mountain air is fresh at the dusk of day;
> The flying birds in flocks return.
> In these things there lies a deep meaning;
> I want to tell it, but have forgotten the words.
>
> (Cited in Schirokauer, p. 93)

In his paintings of "The Admonitions of the Instructress of the Ladies in the Palace," the painter Gu Kaizhi (334–406) kept alive the Confucian teachings of the Han while developing new artistic traditions for a new age. (See Spotlight, pp. 212–3.)

Meanwhile, in the north, China was open to new social and ethnic syntheses. The barbarians were absorbed into the continuing cultural life of China, and, through intermarriage, into its genetic pool as well. When scholars today note the homogeneity of China's population as "95 percent Han" they are referring to cultural rather than ethnic homogeneity and recognizing the openness of

China toward assimilating and accepting neighboring peoples who accept the culture of the "Han." The Chinese themselves echo the importance of this common culture, referring to all who have accepted it as "people of the Han." The nomadic peoples living on the northern borders and settling within the Great Wall at the invitation of the later Han emperors had already begun to absorb Chinese culture. When they became powerful enough to conquer north China, they found that they needed to enlist Chinese bureaucrats to administer their gains. In many regions, the administrators appointed by the new rulers were descendants of families whom the Han had employed. Thus below the surface of foreign rule a powerful stratum of Chinese elites remained in place.

Hill of the Thousand Buddhas, Jinan, Tang dynasty. The increased power of the Buddhist religious establishment in Tang times is reflected in the growth of cave paintings and sculptures. The merchants and missionaries who brought Buddhism to China along the silk route also brought ideas about the iconography of temples and the depiction of the Buddha (see Spotlight, pp. 288–9).

The most powerful and longest ruling of the nomadic conquerors became the most assimilated. These were the Northern Wei dynasty (r. 386–534), also named the Toba Wei after the tribal group that founded it (called the Xianbei in Chinese). The longer they ruled, the more assimilated they became. In 493–494 they moved their capital from the far west to one of the former Han capitals, Luoyang, so as better to control the northeast. But in Luoyang they wore Chinese dress, adopted Chinese names, and many intermarried. The Toba also made their own contributions to China's administrative practices. In Luoyang they instituted a new pattern of urban organization by wards. Subsequent dynasties used this system in laying out the restored capital of Chang'an (see p. 225). Still later, Japanese imperial planners copied it in Nara (see p. 227). Similarly, in their attempts to keep agricultural populations from fleeing north China, the Toba took over all land ownership for the state and continued to redistribute it in "equal fields" as each generation of cultivators died and new ones inherited the land.

The developing, new aristocracy of mixed Chinese-Xianbei blood alienated the unassimilated Xianbei troops who were garrisoning the frontiers. They finally revolted and defeated the Northern Wei government in 534, opening the way to the Sui dynasty, a family of mixed Chinese-foreign (barbarian) parentage, which reunited China.

BUDDHISM REACHES CHINA

During the Han dynasty Buddhism entered China from its birthplace in India. It is first noted in Chinese historical records in the first century C.E. Siddhartha Gautama, the Buddha, "the enlightened one," (c. 563–483 B.C.E.) introduced a religion of compassion in the face of a world of pain; it is discussed at length in Chapter 9. Here, however, we ask why and how this religion that later died out in its own native soil in India took new root in far off China. Indeed, Confucian scholars and bureaucrats and an institutionalized Daoist establishment often opposed Buddhism's early arrival. Over time, however, its very foreignness may have contributed to its success. The nomadic conquerors who succeeded the Han may have felt comfortable accepting, and even sponsoring a religion which, like themselves, came from outside China.

Second, Buddhism arose in India, to a large degree, as an anti-priestly religion favored by the merchant classes. Later, merchants sponsored Buddhist monasteries, convents, and cave temples along the silk routes between India and China, some of which remain impressive today, and Buddhism arrived in China with Indian Buddhist merchants who traveled these routes. The new religion persevered, securing patronage in several regional courts, capturing the hearts of millions of followers, and ultimately becoming one of the unifying elements in Chinese culture. Eventually Buddhism mixed with Confucianism and Daoism, bringing popular new spiritual, intellectual, cultural, and ritual innovations (see Chapter 9).

REUNIFICATION UNDER THE SUI AND TANG DYNASTIES

Despite almost 400 years of imperial fragmentation, many elements of Chinese unity were potentially at hand: language, ideology, culture, administration at the local level, aristocratic families with deep roots, and sufficient imperial prestige and administrative expertise that even China's conquerors were assimilated to it. To reunite the empire required the restoration of military power, economic productivity, and administrative integration. The Sui dynasty (581–618) provided all three. When the Sui fell, after over-extending itself militarily and economically, the Tang dynasty (618–907) continued and even strengthened these attributes of empire. Moreover the Sui and Tang extended China's reign to truly imperial dimensions—that is, beyond China proper to "outer China," Mongolia, Turkestan, and central Asia as far as the frontiers of modern Afghanistan, Pakistan, and Iran. It also held strong cultural sway over Tibet without direct political control. These lands were larger than all of "inner China" in area, although they held only perhaps 5 percent of its population. In addition, Tang China held northern Vietnam and, briefly, northern Korea. China's cultural influence at this time was extremely strong in Japan as well.

The three centuries of Sui and Tang rule consolidated the theory and practice of Chinese imperial rule even to the present (although today there is no emperor). Since 581 C.E. China has been divided into two administrations only once, in 1127–1275, and fragmented into several regions only twice, in 907–959 and 1916–49. Apart from these three periods, totalling 133 years, the Chinese Empire has stood united for a continuous period of more than fourteen centuries.

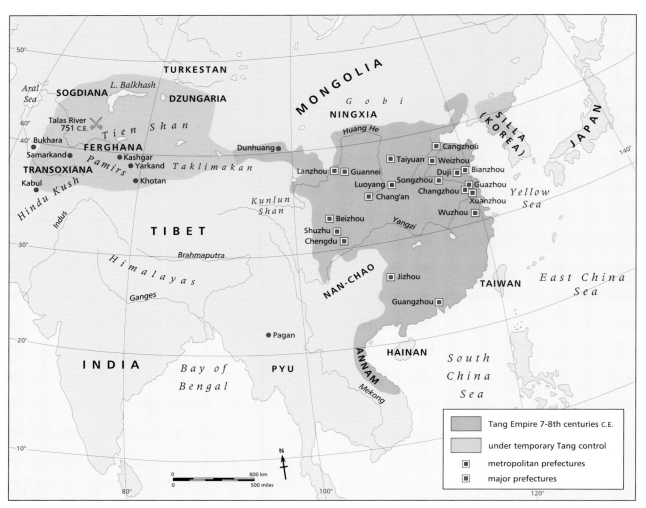

The Tang revival The Sui Dynasty (581–618 C.E.) and its successor, the politically organized Tang, restored the Chinese imperial impulse four centuries after the decline of the Han, extending control along the silk route as far as the Tien Shan mountain range and the arid Ferghana basin. Trade flourished. China finally reached its western limits when its forces were defeated by Arab armies on the Talas River in 751.

The Sui dynasty was founded by the Emperor Wen (581–604), a general of one of the states of north China, who usurped power in his own state and then succeeded in conquering and unifying all of inner China. Militarily he raised the status of the militia, settled them on their own lands, and gave them property rights, thus creating a powerful, committed, and loyal standing army of peasant-farmers. A powerful crossbow, protective body armor, and constant drills to achieve precision in maneuvers and battle made their troops a formidable fighting force. Ideologically, the first Sui emperor and his son, Yang (604–615), who succeeded him, employed a combination of Confucian, Daoist, and Buddhist symbolism and practice in winning popular loyalty.

Administratively, they centralized authority, eliminating a layer of local administrators and transferring their own appointees from one jurisdiction to another every three years to prevent them from establishing their own local power base. They drew up a new centralized legal code which still recognized local customs. Economically, the Sui dynasty completed the Grand Canal from Hangzhou in the south to Kaifeng in the center. The canal linked the Yangzi and Yellow River systems, and extensions connected it to the rebuilt capital in Chang'an and, later, to Beijing. The canal provided for the transportation of the agricultural wealth of the rapidly developing south to the political-military centers of the north.

The expense of mobilizing and dispatching

imperial troops and administrators on their far-flung missions depleted the treasury of the Sui dynasty. The Grand Canal produced many economic benefits, but it cost dearly in manpower. Built in seven years, the canal required the labor of 5.5 million people, and to complete some sections all commoners between the ages of fifteen and fifty-five were pressed into service. Fifty thousand police supervised the construction, flogging and chaining those who could not or would not work, and ordering every fifth family to provide one person to supply and prepare food. In addition to these public works, three disastrous military campaigns in Korea (see pp. 225–6) and in central Asia wasted lives and treasure, and sapped the loyalty of the troops. Finally the leading general of the Sui seized control of the state and under the imperial name Gaozu established the new Tang dynasty in 618 C.E.

Tang policies built on those of the Sui, consolidating and improving them where possible. The Tang dynasty relied more than ever on the imperial examination system to provide its administrators, and in 754 the emperor founded a new Imperial Academy, the Han-Lin Yuan (the Forest of Pens). The arts and technology, often reinforcing one another, flourished under the Tang as never before. The world's first block printing was invented, partly in response to the needs of Buddhists to disseminate their doctrines, for under the Tang the Buddhist religious establishment became increasingly powerful. Buddhist religious art found expression also in further cave sculptures and paintings. New ceramic manufacturing methods led to the production of the first true porcelain, a product of great beauty and durability. For centuries, China alone knew the secret of its manufacture. Millers developed machinery and gears for converting linear and rotary motion, encouraging further development of both water- and windmills. In 659 China produced the world's first pharmacopoeia, or catalog of medicines, listing their contents and uses.

Bridge over the outer moat, a connecting link of the Grand Canal at Suzhou. The engineering feats of the Sui dynasty made significant contributions to the closer integration of the empire. By digging the Grand Canal and building roads in the north China plain, rulers ensured effective communication and the opening of new trade routes between diverse regions.

Finally, Tang era poetry of meditation, nature, politics, fate, suffering, and individual identity transmitted its living legacy even to today's readers in China and beyond. Each of the three most famous Tang poets has been seen as linked to a different cultural tradition: Wang Wei (701–762) to Buddhism; Li Bai (701–761) to Daoism; and Du Fu (712–770) to Confucianism, although each was influenced by all three traditions. Du Fu's "Autumn Meditation" expresses the tension between the high-stakes, hustle-bustle of the imperial court under stress and his own desire for a life of peace within nature:

> I've heard it said Chang'an is like a chessboard, where
> Failure and grief is all these hundred years have brought.
> Mansions of princes and high nobles have new lords.
> New officers are capped and robed for camp and court.
> North on the passes gold drums thunder. To the west
> Horses and chariots rush dispatches and reports.
> Dragon and fish are still, the autumn river's cold.
> My ancient land and times of peace come to my thoughts.

Du Fu's "Ballad of the Army Carts" repeats the heartbreaking pain of war. Du Fu probably wrote it during or following the An Lushan rebellion of 755–763, which the Tang defeated, but from which the dynasty never fully recovered:

> Carts rattle and squeak,
> Horses snort and neigh—
> Bows and arrows at their waists, the conscripts march away.
> Fathers, mothers, children, wives run to say goodbye.
> The Xianyang Bridge in clouds of dust is hidden from the eye.
>
> They tug at them and stamp their feet, weep, and obstruct their way.
> The weeping rises to the sky.
> Along a road a passer-by
> Questions the conscripts. They reply:
> They mobilize us constantly. Sent northwards at fifteen
> To guard the River, we were forced once more to volunteer,

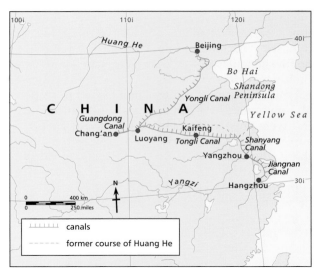

Chinese technology Classical Chinese cultures were administratively and technologically sophisticated. They mastered diplomacy, bureaucracy, navigation, architecture, chemistry, mechanics, astronomy, printing, and, most dramatically, hydrology. Terraced farming, intensive irrigation systems, and the construction of thousands of miles of navigable canals harnessed the often unpredictable rivers of eastern China, and opened up the inland cities to commerce.

> Though we are forty now, to man the western front this year.
> The headman tied our headcloths for us when we first left here.
> We came back white-haired—to be sent again to the frontier.
> Those frontier posts could fill the sea with the blood of those who've died,
> But still the Martial Emperor's aims remain unsatisfied.
> In county after county to the east, Sir, don't you know,
> In village after village only thorns and brambles grow,
> Even if there's a sturdy wife to wield the plough and hoe,
> The borders of the fields have merged, you can't tell east from west.
> It's worse still for the men from Qin, as fighters they're the best—
> And so, like chickens or like dogs, they're driven to and fro.
>
> Though you are kind enough to ask,
> Dare we complain about our task?
> Take, Sir, this winter. In Guanxi
> The troops have not yet been set free.
> The district officers come to press

The land tax from us nonetheless.
But, Sir, how can we possibly pay?
Having a son's a curse today.
Far better to have daughters, get them married—
A son will lie lost in the grass, unburied.

Why, Sir, on distant Qinhhai shore
The bleached ungathered bones lie year on year.
New ghosts complain, and those who died before
Weep in the wet grey sky and haunt the ear.

(Seth)

As Du Fu's poem suggests, the Tang, like the Sui before them, extended their borders too far, pushed the peasants and the conscripts too hard, and, finally, felt the backlash. The Tang dynasty extended China's border farther than any other except the Qing (Manchu), another non-Chinese dynasty from Manchuria, a thousand years later (1644–1912). Its holdings in central Asia flanked and protected the silk route and brought new opportunities for wealth. Ultimately, however, these lands cost more

Ceramic model of a group of musicians seated on a camel, Tang dynasty (618–907 C.E.),
excavated from a tomb in the suburb of Xian. The beards, facial features. and costumes of some
of the musicians in this group suggest that they are from central Asia. Such models, commonly
found in the tombs of the Tang elite, are evidence of a taste for the goods that came along the silk
route from the west and the central Asian music that accompanied them.

than they brought in economically and militarily. In 755 An Lushan, one of China's frontier generals of Turkish extraction, revolted, and although the revolt was put down in 763, the cost of the warfare, and the vulnerability it revealed, weakened the Tang dynasty for the entire century and a half leading up to its fall.

The An Lushan revolt came just four years after the Battle of the Talas River in 751. This battle, 2000 miles (3200 kilometers) from Chang'an, on one of the most distant of China's western frontiers, was won by Arab armies. The combined stresses of military losses abroad and revolt at home led the Tang to withdraw from their "outer China" possessions. They found that the border groups—Turks, Uighurs, Khitans, and other ethnic groups—no longer accepted Chinese domination, but continually probed the Tang border fortifications. China ceded control of central Asia to others. One result was that the silk routes soon became passageways of Islam rather than of Buddhism or Confucianism.

Although both agricultural and commercial wealth in China continued to grow, the government could no longer control them for its own imperial purposes. Regional rulers grew in authority and power. In 907 the Tang finally disappeared as China splintered into ten separate states. Yet the imperial idea and pattern held. In 960 the Song dynasty arose, ruling all of China until 1127, and the south until 1279.

CONNECTION: *From the Mongol Empire to the Ming Dynasty,* pp. 383–94.

GREATER CHINA

PROCESSES OF ASSIMILATION

We opened this part on empires by noting that empire signifies rule by one people over another. Let us examine this definition in relation to China.

Caravanserai, Kirghizstan, Tang dynasty, (618–907 C.E.) The silk route led traders through some inhospitable terrain, such as this barren and mountainous region of Kirghizstan in central Asia. This Tang dynasty-era caravanserai, the oldest complete example in existence, would have protected traders from the elements and from preying bandits.

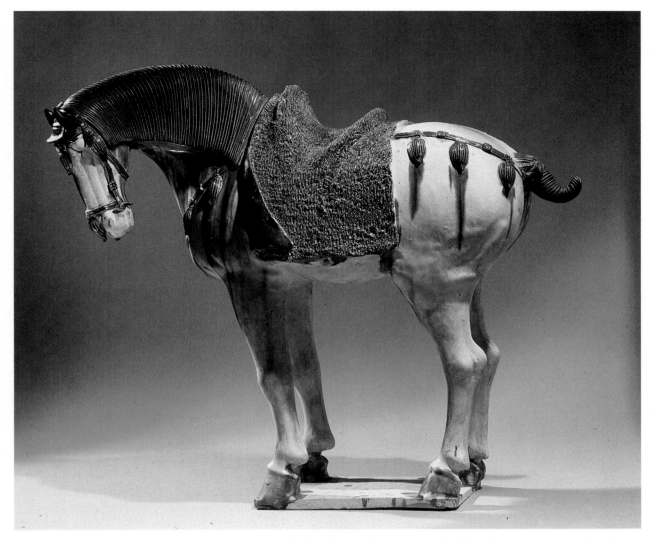

Pottery figure of a Ferghana horse, excavated from a tomb, Tang dynasty (618–907 C.E.). The Tang dynasty opened the Grand Canal, stimulated growth in trade, and expanded the boundaries of the empire. For much of this they were dependent on the mobility of the army, which in turn was dependent for covering great distances on the famed Ferghana horses, immortalized in literature as "the horses that sweated blood." (*Idemitsu Museum of Arts, Tokyo*)

First, within the borders of China, "empire" frequently meant the **assimilation** of others. In the north, many of the tribal groups against which China fought and against which Chinese rulers constructed the Great Wall, nevertheless came to enlist in China's armies, settle its land, assimilate to its culture, adopt its language and calligraphy, and intermarry with its peoples. Both the ethnic Chinese and the Barbarians regarded this process as mutually beneficial. Both also understood the dangers: the "Barbarians" might lose their culture and even find themselves in civil war with others of their ethnic group who rejected assimilation; while the Chinese might be conquered by their new allies.

Indeed, both of these results did occur frequently. Depending on one's point of view, the cultures of both the Barbarians and the Chinese were enriched or diluted by the interchanges.

THE NORTH AND THE NORTHWEST

The most geographically far-reaching of China's expansions beyond the borders of inner China were to the northwest and west. Just as Emperor Han Wudi's expansion into Gansu and beyond did not survive the early Han dynasty, so the Sui–Tang expansion even deeper into central Asia did not survive the Battle of the Talas River and the An Lushan revolt. At other times, China's influence over these regions was cultural and symbolic rather than political, military, or even directly economic.

THE SOUTH AND SOUTHWEST

In south China processes of assimilation took place, but they have made much less of a mark in the records. China as an ethnic, cultural, and political entity developed first in the north, around the Yellow River, but as Chinese peoples moved south of the Yangzi they met people of other ethnic groups. Some moved south to preserve and develop their own separate national identities. The Vietnamese are the clearest example of this pattern. Some remained as distinct, separate tribal groups,

usually in remote areas somewhat difficult to access. Occasionally these peoples revolted against the Chinese invasion and take-over of their land. The Miao gave the clearest example of this response. Most of the rest assimilated, including some Vietnamese and Miao, without making a lasting impression on the historical records.

VIETNAM

For a thousand years China held Annam (North Vietnam) as a colony. Conquered by the Han dynasty and incorporated as a province of China in 111 B.C.E., Annam remained part of China until the Vietnamese rebel Ngo Quyen declared himself the king of the independent state of Dai Viet in 939 C.E. after the collapse of the Tang. During and after the Chinese colonization, the Vietnamese were locked in a love-hate relationship with Chinese culture and politics. Chinese scholars and officials, many of them fleeing imperial policies in China, brought to Vietnam their own ideographic script, Confucian ethical principles, and the Confucian literary classics. The Vietnamese adopted them all. Buddhism also arrived in Vietnam via China. The rest of southeast Asia absorbed Buddhism in its Theravada form from India; Vietnam adopted Mahayana Buddhism as it had developed in China, after about the fifth century C.E. These cultural innovations appealed primarily to the upper class aristocracy. At the level of practical technology, the Chinese also introduced a number of valuable agricultural innovations: the collective construction of the huge network of dams and waterworks that protect against the monsoon flooding every year; the use of human excrement as fertilizer; market gardening; and intensive pig farming.

Despite having adopted many Chinese customs, the Vietnamese resented foreign hegemony by the colossus to its north. For example, the two Trung sisters led a military revolt in 39 C.E., succeeded in evicting the Chinese, ruled jointly over Vietnam for two years, and then committed suicide when the revolt was crushed. They are revered in Vietnam to this day. Leaders of numerous, less dramatic revolts that took place during the period of Chinese rule are also viewed as national heroes. Yet the most profound adoption of Chinese administrative reforms took place paradoxically in the fifteenth century, when Vietnam was independent. As a result of Chinese direct rule in the earlier period and Chinese power and proximity during later periods of Vietnamese independence, the country

CHINESE DYNASTIES

Listed below are all the imperial dynasties, starting with the Qin, and the two major pre-imperial ruling houses. Gaps in the date sequences mark those periods when the country was divided between two or more rulers.

Shang	c. **1600–1100** B.C.E.
Zhou	c. **1100–256**
Qin	**221–206**
Han	**202** B.C.E.–**220** C.E.
Three Kingdoms (Kingdom of Shu Han, Kingdom of Wei, Kingdom of Wu)	**220–65**
Northern and Southern Dynasties	**265–589**
Western Jin	265–317
Eastern Jin	317–419
Northern Wei	424–535
Sui	**202–618**
Tang	**618–907**
Song	**960–1279**
Yuan (Mongol)	**1279–1368**
Ming	**1368–1644**
Manchu (Qing)	**1644–1911**

became a Confucian state, with an examination system, an intellectually elitist administration somewhat aloof from the masses, and an intense desire for independence from China.

KOREA

Korea came under Chinese direct rule only very briefly, but Chinese cultural hegemony profoundly influenced the peninsula. Northern Korea was first conquered by the Emperor Han Wudi in 109–108 B.C.E., along with Manchuria. Military garrisons established Chinese control and influence. Korea, like Vietnam, had borrowed heavily from prehistoric China, including much of Shang technology and, later, iron technology, paper production, printing, lacquerwork, porcelain (although Korean celadon ware had a distinct beauty all its own), wheat and rice agriculture, and the ideographs of written language. (Later, the Koreans developed a written system called *han'gul* based on phonetics.) After the collapse of the Han in 220 C.E., Korea broke free of direct control, although it remained a vassal of the Chinese. Some of China's colonies remained in place, but without military capacity. The Sui dynasty sent three expeditions to conquer Korea, but all ended in disaster. The expansive Tang dynasty also tried to retake Korea in the seventh century, occupying much of the peninsula during 668–676. Ultimately Korea regained and maintained its independence, although it was often forced to accept tributary status.

China's power over Korea can be seen far more in terms of cultural hegemony than in political-military rule. Confucianism, law codes, bureaucratic administration, literature, art, and Mahayana Buddhism all entered Korean life from China, independent of government pressure. In 935 C.E., after the fall of the Tang, Korea's Silla dynasty also fell. The Koryo dynasty, which took its place, built a new capital at Kaesong, just north of today's South Korean capital at Seoul, and modeled it on Chang'an, the Tang capital in China. Both China and Korea spoke of a "younger brother/older brother" relationship between the two countries.

JAPAN

China never conquered Japan, but Japan did accept China's cultural hegemony. Indeed, through the seventh and eighth centuries C.E. Japan actively and enthusiastically attempted to model its state, religion, technology, art, and language on those of

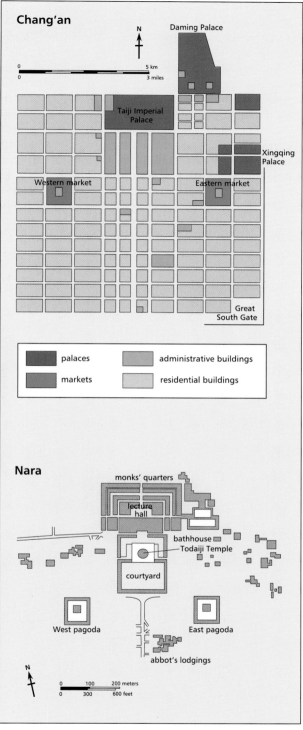

Asian imperial capitals The Tang capital of Chang'an was grid-planned as a massive rectangle over 5 miles (8 km) square, focusing on the imperial quarters and housing about a million people within its walls. The newly centralized Japanese Yamato state built Nara in imitation of Chang'an: a grid plan incorporated the Todaiji Temple complexes.

China. As the Korean peninsula stands between the Chinese mainland and the four major islands of Japan, much of the importation of Chinese forms came through Korea.

Although archaeological records show that Japan was populated by the Jomon people of the coastal regions at least as early as 10,000 B.C.E., rice agriculture, introduced from south China, seems to have begun only about 300 B.C.E. Bronze tools and weapons arrived about the first century B.C.E. and the technology for making iron tools about 200 years later. Waves of immigrants from Korea and China arrived in Japan between *c.* 200 B.C.E. and *c.* 500 C.E. By 500 C.E., about one-third of Japan's nobility claimed Korean or Chinese descent, and many artisans and metal workers in Japan had

come from Korea. All was not peaceful between Japan and Korea, however, and invasions and raids broke out in both directions. In 405 C.E. a Korean scribe, named Wani, came to teach the Chinese script, and this became Japan's earliest written language. In this period the Chinese represented the Japanese by an ideograph that means "dwarf." Japan's recorded history begins only in the eighth century C.E., and most of our knowledge of these earlier years comes either from archaeological records or from references in the literatures of China and Korea.

The formation of a state began about the third century C.E., when a clan of people worshiping the sun-goddess established its rule over the Yamato Plain in central Honshu Island. Ultimately, the

The Nandaimon, or "Great South Gate," of the Todai Buddhist temple, 745–752 C.E. The first Japanese Buddhist temples—modeled on the Buddhist temples of China—are among the oldest surviving timber buildings in the world. So faithful and enduring are they that they have become our best examples of *Chinese* architecture for the period (contrast with picture, p. 287).

imperial line of Japan would claim its descent from this group. They used Chinese written characters and accepted elements of both Confucianism and Buddhism to enrich the practices of the indigenous religion, Shinto. After China succeeded in re-establishing its own powerful empire under the Sui and Tang dynasties, the Japanese rulers dispatched numerous delegations of hundreds of members each to China to learn and adopt Chinese models. The Chinese calendar and many methods of government were introduced. In 604 a new seventeen-point "constitution" was introduced, a guide that was modeled on Chinese practice. The document included reverence for Confucianism and Buddhism, and for the sovereign of Japan, and, on a more mundane level, asserted the government's monopoly over the collection of taxes.

Bloody struggles for control of the court in Japan brought Nakatomi no Kamatari to power in 645. He took the surname Fujiwara, and under this name his family dominated the politics of Japan for centuries to come. (One descendant, Prince Konoe Fumimaro, served as prime minister in 1937–9 and again in 1940–1.) Fujiwara adopted Chinese culture, religion, and government as the way to centralize and unify Japan and to assert his own control. He proclaimed the Taika ("great change") reforms in 646, consolidating provincial administration and constructing an extensive road system. The reforms also abolished private ownership of land and, following the Chinese "equal field system," redistributed land at each generational change.

In 710 two acts further consolidated centralized rule. First, a new capital, modeled on Chang'an, was built at Nara. Second, the Japanese ruler now claimed to rule through divine mandate, which, unlike the Chinese concept, could never be revoked. (To this day, the same family occupies the imperial throne, although after World War II, its divinity was officially repudiated; see Chapter 19.) The emperor continued to serve as the chief priest of Japan's Shinto faith, but as Shinto is a religion that worships the gods of nature—streams, trees, rocks—it can be practiced anywhere. Buddhism, by contrast, although it, too, can be practiced everywhere, provides a much more centralized form of organization, through monasteries and temples. Many new Buddhist temples were, therefore, constructed in Chinese form at Nara to centralize worship in Japan. From this time onward Buddhism and Shinto have coexisted in Japan, with millions of Japanese declaring themselves devotees of both faiths.

Following the Chinese model, the Japanese began to record their history for the first time in the *Nihon Shoki*, which was in Chinese, and their legends in the *Kojiki*, written in a mixture of Chinese and Japanese forms. As centuries passed and Japan became more secure in its own political organization and cultural identity, the reliance on Chinese models declined. But in the centuries in which its basic cultural and political identity was formed, Japan had followed carefully and devotedly the hegemonic examples of China, without compulsion or force of any sort.

CHINA AND ROME: HOW DO THEY COMPARE?

DIFFERENCES

Geopolitical

China's heartland was far larger and more cohesive, geographically and culturally, than Rome's. Rome had as its heartland only central Italy, and even after conquering Italy, it held just that single peninsula bounded by the Alps Mountains and the Mediterranean Sea. In the time of Augustus in Rome and the Han dynasty in China, the Roman and Chinese empires each held about 60 million people, but in Rome only a few of these millions were in Italy. In China virtually all were in "inner China," 90 percent of them in the North China Plain.

Ideological

Although Confucian China spoke of a mythological golden age of equality among people in harmony with each other and with nature, realistically the Confucians believed that the best possible government was a well-ordered empire. Imperial Rome knew of its actual, historical republican past and always looked back to it as a golden age. Roman imperial expansion and stratification were often regarded as violations of the earlier republican ideals.

Longevity and Persistence

Rome's empire rose, fell, and was gone, although it lived on as a concept. China's empire has lasted for the last two thousand years. Dynasties have come and gone, and sometimes the empire has broken into fragments, but finally the empire endured as a single political entity. Today, although without an emperor, China's geopolitical unity continues.

Policy and Powers of Assimilation

As China moved both north and south, it assimilated a great number of the peoples it invaded and conquered. Non-ethnic Chinese were absorbed culturally and biologically. Many of the 95 percent of today's Chinese population who are called "Han" are descended from ancestors who were not. The empire was held together by Confucian and Buddhist ideology, supported by the power of the emperor and his armies. Rome's empire was held together by law and backed by military power. Selected non-Romans could gain citizenship under law, but ethnically and culturally the conquered peoples remained "other." Intermarriage with non-citizens was usually forbidden. Rome maintained the cultural distinctions far more than did China.

Language Policy

The Chinese language unified the Chinese Empire across space and through time, to today, far more than Latin did the Roman Empire. Chinese was never subordinated to another language and culture, as Latin was to Greek for many years and in many regions. Nor did Chinese compete with regional languages as Latin ultimately did. Indeed Chinese helped to bring even neighboring countries, Vietnam, Korea, and Japan, together into a single general cultural unit. Latin was gradually supplanted as a spoken tongue by its successor Romance languages: Italian, French, Spanish, Portuguese, Catalan, and Romanian.

Ideology and Cultural Cohesion

China's cultural, Confucian bureaucracy provided a core cultural identity throughout the empire and beyond. Even the alternative political-cultural philosophies of China, such as Daoism, Legalism, and later Buddhism, usually (but not always) served to broaden and augment the attraction of Confucianism. Rome's principal philosophies of paganism, Stoicism and, later, Christianity did not significantly buttress and augment its imperial rule, and the latter two may even have diminished popular loyalty to the empire.

Influence on Neighbors

The Roman Empire influenced the lands it conquered, but had less influence on those outside its boundaries. China exercised lasting hegemonic influence even on neighbors it did not conquer, such as Japan, or conquered only briefly, such as Korea. A considerable part of this legacy was religious and cultural as well as political, economic, and administrative.

SIMILARITIES
Relations with Barbarians

Both empires faced nomadic groups from central Asia who threatened and penetrated their boundaries. Indeed, the Huns, who invaded Europe, and the Xiongnu, who invaded China, may have belonged to the same ethnic group (compare maps on p. 187 and p. 208). Both empires settled the "Barbarians" near their borders and enlisted them in the imperial armies. In both cases, the Barbarians came to hold great power. Ultimately, however, they dismembered the Roman Empire while they were absorbed by the Chinese.

Religious Policies

Both empires incubated foreign religions, especially in times of imperial disorder, but in Rome, Christianity did not save the empire, and by challenging the significance of earthly power it may even have contributed to the empire's weakness. In China, Buddhism was absorbed into Confucianism and Daoism and helped to sustain the national culture in times of political trouble.

The Role of the Emperor

Both empires ascribed divine attributes to the emperor, and both frequently had difficulty in establishing rules for imperial succession. The Romans often attempted to choose their best general, while the Chinese selected a man who could control the imperial family and court. Neither empire believed that a single imperial family should rule forever.

Gender Relationships

Both empires subordinated women to men at all stages of life, and both drew analogies between hierarchies and loyalties in a well-run family and those in a well-run empire. Both empires used marriages as means of confirming political alliances with foreign powers. Both periodically felt that excessive concern with sexual relationships was distracting energy away from the demands of sustaining the empire and instituted strict codes of sexual morality. In China, far more than in Rome, women of the imperial family played an important role in politics behind the scenes, particularly in terms of determining succession. One woman, the Empress Wu (r. 690–705), took the throne herself.

The Significance of Imperial Armies

In both empires, the army was crucial in creating and sustaining the political structure in the face of domestic and foreign enemies. The Roman Empire was established and ruled by generals, as were the Qin, Han, Sui, and Tang dynasties in China. Both empires were periodically threatened and usurped by rebel generals asserting their own authority. The cost of the armies, especially on distant, unprofitable expeditions, often bankrupted the government and encouraged its subjects to evade taxes and military service and even to rise in revolt.

The Deployment of Armies of Colonization

Both empires used colonies of soldier-colonizers to garrison and develop remote areas while simultaneously providing compensation and retirement benefits for the troops.

Overextension

Both empires suffered their greatest challenges in confronting simultaneously the strains of overexpansion and the subsequent internal revolts that were triggered by the costs. In Rome these dual problems, along with the Barbarian invasions, finally precipitated the end of the empire in the west. In China they led to the loss of the Mandate of Heaven and the downfall of dynasties. The external battles against Qin-Jurchen border tribes, for example, combined with the revolt of the Yellow Turbans brought down the later Han; the loss of the distant Battle of the Talas River, combined with the internal revolt of An Lushan, sapped Tang power.

Public Works Projects

Throughout their empire the Romans built roads, aqueducts, public monumental structures, administrative/military towns, and the great capital cities of Rome and Constantinople. The Chinese built the Great Wall, the Grand Canal, systems of transportation by road and water, public monumental structures, administrative/military towns throughout the empire, and several successive capitals, especially Chang'an and Luoyang.

The Concentration of Wealth

In both empires, the benefits of imperial wealth tended to flow toward the center, to the elites in the capital cities. The capitals grew to unprecedented size. Both Chang'an and Rome housed more than one million people.

Policies For and Against Individual Mobility

In order to maintain power and stability in the face of demands for change, both empires periodically bound their peasantry to the soil and demanded that the sons of soldiers follow their fathers' occupations. Both found these policies difficult to enforce. Both offered some individual mobility through service in their armies. In addition, the Chinese examination system provided for advancement within the imperial bureaucracy.

Revolts

Both empires experienced frequent revolts against the emperor and his policies. In Rome, which housed a much larger slave population, many of the revolts were led by slaves. In China they were more typically initiated by peasants. Rome attempted to forestall mass revolts in the capital and other large cities through the provision of so-called "bread and circuses."

Peasant Flight

In both empires, during times of upheaval, peasants sought to evade taxes and conscription by finding refuge as tenants on large, landed estates. In times when imperial government was weak, the largest of these estates challenged the power of the central government.

BIBLIOGRAPHY

Andrea, Alfred and James H. Overfield, eds. *The Human Record:* Vol I (Boston: Houghton Mifflin Co., 3rd ed., 1998).

Blunden, Caroline and Mark Elvin. *Cultural Atlas of China* (New York: Facts on File, 1983).

Bodde, Derk. *Essays on Chinese Civilization*, ed. Charles Le Blanc and Dorothy Borei (Princeton: Princeton University Press, 1981).

Cotterell, Arthur, ed. *The Penguin Encyclopedia of Ancient Civilizations* (London: Penguin Books, 1980).

Creel, H.G. *Confucius: The Man and the Myth* (Westport, CT: Greenwood Press, reprinted 1972 from 1949 ed.).

deBary, William Theodore and Irene Bloom, eds., *Sources of Chinese Tradition, Vol.I: From Earliest Times to 1600* (New York: Columbia University Press, 1999).

Ebrey, Patricia Buckley, ed. *Chinese Civilization: A Sourcebook* (New York: The Free Press, 2nd ed., 1993).

Elvin, Mark. *The Pattern of the Chinese Past* (Stanford: Stanford University Press, 1973).

Fairbank, John K., Edwin O. Reischauer, and Albert M. Craig. *East Asia: Tradition and Transformation* (Boston: Houghton Mifflin, rev. edn, 1989).

Friedman, Edward. "Reconstructing China's National Identity: A Southern Alternative to Mao-Era Anti-Imperialist Nationalism," *Journal of Asian Studies* LIII, No. 1 (February 1994), 67–91.

Han Fei Tzu. *The Complete Works of Han Fei Tzu*, 2 Vols. trans. W.K. Liao (London: Arthur Probsthain, 1959).

Hughes, Sarah Shaver and Brady Hughes, ed. *Women in World History*, Vol. I (Armonk, NY: M.E. Sharpe, 1995).

Lockard, Craig A. "Integrating Southeast Asia into the Framework of World History: The Period Before 1500," *The History Teacher* XXIX, No. 1 (November 1995), 7–35.

McGovern, William Montgomery. *The Early Empires of Central Asia* (Chapel Hill: University of North Carolina Press, 1939).

Murphey, Rhoads. *East Asia: A New History* (New York: HarperCollins, 1997).

Needham, Joseph. *The Shorter Science and Civilization in China*, Vol. I, abridged by Colin A. Ronan (Cambridge: Cambridge University Press, 1978).

Parker, Geoffrey, ed. *The (London) Times Atlas of World History* (London: Times Books, Ltd., 4th ed., 1993).

Past Worlds: The (London) Times Atlas of Archaeology (Maplewood, NJ: Hammond, 1988).

SarDesai, D.R. *Southeast Asia: Past and Present* (Boulder, CO: Westview Press, 3rd ed., 1994).

Schirokauer, Conrad. *A Brief History of Chinese and Japanese Civilizations* (Fort Worth: Harcourt Brace Jovanovich, 2nd ed., 1989).

Schwartz, Benjamin I. *The World of Thought in Ancient China* (Cambridge: Harvard University Press, 1985).

Seth, Vikram. *Three Chinese Poets: Translations of Poems by Wang Wei, Li Bai, and Du Fu* (New York: HarperCollins, 1993).

Sima Qian. *Historical Records*, trans. Raymond Dawson (New York: Oxford University Press, 1994).

Sima Qian. *Records of the Historian: Chapters from the Shih Chi of Ssu-ma Ch'ien*, trans. Burton Watson (New York: Columbia University Press, 1969).

Sullivan, Michael. *The Arts of China* (Berkeley: University of California Press, 1984).

Time-Life Books. *Time Frame. 400 BC–AD 200: Empires Ascendant* (Alexandria, VA: Time-Life Books, 1988).

——. *Time Frame AD 200–600: Empires Besieged* (Alexandria, VA: Time-Life Books, 1988).

——. *Time Frame AD 600–800: The March of Islam* (Alexandria, VA: Time-Life Books, 1989).

Twitchett, Denis and Michael Lowe, eds. *The Cambridge History of China*, Vol. I: *The Ch'in and Han Empires, 221 B.C.–A.D. 220* (Cambridge: Cambridge University Press, 1986).

Twitchett, Denis, ed. *The Cambridge History of China*, Vol. III: *Sui and T'ang China, 589–906*, Part I (Cambridge: Cambridge University Press, 1979).

CHAPTER

INDIAN EMPIRES

8

1500 B.C.E.–1100 C.E.

*" When one king is weaker than the other, he should make peace with him.
When he is stronger than the other, he should make war with him."*

KAUTILYA, *ARTHA–SASTRA*

CULTURAL COHESION IN A DIVIDED SUBCONTINENT

What do we mean by "India"? In this chapter we include the entire subcontinent of south Asia, which includes not only the present-day country of India, but also its neighbors: Pakistan, Afghanistan, Bangladesh, Nepal, and Bhutan. Geographers call the entire region a subcontinent because it is so clearly bounded by powerful natural borders. Along its entire southern perimeter it is surrounded by oceanic waters: the Arabian Sea to the west and the Bay of Bengal to the east. To the north, the Himalayan Mountains, the highest in the world, form an almost impenetrable barrier. To the east and west, spurs of the Himalayas complete the ring of demarcation, but these mountain ranges are lower and more negotiable. Passes through the northwest mountains, like the Khyber Pass, make entrance possible, as does a route through the desert along the western Makran coast. The peoples who came to India before 3000 B.C.E., for whom we have no historical record, seem to have arrived from a variety of approaches, probably including some by sea voyages from Africa, southeast Asia, and the islands of the Pacific. Since then, all the major immigrations have come from the northwest. In modern times British traders and rulers also came by sea (Chapters 13 and 16). They had an important impact on the subcontinent, but they did not stay.

The entire Indian subcontinent has never been unified into a single empire (although in the nineteenth and twentieth centuries, the British lacked only formal control of Afghanistan). Asoka Maurya (r. *c.* 265–38 B.C.E.) was the first person to come close to achieving that goal, but even he never captured the far south. Usually, as today, a variety of rulers controlled different regions of the subcontinent.

India might, in fact, be regarded more as a continent than as a single country. The geographical area of the subcontinent is equal to about half the size of Europe. It is not surprising, then, that Indian empires did not last more than a few hundred years. Yet unlike Rome, and much more like China, India has maintained a persistent cultural unity over several thousand years. In this chapter we will begin to consider why India dissolved politically into many separate states, and in Chapter 9 we will consider the religious and cultural institutions that nevertheless served to bring a loose unity to the subcontinent.

Lion capital of the pillar erected by Asoka at Sarnath, Mauryan, *c.* **250 B.C.E.** The polished sandstone columns erected by the Emperor Asoka at places associated with events in the Buddha's life, or marking pilgrim routes to holy places, are of special interest for their 7-foot-tall (2.1 m) capitals. These provide us with the best remaining examples of Mauryan imperial art and are rich in symbolism. For instance, the Buddha was spoken of as a "lion" among spiritual preachers, whose sermon penetrated to all four corners of the world, just as the lion's roar established his authority in the forest.

SETTLEMENT IN SOUTH ASIA

In Chapter 3 we read of the civilization of the Indus valley, which began with the appearance of the first cities of south Asia in about 2500 B.C.E. That civilization began to fade about 1500 B.C.E. for reasons that are not entirely understood. It is thought, however, that as the people of the Indus civilization struggled in and emigrated from their home base in the Indus valley, new waves of "Aryan" immigrants arrived. These new arrivals are named not for their race, but for Sanskrit and the other related **Indo-Aryan** languages they spoke. Archaeologists are not certain of the geographical origins of the new arrivals; some claim they came from central Asia, others from the Iranian plateau, while a few suggest Europe.

In successive waves of immigration, the nomadic and pastoral Aryans, mixing with indigenous peoples, migrated slowly eastward, reaching the Ganges valley about the year 1000 B.C.E. As they settled, they began to build a new urban civilization and to form new states. By about 700–600 B.C.E., numerous political groupings, called *janapadas* (populated territories), began to emerge. The leadership of the territories was centered in specific family lineage groups, and as these lineages grew in size, and as they cleared more forest land to expand their territorial control, the *janapadas* began to take on the political forms of states with urban capitals and political administrations. Some constituted themselves as republics, others as monarchies. By 500–400 B.C.E., about the time the Persian armies of Darius reached the Indus, sixteen large *maha-janapadas* had emerged in northern India. By the time Alexander arrived in 326 B.C.E., four of these large states dominated the rest, and one, Magadha, was beginning to emerge as an imperial power over all. One family dynasty, the Nandas, established limited imperial supremacy at Magadha, but its power lasted for only one generation, from *c.* 364 to 324 B.C.E.

The Maurya family dynasty, which succeeded to the throne of Magadha in 324 B.C.E., remained in power for almost a century and a half, until 185 B.C.E. Its founder, Chandragupta Maurya (r. *c.* 321–297 B.C.E.), may have conceived the idea of an India-wide empire from a possible meeting with Alexander the Great. As we saw in Chapter 5, Alexander had reached the Indus in 326 B.C.E. and had wanted to continue his sweep all the way across the subcontinent to the ocean that he believed to be at the end of the world. His troops, however, mutinied with the famous words of caution: "Sir, if there is one thing above all others a successful man should know, it is when to stop" (cited in Green, p. 410). His army's refusal to go forward forced Alexander to leave India.

Soon thereafter Chandragupta marched his own troops from Magadha into northwest India to fill the power vacuum. Chandragupta's son, Bindusara

INDIAN EMPIRES

DATE	POLITICAL	RELIGION AND CULTURE	SOCIAL DEVELOPMENT
600 B.C.E.	• *Janapadas* established		
500 B.C.E.	• Gandhara and Sind held by Persian Empire (*c.* 518) • *Maha-janapadas* established (500–400)	• Buddha, Siddhartha Gautama (*c.* 563–483) • Puranas written (*c.* 500 B.C.E.–500 C.E.) • Vedic period ends (1500–500)	
400 B.C.E.	• Nanda dynasty in Magadha (*c.* 364–324)		
300 B.C.E.	• Alexander the Great in south Asia (327–325) • Chandragupta Maurya (*c.* 321–*c.* 297) founds Mauryan dynasty (324–185) in Magadha • Kautilya wrote *Artha–sastra* (*c.* 300)		
250 B.C.E..	• Bindusara Maurya (*c.* 297–*c.* 272) • Asoka Maurya (*c.* 265–238)	• Rock inscriptions of Asoka • Buddhism organized as state religion • Asokan lion column (see p. 232)	• Mauryan empire extended from Afghanistan to Bay of Bengal to Deccan
200 B.C.E.	• Sunga dynasty (185–73) • Mauryan Empire fractures, along with unity of India (185)	• Jain influence increases	
150 B.C.E.		• Sanchi stupa (p. 276) • Menander (Milanda) king of Indo–Greek Empire (*c.* 160–135)	• Trade contacts with S.E. Asia
100 B.C.E.	• First Shaka king in western India (*c.* 94)	• Sangam poetry from Tamil culture	
50 C.E.	• Height of Kushana power under Emperor Kanishka (*c.* 78–*c.* 103)	• Bhagavad-Gita	
100 C.E.		• Gandhara Buddha (pp. 243 and 288) • Rise of Mahayana Buddhism	• Trade flourishes between India and the Central Asian trade routes
200 C.E.		• Beginning of Hindu–Buddhist influence on southeast Asia	

(r. *c.* 297–*c.* 272 B.C.E.), expanded still further the empire that his father had created, and Bindusara's son, Asoka (r. *c.* 265–238 B.C.E.), brought the empire of the Mauryas to its greatest extent, ruling from modern Afghanistan in the northwest to the Bay of Bengal in the east and well into the Deccan penin-sula in the south. By this time India may have held as many as 100 million people.

The record of Asoka's rule, lost for many centuries, was rediscovered by scholars only about a hundred years ago, and today he is considered the greatest of the emperors of the Mauryan dynasty,

INDIAN EMPIRES

DATE	POLITICAL	RELIGION AND CULTURE	SOCIAL DEVELOPMENT
300 C.E.	• Gupta Empire (c. 320–540) established by Chandra Gupta (320–c. 330)	• Sanskrit used for official business • Hindu ascendancy over Buddhism	• Indian trade contacts with Oc Eo, Funan (300–600)
350 C.E.	• Samudra Gupta (c. 330–c. 380) expands dynasty throughout north and into south		
400 C.E.	• Chandra Gupta II (c. 380–c. 415) expands empire to maximum • Kumara Gupta (c. 415–455)	• Cultural "golden age" • Panini, Sanskrit grammarian (fl. 400) • Faxian, Buddhist pilgrim • Ajanta caves (5th–8th c.) (p. 245)	
450 C.E.	• Skanda Gupta (455–467) repulses Huna invasion from central Asia (c. 460) • Budha Gupta (467–497)	• Kalidasa composes "Meghaduta" and *Shakuntala*	• Sanskrit in S.E. Asia; Indian gods; Buddhism
500 C.E.	• Hunas gain control of north India	• Classical urban culture declines	
600 C.E.	• Pallavas rise to power at Kanchipuram under Mahendravarman I (c. 600–c. 611) • Harsha-vardhana (606-647) rules north India from Kanauj • Chalukyas rule central India under Pulakeshin II at Badami (608-642)	• Xuanzang, Buddhist pilgrim	
700 C.E.	• Arabs conquer Sind (712)	• Ellora temple complex (p. 271) (757-790) • Borobudur, Java (p. 250) (778-824) • Khajuraho temple complex (p. 270) (1025-1050) • Vedantic philosophy flourishes	
1100 C.E.	• Cholas defeat Srivijaya Empire, Sumatra	• Angkor Wat, Cambodia (p. 251)	

See also Hinduism and Buddhism timechart, p. 258

the first imperial dynasty to rule over most (but not all) of the Indian subcontinent. Asoka's fame rests not only on his conquests, but also on his conversion to Buddhism and his subsequent activities in spreading that faith throughout India (see Profile, p. 240) and beyond (see Chapter 9).

Following Asoka's death in 238 B.C.E., no emperor was strong enough to maintain centralized power, and the Mauryan Empire went into a half century of decline. The last Mauryan king was assassinated by one of his military commanders in 184 B.C.E., and India subsequently divided among many regional rulers, including some rulers who invaded and seized control of large territories. Finally, the Gupta dynasty brought all of north India under its control in 320 C.E., and presided over a great flowering of Sanskritic and Hindu culture (see Chapter 9). After the collapse of the Gupta dynasty in 497 C.E. the subcontinent was once again politically divided and subject to one wave of invader-rulers after another. These internal divisions and conquests by outsiders continued until the modern independence of India and Pakistan in 1947, and of Bangladesh in 1971.

THE INDIAN EMPIRES: HOW DO WE KNOW?

ARCHAEOLOGY AND PHILOLOGY

Archaeology has contributed greatly to our understanding of the earlier Indus valley. Its sparsely populated desert sites facilitated relatively easy excavation, but the later settlements in the Ganges valley have not been so accessible. This is a humid, subtropical region, where heavy monsoon rains have not allowed ancient settlements to endure. It is also densely settled, making archaeological excavation impracticable if not impossible. The distribution of pottery, painted gray ware dating primarily before 500 B.C.E., and northern black polished ware from after that date, helps us to identify and follow the waves of Aryan immigration into the Ganges valley. The more recently discovered ocher-colored pottery in the western Ganges valley and the presence of black and red ware further east suggest that by the time the Aryans arrived indigenous peoples had already settled on the land. Since the late 1970s archaeological digs have uncovered small settlement sites dating from 1000 to 600 B.C.E. throughout the Ganges valley, but without additional excavations of many other cities and small towns it is difficult to trace archaeologically in any detail the spread and nature of early Aryan civilization. The very large city-site of Taxila (Takshasila), in what is now northwestern Pakistan, which served as a regional capital for Persian, Greek, and Indian rulers, has been extensively and continuously excavated since John Marshall's first expedition in 1913. It is a very rich source of information, but only for a later period.

Philology helps to establish the dispersion of Indo-Aryan peoples by tracking the spread of their languages. The first known remaining specimens of writing in the Ganges valley are Asoka's rock and pillar inscriptions in Brahmi script, which date to the third century B.C.E. To track the oral transmission patterns of earlier centuries, anthropologists study texts that recorded them in written form at a much later time, and compare them with the distribution and evolution of today's spoken languages.

WRITTEN TEXTS

The greatest sources of information for the Aryan invasions, settlements, and empires are written materials, of which there are many. A special group of bards and chroniclers was responsible for collecting and composing these materials, although they did not attempt to establish a direct chronological, interpretive record of the sort found in Greece or Rome (see p. 143 and p. 166–9) or in China (see pp. 196–9). The **Puranas**, or legends and folk tales from earliest times, which were finally collected and written down between *c.* 500 B.C.E. and 500 C.E., contain genealogical lists of rulers from before the first humans were born to historic times, mixing fact and fable and making no attempt to distinguish between them. The earliest existing source is the *Rigveda*, 1028 hymns composed in Sanskrit about 1500–1200 B.C.E. The **Veda** are religious reflections rather than historical accounts, but to the extent that they refer to the life of the Aryan peoples who wrote them, their accounts are probably reliable. Three other Veda, the *Samaveda*, *Yajurveda*, and *Atharva Veda*, were composed some centuries later. Other religious literature of the Vedic period (1500–500 B.C.E.) include the Brahmanas, which give instructions on rituals and sacrifices, and the Upanishads, which are mystical speculations. These were composed *c.* 700 B.C.E. and afterwards.

The *Mahabharata* and the *Ramayana*

India's two great epics, the *Mahabharata* and the *Ramayana*, recount events that took place between 1000 and 700 B.C.E., although the texts themselves place the action in earlier mythic times. Neither is a historical account, but both provide valuable information on the social structures, the ways of life, and the values of the time in which they were written. The *Mahabharata* is the longest single poem in the world, some ten times longer than the Bible. Its central story is of a great civil war fought between two branches of the same family. In its tales, subplots, and asides are woven myth, speculation, folklore, moral teaching, and political reflection that are central to India's living culture. The intermingling of the great themes of life, death, family, warfare, duty,

Ahmad Kashmiri, Mughal School, scene from the *Mahabharata*, 1598 C.E. In this painting from an illustrated manuscript, one of the earliest such depictions of the great Indian epic, the god Agni is shown creating fire as a smokescreen to assist his father-in-law, while Arjun quells the flames with magic arrows that release springs of water. (*Oriental & India Office, London*)

and power give the *Mahabharata* continuing universal appeal. In 1985–8 the British theatrical producer Peter Brook produced a nine-hour version of the *Mahabharata* in English and in French and won numerous awards as he staged it in theaters around the world. (It is now available also on video.) The most famous single segment of the *Mahabharata* is the profound religious meditation and instruction called the *Bhagavad-Gita*, or "Song of God." (see Source, p. 266).

The *Ramayana*, which is much shorter, refers to somewhat later times, and there are many versions. The first known written version was in Sanskrit, composed by Valmiki about 700 B.C.E. Its core story tells of the mythical god-king Rama's victory over Ravana, the demon king of Sri Lanka, who had kidnapped his wife, Sita. The diverse versions of the *Ramayana* indicate its great popularity and the variety of its uses. Some focus on the battles between north and south, perhaps a reference to the first Aryan invasions of the south about 800 B.C.E. Some southern versions, however, tend to justify Ravana as defending the south against Rama's invasions from the north. The role of Sita is also told in different ways. Men more frequently praise Sita for her adoration of Rama and her willingness to renounce even her life so that his reputation might remain intact. Women, however, are often critical of Rama for inadequately defending Sita in the first place, then for doubting her fidelity to him during her captivity in Lanka, and, finally, for bowing to public skepticism of her loyalty by exiling her from his royal court.

As Indian sailors, merchants, and priests carried their culture to southeast Asia (see p. 249), the *Ramayana* has become a national epic in several of the countries of that region, especially in Thailand and Indonesia, where it is often dramatized by live actors and through puppetry. In India, the story is retold each year on the holiday of Dussehra, which celebrates the victory of good over evil with great color and pageantry. Broadcast on Indian national television in serialized form for about a year each, the *Mahabharata* and the *Ramayana* drew audiences of hundreds of millions for each weekly episode in the mid-1980s.

Even during the period of our central concern, historical records were not written:

> Throughout the period from the rise of the Mauryan empire in the fourth century B.C. to the establishment of the Gupta kingdom in the fourth century A.D.

Indian School, scene from the *Ramayana*, 1713 C.E. This painting from the *Ramayana* is remarkable for its exquisitely rich gouache illustration. Among the heroes depicted are Rama, his faithful wife Sita, his loyal brother Laxman, and the army of monkey warriors who accompany him in his battle against Ravana, the Lord of Lanka. (*Oriental & India Office, London*)

there is, as far as we know, no evidence of any purely historical writing, and this, in spite of the fact that the period was germane to the evolution of the major political and social institutions in ancient India. (Thapar, *Social History*, p. 271)

Other records do, however, begin to appear that cast light on changes taking place. Codes of law and statecraft, such as the *Artha-sastra*, which is attributed to Chandragupta Maurya's minister Kautilya (*fl.* 300 B.C.E.), and Asoka's own rock inscriptions (see Profile, p. 240), illuminate politics and imperial ideology. Many more such codes appeared in later times, together with Buddhist and Jain texts (see Focus, p. 279), which usually include chronologies and some interpretation.

Visitors from outside also give periodic "snapshot" accounts of India. These include the observations by Megasthenes (*c.* 350–*c.* 290 B.C.E.), a Greek ambassador and historian, sent to the court of Chandragupta Maurya about 300 B.C.E., and Menander (Milinda; *fl.* 160–135 B.C.E.), the Greek king of northwest India, who became a Buddhist. Later, about 400–700 C.E., further observations were recorded by Buddhist pilgrims from China, notably Faxian (Fa-hsien) (*fl.* 399–414 C.E.) and Xuanzang (Hsuan-tsang) (602–664 C.E.).

FAMILIAL, SOCIAL, ECONOMIC, AND RELIGIOUS INSTITUTIONS

Throughout fifteen centuries of decentralized and often weak rule, India nevertheless retained a strong sense of cultural cohesion. The leading Indian historian of the ancient period, Romila Thapar, emphasizes the intermediate familial, social, economic, and religious institutions that brought cohesion to both ancient and modern India:

Indian social history at the moment has one basic pre-occupation: an inquiry into the precise nature of social relationships in the structure of early Indian society. (Thapar, *Social History*, p. 20)

In the following pages, therefore, we analyze not only the two major imperial dynasties of ancient India, the Mauryas and the Guptas, but also the more permanent institutions that mediated between the individual and the state. The religious

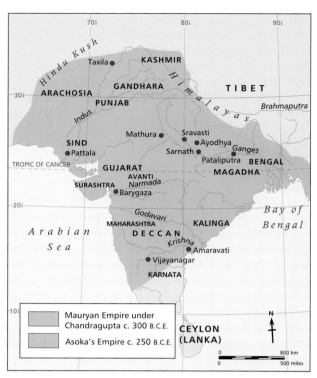

Mauryan India A contemporary of Alexander the Great, Chandragupta Maurya seized control of the kingdom of Magadha and annexed lands to the west, eventually controlling by 300 B.C.E. the strategic trade routes of the Ganges and Indus basins. His grandson Asoka extended the empire west into Seleucid Persia, and south via the wealthy kingdom of Kalinga to gain control of the Deccan by 250.

philosophies and social practices of Hinduism that inspire much of the statecraft of these dynasties are discussed briefly here, and are treated much more fully in Chapter 9. This separation in the discussion of political and religious practices is somewhat artificial, but it allows us to recognize the importance of each system separately as well as to see them interacting in support of one another.

STATECRAFT UNDER THE MAURYAS AND GUPTAS: WHAT DO WE KNOW?

THE MAURYAN EMPIRE

The Maurya dynasty created an imperial government that ruled over or displaced earlier political structures based only on family lineage. Hereditary family lineage did not cease to be important—after all, the imperial ruling dynasty itself was a lineage—but a new state apparatus stood above it in authority and power. The *Mahabharata* told of a large family of cousins falling into intra-family war over issues of inheritance of power, but by the time of the Mauryans, the state stood above such individual families and lineages.

The new empire expressed its theory of politics in the *Artha-sastra*, or science of politics and economics, which has been attributed to Kautilya, the minister of King Chandragupta Maurya. (The date of composition is not certain, and the text may actually have been written down later, but its ideas were current under the Mauryas. The *Artha-sastra* text had been lost to historians and was rediscovered only in 1909.) The text spoke of *danda niti*, translated into English alternatively and provocatively as the "policy of the scepter" or the "policy of the big stick." It had a cut-throat view of inter-state competition. Even in the earlier age of the *janapadas* (smaller political groupings), Indian political thought had already begun to think in terms of *matsyanyaya*, the "justice of the fish"—that is, larger states swallowed smaller ones. The *Artha-sastra* now postulated that every state must be on constant guard against all its neighbors, for all were potential enemies. It counseled that the power of strong states be neutralized through mutual treaties, while weak states should be attacked and conquered. The *Artha-sastra* regarded the immediate circle of neighbors as potential enemies but the next circle beyond them as potential allies, in keeping with the doctrine that the "enemy of my enemy is my friend." In this competitive world of constant warfare, the state had come into its own.

The state had many internal regulatory functions as well. First among these was the requirement to provide a powerful setting in which people had the opportunity to seek the four major goals of life in accord with Hindu philosophy: *artha* (wealth), *kama* (sensual pleasure), *dharma* (the fulfillment of social and religious duties), and *moksha* (the release from earthly existence and union with the infinite power of the universe, achieved, if at all, at the time of death). (see pp. 265–6).

The state helped to enforce rules of behavior between males and females. This relationship charged men with power over women and the responsibility for protecting them, while women were expected to run the household in accordance with the wishes of men and to be available for the pleasure of men. Women's property rights were always very limited, and at some periods they had

none. Hindu views of women's proper role and behavior are discussed briefly on page 281.

The state also regulated the behavior of its subjects in terms of the rules of **caste**. In Hindu belief each person has a social, economic, and ritual position, which was inherited at birth directly from his or her parents. Although this status may, in practice, be changed with considerable difficulty, in theory it remains for life and on into future generations. Caste status not only governs private behavior, it also gives people different, unequal status under law. (The origins and rationale of the caste system as part of Hindu religious belief are discussed in detail on pages 263–4.) It was the task of the state to enforce these caste distinctions, especially their differential rankings, liabilities, and rights in legal proceedings.

The state also regulated religious establishments. The larger Hindu temples and Buddhist monasteries developed considerable economic and political power based on the land and resources that were donated to them by devout followers, especially wealthy landlords, businessmen, and often by kings themselves. They also influenced a wide range of public and private decisions made by their devotees, and the state attempted to regulate the use of this wealth and power.

The state also enforced rules developed by India's **guilds**, associations of businessmen and producers. These mostly urban groups convened to set work rules, prices, and weights and measures, and to enforce quality control. Independent of the state, the guilds could nevertheless call on the state to enforce the regulations they had agreed on. Some students of Indian social structures have asked why the business guilds never seem to have made an attempt to gain direct control of the government in India as they did in medieval Europe (see p. 399). The answer is not entirely clear, but caste distinctions designated some people for government and military careers, others for business, separating those who were permitted to take up the bow and the sword in using force to gain government control from those who could only wield influence through wealth. In Europe businessmen both armed themselves and hired troops; in India, it seems, they did neither.

With so many responsibilities for regulating the interests of conflicting groups internally, and recognizing the need to remain constantly vigilant against powerful neighbors, Chandragupta Maurya and his son Bindusara attempted to build a highly centralized administration with a group of well-

PROFILE
Asoka
INDIA'S BUDDHIST EMPEROR

Until just over a hundred years ago, little was known about Asoka, the Mauryan emperor who held sway over the bulk of the Indian subcontinent from 265 to 238 B.C.E. In the nineteenth century, however, inscriptions that Asoka had made on pillars and rocks to spread his name and ideals were deciphered, and for the first time in modern history Asoka's identity and teachings were understood.

Asoka had constructed at least seven pillar edicts and had inscribed at least fourteen major and numerous minor rock edicts which have been discovered and excavated across many regions of India. Most are written in Brahmi script and are the oldest existing writing in India. The script, although an early variant of Sanskrit, had been lost for centuries until a British official, James Prinsep, redeciphered it in 1837. He also analyzed the collective significance of the rock and pillar edicts discovered up to his time along with materials on Asoka found in early chronicles in Ceylon (modern-day Sri Lanka).

Asoka's famed conversion to Buddhism, a dramatic turning-point in his life, is described in the Thirteenth Major Rock Edict. The carnage he had created in his military victory at Kalinga and the suffering of his victims had left Asoka with a terrible sense of remorse. As reparation for his actions, he proclaimed his renunciation of violence and acceptance of *Dhamma*, the teachings of the Buddha that promote compassion, tolerance, and honesty:

> A hundred and fifty thousand people were deported, a hundred thousand were killed and many times that number perished. Afterwards, now that Kalinga was annexed, the Beloved of the Gods [Asoka] very earnestly practiced *Dhamma*, desired *Dhamma*, and taught *Dhamma*. (Thapar, *Asoka*, p. 255)

He did not however renounce the conquest and annexation of Kalinga, and while he disavowed violence as a general principle, he seemed to retain

paid central ministers and bureaucrats, a powerful military, and an efficient system of spies dispersed throughout the empire.

At first Asoka followed similar policies, and he was especially effective at enlarging the empire through military force, but nine years into his administration, he abruptly changed course. In 260 B.C.E. Asoka defeated Kalinga (now Orissa), incorporating this eastern kingdom into his empire. The killing and chaos required to win the victory soured his heart, and he determined to become a different person and a different ruler. He converted to Buddhism, a religion firmly committed to nonviolence, and began to dispatch missionaries throughout his realm as well as to parts of south India beyond his own borders, and to Syria, Greece, Egypt, and, probably, southeast Asia. He sent his own son on a mission to Sri Lanka and the island kingdom permanently converted to Buddhism.

For thirty years after the battle of Kalinga Asoka's reign brought general peace to India and the further expansion of a new, more universalist ethic for a people who were increasingly settling down from nomadism into stable agricultural and urban life. Buddhism, diminishing the importance of the *brahmin* castes, was especially attractive to merchant castes and guilds, and Asoka's patronage was apparently also good for business. But in 185 B.C.E., fifty-three years after Asoka's death, the Mauryan dynasty came to an end, and with it the unity of India. The Mauryas still depended on the power of their lineage as the core of their rule, but they had not continued to produce emperors of the power and charisma of Chandragupta, Bindusara, and Asoka. The Mauryan lineage had not institutionalized its state into a permanent form. India dissolved again into a variety of contesting states.

The core region that remained from Magadha was ruled by the Sunga dynasty, 185–73 B.C.E. With Indian governments faltering, Indo-Greeks, the

it as an option of state policy, especially in dealing with the tribal people of the hills:

> the Beloved of the Gods conciliates the forest tribes of his empire, but he warns them that he has power even in his remorse, and he asks them to repent, lest they be killed. (Thapar, *Asoka*, p. 256)

To spread his message and promote a universal faith, Asoka dispatched missionaries throughout his empire and beyond. He also made his own journeys to practice *Dhamma* and help alleviate suffering, especially in rural areas. The Sixth Major Rock Edict proclaims Asoka's dedication to public welfare:

> I consider that I must promote the welfare of the whole world, and hard work and the dispatch of business are the means of doing so. Indeed there is no better work than promoting the welfare of the whole world. And whatever may be my great deeds, I have done them in order to discharge my debt to all beings. (Thapar, *Asoka*, p. 253)

Asoka, as depicted in a nineteenth-century engraving.

Projects implemented by Asoka to improve the welfare of his people included the founding of hospitals, the planting of medicinal plants and trees, and the building of some 84,000 stupas (Buddhist burial mounds) and monasteries. In his bid to create a more tolerant, compassionate society, Asoka granted religious groups outside of Buddhism the freedom to worship, but at the same time encouraged them to respect the beliefs and practices of other sects. The sacrificial use of animals was banned.

Asoka's active contribution to the spread of Buddhism had a lasting impact. His inscriptions offer us tangible evidence of the great influence Buddhism had not only on his own life but on Indian life and thought as a whole.

---

inheritors of Alexander's empire stationed in Afghanistan and Bactria, invaded in 182 B.C.E., capturing the northwest all the way south to the coastal cities of Gujarat. They produced a hybrid culture with the Indians they conquered. King Menander (*fl.* 160–135 B.C.E.), an Indo-Greek, carried on a profound conversation with the Buddhist monk Nagasena who introduced the king to his religion. Their dialogue is still studied today as the *Questions of King Milinda*. Gandharan art, synthesizing Greek and Indian contributions, flourished in this period (see Spotlight, p. 242–3), as did the city of Taxila, the great center of trade, culture, and education in the northwest. Finally, large caches of Indo-Greek coinage reflect the importance of trade routes running through the northwest and linking India to the great silk routes of central Asia.

Indo-Greek coin (obverse and reverse), central Asia.
The Indian subcontinent was linked to the silk route by trade routes that passed through Afghanistan and the Kushan Empire and continued westward. These economic connections account for the large quantity of Indo-Greek coinage, like this example showing the Macedonian king Demetrius I (*c.* 337–283 B.C.E.), (see map, p. 272). (*British Museum, London*)

New invaders conquered and displaced the old. In Chapter 7 we read of tribal wars in east Asia, on the borders of China, which pushed Mongol groups westward to Rome. The Shakas, who invaded and ruled parts of northwest and western India for about a century, *c.* 94 B.C.E. to *c.* 20 C.E., were one of these tribal groups. They, in turn, were displaced by

SPOTLIGHT
Gandharan Art

Gandhara, the northern part of Pakistan and northeast Afghanistan, has been a crossroads of warfare, empire, trade, religion, and art at least since the Aryans invaded India, *c.* 1700 B.C.E. Much later, on his way to the Indus Valley, 330 B.C.E., Alexander the Great conquered it, leaving a legacy of Hellenistic influence on local art forms which endured for centuries. **Figure 1** presents one of the most striking examples. This frieze of the Trojan horse, found in northern Pakistan, dates to the second or third century C.E. Cassandra stands in a doorway attempting to block the horse's entry while Laocoön holds a spear to its chest. The subject matter, the draped clothing, and Laocoön's posture derive from Hellenistic culture. The fullness of Cassandra's figure, the form of the chariot wheels, and a general solidity of form reflect local traditions.

As the Greeks left Gandhara, the Mauryan dynasty from the Ganges valley moved in. The emperor Asoka Maurya (265–238 B.C.E.) embraced Buddhism and used his power to broadcast its message. Gandhara was receptive. In addition, many of Buddhism's early supporters were businessmen, some of

Figure 1 Trojan horse frieze, from Mardan district, Gandhara, second to third century C.E. (*British Museum, London*)

Figure 2 "The Bimaran reliquary," Gandhara, first century C.E.

whom must have propagated their faith through Gandhara, for this is the principal corridor linking Indian commerce with the silk routes of central Asia. Gandharan art, as **figures 2** and **3** suggest, became Buddhist art.

Gandharan art began to reach its apogee after Kanishka, emperor of the Kushana invaders, began to rule about 78 C.E. Kanishka, too, was a Buddhist and provided royal patronage to Buddhism. He favored the newly emerging Mahayana form of Buddhism, which for the first time represented the Buddha's human form in artistic images. The Kushanas had migrated from central Asia, and in their travels they had absorbed some Hellenistic perspectives. Their rule within India extended to the Ganges valley as far east as Mathura, Varanasi, and Sarnath, where the Buddha had preached his first sermon. Buddhism and its representation in Hellenistic forms continued through the classical period of the Gupta dynasty (320–480 C.E.). After the "White Huns" invaded, however, at the end of the fifth century, Gandharan art survived only in pockets in Afghanistan and Kashmir until perhaps the eighth century.

Art historians debate the date of the brilliant gold and ruby reliquary, or container for the fragments of Buddhist relics, in **figure 2**. Some argue that its arcade of the Buddha flanked by the gods Indra and Brahma, each in its own arched niche, must be modeled on a style of Roman sarcophagus that did not appear

until the second century C.E. Others assert that Indian artists did not require tutelage from Rome and that it may date from the first century C.E.

Figure 3 from about the third or fourth century C.E. represents the Buddha as rather stiff, his Hellenistic clothing falling in rigid lines, and the expression on his face rather flat. His right hand is posed in the *abhaya mudra* or the hand position

expressing reassurance. His palm shows the Wheel of the Buddha's Doctrine, which enlightens the entire world with its message of the eternal cycle of birth, maturity, and death. Above his head are two *yakshis* or heavenly beings, and to his left and right are Bodhisattvas, newly emerging Buddhas, who, according to Mahayana Buddhism, forsake nirvana to stay on earth and help other humans.

Figure 3 Buddha of the "great wonders," Gandhara, third to fourth century C.E.

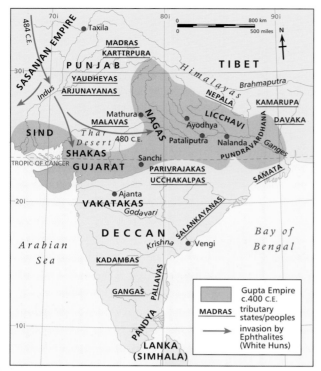

Gupta India In the fourth century C.E. the indigenous Gupta dynasty gained control of the middle Ganges and rapidly built an empire straddling the subcontinent from Sind to the Ganges delta, augmented by a web of treaty and tributary arrangements with neighboring powers. This classical age of Indian civilization was destroyed by invasions of central Asian peoples in the fifth century.

yet another, larger nomadic tribal group from east Asia, known in India as the Kushanas. The geographical extent of Kushana rule is not entirely known, but it seems to have included today's Afghanistan, Pakistan, Kashmir, and India as far south as Gujarat and its ports. The most outstanding Kushana king, Kanishka (r. *c.* 78–*c.* 103 C.E.), seems also to have promoted Buddhism and may have adopted it himself. With a single ruler controlling all these lands, trade between the subcontinent and the central Asian silk routes flourished.

THE GUPTA EMPIRE

In 320 C.E. a new dynasty began its rise to power in the Ganges valley, apparently through a fortunate marriage. The founder, Chandra Gupta I (r. 320–330), came from a dynasty of no historical fame but he married a princess of the powerful Licchavi lineage. Their son, Samudra Gupta (r. *c.* 330–*c.* 380), earned a reputation as one of India's greatest military conquerors. The record of his battles, inscribed on an old Asoka pillar at Allahabad, touches all regions of India: the far south, the east to Bengal and even Assam, the north to Nepal, and the mountain kingdoms of central India, which had often remained independent in their inaccessibility. Samudra's son and successor, Chandra Gupta II (r. *c.* 380–*c.* 415), conquered the Shakas and annexed western India, including prosperous Gujarat and

Plaque of musician with lyre, central India, fifth century C.E. During the Gupta period terra cotta plaques, such as this cross-legged lyre-player, were used to adorn the exterior of temples. It comes from one of the few surviving examples of free-standing brick temples decorated in this way at Bhitargaon in the Gupta heartland. (*British Museum, London*)

Wall-painting illustrating the _Vishvantara Jataka_, Cave 17, Ajanta. Gupta period, fifth century C.E. The rock-cut sanctuaries of Ajanta in northwest Deccan were abandoned for centuries until they were rediscovered in 1817 by British soldiers hunting tigers. The twenty-nine temple caves contain some of the earliest surviving Indian painting and mark the last true flowering of Buddhist art in the subcontinent prior to the ascendancy of Hinduism. This erotic fresco, taken from a folk tale, portrays Prince Vishvantara informing his queen that he has been banished from his father's kingdom.

its Arabian Sea ports, for the first time in five centuries. By marrying his daughter to the head of the Vakataka lineage, he solidified an alliance with his kingdom in central India. Other Gupta alliances were established through marriages with other powerful lineages in the Deccan. The fourth Gupta emperor, Kumara Gupta (r. _c._ 415–455), presided over a great empire now at peace.

Gupta rule was often indirect. Following many of their distant military victories the Gupta emperors abdicated the tasks of administration and withdrew, demanding only tribute payments. Nor did their alliances with other kingdoms and lineages call for direct rule. In the Ganges valley heartland of the empire, the Gupta emperor himself appointed governors at provincial levels, and sometimes even at the district level. At the most local level of the village and the city, however, the Guptas allowed considerable independence to local administrators. The area they administered directly was much smaller than the Mauryan Empire, and the two centuries of Gupta rule and influence are considered India's "golden age" even more for their cultural brilliance than for their political power.

The Guptas presided over a resurgence of Sanskrit literature and Hindu philosophy. The great playwright Kalidasa (fifth century C.E.) composed two epic poems, a lyrical poem "Meghaduta," and the great drama *Shakuntala,* the first Sanskrit drama translated into a western language in modern times. (This 1789 translation by the English judge and Sanskrit scholar William Jones went through five editions in twenty years.) Much of the important literature that had been transmitted orally was now transcribed into writing, including the Purana stories of legend and myth. Further emendations were made to the great epics, the *Mahabharata* and *Ramayana* (see p. 235).

The Gupta Empire began to use Sanskrit for its official correspondence. The great grammarian Panini (*fl. c.* 400 B.C.E.) had fixed the essentials of Sanskrit grammar in *Astadhyayi,* but the Mauryas and most other earlier rulers had used Prakrit, a variant of Sanskrit that was closer to the common language of the people. Now Sanskrit law codes, such as the *Manusmriti,* and principles of statecraft, such as Kautilya's *Artha-sastra,* were studied, revised, and further codified. Many locally powerful officials patronized scholars, humanists, and artists. Important academic centers for Buddhist learning flourished at Taxila in the northwest and Nalanda in the Ganges valley. Chinese Buddhist scholars visited and described these academies, although descriptions of Hindu academies have not been transmitted to the present.

This was especially an age of the resurgence of Hindu religious authority, and major systems of Hindu philosophy were articulated. The most influential, Vedanta, which developed the teachings of the Upanishads, posed a powerful, attractive alternative vision to Buddhism, and in this period Hinduism began to regain ascendancy over Buddhism in India. This was also the period in which the caste system was elaborated and enforced in more detail. *Brahmin* received patronage from rulers, high-level administrators, and wealthy landlords in the form of land grants and court positions. *Brahmin* priests also asserted their role in ritual performance. Buddhism, which had flourished through the patronage of earlier empires, ceded the performance of many of its own rituals to *brahmin* priests, and began to decline (see p. 280).

HUNA INVASIONS AND THE END OF THE NORTH INDIAN EMPIRE

In the fifth century, however, new conquerors came through the passes of the northwest, overthrowing the Gupta Empire and establishing their own headquarters in Bamiyan, Afghanistan. The Hunas were a branch of the Xiongnu, the nomadic Mongol tribes which roamed the regions north of the Great Wall of China. In previous expansions, they had driven other groups west, even into the Roman Empire, as we saw in Chapter 6. Domino fashion, these groups pushed one another westward. The Shakas had invaded India as a result of this sequence in about 94 B.C.E. The Kushanas followed about a century later, driven out of northeast Asia by the Hunas. Now the Hunas themselves arrived in force. These same ethnic peoples were called Huns in the Roman Empire, which they invaded under Attila in 454 C.E.

The first Huna invasions, which occurred about 460 C.E., were repulsed by Skanda Gupta (r. 455–467), but the continuing Huna presence across India's northwest border seems to have disrupted international trade and reduced Gupta wealth. Skanda's successor apparently could not hold the empire together. Regional strongmen began to assert their independence. With central control thus weakened, Huna armies invaded again in about 500 C.E., and for the next half century they fought in, and controlled, much of northern and central India. From their capital in Bamiyan, Afghanistan, the Hunas ruled parts of India as their own imperial provinces. As in Rome, they earned a reputation for great cruelty, reported not only by Indians but also by Chinese and Greeks who visited the region. Huna rule proved brief, however. In 528 C.E. Indian regional princes drove them northwest as far as Kashmir. About a generation later Turkic and Persian armies defeated the main Huna concentrations in Bactria, removing them as a force in India.

Although it was shortlived, the Huna impact on India was considerable. Their invasion further weakened the Gupta Empire, enabling regional powers to dismember it and to declare their own independence. Except for a brief reign by Harshavardhana (r. 606–647), king of the north Indian region of Kanauj, no further unification of all of India was ever seriously attempted from inside the subcontinent until the twentieth century. (The Moghul and British empires, discussed in Chapters 14 and 16, were created by invasions from outside, although the Moghuls later settled within the subcontinent.) The urban culture of north India dimmed. The Buddhist monasteries, which the Hunas attacked with especial force, never recovered. By opening up their invasion routes the

Hunas indirectly enriched India's population pool. Gurjaras and Rajputs entered western India more or less along with the Hunas, and settled permanently. The modern Indian states of Gujarat and Rajasthan are named for them and their descendants.

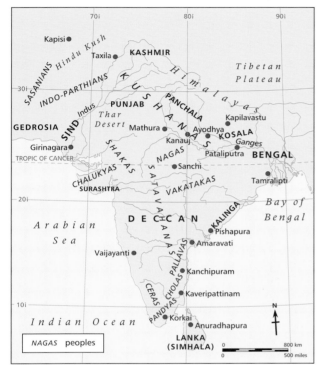

Classical South Asia As kingdoms rose and fell, India had no centralized empire for almost a thousand years. Local powers grew up, often based on different languages and ethnicities. More powerful groups occupied the richest lands, while the weaker were forced into the hills. The roots of today's separate states of India lie in some of these early ethnic kingdoms.

LEGACIES OF THE HUNAS

The legacies of the Hunas in India—the destruction and dismemberment of the Gupta Empire, the reduction in inter-regional trade, the decline of culture, and the introduction of new nomadic groups into already settled imperial lands—quite closely mirror those of their Hun brothers in the Roman Empire. Even the timings were similar, products of the same emigration from east Asia. Of the great empires of the ancient world, only China was capable of defeating or assimilating these invaders without losing its own coherence and identity.

REGIONAL DIVERSITY AND POWER

The history of the Indian subcontinent tends to be written from the perspective of the Ganges valley as the center of political power and influence. (The settlements of the central Indus valley [Chapter 3] did not endure and the region is now a desert.) The Aryans established their centers in the Ganges region; the Mauryans continued the pattern; so did the Guptas; the later Moghuls established their capitals there; the British ultimately followed Moghul patterns by also placing their capital at Delhi; and today's government of independent India has also followed suit. But other regions of India have always been important, too. Even at times when India has been unified, regional powers have regularly challenged the supremacy of the Ganges heartland. In periods such as the

Earthenware sculpture, Nilgiri Hills, south India, early centuries C.E. The Tamil culture of southern India generated not only a separate language and an expressive literary tradition, but also distinctive artifacts. A buffalo cult among the Todas, the largest of the Nilgiri Hills tribal groups, led to the creation of this characterful figurine, made to decorate the lid of an urn containing ashes. (*British Museum, London*)

millennium from 500 C.E. to 1500 C.E., when India had no central empire, the outlying regions asserted their status as independent states.

The major regions of India speak different languages from one another, although imperial rulers have usually introduced a unifying link language for inter-regional communication: Prakrit under Asoka; Sanskrit under the Guptas; and, later, Persian under the Moghuls; and English under the British. Today, two languages are used in India, Hindi and English, while Pakistan uses Urdu and Bangladesh, Bengali. The peoples of different

---

SOURCE
Tamil Culture in Southeast India

The dominant language of the southeast was Tamil and it developed an especially expressive literature. The poetry of the southern Tamilian academies, called *sangam* poetry, written about 100 B.C.E.–250 C.E., set in counterpoint the private, bittersweet play of love against a public atmosphere of warfare and strife. This poetry was lost until it was rediscovered by scholars in the later decades of the nineteenth century. It has been brought to the attention of the English-speaking world by the efforts of the late A.K. Ramanujan.

A King's Double Nature

His armies love massacre,
he loves war,
yet gifts
flow from him ceaselessly.

Come, dear singers,
let's go and see him in Naravu

    where, on trees
    no axe can fell,
    fruits ripen, unharmed
    by swarms of bees,
    egg-shaped, ready
    for the weary traveller
    in the fields of steady, unfailing harvests;
    where warriors with bows
    that never tire of arrows
    shiver
    but stand austere
    in the sea winds
    mixed with the lit cloud
    and the spray of seafoam.

There he is,
in the town of Naravu,
tender among tender women.

Harvest of War

Great king,

you shield your men from ruin,
so your victories, your greatness
are bywords.

Loose chariot wheels
lie about the battleground
with the long white tusks
of bull-elephants.

Flocks of male eagles
eat carrion
with their mates.

Headless bodies
dance about
before they fall
to the ground.

Blood glows,
like the sky before nightfall,
in the red center
of the battlefield.

Demons dance there.
And your kingdom
is an unfailing harvest
of victorious wars.

(trans. by A.K. Ramanujan, pp. 131, 115)

regions have immigrated into the subcontinent from different places and at different times. Throughout their history, when not consolidated into larger empires, they have had their own political-cultural administrations and have often fought one another. The indigenous tribal peoples whose immigration predates any historical records, referred to today as "native Indians" or "**tribals**," generally inhabit less accessible areas, frequently in hilly tracts not easy to farm. They have attempted to protect their independence from outside exploitation by maintaining inaccessibility.

The peoples of Gujarat in the west and of Bengal and Orissa in the east have all seen themselves as distinct when they were ruled from the north, and as independent when that rule was broken. Regional dynasties came and went. The most distinct and separate region was the far south. Here, several lineage and ethnic groups fought to maintain their independence: in the extreme southeast the Pandyas; just north of them along the coast, the Pallavas; still further north, the Colas; and then still further north, along the coast, the Chalukyas. Along the southwest coast, the Perumal and Cera lineages dominated.

SEA TRADE AND CULTURAL INFLUENCE: FROM ROME TO SOUTHEAST ASIA

Imperial governments based inland in the Ganges valley and even further to the northwest tended to draw their economic power from their control over that rich land and from trade through the mountain passes connecting to the silk routes. Many of the regional, coastal powers, on the other hand, traded by sea. This gave them wide ranging external connections to the Roman Empire in the west and to southeast Asia in the east.

Under the Roman emperor Caesar Augustus (r. 27 B.C.E.–14 C.E.) Rome annexed Egypt, opening up a trade route to the east via the Red Sea. Rome controlled enormous wealth, generating a powerful economic demand for goods from Asia. Roman traders learned from the Arabs before them to sail with the southwest monsoon winds from the Red Sea to the west coast of India in about two weeks; about six months later they could sail back with the northeast monsoon. About 50 C.E., a Greek merchant wrote of the Roman trade with Malabar, the southwest coast of India, in his great compendium of trade in the Indian Ocean, *The Periplus of the Erythraean Sea*:

They send large ships to the market-towns on account of the great quantity and bulk of pepper and [cinnamon]. There are imported here, in the first place, a great quantity of coin; topaz, thin clothing, not much; figured linens, antimony, coral, crude glass, copper, tin, lead, wine, not much, but as much as at Barygaza [the flourishing port of Gujarat, further north] . . . There is exported pepper, which is produced in quantity in only one region near these markets. . . . Besides this there are exported great quantities of fine pearls, ivory, silk cloth, spikenard from the Ganges, [cinnamon] from the places in the interior, transparent stones of all kinds, diamonds and sapphires, and tortoise shell. (Cited in Kulke and Rothermund, p. 106)

Numerous hoards of Roman gold coins throughout south India provide archaeological evidence of this trade. Eleven such deposits were found near Coimbatore alone, the area through which trade routes led inland from the Malabar coast, and many others have been discovered near the major ports on the west and east coasts. In 1945, the British archaeologist Sir Mortimer Wheeler discovered the remnants of a Roman trading post at Arikamedu, a fishing village adjacent to Chennai (formerly Madras), and he excavated the brick foundations of large halls and terraces, cisterns, fortifications, and ceramics that had been produced in Italy between 30 B.C.E. and 35 C.E. This outpost suggests that it was likely that the traders actually carrying the goods across the Arabian Sea were foreign rather than Indian: Arabs, Jews, and Romans. Pliny, the Roman historian, complained that Rome was sending around 50 million sesterces a year to India to buy its luxuries, although he noted that they sold in Rome for one hundred times that amount.

CONNECTION: *The Roman Empire and intercontinental trade, pp. 178–81*

SOUTHEAST ASIA: "GREATER INDIA"

Some of the luxuries shipped to Rome were first brought to India from southeast Asia. Indian sailors traveled to all the coastal countries of modern southeast Asia: Myanmar (formerly Burma), Thailand, Cambodia, Vietnam, Malaysia, and Indonesia. To anchor this trade, they established settlements in port cities like Oc Eo in Funan, in the southernmost part of modern Vietnam. *Brahmin* priests and Buddhist monks settled along with the traders, serving the Indian expatriates and attracting local converts at the same time.

At first the impact of Hinduism was more powerful. Both Funan, the present-day Mekong delta region of southern Vietnam and Cambodia, and Champa, further north along the coast of Vietnam, became Hindu kingdoms. Local mythology and Chinese historical records tell quite different stories of the arrival of a *brahmin* priest named Kaundinya. As a result of his activities, Funan adopted Sanskrit as the language of the court and encouraged Hinduism and later Buddhism, as well. But Funan remained an independent state, not an Indian province. Indeed, in the third century C.E. Funan extended its own rule to South Vietnam, Cambodia, central Thailand, northern Malaya, and southern Myanmar from its capital at Vyadhapura, near present-day Phnom Penh. Wherever it went, it encouraged the adoption of Indian culture. Ironically, it infused Indian culture even into states that conquered it. When Champa expanded southward into Funan lands, the kings of Champa began to adopt the cultural, linguistic, and architectural styles of the Pallavas of south India which were then current in Funan. Bhadravarman, a Champa king, built the first Champa temple to the Hindu god Shiva.

Two additional kingdoms under Funan hegemony later established independent states with

Borobudur, Java, late eighth century. This monument, the supreme example of Buddhist art in southeast Asia and Indonesia, is a fantastic microcosm, reproducing in miniature the universe as it was known and imagined in the Mahayana school of Buddhist theology. The relief sculptures, of which there are some 10 miles (16 km), represent the doctrine of karma, the cycle of birth and rebirth, of striving, and release from the Wheel of Life (also shown on the Asokan capital, p. 232).

Angkor Wat, Angkor, Cambodia, early twelfth century C.E. Dedicated to the Hindu god Vishnu, this huge, jungle-bound temple complex once served as the centerpiece of the Khmer Empire, originally founded in 880. Decorated with extensive relief sculpture, the temples of Angkor Wat were intended to emulate mountains in dressed stone.

strong Hindu and Buddhist cultural elements: Java, which was ruled by the Sailendra lineage, and the kingdom of Srivijaya in Sumatra. They, in turn, further spread Indian influences. When the Sailendras attacked the Khmer peoples of present-day Cambodia, the Khmers unified their defenses under King Jayavarman II (r. 790–850). He established a new capital and introduced Hindu temples and philosophies into the whole region around it at Angkor, which was later the location of one of Hinduism's greatest temples constructed by Jayavarman VII (r. 1181–1219). In Java, the Sailendras built an equally extraordinary Buddhist temple at Borobudur in 778–824.

The diffusion of Indian religious and cultural forms continued for centuries throughout southeast Asia. It proceeded almost entirely peacefully, spread by priests and traders, but there were a few exceptions. The Pallava king, Nandivarman III (r. *c.* 844–866), supported a military camp on the Isthmus of Siam in order to protect a group of south Indian merchants who were living and working there. The Chola king, Rajendra I (r. 1014–47), dispatched a fleet to Sumatra and Malaya and defeated the Srivijaya Empire. It appears that his goal was to keep the trade routes open and to support India's shippers on the competitive sea lanes; he claimed no territory. In 1068–9, the

Cholas apparently intervened in a dispute among rival claimants to rule in Malaya, conquered a large part of the region, but then turned it over to their local client. Long before any of these trade ventures, in the third century B.C.E. King Asoka had dispatched missionaries to Sri Lanka and to Myanmar to begin the process of converting these lands to Buddhism.

INDIA, CHINA, AND ROME: EMPIRES AND INTERMEDIATE INSTITUTIONS
HOW DO THEY COMPARE?

SOURCES

Comparing India, China, and Rome is not straightforward. To begin with, in terms of sources of information, India lacks the detailed political, military, economic, administrative, and personal records that would facilitate comparison in any detail. Rome and China compiled official histories as well as a wide variety of personal accounts that have survived to the present. For India, on the other hand, we are often reliant for our best accounts on the observations of foreign visitors. Even the life, writings, and policies of Asoka, now regarded as ancient India's greatest emperor, were lost from historical consciousness for centuries until his rock and pillar edicts were deciphered in the nineteenth century.

ADMINISTRATION

Second, while both Rome and China built institutionalized bureacracies and systems of administration, lasting for centuries in Rome and millennia in China, India's states and empires generally seemed to be extensions of family lineages. Even the most powerful of ancient India's empires, the Mauryan and Gupta, were family holdings. Despite the administrative rigor suggested by Kautilya's *Artha-sastra*, even Chandragupta Maurya's dynasty began to weaken after the death of his grandson Asoka.

INTERNATIONAL RELATIONS

The *Artha-sastra* characterized inter-state relations by the law of the fish, *matsyanyaya*, the large swallow the small. Despite Asoka's renunciation of the excessive use of force, the constant rise and fall of kingdoms and small empires throughout India suggest that Kautilya's view generally prevailed. We do not have records of internal revolts against states and empires in India. Instead, dissidents would abscond to a neighboring state where they felt they could live more freely. Then they might join the official military to fight against their former ruler.

INVASION OF THE HUNAS

Indian empires did not expand beyond the borders of the subcontinent. Indian trade missions in southeast Asia exported cultural and religious innovations along with their material cargo, but almost without exception they made no attempt to establish political rule. On the other hand, outsiders frequently invaded the subcontinent. Remarkably, the one political experience that the empires of India, Rome, and China all shared was invasion and at least partial conquest by the Hunas (Huns, Xiongnu) and by the peoples they displaced. Indeed, all three of these last chapters point to the great importance of the Hunas/Huns in world history, especially from the third through the sixth centuries C.E. Historical records include not only the builders and sustainers of sedentary empire, but also their nomadic challengers. (We will explore this issue further in considering the Mongols in Chapters 12 and 14.)

LOCAL INSTITUTIONS AND THE STATE

In Rome and China, government touched much of the population directly, through taxes, military conscription, imperial service, and aggressive bureaucracies. The state was fundamental to all areas of life. The state in India, on the other hand, seemed to preside over a set of social institutions that had existed prior to it, were more deeply rooted, and were more persistent through time. These institutions included family lineages, aware and proud of their histories; caste groups, each presiding over its own occupational, ritual, and ethnic niche; guild associations, overseeing the conditions of economic production and distribution; local councils, providing government at the village and town level; and religious sects, which gave their members a sense of belonging, identity, and purpose. The state was important in overseeing the activities of all of these groups, but it existed only in the context of their existence. States and empires came and went, but these varied, pervasive institutions carried on in their own rhythms. In the words of historian Romila Thapar:

> The understanding of power in India lies in analyses of the caste and sub-caste relationships and of institutions such as the guilds and village councils, and not merely in the survey of dynastic power. (Thapar, *History*, vol. I, p. 19)

In India political authority was intimately connected, and sometimes subordinated, to familial, cultural, and religious power. In the next chapters on religion in world history, and especially in Chapter 9 on Hinduism and Buddhism, we will explore these connections.

BIBLIOGRAPHY

Allchin, F.R., *et al. The Archaeology of Early Historic South Asia: The Emergence of Cities and States* (Cambridge: Cambridge University Press, 1995).

Basham, A.L. *The Wonder That Was India* (New York: Grove Press, 1954).

Cotterell, Arthur, ed. *The Penguin Encyclopedia of Ancient Civilizations* (London: Penguin Books, 1980).

Craven, Roy C. *A Concise History of Indian Art* (New York: Oxford University Press, n.d.).

Embree, Ainslee, ed. and rev. *Sources of Indian Tradition*, Vol. I: *From the Beginning to 1800* (New York: Columbia University Press, 2nd ed., 1988).

Green, Peter. *Alexander of Macedon, 356–323 B.C.* (Berkeley: University of California Press, 1991).

Hughes, Sarah Shaver and Brady Hughes, eds. *Women in World History*, Vol. I: *Readings from Prehistory to 1500* (Armonk, NY: M.E. Sharpe, 1995).

Kulke, Hermann and Dietmar Rothermund. *A History of India* (Totowa, NJ: Barnes and Noble Books, 1986).

Lockhard, Craig A. "Integrating Southeast Asia into the Framework of World History: The Period Before 1500," *The History Teacher* XXIX, No. 1 (November 1995), 7–35.

The (London) Times Atlas of World History (London: Times Books, 4th ed., 1993).

Past Worlds: The Times Atlas of Archaeology (Maplewood, NJ: Hammond, 1988).

Ramanujan, A.K., ed. and trans. *Poems of Love and War: From the Eight Anthologies and the Ten Long Poems of Classical Tamil* (New York: Columbia University Press, 1985).

Richman, Paula, ed. *Many Ramayanas: The Diversity of a Narrative Tradition in South Asia* (Berkeley: University of California Press, 1991).

Rowland, Benjamin. *The Art and Architecture of India: Buddhist/Hindu/Jain* (New York: Penguin Books, 1977).

SarDesai, D.R. *Southeast Asia: Past and Present* (Boulder, CO: Westview Press, 1994).

Schwartzberg, Joseph E., ed. *A Historical Atlas of South Asia* (Chicago: University of Chicago Press, 1978).

Spodek, Howard, "Studying the History of Urbanization in India," *Journal of Urban History* VI, No. 3 (May, 1980), 251–95.

Spodek, Howard and Doris Srinivasan, eds. *Urban Form and Meaning in South Asia: The Shaping of Cities from Prehistoric to Precolonial Times* (Washington: National Gallery of Art, 1993).

Thapar, Romila. *Ancient Indian Social History* (New Delhi: Orient Longman, 1978).

——. *Asoka and the Decline of the Mauryas* (Delhi: Oxford University Press, 1963).

——. *A History of India*, Vol. I (Baltimore, MD: Penguin Books, 1966).

——. *Interpreting Early India* (New York: Oxford University Press, 1992).

Tharu, Susie and K. Lalita, eds. *Women Writing in India 600 B.C. to the Present*, Vol. I (New York: The Feminist Press, 1991).

The Rise of World Religions

600 B.C.E.–1500 C.E.

NOT BY BREAD ALONE: HOW DO HISTORIANS UNDERSTAND RELIGION IN WORLD HISTORY?

Religion is the sense of human relationship with the sacred, with forces in and beyond nature. Throughout history people have felt the need to establish such relationships with powers that they believed capable of protecting and supporting them and capable of providing a deeper sense of significance to life and the possibility of some form of existence after death. Some people have thought of these forces as abstract and remote; others have regarded them as having personalities, as gods. Some people, of course, do not believe in such powers at all, or they are skeptical.

Mircea Eliade (1907–86), perhaps the leading historian of religion in the mid- and late twentieth century, wrote:

In the most archaic phases of culture, *to live as a human being* was in itself *a religious act*, since eating, sexual activity, and labor all had a sacramental value. Experience of the sacred is inherent in man's mode of being in the world.

When we think of the sacred we must not limit it to divine figures. The sacred does not necessarily imply belief in God or gods or spirits ... it is the experience of a reality and the source of an awareness of existing in the world. . . . The sacred cannot be recognized "from outside." It is by means of internal experience that each individual will be able to recognize it in the religious acts of a Christian or a "primitive" man. (Eliade, *Ordeal by Labyrinth*, p. 154)

Dome of the Rock, Jerusalem, 692 C.E.

From the earliest human records we have encountered such religious needs. More than 100,000 years ago Neanderthals buried their dead in anticipation of their journey to an afterlife. Archaeologists have found Neanderthal burials with flint tools, food, and cooked meat at Teshik-Tash in Siberia; the burial of a man with a crippled right arm at the Shanidar cave in the Zagros Mountains of Iraq; and graves covered with red ocher powder, including some group burials, in France and central Europe.

Burial rituals—the formal recognition of our common mortality—suggest that the earliest humans thought about the significance of their lives. They hoped that life might continue in some form, even after death, and they must also have dedicated a part of their energies to transmitting values that would continue after they died and to creating institutions to perpetuate those values.

In Part 2 we saw that many early cities and states were dedicated to particular gods or goddesses, sometimes even carrying their names. Gilgamesh, builder of the city of Uruk in Mesopotamia, was two-thirds a god and sought eternal life. In Babylon, Hammurabi transmitted his legal code in the name of the god Shamash. Egyptian hymns proclaimed the divinity of the pharaohs. Chinese of the Shang dynasty used oracle bones to augur the will of transcendent powers. Athens was named for the goddess Athena.

The empires we discussed in Part 3 sought the validation provided by religious leaders and, in exchange, gave financial and political backing to religious institutions. The emperors of Rome and China served also as high-priests for their people. When the Roman emperor Constantine believed that he had been miraculously assisted by Jesus, he transferred his allegiance from paganism to the embattled Christian church. Hinduism and its caste system provided India with a sense of unity and continuity. In several states of south and southeast Asia, Buddhist priests were called upon to validate the authority of rulers. Confucianism, which was discussed in Chapter 7 as one of the pillars of the Chinese imperial system, presents a profound theory of ethical human relationships. Unlike the religions just mentioned, however, Confucianism has very little other-worldly focus.

This part focuses in greater depth on the role of religion in human history. Chronologically, the part spans the entire period, from earliest humans to about 1500 C.E. Its key focus, however, is from *c.* 300 C.E. to *c.* 1200 C.E. In this period Hinduism became more fully defined and systematized throughout India; Buddhism rose to great importance in China, Japan, and southeast Asia; Judaism, exiled from its original home in Israel, spread with the exiles throughout much of west Asia, the Mediterranean basin, and northern Europe; Christianity grew into the great cultural system of Europe; and Islam radiated outward from the pivotal center of Afro-Eurasia to the far corners of the eastern hemisphere. These five religions often confronted one another, sometimes leading to **syncretism**, the borrowing and adaptation of ideas and practices; sometimes to competition; and sometimes to direct conflict.

HINDUISM AND BUDDHISM

300 B.C.E.—1200 C.E.

" Empires crumble: Religion alone endures."

JACQUES BENIGNE BOSSUET,

UNIVERSAL HISTORY (1681)

THE SACRED SUBCONTINENT: THE SPREAD OF RELIGION IN INDIA AND BEYOND

This chapter begins with a definition of religion and a description of early religious practices. It proceeds to a brief history of early Hinduism, the most ancient of existing major religions, and analyzes its evolution as the principal cultural system of the Indian subcontinent. Buddhism emerged out of Hinduism in India and spread throughout central, eastern, and southeastern Asia, defining much of the cultural and religious life of this vast region. Its history concludes this chapter.

THE HISTORIAN AND RELIGIOUS BELIEF: HOW DO WE KNOW?

Organized religious groups usually build on the religious experiences proclaimed by their founders and early teachers. All five of the religions we study in this part grew from such experiences, and many of the experiences were miraculous—that is, they are contrary to everyday experience, and they can be neither proved nor disproved. For example, most Hindus believe that gods have regularly intervened in human life as Krishna is said to have done at the Battle of Kurukshetra (see Source, p. 266). They also believe in the reincarnation of all living creatures, including gods. Buddhists believe in the revelation of the Four Noble Truths and the Eightfold Path to Siddhartha Gautama (the Buddha) under the bodhi (bo) tree at Bodh Gaya in northern India; most also believe that Siddhartha was a reborn soul of an earlier Buddha and would himself be born again. Most Jews have believed in special divine intervention in the lives of Abraham and his descendants, a special divine covenant with the Jewish people, and a revelation of divine law at Mount Sinai. Most Christians have believed in the miracle of Jesus' incarnation as the Son of God and his resurrection after death. Most Muslims believe that God revealed his teachings to Muhammad through the angel Gabriel, and that these were later transcribed in the **Quran**.

Historians, however, cannot study miracles. Historical study seeks proof of events, and such proof is not usually available for miracles. Almost by definition, a belief in miracles is a matter of faith, not of proof. Moreover, history is the study of the regular processes of change over time, and miracles, again by definition, are one-time-only events, which stand outside and defy the normal processes of change.

What can be studied are the manifestations and effects of religious beliefs on people's behavior. Sincere believers in religious miracles restructure their lives accordingly, creating and joining religious organizations to spread the word about these miracles and about their own experiences with them. These new organizations formulate rules of membership, and they infuse their beliefs into everyday life by establishing sacred time, sacred

HINDUISM AND BUDDHISM

DATE	POLITICAL/SOCIAL EVENTS	LITERARY/PHILOSOPHICAL EVENTS
1500 B.C.E.	● Caste system	● *Rigveda* (1500–1200)
900 B.C.E.		● Brahmanas (900–500)
800 B.C.E.		● Upanishads (800–500)
500 B.C.E.	● Siddhartha Gautama (Buddha) (*c.* 563–483) ● Mahavir (*b.* 540), Jain teacher	● Buddha delivers sermon on the Four Noble Truths and the Noble Eightfold Path
300 B.C.E.		● *Mahabharata* (300–300 C.E.) ● *Ramayana* (300–300 C.E.)
200 B.C.E	● Buddhism more widespread than Hinduismin India (until 200 C.E.); spreading in Sri Lanka ● Mahayana Buddhism growing in popularity	
10 C.E	● 4th general council of Buddhism codified Theravada doctrines ● Buddhist missionaries in China (65 C.E.)	● Nagarjuna (50–150 C.E.), philosopher of Mahayana Buddhism
300 C.E	● Spread of Hinduism to southeast Asia	
400 C.E.	● Hindu pantheon established ● Buddhism declining in India	● Puranas written (400–1000) ● Faxian's pilgrimage to India ● Sanskrit; Hindu gods, temples, and priests in southeast Asia; Buddhism in southeast Asia
500 C.E.	● Bhakti begun in south India ● Buddhist monks to Japan	
600 C.E.	● Buddhist monks to southeast Asia ● Buddhism flourishes under Tang dynasty (618–907)	● Xuanzang's pilgrimage to India
700 C.E.	● Hindu temples and shrines begin to appear in India ● Buddhism begins to decline in China ● Buddhism becoming established in Japan	● Hindu philosopher Shankaracharya (788–820) ● Saicho (767–822), Japanese Buddhist priest ● Kukai (774–835), Japanese Buddhist priest
800 C.E.	● Hindu priests in southeast Asia ● Emperor Wuzong attacks Buddhism in China	● Earliest printed book: (*The Diamond Sutra*) (868)
1000 C.E.	● Muslim invasion of India (1000–1200) ● Buddhist institutions close in India	● Hindu philosopher Ramanuja (1017–1137)

See also Indian Empires timechart, pp. 233–4

CHRONOLOGY OF THE WORLD'S RELIGIOUS CULTURES

CULTURE	3000 B.C.E.	2500	2000	1500	1000	500	0	500 C.E.	1000	1500	2000
SUMERIAN	████████████████										
AKKADIAN/BABYLONIAN		███████████████████████████									
HITTITE/HURRIAN		██████████									
EGYPTIAN	███										
GREEK				••••••••••							
ROMAN						████████████████					
JEWISH			••••███								
CHRISTIAN							████████████████████████████				
ISLAMIC								████████████████			
HINDU				██							
BUDDHIST						████████████████████████████████████					
INCAN								█████████████			
MAYAN							████████████				
AZTEC								███████████████			
CELTIC							██████████				
NORDIC/ICELANDIC								███████████			

space, sacred liturgy, and sacred literature and culture. Historically, when religious identity combined with political power, group boundaries became even more important, marking in-group from out-group, separating "us" from "them," sometimes even leading to violent conflict. Historians *do* study these manifestations and effects of religious beliefs:

- **The sanctification of time** Each religion creates its own sacred calendar, linking the present with the past by commemorating each year the key dates in the history of the religion and in the life of its community. It marks dates for the performance of special rituals, celebrations, fasts, and community assemblies. In addition to the community calendar, members of religious organizations create their own individual and family calendars to mark the rites of passage—the great lifecycle events of birth, puberty, marriage, maturity, and death—so that each event has its own ritual observance. Religions especially formulate rules of marriage in an attempt to channel the raw, powerful, mysterious, and often indiscriminate forces of youthful sexuality to conform to the norms of the group.

- **The sanctification of space** Each religion creates its own sacred geography by establishing shrines where miraculous acts are said to have occurred; where saints had been born, flourished, or met their deaths; and where relics from the lives of holy people are preserved and venerated. The most sacred of these sites become centers of pilgrimage. As we have seen in earlier chapters (see for example the Focus, p. 48), whole cities, and especially their sacred quarters, were dedicated to gods and goddesses, and thought to be under their special protection.

- **The sanctification of language and literature** Each religion shapes its own use of language, literature, and artistic imagery. The Hebrew **Bible,** the Greek **New Testament,** the Arabic Quran, the Sanskrit Veda and epics, and the Pali Buddhist **Tripitaka** have provided linguistic and literary canons across the millennia. In translation these texts have given character to new languages. For example, translations of the Bible by Saint Jerome (c. 347–419), William Tyndale (c. 1494–1536), and Martin Luther (1483–1546) have enriched Latin, English, and German, respectively. The retelling in Hindi by Tulsidas (c. 1543–1623) of the Sanskrit Ramayana helped to establish the importance of that modern language in north India. This religious literature usually provides the core of religious liturgy and thus becomes part of the daily expression of faith of the common people. Part 4 quotes religious scriptures extensively because of their centrality to the world's languages, literatures, and imagery.

- **The sanctification of artistic and cultural creativity**
  Religious sensibilities often inspire specific creative efforts, and religious groups often encourage the creation of art and music to express and enhance their message.

- **The creation of religious organization**
  As religion moves from individual experience to group membership, organization develops. At one extreme this may be a hierarchical structure with a single leader at the apex and an array of administrative and spiritual orders down to the most local level, the form of the Roman Catholic Church. At another extreme there may be no formal overall organization, and no formal set of rules and regulations, but instead a loose association of local communities related to one another through common beliefs and social structures, the form of Hinduism.

If a religious group grows to include a sizable proportion of the population, some relationship must be negotiated between its organization and the state. We have already noted some examples of close relationships between religion and government—for example, in Sumer (Chapter 2) and in Aryan India (Chapter 8). We shall see more. We shall also see antagonistic relationships between religions and governments. In Chapter 10, for example, we shall see Jewish prophets call Jewish kings to a moral accounting, and in Chapter 11 we shall see Muslim religious authorities fight for their independence from the caliph, the political ruler.

Religious networks and political networks frequently intersected the same geographical space, each growing up in the soil plowed by the other. Both the Roman Catholic and Eastern Orthodox churches, for example, grew up largely in the territory dominated by the Roman Empire—the Roman church in the west, the Orthodox church in the east. Islam flowered especially in the lands once conquered by Alexander and ruled by his successors, except in the Greek homelands themselves. Buddhism spread across India after the Emperor Asoka made it his state religion, while Hinduism developed as the dominant religion of many of India's subsequent governments. The intersection of major religions with powerful states has created world civilizations of great depth, power, and longevity.

MAJOR RELIGIONS OF THE WORLD, 1998

Religion	Number of followers	Percentage of world population
Christians	1,943,038,000	32.8
Roman Catholics	1,026,501,000	17.3
Protestants	316,445,000	5.3
Orthodox	213,743,000	3.6
Anglicans	63,748,000	1.1
Other Christians	373,832,000	6.3
Unaffiliated Christians	107,686,000	1.8
Muslims	1,164,622,000	19.6
Hindus	761,689,000	12.8
Nonreligious	759,655,000	12.8
Chinese folk religionists	379,162,000	6.4
Buddhists	353,794,000	6.0
Ethnic religionists	248,565,000	4.2
Atheists	149,913,000	2.5
New religionists	100,144,000	1.7
Sikhs	22,232,000	0.4
Jews	14,111,000	0.2
Baha'is	6,764,000	0.1
Confucianists	6,241,000	0.1
Jains	3,922,000	0.1
Shintoists	2,789,000	0.0
Zoroastrians	274,000	0.0

(*Encyclopedia Britannica Book of the Year, 2000, p. 315*).

HINDUISM

THE ORIGINS OF HINDUISM: HOW DO WE KNOW?

Hinduism began before recorded time. The other major religions of the world were inspired by a specific person or event: Abraham's covenant; the Buddha's enlightenment; Jesus' birth; Muhammad's revelation. Hinduism, by contrast, emerged through the weaving together of many diverse, ancient religious traditions of India, some of which precede written records. Hinduism evolved from the experience of the peoples of India.

Because Hinduism preserves a rich body of religious literature written in Sanskrit, the language of the Aryan invaders of 1700–1200 B.C.E., scholars believed until recently that Hinduism was a product of that invasion. Even the excavations at Mohenjo-Daro and Harappa, which uncovered a pre-Aryan civilization (see Chapter 3), did not at first alter these beliefs. But as excavation and analysis have continued, many scholars have come to believe that the Indus valley civilization may have contributed many of Hinduism's principal gods and ceremonies. Excavated statues seem to represent the god Shiva (see p. 84), the sacred bull Nandi on which he rides, a man practicing yogic meditation, a sacred tree, and a mother goddess. Archaeologists increasingly argue that the invading Aryans absorbed religious beliefs and practices, along with secular culture, from the Indus valley.

Contemporary anthropological accounts support the idea that Hinduism is an amalgam of beliefs and practices. These accounts emphasize Hinduism's remarkable ability to absorb and assimilate tribal peoples and their gods. Today, about 100 million of India's 1000 million people are officially regarded as "tribals." These peoples were living in India before the arrival of the Aryans, and they have largely attempted to escape Aryan domination by retreating into remote hilly and forested

Gouache illustration from Bhanudatta's *Rasamanjari*, 1685. Krishna, the eighth *avatar* (incarnation) of Vishnu, is always depicted with blue/black skin and is renowned for his prowess as a warrior and a lover. In this scene from one of his amorous adventures, a woman hinders a forester from felling the tree under which she has arranged to meet Krishna for a romantic tryst.

regions, where they could preserve their own social systems. Hindus have, however, pursued them and their lands, building temples in and around tribal areas. These temples recognize tribal gods and incorporate them with the mainstream deities in an attempt to persuade the tribals to accept Hindu religious patterns. Indeed, one of Hinduism's greatest gods, Krishna, the blue/black god, was apparently a tribal god who gained national recognition.

As India's peoples have been diverse, so its evolving religious system is diverse. The concept of "Hinduism" as a unified religion comes from outsiders. Greeks first encountering India, and especially Alexander the Great, who arrived in 327 B.C.E., spoke of India's belief systems and practices collectively as "Hinduism," that is, the ways of the peoples on the far side of the Indus River. When Muslims began to arrive in India, beginning in the eighth century C.E., they adopted the same terminology.

SACRED GEOGRAPHY AND PILGRIMAGE

More than any other religion, Hinduism is associated with a specific territory, India. Almost all Hindus live in India or are of Indian descent. Within India itself a sacred geography has developed. Places visited by gods and by saints, as well as places of great natural sanctity, have become shrines and pilgrim destinations. Pilgrims traveling these routes have created a geography of religious/ national integration, and modern transportation, in the form of trains, buses, and airplanes, has increased the pilgrim traffic throughout India. Some of the most important shrines are at the far corners of India, such as Somnath on the far west coast, Haridwar and Rishikesh in the far north on the upper Ganges, Puri on the east coast, and Kanya Kumari (Cape Comorin) at the extreme southern tip. Travel to all of these shrines would thus provide the pilgrim with a "Bharat Darshan," a view of the entire geography of India. Such pilgrimage routes have helped to unify both Hinduism and India.

Each locality in city and village is also knit together by religious shrines, ranging from the simple prayer niche, containing pictures and statues of the gods of the kind found in even the most humble home; through neighborhood shrines, nestled perhaps into the trunk of an especially sacred tree; to local and regional temples.

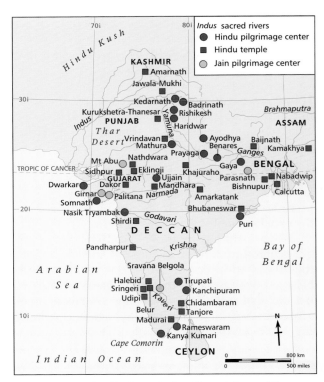

Hindu South Asia Hinduism is the oldest of the world's leading religions, although its geographic range is confined to the peoples of South Asia. Here its impact has been profound, exemplified by the sacred geography of the subcontinent; rivers, mountains, and regions associated with divine mythology are important, and networks of pilgrimage centers and temples provide cultural unity.

THE CENTRAL BELIEFS OF HINDUISM

Hinduism has none of the fixed dogmas of most other world religions, and great flexibility and variety of beliefs exist under the general term "Hindu." Nevertheless, sacred texts do provide a set of beliefs and orientations toward life that are very widely shared. Over time, the introduction of new texts to the Hindu legacy marked the evolution of Hinduism as a living, changing system of beliefs and practices.

The *Rigveda*

Between *c.* 1500 and 1200 B.C.E. *brahmin* priests of the nomadic pastoralist Aryan peoples entering India composed the *Rigveda*, a collection of 1028 verses of Sanskrit poetry, the oldest and most venerated of the four books called, collectively, Veda. These verses invoke many early gods, including

Agni, the god of various kinds of fire; Indra, a phallic god of rain and fertility; Surya, god of the sun; and the goddess Dawn, who ushers in the sun each day. They include references to music, dance, and acting as modes of worship. Vedic worship also takes the form of animal sacrifice offered on sacred altars. The *Rigveda* speculates on the creation of the world and on the significance of life in this world, but it pretends to no conclusive answers:

> Who really knows? Who shall here proclaim it? whence things came to be, whence this creation. . . . This creation, whence it came to be, whether it was made or not—he who is its overseer in the highest heaven, he surely knows. Or if he does not know . . . ? (X:129, Embree, p. 21)

Prayer room and shrine, India. Nearly every Hindu home in India has a shrine with pictures or small statues of various deities, and many have a special prayer room set aside for their worship. For *puja*, or worship, which is observed every day, ritual purity is emphasized; the time for offerings to the gods is after the morning bath or evening wash.

Caste

The *Rigveda* also introduces the mythic origin and rationale of the caste system, one of the most distinctive features of Hindu life. Caste began, the *Rigveda* suggests, in a primeval sacrifice of a mythical creature, Purusha. He was carved into four sections, each symbolizing one of the principal divisions of the caste system:

> When they divided Purusha, in how many different portions did they arrange him? What became of his mouth, what of his two arms? What were his two thighs and his two feet called? His mouth became the *brahman* [priest]; his two arms were made into the *rajanya* [or *kshatriya*, warrior]; his two thighs the *vaishyas* [business people and farmer/landlords]; from his two feet the *shudra* [person of the lower working class] was born. (X:90 Embree, 18–19)

Apparently, the Aryan invaders were even then thinking of a social system that separated people by occupation and sanctioned that separation through religion. The caste system that developed in India was probably the most rigidly unequal and hierarchical of any in the world. Caste status was hereditary, passing from parent to child at birth. Each caste was subject to different local legal rules, with upper castes being rewarded more generously and punished less severely than lower. Only upper castes were permitted to receive formal education, and the separate castes were not to inter-marry nor even to inter-dine. Their vital fluids were distinct and different, and the blood and semen of one group were not to mingle with those of another. The food fit for one group was not necessarily appropriate for others: *brahmin* priests were to be vegetarians, but *kshatriya* warriors were to eat meat.

Commentators throughout the centuries have searched for additional roots of the caste system, more grounded in social, economic, and political rationales. Many have seen India's caste system as a means of ordering relationships among the multitude of immigrant groups in India's multi-ethnic population, consolidating some at the top and relegating others to the bottom. Others have seen caste as the result of a frozen economic system, with parents doing all they could to make sure that their children maintained at least the family's current occupational status. They sacrificed the possibility of upward mobility in exchange for the security that they would not fall lower on the social scale. Many suggested that the system was

MAJOR HINDU GODS

A shrine with images of one or more of the thousands of gods in the pantheon can be found in every devout Hindu home. Shiva and Vishnu are the two major gods, and we also list others that are widely worshiped.

Brahma   The creator god, whose four heads and arms represent the four veda (scriptures), castes, and yugas (ages of the world).

Ganesh   The elephant-headed god, bringer of good luck.

Kali   Shiva's fierce consort—the goddess of death—is shown as a fearsome, blood-drinking, four-armed black woman.

Krishna   The eighth avatar (incarnation) of Vishnu, depicted with blue or black skin. He is honored for his skills as a lover and a warrior; with his consort **Radha**.

Rama   The personification of virtue, reason and chivalry; with his consort **Sita**, revered for her loyalty.

Shiva   God of destruction, whose dancing in a circle of fire symbolizes the eternal cycle of creation and destruction.

Sitala   Mothers traditionally pray to this goddess to protect their children from disease.

Vishnu   The preserver, a kindly god, who protects those who worship him, banishes bad luck, and restores good health; with his consorts **Lakshmi**, the goddess of wealth, and **Saraswati**, the goddess of wisdom and the arts.

ical observation shows that the four castes of the Veda do not exist in practice today. Instead, India has tens of thousands of castes—indeed, there are thousands of different *brahmin* groups alone. In practice, caste is lived in local groupings, in the 750,000 villages, towns, and cities of India. From customary law to dining patterns to marriage arrangements, caste relationships are determined locally, and there is no national over-arching religious system to formulate and enforce rules. In any given village, for example, some twenty to thirty castes may be represented, including all the various craftspeople and artisans. There may be more than one caste claiming *brahmin* status, or *kshatriya*, or *vaishya*, or *shudra*. Anthropologists differentiate between the mythological four *varna* groups of the Vedic caste system and the thousands of *jati* groups through which caste is actually lived in India. Both historians and anthropologists are convinced that the same multitude of castes that they find "on the ground" today existed also in the past.

Throughout Indian history there have been revolts against the hierarchy of the caste system. Throughout the twentieth century the government of India has acted assertively to eliminate the historic discrimination of the caste system (as we shall see in Chapter 20). Nevertheless, through the millennia, caste has usually been more important than government in determining the conditions of life of most people. As historian Romila Thapar has written:

> At the basic level of everyday life interrelationships between the sub-castes within the community were the most influential factor in village life, and this tended to divert attention from political relationships and loyalties to local caste relationships and loyalties. Central political authority became more and more remote. (Thapar, *A History of India*, Vol. I, p. 48)

The Brahmanas and Upanishads

A second collection of Sanskrit religious literature, dating from *c.* 900–500 B.C.E., sets out rules for *brahmins*, including procedures for sacrifice and worship. These scriptures, the Brahmanas, include discussions of the origins of various rituals and myths of the immortal gods. Among the rituals, the *Ashwamedha*, or horse sacrifice, most strongly demonstrates the historic link between *brahmin* priests and *kshatriya* warriors. Truly powerful kings were to allow a horse to roam freely for a year. At

imposed on the rest of the population by an extremely powerful coalition of *brahmin* priests and *kshatriya* warrior-rulers. Such a dominant coalition is common in world history, and the Indian situation was simply more entrenched than most.

Historians employ the insights of anthropologists as they attempt to understand the historical origins and basis of the caste system. Anthropolog-

the end of the year, the king was to enforce his own authority over all this land, and to sacrifice the horse. Some of India's most powerful rulers actually did perform this ritual, although historians suggest that the horses may have been discreetly guided and restricted in their travels by an accompanying retinue of priests.

The Upanishads, composed about 800–500 B.C.E., are devoted primarily to mystical speculation. They proclaim the oneness of the individual and the universe. The universal spirit, Brahman, and the soul of each individual, *atman*, are ultimately the same substance, just as individual sparks are the same substance as a large fire. In time, each *atman* will be united with the universal Brahman. To reach this unity, each soul will be reincarnated (*samsara*) in a series of bodies, until it is purged of its attachments to the physical world and achieves pure spirituality. Then, at this death of this

SACRED WRITINGS OF HINDUISM

Veda The most sacred of the Hindu scriptures, meaning "divine knowledge." They consist of collections of writings compiled by the Aryans: *Rigveda* (hymns and praises), *Yajurveda* (prayers and sacrificial formulas), *Samaveda* (tunes and chants), and *Atharva-Veda* (Veda of the Atharvans, the priests who officiate at sacrifices).

Upanishads Philosophical treatises, centering on the doctrine of Brahma.

Brahamanas Instructions on ritual and sacrifice.

Ramayana An epic poem, telling how Rama (an incarnation of the god Vishnu) and his devotee Hanuman, the monkey god, recover Rama's wife, Sita, who has been abducted by the demon king Ravana.

Mahabharata ("Great Poem of the Bharatas") It includes the *Bhagavadgita* ("Song of God") and consists of eighteen books and 90,000 stanzas.

final body, the *atman* is finally released to its union with the Brahman.

The Upanishads introduce several concepts fundamental to almost all strands of Hinduism. *Dharma* is the set of religious and ethical duties to which each living creature in the universe is subject. These duties are not the same, however, for each creature; they differ according to ritual status. *Karma* is the set of activities of each creature and the effects that these activities have on its *atman*. Each action has an effect on the *atman*; activities in accord with one's *dharma* purify the *atman*; activities in opposition to one's *dharma* pollute it. "Good *karma*," the good effects brought about by actions in accord with *dharma*, will finally enable the *atman* to escape *samsara*, or reincarnation, and reach *moksha*, release from the travails of life on earth and ultimate union with the Brahman. Thus Hinduism sees reward and punishment in the universe as a natural consequence. Good, *dharmic* actions carry their own reward for the *atman*; activities opposed to *dharma* carry their own negative consequences. Activities in this life earn good or bad *karma*.

Hinduism sees life on this earth as *maya*, illusion, compared to the reality beyond, but it also teaches the importance of taking life seriously and living in accordance with *dharma*. Hinduism teaches four goals in life. Two are *dharma* and *moksha*. The other two are *kama*, or physical pleasure, and *artha*, wealth and power (which we considered in Chapter 8). Activity on earth is only *leela*, or play—but the play is important.

The Upanishads also introduce the concept of the lifecycle, with its different duties at each stage. The first stage, *brahmacharya*, is the youthful time of studies and celibacy; the second, *gruhasta*, the householder stage, is for raising a family; the third, *vanaprastha*, literally forest-wandering, is for reflection outside the demands of everyday life; and the last, *sunnyasin*, is for total immersion in meditation in preparation for death and, ideally, for *moksha*.

These early scriptures established a set of principles that constitute the core of Hindu belief: caste, *dharma*, *karma*, life stages, *samsara*, and, ultimately, *moksha*, the union of *atman* and Brahman. They represent a rational system of order in the universe and in individual life. They teach the importance of dharmic activities in this world in order to reach *moksha* in the deeper reality beyond. They are transmitted from *guru*, or teacher, to *shishya*, or student. Although it reveres the *brahmin* priest (not to be confused with the Brahman spirit of the universe), Hinduism is ultimately accessible to each

The Bhagavad-Gita *from the Mahabharata*

The *Bhagavad-Gita* opens on the field of Kuruk-shetra before the final battle between the two branches of the Bharata family, the Kauravas and the Pandavas. Arjun, leader of the Pandavas, despairs of his choices: if he fights, he kills his cousins; if he does not fight, he dies. He turns to his chariot driver, the Lord Krishna, for advice. Krishna's reply incorporates many fundamental principles of Hindu thought. First, Krishna speaks of the duty of Arjun, a *kshatriya* by caste, to fight: "For a *kshatriya* there does not exist another greater good than war enjoined by *dharma*" (II: 31). Each person has a unique *dharma*, largely determined by caste. In this philosophy, changing one's occupational duty is no virtue:

> Better is one's own *dharma* that one may be able to fulfill but imperfectly, than the *dharma* of others that is more easily accomplished. Better is death in the fulfillment of one's own *dharma*. To adopt the *dharma* of others is perilous. (III:35)

Krishna counsels Arjun to action. He notes three kinds of yoga, or discipline, which bring people to spiritual liberation: the yoga of knowledge; the yoga of devotion; and the yoga of action. (The yoga of physical discipline and meditation, known widely today in the West, is yet another form.) In this case, Krishna tells Arjun, the yoga of action is required:

> Do your allotted work, for action is superior to nonaction. Even the normal functioning of your body cannot be accomplished through actionlessness. (III:8)

The key, however, is performing the action because it is right, without concern for its results or rewards:

Action alone is your concern, never at all its fruits. Let not the fruits of action be your motive, nor let yourself be attached to inaction. . . . Seek refuge in the right mental attitude. Wretched are those who are motivated by the fruits of action. (II:49)

Non-attachment is the ideal:

> He who feels no attachment toward anything; who, having encountered the various good or evil things, neither rejoices nor loathes—his wisdom is steadfast. (II:59)
> He who behaves alike to foe and friend; who, likewise is even-poised in honor or dishonor; who is even-tempered in cold and heat, happiness and sorrow; who is free from attachment;
> who regards praise and censure with equanimity; who is silent, content with anything whatever; who has no fixed abode, who is steadfast in mind, who is full of devotion—that man is dear to me. (XII:18–19)

In reply to Arjun's specific anxiety about killing his cousins, Krishna reminds him of the doctrine of reincarnation:

> As a man discards worn-out clothes to put on new and different ones, so the disembodied self discards its worn-out bodies to take on other new ones.
> Death is certain for anyone born, and birth is certain for the dead; since the cycle is inevitable, you have no cause to grieve! (II:22, 27)

Krishna also assures Arjun of his abiding concern for him, and of the god's power to help him: "If I am in your thought, by my grace you will transcend all dangers" (XVIII:58). Arjun does fight, and wins, and in the end all the warriors who die are reborn.

individual, even to those of low caste. Despite the hierarchy of the caste system, Hinduism allows enormous spiritual scope to each individual. It has no core dogma that each must affirm. Each individual Hindu frequently has his or her own sense of spirituality. This universal accessibility of Hinduism is most clear in three later forms of literature that have become a kind of folk treasury (in contrast to the Veda, Brahmanas, and Upanishads, which are the province of the *brahmin* priests).

In the last chapter (see p. 235) we discussed India's two great epic poems, the *Ramayana* and the *Mahabharata*. The latter's central story revolves around the civil war between two branches of the family of the Bharatas (from whom India derives its current Hindi name, Bharat). Like the *Ramayana*, the *Mahabharata* presents moral conflicts, the dilemma of taking sides, and the necessity of acting decisively. At its center stands the *Bhagavad-Gita* ("Song of God"; see Source, opposite), a philosophical discourse on the duties and the meaning of life and death.

The *Bhagavad-Gita* summarizes many of the key doctrines of Hinduism. Lord Krishna promises to help people who do their duty, and points the way toward spiritual fulfillment. The text demonstrates considerable assimilation within Hinduism, for the Lord Krishna is a dark-skinned, non-Vedic, non-Aryan tribal god, perhaps from the south. His centrality in this most revered Sanskrit text suggests the continuing accommodation between the Aryans and the indigenous peoples of India.

The two epics generally also reflect greater prestige for women than did earlier Sanskrit texts. In the *Ramayana*, Sita is presented as a

traditionally subordinate wife to Rama: her commitment to honor and duty surpasses even his; she defends Rama's honor even when he fails to defend hers. She is more heroic than he, although her heroism is defined by her role as dutiful wife. Rama is implicitly criticized for his inability to defend her both from Ravana and from the gossip of his own subjects. In some versions, the criticism is made explicit. In the *Mahabharata*, by contrast, Draupadi is the wife of all five of the Pandava brothers, and she protects, defends, and inspires them in their struggles, going far beyond the subservient role that women play in the majority of Aryan literature. In the epics, the female force, *shakti*, has gained recognition.

Scene from a dramatization of the *Ramayana.* During the north Indian festival of Dussehra, the Ram-leela, the play of the Lord Rama, is enacted in huge public spectacles. Scenes from the *Ramayana*, with its epic tale of the victory of good over evil, are performed by exotically costumed actors, and giant effigies of demons from the epic are dramatically burnt to the delight of the crowds.

The Puranas

The Puranas, ancient stories, are eighteen major and eighteen minor collections of folk tales of the people. These are legends of gods and kings, of the creation and destruction of the universe. Here emerge in central positions the most popular of the gods of Hinduism, Vishnu and Shiva. Here, too, appear female goddesses, often as consorts of the principal gods, such as Lakshmi and Saraswati with Vishnu; and Parvati, Durga, and Kali with Shiva. These goddesses also help to balance the rather suppressed position of females evident in the earlier Aryan literature. The Puranas were transmitted orally, usually in popular vernacular languages, until, beginning about 450 C.E., in recognition of their popularity, they were translated and recorded in Sanskrit and became part of Hinduism's informal literary canon.

TEMPLES AND SHRINES

By the seventh century C.E. fundamental changes had taken place in the form of Hindu worship. Personal prayer, often addressed to representations of the gods in statues and pictures, displaced sacrifice. Temples of great beauty were built. The caves at Ellora in western India were fashioned into temples in the eighth century, reflecting the early importance of caves in Hindu worship. Within the temples, sculpture and painting demonstrate the artistic development in religious worship. The bas reliefs and artwork in the temples at Kanchi and Mahabalipuram in the south, also built in the eighth century, continue to dazzle viewers today. Sexual passion and the union of male and female entered into forms of worship, symbolically representing passion for, and union with, god, as the temple sculptures at Khajuraho in north India about 1000 C.E. illustrate.

Magnificent temples flourished everywhere in India, but especially in the south of the subcontinent. University of Chicago anthropologist Arjun Appadurai writes of the diverse array of temples that mark the Indian landscape:

> In many ways the Hindu temple is the
> quintessentially South Indian institution. . . .
> Temples come in every size and scale, from small
> family shrines to village temples, to lineage temples,
> to regional temples, to great pan-regional
> pilgrimage centers. (pp. 8–9)

Bronze sculpture of Vishnu, early Chola period, first half of tenth century. Vishnu is beloved as the tender, merciful deity—the Preserver—and as the second member of the Hindu trinity he complements Brahma the Creator and Shiva the Destroyer. He is said to come to earth periodically as an *avatar*, an incarnation in various forms, to help humankind in times of crisis. (*Metropolitan Museum of Art, New York*)

FOCUS
Bhakti: The Path of Mystical Devotion

About 500 C.E., beginning in south India and spreading northward, a powerful new strand of mystical devotion enriched Hinduism. It continues today in the multitudes of devotional prayer meetings in every corner of India. Bhakti built on classical texts such as the *Gita* that promised: "No one devoted to me is lost. . . . Keep me in your mind and devotion, sacrifice to me, bow to me, discipline your self toward me, and you will reach me." (IX:31, 34)

Bhakti was a revolt within Hinduism against formality in religion, against hierarchy, and against the power of the *brahmin* priesthood. It often found expression in poetry composed in the everyday vernacular local language by common people, including washermen, potters, fishermen, hunters, and producers of home-made liquor, as well as by a few kings and princes.

Basavanna (1106–68), declaring that "Love of Shiva cannot live with ritual," left his home at the age of sixteen and wandered until he received a message from Shiva at a place "where three rivers meet." He devoted himself to the Lord Shiva, advocated equality, spoke for the poor, attacked orthodox Brahminism, and founded the Virashaiva movement dedicated to these principles. He composed his poetry in Kannada, one of the vernacular languages of south India. Here it is translated by A.K. Ramanujan in his beautiful, brief anthology of four south Indian Bhakti poets, *Speaking of Siva*:

> The rich
> will make temples for Shiva.
> What shall I,
> a poor man,
> do?
>
> My legs are pillars,
> the body the shrine,
> the head a cupola
> of gold.
>
> Listen, O lord of the meeting rivers,
> things standing shall fall,
> but the moving ever shall stay.
>
> (Ramanujan, p. 88)

Some of the most inspired and popular of the Bhakti poets, like Mahadeviyakka in twelfth-century south India and Mirabai in sixteenth-century west India, were women who expressed their religious passion in overtly sexual terms. Mahadeviyakka wrote in the Kannada vernacular of her longing for God: "Night and day in your worship I forget myself."

> He bartered my heart,
> looted my flesh
> claimed as tribute
> my pleasure,
> took over
> all of me.
>
> I'm the woman of love
> for my lord, white as jasmine.
>
> (Ramanujan, p. 125)

Mirabai, who left a marriage with a prince in order to follow her religious passion, wrote in Hindi of her love for Lord Krishna:

> Let us go to a realm beyond going,
> Where death is afraid to go
> Where the high-flying birds alight and play,
> Afloat in the full lake of love.   (Embree, p. 369)

Writing also in a Hindi dialect, also in the sixteenth century, the blind poet Surdas sang of Krishna's steadfast concern for each person:

> Listen, ingrate, who then do you think has stayed
>   by you both day and night,
> Befriending you—though you long ago forgot, if
>   ever, that is, you knew?
> Even today he stands at your side, ready to bear
>   your birth-born shame,
> Always wanting for life to go well, and loving you
>   as his own.   (Embree, 360–61)

RELIGION AND RULE

Temples were often patronized by wealthy land-owners and rulers who sought validation of their power and rule through the prestige of *brahmin* priests. As in many religions, rulers supported priests, while priests affirmed the authority of the rulers. This was especially true in the south. At least as early as the eighth century, new rulers who seized lands occupied by indigenous tribal peoples often imported *brahmin* priests to overawe the tribals with their learning, piety, and rituals. The priests were to persuade the tribals of the proper authority of the king. In order to pacify the tribals, their gods might be incorporated into the array of gods worshiped in the temple by the priests, just as the tribal peoples would begin to worship the major gods of Hinduism. Anthropologists describe this process as an interplay between the "great" national tradition and the "little" local tradition. As new lands were opened, and tribals were persuaded to accept the new ruling coalition, the temples grew larger and more wealthy.

In exchange for their support, kings rewarded priests with land grants, court subsidies, and temple bequests. *Brahmin* priests and Tamil rulers prospered together. Historian Romila Thapar reports the temples "financing various commercial enterprises and acting as banker and money-lender to village assemblies and similar bodies" (*History of India*, p. 211). Hindu colleges, rest-houses for pilgrims, centers of administration, and even cities grew up around some of these temples.

Kandariya Mahadeo Temple at Khajuraho, Chandela, *c.* 1025–1050 C.E. The twenty surviving temples at Khajuraho, though maimed by time, are still among the greatest examples of medieval Hindu architecture and sculpture in north India. Beneath the soaring towers, multilayered bands of sculptures writhe in a pulsating tableau of human and divine activity. The depictions of athletic lovemaking, which so scandalized nineteenth-century European travelers, can be linked to Tantric sects of Hinduism, then prevalent in the Chandela region.

Kailasanatha Temple at Ellora, Rashtrakuta, c. 757–790 C.E. Carved into an escarpment of volcanic stone, the thirty-three shrines of Ellora have for centuries been a pilgrimage center for Hindus, Buddhists, and Jains (see Focus, p. 279). The monolithic stone shaft in the foreground, 60 feet (18 m) high, would have originally supported a trident symbol of Shiva, to whom this temple is dedicated.

HINDUISM IN SOUTHEAST ASIA

Hinduism did not generally attract, nor seek, converts outside of India, but southeast Asia was an exception. Here, the initiative for conversion grew out of politics, as it had in southern India. The powers of the Hindu temple and the *brahmin* priesthood were imported to validate royal authority in southeast Asia from as early as the third century C.E. to as late as the fourteenth century.

Trade contacts between India and southeast Asia date back to at least 150 B.C.E. Indian sailors carried cargoes to and from Myanmar, the Straits of Malacca, the Kingdom of Funan in modern Cambodia and Vietnam, and Java in modern Indonesia. By the third century C.E., Funan had accepted many elements of Indian culture, religion, and political practice. Chinese envoys reported a prosperous state with walled cities, palaces, and houses. Sanskrit was in use, as was some Indian technology for irrigation and farming. By the fifth century it appears that Sanskrit was in widespread official

use, Indian calendars marked the dates, and Indian gods, including Shiva and Vishnu, were worshiped, as were representations of the Buddha (see Spotlight, pp. 288–9). Hindu temples began to appear with *brahmin* priests to staff them.

Hinduism in Southeast Asia: How Do We Know?

Even today the historical stamp of Hinduism endures in southeast Asia in the names of cities like Ayuthia in Thailand, derived from Ayodhya in northern India; in the influence of Sanskrit on several southeast Asian languages; in the popularity of the *Ramayana* and other Hindu literature in the folklore and theater of the region. Moreover, Hindu temples still stand, most spectacularly the Angkor Wat temple complex in Cambodia. Evidence of Hindu influence in southeast Asia appears also in early reports of Chinese visitors, archaeological remains, and **epigraphy** (inscriptions on metal and rock). These records are, nevertheless, sparse. *Brahmin* priests appear in the southeast-Asian records only after 800 C.E. It is, therefore, difficult to answer the question: "What brought Indian power and prestige into southeast Asia from about the third century to about the fourteenth century?"

Three theories explaining the appearance of Indian influence in southeast Asia have been suggested. The first two, originally advocated by historian George Coedes in the early twentieth century, argued that Indians initiated contact and attempted to introduce their religion and culture into southeast Asia. His first theory, which stressed the use of military might, is no longer accepted. As noted in Chapter 8, there is very little record of Indian mili-

tary action in the area, and none suggesting a desire for conquest. His second theory—that Indian traders brought their culture with them—has wider acceptance, but it also encounters serious opposition. Trade connections between India and southeast Asia were numerous, long-standing, and intense. Some cultural and religious influence must have accompanied them, but these contacts were by sea, while much of the Hindu influence was manifest inland.

The third theory, advocated by J.C. van Leur in the 1950s and by O.W. Wolters a generation later, argued that local rulers invited *brahmin* priests to come from India to southeast Asia to build temples, to promote agricultural development on land

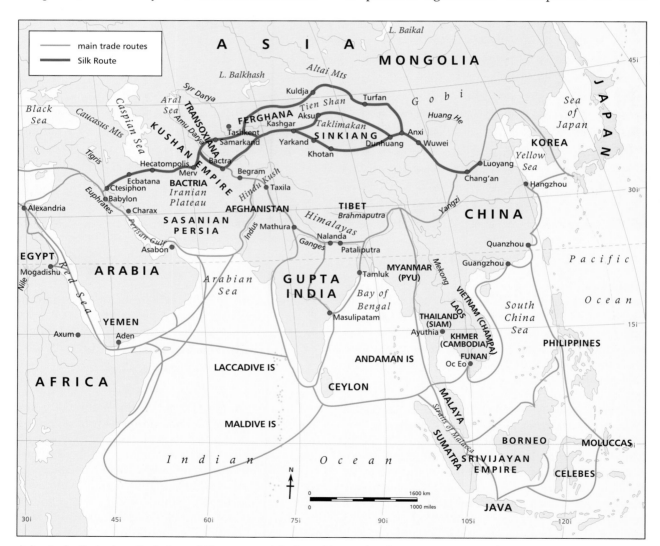

Asian trade Ports along the Indus and Ganges served Arab maritime traders for many centuries, and provided links to the kingdoms of southeast Asia and the South China Sea. To the north, roads following river valleys and passes through the towering Himalayas and the Hindu Kush provided contact with China and the silk route respectively.

specially granted to them, to invoke the Hindu gods to validate the authority of the rulers, and to convince the local population of this divine validation. In the words of historian Kenneth R. Hall, these priests were to serve as "development planners." They brought with them from India principles of government, religious law, administration, art, and architecture. In promoting these religious/political practices through the priests, southeast Asian rulers were emulating the policies of the Pallava and Chola kings of southern India. But Hinduism did not survive in southeast Asia. It was superseded by Buddhism and, later, by Islam.

HINDUISM AND BUDDHISM IN SOUTHEAST ASIA

Buddhist monks as well as Hindu priests were invited to southeast Asia to help establish and consolidate the power of local kings, and southeast Asian rulers found the Buddhist monks as useful as the Hindu *brahmins,* for they served similar political and administrative functions, but in the name of Buddhism. For example, the ruler of the Srivijaya Empire in the East Indies welcomed 1000 Buddhist monks to his kingdom in the late seventh century C.E. Jayavarman VII, the Buddhist ruler of the Khmer kingdom at the end of the twelfth century, added Buddhist images in the great temple of Angkor Wat, which had been built earlier in the century to honor the Hindu god Vishnu.

By about the fourteenth century, Hinduism had died out in southeast Asia, while Buddhism continued to thrive. In India, on the other hand, Buddhism withered away, while Hinduism flourished. In fact, except for its temporary success in southeast Asia, Hinduism has never attracted, nor welcomed, many converts outside of India and its neighbor, Nepal. Buddhism, on the contrary, became an enormously successful proselytizing religion throughout Asia.

BUDDHISM

Buddhism was born in India, within the culture of Hinduism, and then charted its own path. Like Hinduism, it questioned the reality of this earthly world and speculated on the existence of other worlds. Unlike Hinduism, however, Buddhism had a founder, a set of originating scriptures, and an order of monks. In opposition to Hinduism, it renounced hereditary caste organization and the supremacy of the *brahmin* priests. Budhism spread to southeast Asia along with Hinduism, but Buddhism became more popular, gaining acceptance as the principal relgion of Myanmar, Thailand, Cambodia, Laos, Vietnam, Sri Lanka, and Tibet until today. It won multitudes of adherents throughout the rest of Asia as well, in Sri Lanka, Tibet, China, Korea, and Japan. Yet in India itself, Buddhism lost out in competition with Hinduism and its priesthood, virtually vanishing from the subcontinent by about the twelfth century C.E.

Bronze Dancing Shiva, eleventh century. Shiva is a god of destruction whose frenzied dancing—usually, as here, enacted on the body of a dwarf demon—symbolizes the eternal cycle of creation and destruction. Craftworkers of the South Indian Chola dynasty molded bronze into forms of exquisite grace and power (see also picture, p. 268). (*Musée Guimet, Paris*)

THE BUDDHA

Born about 563 B.C.E. as a prince, Siddhartha Gautama was shielded from normal life until at the age of twenty-nine he emerged from his palace and confronted for the first time the reality of the pain of everyday life. He identified human suffering as the key problem of life and sought a means of emancipation from it. Following a long quest, he found his enlightenment through meditation, becoming the Buddha, the enlightened one, and began to preach his new understanding. The source of suffering, he taught, was personal desire and passion; they could be overcome by proper living. A new consciousness could be achieved by a combination of disciplining the mind and observing ethical precepts in human relationships. In the face of continuing rebirths into the pain of life, the Buddha taught that right living could bring release from the cycle of mortality and pain, and entry into *nirvana,* a kind of blissful nothingness. On the metaphysical plane, the Buddha taught that everything in the universe is transient; there is no "being." There exists neither an immortal soul nor a god, neither *atman* nor Brahman. The Buddha's teachings about the illusion of life and about rebirth and release were consistent with Hindu concepts of *maya, samsara,* and *moksha,* but the Buddha's denial of god put him on the fringes of Hindu thought. His rejection of caste as an organizing hierarchy and of the Hindu priests as connoisseurs of religious truth, won him powerful allies—and powerful opponents. A band of disciples, monks, the *Sangha,* gathered around him to learn his message and to teach it.

The three-fold motto of all devout Buddhist was: "I seek refuge in the Buddha; I seek refuge in the Doctrine; I seek refuge in the Sangha (order of monks)."

SOURCE
The Address to Sigala: Buddhism in Everyday Life

Much of the Buddha's moral and ethical instruction is directed to the monks of the Sangha. In the Address to Sigala, however, he speaks to laypeople about their relationships and responsibilities toward one another. The address includes practical advice to husbands and wives, friends, employers, and employees. The lengthy address is translated and summarized here by A.L. Basham.

> Husbands should respect their wives, and comply as far as possible with their requests. They should not commit adultery. They should give their wives full charge of the home, and supply them with fine clothes and jewellery as far as their means permit. Wives should be thorough in their duties, gentle and kind to the whole household, chaste, and careful in housekeeping, and should carry out their work with skill and enthusiasm.

> A man should be generous to his friends, speak kindly of them, act in their interest in every way possible, treat them as his equals, and keep his word to them. They in turn should watch over his interests and property, take care of him when he is "off his guard" [i.e., intoxicated, infatuated, or otherwise liable to commit rash and careless actions], stand by him and help him in time of trouble, and respect other members of his family.

> Employers should treat their servants and workpeople decently. They should not be given tasks beyond their strength. They should receive adequate food and wages, be cared for in time of sickness and infirmity, and be given regular holidays and bonuses in times of prosperity. They should rise early and go to bed late in the service of their master, be content with their just wages, work thoroughly, and maintain their master's reputation. (Digha Nikaya, iii:161; cited in Basham, p. 286)

PROFILE

Siddhartha Gautama

THE BUDDHA

A.L. Basham (1914–86), the most influential interpreter of ancient India of his generation, wrote that all we know of the Buddha's life and teaching comes from much later accounts, embellished by his followers. "Much doubt now exists as to the real doctrines of the historical Buddha, as distinct from those of Buddhism" (p. 256). The accounts that exist tell the following story.

Siddhartha Gautama was born *c.* 563 B.C.E. in the foothills of the Himalayan mountains of what is now Nepal. His father, a *kshatriya* warrior caste chief of the Shakyas, a republican tribe, received a prophecy that Siddhartha would become either a great emperor or a great religious teacher. Hoping that his son would follow the former vocation, the chief sheltered him as best he could so that he would experience neither pain nor disillusionment.

At the age of twenty-nine, Siddhartha started to grow curious about what lay beyond the confines of his father's palace. Leaving his wife, Yasadhara, and their son Rahula, he instructed his charioteer to take him to the city. Here he came across a frail, elderly man. Never having encountered old age, Siddhartha was confused. His companion explained that aging was an inevitable, and painful, part of human experience. As Siddhartha took further excursions outside the palace he soon came to see that pain was an inevitable part of life, experienced in illness, aging, death, and even birth.

On his fourth and final trip he met a wandering holy man who had shunned the trappings of wealth and material gain. Siddhartha decided to do likewise. Bidding farewell to his family for the last time, he set out on horseback in search of an antidote to sorrow and a means of teaching it to others.

For six years Siddhartha wandered as an ascetic. Nearing starvation, however, he gave up the path of asceticism. Determined to achieve enlightenment, he began to meditate, sitting under a tree at Bodh Gaya near modern Patna, in India. His concentration and fortitude were tested by Mara, the spirit of this world, who tempted him to give up his meditation with both threats of punishment and promises of rewards. Touching the ground with his hand in a gesture, or *mudra*, repeated often in sculptures of the Buddha, Siddhartha revealed these temptations to be illusions. On the forty-ninth day of meditation he reached enlightenment, becoming the Buddha, He Who Has Awakened. He had found an antidote to pain and suffering. He proceeded to the Deer Park at Sarnath, near Banaras, where he delivered his first sermon setting forth the Four Noble Truths and the Noble Eightfold Path (see Source, p. 276).

Although much of the Hindu priesthood opposed the Buddha's teachings, the kings of Magadha and Koshala, whose territories included most of the lower Gangetic plain, befriended and supported him and the small band of followers gathered around him. The Buddha taught peacefully and calmly until about 483 B.C.E., when, at the age of eighty, he died, surrounded by a cadre of dedicated monks and believers, the original Buddhist Sangha (order of monks).

Teaching Buddha, **from Sarnath, India, Gupta dynasty, fifth century** C.E. (*Archeological Musem, Sarnath*)

SOURCE

The Four Noble Truths and the Noble Eightfold Path

This is the Noble Truth of Sorrow. Birth is sorrow, age is sorrow, disease is sorrow, death is sorrow, contact with the unpleasant is sorrow, separation from the pleasant is sorrow, every wish unfulfilled is sorrow—in short all the five components of individuality are sorrow.

And this is the Noble Truth of the Arising of Sorrow. [It arises from] thirst, which leads to rebirth, which brings delight and passion, and seeks pleasure now here, now there—the thirst for sensual pleasure, the thirst for continued life, the thirst for power.

And this is the Noble Truth of the Stopping of Sorrow. It is the complete stopping of that thirst, so that no passion remains, leaving it, being emancipated from it, being released from it, giving no place to it.

And this is the Noble Truth of the Way which Leads to the Stopping of Sorrow. It is the Noble Eightfold Path—Right Views, Right Resolve, Right Speech, Right Conduct, Right Livelihood, Right Effort, Right Recollection and Right Meditation. (Basham, p. 269)

Great Stupa, Sanchi, third century B.C.E.–first century C.E. With its four gloriously carved gates and majestic central hemisphere, the Great Stupa of Sanchi is the most remarkable surviving example of the 84,000 such Buddhist burial mounds reputedly erected by the emperor Asoka during the Mauryan Empire. This "world mountain," oriented to the four corners of the universe, contained a holy relic, the object of pilgrims' devotion, and is topped by a three-tiered umbrella representing the Three Jewels of Buddhism: the Buddha, the Law, and the community of monks.

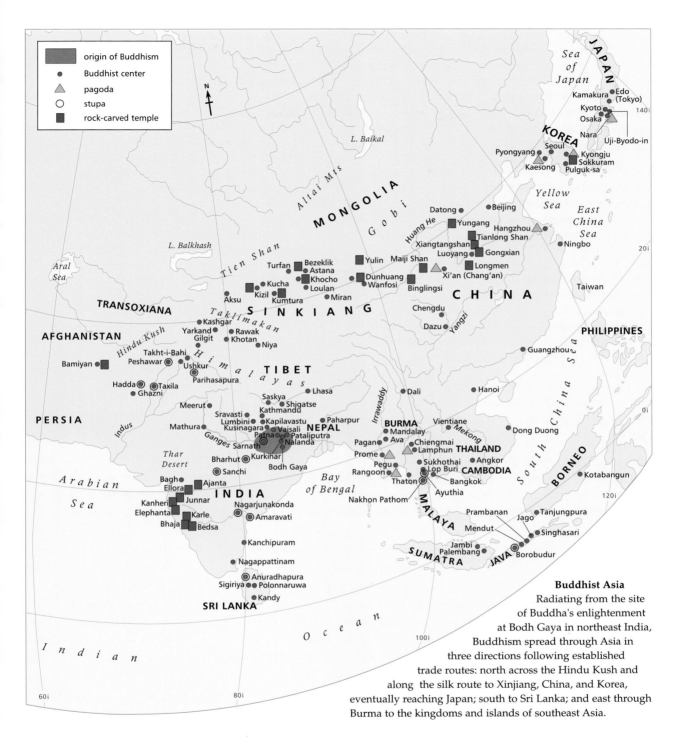

Buddhist Asia
Radiating from the site of Buddha's enlightenment at Bodh Gaya in northeast India, Buddhism spread through Asia in three directions following established trade routes: north across the Hindu Kush and along the silk route to Xinjiang, China, and Korea, eventually reaching Japan; south to Sri Lanka; and east through Burma to the kingdoms and islands of southeast Asia.

The Sangha and the Doctrine

The Sangha was open to all men regardless of caste and thus drew the antagonism of *brahmins*, although some did join. For a time, women were permitted to form their own convents, but only under special restrictions. (Today Buddhist nuns exist only in Tibet.)

The monks wore saffron robes and shaved their heads. They practiced celibacy and renounced alcohol, but no vow of obedience to the order was required. The monks were intellectually and spiritually free. Decisions were made through group discussion, perpetuating the pattern of the early republics of the north Indian hills. Monks studied, disciplined their spirits, meditated, and did the physical work of their monasteries. At first, they were to wander, begging for their living, except during the rainy months of the monsoon, but as monasteries became richer through donations of money and land, the monks tended to settle down. They also tended to give up begging, which diminished their contact with the common people to some degree.

A series of general councils began to codify the principles, doctrines, and texts of the emerging community. The first, convened shortly after the Buddha's death, began the continuing process of collecting his teachings. The second, about a century later, began to dispute the essential meaning of Buddhism. The third, convened at Pataliputra, Asoka's capital, revealed more of the differences that would soon lead to a split over the question of whether the Buddha was a human or a god. By this time an array of Buddhist *caityas*, or shrines, was growing. In addition to monasteries, great *stupas*, or burial mounds, of Buddhist relics were built at Barhut, Sanchi, and Amaravati. Between 200 B.C.E. and 200 C.E. there were more Buddhist than Hindu shrines in India. Theological discussion flourished, with a heavy emphasis on *metta*, or benevolence; non-violence; *dharma*, or proper behavior, although not related to caste since Buddhism rejected hereditary caste; and tolerance for all religions.

Mahayana Buddhism

The fourth general council, convened in the first century C.E. in Kashmir, codified the key doctrines of Buddhism as they had developed from earliest times. These were the principles of the Theravada ("Doctrine of the Elders") branch of Buddhism, which we have been examining and which is today the prevailing form in Sri Lanka and southeast Asia, except for Vietnam. But by now a newer school of Mahayana Buddhism had been growing for perhaps two centuries and had become a serious challenge to Theravada. Mahayana means "the Greater Vehicle," and its advocates claimed that their practices could carry more Buddhists to nirvana because they had bodhisattvas to help. A bodhisattva was a "being of wisdom" on the verge of achieving nirvana but so concerned about the welfare of fellow humans that he postponed his entrance into nirvana to remain on earth, or to be reborn, in order to help others.

In addition, Mahayana Buddhism taught that religious merit, achieved through performing good deeds, could be transferred from one person to another. It embellished the concept of nirvana with the vision of a Mahayana heaven, presided over by Amitabha Buddha, a form of the Buddha who had lived on earth and had now become a kind of father in heaven. Subsequently, Mahayanists developed the concept of numerous heavens with numerous forms of the Buddha presiding over them. They also developed the concept of the Maitreya Buddha, a suffering servant who will come to redeem humanity.

Some theologians note the similarity of the concept of this Maitreya Buddha to the Christian

SACRED WRITINGS OF BUDDHISM

Tripitaka	"The Three Baskets": **Vinaya**, on the proper conduct of Buddhist monks and nuns; **Sutta**, discourses attributed to the Buddha; and **Abhidhamma**, supplementary doctrines. Written in Pali.
The Mahayanas	(Mahayana is Sanskrit for "Greater Vehicle.") The body of writings associated with the school of Buddhism dominant in Tibet, Mongolia, China, Korea, and Japan. Includes the famous allegory, the Lotus Sutra, the Buddhist Parable of the Prodigal Son.
Milindapanha	Dialogue between the Greek king Milinda and the Buddhist monk Nagasena on the philosophy of Buddhism.
Buddha's Four Noble Truths	Suffering is always present in life; desire is the cause of suffering; freedom from suffering can be achieved in nirvana (perfect peace and bliss); the Eightfold Path leads to nirvana.

FOCUS
Jainism

India has given birth to several religions, and Jainism is one of the oldest still existing. It shares many characteristics with Buddhism. At about the time of the Buddha, the teacher Mahavir (b. *c.* 540 B.C.E.), the twenty-fourth in a long lineage of Jain religious leaders, guided the religion into its modern form. The religion takes its name from Mahavir's designation *jina*, or conqueror. Like Theravada Buddhists, Jains reject the caste system and the supremacy of *brahmin* priests, postulating instead that there is no god, but that humans do have souls that they can purify by careful attention to their actions, and especially by practicing non-violence. If they follow the eternal law of ethical treatment of others and devotion to the rather austere rituals of the faith, Jains believe they will reach nirvana, which is an end to the cycle of rebirths rather than a rewarding afterlife.

Jainism's emphasis on non-violence is so powerful that Jains typically do not become farmers lest they kill living creatures in the soil. In a country overwhelmingly agricultural, Jains are usually urban and often businessmen. Jainism did not spread outside India, and its 4 million adherents today live almost entirely in India. Because Jains, like earlier Buddhists, employ *brahmin* priests to officiate at their lifecycle events, and because Jains intermarry freely with several Hindu *vaishya* (business) sub-castes, some consider them a branch of Hinduism, although they do not usually regard themselves as Hindus. One of the regions of Jain strength in India is western Gujarat, the region where Mahatma Gandhi grew up (see Chapter 20). The Mahatma attributed his adherence to non-violence in large part to the influence of Jainism.

Jainist nuns on their way to worship. Although most Jains are laypersons, important monasteries house priests and nuns. These nuns wear mouth-cloths to prevent injury to insects that might otherwise be inhaled.

Messiah, and some suggest that the Buddhists may have borrowed it. They also suggest that Christians may have borrowed the narratives of the virgin birth of the Buddha and of his temptation in his search for enlightenment, and applied them to Jesus. There are significant similarities in the stories of these two men/gods and their biogra-

phies. Further, Mahayanists spoke of three aspects of the Buddha: Amitabha, the Buddha in heaven; Gautama, the historical Buddha on earth; and the most revered of all the bodhisattvas, the freely moving Avalokiteshvara. Theologians ask: To what degree do these three Buddhist forms correspond to the Father, Son, Holy Spirit of Christianity as it was developing at the same time? How much borrowing took place between India and the Mediterranean coast, and in which direction?

Within India, Mahayana Buddhism began to challenge Hinduism more boldly than Theravada had. Wishing to compete for upper caste and upper class audiences, Mahayanists began to record their theology in Sanskrit, the language of the elites, rather than the more colloquial Pali language, which Theravada had preferred. Mahayana theologians, most notably Nagarjuna (*fl. c.* 50–150 C.E.), began to elaborate Buddhist philosophy and debate directly with *brahmin* priests. Buddhist monasteries established major educational programs, especially at Nalanda in Bihar, where the Buddha had spent much of his life, and at Taxila, on the international trade routes in the northern Punjab.

To spread the new faith, Buddhist missions traveled to southeast Asia and, increasingly, overland via the silk routes to central Asia and China. The first Buddhist missionaries are mentioned in Chinese records about 65 C.E. They established their first monastery at Luoyang. Over the centuries, many more were built within China and along the silk route. Chinese pilgrims traveled the silk route in the opposite direction to visit and study in the land of the Buddha, and some, most notably Faxian, who visited in 399–414, left important records of their observations. Thousands came from throughout the Buddhist world to study at Taxila and Nalanda.

THE DECLINE OF BUDDHISM IN INDIA

From its beginnings in India, Buddhism's strongest appeal had been to *kshatriya* rulers and *vaishya* businessmen, who felt that *brahmin* priests did not respect them. The Buddha himself came from a *kshatriya* family, and his early friendship with the *kshatriya* kings of Magadha and Koshala had ensured their early support for his movement. Later kings and merchants also donated huge sums of money to support Buddhist monks, temples, and monasteries. Many people of the lower castes, who felt the weight and the arrogance of all the other castes pressing down on them, also joined the newly forming religion. They were especially attracted by the use of the vernacular Pali and Magadhi languages in place of Sanskrit, and the absence of the financial demands of the *brahmins*. (In the 1950s, almost a thousand years after Buddhism's demise in India, about 5 million "out-

castes," people whose caste ranked below the bottom, revived Buddhism in India in protest at the inequalities of the caste system and declared their allegiance to the old/new religion. These "neo-Buddhists" are virtually the only Buddhists to be found in India today [see Chapter 20].)

By the fifth century C.E., however, the Chinese Buddhist pilgrim Faxian noted weaknesses in Indian Buddhism. The religion continued to exist in India for another six centuries, so his observation was hardly definitive, but Buddhism did die out in India, losing strength from the time of the decline of the Gupta Empire (*c.* 320–550 C.E.; see p. 246). Regional rulers began to choose Hinduism over Buddhism, and alliances with priests rather than with monks. Perhaps such choices strengthened the rulers' standing with their subjects, since Hinduism always seemed closer to the common people. Also, without imperial assistance, merchants' incomes may have decreased within India, reducing their contributions to Buddhist temples. Trade with southeast Asia continued to be lucrative, however, and the Buddhist presence there remained strong.

At the popular level, lower castes who had found the anti-caste philosophy of Buddhism attractive, apparently also began to shift their allegiances back toward more orthodox Hinduism as an anchor in a time of political change. In any case, Mahayana Buddhism, with its many god-like Buddhas and bodhisattvas inhabiting a multitude of heavens, seemed so close to Hinduism that many Buddhists must have seen little purpose in maintaining a distinction. Finally, Buddhists throughout their history in India had relied upon Hindu *brahmin* priests to officiate at their lifecycle ceremonies of birth, marriage, and death, so Hindu priests could argue that they always had a significant claim on Buddhist allegiance.

Readers who are accustomed to the monotheistic pattern of religions claiming the undivided loyalty of their followers will recognize here a very different pattern. Many religions, especially polytheistic religions, expect that individuals will incorporate diverse elements of different religions into their personal philosophy and ritual. We will see more examples of this personal syncretism and loyalty to multiple religions as we examine Buddhism's relationship with Confucianism in China and with both Confucianism and Shinto in Japan.

As Hinduism evolved, it became more attractive to Buddhists. Theologians like Shankaracharya (788–820) and Ramanuja (1017–1137) advanced philosophies based on the Vedic literature known to the common people and built many temples and schools to spread their thought. Hindu *bhakti* devotionalism (see Focus, p. 269) also attracted followers to its mystical, ecstatic forms. At the same time, Hinduism, following its tradition of syncretism, incorporated the Buddha himself within its own polytheistic universe as an incarnation of Vishnu. A devotee could revere the Buddha within the overarching framework of Hinduism. Finally, although neither Buddhism nor Hinduism gave much scope to women within their official institutions of temples, schools, and monasteries, for Hinduism the home was much more central than the public institution, and here women did have a central role in worship and ritual. Buddhism was much more centered on its monasteries and monks. The comparative lack of a role for women, and the comparative disinterest in domestic life generally, may have impeded its spread.

The end of Buddhism in India came with the arrival of Muslims during the first two centuries of their major invasions into India, between 1000 and 1200 C.E. Muslims saw Buddhism as a competitive proselytizing religion, unlike Hinduism, and did not wish to coexist with it. Because Buddhism was, by this time, relatively weak and relatively centralized within its monasteries and schools, Muslims were able to destroy the remnants of the religion by attacking these institutions. Buddhist monks were killed or forced to flee from India to centers in southeast Asia, Nepal, and Tibet. Hinduism was equipped to survive the challenge because it was much more broadly based as the religion of home and community and far more deeply rooted in Indian culture.

Guanyin, Buddhist deity, Northern Song dynasty, China, *c.* **1200** C.E. Guanyin, a bodhisattva, or enlightened being, who remains in this world to relieve human suffering, was a very popular subject in Chinese art: this painted-wood example is particularly sensuous and refined. Buddhist deities are considered to have the spiritual qualities of both genders and by this date the feminine qualities were accentuated. (*Nelson-Atkins Museum of Art, Kansas City, Missouri*)

BUDDHISM IN CHINA AND JAPAN

Early Buddhism Outside India: How Do We Know?

Because Buddhism has no single central organization, our knowledge of its spread is gained by studying the works of the monks, missionaries, poets, architects, and sculptors who spread the faith. This decentralization and vast geographical diffusion mean that Buddhism has taken on different forms from place to place, time to time, and state to state. It arrived in foreign form, but over time each regional culture has put its own stamp on Buddhism. We must, therefore, examine the faith and practice of Buddhism in each region separately.

Arrival in China: The Silk Route

The thin line of communication over which pilgrims and missionaries carried the message of the

Diamond Sutra, 868 C.E. This superb frontispiece, showing the Buddha preaching to an elderly disciple, comes from the *Diamond Sutra*, a Sanskrit tale transmitted along the silk route and translated into Chinese in the fifth century. Produced by woodblock to a high standard of technical and artistic achievement, the 17-foot-long (5.2 m) sutra is the world's earliest dated printed book. (*British Library, London*)

Buddha from India to China and beyond was the silk route, the same route that carried luxury products between China and India and then on to the West. Several of the pilgrims who traveled these routes, especially Faxian, in the early years of the fifth century C.E., and Xuanzang, in the early years of the seventh, brought back both Buddhist texts and important first-hand information from India and the lands along the silk routes. Turning north from India through Kashgar, and then east to Khotan, Turfan, Dunhuang, and on to Chang'an in the heart of China, Buddhist pilgrims improved these trade routes with rest-houses (see picture, p. 222), temples, and monasteries, some built into caves.

Although Buddhism first appeared in China in the first century C.E., at the height of the Han dynasty, it took firmer root after the dynasty fell (see p. 217). Confucianism, China's dominant philosophy, was intimately tied to the fate of the imperial government, and only after this central political structure collapsed could Mahayana Buddhism find a place. The mystical character of Mahayana Buddhism especially attracted Daoists. To some degree, the two beliefs competed, but some of the competition eventually led to each validating the other. For example, some Daoists claimed that the Buddha was actually Laozi as he appeared in his travels in India. Many Buddhists, in turn, accorded to Laozi and Confucius the status of bodhisattva. In this way, competition sometimes turned into mutual recognition.

As a foreign religion, Buddhism also had special appeal for some of the rulers of northern China in the third through the sixth centuries, since they, too, were outsiders. The Toba rulers of the Northern Wei dynasty (386–534) occasionally persecuted Buddhists as a threat to the state, but mostly they felt some kinship to this religion of outsiders. They patronized Buddhist shrines and monks, but they also regulated them.

In the south, with its abundance of émigrés from the northern court, Confucianism was crippled by the severance of its connection with the government. In contrast, newly arriving Buddhists won followers by proposing an organized, aesthetic philosophy for coping with the hazards of life in semi-exile. In southern China Buddhist arts of poetry, painting, and calligraphy flourished, and monasteries in the south offered refuge to the men who might have been part of the governing Confucian aristocracy in other times. In the southern state of Liang, the "Emperor" Wu (r. 502–549) declared Buddhism the official state religion, built temples, sponsored Buddhist assemblies, and wrote Buddhist commentaries.

Doctrinally, Buddhism had important differences from Confucianism, but the two world perspectives seem to have reached mutual accommodation. For example, Confucianism encouraged family cohesion and the veneration of ancestors, while Buddhist monks followed lives of celibacy; but Buddhist laypeople also valued family (see Source, p. 274), and the monks themselves venerated the Buddha and bodhisattvas as their spiritual ancestors. Nevertheless, tension between the two belief systems and organizations never completely dissipated. Confucians thought in terms of government order and control, while Buddhists tended toward decentralized congregational worship within a loose doctrinal framework. In many areas of China, as Buddhist monasteries became wealthy from the donations of local magnates and landlords, Confucian governments moved to regulate their power.

Buddhism's network of pilgrims and monks crisscrossed China, helping to integrate the nation. Through almost four centuries of division in China, from the fall of the Han (220 C.E.) to the rise of the Sui (581), Buddhism continued to grow in both north and south. Indeed, the founder of the Sui dynasty, a Buddhist himself, also patronized Confucianism and Daoism, seeing all these belief systems as vital to earning legitimacy for his government. The Tang extended this veneration. The only woman ever to rule China in her own name, the "Emperor" Wu, was a great patron of Buddhism. First ruling indirectly through the Emperor Gaozong (d. 683), whose concubine she was, and then, after his death, through two of their sons, in 690 she proclaimed herself the emperor of a new dynasty, the Zhou. She patronized Buddhism as a means of legitimizing her rule, declaring herself a reincarnation of Maitreya, the Buddha of future salvation. The empress built temples in every province of China. Before she was deposed in 705, she had overseen the warfare that expanded the Tang to its greatest geographical extent, including Xinjiang and Tibet.

Buddhism under the Tang Dynasty

Under the Tang dynasty (618–907) the intellectual, spiritual, and artistic life of Buddhism flourished. Eight major sects developed, each with a different interpretation of the original message of the Buddha, the importance of rules and regulations, rituals, meditation, scholarship, disciplinary exercises, and devotion. Among the larger and more significant schools was the Pure Land Sect. Its devotees believed that anyone could reach the Pure Land of paradise after death through faith in the Buddha Amitabha, the presiding authority in that realm. Members of the sect demonstrated their faith by continuously repeating the name Amitabha. Devotees also meditated on the Bodhisattva Guanyin, the bodhisattva of mercy (see picture, p. 281).

Another sect, Chan Buddhism, taught the importance of meditation. Some followers believed in lengthy disciplines of meditation, which would gradually lead to enlightenment; others in spontaneous flashes of insight, which would lead to the same goal. Both Pure Land and Chan were adopted in Japan as well, where the meditative exercises of Chan became known as Zen.

Buddhists are credited with inventing woodblock printing as a means of reproducing their sacred texts. The earliest woodblock print known is an illustrated copy of the *Diamond Sutra* from 868 C.E., discovered in the Dunhuang Caves. Most of the Buddhist art and architecture of Tang China was destroyed in later persecution, confiscation, and warfare. Its leading representations are now seen in Japan, which at just about this time adopted much of Chinese Buddhism as its own and then modified it (see pictures, pp. 226 and 286).

Political and military defeats started Buddhism on its decline in China. In far-off central Asia Muslim forces defeated Chinese forces in the decisive Battle of the Talas River in 751. Four years later, the revolt of General An Lushan in northeast China occupied the imperial armies for eight years. China's power in central Asia was broken, and with it the power of Buddhism in these regions. Islam would become the world religion of most of central Asia (see Chapter 11).

Almost a century later, the Tang emperor, Wuzong (r. 840–846), attacked Buddhism and its monasteries. Wuzong was a Daoist, personally opposed to Buddhism. He feared the power of the Buddhist establishment, the wealth and influence of its various monasteries especially when the Tang had been weakened by external defeats and internal revolts. Wuzong confiscated the lands and wealth of the Buddhist monasteries. He forced monks and nuns to leave the monasteries, claiming that he personally had defrocked 260,500 monks and nuns. He destroyed sacred texts, statues, and shrines, leaving only 49 monasteries and 800 monks in all of China. Later rulers alternated between reversing and re-imposing Wuzong's policies, and although Buddhism has remained a presence in China, even to today, it never recovered its numbers, vitality, or influence.

Buddhism in Japan

Long before "The Way of the Buddha" arrived in Japan, *c.* 552 C.E., the people of Japan followed "The Way of the *Kami*," later called Shinto. *Kamis* were the powers and spirits inherent in nature. Found everywhere, they could be called upon to help in time of human need. Shrines to the *kami* were built everywhere, always including a mirror in tribute to the sun-goddess, a sword, and a jewel. According

The Transience of Life: A Woman's Perspective from the Tang Dynasty

This anonymous poem of the Tang dynasty, discovered in the Dunhuang cave and translated by Patricia Ebrey and Lily Hwa, illuminates the Buddhist sense of the transience of life as experienced by a woman of high status.

A Woman's Hundred Years

At ten, like a flowering branch in the rain,
She is slender, delicate, and full of grace.
Her parents are themselves as young as the
rising moon
And do not allow her past the red curtain
without a reason.

At twenty, receiving the hairpin, she is a spring
bud.
Her parents arrange her betrothal; the matter's
well done.
A fragrant carriage comes at evening to carry her
to her lord.
Like Xioshi and his wife, at dawn they depart
with the clouds.

At thirty, perfect as a pearl, full of the beauty of
youth,
At her window, by the gauze curtain, she makes
up in front of the mirror.
With her singing companions, in the waterlily
season,
She rows a boat and plucks the blue flowers.

At forty, she is mistress of a prosperous house
and makes plans.
Three sons and five daughters give her some
trouble.
With her lute not far away, she toils always at her
loom.
Her only fear that the sun will set too soon.

At fifty, afraid of her husband's dislike,
She strains to please him with every charm.
Trying to remember the many tricks she had
learned since the age of sixteen.
No longer is she afraid of mothers- and sisters-
in-law.

At sixty, face wrinkled and hair like silk thread,
She walks unsteadily and speaks little.
Distressed that her sons can find no brides,
Grieved that her daughters have departed for
their husbands' homes.

At seventy, frail and thin, but not knowing what
to do about it,
She is no longer able to learn the Buddhist Law
even if she tries.
In the morning a light breeze
Makes her joints crack like clanging gongs.

At eighty, eyes blinded and ears half-deaf,
When she goes out she cannot tell north from
east.
Dreaming always of departed loves,
Who persuade her to chase the dying breeze.

At ninety, the glow fades like spent lightning.
Human affairs are no longer her concern.
Lying on a pillow, solitary on her high bed,
She resembles the dying leaves that fall in
autumn.

At a hundred, like a cliff crumbling in the wind,
For her body it is the moment to become dust.
Children and grandchildren will perform
sacrifices to her spirit.
And clear moonlight will forever illumine her
patch of earth.

(Ebrey, p. 104)

to the earliest Japanese records, the *Kojiki* (712 C.E.) and *Nihon shoki* (720 C.E.), the highest of the *kami* were Amaterasu, the sun-goddess and her obstreperous brother Susa-no-o. Amaterasu's grandson Niniqi descended to earth and set out to conquer Japan. He established himself as Japan's first emperor in 660 B.C.E., and all subsequent emperors trace their lineage directly back to this mythological founder. With the later arrival of Buddhism, the *kami* continued to have a distinguished and venerated position, often as minor Buddhas or bodhisattvas. Conversely, the Buddhas and bodhisattvas were accepted as especially powerful and exalted *kami*, capable of helping those in adversity. The royal family in Japan knew that the Emperor Asoka in India had adopted Buddhism and they emulated his decision.

BUDDHISM'S ARRIVAL IN JAPAN: HOW DO WE KNOW?

The semi-mythological *Nihon shoki* and *Kojiki* give a basic history of early Japan, but these records—and all accounts of Buddhist saints—must be read with some caution since they blend myth with factual record. Chinese histories occasionally discuss conditions in Japan; temples in Japan are themselves models of the development of Buddhism in the nation; and the treasures of art and documents housed in the temples enhance that perspective. For example, inside the Todaiji Temple in Nara, the Shosoin storehouse is one of the world's great repositories of art, holding several thousand treasures from the eighth century, including paintings, sculptures, calligraphy, textiles, ceramics, jade, metal and lacquer work, masks for drama, and musical instruments. Some were imported from regions throughout Asia and demonstrate Japan's position as eastern terminus of one great trans-Asian silk route. For later times, after the eighth century C.E., literature as well as personal diaries and records help to fill out the more formal accounts.

BUDDHISM'S ARRIVAL IN JAPAN: WHAT DO WE KNOW?

Buddhism first came to Japan from China via the Paekche kingdom of southwest Korea in 552 C.E. The *Nihon shoki* tells of the Paekche king sending Buddhist texts and statues and asking help in a war against another Korean kingdom, the Silla. From the very beginning, Buddhism had political as well as religious implications. Clans close to the Japanese emperor were divided in their reception of the foreign religion, with those who accepted it regarding Buddhism as a force for performing miracles, especially healing the sick, and many Buddhist monks were especially skilled in medicine. A minority, however, thought the new religion ought to be banned.

Buddhism found acceptance at a political level in Japan a half century later under Prince Shotoku Taishi (573–621). The prince effectively ruled the country as the regent to the ruler of the Yamato Plain, the western region of Japan. An enthusiastic Buddhist, Shotoku built many temples, including the Horyuji in the capital city of Nara. A scholar of Buddhist theology, he invited Buddhist clergy from Korea, and dispatched four Japanese missions to Sui China to learn more about Buddhism, both as a religious system and as a model for centralizing his political rule. At this time China was the premier state of eastern Asia, and Buddhism was seen as one of the principal constituents of its power. In 604, Prince Shotoku introduced a kind of constitution to centralize and strengthen the Japanese government. Among its seventeen articles, the first promoted Confucian principles of social organization and the second declared that the Japanese people should "Sincerely reverence the three treasures . . . the Buddha, the Law, and the Monastic orders" (Embree, p. 50).

A century later, in 710, the ruling clans of Japan moved their capital to Nara, then called Heijo. Continuing to regard China as the model state of their day, the Japanese rulers copied much of the Chinese structures of authority and administration. They used Chinese ideographs as their written language, and adopted Chinese patterns of bureaucracy, tax systems, architecture, and land reforms. They modeled their new capital on the city plan of Chang'an, building a smaller version of that Chinese capital at Nara. Within Nara they built numerous Buddhist temples, including several of national significance. They encouraged the creation of a system of monasteries and convents throughout the provinces, with the Todaiji monastery, built by the Emperor Shomu (r. 724–749), at the apex. Buddhism became a pillar in the structure of national unity and administration. Buddhism did not replace Shinto, the indigenous worship of spirits, especially spirits of nature. Rather, it complemented the indigenous system. The emperor performed the official rituals of both Shinto and Buddhist worship.

Buddhism introduced a measure of centralization. Shinto, a looser system of belief and worship, had spread throughout all of Japan with no need of a central shrine for its worship of nature. By contrast, the Horyuji Temple near Nara became a central shrine for all of Japan. In 741 the rulers ordered that a Buddhist temple and pagoda be established in each province. Buddhism and Shinto co-existed in Japan in a pattern that continues even today.

As in China, the power and wealth of Buddhist monasteries and temples in Japan, and especially in Nara, alarmed some members of the court. To reduce the power of the Buddhist clergy and to increase the power of his own lineage, the Emperor Kammu (r. 781–806) moved the capital again, from Nara to Heian (modern Kyoto) in 794. This move initiated the Heian period in Japanese history and coincided with the decline of the Tang Empire in China. The Japanese government dispatched its last official mission to China in 838. With Japan on the ascendant and China in decline, Japan's Buddhism developed along its own paths, helped by substantial imperial patronage. The Emperor Kammu himself patronized two young Japanese monks who founded the Tendai and Shingon schools of Buddhism, the two most powerful and enduring Buddhist movements in Japan.

The Buddhist priesthood itself became increasingly Japanese, no longer reliant on priests from the mainland. It also entered more profoundly into politics. The priest Saicho (767–822) studied Tiantai (*Tendai* in Japanese) Buddhism in China and introduced it into Japan. Based on the Lotus Sutra, Tendai taught that each person could achieve enlightenment through sincere religious devotion. On Mount Hiei, northeast of Kyoto, Saicho built the Enryakuji monastery, which grew rapidly and steadily into one of the most important temple communities in Japan.

Horyuji Temple, Nara, Japan, 670 C.E. Through the seventh and eighth centuries the Japanese court enthusiastically welcomed Chinese political and artistic forms (Chapter 7). This is Japan's earliest surviving example of Buddhist architecture, which was adopted along with Chinese writing, painting, and sculpture. It became a central shrine for all of Japan.

Hoodo (Phoenix Hall), Byodoin Temple, Uji, Japan, eleventh century. The Phoenix Hall of the Byodoin Temple, with its jauntily uplifted roof-corners, indicates how over time the Buddhist style took on a distinctively Japanese flavor and shed its Chinese influence (contrast with picture, p. 286).

Saicho had intended his monastery to remain aloof from politics, and he therefore built it far from the national capital in Nara. Ironically, however, when the capital was moved to Kyoto, the monastery again found itself geographically close to the national political center. Saicho encouraged the monks to add teaching, administration, and social work in the service of the nation to their religious duties, merging Confucian and Buddhist value systems. His monastery grew to house tens of thousands of monks in some 3000 buildings. By the eleventh century, an era of deep and violent political fissures in Japanese political life, many Shinto and Buddhist temples supported standing armies to protect themselves and their extensive land holdings and branch temples. Troops from the Mount Hiei monastery began to enter the capital, demanding additional lands and thus completely reversing Saicho's original wishes. The Buddhist clergy thereafter became increasingly intertwined with Japanese politics.

Kukai (774–835), another Japanese Buddhist priest who studied in China, also returned home to preach a new form of Buddhism. He became abbot of the monastery of the great Toji temple at Kyoto, where he introduced Shingon ("True Word") Buddhism. Shingon emphasizes the repetition of mystic incantations or **mantras**; meditation on col-orful, sometimes stunning, geometrically ordered religious paintings, called **mandalas**, of Buddhas and bodhisattvas in their heavens; complicated rituals; music; and ecstatic dancing. Because the transmission of these forms was closely guarded among believers, Shingon was also called Esoteric Buddhism. Creating more accessible forms as well, Kukai introduced rituals, such as the austere and beautiful tea ceremony, in which a formal ritual surrounding the serving and drinking of tea invites deep meditation. Kukai is also credited with inventing the *kana* **syllabary**, a Japanese script in phonetic letters rather than **ideograms**. These innovations, in addition to mysterious, secret rituals, use of herbal medicines, and the elegant pageantry of Shingon, gave Kukai's monastery great popularity and power.

Another Chinese form of Buddhism that deeply influenced Japan was dedicated to Amida, or, in Sanskrit, Amitabha, the Buddha of the Infinite Light. In the tenth century, two priests, Kuya (903–972) and Genshin (942–1017), popularized this sect, which taught the importance of chanting the mantra *nembutsu*, "Praise to Amida Buddha." Amidism grew in subsequent generations through the organizational abilities of a series of monks, including Ryonin (1072–1132), who taught the counting of rosary beads to accompany the

SPOTLIGHT

Images of the Buddha

Monks and merchants carried the Buddha's message throughout Asia. He had taught that humans could cope with the suffering of life, illness, aging, and death by cultivating proper understanding of these normal processes and by curbing excessive expectations and desires for unrealistic alternatives. This message remained the core of Theravada Buddhism, the form practiced in Sri Lanka and southeast Asia. Other devotees accepted this profound message of simplicity but elaborated it into new forms. The greatest theological change, the development of Mahayana Buddhism, introduced the concept of the Bodhisattva, the saintlike person so dedicated to humanity that he would choose to be reborn to help others rather than enter nirvana (see picture, p. 281). For Mahayanists the Buddha himself was seen as a Bodhisattva who had lived on earth before his known lifetime, 563–483 B.C.E., and would be reborn again. This and related new

concepts were transmitted across the silk route to China, Korea, and Japan and proved attractive to hundreds of millions of people. The three pictures in this Spotlight illustrate the increasing elaboration of the message of the Buddha in its manifestations across two millennia of time and a continent of space. Because they all represent the same event, the death of the Buddha, we can compare these transformations directly.

Figure 1 Dying Buddha, Gandhara, Afghanistan, second century C.E.

Figure 1 from Gandhara in northern Pakistan–Afghanistan in the second century C.E. (see Spotlight, pp. 242–3) gives one of the early representations of the Buddha in human form. Previously art had represented him through the icon of a wheel, a reference to his message of the wheel of life, death, and rebirth. Here he is shown dying, surrounded by a small group of grieving monks and devotees. The Buddha has a halo around his head. The Gandharan artist fuses Hellenistic styles, as in the clothing, with Indian, as in the forms of the bodies.

Figure 2 is a painting from a wall in the Buddhist cave complex at Dunhuang (Cave 428) from the early sixth century C.E. Monks and merchants transmitting the message of the Buddha along the silk route and into China constructed numerous monasteries and caravan halts along the way. Dunhuang, situated just west of the end of the Great Wall, marked the ecological boundary between the great Lop and Taklamakan deserts to the west and the Gansu corridor leading into China to the east and provided the site for one of the most important of these complexes. The walls of 460 of its caves are painted with Buddhist scenes. In **figure 2** many devotees, as well as the Buddha, are crowned with halos, suggesting their bodhisattva status. The artwork differs sharply from the one from Gandhara, with the faces and bodies far more sketchy, and the background as well as the facial markings far more abstract and enchanted.

As Buddhism reached Japan in the seventh century C.E., the elaboration of immortal beings continued to multiply along with representations of a heavenly life. **Figure 3**, a Japanese painting on silk from the seventeenth/eighteenth century, portrays the dying Buddha in a grove of sal trees, attended by human disciples, bodhisattvas, grieving animals, and representatives of other worlds. From across the river, another disciple leads the Buddha's mother and her retinue down from heaven to attend his last teaching. The specific mixture of populations as well as the aesthetic style of this picture, quite different from those at Dunhuang and Gandhara, are products of the Japanese imagination. This variety is the mark of a living, expanding, diversifying religious system engaging the needs of its growing population across time and space.

Figure 2 Dying Buddha, Cave 428, Dunhuang, China, early sixth century C.E.

Figure 3 Dying Buddha, Japanese scroll, seventeenth to eighteenth century C.E.

repetition of the *nembutsu*, a practice that spread to most sects of Japanese Buddhism. By the late twelfth century Amidism established its independence of other Buddhist sects and at last reached a mass audience for whom its message of uncomplicated, universal access to salvation had great appeal.

Three other elements gave Buddhism a prominence and significance in Japanese life that has continued till today. First, Japanese Buddhism cultivated an especially pure aesthetic dimension, which we have seen here in the representations of the Buddha and bodhisattvas and of the architecture and art of the Japanese Buddhist temples. This appreciation of artistic creativity is apparent throughout Japan in formal gardens, in painting and calligraphy, and in the art of presentation of everything from self, to gifts, to tea, to food. Second, Buddhism's emphasis on the transience of all life has inspired much of the greatest Japanese literature, from the *Tale of Genji*, written by Lady Murasaki (c. 978–c. 1015) at the Japanese court a thousand years ago, to the novels of Mishima Yukio (1925–70), who committed *seppuku*, ritual suicide, immediately after completing his last novel. Third, Buddhism has coexisted and even merged to some degree with indigenous Shinto worship and belief.

By the twelfth century Japan had entered its Buddhist Age. Despite occasional attacks on Buddhism as a foreign religion and as an excessively wealthy and powerful organization, Buddhism has remained one of the two national religions of Japan. Most Japanese continue to mingle Buddhism and Shinto in their aesthetic and spiritual lives as well as in their ritual practices.

HINDUISM AND BUDDHISM: HOW DO THEY COMPARE?

Hinduism and Buddhism have undergone enormous transformations through their thousands of years of history. Geographically, Hinduism spread across the Indian subcontinent from its roots in the encounter between Aryan invaders and the indigenous peoples of the Indus valley and north India. It extended briefly even to southeast Asia (where a single Hindu outpost still remains on the Indonesian island of Bali). Buddhism spread from the Buddha's home region in the Himalayan foothills throughout India, where it subsequently died out, and most of east and southeast Asia, where it flourishes (see map, p. 277). Buddhism's array of monasteries and temples, and its venera-

tion of the homeland of the Buddha himself, mark its sacred geography.

Both religions established their own sacred calendars and their control over lifecycle events. In this, Hindu priests took a commanding position since even Buddhists employed them to officiate. Within India this continuing role of the *brahmin* priests ultimately helped Hinduism to absorb Buddhism. Outside India, where no other major religion was already in place, Buddhist priests performed their own rituals, and came to predominate.

Both groups developed sacred languages. Buddhists felt that Sanskrit was narrowly limited to Hindu priests and so used Pali, a language closer to the vernacular. Over time, as the common people expressed their own religious feelings in their own languages, the leaders of both religions responded by also using the vernacular. Both religions inspired extensive literatures, including philosophy, mystical poetry, drama, and folk tales. Both generated their own artistic traditions in painting, sculpture, and temple architecture.

Organizationally, Buddhism, especially in its early Theravada form, was seen as a religion of its monks. Many of the common people found comfort and meaning in their philosophy and supported them, but ultimately they turned to *brahmin* priests for their ritual needs. Within Hinduism the caste system structured all classes and occupations into a single framework of relationships, with *brahmins* and *kshatriyas*, and, in a few more commercial locations, *vaishyas*, predominating. Buddhism's later Mahayana form, with its multitudes of gods, bodhisattvas, and heavens, did reach out to more people ritually as well as emotionally.

The evolution of Hinduism and Buddhism demonstrates the flexibility of great world religions. A small sect may define itself narrowly, proclaiming a core set of principles and practices and adhering to them rigidly. For its small membership, these restrictions may be the very attraction of the sect. But for a religion to grow in numbers, it must be open organizationally, doctrinally, and ritually to the varied spiritual, psychic, and social needs of diverse peoples. Like the empires we studied in Part 3, a world religion must be able to accommodate, satisfy, and absorb people of various languages, regions, classes, and previous spiritual beliefs and practices. World religions expand their theologies and practices to incorporate ever more members, until they reach their limits of flexibility.

Finally, religions and governments have been historically interdependent. Buddhism flourished thanks to the early support of the Buddha's royal allies and later through the backing of the Emperor Asoka. It spread to southeast Asia and to Japan as kings offered their support in exchange for Buddhist legitimation. In China, Buddhism found its opening after Confucian dynasties fell and people searched for new belief systems and new leaders. Hinduism flourished as kings in India struck their own agreements with *brahmin* priests. Conversely, when governments turned against particular religious groups, they could devastate them. And when sizable religious groups shifted their support away from a ruler, they undermined his authority. We shall find more of this mutual antagonism in the next chapters.

We turn now to three religions—Judaism, Christianity, and Islam—which have been militantly monotheistic. Although Judaism has remained quite small, Christianity and Islam have been aggressive in their desire to win converts, and have become today the largest of the world's religions, with almost two billion and one billion followers, respectively. Their relationships with the governments alongside which they exist have been checkered. Their impact on spiritual, cultural, social, and aesthetic life has been immense.

BIBLIOGRAPHY

Allchin, F.R., *et al. The Archaeology of Early Historic South Asia: The Emergence of Cities and States* (Cambridge: Cambridge University Press, 1995).

Andrea, Alfred and James Overfield, eds. *The Human Record*. Vol. I (Boston: Houghton Mifflin Company, 3rd ed., 1998).

Appadurai, Arjun. *Worship and Conflict under Colonial Rule* (Cambridge: Cambridge University Press, 1981).

Basham, A.L. *The Wonder That Was India* (New York: Grove Press, 1954).

Berger, Peter L. *The Sacred Canopy* (New York: Anchor Books, 1967).

Bhagavad Gita, trans. Barbara Stoler Miller (New York: Bantam Books, 1986).

Bhattacharya, Haridas, ed. *The Cultural Heritage of India*. Vol. III: *The Philosophies* (Calcutta: The Ramakrishna Mission Institute of Culture, 1953).

Holy Bible, New Revised Standard Version (Grand Rapids, MI: Zondervan Publishing House, 1989).

Blunden, Caroline and Mark Elvin. *Cultural Atlas of China* (New York: Facts on File, 1983).

Bodde, Derk. *Essays on Chinese Civilization*, ed. Charles Le Blanc and Dorothy Borei (Princeton: Princeton University Press, 1981).

Britannica Book of the Year 2000 (Chicago: Encyclopedia Britannica, Inc., 1999)

Conze, Edward. *Buddhist Scriptures* (New York: Penguin Books, 1959).

Cotterell, Arthur, ed. *The Penguin Encyclopedia of Ancient Civilizations* (London: Penguin Books, 1980).

Craven, Roy C. *A Concise History of Indian Art* (New York: Oxford University Press, n.d.).

deBary, William Theodore and Irene Bloom, eds., *Sources of Chinese Tradition, Vol. I: From Earliest Times to 1600* (New York: Columbia University Press, 2nd ed., 1999).

The Dhammapada, trans. by Juan Mascaro (New York: Penguin Books, 1973).

Dimmitt, Cornelia and J.A.B. van Buitenen, ed. and trans. *Classical Hindu Mythology* (Philadelphia: Temple University Press, 1978).

Eberhard, Wolfram. *China's Minorities: Yesterday and Today* (Belmont, CA: Wadsworth Publishing, 1982).

Ebrey, Patricia Buckley, ed. *Chinese Civilization: A Sourcebook* (New York: The Free Press, 2nd ed., 1993).

Eliade, Mircea. *Ordeal by Labyrinth* (Chicago: University of Chicago Press, 1982).

——. *The Sacred and the Profane* (New York: Harper Torchbooks, 1959).

——. *Yoga: Immortality and Freedom* (Princeton: Princeton University Press, 1969).

Elvin, Mark. *The Pattern of the Chinese Past* (Stanford: Stanford University Press, 1973).

Embree, Ainslee, ed. and rev. *Sources of Indian Tradition*, Vol. I: *From the Beginning to 1800* (New York: Columbia University Press, 2nd ed., 1988).

Friedman, Edward. "Reconstructing China's National Identity: A Southern Alternative to Mao-Era Anti-Imperialist Nationalism," *Journal of Asian Studies* LIII, No. 1 (February 1994), 67–91.

Green, Peter. *Alexander of Macedon, 356–323 B.C.* (Berkeley: University of California Press, 1991).

Hall, Kenneth R. *Maritime Trade and State Development in Early Southeast Asia* (Honolulu: University of Hawaii, 1985).

Hall, Kenneth R. and John K. Whitmore, eds. *Explorations in Early Southeast Asian History: The Origins of Southeast Asian Statecraft* (Ann Arbor: Center for South and Southeast Asian Studies, University of Michigan, 1976).

Honour, Hugh and John Fleming. *The Visual Arts: A History* (Englewood Cliffs, NJ: Prentice-Hall, 1995).

Hopfe, Lewis M. *Religions of the World* (New York: Macmillan Publishing Company, 5th ed., 1991).

Hughes, Sarah Shaver and Brady Hughes, eds. *Women in World History*, Vol. I: *Readings from Prehistory to 1500* (Armonk, NY: M.E. Sharpe, 1995).

Kulke, Hermann and Dietmar Rothermund. *A History of India* (Totowa, NJ: Barnes and Noble Books, 1986).

Lockard, Craig A. "Integrating Southeast Asia into the Framework of World History: The Period Before 1500," *The History Teacher* XXIX, No. 1 (November 1995), 7–35.

Martin, Rafe. *The Hungry Tigress: Buddhist Legends and Jataka Tales* (Berkeley, CA: Parallax Press, 1990).

McGovern, William Montgomery. *The Early Empires of Central Asia* (Chapel Hill: University of North Carolina Press, 1939).

McManners, John, ed. *The Oxford Illustrated History of Christianity* (New York: Oxford University Press, 1990).

Murphey, Rhoads. *A Brief History of Asia* (New York: HarperCollins, 1992).

Needham, Joseph. *The Shorter Science and Civilization in China*, Vol. I, abridged by Colin A. Ronan (Cambridge: Cambridge University Press, 1978).

Nelson, Lynn and Patrick Peebles, eds. *Classics of Eastern Thought* (San Diego: Harcourt Brace Jovanovich, 1991).

Parker, Geoffrey, ed. *The (London) Times Atlas of World History* (London: Times Books, 4th ed., 1998).

Past Worlds: The (London) Times Atlas of Archaeology (Maplewood, NJ: Hammond, 1988).

Ramanujan, A.K., ed. and trans. *Poems of Love and War: From the Eight Anthologies and the Ten Long Poems of Classical Tamil* (New York: Columbia University Press, 1985).

Ramanujan, A.K., trans. *Speaking of Síva* (Harmondsworth, England: Penguin Books, 1973).

Richman, Paula, ed. *Many Ramayanas: The Diversity of a Narrative Tradition in South Asia* (Berkeley: University of California Press, 1991).

Rowland, Benjamin. *The Art and Architecture of India: Buddhist/Hindu/Jain* (New York: Penguin Books, 1977).

SarDesai, D.R. *Southeast Asia: Past and Present* (Boulder, CO: Westview Press, 3rd ed., 1994).

Schirokauer, Conrad. *A Brief History of Chinese and Japanese Civilizations* (Fort Worth: Harcourt Brace Jovanovich, 2nd ed., 1989).

Schwartz, Benjamin I. *The World of Thought in Ancient China* (Cambridge: Harvard University Press, 1985).

Schwartzberg, Joseph E., ed. *A Historical Atlas of South Asia* (Chicago: University of Chicago Press, 1978).

Seth, Vikram. *Three Chinese Poets: Translations of Poems by Wang Wei, Li Bai, and Du Fu* (New York: HarperCollins, 1993).

Sima Qian. *Historical Records*, trans. Raymond Dawson (New York: Oxford University Press, 1994).

Sima Qian. *Records of the Historian: Chapters from the Shih Chi of Ssu-ma Ch'ien*, trans. Burton Watson (New York: Columbia University Press, 1969).

Smart, Ninian. *The World's Religions* (Cambridge: Cambridge University Press, 1989).

Spodek, Howard. "Studying the History of Urbanization in India," *Journal of Urban History* VI, No. 3 (May, 1980) 251–95.

Spodek, Howard and Doris Srinivasan, eds. *Urban Form and Meaning in South Asia: The Shaping of Cities from Prehistoric to Precolonial Times* (Washington: National Gallery of Art, 1993).

Ssu-ma Ch'ien. *The Grand Scribe's Records, Vol. I: The Basic Annals of Pre-Han China*, ed. William H. Nienhauser, jr., trans. Tsai-fa Cheng, *et al* (Bloomington: Indiana University Press. 1994).

Stein, Burton. *Peasant State and Society in Medieval South India* (New Delhi: Oxford University Press, 1980).

Sullivan, Michael. *The Arts of China* (Berkeley: University of California Press, 1984).

Thapar, Romila. *Ancient Indian Social History* (New Delhi: Orient Longman, 1978).

——. *Asoka and the Decline of the Mauryas* (New Delhi: Oxford University Press, 1963).

——. *A History of India*, Vol. I (Baltimore, MD: Penguin Books, 1966).

——. *Interpreting Early India* (New York: Oxford University Press, 1992).

Tharu, Susie and K. Lalita, eds. *Women Writing in India 600 B.C. to the Present*, Vol. I (New York: The Feminist Press, 1991).

Tsunoda, Ryusaku, William Theodore deBary, and Donald Keene, comps. *Sources of Japanese Tradition* (New York: Columbia University Press, 1958).

Twitchett, Denis and Michael Lowe, eds. *The Cambridge History of China*, Vol. I: *The Ch'in and Han Empires, 221 B.C.-A.D. 220* (Cambridge: Cambridge University Press, 1986).

Twitchett, Denis, ed. *The Cambridge History of China*, Vol. III: *Sui and T'ang China, 589–906*, Part I (Cambridge: Cambridge University Press, 1979).

Warren, Henry Clarke. *Buddhism in Translations* (New York: Atheneum, 1963; first published Cambridge: Harvard University Press, 1896).

Weins, Herold J. *Han Expansion in South China* (N.P.: The Shoe String Press, 1967).

Zimmer, Heinrich. *Philosophies of India* (New York: Meridian Books, 1956).

JUDAISM AND CHRISTIANITY

600 B.C.E–1100 C.E

"Love your neighbor as yourself."

LEVITICUS 19:18, MATTHEW 19:19

"Love the Lord your God with all your heart, and with all your soul, and with all your might."

DEUTERONOMY 6:5, MARK 12:33

PEOPLES OF THE BIBLE:
GOD'S EVOLUTION IN WEST ASIA AND EUROPE

JUDAISM

The story of Judaism begins some 3800 years ago with one man's vision of a single, unique God of all creation. God and Abraham sealed a covenant stating that Abraham's descendants would forever revere and worship that God, and God, in turn, would forever watch over and protect them. From then until now Judaism has remained a relatively small, family-based religion, focused in part in Israel, the land promised by God to Abraham, with branches throughout the world. Today there are only about 14 million Jews worldwide, but their role in world history has been disproportionate to their numbers.

The Jewish belief in one god, **monotheism**, was not simply a reduction in the number of gods from many to one. Historian–theologian Yehezkel Kaufmann explains that monotheism presented "a new religious category . . . of a God above nature, whose will is supreme, who is not subject to compulsion and fate,

who is free of the bonds of myth and magic" (p. 227). Into a world that believed in many gods who often fought with one another and interfered capriciously in human life, Abraham and his family introduced and perpetuated the concept of a single god whose rule was both orderly and just. (The Pharaoh Akhenaten in Egypt had proposed a single god [see Profile, p. 70], but later rulers obliterated his teachings and institutions.) In contrast with paganism's many gods of diverse temperaments, the new monotheism provided a much more definitive statement of right and wrong. At the same time it demanded much greater conformity in both faith and action, calling for adherence to a strict code of ethics within a community governed by laws proclaimed by God.

Although the number of Jews has always been small, many of Judaism's core beliefs were later incorporated into Christianity and Islam, the two great monotheistic faiths that have come to

JUDAISM AND CHRISTIANITY

DATE	POLITICAL/SOCIAL EVENTS	LITERARY/PHILOSOPHICAL EVENTS
1700 B.C.E.	● Abraham travels from Mesopotamia to Israel (c. 1750)	
1600 B.C.E.	● Hebrew slavery in Egypt	
1200 B.C.E.	● Moses (?1300–?1200) ● Exodus from Egypt; legal codes formulated; return to Palestine; tribal government under Judges	
1000 B.C.E.	● Period of Kings begins with Saul, David, and Solomon ● First temple in Jerusalem	
900 B.C.E	● Jewish kingdom divides into Israel and Judaea	
800 B.C.E.	● Prophets exhort Jewish nation (800–500) ● Assyrians conquer Israel and exile Jews (721)	● Numbers (850–650) ● Genesis (mid 8th century) ● Prophets Isaiah, Amos, Micah
700 B.C.E.		● Josiah begins to write down Torah (640) ● Deuteronomy (mid 7th century) ● Leviticus (mid 7th century) ● Jeremiah
600 B.C.E.	● Babylonians conquer Judaea, exile the people, and destroy the first temple (586) ● Jews permitted to return to Judaea and rebuild the temple (538)	● Book of Job (600)
300 B.C.E.		● Books of TaNaKh (the Torah) edited and canonized
100 B.C.E	● Birth and death of Jesus (c. 4 B.C.E.–30 C.E.)	
10 C.E.	● Rome captures Jerusalem (63) ● Christianity emerges from Judaism ● St. Paul, Saul of Tarsus, organizes early Christianity (d. c. 67) ● Rome destroys second temple (70)	● Gospels (70–100) ● Acts (70–80) ● Epistles of Paul (50–120)
100 C.E.	● Rome exiles Jews from Judaea; Jewish diaspora throughout Mediterranean basin and west Asia (135) ● Rabbinical tradition developed (1st to 4th century)	

include half the world's population today. Judaism, however, has tenaciously maintained its own particular rituals and its own sense of family, setting it apart as a distinct religious community. We begin this chapter with a study of Judaism and then proceed to Christianity, which emerged from it, and challenged it. In the next chapter we explore Islam and the interactions among all three of these closely related, but often bitterly antagonistic, monotheistic religions.

EARLY JUDAISM: HOW DO WE KNOW?

Our knowledge of early Jewish history comes from the scriptures known collectively as the **TaNaKh**: Torah (the Five Books of Moses), Nevi'im (the Books of the Prophets), and Ketuvim (additional historical, poetic, and philosophic writings). Christians have incorporated the entire TaNaKh into their Bible, referring to these scriptures

JUDAISM AND CHRISTIANITY

DATE	POLITICAL/SOCIAL EVENTS	LITERARY/PHILOSOPHICAL EVENTS
200 C.E.	● Christians presecuted under Severus, Decius, and Diocletian	● Babylonian and Jerusalem Talmuds edited and published (200–500)
300 C.E.	● Christianity legalized (313) and then declared the official religion of the Roman Empire (392) ● Council of Nicea (325)	● Augustine's *The City of God* and *Confessions*
400 C.E.	● Council of Chalcedon (451)	
500 C.E.	● Monasticism in Europe ● Clovis converted to Christianity ● St. Benedict founds monastery of Monte Cassino	
600 C.E.	● England converted to Christianity	● Venerable Bede, Ecclesiastical *History of the English People*
700 C.E.	● Iconoclastic controversy	
800 C.E.	● Coronation of Charlemagne (800) ● St. Cyril and St. Methodius convert Russia, translate the Bible, and create the Cyrillic alphabet	● Einhard, *Life of Charlemagne*
900 C.E.	● Missionaries proliferate among the Vikings	
1000 C.E	● Christians capture Toledo from Muslim control and begin *reconquista* (1085) ● Split of Western and Eastern Christianity (1054) ● 1st Crusade (1095–9))	
1100 C.E.	● 2nd Crusade (1147–9) ● 3rd Crusade (1189–92)	
1200 C.E.	● 4th Crusade (1202–04) ● Children's Crusade (1212) ● Crusaders capture Constantinople (1204–61) ● 5th–8th Crusades (1218–91)	
1300 C.E.	● Monastic orders proliferate	
1400 C.E.	● Christians capture Granada, Spain, complete the *reconquista* (1492), expel Jews and Muslims	

collectively as the "Old Testament." Because the New Testament is written in Greek and the Old Testament in Hebrew, the TaNaKh is often referred to as the Hebrew Bible. For centuries, Jews and Christians believed that these earliest books of the Bible, which describe the creation of the world and the earliest history of the Jewish people, were the literal word of God. Some still hold to this belief, but during the past two centuries scholarship has undermined it and has given us a new

sense of the historical place of these books. Today historians ask: When and where were the books of the Hebrew Bible composed and how valid are they as historical documents?

Modern scholarly analysis of the TaNaKh texts became a prominent academic enterprise in Germany during the early nineteenth century. The founders of "biblical criticism" argued persuasively that the decision to begin to edit and write down the oral texts that had been passed from

The Kingdom of Israel The first unified Jewish state in Palestine emerged around 980 B.C.E. under King David. He united the tribes of Israel during a period of decline among their more powerful neighbors—Egypt and the Hittites. After the death of his son Solomon (926 B.C.E.), tribal rivalries divided the empire into the kingdoms of Judah and Israel, but the sense of cultural unity survived.

generation to generation was made by Josiah, the king of the Jewish state of Judah (r. 640–609 B.C.E.). The story of Josiah's reign is told in the biblical book of II Kings, chapters 20–21. Struggling to survive in the face of the powerful Assyrian Empire, Josiah was anxious to promote allegiance to the state and its religion. He centralized Jewish worship in the national temple in Jerusalem and collected and transcribed the most important texts of his people. Josiah regarded adherence to the laws laid down in these scriptures as fundamental to the maintenance of the Jewish religion, the Jewish people, and his own Jewish kingdom. From existing literary fragments, folk wisdom, and oral history he had the book of Deuteronomy, the fifth book of the TaNaKh, written down. Soon, additional literary materials from at least three other major interpretive traditions were also woven together to create the books of Genesis,

Exodus, Leviticus, and Numbers. Together with Deuteronomy, these books formed the Torah or "Five Books of Moses."

With the ravages of time, older copies of the Torah, written in Hebrew on parchment scrolls, began to perish and new ones were copied out. The oldest existing Hebrew manuscripts of the entire Torah date only to the ninth to the eleventh centuries C.E., but fragments dating to as early as the second century B.C.E. have been discovered. Stored in caves near the Dead Sea in Israel, these Dead Sea Scrolls have been rediscovered only since 1947. Another very early edition of the Torah is a Greek translation from the Hebrew, the Septuagint. It was prepared for the Greek-speaking Jews of Egypt in the third and second centuries B.C.E. It still exists and is consistent with the Hebrew texts of our own time. In short, the written text of the Torah appears to have been preserved with great fidelity for at least 2600 years. The oral texts on which the written scriptures were based date back much further.

The narratives of the five books of the Torah abound with miracles, as God intervenes continuously in the history of the Jews. The Torah begins with God's creating the world and contracting his covenant with Abraham. Over the next several generations, the Torah continues, famine struck Canaan, the land God promised to Abraham. Abraham's grandson and his family traveled to the Nile valley of Egypt in search of food. At first invited by the Pharaoh to remain as permanent residents, they were later enslaved. After 400 years of slavery, about 1200 B.C.E., the Jews won their freedom and escaped from Egypt under the leadership of Moses through the miraculous intervention of God. During their journey back to Israel through the wilderness of the Sinai Desert, the contentious group of ex-slaves was forged into a small but militant nation. The Torah records a dramatic miracle at Mount Sinai in which God revealed a set of religious and civil laws for them to follow.

The Torah remains one of the greatest examples of mythistory. Its stories are not necessarily to be read as literal, historical records, but their version of events gave birth to the Jewish people's concept of itself and helped to define its character and principal beliefs. The mythological stories of the Torah tell us what the Jewish people, and especially its literate leadership, have thought important about their own origins and mission. They also define images of God that have profoundly influenced the imagination and action of Jews, Christians, and Muslims for millennia.

ESSENTIAL BELIEFS OF JUDAISM IN EARLY SCRIPTURES

The Torah fixes many of the essential beliefs and principles of Judaism:

- A single caring God, demanding obedience, who administers rewards and punishments fairly and in accordance with his fixed laws:

  Hear, O Israel, the Lord is our God, the Lord alone. You shall love the Lord your God with all your heart, and with all your soul, and with all your might. (Deuteronomy 6:4–5)

  Know therefore that the Lord your God is God, the faithful God who maintains covenant loyalty with those who love him and keep his commandments, to a thousand generations, and who repays in their own person those who reject him. (Deuteronomy VII:9–10)

- A God of history, whose power affects the destiny of individuals and nations:

  I am the Lord your God who brought you out of Egypt, out of the land of slavery. (Exodus 20:2–3)

- A community rooted in a divinely chosen family and ethnic group:

  Now the Lord said to Abram, "Go from your country and your kindred and your father's house to the land that I will show you. I will make of you a great nation, and I will bless you, and make your name great, so that you will be a blessing." (Genesis 12:1–2)

Dead Sea Scrolls, Isaiah scroll 1Q Is. 9 verses 58.6–63.4. The five hundred or so documents that make up the Dead Sea Scrolls—which date between about 250 B.C.E. and 70 C.E.—appear at one time to have formed the library of a Jewish community. As well as providing evidence of the accuracy of Hebrew biblical texts, they give information about the life of the community itself. (*Israel Museum, Jerusalem*)

- A specific, "promised," geographical homeland:

  When Abraham reached Canaan, God said to him: "Raise your eyes now, and look from the place where you are, northward and southward and eastward and westward; for all the land that you see I will give to you and to your offspring forever." (Genesis 13:14–15)

- A legal system to guide proper behavior: religious, familial, sexual, commercial, civic, ethical, and ritual. The introduction to this code was the Ten Commandments, revered as the heart of the revelation to Moses at Mount Sinai (see p. 323).

To ground the mystical beliefs and forge the Jewish people into a "kingdom of priests and a sacred nation," rules issued in the name of God forbade intermarriage with outsiders; prohibited eating animals which do not have cloven hooves and chew their cud, and fish which do not have scales and fins (Deuteronomy 14 and Leviticus 11); and centralized worship in the hands of a priestly aristocracy. Animal sacrifices were to be offered, but only by the hereditary priests and only in a single national temple in Jerusalem.

The Jewish Calendar

Jewish religious leaders reconstituted earlier pagan nature celebrations into a calendar of national religious celebration. A spring festival of renewal was incorporated into Passover, the commemoration of the exodus from Egypt; an early summer festival of first harvest was subsumed into Shavuot, a rejoicing in the revelation of the Ten Commandments at Sinai; and an early fall harvest festival became part of Sukkot (Succoth), a remembrance of the years of wandering in the desert. All these festivals were to be celebrated, if possible, by pilgrimage to the central, national temple in Jerusalem. Celebrations of nature, history, and national identity were fused together.

SOURCE
The Ten Commandments

I am the Lord your God who brought you out of Egypt, out of the house of slavery.

You shall have no other gods before me.

You shall not make for yourself an idol, whether in the form of anything that is in heaven above, or that is on the earth beneath, or that is in the water under the earth.

You shall not bow down to them or worship them; for I the Lord your God am a jealous god, punishing children for the iniquity of parents, to the third and fourth generation of those who reject me, but showing steadfast love to the thousandth generation of those who love me and keep my commandments.

You shall not make wrongful use of the name of the Lord your God, for the Lord will not acquit anyone who misuses his name.

Remember the sabbath day, and keep it holy. Six days you shall labor and do all your work. But the seventh day is a sabbath to the Lord your God; you shall not do any work—you, your son or your daughter, your male or female slave, your livestock, or the alien resident in your towns. For in six days the Lord made heaven and earth, the sea, and all that is in them, but rested the seventh day; therefore the Lord blessed the sabbath day and consecrated it.

Honor your father and your mother, so that your days may be long in the land that the Lord your God is giving you.

You shall not murder.

You shall not commit adultery.

You shall not steal.

You shall not bear false witness against your neighbor.

You shall not covet your neighbor's house; you shall not covet your neighbor's wife, or male or female slave, or ox, or donkey, or anything that belongs to your neighbor.

(Exodus 20:2–17; see also Deuteronomy 5)

Moses, mosaic in San Vitale, Ravenna, Italy, sixth century C.E. After he had led the Israelite slaves out of Egypt by the miracle of parting the Red Sea (see picture, p. 302), Moses ascended Mount Sinai. There he received from God the Torah, or sacred teachings, beginning with the two tablets of the Ten Commandments. He led his quarrelsome people across the Sinai desert but died at the border of the promised land.

10: JUDAISM AND CHRISTIANITY (600 B.C.E.–1100 C.E.)   299

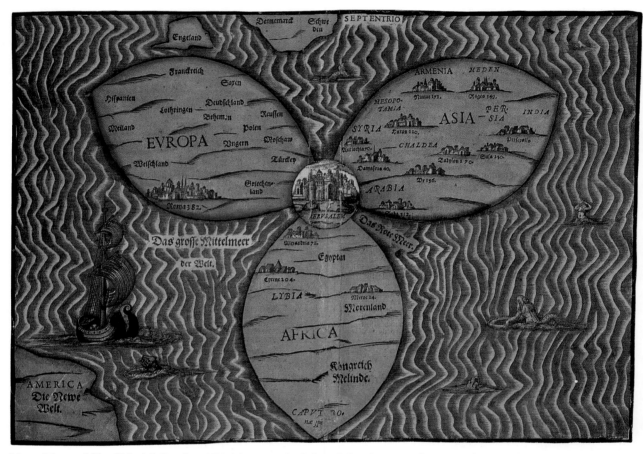

Map of the world by Heinrich Bunting, 1585. Many peoples believed that their capital city was the cosmo-magical axis of the universe (see pp. 48 and 92). This map, shaped like a clover leaf, places Jerusalem at the center, uniting Africa, Asia, and Europe.

THE EVOLUTION OF GOD

The Torah portrays God as an evolving moral force in dialogue with humans. In God's early interactions with humans, his nature is still malleable. Disgusted at human disobedience, he destroys almost all humankind through a flood, but he then pledges never to be so destructive again, creating a rainbow as a kind of treaty of peace with humanity (Genesis 6–8). Still fearful of the collective power of humanity, God confounds their inter-communication by dividing them into separate language groups at the Tower of Babel (Genesis 11). While deciding the fate of the sinful cities of Sodom and Gommorah, God listens to Abraham's plea for the defense: "Far be it from thee to do this—to kill good and bad together; for then the good would suffer with the bad. Far be it from thee. Shall not the judge of all the earth do what is just?" (Genesis 18–19). God apparently bans child sacrifice when he stops Abraham from killing his son Isaac. (The Muslim Quran reports this to be Abraham's son Ishmael; see p. 336.)

When asked by Moses to identify himself by name, God replies enigmatically and powerfully, "I am who I am" (Exodus III:14). The Hebrew designation for God's name is YHWH, "Being." Because Jews have regarded this name as too sacred to pronounce, only the consonants are written; the vowels are unknown. English-speaking readers have usually rendered it either Jehovah or Yahweh. Slowly, God becomes more secure in his own power and more available to dialogue with humans.

In Jewish theology, God is almighty but still accessible through prayer and even through dialogue. Indeed, humans and God come to understand each other by arguing with one another in a process that the contemporary rabbi Arthur Waskow has called "Godwrestling." If Jews are to be God's people and to follow his will, he, in turn, is expected to be a compassionate and attentive ruler. This view challenged the pagan beliefs in self-

Recent academic findings of the past 150 years situate Jewish core beliefs in the geography of the Fertile Crescent. For example, as we know from earlier chapters, some of the pharaohs, notably Amenhotep IV, known also as Akhenaten (see Profile, p. 70), who ruled Egypt at just about the time that the Torah places the Jewish captivity there, also proclaimed a belief in one god:

O sole god, like whom there is no other!
Thou didst create the world according to thy desire,
Whilst thou wert alone:
All men, cattle, and wild beasts,
Whatever is on earth, going upon (its) feet,

And what is on high, flying with its wings.

(Pritchard, p. 370)

And, as we read in Chapter 2, Hammurabi of Mesopotamia had already issued a law code in the name of his god, Shamash, by the year 1750 B.C.E., 500 years before the Torah reported that Moses received the Ten Commandments and the beginnings of the Jewish code of law. These historic precedents must have inspired many of the early Jewish beliefs and practices. Through the centuries, however, the beliefs of Akhenaten and the legal system of Hammurabi were lost, even within their own nations, while Jews kept themselves and their beliefs alive.

willed gods, but it left Judaism with no strong answer to the eternal problem of evil in the universe: "If there is a single God, and if he is good, why do the wicked prosper and the righteous suffer?" One biblical response is found in the Book of Job (*c.* 600 B.C.E.). To the questions of the innocent, suffering Job, God finally responds with overwhelming power:

Who is this whose ignorant words cloud my design
in darkness?
Brace yourself and stand up like a man; I will ask
the questions, and you shall answer.
Where were you when I laid the earth's
foundations?
Tell me, if you know and understand.
Who settled its dimensions? Surely you should
know. . . .
Is it for a man who disputes with the Almighty to be
stubborn?
Should he that argues with God answer back?
(Job 38:2–5; 40:2)

But while God lectures Job for his brashness in questioning his authority and power, he understands Job's anguish at the apparent injustice in the world and ultimately rewards Job with health, a restored family, and abundance for his honesty in raising his questions.

THE LATER BOOKS OF JEWISH SCRIPTURE

The later volumes of the TaNaKh, the books of Nevi'im and Ketuvim, carry the history of the Jewish people to about the fifth century B.C.E. God continues as a constant presence in these narratives, but he intervenes less openly and less frequently. These later records can generally be cross-checked against the archaeology of the region and the history of neighboring peoples, and they seem generally consistent.

These volumes continue the history from about the year 1200 B.C.E., as the Jews returned to Canaan, or Israel, the land promised to them, and made it their home. The biblical account in the Book of Joshua tells of continuous, violent, political and religious warfare between the invading Jews and the resident Canaanite peoples. Modern scholarship suggests, however, that re-entry into the land of Israel was a gradual process, with fewer, more localized battles, and considerably more cultural borrowing among all the groups in the region.

Arriving in Canaan, the Jews first organized themselves in a loose tribal confederacy led by a series of "Judges," ad hoc leaders who took command at critical periods, especially at times of war. Later, despite warnings that a monarchy would lead to increased warfare, profligate leaders,

Crossing the Red Sea, *c.* **245** C.E. **Fresco from the synagogue at Dura Europos.** The Old Testament tells of God's miraculous intervention in helping Moses and the people of Israel escape enslavement in Egypt. Hotly pursued by Pharaoh's soldiers to the banks of the Red Sea, Moses saw the waves draw back in front of him to allow the Jews to pass. When the Egyptians tried to follow, the sea engulfed them and they were drowned. (*National Archaeological Museum, Damascus, Syria*)

extortionate taxes, and the impressment of young men and women into royal service, the Jews anointed a king. For three generations, strong kings, Saul, David, and Solomon (*c.* 1020–950 B.C.E.), ruled and expanded the geographic base of the people. They established a firm national center in Jerusalem, where they united political and religious power by building both palace and temple, exalting both king and priest. The earlier warnings against royal excesses, however, proved correct. Unable to sustain Solomon's legendary extravagances in expenditures and in relationships with 700 wives, many of them foreign princesses, and 300 concubines, the kingdom split in two.

THE TEACHINGS OF THE PROPHETS: MORALITY AND HOPE

Continuing despotism by their kings and greed on the part of their wealthier citizens ripped apart the social fabric of the two splinter kingdoms of Judah and Israel. A group of prophets emerged, demanding reform. In powerful and sublime language these men called for a reinstitution of justice, compassion, and ethics. They introduced permanently into the conscience of mankind their voices, speaking in the name of God and of the people against the hypocritical misuse of religious and political power. The prophet Isaiah, in the eighth century B.C.E., led the charge:

> When you stretch out your hands, I will hide my
> eyes from you;
> even though you make many prayers, I will not
> listen;
> your hands are full of blood.
> Wash yourselves; make yourselves clean;
> remove the evil of your doings
> from before my eyes;
> cease to do evil,
> learn to do good;
> seek justice,

rescue the oppressed,
defend the orphan,
plead for the widow. (Isaiah 1:15–17)

At about the same time, Amos was equally severe and equally eloquent in confronting the northern kingdom of Israel just before its destruction:

You that turn justice upside down and bring righteousness to the ground! . . .
you that hate a man who brings the wrongdoer to court
and loathe him who speaks the whole truth:
for all this, because you levy taxes on the poor and extort a tribute of grain from them,
Though you have built houses of hewn stone, you shall not live in them, though you have planted pleasant vineyards, you shall not drink wine from them. . . .
Hate evil and love good; enthrone justice in the courts. (Amos 5:7–15)

A century later, Jeremiah continued in the same spirit of moral outrage, rebuking the rulers and people of Judah, the remaining southern kingdom:

You keep saying, "This place is the temple of the Lord, the temple of the Lord, the temple of the Lord!" This catchword of yours is a lie; put no trust in it. Mend your ways and your doings, deal fairly with one another, do not oppress the alien, the orphan, and the widow, shed no innocent blood in this place, do not run after other gods to your own ruin. (Jeremiah 7: 4–6; Oxford New English Bible translation)

So even at the time that Israel and Judah developed powerful kingdoms, ironically, the prophets remembered that the beginnings of the Jewish people were in slavery and that a significant part of its mission was to identify with and help the downtrodden. As power and excess multiplied, they echoed the words of Deuteronomy 16:20: "Justice, and only justice, you shall pursue, so that you may live and occupy the land that the Lord your God is giving you." When destruction came, the prophets interpreted it as punishment not *of* their God, as earlier peoples had often done, but *by* their God. Destruction of a corrupt nation indicated not the weakness of its God, but his ethical consistency.

Finally, the prophets not only harangued, blamed, and condemned, they also held up visions of a future to inspire their listeners. They saw God transforming human history. He offered rewards as well as punishments. He offered hope. Micah's prophecy, also in the eighth century B.C.E., is one of the most exalted, and perhaps utopian:

JEWISH FESTIVALS AND FAST DAYS

Hebrew date	Gregorian date	Name of festival
1–2 Tishri	Sept–Oct	Rosh Hashana (New Year)
10 Tishri	Sept–Oct	Yom Kippur (Day of Atonement)
15–21 Tishri	Sept–Oct	Sukkot (Feast of the Tabernacles)
22 Tishri	Sept–Oct	Shemini Atzeret (8th Day of the Solemn Assembly
23 Tishri	Sept–Oct	Simchat Torah (Rejoicing of the Law)
25 Kislev–2–3 Tevet	Nov–Dec	Hannukah (Feast of Dedication)
14–15 Adar	Feb–Mar	Purim (Feast of Lots)
14–20 Nisan	Mar–Apr	Pesach (Passover)
5 Iyar	Apr–May	Israel Independence Day
6–7 Sivan	May–Jun	Shavuot (Feast of Weeks)
9 Av	Jul–Aug	Tisha be–Av (Fast of 9th Av)

For out of Zion shall go forth instruction, and the word of the Lord from Jerusalem.
He shall judge between many peoples, and shall arbitrate between strong nations far away; they shall beat their swords into plowshares, and their spears into pruning hooks; nation shall not lift up sword against nation, neither shall they learn war any more;
but they shall all sit under their own vines and under their own fig trees, and no one shall make them afraid; for the mouth of the Lord of hosts has spoken. (Micah 4:1–4)

Micah closed with a vision of great Jewish religious commitment, balanced by equally great tolerance for the diversity of others:

For all the peoples walk each in the name of its god, but we will walk in the name of the Lord our God forever and ever. (Micah 4: 5)

Gender Relations

The God of the Hebrew Bible is male and alone. His words establish a patriarchal society through Abraham and his descendants. The Torah grants women fewer civil and religious rights (and obligations) than men. They are regarded as ritually unclean each month at times of menstruation and in childbirth. Men may be ritually unclean as a result of wet dreams or sexual diseases (Leviticus 15), but these occur with less regularity. The regulation of sexuality is a fundamental issue in Jewish law, as it is in most religions. Marriage is regarded as the norm, with a strong emphasis on bearing children. Homosexual behavior is strongly rejected. (Today, however, some branches of Judaism have revised gender rules and discarded prohibitions on homosexuality.)

A few women are credited with heroic roles. Sarah, Abraham's wife, forced him to choose her son as his proper successor, and gained God's approval (Genesis 16). Deborah led Israel in peace and war, during the period of conquering the land of Israel (Judges 4–5). Ruth, a convert, taught the importance of openness to the outside world, and became an ancestor of King David and, therefore, in Christian belief, of Jesus (Book of Ruth). Esther, in the Persian diaspora, was married to the king and used her position to block the attempts of a court minister to kill the Jews of the Persian Empire (Book of Esther). Although none of these stories can be authenticated externally, nor dated exactly, they speak to the significance of individual, exceptional women at turning points in Jewish history, and in the collective mind of the Jewish people.

DEFEAT, EXILE, AND REDEFINITION

Jews represent both an ethnic community and a universal religion. This dual identity became especially clear as Jews were exiled by foreign conquest out of the land of Israel as part of a plan to encourage their assimilation and to open up the land of Canaan to foreign immigration. First, the northern kingdom of Israel was exiled by Sennacherib of Assyria in 721 B.C.E. These exiles drifted into assimilation and were subsequently referred to as the "Lost Ten Tribes of Israel." In 586 B.C.E., the temple in Jerusalem was destroyed, and thousands of Jews from the southern kingdom of Judah were exiled to Babylon, but this group remained loyal to its unique identity as a separate community, remembering its homeland:

By the rivers of Babylon—there we sat down and wept when we remembered Zion. . . .
Our captors asked us for songs: "Sing us one of the songs of Zion!"
How could we sing the Lord's song in a foreign land?
If I forget you, O Jerusalem, let my right hand wither!
Let my tongue cling to the roof of my mouth if I do not remember you, if I do not set Jerusalem above my highest joy. (Psalm 137)

When they were permitted to return to Judaea some sixty years later, many Jews left Babylonia, returned to Judaea, rebuilt their temple and reconstructed national life. But many did not. Those who stayed behind did not assimilate into the Babylonian culture, however. They reconstituted their religion, replacing the sacrificial services of the temple with meditation and prayers offered privately or in synagogues. They substituted teachers and rabbis, positions earned through study and piety, for the hereditary priesthood. In academies at Sura and Pumbeditha, towns adjacent to Babylon, rabbis continued the study of the Torah. They interpreted and edited Jewish law based on its teachings, and they elaborated stories and myths, which often conveyed moral principles. The multi-volumed recording of their proceedings, the Babylonian Talmud, was completed about 500 C.E.

So distinguished was the scholarship of Babylonia, that this Talmud was considered superior in coverage and scholarship to the Jerusalem Talmud that was produced at about the same time in academies in Israel.

For several centuries Jews lived in substantial numbers both in Israel and in the diaspora. A census of the Roman Empire undertaken by the Emperor Claudius in 48 C.E. showed 5,984,072 Jews. This figure suggests a total global Jewish population of about 8 million (Baron, pp. 170 and 372, n. 7). At the time, the population of the Roman Empire was perhaps 60 million, and that of the Afro-Eurasian world about 170 million. Most Jews outside Israel seemed to have continued to look to Jerusalem as a spiritual center, and they sent funds to support the temple until its second destruction by the Romans in 70 C.E. The Roman philosopher Seneca (4 B.C.E.–65 C.E.), resentful of the Jewish presence, exaggerated their power: "The customs of this accursed race have gained such influence that they are now received throughout all the world. The vanquished have given laws to their victors" (*De superstitione*, cited in Crossan, p. 418).

The second (Herod's) temple (model), 20 B.C.E. The temple at Jerusalem was originally built in the tenth century B.C.E. by King Solomon as a symbol of national unity and as a religious pilgrimage center. Razed by the Babylonians in 586 B.C.E., it was rebuilt sixty years later. It was finally destroyed by the Romans in 70 C.E. as part of the campaign to crush Jewish rebellion.

Jews were driven out of their promised land into exile several times: by the Assyrians in 721 B.C.E., by the Babylonians in 586 B.C.E., and, following anti-imperial revolts, by the Romans in 135 C.E. In addition, many Jews traveled willingly, by free choice, throughout the trade and cultural networks that had been established by the Persians in the sixth century B.C.E., enhanced by Alexander the Great in the fourth century B.C.E., and extended by the Roman Empire.

The Roman exile of 135 C.E., however, fundamentally and permanently altered Jewish existence. It removed all but a few Jews from their political homeland until the twentieth century. This final exile established the principal contours of Jewish diaspora existence from then on: life as a minority group; dispersed among various peoples of the entire world; with distinct religious and social practices; united in reverence for sacred texts and their teachings; usually dependent on the widely varying policies of the peoples among whom they lived; and sometimes forced to choose between religious conversion, emigration, or death. Jews preserved their cohesion through their acceptance of the authority of the TaNaKh and the importance of studying it, and their persistence in seeing themselves as a special kind of family even in dispersion.

MINORITY–MAJORITY RELATIONS IN THE DIASPORA

In general, Jews remained socially and religiously distinct wherever they traveled. This identification was imposed partially from the outside by others, partially by internal discipline and loyalty to the group, its traditions, and laws. Jewish history becomes a case study also of tolerance and intolerance of minorities by majority peoples around the world. The Book of Esther, written about (and probably during) the Persian diaspora, 638–333 B.C.E., captures the vulnerability of minority existence. A royal minister sees his chance to advance his career and profit and argues to the king:

> There is a certain people, dispersed among the many peoples in all the provinces of your kingdom, who

Menorah procession, Arch of Titus, Rome, *c.* 81 C.E. The Romans put down the Jewish revolt of 70 C.E. by recapturing Jerusalem, destroying the temple, and looting its sacred objects. This relief from Emperor Titus' triumphal arch shows Roman soldiers with the temple *menorah*, a seven-branched candelabrum, which today serves as an official emblem of the state of Israel.

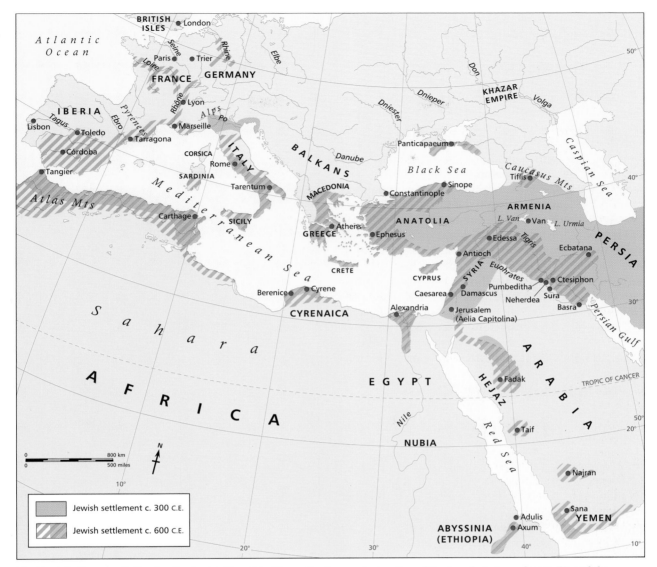

The Jewish diaspora Following the Jewish Revolt in 66 C.E., the Roman destruction of the temple in Jerusalem in 70, and the defeat of the Bar-Cochba revolt in 135, the Roman government expelled the Jews from Judaea. These migrations spread Judaism north into Mesopotamia and Anatolia, followed trade routes throughout the Mediterranean and the Red Sea, and eventually resulted in Jewish communities being established as far afield as northwest Europe and Ethiopia.

keep themselves apart. Their laws are different from those of every other people; they do not keep your majesty's laws. It does not befit your majesty to tolerate them. If it please your majesty, let an order be made in writing for their destruction; and I will pay ten thousand talents of silver to your majesty's officials, to be deposited in the royal treasury. (Esther 3:8–9; Oxford New English Bible)

The king accedes: "The money and the people are yours; deal with them as you wish" (Esther 3:11; Oxford translation). A pattern of official xeno-

phobia and greed, repeated frequently in Jewish history—and in the history of many minorities—is captured in biblical literature.

There were many contrary examples, however. Jewish life in the diaspora survived and often flourished. For example, Rabbi Benjamin of Tudela, Spain, visited Muslim Baghdad in 1160–70 C.E. and reported: "In Baghdad there are about 40,000 Jews, and they dwell in security, prosperity, and honor under the great Caliph, and amongst them are great sages, the heads of Academies engaged in the study of the law. In this city there are ten Academies . . .

and twenty-eight Jewish synagogues" (cited in Andrea and Overfield, pp. 248–9).

CHRISTIANITY EMERGES FROM JUDAISM

At about the time of the destruction of the temple in 70 C.E., a splinter group within the Jewish people was forming around the person and teachings of Jesus of Nazareth. Disdained by segments of the Jewish religious establishment as a heretic and feared by the Roman imperialists as a potential revolutionary, Jesus was exalted by his followers as one specially chosen and anointed by God (*Messiah* in Hebrew, *Christos* in Greek). Jesus said that he had come not to abolish the Jewish law but to fulfill it. His followers ultimately accepted much of the moral core of Jewish teachings but rejected most parts of its legal and separatist covenant. They proclaimed Jesus to be the source of eternal life and accepted him as a miracle-worker and the son of God. Beginning with the early missionary activities of St Paul, they built an entirely new organizational structure and spread the new faith of Christianity among one-third of humankind.

CHRISTIANITY

Jesus Christ (*c.* 4 B.C.E.–*c.* 30 C.E.), the founder of Christianity, was born to an unmarried Jewish woman and her carpenter fiancé in a manger in Bethlehem, 10 miles (16 kilometers) from Jerusalem, some 2000 years ago. Jesus grew into an astonishingly powerful preacher, who promised eternal life and happiness to the poor and downtrodden people of colonial Judaea if only they would keep their faith in God. As Jesus' fame spread, and came to include a reputation for curing the blind and lame, and even raising the dead, the Jewish religious authorities and the Roman colonial administrators feared his attacks on their establishments. To prevent any potential rebellion, the Roman government crucified him when he was thirty-three years old.

But death did not stop Jesus' message. His disciples, and especially Paul, a newcomer to the faith who was converted through a miraculous encounter with the dead Jesus, took his message of compassion, salvation, and eternal life to Rome. Although Jesus had avoided the question during his life, his followers now claimed that he was indeed the son of God, born to his mother Mary through a virgin birth. The upper classes of proud

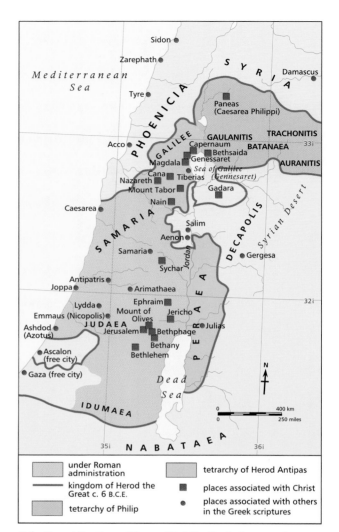

Palestine at the time of Jesus Christianity first emerged as a sect within Judaism when Roman control of Palestine was increasing. Shortly before Jesus' birth, Rome had granted Herod the Great the Kingdom of Judaea as a client ruler. Upon his death in 4 B.C.E. the kingdom was divided among his sons, and Judaea itself came under direct Roman military rule.

Rome scoffed at first, but more and more of the simple people believed. Despite early persecution, Christianity increased in influence, until it became the official religion of the empire. Spread through the networks of the empire, it ultimately became the most important organizing force in post-Roman Europe. The message of compassion and exultation and the organization of the church expanded throughout the world. Today almost 2 billion people, one-third of the world's population, spread among numerous different churches and denominations, declare themselves followers of this son of God, the simple preacher from Judaea.

MYTHISTORY:
HOW DO WE KNOW?

The search for the historical Jesus has become something of a scholarly industry:

> Historical Jesus research is becoming something of a scholarly bad joke . . . There is Jesus as a political revolutionary by S.G.F. Brandon (1967), as a magician by Morton Smith (1978), as a Galilean charismatic by Geza Vermes (1981, 1984), as a Galilean rabbi by Bruce Chilton (1984), as a Hillelite or proto-Pharisee by Harvey Falk (1985), as an Essene by Harvey Falk (1985), as an eschatological prophet by E.P. Sanders (1985). (Crossan, p. xxvii–xxviii)

And as a prophet, exorcist, miracleworker, and marginal Jew by J.P. Meier (1991). It remains inconclusive because the only records of Jesus' life are the four gospels, "the good news accounts," of the New Testament, and they are neither unbiased nor contemporary. These four books are the opening segment of the New Testament, the second section of the Christian Bible, which recounts the life, teachings, and disciples of Jesus. Mark, probably the oldest of the four gospels, dates to 70 C.E., forty years after Jesus' death. Like the later gospels attributed to Matthew, Luke, and John, Mark assembles a collection of traditions about Jesus as they were transmitted among his followers. Despite the gospels' accounts of Jesus' multitudes of followers, he is not discussed in either Roman or Jewish records of the time.

External histories do indicate, however, that Jesus' times were turbulent and difficult. Judaea was a colony of the Roman Empire, taxed heavily and suppressed economically and politically. Jesus' nation, the Jewish people, was divided into at least four conflicting groups. The largest of these groups, the Pharisees, identified with the masses of the population, resented the Roman occupation, and sought comfort in keeping alive and re-interpreting Jewish religious traditions. The Jesus of the gospels wanted much more rapid and radical religious reform and frequently referred to the Pharisees as hypocrites. The more elite Sadducees, the temple priesthood and their allies, had become servants of the Roman state and preached accommodation with it. A much smaller, militant group of Zealots sought, quixotically, to drive out the Romans through violence. A fourth, still smaller group, the Essenes, lived a prayerful existence by the shores of the Dead Sea and preached the imminent end of the world as they knew it. Predictions of a radical reversal of fortune had also been common among the Jewish prophets centuries before, and Jesus' emphasis on the coming of the kingdom of God resonated strongly with these beliefs in a coming apocalypse.

JESUS' LIFE, TEACHINGS, AND DISCIPLES

According to the four gospels, which were written about 70–100 C.E., Jesus' life and message inspired a core of devoted disciples who embraced his concern for the poor and downtrodden and believed that he had accomplished miracles in feeding the multitudes, curing the sick, and even restoring the dead to life. They believed Jesus to be at least in part divine, the son of God, born miraculously through Mary, a virgin betrothed to Joseph, a carpenter from Nazareth. When asked, Jesus did not contradict their assumptions about his identity. After Jesus' death, his followers believed that he had arisen from the grave and ascended to heaven to join God. Their belief contained equal measures of admiration for his message of compassion and salvation and for his ability to perform miracles.

The four gospels present only a sketch of Jesus' life. They chart more fully his teachings and his charismatic power over his disciples, the men and women who created the religious community of Christianity. Despite conventional dating, Jesus must have been born no later than 4 B.C.E., for Herod, king at the time of his birth, died in that year. Jesus' family had been living in Galilee, where his father was an artisan. Taken to Jerusalem when he was twelve years old, Jesus asked precocious and disturbing questions of the temple priests. In Galilee, the beautiful and lush northern region of Judaea, only recently converted to Judaism, he continued his unorthodox search for truth. Toward the end of his life, perhaps frustrated by a lack of success at home, he turned his attentions to Jerusalem, the religious heartland of Judaea. There he continued his preaching, angering both the Jewish religious establishment, which viewed him as a heretic, and the Roman imperial government, which feared his rabble-rousing. The Roman governor of Judaea, Pontius Pilate, had Jesus crucified to avoid possible rebellion.

The Sermon on the Mount: The Beatitudes

Jesus' teaching, powerful in direct address, in parable, and in allegory, established his identification with the poor and oppressed, his disdain for the Roman authorities, and his scorn for the Jewish religious leadership of his time. He sounded much like a latterday Jewish prophet calling his people to reform. The Beatitudes, a list of promises of God's rewards for the simple, righteous people, the first of Jesus' great sermons recorded in the New Testament, was delivered from the top of a hill in Galilee.

Blessed are the poor in spirit, for theirs is the kingdom of heaven.
Blessed are those who mourn, for they will be comforted.
Blessed are the meek, for they will inherit the earth.
Blessed are those who hunger and thirst for righteousness, for they will be filled.
Blessed are the merciful, for they will receive mercy.
Blessed are the poor in heart, for they will see God.
Blessed are the peacemakers, for they will be called children of God.
Blessed are those who are persecuted for righteousness' sake, for theirs is the kingdom of heaven. (Matthew 5:3–10).

He promised that religious sincerity would be rewarded:

Ask, and it will be given you; search, and you will find; knock, and the door will be opened for you. For everyone who asks receives, and everyone who searches finds, and for everyone who knocks, the door will be opened. (Matthew 7:7–8).

He prescribed a form of prayer:

Pray then in this way:
Our Father in heaven, hallowed be your name. Your kingdom come. Your will be done, on earth as it is in heaven.
   Give us this day our daily bread.
   And forgive us our debts, as we also have forgiven our debtors.
   And do not bring us to the time of trial, but rescue us from the evil one. (Here biblical accounts differ, some adding: "For the kingdom, and the power, and the glory are yours forever. Amen.") (Matthew 6:9–13)

Adapting Rituals and Philosophies

Jesus' form of prayer and the Beatitudes that he preached (see Source above) were fully in accord with Jewish tradition, but baptism was marginal to Judaism. By accepting baptism from the desert preacher John the Baptist, Jesus prepared the way for adapting an existing practice and giving it new meaning for his followers. A minor practice within Judaism, baptism would later become in Christianity the central **sacrament** of purification enjoined on all members. As we have seen, newly forming religions often adapt rituals and philosophies from already existing religions, as, for example Buddhism adapted the concept of dharma from Hinduism, and both Buddhists and Jains employed Hindu priests. This borrowing and adaptation can be attractive to members of the existing religion who wish to join the new one, for it assures them that their spiritual customs will be maintained. At the same time, a new interpretation gives the ritual a new meaning for the new faith. At his "last supper," a Passover ritual meal, Jesus had eaten unleavened, flat bread as a symbol of slavery in Egypt, and he had drunk wine that accompanies all Jewish festivals as a symbol of joy. He offered the bread and wine also to his disciples, with the words, "This is my body … this is my blood." Thus he introduced the **Eucharist**, or Holy Communion, a central sacrament, a mystery through which the invisible Christ grants communion to those who believe in him.

In his teachings, Jesus also addressed political and social issues, staking out his own often ambiguous positions in relationship to the contesting philosophies of the day. When Jesus, following John, taught, "Repent; for the kingdom of heaven has come near" (Matthew 4:17), he was not explicit in describing that kingdom or its date of arrival. But in metaphor and parable he preached that life as we know it on earth would soon change dramatically, or even come to an end. His advice was not for a middle-class, bourgeois audience planning carefully for the future:

> Therefore I tell you, do not worry about your life, what you will eat or what you will drink, or about your body, what you will wear. Is not life more than food, and the body more than clothing? Look at the birds of the air; they neither sow nor reap nor gather into barns, and yet your heavenly Father feeds them. Are you not of more value than they? And can any of you by worrying add a single hour to your span of life? And why do you worry about clothing? Consider the lilies of the field, how they grow; they neither toil nor spin,

Silver crucifix from Birka, Sweden, *c.* **900** C.E. The cross—signifying Christ's crucifixion—was adopted by Christians as a symbol of their faith as early as the second century. Making "the sign of the cross" was believed powerful in warding off evil, and, in later centuries, crusaders were said to "take the cross" when they set off on crusade (a word itself derived from the Latin for cross, *crux*). (*Historiska Museet, Stockholm*)

yet I tell you, even Solomon in all his glory was not clothed like one of these. (Matthew 6:25–9)

Jesus' words must have been especially welcome to the poor, as he spoke repeatedly of the "Kingdom of Heaven" in which the tables would be turned:

It will be hard for a rich person to enter the kingdom of heaven. Again I tell you, it is easier for a camel to go through the eye of a needle than for someone who is rich to enter the kingdom of God. (Matthew 19:23–4)

In that Kingdom, Jesus promised much to his devoted followers:

At the renewal of all things, when the Son of Man is seated on the throne of his glory, you who have followed me will also sit on twelve thrones, judging the twelve tribes of Israel. And everyone who has left houses or brothers or sisters or father or mother or children or fields, for my name's sake, will receive a hundredfold, and will inherit eternal life. (Matthew 19:28–9)

The apocalypse would be violent. Jesus had declared that the most important commandment

The four evangelists, from the *Gospel Book of Charlemagne*, early ninth century. With the exception of the cross, the best-known symbols in early Christianity were associated with the four gospels. Based on a text in the Book of Revelation (4:7), Matthew was represented by a man, Mark by a lion, Luke by a winged ox, and John by an eagle. (*Cathedral Treasury, Aachen, Germany*)

was to "Love the Lord your God with all your heart, and with all your soul, and with all your mind," and the second was "Love your neighbor as yourself," both directly cited from the TaNaKh, Deuteronomy 6:7 and Leviticus 19:18. Indeed he had carried these principles to new dimensions, declaring "Love your enemies and pray for your persecutors" (Matthew 5:44). But he also proclaimed a very contrary battle cry: "He that is not with me is against me" (Matthew 12:30):

> Do not think that I have come to bring peace to earth; I have not come to bring peace, but a sword. I have come to set a man against his father, and a daughter against her mother, and a daughter-in-law against her mother-in-law; and one's foes will be members of one's own household.
> (Matthew 10: 34–6)

He reversed Isaiah's prophecy of a world at peace:

> Nation will make war against nation, kingdom upon kingdom; there will be famines and earthquakes in many places. With all these things the birth-pangs of the new age begin. (Matthew 24:7–8; compare Mark 13:8 and Luke 21:10–11)

Jesus and the Jewish Establishment

The gospels depict Jesus' attitude toward Jewish law as ambivalent but often condescending, his relationship toward the Jewish religious leadership as confrontational. He scoffed at Jewish dietary laws: "It is not what goes into the mouth that defiles a person, but it is what comes out of the mouth that defiles" (Matthew 15:11). He constantly tested the limits of Sabbath restrictions, declaring that: "The Sabbath is made for man, not man for the Sabbath." He restricted divorce, announcing that: "If a man divorces his wife for any cause other than unchastity he involves her in adultery; and anyone who marries a divorced woman commits adultery" (Matthew 5:32).

Miracle and Mystery: Passion and Resurrection

Throughout his ministry Jesus had performed miracles—healing the sick, restoring sight to the blind, feeding multitudes of followers from just a few loaves and fishes, walking on water, calming storms, even raising the dead. These miracles, perhaps even more than his ethical teachings, brought followers flocking to him. The gospel narrative of Jesus' Passion, his suffering on the cross, presenting himself at this final moment of his life as both human and divine in one personage, and finally his miraculous resurrection from the grave, his appearances to his disciples, and his ascent to heaven, complete the miracle and the majesty.

The stories of Jesus' life and death, message and miracles, formed the basis for Christianity, at first a new sect located within Judaism. Although different followers attributed more or less divinity and greater or lesser miracles to him, apparently all accepted Jesus as a new, reforming teacher. Many saw him as the long-awaited "messiah," a messenger and savior specially "anointed" by God. His apostles, especially Paul of Tarsus (d. 67), now refocused Jesus' message and built the Christian sect into a new, powerful religion. The apostles' preaching, organizational work, and letters to fledgling Christian communities fill most of the rest of the New Testament.

CHRISTIANITY ORGANIZES

The Early Disciples

Peter, described in the gospels as Jesus' chosen organizational leader, first took the Christian message outside the Jewish community (Acts 10). Declaring circumcision unnecessary for membership, he welcomed gentiles into the new church. James, Jesus' brother and leader of the Christian community of Jerusalem, abrogated most of the Jewish dietary laws for the new community (Acts 15). These apostles believed that the rigorous ritual laws of Judaism inhibited the spread of its ethical message. Instead, they chose to emphasize the miraculous powers of Jesus and his followers. They spoke little of their master's views on the coming apocalypse, but stressed his statements on the importance of love and redemption.

Paul Organizes the Early Church

Tensions continued to simmer between mainstream Jewish leaders and the early Christians. One of the fiercest opponents of the new sect, Saul from the Anatolian town of Tarsus, was traveling to confront the Christian community in Damascus, when he experienced an overpowering mystical vision of Jesus that literally knocked him to the ground. Reversing his previous position, Saul now affirmed the authenticity of Jesus as the divine

Son of God. In speaking within the Jewish community, he had preferred his Hebrew name Saul. Now, as he took his new message also to gentiles, he preferred his Roman name Paul. He dedicated himself to establishing Christianity as an independent, organized religion. Jewish by ethnicity and early religious choice, Roman by citizenship, and Greek by culture, Paul was ideally placed to refine and explicate Jesus' message. He became the second founder of Christianity.

To link the flourishing, but separate, Christian communities, Paul undertook three missionary voyages in the eastern Mediterranean, and he kept in continuous communication through a series of letters, Paul's "Epistles" of the New Testament. He advised the leadership emerging within each local church organization: the presbyters, or elders; the deacons above them; and, at the head, the bishop. He promised eternal life to those who believed in Jesus' power. He declared Jewish ritual laws an obstacle to spiritual progress (Galatians 5:2–6). Neither membership in a chosen family nor observance of laws or rituals was necessary in the new religion. Faith alone was sufficient.

> The law was our disciplinarian until Christ came, so that we might be justified by faith. But now that faith has come, we are no longer subject to a disciplinarian, for in Christ Jesus you are all children of God through faith. (Galatians 3:24–6)

Paul proclaimed a new equality in Christianity:

> There is no longer Jew or Greek, there is no longer slave or free, there is no longer male or female; for all of you are one in Christ Jesus. (Galatians 3:28)

Recalling Jesus' resurrection, Paul's greatest promise was eternal life, the miraculous triumph over death. All Christians could achieve it:

> Listen, I will tell you a mystery! We will not all die but we will all be changed, in a moment, in the twinkling of an eye, at the last trumpet. For the

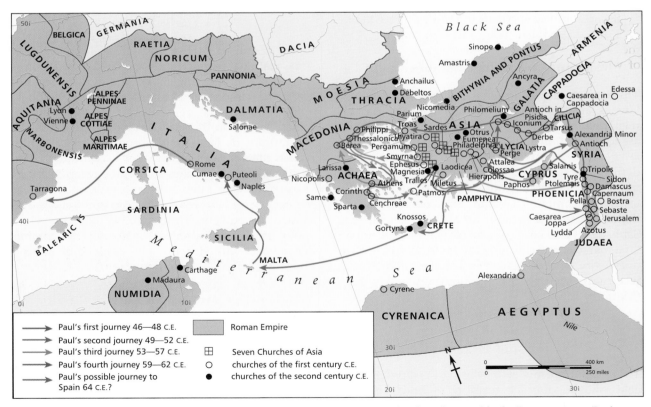

Paul's missionary journeys Following Jesus' trial and crucifixion, about 29 C.E., his disciples, notably the Roman convert Paul, set out to convert non-Jews or gentiles. Paul's journeys took him throughout the Greco-Roman east Mediterranean, and beyond. These journeys and the epistles Paul wrote began to weave struggling Christian groups into a new religious organization, the Roman Catholic Church. Paul died in Rome, apparently a martyr to the Emperor Nero.

trumpet will sound, and the dead will be raised imperishable, and we will be changed. For this perishable body must put on imperishability, and this mortal body must put on immortality. (1 Corinthians 15:51–3)

Paul formulated a new concept of "original sin" and redemption from it. Jews had accepted the Genesis story of Adam and Eve's disobedience in the Garden of Eden as a mythical explanation of some of life's harsh realities: the pain of childbirth, the struggle to earn a living, the dangers of wild beasts, and, most of all, human mortality. Paul now proclaimed that Adam and Eve's "original sin" could be forgiven. Humanity could, in a sense, return to paradise and eternal life. Jesus' death on the cross was atonement for original sin. According to Paul, those who believed in Jesus and accepted membership in the new Christian community would be forgiven by God and "saved." Although they would still be mortal, at the end of their earthly lives they would inherit a life in heaven, and, much later, would even be reborn on earth (Romans 5–6).

Paul re-affirmed existing mystical rights, like baptism, and created new ones like the eucharist, the ritual eating of unleavened bread and drinking of wine. The eucharist recalled Jesus' last supper with his disciples at the Passover Seder meal before he was taken to his final trial and crucifixion. Many Christians said the eucharist represented the body and blood of Jesus himself, now consumed and incorporated by his followers. (Some pagans satirically called it cannibalism.)

The Christian Calendar

Pagans had celebrated the winter solstice; Christians now fixed the observance of Jesus' birth, **Christmas**, at that time of year, although no one knew the actual date of his birth. Good Friday, at about the time of Passover, mourned Jesus' crucifixion and death; three days later his resurrection was celebrated in the joyous festival of **Easter**. Corresponding to the Jewish holiday of **Pentecost**, the anniversary of receiving the Ten Commandments fifty days after the Passover, Christianity introduced its own holiday of Pentecost. It commemorates the date when, according to the book of Acts, chapter 2, the "Holy Spirit," the third element of the Trinity along with God the Father and Jesus the son, filled Jesus' disciples and they "began to talk in other tongues, as the Spirit gave them power of utterance,"

MAJOR CHRISTIAN FESTIVALS

January 6	Epiphany
February–March	Shrove Tuesday, or Mardi Gras (day before Ash Wednesday)
February–March	Ash Wednesday (first day of Lent)
February–April	Lent
February 2	Candlemas Day
March–April	Easter
March 25	Feast of Annunciation
April–June	Ascension (40 days after Easter)
May–June	Pentecost/Whit Sunday (50 days after Easter)
May–June	Trinity Sunday (Sunday after Pentecost)
November–December	Advent
December 24	Christmas Eve
December 25	Christmas Day

enabling them to preach to the various peoples of the world. (Modern day Christian Pentecostals "speak in tongues," praying and uttering praises ecstatically, healing through prayer and laying on of hands, and speaking of experiencing spiritual miracles.)

Special saints' days were designated to mark the lives and deaths of people who helped to spread the new religion. The new Christian calendar, which has become the most widely used in the world, fixed its first year at the approximate date of Jesus' birth. The Jewish Sabbath, a weekly day of rest and reflection, was transferred from Saturday to Sunday.

Gender Relations

Although Paul had proclaimed that in Jesus "There is no longer male or female," he seemed to distrust sexual energies. Like Jesus he was unmarried. He recommended celibacy and, for those unable to meet that standard, monogamous marriage as a means of sexual restraint:

> It is well for a man not to touch a woman. But because of cases of sexual immorality, each man should have his own wife and each woman her own husband. The husband should give to his wife her conjugal rights, and likewise the wife to her husband. (1 Corinthians 7:1–3)

In addition, Paul moved to subordinate women, first at home:

> I want you to understand that Christ is the head of every man, and the husband is the head of the wife. . . . he is the image and reflection of God; but woman is the reflection of man. Indeed, man was not made from woman, but woman from man. Neither was man created for the sake of woman, but woman for the sake of man. (1 Corinthians 11:3–9)

Then in the church:

> Women should be silent in the churches. For they are not permitted to speak, but should be subordinate, as the law also says. If there is anything they desire to know, let them ask their husbands at home. (1 Corinthians 14:34–5)

On the other hand, women served as deaconesses and abbesses in some of the early churches, and Paul welcomed them warmly and treated them respectfully. So it is difficult to understand the relationship between Paul's theory and his practice with regard to women in the Church.

Slavery

Paul had also declared that spiritually "There is no longer slave or free," but in practice he accepted slavery, saying, "Slaves, obey your earthly masters with fear and trembling." He did urge masters to be kind to slaves and to "stop threatening them for you know that both of you have the same Master in heaven, and with him there is no partiality" (Ephesians 6:5–9).

Struggle for Survival in Rome

Having established the central doctrines of the new religion, and stabilized its core communities, both Peter and Paul moved to expand its geographical scope. Both saw Rome as the capital of empire and the center of the international communication network of the time. Both traveled to Rome to preach and teach, and tradition holds that both were martyred there in the persecutions of the Emperor Nero, about 67 C.E. and that both are entombed and enshrined there.

In this capital of empire, Christianity appeared as one of several mystery religions, all of which were based on beliefs in supernatural beings. They included the religion of Mithras, a Persian sun god; Demeter, a Greek goddess; YHWH of the Jews; and an eclectic mixture of beliefs called Gnosticism. Romans seemed to be in search of a more inspiring, other-worldly faith than paganism provided, but at the time of the deaths of Peter and Paul, Christianity was still a relatively weak force.

Paradoxically, because they refused to worship the Emperor or to take oaths in his name, Christians were viewed by official Rome as atheists. Their emphasis on other-worldly salvation and their strong internal organization were seen as threats to the state's authority. Official treatment of Christianity was erratic but was often marked by severe persecution. The first Christians, Jews by nationality, were scorned as provincial foreigners. Some Roman authorities thought that Christian beliefs in resurrection and an afterlife undermined pride in citizenship and willingness to serve in the army. About the year 100, the historian Tacitus wrote of:

> a class of persons hated for their vices whom the crowd called Christians. Christus, after whom they were named, had undergone the death penalty in the reign of Tiberius, by sentence of the procurator Pontius Pilate, and the pernicious superstition was checked for a moment only to break out once more, not only in Judaea, the home of the disease, but in the Capital itself, where everything horrible or shameful in the world gathers and becomes fashionable. (Tacitus, *Annales* XV:44, cited in Honour and Fleming)

Nero (r. 54–68) scapegoated the Christians, blaming them for the great fire in 64, apparently executing both Peter and Paul among his victims, and sending hundreds of Christians to die in public gladiatorial contests and by burning. Edicts of persecution were issued by Emperors Antoninus Pius (r. 138–161), Marcus Aurelius (r. 161–180), Septimius Severus (r. 193–211), and Diocletian (r. 284–305). In 257 the Emperor Valerian (r. 253–

260) was prepared to launch a major persecution of Christians, but he was captured in battle by Persians. In these early years of persecution, thousands of Christians suffered martyrdom.

CHRISTIANITY TRIUMPHANT

Despite the scorn and the persecution, Christianity continued to grow. Its key doctrines and texts were written, edited, and approved by leaders in the network of Christian churches. The contents of the New Testament were agreed upon by about 200, and by 250 the city of Rome alone held about 50,000 Christians among its million inhabitants. Most were of the lower classes, attracted by Jesus' message to the poor, but middle- and upper-class Romans had also joined. In particular, Christianity proved attractive to the wives of Roman leaders, perhaps drawn by its emphasis on monogamy. Many brought their husbands into the Church. About the year 200, the Church leader Tertullian exulted, with some exaggeration, "We are but of yesterday, and already we have filled your world: cities, islands, fortresses, towns, marketplaces, the camp itself, tribes, companies, the palace, the senate, the forum. … We have left you nothing but your temples only!" (*Apology* 37.4, cited in Kee (1995), p. 213). By the reign of Constantine, one out of five inhabitants of the Roman Empire was a Christian.

The Conversion of Constantine

Helena, the mother of the Emperor Constantine (r. 306–337), had churches built in Asia Minor and the Holy Land and traveled to Jerusalem, seeking the cross on which Jesus died. In 313, Constantine himself had a vision in which a cross with the words *in hoc signo vinces* (in this sign you will be victorious) appeared to him the night before he won the critical battle that made him sole emperor in the Western Empire. He immediately declared Christianity legal. He funded Christian leaders and their construction of churches while he withdrew official support from the pagan churches, making Christianity the *de facto* official religion of the Roman Empire. Constantine sponsored the Council of Nicea in 325, the largest assembly of bishops of local Christian churches up to that time. He convened the Council primarily to establish the central theological doctrines of Christianity, but it also established a Church organization for the Roman Empire, a network of urban bishoprics

Marble head of Constantine, Palazzo dei Conservatori, Rome, 313 C.E. This gigantic bust—the head is over 8 feet (2.4 m) tall—exhibits a stark and expressive realism that verges on caricature. Coming after Diocletian (r. 284–305) insisted on being worshiped as divine, the bust represents a returning awareness that people—even Roman emperors—are humans not gods.

grouped into provinces, with each province headed by the chief bishop of its largest city. In 337, on his deathbed, Constantine accepted baptism.

In 392, the Emperor Theodosius (r. 379–395) declared Christianity the official religion of the Roman Empire. He outlawed paganism and severely restricted Judaism, initiating centuries of bitter Christian persecution of both traditions.

How Had Christianity Succeeded?

How had Christianity, once scorned and persecuted, achieved such power? Christian believers attributed the success to divine assistance. Historians seek more earthly explanations. Let us consider two approaches.

Beginning in 1776, Edward Gibbon began the publication of his six-volume masterpiece, *The History of the Decline and Fall of the Roman Empire.* A child of the enlightenment philosophy of his time, which rejected supernatural explanations (see Chapter 15), Gibbon rather sarcastically presented five reasons for Christianity's victories. But beneath his sarcasm Gibbon revealed the profound strengths of the new religion:

- Its "inflexible and intolerant" zeal, derived from its Jewish roots.

- Its promise of resurrection and a future life for believers, soon augmented by the threat of eternal damnation for nonbelievers; Cyprian, Bishop of Carthage (d. 258) declared, for example, "Outside the church there is no salvation." (McManners, p. 37)

- Its assertion of miraculous accomplishments, including exorcisms. Gibbon, always seeking the exaggeration, cited the paradoxical claim of Tertullian: "I believe because it is absurd!" (Gibbon, p. 206)

- The austere morals of the first Christians. The Christian search for spiritual perfection, monogamous sexual code, rejection of worldly honor, and general emphasis on equality attracted many converts. In the extreme case, martyrdom won admiration, sympathy, and followers. Tertullian asserted "The blood of martyrs is seed." (McManners, p. 43)

- The Church generated a state within a state through the decentralized leadership of its local bishops and presbyters, the structure Paul had begun to knit together. As imperial structures weakened, the Church provided an alternative community. This Christian community distributed philanthropy to needy people within and even outside the Church. It also publicized its message effectively—in Greek, the language of the eastern part of the empire.

Many historians of our own time accept the thrust of Gibbon's explanations, but tend to emphasize more the importance of community within the Church.

"From the outset, the major goal of the Jesus movement was to call into existence a new kind of inclusive community that might arch over all the ordinary human distinctions of race and religion," writes Howard Clark Kee (1991, p. 2). Kee analyzes five different kinds of community that were active in the Roman world during the first two centuries of the Christian era and suggests that Christianity developed an appeal to each of them: The community of the wise, seeking special knowledge of the future; the community of the law-abiding, seeking appropriate rules of guidance in the present; the community where God dwells among his people, seeking assurance that it was specially selected and cared for; the community of mystical participation, influenced by the mystery religions of the time; and the ethnically and culturally inclusive community, outsiders seeking a place of belonging. Different aspects of the Christian message, developed by different Church leaders, spoke to each of these communities and succeeded in drawing them in (Kee, 1995).

Historical sociologist Michael Mann cites the psychological and practical rewards of the growing Christian "ecumene," the worldwide community of the Church, with its comprehensive philosophy for living and organizing. Although much of Christianity's message targeted the poor, Mann notes that the religion also drew a large following of urban artisans, whom the aristocratic Roman Empire devalued. Excluded from political power, these working-class people were in search of a comprehensive and welcoming community. They wanted to recreate an earlier, simpler, more participatory era and they became Christians. As imperial power became increasingly centralized, remote, insensitive, and later unstable, "In many ways Christianity represented how Rome liked to idealize its republican past" (Mann, p. 325).

PROFILE
St. Augustine
BISHOP OF HIPPO

With the declaration that "the true philosopher is the lover of God," Augustine (354–430) aptly described his own position within the early Christian Church. Brought up by a devout Christian mother and pagan father in the Roman province of Numidia (modern-day Algeria), Augustine displayed a devotion to intellectual pursuits from an early age. In Carthage, where he was a student, he became deeply involved in Manichaeism, a philosophy that combined Christianity with elements of other religions and encouraged its adherents to a life of asceticism and celibacy. Unfortunately, Augustine was only permitted to join the lower order of the Manichaean Church because of his romantic attachment to a woman of low birth, with whom he had a son, and it was not long before he decided to look elsewhere for intellectual and spiritual fulfilment. An official professorship at Milan brought Augustine into contact with the writings of Plotinus, the third-century philosopher and founder of Neoplatonism. According to Neoplatonic thought, the way to experience ultimate reality or truth was by returning to one's inner self. Through such an act of introspection Augustine discovered God. The incident, which is described in terms of a mystical experience in the *Confessions*, came about just as Augustine was bemoaning his past actions:

> I was saying these things and weeping in the most bitter contrition of my heart, when lo, I heard the voice of a boy or girl, I know not which, coming from a neighbouring house, chanting, and oft repeating, "Take up and read; take up and read." Immediately my countenance was changed. . . . I rose up, interpreting it no other way than as a command to

> me from Heaven to open the book, and to read the first chapter I should light upon
>
> [Augustine, *Confessions*, I; ed. J. G. Pilkington, 1896]

The book that Augustine opened was the New Testament Letters and the first words he read were from the Letter of Paul to the Romans: ". . . put ye on the Lord Jesus Christ, and make not provision for the flesh, to fulfil the lusts thereof." Knowledge of God, Augustine discovered, only became possible through a renunciation of the body and a profound identification with one's own soul—an idea that fused Christian theology with Platonic philosophy.

Shortly after his conversion to Christianity—he was baptized in 386 with his son—Augustine returned to Tagaste in North Africa, the place of his birth, and established a small religious community. In 396 he became Bishop of Hippo, a role that necessitated his active participation in the struggle to end the schism in the African Church and control the various heretical schools. Augustine's belief that all moral activity was ultimately dependent on the grace of God was deemed extreme by some of his contemporaries and his personal understanding of the doctrines of original sin and free will was never fully accepted by the Church. Despite this, Augustine's enormous literary output continued as a significant source of inspiration for later generations of theologians and his legacy to Christian thinking on the relationship between politics and religion was profound.

Augustine died on August 28, 430 just as Rome's dominance in north Africa was drawing to its close.

St. Augustine of Hippo as represented by El Greco, 1590. (*Museum of Santa Cruz Toledo*)

DOCTRINE: DEFINITION AND DISPUTE

As it grew after receiving official recognition, institutional Christianity refined its theology. The most influential theologian of the period, Augustine (354–430), Bishop of Hippo in north Africa, wrote *The City of God* to explain Christianity's relationship to competing religions and philosophies, and to the Roman government with which it was increasingly intertwined. Despite Christianity's designation as the official religion of the empire, Augustine declared its message to be spiritual rather than political. Christianity, he argued, should be concerned with the mystical, heavenly City of Jerusalem rather than with earthly politics. His theology supported the separation of Church and state that came to characterize western Europe fourteen centuries later, after the French Revolution (see Chapter 15).

Augustine built philosophical bridges to Platonic philosophy, the dominant system of the Hellenistic world of his time and place. Christianity envisioned Jesus, God's son, walking the earth and suffering for his people. He was, literally, very down to earth. God, the Father, had more transcendent characteristics, but they were less emphasized in Christian theology at the time. Plato (*c.* 429–*c.* 347 B.C.E.; see p. 145) and later **Neoplatonic** philosophers, however, provided the model of a more exalted, more remote god, a god that was more accepted among the leading thinkers of Augustine's time. According to Augustine, Plato's god was:

> the maker of all created things, the light by which things are known, and the good in reference to which things are to be done; . . . we have in him the first principle of nature, the truth of doctrines, and the happiness of life. (p. 253)

In addition, Plato's god existed in the soul of every person, perhaps a borrowing from Hinduism (see Chapter 9).

Augustine married these Platonic and Neo-Platonic views to the transcendent characteristics of God in Christian theology. This provided Christianity with a new intellectual respectability, which attracted new audiences in the vast Hellenistic world. He also encouraged contemplation and meditation within Christianity, an important element in the monastic life that was beginning to emerge. Augustine himself organized a community of monks in Tegaste (now Souk-Ahras), the city of his birth.

Augustine believed that Christians should subordinate their will and reason to the teachings and authority of the Church:

> Man was made upright that he might not live according to himself, but according to Him that made him—in other words, that he might do His will and not his own. (p. 445)

Judgment and salvation were in the hands of God alone.

> The source of man's happiness lies only in God, whom he abandons when he sins, and not in himself, by living according to whom he sins. (p. 445)

Some Church theologians, such as Pelagius (*c.* 354–after 418), feared that Augustine's elevation of the majesty and authority of the Church would devalue both public service for the poor and private initiative by less disciplined Christians, but Augustine's views prevailed.

Original Sin, Sexuality, and Salvation

In his earlier *Confessions*, Augustine had written of his personal life of (relatively mild) sin before his conversion to Christianity. Now he warned Christians that Adam and Eve's willfulness had led to original sin; sin had unlocked the forces of lust, turning the flesh against the spirit; and lust had called forth a death sentence on all humans in place of the immortality originally intended for them:

> As soon as our first parents had transgressed the commandment, divine grace forsook them, and they were confounded at their own wickedness. . . . They experienced a new motion of their flesh which had become disobedient to them, in strict retribution of their own disobedience to God. . . . Then began the flesh to lust against the Spirit. . . . And thus, from the bad use of free will, there originated the whole train of evil . . . on to the destruction of the second death, which has no end, those only being excepted who are freed by the grace of God. (p. 422–3)

For Augustine, and for the Church, sexuality was perilous and woman suspect. In Roman Catholic theology, profane flesh and divine spirit confronted each other uneasily.

Church Dogma: Discipline and Battles

Some theological disputes led to violence, especially as the Church attempted to suppress doctrinal disagreement. The most divisive concerned the nature of the divinity of Jesus. The theologian Arius (c. 250–336) taught that Christ's humanity limited his divinity; God the father, wholly transcendent, was more sacred than the son who had walked the earth. The Council of Nicea, which was convened in 325 to resolve this dispute, issued an official statement of creed affirming Jesus' complete divinity and his indivisibility from God. The Arian controversy continued, however, especially on the fringes of empire, where Arian missionaries converted many of the Gothic tribes to their own beliefs.

Pope Leo I (440–461) demanded unquestioning obedience: "Truth, which is simple and one, does not admit of variety" (Grant, *Rome*, p. 458). Wars between the new Arian converts and the Roman Church ensued, until finally Arianism was defeated in battle. Of these struggles the historian Ammianus Marcellinus (c. 330–395) wrote, "No wild beasts are such enemies to mankind as are most of the Christians in the deadly hatred they feel for one another" (Grant, *Rome*, p. 457). A recent (1999) book by Richard L. Rubenstein, *When Jesus Became God*, explores the Arian controversy and the use of violence to suppress dissent within the early Church.

In the eastern Mediterranean, bitter and violent conflicts broke out among rival Christian theological factions, again, over the precise balance between Jesus' divinity and his humanity. Persecution of dissidents by the Orthodox Church in Carthage, Syria, and Egypt was so severe that the advent in the seventh century of Muslim rule, which treated all the Christian sects equally, was often welcomed as a respite from the struggles (Matthew, p. 49).

OFFICIAL CHRISTIANITY IN THE WAKE OF EMPIRE

Christianity spread to western and northern Europe along the communication and transportation networks of the Roman Empire. Born in Judaea under Roman occupation, Christianity now spread throughout the empire, spoke its languages of Greek and Latin, preached the gospel along its trade routes, and constructed church communities in its cities. As the empire weakened and dissolved, Christianity emerged and flourished.

Thanks to official recognition and patronage, the Church grew steadily. As the Roman imperial government weakened (see pp. 185–90), it enlisted the now official Church as a kind of department of state. Roman Catholic bishops now came "from the ranks of the senatorial governing class . . . they stood for continuity of the old Roman values. . . . The eventual conversion of the barbarian leaders was due to their influence" (Matthew, p. 21). Through a variety of educational institutions the churches, monasteries, convents, and bishops kept Rome's culture alive in northern and western Europe. In more remote areas these were virtually the only centers of literacy and through them Christianity spread its message aggressively and effectively: "None of the major Germanic peoples who entered the Roman provinces in the fourth and fifth centuries remained pagan for more than a generation after they crossed the frontier" (Mann, p. 335). About 507 Clovis, chief of the Merovingian Franks, converted to Christianity, the first barbarian to accept the religion of the empire. He established his capital in Paris and had thousands of his tribesmen converted, for, in general, followers accepted the religion of their leader.

Monasteries and Missionaries

Decentralized Leadership Christianity spread in urban areas through its bishops in their large churches. In rural and remote areas, monks, acting as missionaries, carried the message. Monasteries, which were small, isolated communities, each under the local control of a single abbot, modeled the spirituality and simplicity of the earliest Christian communities. Because sexual activity was ruled out, monasticism became as accessible to women in convents as to men in monasteries, and was equally valued by both. Many monasteries contained both men and women, each living in celibacy. The most famous of the early monastics, St. Benedict (c. 480–547), founded a monastery at Monte Cassino, about 100 miles (160 kilometers) southeast of Rome. The writings of Pope Gregory I (r. 590–604) give us the most detailed information on the life, regulations, and discipline of that exemplary institution, although each monastery had its own variations in administration and practice.

Gregory saw the usefulness of the monasteries and monks in converting and disciplining the barbarians, and he began to direct their activity from Rome. By the year 600 there were about

200 monasteries in Gaul alone, and the first missionaries dispatched by Rome arrived in England *c.* 597. By 700 all of England had been converted. Linguistic and cultural development accompanied the Church's teaching; in Northumbria, for example, the Venerable Bede (*c.* 673–735) translated the gospels into English and wrote *The Ecclesiastical History of the English People*. In the ninth, tenth, and eleventh centuries, missionary activity was directed toward the "Northmen," the Vikings, from Scandinavia, who raided and traded for goods and slaves from North America and Greenland, through the North Sea and the Baltic, down the Volga River, across the Caspian Sea, and on as far as Baghdad. The Vikings came into the Christian fold with only a tenuous link to Rome and a strong admixture of pagan ritual.

By this time Christians had far surpassed Jews in numbers, geographical spread, power, and influence. Christian missionaries continued their attempts to convert Jews, often by coercion. In 576, for example, a Gallic bishop gave the Jews of his city the choice between baptism and expulsion (McManners, p. 85), a pattern that was repeated periodically, although Jews had not yet immigrated into western Europe in large numbers.

In much of rural western Europe local authorities valued the monks both as the only literate people in the region and as the most capable persons in administering land and agriculture. These authorities also sought an alliance with the prestige and power of the Church. They granted land and administrative powers to nearby monasteries, transforming them into important local economic forces. (Compare the administrative roles of Hindu priests and Buddhist monks in south and southeast Asia; Chapter 9.) Monks became courtiers and bishops as well as missionaries as they expanded the geographic, social, and economic dimensions of the Church. Until the Lateran Declaration of 1216 under Pope Innocent III (r. 1198–1216), monasteries could form and dissolve at local initiatives, so we have no record of their exact numbers in the early centuries. A history of the very decentralized Church of this time would have to be written from the bottom up.

The Church in the West was decentralized partly because the Roman Empire was decentralized, having lost its administrative power. There was no longer an emperor in Rome. The Church and what was left of the government groped toward a new mutual relationship. In 496, Pope Gelasius I (r. 492–496) saw the mutual dependence of Church and state, and he wrote: "Christian emperors would need priests for attaining eternal life and priests would avail themselves of imperial regulations in the conduct of temporal affairs" (Tierney, p. 15). Gelasius, who wanted each institution to keep to its own domain, supported St. Augustine of Hippo in advocating an early separation of Church and state.

The Church East and West

In the far more literate and sophisticated Byzantine Empire, political leaders did not relinquish their power to Church authorities. Indeed, the emperor at Constantinople served as administrative head of the Church, a pattern that had been set by Constantine when he presided over the Council of Nicea, outside Constantinople.

Today, Eastern Orthodoxy and Roman Catholicism share the same fundamental faith and scripture and they maintain official communication with each other, but they developed many historic differences over church organization, authority, aesthetics, and language. In the East, the Church remained far more urban, as did the entire region. The West had so few roads and so little trade that it was held together organizationally by its urban military and ecclesiastical strongholds. The Council of Chalcedon (451) recognized four centers of church organization, or sees: Antioch, Jerusalem, Alexandria, and Constantinople, with Constantinople predominating—and having the same leadership role in the East as Rome had in the West. Rome, still under its own emperor, and with its own bishop, was deemed an entirely separate administrative center.

Rome and Byzantium have remained divided over the authority of the bishop of Rome to the present. From the sixth century, he has claimed to be pope, *pappa*, father of the (Roman) Catholic Church, the direct organizational successor of the apostle Peter. Eastern Orthodox Christianity, however, has never recognized the pope's claim to preeminent authority. Also, unlike the Roman practice, all but the highest clergy in Eastern Orthodoxy are permitted to marry, so here again the two clergies have not accepted each other's authority. The language of Rome is Latin, while the East uses Greek and the various Slavic languages of eastern Europe. Their aesthetics for religious art are also different (see Spotlight, pp. 324–5). Friction between the two groups has waxed and waned over time, with the most direct confrontation coming in 1204, when crusaders dispatched by Rome to fight against Muslims in Jerusalem (see pp. 360–3) turned northward and sacked Constantinople instead.

As in the West, monastic life flourished in the Byzantine Empire, with exemplary institutions at remote, starkly beautiful sites such as Mount Sinai and Mount Athos. The greatest missionary activity of the Eastern monks came later than in the West. Hemmed in by the Holy Roman Empire and the barbarians to the west and by the growing power of Islam to the east after about 650, Byzantium turned its missionary efforts northward, toward Russia. The brothers St. Cyril (c. 827–869) and St. Methodius (c. 825–884) translated the Bible into Slavonic, creating the Cyrillic alphabet in which to transcribe and publish it. When Russia embraced Orthodox Christianity in the tenth century it also adopted this alphabet. In the late fifteenth century, after the fall of Constantinople to the Turks (1453), Moscow began to refer to itself as the "Third Rome," the spiritual and political heir to the Caesars and the Byzantine Empire.

Monastery of St. Catherine, Mount Sinai, 557 C.E. According to the Torah, Moses received the tablets of the law from God on Mount Sinai. It was for this reason that the Byzantine emperor Justinian I (r. 527–565) chose to found the monastery of St. Catherine here. The remote beauty of the place also made it ideal for spiritual meditation.

SPOTLIGHT
Icons and Iconoclasm

"What the written word is to the literate, the icon is to the illiterate. What speech is to the ear, the icon is to the eye." With these words St. John of Damascus (*c.* 657–*c.* 749) explained the importance of **icons** in Eastern Orthodox Christianity. Icons—sacred images of Jesus, Mary, angels, and saints, often paintings on gold backgrounds—are of central importance in Eastern Orthodox Christian worship. Incense is offered to them, candles are lit before them, they are carried in processions in the church and accorded a place of honor in the home. Legends report that Christ and the Virgin Mary appeared after their deaths to St. Luke so that he might paint them and thus provide an accurate representation of their likeness. **Figure 1**, an icon of Mary holding the infant Jesus in her lap, flanked by SS. Theodore and George and overseen by angels, was probably painted in Constantinople in the sixth or seventh century and is one of the oldest

remaining icons.

This heritage from the earliest icons to their central position today might appear to be a straight-line development, but, in fact, for more than a century, between 726–843, fierce controversy over the place of icons divided Eastern Orthodoxy

Figure 1 Icon of Mary, Jesus, and SS. Theodore and George, St Catherine's Monastery, Israel, sixth to seventh century C.E.

and created tensions with the Roman Church as well. In 726 the Emperor Leo III took the side of the **iconoclasts**, the breakers of icons, in ordering the destruction of all images that depicted Jesus, Mary, saints, or angels in human form. The representation of Christ was especially targeted.

Those who kept such icons were to be physically punished. **Figure 2** from an eleventh-century manuscript portrays an iconoclast destroying an image of Jesus.

Historians cite multiple reasons underlying the emperor's order. Theologically, iconoclasts argued that Jesus' divine nature could not be painted. **Iconodules**, people who venerated the icons, replied that Christ's human presence was real and significant, and paintings were needed to capture it. Politically, Emperor Leo III was asserting his power in a struggle with Church authorities. Culturally, iconoclasts were accepting the Islamic (and Jewish) reading of the biblical prohibition against creating images of humans or gods for worship. From its founding in 622 C.E. (see Chapter 11), Islam defeated a series of Christian armies and was gaining whole nations of converts, while the Byzantine empire itself was reduced to Constantinople, its European provinces, and Asia Minor. Some Church leaders may have reasoned that biblical bans against the use of images in worship should be enforced. As in Islam, Eastern Orthodoxy did continue to produce an abundance of art that did not reproduce the human figure. The western regions of the empire did not cease creating religious images, and the pope and Western Christendom repudiated the edict altogether.

Iconoclasm raged for over a century as art forms became the focal center of theological, political, and cultural struggles. In 843 the Empress Theodora restored the use of icons in an act called "The Triumph of Orthodoxy," an event still celebrated in the Eastern Church on the first Sunday in Lent. **Figure 3**, an icon entitled "The Triumph of Orthodoxy," painted in Constantinople in the late fourteenth or early fifteenth century, commemorates the victory. In the top center stands the Virgin Mary holding the infant Jesus; on the left, Theodora and her young son, the emperor Michael III; to the right, the Patriarch of Constantinople, Methodius, and three supporters of the iconodule position. The lower register includes eleven additional iconodules.

Figure 2 Iconoclast churchmen spearing an image of Christ, illumination, The Chludov Psalter, eleventh century C.E.

Figure 3 Icon of the "Triumph of Orthodoxy," Constantinople, late fourteenth/early fifteenth century C.E.

The spread of Christianity The disciples and early missionaries established Christian communities in southwest Asia, Greece, Italy, north Africa, and India. On the other hand, Roman persecution, the decline of western Rome, and the rise of Islam (see map, p. 341) hindered its dissemination. The Orthodox Church of Constantinople converted eastern Europe, penetrating Russia; Rome became reestablished as a powerful center; and Celtic missionaries traveled throughout northwest Europe.

In other regions of east-central Europe, Rome and Byzantium competed in spreading their religious and cultural messages and organizations. Rome won out in Poland, Bohemia, Lithuania, and Ukraine; the Eastern Church in Bulgaria, Romania, and Serbia. In the Great Schism of 1054 the two Churches divided definitively into the Latin or Roman Catholic Church, predominant in western Europe, and the Greek Orthodox Church, which prevailed in the east. Other national Churches, among the world's oldest, had also grown up beyond Rome's jurisdiction, including the Armenian, the Coptic in Egypt, and the Ethiopian. They now asserted their independence from

Constantinople as well, creating a pattern of distinct national Churches that the Protestant Reformation would later adopt (see Chapter 13).

CHRISTIANITY IN WESTERN EUROPE

The abrupt, dramatic rise of Islam throughout the Middle East and into the Mediterranean, which we will examine in the next chapter, had an immediate and profound influence on Christianity. By the year 700, Islam had won the eastern Mediterranean and the north coast of Africa, key regions of both Christianity and the former Roman Empire. The Muslim Umayyad dynasty pushed on into Spain and crossed the Pyrenees. Stopped only in southern France by Charles Martel (c. 688–741) at the Battle of Tours in 732, the Umayyad forces returned to Spain. Muslim troops captured segments of the southern Italian peninsula, Sicily, and other Mediterranean islands. Geographically cut off from the lands of its birth and early vigor, Christianity became primarily a religion of Europe, where many of its members were recently converted warrior nobles.

In western Europe outside of Rome, Christianity developed a multitude of local institutions. Churches, monasteries, and convents were established, and leadership was decentralized. In regions which lacked organized government and administration, local church leaders and institutions provided whatever existed of order, administration, and a sense of larger community. For several centuries, "Christendom was dominated by thousands of dedicated unmarried men and women" (McManners, p. 89), the clergy of the Church. Among lay people as well as among the clergy, the period from the sixth through the tenth centuries was a lengthy era of faith, prayer, and meditation. Quiet piety and spiritualism gave meaning to life. Christians

Christ triumphing over evil, Frankish terra cotta plaque, Merovingian era.
It was not unusual for western Europeans to represent Christ in contemporary local costume (compare the Spotlight on Buddhas, pp. 288–9). Here, dressed as a member of the German warrior nobility, he treads the serpent, an emblem of the devil, underfoot. (*Musée des Antiquités, St-Germain-en-Laye, France*)

sought eternal salvation within the Church, and feared eternal damnation outside it. Missionary activity continued enthusiastically, now turned northward toward the Vikings and the Slavs, as other geographical doors had been forcibly shut.

In the Byzantine Empire, the state became in effect an armed force. In Rome, the pope felt surrounded by the hostile powers of Constantinople and Islam to the east and south, and several Gothic kings to the north and west. Seeking alliances with strongmen, he turned to a Frank, Charles (Carolus) Martel, who gave his name to the Carolingian family. As we have seen, Martel had repulsed the Muslims at Tours in 732. In 754 his son Pepin III (r. 751–768) answered the call of Pope Stephen II (r. 752–757) for help in fighting the Lombard Goths who were invading Italy and threatening the papal possessions. Pepin secured a swath of lands from Rome to Ravenna and turned them over to papal rule. In exchange, the pope anointed Pepin and his two sons, confirming the succession of his family as the royal house ruling the Franks.

THE CAROLINGIAN DYNASTY

751	Pepin III "the Short" becomes King of the Franks
755	Franks drive Lombards out of central Italy; creation of Papal States
768–814	Charlemagne rules as King of the Franks
774	Charlemagne defeats Lombards in northern Italy
800	Pope Leo III crowns Charlemagne
814–840	Louis the Pious succeeds Charlemagne as "emperor"
843	Treaty of Verdun partitions the Carolingian Empire
870	Treaty of Mersen further divides Carolingian Empire
875–950	New invasions of Vikings, Muslims, and Magyars
962	Ottonian dynasty succeeds Carolingian in Germany
987	Capetian dynasty succeeds Carolingian in France

Bronze and gilt statuette of Charlemagne, *c.* 860–870 C.E. Charlemagne's ceaseless warfare spread Christianity and Frankish rule across western Europe, while repelling barbarian intruders and enemies of Rome. In 800 C.E. Pope Leo III showed his gratitude by crowning him Holy Roman Emperor. (*Louvre, Paris*)

Charlemagne

Pepin's son Charles ruled between 771 and 814 as Charles the Great, Charlemagne, and was crowned Roman Emperor by Pope Leo III on Christmas Day 800, in Rome. Emperor and pope set out to attempt to reconstruct the historic Roman Empire, and to achieve this goal Charlemagne spent all his adult lifetime in warfare (see Source below), continuing the military expeditions of his father and grandfather. He reconquered the north-eastern corner of Spain from its Muslim rulers, defeated the Lombard rulers of Italy and relieved their pressure on the pope, seized Bavaria and Bohemia, killed and looted the entire nobility of the Huns in Pannonia (modern Austria and Hungary), and subdued the German Saxon populations along the Elbe River after thirty-three years of warfare. Himself a German Frank, Charlemagne offered the German Saxons a choice of conversion to Christianity or death. With Charlemagne's victories the borders of his kingdom came to match the borders of the dominance of the Church of Rome, except for the British Isles, which he did not enter. The political capital of western Europe passed from Rome to Charlemagne's own palace in Aix-la-Chapelle (Aachen) in modern Germany. Although Charlemagne was barely literate, he established within this palace a center of learning that attracted Church scholars from throughout Europe, initiating what historians call the Carolingian Renaissance.

"For good or ill, a peculiarly determined form of Catholic Christianity became the mandatory faith of all the regions, Mediterranean and non-Mediterranean alike, that had come together to form a post-Roman western Europe." (Brown, p. 17)

SOURCE
Charlemagne and Harun-al-Rashid

Charlemagne spent his lifetime fighting in the name of the pope and on behalf of Christianity. In 777 he invaded Muslim Spain and by 801 had captured Barcelona. (His campaigns in Spain gave rise to the epic poem *The Song of Roland* about the defeat of his rearguard in the pass of Roncesvalles. This became the most celebrated poem of medieval French chivalry.)

Yet Charlemagne carried on a valued diplomatic friendship with the most powerful Muslim ruler of his day, Harun-al-Rashid, Caliph of Baghdad (r. 786–809). Charlemagne's adviser, friend, and biographer Einhard (*c.* 770–840) describes the friendship:

With Harun-al-Rachid [sic], King of the Persians, who held almost the whole of the East in fee, always excepting India, Charlemagne was on such friendly terms that Harun valued his goodwill more than the approval of all the other kings and princes in the entire world, and considered that he alone was worthy of being honoured and propitiated with gifts. When Charlemagne's messengers, whom he had sent with offerings to the most Holy Sepulchre of our Lord and Saviour and to the place of His resurrection, came to Harun and told him of their master's intention, he not only granted all that was asked but even went so far as to agree that this sacred scene of our redemption should be placed under Charlemagne's own jurisdiction. When the time came for these messengers to turn homewards, Harun sent some of his own men to accompany them and dispatched to Charlemagne costly gifts, which included robes, spices and other marvels of the lands of the Orient. A few years earlier Harun had sent Charlemagne the only elephant he possessed, simply because the Frankish King asked for it. (Einhard, p. 70)

Einhard does not note what gifts Charlemagne might have sent to Baghdad in return, nor does he comment on the political benefits of this interfaith diplomacy between the two great empires—empires that flanked, and confronted, the Byzantine Empire lying between them.

Charlemagne's coronation challenged the authority of the Eastern emperor in Constantinople, but during the next years Charlemagne managed, through negotiation and warfare, to gain Constantinople's recognition of his title. There were once again two emperors, east and west.

The Carolingian family remained powerful until about the end of the century, but then could no longer fight off the new invasions of the western Christian world by Magyars (Hungarians), Norsemen, and Arabs. Internally, regional administrators, emboldened by weakness at the center, began to act independently of the emperor's authority. Only after yet another century could militarily powerful leaders begin to cobble together loosely structured kingdoms in northwest-

ern Europe. Meanwhile, political leadership in Europe was generally decentralized in rural manor estates controlled by local lords. Religious leadership in the cathedrals, churches, monasteries, and convents filled the gap, providing a greater sense of overall community and order. In this era, 600–1100 C.E., the Church gave Europe its fundamental character and order. The Magyar and Norse invaders, like the Germans before them, converted to it. By the end of the eleventh century, the Roman Catholic Church, as well as the political authorities of western Europe, were preparing to confront Islam.

CONNECTION: *The Crusades (1095–1291), pp. 360–3*

TRANSITIONS

During the European high middle ages Christianity completed its first millennium. It had originated in the eastern Mediterranean and spread throughout Europe. It had begun with the teachings of one man preached by a handful of disciples and institutionalized through the zeal of a single missionary, and had flowered into two separate, far-flung Church hierarchies and several localized Church structures. It had begun with a membership of downtrodden Jews, added middling-level gentiles, attracted some of the elites of Rome, and finally converted multitudes of Europe's invading barbarians. It had expanded its own organizational establishment via the network of transportation, communication, and trade put in place by the Roman Empire, and when that empire dissolved and contracted it maintained and consolidated its position within the remains of those old Roman administrative and market centers. As European society became more rural, Christian monasteries and convents were founded in the countryside and often took on administrative and developmental roles alongside their spiritual missions. In short, the Church, like the empire, was much transformed.

The transformations of both the Christian religious world and the European political world continued after 1000 with extraordinary developments in crusading vigor, trade and commerce, urbanization, intellectual and artistic creativity, and religious reform. We will explore these transformations in Chapter 12. (Readers who wish to follow those events may skip ahead to that chapter.) First, however, we turn to equally startling and revolutionary

Laon Cathedral, west front, c. 1190–95. Gothic architecture was the dominant style in Europe after the twelfth century and was based on northern European models. Gothic churches were built to communicate, announcing the glories of heaven with their confident mastery of space and light and, at the same time, heralding the wealth and power of the Church.

developments that had created another world religion, originating in the Arabian peninsula only a few hundred miles from the birth place of both Judaism and Christianity. By the year 1000 it had spread across north Africa, northward into Spain, throughout the Middle East, and on through Iran and Afghanistan into India. Our study of Islam in Chapter 11 will complete our introduction to the origins and early life of the three major monotheistic religions.

BIBLIOGRAPHY

Andrea, Alfred and James Overfield, eds. *The Human Record*, Vol. I (Boston: Houghton Mifflin Company, 3rd ed., 1998).

Armstrong, Karen. *A History of God* (New York: Knopf, 1993).

Augustine. *The City of God*, trans. Marcus Dods (New York: Modern Library, 1950).

Baron, Salo Wittmayer. *A Social and Religious History of the Jews*, Vol. 1 (New York: Columbia University Press, 1952).

Brown, Peter. *The Rise of Western Christendom* (Malden, MA: Blackwell Publishers, 1996).

Holy Bible. New Revised Standard Version (Grand Rapids, MI: Zondervan Publishing House, 1989).

Crossan, John Dominic. *The Historical Jesus. The Life of a Mediterranean Jewish Peasant* (San Francisco: HarperCollins, 1991).

de Lange, Nicholas. *Atlas of the Jewish World* (New York: Facts on File, 1984).

Einhard and Notker the Stammerer. *Two Lives of Charlemagne*, trans. Lewis Thorpe (Harmondsworth, England: Penguin Books, 1969).

Eliade, Mircea. *Ordeal by Labyrinth* (Chicago: University of Chicago Press, 1982).

——. *The Sacred and the Profane* (New York: Harper Torchbooks, 1959).

Gibbon, Edward. *The History of the Decline and Fall of the Roman Empire*, 3 vols., abridged by D.M. Low (New York: Washington Square Books, 1962).

Grant, Michael. *History of Rome* (New York: Charles Scribner's Sons, 1978).

——. *Jesus: An Historian's Review of the Gospels* (New York: Touchstone, 1995).

Halpern, Baruch. *The First Historians: The Hebrew Bible and History* (San Francisco: Harper and Row, 1988).

Honour, Hugh and John Fleming. *The Visual Arts: A History* (Englewood Cliffs, NJ: Prentice-Hall, 4th ed., 1995).

Hopfe, Lewis M. *Religions of the World* (New York: Macmillan Publishing Company, 5th ed., 1991).

Kaufmann, Yehezkel. *The Religion of Israel* (Chicago: University of Chicago Press, 1960).

Kee, Howard Clark. *Who Are The People of God: Early Christian Models of Community* (New Haven: Yale University Press, 1995).

Kee, Howard Clark, et al. *Christianity: A Social and Cultural History* (New York: Macmillan Publishers, 1991).

Mann, Michael. *A History of Power from the Beginning to A.D. 1760* (Cambridge: Cambridge University Press, 1986).

Matthew, Donald. *Atlas of Medieval Europe* (New York: Facts on File, 1983).

McManners, John, ed. *The Oxford Illustrated History of Christianity* (New York: Oxford University Press, 1990).

Meier, John P. *A Marginal Jew: Rethinking the Historical Jesus* 2 vols. (New York: Doubleday, 1991, 1994).

Momigliano, Arnaldo. *On Pagans, Jews, and Christians* (Hanover NH: University Press of New England for Wesleyan University Press, 1987).

The New English Bible with the Apocrypha. Oxford Study Edition (New York: Oxford University Press, 1970).

Palmer, R.R. and Joel Colton. *A History of the Modern World*, 8th ed. (New York: Knopf, 1984).

Pritchard, James B., ed. *Ancient Near Eastern Texts Relating to the Old Testament* (Princeton: Princeton University Press, 3rd ed., 1969).

Rosenberg, David and Harold Bloom. *The Book of J* (New York: Grove Weidenfeld, 1990).

Rubenstein, Richard L. *When Jesus Became God* (New York: Harcourt Brace, 1999).

Smart, Ninian. *The World's Religions* (Cambridge: Cambridge University Press, 1989).

Smart, Ninian and Richard D. Hecht, eds. *Sacred Texts of the World: A Universal Anthology* (New York: Crossroad Publishing, 1982).

Smeltzer, Robert M. *Jewish People, Jewish Thought* (New York: Macmillan Publishing Co., Inc., 1980).

Tierney, Brian. *The Crisis of Church and State 1050–1300* (Englewood Cliffs; Prentice-Hall, 1964).

CHAPTER
11

ISLAM

570 C.E.–1500 C.E.

"For much of the period from the eighth to the eighteenth century the leading civilization on the planet in terms of spread and creativity was that of Islam."

FRANCIS ROBINSON

SUBMISSION TO ALLAH: MUSLIM CIVILIZATION BRIDGES THE WORLD

Islam, in Arabic, means submission. Islam teaches submission to the word of the one God, called "Allah" in Arabic. Muslims, those who submit, know God's word primarily through the Quran, the Arabic book that records the teachings of God as they were transmitted through the angel Gabriel to the Prophet Muhammad (570–632). Stories of Muhammad's life, words, and deeds *(hadith)* carefully collected, sifted, and transmitted over many generations, and the biography of the Prophet compiled by Ibn Ishaq (d. 767) and revised by Ibn Hisham (d. 833–4), provide models of the righteous life and how to live it. Muhammad was the most recent, and the final, prophet of God's message of ethical monotheism. Devout Muslims declare this belief in prayers, which are recited five times each day: "There is no God but God, and Muhammad is his Prophet."

As Christians begin the year 1 of their calendar with an event in the life of Jesus, so Muslims begin theirs with an event in the life of Muhammad. The event, however, is not the birth of Muhammad, nor the revelation to him of the Quran, but his **hijra**, the journey from the city of his birth, Mecca, where he was harassed for his beliefs, to

Medina some 200 miles (320 kilometers) away. City leaders in Medina invited Muhammad to establish a new form of government. For Islam the teachings of the Quran and of Muhammad's life are fulfilled only with the creation of a community of believers, the **umma**, and its proper regulation through political structures. The *hijra* and Muhammad's assertion of governmental leadership in Medina therefore mark the year 1 on the Muslim calendar, corresponding to the year 622 on the Christian calendar.

Through its early centuries, Islam established administrative and legal systems in the areas to which it spread: Arabia, western Asia, northern Africa, and Spain. As Islam spread later to eastern Europe, central Asia, south Asia, and sub-Saharan Africa, it arrived sometimes with government backing, sometimes without. Islam is considered in this part on the spread of world religions, but because it often unified government and religion into a single system, it may also be compared with the materials in Part 3 on the expansion of world empires. After the twelfth century, Islam extended into China and southeast Asia as a religious and cultural system without government support. In this chapter, however, we shall trace the growth and spread of Islam as a religious, governmental, and cultural system. We shall also examine its encounters with other religions and empires.

PERSPECTIVES ON ISLAM: HOW DO WE KNOW?

A 1993 essay by Richard Eaton, historian at the University of Arizona, explores many of the key historiographical problems in Islamic history. Eaton notes that much of the historical writing on Islam is based on orthodox Islamic sources or, conversely, on the writings of their opponents. Such sources are not unbiased. In addition, several key documents were written down long after the events they describe, allowing possible alterations in the text.

The Quran itself, for example, was compiled some fifty years after Muhammad received his first revelation. The first Arabic biography of the Prophet was written by Muhammad ibn Ishaq (d. 767) more than a century after the Prophet's death. Moreover, Islam suffered three civil wars in its first 120 years, and considerable internal fighting thereafter, and many of the "official" histories were prepared in support of one position or another. Finally, as Islam confronted other religious civilizations, the accounts of its history were frequently tendentious, again supporting one side or another.

In their search for unbiased information, recent historians have made use of sources that were not recorded as historical narratives but that provide data from which history can be written:

The new generation of historians thus uncovered an impressive variety of sources: commercial

ISLAM		
DATE C.E.	POLITICAL/SOCIAL EVENTS	LITERARY/PHILOSOPHICAL EVENTS
500	• Muhammad (570–632)	
600	• Hijra (622) • Muslim conquest of Mecca • Orthodox or Rightly Guided Caliphs (632–661) • Muslim conquest of Iraq, Syria, Palestine, Egypt, western Iran (632–642), Cyprus (649), and Persian Empire (650s) • Umayyad caliphate (661–750); capital in Damascus • Muslim conquest of Carthage (698) and central Asia (650–712) • Husayn killed at Karbala (680); Sunni–Shi'ite split	• Revelation of the Quran to Muhammad (610) • Persian becomes second language of Islam
700	• Muslim conquest of Tunis (700), Spain (711–716), Sind and lower Indus valley • Muslim defeat at Battle of Tours (732) • Muslims defeat Chinese at battle of Talas River (751) • Abbasid caliphate (750–1258) • Baghdad founded (762)	• Biography of Muhammad by Ibn Ishaq (d. 767) • Formulation of major systems of Islamic law
800	• Divisions in Muslim Empire (833–945) • Fez founded (808)	• al–Tabari, *History of Prophets and Kings* • al–Khwarazmi develops algebra • Abbasid caliphate establishes "House of Wisdom" translation bureau in Baghdad • Sufi tariqat
900	• Persians seize Baghdad (945) • Cairo founded (969)	• Ferdowsi, *Shah Nama* • al–Razi, *Encyclopedia of Medicine* • Turkish becomes third language of Islam • Mutazilites challenge Islamic orthodoxy

ISLAM

DATE C.E.	POLITICAL/SOCIAL EVENTS	LITERARY/PHILOSOPHICAL EVENTS
1000	• Seljuk Turks dominate Abbasid caliphate (1038) • Almoravid dynasty in north Africa and Spain (1061–1145) • Battle of Manzikert (1071) • 1st Crusade (1095–9)	• Ibn Sina (Avicenna), philosopher, produces "Canon of Medicine" • al–Biruni writes on mathematics and astronomy (d. 1046)
1100	• Almohad dynasty rules north Africa and Spain (1145–1269) • 2nd Crusade (1147–9) • Salah al–Din (Saladin) recaptures Jerusalem (1187) • 3rd Crusade (1189–92)	• al–Ghazzali (d. 1111), Muslim philosopher and theologian • Ibn Rushd (Avarroes; 1126–98) • Maimonides (1135–1204), Jewish physician, philosopher, and theologian
1200	• 4th Crusade (1202–04) • Sultanate of Delhi (1211–1526) • Children's Crusade (1212) • 5th–8th Crusades (1218–91) • Crusaders driven from west Asia (1291) • Fall of Baghdad to Mongols (1258); end of Abbasid Caliphate	• Jalal al–Din Rumi, *Mathnawi* • al–Juvaini, *History of the World Conquerors* • Rashid al–Din, *World History*
1300	• Mansa Musa's pilgrimage to Mecca (1324) • Conversion of Malayans and Indonesians to Islam	• Ibn Battuta (1304–68), traveler • Ibn Khaldun, *Universal History*
1400	• Ottoman Turks conquer Constantinople (1453) • Christians capture Granada, Spain, and complete the *reconquista* (1492)	

documents, tax registers, official land grants, administrative seals, census records, coins, gravestones, magical incantations written on bowls, memoirs of pilgrims, archeological and architectural data, biographical dictionaries, inscriptional evidence, and, more recently, oral history. (Eaton in Adas, p. 4)

From these records has emerged a deeper understanding of the culture of Muhammad's homeland in Arabia and of the adjacent Byzantine and Sassanian Persian Empires. These records suggest that Islam did not develop within a national vacuum. It incorporated religious, cultural, and social structures that were already present among its neighbors. Further, in contrast to the view that Islam was spread by the sword, new information suggests that the early rapid military expansion of the Islamic Empire was not motivated by a desire to win converts to the new faith but rather by political, economic, and military goals. Indeed, at first non-Arabs were not encouraged to join the ranks of Muslim believers.

People converted to Islam not primarily under threat of the sword, nor even necessarily because of devout belief in the Muslim creed, but because participation in Islam widened their religious, political, social, economic, and cultural horizons. To convert to Islam was to access world civilization. (On p. 318 we noted a similar rationale inspiring the spread of Christianity.) Islam was not only a faith, not only a system of government, not only a social and cultural organization, but a combination of all four. For ten centuries Islam represented the world's most cosmopolitan civilization.

Another area of intense concern and reinterpretation is the status of women in early Islam. Here, Eaton's insights are supplemented by those of scholars such as Judith Tucker, Nikki Keddie, Beth Baron, and Leila Ahmed, who have enriched our understanding of gender roles in pre-Islamic Arabia. These scholars differ in their evaluations of the impact of early Islam on women because they differ in their evaluation of the status of women in Arabia and in the neighboring Byzantine and Sassanian Empires in the period before

Muhammad. Some see the treatment of women advocated by Muhammad as an improvement in that status, some as a decline. All, however, agree that the status of women was affected less by the teachings of Muhammad, which are ambiguous, than by contact with the Sassanian and Byzantine Empires. Seclusion from men, the wearing of the veil, practices of marriage and divorce, and the legal and economic status prescribed for women were adapted from these areas of conquest.

THE PROPHET: HIS LIFE AND TEACHING

Born in 570 to parents eminent in the Quraysh tribe of Arabia, Muhammad was a deeply meditative person, retreating regularly to a nearby hill to pray and reflect. In 610, when he was forty years old, his reflections were interrupted by the voice of the angel Gabriel, who instructed him: "Recite: In the name of the Lord who created Man of a blood-clot." For the next two decades, God continued to reveal his messages to Muhammad through Gabriel. Muhammad, who could not write, dictated these messages to a scribe. During the Prophet's lifetime, the verses were written down on palm leaves, stone, and other materials. The collection was completed during the rule of Umar, the second caliph (r. 634–644), and under Uthman, the third caliph (r. 644–656), an officially authorized edition was issued. By the middle eighth century, as Arab armies defeated Chinese forces in central Asia, the Muslim victors learned from their prisoners of war the technology of papermaking. By the end of the eighth century Baghdad had a paper mill; Egypt by 900; Morocco and Spain by 1100. Turks brought the art of papermaking to north India in the twelfth century. One use of paper was, of course, in the administration of the government bureaucracy. Another, perhaps even more important, was in the printing and diffusion of the Quran.

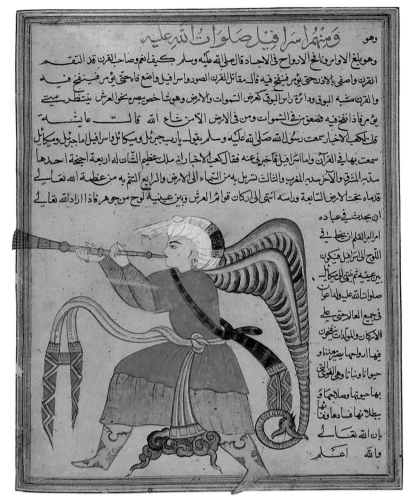

Trumpet call of the archangel Gabriel. Muhammad's religious career as a prophet seems to have been inspired by his early supernatural experiences. Once, he encountered a mighty being, the archangel Gabriel, on the horizon, who commanded him to recite . . . This was the first *surah* (section from the Quran) revealed to humanity, and is symbolized here by Gabriel's blowing on a trumpet. (*British Library, London*)

Approximately the length of the Christian New Testament, the Quran is considered by Muslims the absolute, uncorrupted, word of God. Composed in poetic form, the Quran helped to define the literary standards of the Arabic language. Muslims chant and study its text in Arabic, considering each syllable sacred. Even today many Muslims reject translations of the Quran into other languages as inadequate. (In this text we follow the translation of A.J. Arberry, the version most acceptable to Muslim scholars. The translation by N.J. Dawood is somewhat more accessible and reads more smoothly.) Reverence for the language, poetry, and message of the Quran brings unity to all Muslims throughout the world. The Quran provides the basis not only of the Islamic faith but also of its principles of government, law, and social cohesion.

According to the Quran, Muhammad was only a messenger of God, not the originator of a new doctrine. Indeed, he was not even the founder of Islam. Several prophets came before him, including Adam, Noah, Abraham, Moses, and Jesus:

> We believe in God, and in that which has been sent down on us and sent down on Abraham, Ishmael, Isaac and Jacob, and the tribes, and that which was given to Moses and Jesus and the Prophets, of their Lord; we make no division between any of them, and to Him we surrender. (Quran, 2:130–32)

Muslims claim Abraham, the father of Jewish monotheism, as the first Muslim: "Abraham in truth was not a Jew, neither a Christian; but he was a Muslim and one of pure faith" (Quran, 3:60).

The teachings of each of the earlier prophets, however, were corrupted over time by their followers. Christians, for example, mistakenly considered Jesus to be the son of God, and perverted the message of pure monotheism. The Quran deplored this heresy, declaring, "It is not for God to take a son unto Him" (19:36). The Jews' error was in refusing to accept the Quran as a revised and updated version of the truth already given to them:

> When they were told, "Believe in that God has sent down," They said, "We believe in what was sent down on us"; and they disbelieve in what is beyond that. (2:85)

The message delivered to Muhammad was final, uncorrupted, and true. Muhammad did not formulate this message; he only transmitted it as received. In the chain of prophets, Muhammad is the last and final link.

THE FIVE PILLARS OF ISLAM:

The Quran reveals the "five pillars" of Islam, the five ritual expressions that define orthodox Muslim religious belief and practice:

- Declaration of the creed, "There is no god but God, and Muhammad is his Prophet"

- Prayers to be recited five times daily while facing Mecca (2:144), and, if possible, to be recited in public assembly at midday each Friday

- Alms to be donated to the poor in the community, especially to widows and orphans (2:212 ff.), later recommended at 2½ percent of income

- The month of Ramadan to be observed by fasting each day, although eating is permitted at night, with a major feast marking the month's end (2:179–84)

- The *hajj*, a pilgrimage to Mecca to be undertaken, where possible, at least once in a lifetime (2:185 ff.).

A sixth pillar, **jihad**, or sacred struggle (2:187), was less stringently required and has been interpreted in different ways. Some scholars interpret *jihad* as a call to physical warfare to preserve and extend the **dar al-Islam**, the political rule of Islam. Even then, *jihad* should be pursued only in self-defense, for "God loves not the aggressors" (2:187). Others understand *jihad* as a call to internal spiritual struggle to live Islam as fully as possible. The Quran gives a capsule description of this proper life:

> True piety is this: to believe in God, and the Last Day, the angels, the Book, and the Prophets, to give of one's substance, however cherished, to kinsmen, and orphans, the needy, the traveller, beggars, and to ransom the slave, to perform the prayer, to pay the alms. And they who fulfil their covenant, and endure with fortitude misfortune, hardship and peril, these are they who are true in their faith, these are the truly godfearing. (2:172–3)

Finally, the Quran promises repeatedly that those who observe Islam faithfully will find their reward in paradise:

> And those that believe, and do deeds of righteousness, them We shall admit to gardens underneath which rivers flow, therein dwelling forever and ever; therein for them shall be spouses purified, and We shall admit them to a shelter of plenteous shade. (4:60)

On the other hand, those who reject the opportunity to fulfill the teachings of Islam will burn in Hell:

> Who earns evil, and is encompassed by his transgressions—those are the inhabitants of the Fire; there they shall dwell forever. (2:75)

Humans are to choose between doing good and evil, but the Quran asserts that our free will is limited: "God has power over everything" (4:87).

Historian Michael Morony demonstrated that many of Islam's beliefs and practices were consistent with the rituals of peoples in the regions into which Islam spread, and this made acceptance of the new religion easier. For example, regular prayer times and recitals of creed were also central to Judaism and Christianity, as was institutionalized charity. Animal sacrifice was a part of pagan and Zoroastrian religions, as it was of Islam. Ritual slaughter of animals for food mirrored Jewish practice, as did male circumcision. Ritual washing before public prayers was also practiced by Zoroastrians. In this sense, Islam fit into its cultural setting, facilitating assimilation in both directions.

WOMEN: DEBATES OVER THE EFFECTS OF ISLAM

The Quran speaks extensively of women, establishing a pattern of gender relations that clearly places men above them.

> Men are the managers of the affairs of women for that God has preferred in bounty one of them over another, and for that they have expended of their property. Righteous women are therefore obedient, guarding the secret for God's guarding. And those you fear may be rebellious admonish; banish them to their couches, and beat them. If they then obey you, look not for any way against them; God is All-high, All-great. (4:38)

Women are placed on earth, in part, to satisfy men's sexual desires:

> Your women are a tillage for you; so come into your tillage as you wish. (2:223)

Women are also considered sexually seductive, and the Quran therefore urges the Prophet to

> Say to the believing women, that they cast down their eyes and guard their private parts, and reveal not their adornment save such as is outward; and let them cast their veils over their bosoms, and not reveal their adornment save to their husbands [close relatives, and the very old and very young]. (24:31)

As witnesses in legal matters, the testimony of two women is equal that of a single man (2:282). Similarly in matters of inheritance, "to the male the like of the portion of two females" (4:11).

Despite these apparently demeaning exhortations, some modern scholars assert that Islam actually introduced "a positive social revolution" (Tucker, p. 42) in gender relations. Compared to what came before, Islam introduced new rights and security in marriage. Islamic law, **shari'a**, safeguarded the rights of both partners in marriage through contractual responsibilities: it insisted on the consent of the bride; it specified that the dowry, or bridal gift, go to the bride and not to her family; and it spelled out the husband's obligations to support his wives and children. Although men were allowed to take up to four wives, the Quran added, "if you fear that you will not be equitable, then one only" (4:3), so in practice only one wife was normally permitted. These scholars note also that in the life of Muhammad, three women played exemplary roles: his first wife, Khadija, who supported him economically and emotionally when the revelations he received brought him scorn from others; Aisha, the most beloved of the wives he took after Khadija's death, and the daughter of Abu Bakr, Muhammad's successor as **caliph** or leader of the Muslim community; and Fatima, the daughter of the Prophet and wife of the fourth caliph, Ali. Nevertheless, these women drew their importance from their service to prominent men, and were criticized when they asserted more independent roles.

Other scholars have argued that Islam made the plight of women worse than it had been before. These scholars argue that in pre-Islamic Arabia, women could initiate marriage, they could have more than one husband, they could divorce their husbands, they could remain in their parents' home area and have their husbands come to live with them, and they could keep custody of their children in case of divorce. In pre-Islamic Arabia, some pagan goddesses were worshipped, suggesting that there was considerable respect for females.

Of those scholars who feel that the position of women declined under Islam, some put the blame on Islam itself, but others suggest that the teachings of Islam were actually comparatively liberal. These scholars argue that it was contact with the Byzantine and Sassanian Empires that reduced their status. Tribal, nomadic Arabia treated women with relative equality, but the neighboring empires, with their settled, urban civilizations, veiled women and kept them home under male domination. The Arabs adopted these practices. In effect, this group of scholars is also saying that the more liberal Quranic rules regarding women were reinterpreted after contact with societies outside Arabia.

MUHAMMAD IN WAR AND PEACE

Muhammad created the original *umma* or Muslim community. In his home town of Mecca, Muhammad became the leader of a sect of about 100 followers, but many people thought Muhammad mad because of his reports of revelations from God, and some apparently tried to assassinate him. Then, in 622, the elders of the city of Medina, some 200 miles (320 kilometers) to the north, invited him to adjudicate bitter disputes among local tribes and to take over the reins of government. Muhammad accepted, confirming the principle that the teachings of Islam were best implemented under an Islamic government, a *dar al-Islam* ("an abode of Islam"). In Medina Muhammad promulgated Quranic business ethics as well as family laws of marriage, divorce, and inheritance.

After establishing his authority in Medina, Muhammad turned his ambition and his troops back towards Mecca. In 624 he successfully raided a large Meccan caravan train, reducing Mecca's prosperity by cutting important trade routes and winning local fame for himself. In 625 the Meccans fought back, defeating Muhammad at Uhud. In 627 the two sides fought to a draw at the Battle of the Ditch, but Muhammad's reputation grew as he stood up to the proud and powerful Meccans. In 630, following a dispute between the tribes of the two cities, Mecca surrendered to Medina.

Christian Arabs remained largely aloof from Muhammad's alliances, while some Jews actively opposed his political goals and rejected his claims to religious prophecy. Disappointed in his wish to unite the members of the two monotheistic religions of the region under his leadership, and especially infuriated that some Jewish families had even joined the Meccan enemy in war, he had the Jewish men of the Banu Qurayza clan executed, and the women and children enslaved. On the other hand, in other parts of Arabia Jews and Christians, though subject to a special tax, were free to practice their religion.

By the time he died in 632, Muhammad was well on his way to creating from the warring tribes an Arabia-wide federation dedicated to the faith and the political structure of Islam.

SUCCESSION STRUGGLES AND THE EARLY CALIPHS

When the Prophet died leaving no male heir, the Muslim community feared that the *umma* and its political organization would break up. To preserve them, the Muslim leadership elected Abu Bakr (r. 632–634), one of Muhammad's closest associates and the father of his wife Aisha, as caliph—that is, successor to the Prophet and head of the Muslim community. The next three caliphs were similarly elected from among Muhammad's relatives and companions, but amidst much more dissension.

Abu Bakr mobilized to prevent Muslims from deserting their new religion and the authority of its government, attacking those who tried. Arabia was convulsed in tribal warfare. The contending tribes fought for power and looted one another. Their battles spilled over the borders of the Arabian peninsula, as did their search for allies. The Byzantine and Sassanian Empires saw the Arab troops encroaching on their territories and fought back, but in the Battle of Ajnadayn (634), in southern Palestine, the Arab clans combined to form a unified army and defeated the Byzantine army.

> With this victory their ambitions became boundless; they were no longer raiders on the soil of Syria seeking booty, but contenders for control of the settled empires. What began as large-scale intertribal skirmishing to consolidate a political confederation in Arabia ended as a full-scale war against the two empires. (Lapidus, p. 39)

Conquest followed conquest—Damascus in 636; Jerusalem in 638. But the northward march stopped as Byzantine troops held fast at the borders of the Anatolian peninsula. The Byzantine Empire defended its Anatolian borders for another four centuries, and its Balkan territories for eight. But the Sassanian Empire collapsed almost immediately. In 637 Arab armies defeated the Persians in battle, seized their capital, Ctesiphon, and forced the last emperor to flee. Meeting little opposition, Arab armies swept across Iraq, Iran, Afghanistan, and central Asia. Other Arab armies now turned toward northern Africa, taking Egypt in 641–643 and Tripoli in 643.

The second caliph, Umar I (r. 634–644), established the early principles of political administration in the conquered territories. The troops were not to interfere with the way of life of the conquered populations. The early caliphs did not encourage conversion to Islam, lest the political and social status of conqueror and conquered become confused. Also, since Muslims were exempted from land taxes and poll taxes, the conversion of the conquered peoples would cause considerable loss of tax revenue to Umar's government. To prevent the armies and the administrators from interfering with the economy and the social traditions of the newly conquered territories, Umar ordered the occupiers to live in garrison cities somewhat apart from the conquered populations. New garrison cities, such as Basra, Kufa, Fustat, and Merv, were built, and new neighborhoods for the foreign troops and administrators were added to existing cities. Local systems of taxation and administration were largely left in place, and incumbent personnel

Stone statue of the caliph al-Walid II, Khirbat al-Mafjar, Syria, *c.* eighth century. Arab conquerors, as rulers of west Asia, could pick and choose between the artistic styles of the region. Artworks from the palaces built by Umayyad princes in the Syrian desert combine Iranian and Byzantine influences, as can be seen in this statue of an early caliph. (*Israel Antiquities Authority, Jerusalem*)

often kept their jobs, but lands that had been owned by the state and its officials were confiscated and claimed for the new government.

These new arrangements proved unstable. In the new garrison cities, conqueror and conquered lived side by side, and they could not effectively be segregated socially and culturally. In addition, the troops soon argued that their pay was not adequate. Their incomes lagged, even as the new conquests enriched the top-level administrators. What had become of Islam's call for a more egalitarian society? In essence, the imperial aims of the ruling class and the religious goals of Islam were pulling in opposite directions.

THE FIRST CIVIL WAR; UMAYYAD VICTORY

The jockeying for power among various political, economic, tribal, and religious interest groups precipitated a series of civil wars. The third caliph, Uthman (r. 644–656), was assassinated by a contingent of Arab troops from Egypt, who complained that their governors were cruel, their pay was inadequate, and that class divisions were destroying Arab unity. Uthman's successor, Ali (r. 656–661), was assassinated by a group that found him too soft on the Umayyad family, which was claiming the caliphate for itself. After Ali's assassination, the Umayyad leader, Mu'awiya, declared himself caliph and began the ninety-year rule of the Umayyad caliphate. Moving the capital out of Arabia to Damascus, Syria, Mu'awiya (r. 661–680) distanced himself from the original Muslim elite of the Arabian peninsula. He opened Islam to more cosmopolitan influences and a more professional style of imperial administration.

Life in the cities was eroding the solidarity of tribal society. A new social structure was developing that would divide the Arab upper and lower classes while mixing together the Arab and non-Arab elites. The caliphs looked to Islam as the glue that could bind the emerging society together, and they abandoned the policy of Muslim Arab rule over non-Muslim, non-Arab peoples. Instead they sought to assimilate the conquered peoples into a single Muslim *umma*. By the middle of the eighth century, conversions to Islam were increasing among the urban populations, as was the use of Arabic as the language of administration, literature, and everyday speech. These changes in religion and language had not yet affected the rural areas very deeply.

THE SECOND CIVIL WAR; SUNNI, SHI'A, AND ISMAILI DIVISIONS

Tension nevertheless remained high among the various religious and tribal factions, and war broke out again on Mu'awiya's death in 680. His son, Yazid I (r. 680–683), claimed the caliphate, but Husayn, the son of Ali, took the field against him. When Husayn was killed in battle at Karbala, Iraq, in the year 680, he joined his father as the second martyr of the Shi'a ("partisans" of Ali; also Shi'ite) branch of Islam. The Shi'as, who stressed the importance of religious purity, wanted the caliph to represent Islam's religious principles rather than imperial aspirations. They felt that Ali had represented that purer orientation and they would recognize only descendants of Ali as **imam**, or rightful caliph. From this time onward, Shi'as campaigned for the appointment of their imam to fill the position of caliph.

One after another, all of the first eleven imams were assassinated. After the death of the eleventh imam in 874 and the disappearance of his son, the hereditary line ended. From this time onward, "twelver" Shi'as have looked forward to the reappearance of the "hidden" twelfth imam, referred to as the **mahdi**, or the "rightly guided one," a messiah, to usher in a new age of Islam, truth, and justice. Meanwhile, they have usually been willing to accept the authority of the current government, while stressing matters of the spiritual rather than the temporal world.

An earlier split had occurred among the Shi'as at the death of the sixth imam in 765. While most accepted the accession of his younger son, Musa al-Kazim, a minority called "seveners" followed the elder son Ismail. These Ismailis led active proselytizing campaigns among tribals and peasants in Arabia, Syria, Iraq, central Asia, and northern Africa, and in the towns of Iran. They led frequent rebellions against the caliphate. This group, too, later split. One branch of Ismailis lives on today, revering the Aga Khan as its leader.

The great majority of Muslims, however, regarded the caliph as primarily a political official, administering the empire of Islam, and they accepted the

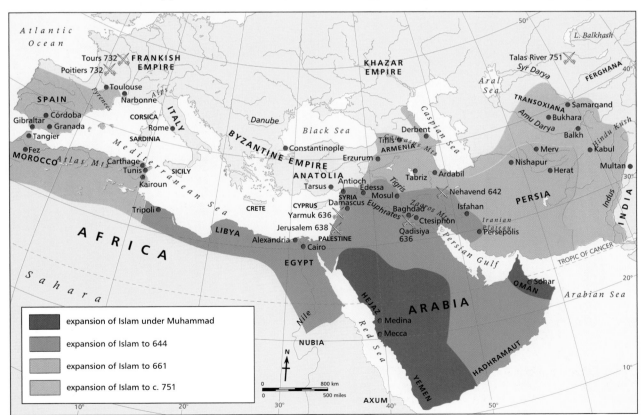

The expansion of Islam The Muslim faith spread with astonishing speed from its center at Mecca, exploiting the vacuum left by the collapse of Rome and Seleucid Persia. Within a century of the death of the Prophet Muhammad in 632 C.E., Arab armies had reached the Atlantic coast in the west, and the borders of India and China in the east.

rule of the Umayyads. They called themselves Sunnis, or followers of "the Prophet's example." The division between Sunni and Shi'a, which began over the proper succession to the caliphate, has continued to the present, long after the caliphate has ceased to exist, as the principal sectarian division within Islam. Some 83 percent of the world's Muslims today are Sunnis, 16 percent Shi'as. The split is largely geographical with Shi'as forming 95 percent of the population of Iran and about 60 percent of Iraq. Ismailis, a branch of Shi'as, are found mostly in Pakistan and India. Elsewhere Sunnis are the overwhelming majority.

THE HEIGHTS AND DEPTHS OF THE UMAYYAD DYNASTY

After the succession struggle on Mu'awiya's death, the Umayyads consolidated their rule and embarked on wars of imperial conquest. Arab armies conquered the entire northern coast of Africa by 711. They crossed the Straits of Gibraltar and completed the conquest of Spain between 711 and 756. Raiders into France were pushed back south of the Pyrenees in 732, however, by the armies of Charles Martel at the Battle of Tours. Other armies marched eastward, capturing large parts of central Asia, and raiding repeatedly in the Indus valley region of Sind.

To symbolize their imperial power, the Umayyad caliphs constructed elegant, monumental mosques in Jerusalem in 691 (the Dome of the Rock; see picture below); in Medina, 706–710; Damascus, 706–714; and, again, Jerusalem (the al-Aqsa), 709–715. They began also to create an imperial bureaucracy which owed its allegiance to the state rather than to the current ruler personally.

The Umayyads copied the imperial structures of the Byzantine and Persian Empires: wars of imperial conquest, bureaucracy in administration, monu-

The exterior of the Dome of the Rock, Jerusalem, first constructed in 692 C.E. The first Umayyad caliph, Abd al-Malik (r. 685–705) built this shrine as the first major monument in Islamic history. It celebrates the triumphal conquests of the Umayyad dynasty as it emerged from Arabia and defeated both the Byzantine and Persian empires to carve out a new empire of its own.

mentality in architecture, and regal opulence at court. They used Arabic as their language of administration. Under Caliph Umar II (717–720), the Umayyads turned to Islam to provide the spiritual and ideological glue of their empire. Recognizing that they could no longer administer so large and sophisticated an empire from their narrow base as foreign conquerors, they encouraged their subjects to convert to Islam and create a universal empire based on a common faith. Arabs and non-Arabs would be equal in the eyes of Islam. Access to both military and civilian office would be equalized, as would taxes.

The Umayyads were raising conflicting aspirations. Worse, Umar's successors were not so committed to the program of equality under Islam as he was, so implementation was inconsistent and various interest groups were frustrated by the vagaries of their changing fortunes. Many Sunni religious leaders, although pleased with the new emphasis on Islam, were offended by the imperial pomp of the Umayyads and their use of religion for blatantly political purposes. Many Shi'as continued to nourish the hope that one of their imams would displace the Umayyads and take his rightful place as caliph. In Kufa, Iraq, Shi'as revolted in 740, but the revolt was suppressed, and its leaders were executed. Non-Arab Muslims whose taxes were not lowered, or were lowered only temporarily, railed against the government that had not delivered on its promises. Arabs were unhappy that their own taxes were being raised to compensate for the reductions offered to others.

The Umayyad armies were overextended and exhausted and began to lose major battles. The Turks drove them from Transoxiania, central Asia; the Khazars stopped them in Armenia in 730; the Greeks destroyed a major Syrian army in Anatolia in 740; Charles Martel halted the Umayyad advance in France in 732; in north Africa Berber rebels, although defeated in 742, destroyed a Syrian army of 27,000 in the process. Umayyad forces did win the critical Battle of the Talas River in 751, halting the advance of Chinese forces westward and opening central Asia and its silk routes to Islamic religious and cultural missions, but they did not push forward. Military advances stopped. Pulled in many conflicting directions, without the strength to reply, the caliphate was drawn into the third civil war.

THE THIRD CIVIL WAR; ABBASID VICTORY

The Abbasid clan in northern Iran—descended from an uncle of Muhammad named Abbas, and also claiming support from descendants from the line of Ali—revolted against the Umayyads. Supported by Arab settlers in Iran who were protesting against high and unjust taxes, by Shi'as who were seeking their own rule, and also by a faction from Yemen, they overthrew the Umayyad caliphate. In 750, Abu al-Abbas al-Saffah initiated the new Abbasid caliphate, which ruled in reality for a century and a half and in name until 1258. Signaling new policy directions, the new Abbasid caliph built a new capital, Baghdad, 500 miles (800 kilometers) to the east of Damascus, along the banks of the Tigris River, in the heart of the historic Fertile Crescent.

THE ABBASID CALIPHATE

The Abbasid caliphs continued the tasks of the Umayyads in trying to bring order and unity to an empire of heterogeneous peoples, and they followed many of the principles attempted by Umar II. They used Arabic as a unifying language of official communication and administration, and they continued to urge non-Muslims to convert. They recruited widely among all the peoples of the empire to fill admin-

Clay figurine of a female slave from Khirbat al-Mafjar, Syria, *c.* eighth century. Female slaves had their place in the world of the Umayyad dynasty and beyond. Often the objects of passionate love, many were accomplished singers and highly educated.

istrative and military positions. As the bureaucracy expanded Nestorian Christians, Jews, Shi'as, and numerous ethnic groups were prominent in their administration.

For a century the Abbasids succeeded—to a surprising degree—in solving the problems of administering large empires. They kept their administration cosmopolitan and centralized, yet at the same time in touch with local communities. They rotated their officers so that none could become entrenched and semi-independent in a distant posting. They regularized taxes. They employed spies as well as troops of soldiers and armed police. They also attempted to maintain good relations with the local notables, such as village headmen, large landowners, *qadis* or judges, officials of local mosques, religious teachers, moneylenders, accountants, merchants, and family patriarchs, who were the critical sources of information and power in the villages and towns.

STRESS IN THE CALIPHATE

Difficulties in the caliphate became apparent early on, however. The process of choosing a successor to the caliph remained unresolved. At the death of Caliph Harun-al-Rashid (786–809), his two sons fought for the throne, provoking a fourth civil war. Recruiting troops proved an even bigger problem. Throughout the empire, local strongmen were invited to ally their troops to the caliph's armies, but these military contingents naturally owed their allegiance not to Baghdad but to the local potentate.

The caliphs expanded sharply the use of slave troops in their armies. The Umayyads and some peripheral administrations had already set the example of using slaves to staff their armies, but slave troops were often poorly disciplined. Sometimes various contingents turned on one another, and reliance on slaves isolated the caliphs from their own civilian populations. The rulers became increasingly remote from the people they ruled—the more imperial the caliphate, the more distant it became from the original Islamic ideals of equality and simplicity.

THE EMERGENCE OF QUASI-INDEPENDENT STATES

At the same time the civilian bureaucracy became more corrupt and more distant from the general population, and tax collection was increasingly turned over to exploitative, semi-independent tax farmers. In 868 Ahmad ibn Tulun, a Turkish commander, established a virtually independent dynasty ruling over Egypt and Syria, until the caliph, al-Muktafi (r. 902–908), brought them back into line in 905. The slaves in the salt mines of southern Iraq waged a successful revolt for fifteen years, 868–883. In 867, frontier troops in central Iran revolted and won control of southern and western Iran.

Ismaili and Shi'a religious leaders organized revolts throughout the empire. Denying the legitimacy of Abbasid claims to rule and highlighting the exploitation of the village and tribal masses by the distant and corrupt administration in Baghdad, they won many victories in the name of their own views of Islam. Inspired by the Ismailis, peasant and Bedouin raiders raided Mecca, briefly carrying away the sacred Ka'aba stone, the most venerated shrine in the holy city.

The Fatimid clan, claiming to be the rightful successors of the Prophet, conquered Egypt and much of northern Africa. They broke openly with Baghdad, declaring themselves the legitimate caliphs. In Iraq, other rebels took control first of the regions around Baghdad and then, in 945, of Baghdad itself. The caliph was permitted to continue to rule in name, but in effect the empire as a unified, centralized administration was finished.

ISLAM EXPANDS

The functional end of the caliphate did not mean the end of the spread of Islam. Quite the contrary. Regional rulers, finding themselves more independent, pursued policies of political and military expansion while proclaiming the religion and culture of Islam as their own. Sometimes they claimed to act in the name of the caliph; sometimes they claimed complete independence.

INDIA

In northern Iran and Afghanistan, a government run by slave soldiers who had earned their freedom established itself in Ghazni, Afghanistan, in 962. These Ghaznavids launched raids into north India, 999–1026, and finally established their rule over the Punjab, 1021–1186. They were followed by the Ghurids, who were also at first more raiders from Ghur than rulers of India. In 1211, however, the Ghurid general who conquered Delhi declared himself an independent sultan, initiating a series of five dynasties, which are known collectively as the

Portrait of Mahmud of Ghazni, from Rashid al-Din's *World History*, 1306–7. Mahmud (998–1030), a Sunni Muslim prince, is shown putting on the traditional diplomatic gift of a robe of honor, bestowed by the Abbasid caliph. Regional rulers sometimes declared their independence from central control, but Mahmud of Ghazni was careful to include the caliph's name on his coinage, thereby presenting himself as a loyal subject. (*Edinburgh University Library*)

Sultanate of Delhi (1211–1526). By 1236 they controlled north India; by 1335, almost the entire subcontinent. When Delhi's power dimmed, numerous Muslim rulers controlled other regions of India. These regional governments, in particular, stayed close to their subjects, encouraged the development of regional languages, and provided new opportunities to **Sufis**, Muslim mystics and teachers, to introduce and practice Islam in new areas. In 1526, temporarily, and in 1556, more permanently, a mixture of Mongol and Turkish Muslim invaders conquered India, heralding the start of a new era, the Mughal Empire.

Most, but not all, of the Muslim rulers recognized the importance of a respectful religious accommodation with the overwhelming Hindu majority. The first Muslim invaders in Sind in the

The rise of the Delhi Sultanate The Muslim Afghan Ghaznavid Empire was the first of a number of Afghan and Turkic powers who, exploiting divisions among local Hindu rulers, established their hegemony in northern India. Based at Delhi, six successive Muslim dynasties commanded varying territorial extents, but only briefly in the mid-fourteenth century did they completely control the Deccan.

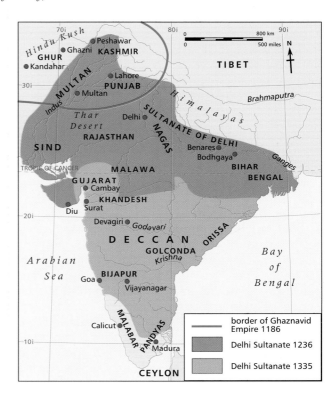

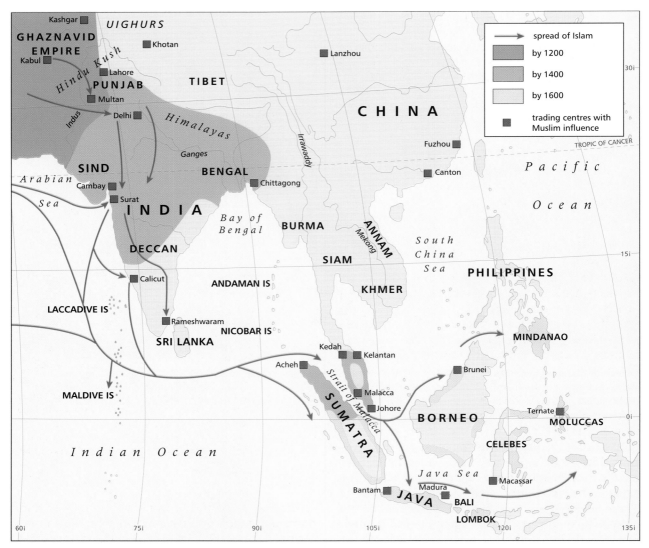

Islam in south and southeast Asia The disruption of centralized political power in the Muslim world did not stop the expansion of Islam in Africa and southern Asia. Arab maritime traders carried their faith to the shores of India and onward throughout maritime southeast Asia. The Indian heartland was conquered by successive waves of Muslim invaders, who, by 1400, secured the key Indo-Gangetic plain.

eighth century extended **dhimmi** status (see Focus, p. 361) to Hindus, arguing that behind the many forms of god in Hinduism there was just one reality, and also recognizing that warfare against so large a majority of Hindus was impossible. Muslims often did deface Hindu and Buddhist shrines. For example, they destroyed the famous Shaivite temple at Somnath, western India, in 1024, and the Turkish forces occupying Bengal and Bihar also destroyed the last remaining libraries and monasteries of Buddhism in that region, delivering the final death blow to a religion that had already seen most of its following in India disappear.

The Muslim conquest of India opened the subcontinent to Persians, Afghans, Turks, and Mongols seeking jobs with the new governments (see Chapter 14). This immigration brought a variety of Islamic practices to India, where no single orthodoxy prevailed. Diverse Muslims coexisted with diverse Hindus, venerating some saints and sharing some devotions in common. India's population became 20–25 percent Muslim. Many were descendants of Muslim immigrants near the top of the social hierarchy; others were converts, escaping untouchability at the bottom of the caste system. The majority of India's population, however, remained Hindu.

SOUTHEAST ASIA

The beginning of mass conversions of southeast Asians to Islam came in the fourteenth and fifteenth centuries, and today, Malaysia and Indonesia are overwhelmingly Muslim. Ocean traders and Sufis from India seem to have accomplished most of the missionary work. The traders offered increased economic opportunities to local people who would adopt Islam, while the Sufis and the regional kings of southeast Asia exchanged support for one another in a familiar pattern of interdependence between religious and political leaders. We will consider this further in Chapter 12.

MOROCCO AND SPAIN

The Arab Umayyads had carried Islam across northern Africa and into Spain by 711. In north Africa, after initial resistance, most of the conquered Berbers converted to Islam. At one extreme, conversion was accompanied by intermarriage, and some of the Arab conquerors and Berber peoples intermingled to the point where it was no longer possible to distinguish among them ethnically. In other cases, whole tribes converted. They became part of the Islamic world, but they remained in their tribal groupings. Often they conducted their own internal administration like a small state.

In 786 Idris (d. 791), a descendant of Ali and Fatima, in rebellion against the Umayyads, led an Arab-Berber coalition and founded the first Moroccan-Islamic state. Other small Berber-Muslim states also sprang up. In the tenth century a coalition of Muslim Berbers founded the Almoravid dynasty. They conquered Morocco, crossed the Straits of Gibraltar, and captured southern Spain, which had been ruled by the Umayyads but was now threatened by Christian powers. By the mid-twelfth century the Almoravids weakened. A new dynasty, the Almohads, followed, also rooted in ascetic Islam and imposing a religious hierarchy on a tribal society. They conquered both Morocco and Spain, but were driven from Spain by Christian forces in 1212 and collapsed in Morocco in 1269, leaving the region with localized governments.

SUB-SAHARAN AFRICA

As in southeast Asia, Islam was carried to sub-Saharan Africa by traders and Sufis from the north. The Arab conquest of north Africa multiplied contacts between Arab and Black Africans, and south

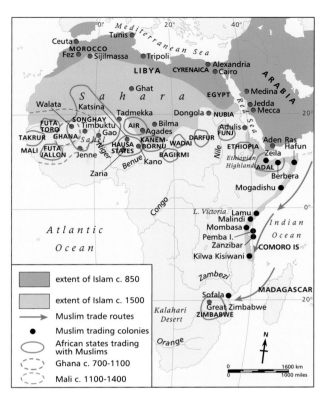

Islam in Africa Islam entered sub-Saharan Africa as a result of trade. Trans-Saharan caravans from Egypt, Libya, and Morocco gradually introduced the faith overland among the trading kingdoms of west Africa, while the Arab traders of the Indian Ocean carried the message south by sea along the east coast of the continent.

of the Sahara new kingdoms were growing, their power derived from their control of the trade routes across the desert. The southern states sent gold, slaves, hides, and ivory to the north in exchange for copper, silver, dried fruit, cloth, and salt. The largest of the states, Ghana, had been founded about 300 C.E., and by the tenth century it was both a partner and a rival of the Berbers for control of the trade. Other nearby states, including Kawkaw, Takrur, and Bornu also participated in this trade. All of them invited Muslim administrators from the north to join their courts. Traders from the north invited their southern counterparts to adopt their religion, and Sufis came to establish new communities of faith and good works. Although the common people were not much affected until the nineteenth century, leading traders and rulers began to convert to Islam, and many participated in both Islamic and indigenous religious practices. Throughout the region, Islam served commercial and administrative as well as religious purposes.

From about 1200 to about 1600, Mali succeeded Ghana as the dominant state of sub-Saharan Africa, and as the center of Islam in the region. Mali's most famous ruler, Mansa Musa (r. 1307–32), made the *hajj* (pilgrimage) to Mecca in 1324, disbursing legendary amounts of gold along the way. By this time, Muslim rulers sought prestige through public affiliation with, and support for, Islamic institutions. They built up Timbuktu, the most important trading city on the Niger River, at its northern bend near the Sahara, into a major center of Arabic and Muslim studies. Through the eighteenth century, Timbuktu remained the focus of Islamic scholarship in sub-Saharan Africa.

SELJUK TURKS AND THEIR SULTANATE

In the seventh and eighth centuries, the consolidation of the Tang dynasty in China revived the pressure on the pastoral, nomadic peoples of inner Asia, pushing them westward, just as the Han had done centuries before (see Chapters 7 and 8). This time the pastoral nomads encountered peoples who had been converted to Islam. As a result of contacts with Muslim scholars and mystics, many of the nomadic peoples converted as well. One of these groups, the Turkish-speaking Qarluq peoples, gained control of Bukhara (992) and Samarqand (999) in modern Uzbekistan. They propagated Islam and began to sponsor the development of the Turkish language and a Turkish-Islamic civilization.

Another Turkish-speaking group, led by the Seljuk (or Saljuq) family, entered central Asia, conquered Afghanistan and Iran, and seized Baghdad in 1055. They proceeded to defeat the Byzantine Empire at Manzikert in 1071, opening Anatolia to further invasion.

In Baghdad, the Seljuk Turks kept the caliph on his throne and ruled in his name. They titled themselves sultans, claiming authority over the secular side of government, while leaving the administration of religious affairs to the caliph. Several of the provincial governments that had already won effective control over their own affairs now also called themselves sultanates. The unity of the Abbasid state dissolved, although the nominal authority of the caliph was still accepted everywhere.

MONGOLS, TURKS, AND THE DESTRUCTION OF THE CALIPHATE

In Karakorum, Mongolia, Temujin (*c.* 1162–1227), later called Genghis Khan ("Universal Ruler"),

Byzantium and Islam The Byzantine Empire remained the bastion of Christian political power in Asia Minor for a thousand years after the fall of Rome. A powerful new force for Islam, the Seljuk Turks, appeared out of central Asia in the eleventh century. After invading Persia and Syria, they defeated a Byzantine army at Manzikert in 1071 and began to infiltrate the Byzantine heartland.

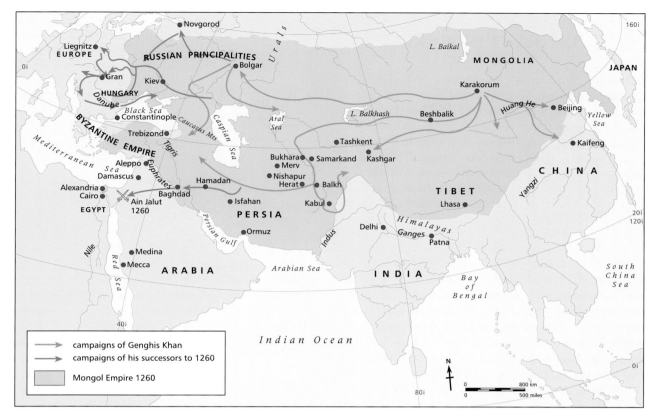

The Mongol world The irruption across Eurasia of the Mongols, an aggressive steppe nomad people, remains one of the most successful military undertakings of all time. Within thirty years the campaigns of Genghis Khan took the Mongol cavalry east to the Chinese heartland and west to Kievan Russia, the Caucasus, and Persia. His immediate successors consolidated China, entered Europe, and went on to establish a network of trans-Asian empires.

forged a confederation of Mongol and Turkish peoples which rode outward, east and west, creating the largest land-based empire in history. The story of the Mongol expansion is told in Chapter 12. Muslims whose lands he conquered felt especially devastated. An eyewitness observer, Ibn al-Athir, records his response to the early waves of invasions in 1220–1:

> For some years I continued averse from mentioning this event, deeming it so horrible that I shrank from recording it. To whom, indeed can it be easy to write the announcement of the death-blow of Islam and the Muslims, or who is he on whom the remembrance thereof can weigh lightly? O would that my mother had not born me, or that I had died and become a forgotten thing ere this befell. …
>
> These [Tartars] spared none, slaying women and men and children, ripping open pregnant women and killing unborn babes. … For these were a people

who emerged from the confines of China, and attacked the cities of Turkistan, like Kashghar and Balasahun, and these advanced on the cities of Transoxiana, such as Samarqand, Bukhara, and the like …

Therefore Islam and the Muslims have been afflicted during this period with calamities wherewith no people hath been visited. (McNeill and Waldman, pp. 249–51).

In 1258, Genghis' grandson Hülegü (c. 1217–65) conquered Baghdad and executed the caliph, ending the Abbasid empire. The Mongols might have continued further on their conquests in west Asia, but the death of Hülegü's brother in China diverted their attention. Meanwhile, the sultan in Cairo defeated the Mongol troops at the Battle of Ain Jalut (1260), near Nazareth, ending their threat of further advance. Mongol rule in west Asia continued, however, until 1336.

SPIRITUAL, RELIGIOUS, AND CULTURAL FLOWERING

When the caliphate fell, the universal Muslim community, the *umma*, seemed to fall with it. Its central political focus was destroyed. Earlier historians have therefore characterized 1258 as a downward turning point, ushering in a protracted decline. More recent writers, however, especially Marshall Hodgson, in his monumental three-volume *The Venture of Islam*, emphasize the continuing growth of Islam outside the Arab world. After 1258 Islam "as a belief system *and* as a world civilization, grew among the peoples of Asia and Africa" (Eaton, p. 24). The descendants of the Mongols themselves converted to Islam within a century of their arrival in Islamic lands. Muslim scholars, mystics, and merchants carried Islam throughout the entire region of the Indian Ocean by sea, and along the length of the silk routes by land. When Timur the Lame (Tamerlane or Tamburlane; 1336–1405) led his Turkish invaders along many of the routes and in many of the same kinds of campaigns as Genghis Khan had done, sacking or capturing Delhi (1398), Aleppo (1400), Damascus (1401), Ankara (1402), and Bukhara (1402), he had the support of Islamic scholars (*ulama*) and mystics (Sufis). Timur's descendants patronized Islamic scholarship and within a century Samarqand and Bukhara had become major capitals of Islamic culture. They also patronized Turkish as a literary language, encouraging its development as the third language of Islam along with Arabic and Persian.

Today, approximately 17 percent of the world's Muslim population lives in southeast Asia, an area never subject to the rule of the caliphate; 30 percent lives in south Asia, where conversion took place almost entirely after its fall; 12 percent lives in sub-Saharan Africa, again virtually untouched by the caliphate. In short, some 60 percent of today's Muslims are descended from peoples who had no connection to the Abbasid caliphate in Baghdad. In the following pages we consider the factors that enabled Islam to flourish and spread as a religion and a civilization even after its historic political center collapsed.

LAW

First, the legal systems of Islam, *shari'a*, lived on. For Muslims, as for Jews, law expresses in formal terms the standards of proper conduct. Law sup-

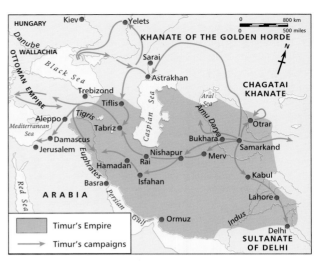

The Empire of Timur The final stage of Mongol power was inspired by Timur's ambitions. Originating in Samarqand, his armies struck east to India, north to the Khanate of the Golden Horde, and west against the Ottoman and Egyptian Mameluke empires. Despite brilliant, brutal, early successes, the empire was unable to sustain its internal dynamics, and its collapse saw the exit of Mongol power from the world stage.

ports the fundamental Islamic duty of *hisba*, "to promote what is right and to prevent what is wrong" (Musallam in Robinson, p. 175). Muslims encounter their legal system in the regulation of public life; in family matters of marriage, divorce, parental responsibilities, and inheritance; and in the *shari'a's* advice on daily activities such as eating, dressing, and housekeeping. As the early caliphs and the Abbasids began to confront legal questions, they appointed *qadis*, or judges, to resolve them. The *qadis* searched the classical texts of the Quran, the *hadith,* and biographies of the Prophet for their core teachings, and then relied on a combination of local custom and their own deliberation and judgment (*ijtihad*) in rendering final decisions.

Seeking to overcome wide differences in local practices, four great legal scholars of the eighth and ninth centuries formulated the major systems of Islamic law that endure till today: the system of Abu Hanifah (699–767) is in use mostly in the Arab Middle East and south Asia; of Malik ibn Anas (*c.* 715–795) in north, central, and west Africa; of Muhammad al-Shafii (767–820) in east Africa, southern Arabia, and southeast Asia; and of Ahmad ibn Hanbal (780–855) in Saudi Arabia. Although most localities have followed one or another of these systems since about the tenth century, the existence of multiple systems has allowed flexibility in interpretation. Under certain circumstances, local legal experts have the option of drawing on any of the four texts. Because Shi'a maintain different traditions of authority, encompassing the teachings of Ali and the early imams, they have also developed different schools of law. The most widespread is that of Jafar al-Sadiq (d. 765).

The *Ulama:* the Scholars and Jurists of Islam

The personnel of the legal system are the **ulama** (singular *alim*), the religiously trained scholars of Islam who interpret and implement the law. The *ulama* constitute a class that includes *qadis* and their assistants, Quran reciters, prayer leaders, and preachers. The *ulama* are sometimes trained in formal theological schools or, more frequently, are simply apprenticed to senior *ulama*. Islam has no formal hierarchical, bureaucratic institution of *ulama*—indeed, it has no official church. Informal networks of respected *ulama* have provided cohesion, stability, and flexibility within Islam, regardless of the changing forms of government.

Ideally, *ulama* and ruler worked together to decide and implement religious policy, but when Caliph al-Mamun (r. 813–833) proclaimed that he had the right to give authoritative interpretations of the Quran, the *ulama* mobilized the population of Baghdad against him. He responded with an inqui-

sition to root out these opponents. The only major leader who stood up to him was Ahmad ibn Hanbal, the greatest *hadith* scholar of his generation, who argued that only the scholars had the authority to interpret Quranic text. The people supported him, and to escape the continuing popular protest, Caliph al-Mutasim (r. 833–842) moved his capital from densely populated Baghdad to Samarra, 60 miles (97 kilometers) away.

In 848–849 the Caliph al-Mutawakkil (d. 861) withdrew the claim of caliphal authority in religious matters. The *ulama* had won, but the battle had so embittered relations between caliph and *ulama* that their spheres of influence were forever separated: the caliph had authority over matters of state; the *ulama* over matters of religion. The caliphs came to represent the imperial aspirations of the state, while the *ulama* represented the everyday needs and wishes of the people. Losing touch with their own people, caliphs employed armies of slaves and of Turkish mercenaries. Over time, such departures from popular accountability cost them the caliphate. But the *ulama* endured, in touch with the people, and serving as their guides.

SUFIS, THE MYSTICS OF ISLAM

Law brings order to life. It makes concrete the responsibilities of one individual to another and to society in general. In Islam it also fixes the formal

Divorce proceedings. A scribe records the accusations of a husband and wife as they petition for a divorce in front of a *qadi*, or judge. A woman had limited rights to divorce her husband, but a man could divorce his wife without stipulating a reason, though in practice matters were rarely this simple. A *qadi* would bring to bear the combined wisdom of scriptural knowledge, local custom, and his own judgment in making an adjudication. (*Bibliothèque Nationale, Paris*)

Delivering a lecture. A traditional saying—"Kings are the rulers of the people, but scholars are the rulers of kings"—indicates the esteem in which learning is traditionally held by Muslims. Moreover, the transmission of knowledge was deemed a major act of piety. A well-stocked library serves as the backdrop for a lecture, in which a teacher would first dictate a text, then discourse upon it. (*Bibliothèque Nationale, Paris*)

obligations due to God; the *ulama* convey and interpret this message.

Sufis, on the other hand, reveal the inner, mystical path to God. Early Sufis found and transmitted the inner disciplines of mind and body, the purifications of the heart that enabled their followers to experience God directly as the ultimate reality. They usually disdained worldly pleasures. One of the earliest of the Sufis, Hasan al-Basri (643–728), concluded: "This world has neither worth nor weight with God, so slight it is" (cited in Esposito, p. 102). Though most Sufis were men, some, like Rabi'a al-Adawiyya (d. 801), were women. Rabi'a, like the Hindu Mirabai (see p. 269), rejected marriage to devote herself to God: "Love of God hath so absorbed me that neither love nor hate of any other thing remain in my heart" (Embree, p. 448).

As we have seen throughout this part, every theistic religion has an aspect of devotional love of god, spontaneous prayer, private meditation, fasting and asceticism, and, often, of physical disciplines, music, dance, and poetry. In Islam these aspects were adopted by the Sufis, who also absorbed influences from the mystics of other religions, especially monasticism from Christianity and Buddhism, and ecstasy in prayer (bhakti, see Source, p. 269) from Hinduism.

Through their lives of exemplary devotion to God and people the Sufis enhanced the message of Islam, as J.S. Trimingham has written in *Sufi Orders in Islam*. They attracted people through the simplicity of their piety, their personal love of God, and their dedication to the needs of others. Some developed reputations for magical powers.

The mosques where they lived and prayed, and the mausolea in which they were buried, were revered as sacred shrines (see Focus, p. 359). Eaton cites such a Sufi saint in a sixteenth-century folk ballad of eastern Bengal:

At that time there came a Mahomedan *pir* [Sufi] to that village. He built a mosque in its outskirts, and for the whole day sat under a fig tree. . . . His fame soon spread far and wide. Everybody talked of the occult powers that he possessed. If a sick man called on him he would cure him at once by dust or some trifle touched by him. He read and spoke the innermost thoughts of a man before he opened his mouth. . . . Hundreds of men and women came every day to pay him their respects. Whatever they wanted they miraculously got from this saint. Presents of rice, fruits, and other delicious food, goats, chickens, and fowls came in large quantities to his doors. Of these offerings the *pir* did not touch a bit but freely distributed all among the poor. (Adas, pp. 21–2)

Individual mystics appeared in Islam from its earliest days, drawing their inspiration directly from the Quran: "I am near to answer the call of the caller, when he calls to Me" (2:182); "We indeed created man; and We know what his soul whispers within him, and We are nearer to him than the jugular vein" (L:15). Centuries later, they began to form **tariqas**, or mystical brotherhoods, often located at the mosque or mausoleum of an especially revered saint. Some *tariqas*, like that attributed to Abu Yazid al-Bistami (d. 874), emphasized ecstatic practices; others, like that of the even more famous Abu'l Qasim al-Junayd (d. 910), were more sober and meditative. The *tariqa mawlawiya* was founded by Jalal-al-Din Rumi (1207–73) in Konya, Turkey. Rumi is most famous for his expression of ecstatic worship through dance. Rumi's Persian language text, the *Mathnawi*, expressed in rich and evocative lyrics his love of God: "The result of religion is nothing but rapture" (Rumi, *Mathnawi* 1:312, cited in Vitray-Meyerovitch, p. 83).

The more solemn *ulama* and the more emotional Sufis were often suspicious of one another. Deeply

Whirling Dervishes. Sufism represents the mystical, contemplative strand of Islam—a strand that is captured vividly by the "Whirling Dervishes," a religious order closely linked to the teachings of the thirteenth-century Persian poet Jalal al-Din Rumi. Their slow, revolving dance helps to create higher states of consciousness, while being a ceremonial ritual in its own right.

PROFILE
Al-Ghazzali
"RENEWER OF ISLAM"

Born and educated in Iran, Abu Hamid Muhammad al-Ghazzali (1058–1111) was appointed at the age of thirty-three to teach philosophy at the leading *madrasa*, or theological institute, in Baghdad. During four years there Ghazzali began to doubt the role of rationality in life and searched for more holistic ways of experiencing the world. Torn between holding his prestigious tenure at the *madrasa* or giving it up to pursue new roads toward truth, Ghazzali was on the verge of breakdown:

> For nearly six months . . . I was continuously tossed about between the attractions of worldly desires and the impulses towards eternal life. In that month the matter ceased to be one of choice and became one of compulsion. God caused my tongue to dry up so that I was prevented from lecturing. One particular day I would make an effort to lecture in order to gratify the hearts of my following, but my tongue would not utter a single word nor could I accomplish anything at all. This impediment in my speech produced grief in my heart, and at the same time my power to digest and assimilate food and drink was impaired; I could hardly swallow or digest a single mouthful of food.
> (al-Ghazzali, p. 57)

In 1095 Ghazzali resigned his post. He traveled to Damascus, Jerusalem, and Mecca, and then returned to his home town, where he lived the monastic life of a Sufi mystic, for ten years:

> I learnt with certainty that it is above all the mystics who walk on the road of God; their life is the best life, their method the soundest method, their character the purest character. (p. 60)

During his time of contemplation, Ghazzali wrote a great number of philosophical and theological works, including the influential *Revival of the Religious Sciences*, exploring the relationship between religion and reason. He asserted the importance of mystical experience and a direct, personal understanding of God, while at the same time defending the doctrine and authority of the Islamic faith.

In 1106 Ghazzali was persuaded to return to teaching, now proclaiming the complementarity of Sufism and rationality:

> Just as intellect is one of the stages of human development in which there is an "eye" which sees the various types of intelligible objects, which are beyond the ken of the senses, so prophecy also is the description of a state in which there is an eye endowed with light such that in that light the unseen and other supra-intellectual objects become visible. (p. 65)

By the end of his life, Ghazzali's reconciliation of Sufism and rationality within Islam had earned him the title "Renewer of Islam."

---

disturbed by the tension between the two perspectives, almost to the point of emotional and psychological breakdown, Abu Hamid Muhammad al-Ghazzali (1058–1111) finally formulated a synthesis of the intellectual and the mystical sides of Islam that has proved satisfying to Muslims ever since (see Profile above).

INTELLECTUAL SYNTHESES

As the *ulama* provided order to the social structures of Islam, and the Sufis spread its spiritual powers, other intellectuals further enriched its cultural depth. The historian and theologian al-Tabari (*c.* 839–923) introduced formal historical writings with his *History of Prophets and Kings*. The segment on prophecy recorded the contributions from Abraham through Muhammad; the record of kings covered rulers from biblical times to his own and included eyewitness reports of relatively recent events.

With the conquest of Iran in the mid-seventh century, Persian became the second language of Islam. (The arrival of the Turks in 923 introduced Turkish as the third.) The Persian poet Ferdowsi (940–1020) wrote an epic poem on the mythical origins of the Persian peoples, in which one of his central themes is the tragedy that befalls "a good man whose king is a fool."

The Mongols also supported historical writing, including al-Juvaini's (1226–83) *History of the World Conquerors,* which told of Genghis Khan's conquests, especially in Iran. Rashid al-Din (1247–1318) wrote *World History*, which many regard as the first attempt at a history of humanity, as it integrates Chinese, Indian, European, Muslim, and Mongol history into a single cosmopolitan perspective.

Ibn Khaldun (1332–1406) of Tunis is often viewed as the first to apply social science theory to the study of history. His *Universal History* stressed a cyclical theory of history, in which vigorous nomadic peoples regularly conquered urban peoples who were settled, cultured, and contented, took over their cities, settled into lives of luxury, and then themselves fell prey to the next round of invasion from more robust nomads. The theory seemed to fit the coming and going of invaders from Arabia, Mongolia, and central Asia that characterized his times. Among Ibn Khaldun's other interpretive themes that still seem insightful today are: "The differences between Easterners and Westerners are cultural [not innate]"(p. 51); "The differences between peoples arise principally from the differences in their occupations" (p. 80); and, perhaps, "Scholars are of all men those least fitted for politics and its ways" (p. 64).

Theology and philosophy had been regarded as inferior to revelation in early Islam, but as Muslims came into contact with the philosophies of the Hellenistic and Indian worlds, they were drawn to concepts of Platonism and Neoplatonism in particular. The caliphate established in Baghdad a "house of wisdom," a translation bureau under Hunayn ibn Ishaq (d. 873). In the next 200 years some eighty Greek authors were translated, including Aristotle, Plato, Galen, and Euclid. So, too, were writings from Syriac, Sanskrit, and Persian.

A group of Islamic philosophers, called *Mutazilites,* "those who keep themselves apart," began to challenge orthodox Islamic belief, arguing that the attributes of God in the Quran were not literal but metaphorical, that human actions and life were not pre-determined, and that the Quran had not existed eternally. Their style of rational argument, called *kalam*, was deeply suspect among most Muslims. One of these men, al-Ashari (873–935), began in the *Mutazilite* camp, but when he was about forty years old, he turned to the orthodox belief that the Quran was indeed the revealed word of God, that only authentic traditions about the Prophet were trustworthy, and that, while rationality was useful within certain limits, it could not equal the truths revealed by God.

Other *Mutazilites* rejected this position. Al-Farabi (*c*. 870–950) argued that philosophical knowledge gained through study and thought was of higher value than revelation from God. Similar notions of the supremacy of philsophy were expressed by al-Kindi (d. 870), Ibn Sina (Avicenna; d. 1037), and Ibn Rushd (Averroes; 1126–98). Such philosophical speculation was marginal to mainstream Islamic thought and actually found more resonance among Christian and Jewish philosophers of the time.

The European Christian thinkers were indebted to the Muslims for keeping alive the Hellenistic traditions, for with the fall of the Roman Empire in the West the intellectual traditions and resources of Christianity had been neglected and forgotten. Now, thanks to Arabic translations and Islamic thought, Christian and Jewish philosophers grappled both with the original texts from Greece and India, and with the newer concepts introduced by Muslim thinkers.

The intersection of intellectual traditions also enriched mathematics, astronomy, and medicine. Indian scholars brought their texts on astronomy to Baghdad as early as 770. The caliph had them translated into Arabic, which was becoming the common language of scholarship throughout the empire. Arabs adopted and transmitted Hindi numerals and the decimal system, including the zero, throughout the empire and on into Europe, where they were (mis)named "Arabic" numerals. A few decades later, al-Khwarazmi (d. *c*. 846) used Indian texts in conjunction with scholarship from Greece and Iran to develop algebra (from the Arabic *al-jabr*, "restoration"). (The word algorithm comes from al-Khwarazmi's name.) Al-Biruni (d. 1046) wrote extensively on number theory and computation, and later scholars developed the trigonometry we study today. Al-Biruni also wrote *al-Qanun al-Mas'udi*, a compendium of Islamic astronomy, which incorporated findings from throughout the empire. Arabic mathematical and astronomical theories apparently informed Copernicus as he proposed a **heliocentric** universe in the sixteenth century (see Chapter 13).

Medical wisdom and herbal remedies were transmitted from one end of the empire to the other. Al-Razi (d. 925) compiled an encyclopedia of medicine, *al-Hawi*, giving the views of Greek, Syrian, Indian, Iranian, and Arab writers on each disease, and including his own clinical observations and opinions. The book was translated into Latin as *Continens*. Ibn Sina, noted above for his contributions to philosophy, produced the even more encyclopedic *Qanun fi'l-tibb* ("Canon of Medicine"), which included volumes on the pharmacology of herbs, the functioning of organs, fevers, and surgery. The *Qanun* was translated into Latin and dominated medical thinking for 300 years.

THE GLOBAL TRANSMISSION OF TECHNOLOGY

By 751, at the end of the Umayyad dynasty, Islam served as a network of communication that linked all the major civilizations of Eurasia. For example, as we noted above on p. 335, Muslims learned paper-making from the Chinese and transmitted the technology throughout their domain. European Christians learned the art from Muslims in Spain.

Andrew Watson's *Agricultural Innovation in the Early Islamic World* discusses the agricultural exchanges and innovation that enriched the world of Islam. Between the eighth and tenth centuries Arabs brought from India hard wheat, rice, varieties of sorghum, sugarcane, bananas, sour oranges, lemons, limes, mangoes, watermelon, coconut palm, spinach, artichokes, eggplants, and the key industrial crop, cotton. All these crops were introduced throughout the empire, wherever climatic conditions were favorable. Watson suggests that this was the largest agricultural exchange in world history up to that time. Because most of these crops from India were warm weather crops, many of them facilitated summer cropping in areas that had previously lain fallow in that season. To replicate the monsoon climate of India, Muslim officials improved existing forms of irrigation (underground water canals and water-lifting mechanisms) and invented new ones (certain kinds of cisterns).

Agricultural productivity diversified and increased, encouraging population increase in general and urban growth in particular.

CITY DESIGN AND ARCHITECTURE

Muslim governments built great cities and adorned their public spaces lavishly and often exquisitely. The largest of the cities were the political capitals. Baghdad was built along the west bank of the Tigris River in 762 to serve as the capital of the Abbasid dynasty, and it served that purpose for almost 500 years. In the ninth century, with between 300,000 and 500,000 people in 25 square miles (65 square kilometers), Baghdad became the largest city in the world west of China. As the caliphate declined, and Baghdad with it, regional capitals grew in importance: Bukhara, Nishapur, and Isfahan in the east, and Cairo, Fez, and Cordoba in the west. The Fatimid rulers of Egypt began their administration in Fustat and expanded that already existing city into al-Qahira, Cairo, in 969. In Morocco, Idris II (r. 791–828) built Fez in 808 as the capital of the Idrisid dynasty, which had been founded by his father. A later dynasty, the Almoravids, built their capital Marrakesh in 1070. In Andalusia, southern Spain, the Umayyads developed Cordoba into one of the most cosmopolitan cities of the Islamic world. It achieved its greatest splendor in the midtenth century, but was sacked by Berbers in 1013 and never fully recovered.

The architecture of these cities proclaimed the splendor of Islam and the power of the Muslim ruler. Although the daily prayers in Islam may be performed privately, Friday noon prayers require collective assembly, so all cities and most neighborhoods within cities also construct mosques for public services. Wealthy rulers proclaimed their power and piety by building monumental central mosques, as they did early on in Jerusalem, Medina, and Damascus. The Abbasids constructed an enormous central mosque in Baghdad, and during the years that Samarra served as their capital a huge mosque was constructed there, too (848–52). Great mosques were also built at Qayrawan in Tunisia, Fez in Morocco, and Cordoba in Spain.

As the Seljuk Turks conquered and then joined the world of Islam, they built an especially monumental mosque at Isfahan in the late eleventh century, and then rebuilt it fifty years later after Ismaili Shi'as burned it down. Ottoman architects, most notably Hoja Sinan (1490–1578), constructed magnificent mosques, such as the Selimiye at Edirne

Mihrab **in the Great Mosque, Cordoba, Spain,** *c. 961–976.* Under the Umayyads, Cordoba grew to be by far the most prosperous city in western Europe, second only to Baghdad in the Islamic world. At its height, the city is said to have contained some 300 public baths and 3000 mosques within its walls. Shown here is the most important surviving example. Great attention was lavished on the decoration of the Great Mosque, and the *mihrab,* a small domed chamber indicating the direction of Mecca, is considered unique for its horseshoe-shaped doorway, a stylistic innovation of the Muslims in Spain.

The Great Mosque and minaret of al-Mutawakkil, Samarra, Iraq, 848–52. Though now only a shadow of its former glory, this 1150-year-old mosque remains the largest of its kind in the world. The three essential elements of simple mosque architecture emerge clearly through the ruins: a central courtyard or atrium, a (formerly) covered sanctuary inside the perimeter walls, and a minaret, or tower, from which the *muezzin* (crier) summons the community to worship.

and the Sulaymaniye in Istanbul, and other public buildings which incorporated Byzantine and Islamic forms. When Islam crossed the Sahara desert, a new architectural form developed, the Sahelian mosque. When Mansa Musa returned from his trip to Mecca in 1325 (see p. 348), he brought with him an Arab architect to supervise the construction of mosques and **madrasas** (theological schools) especially in Timbuktu.

The public architecture of mosques, mausolea, and, to a lesser extent, the royal and governmental buildings that frequently adjoin them, anchored the formal religious and political institutions of the Islamic city. The bazaar, or market area, was home to the business activities. Business in Islam was an honored profession. Muhammad himself had been a caravan operator, and his first wife, Khadija, had been a businesswoman. Even today mosques often control the land immediately adjacent to them and lease it out to businesses so that the rents can support the mosques. Islamic cities were, in effect, nodes on international trade routes linking the Islamic world from China to Morocco and Spain. These trade routes enabled the movement not only

of goods but also of people and ideas from one end of Eurasia to the other (see Chapter 12). The *hajj* (pilgrimage) to Mecca was also instrumental in creating a communication network among the regions and peoples of Islam.

The *Rihla* or travelogues of Ibn Battuta (1304– c. 1368; see Source, p. 360) demonstrate the opportunities for travel open to a person of culture. In thirty years of traveling from his home in Tangier, he traversed approximately 73,000 miles (117,000 kilometers) of territories that today belong to some fifty different countries. Thanks to his mastery of Arabic and his knowledge of *shari'a*, he found a welcome reception, and frequently temporary employment and gifts of wives and wealth in the lands he traversed. Muhammad Tughluq, sultan of Delhi, appointed him a *qadi* and, later, his envoy to China. Ibn Battuta's tales of adventure reflect the unity of the Islamic world. Despite its diversity, this world was held together by reverence for the Quran, the *shari'a*, the Arabic language (supplemented by Persian and Turkish), the rulers who ruled in its cities, and the scholars and merchants who traveled through them.

Mausolea in Islam

Because Islam teaches that all the dead should be honored, and that the saintly among them could confer blessings, mausolea have a special significance and sanctity. The followers of Timur (Tamerlane), for example, built for him an enormous tomb at Samarqand in 1405. Some mark personal love and devotion. Perhaps the best known of all Islamic buildings, the Taj Mahal in Agra, India, was built by the Emperor Shah Jahan as a mausoleum for his wife Mumtaz Mahal, who died giving birth to their fifteenth child. At a much more humble level, simple tombs of local saints are found throughout the Islamic world, attracting followers, especially women, who pour out their hearts in prayer, trusting that the sanctity of the saint will carry it to God.

The Taj Mahal, Agra, India, 1632–48.

Bronzesmith, Isfahan bazaar, Iran. In Islam religion and business are integrally linked, in that the land adjoining mosques is often leased to market traders whose rents support the buildings and their activities. Here a bronzesmith works outside his shop in the bazaar at Isfahan, which has been thriving since the third century C.E.

RELATIONS WITH NON-MUSLIMS

ISLAM AND THE SWORD

Early Islamic governments spread by the sword. As a result, popular belief in the West has held that the religion of Islam spread in the same way. Although conversion by force was practiced occasionally, by and large it was not. For example, as we have noted, the early "rightly guided" caliphs and the early Umayyads did not seek to convert the people they conquered. They wanted to rule as Arab Muslim conquerors over non-Arab, non-Muslim subjects. Only when the later Umayyads feared that they could not continue minority rule over so large a majority, did they decide actively to seek

Ibn Battuta's Observations on Gender Relations

Ibn Battuta (1304–c. 1368) learned his concepts of gender relations in the Arab heartland of Islam. As he traveled he was often astonished, and sometimes shocked, by the status of women in other Islamic countries. In the Turkish and Mongol regions between the Black and Caspian Seas, wives of local, ruling khans (sultans) owned property. When the senior wife appeared at the khan's residence, Ibn Battuta observes, the khan (sultan)

> advances to the entrance to the pavilion to meet her, salutes her, takes her by the hand, and only after she has mounted to the couch and taken her seat does the sultan himself sit down. All this is done in full view of those present, and without any use of veils.
> (Dunn, p. 168)

In the Maldive Islands, in the Indian Ocean, Ibn Battuta was even more scandalized:

> Their womenfolk do not cover their hands, not even their queen does so, and they comb their hair and gather it at one side. Most of

them wear only an apron from their waists to the ground, the rest of their bodies being uncovered. When I held the *qadiship* there, I tried to put an end to this practice and ordered them to wear clothes, but I met with no success. No woman was admitted to my presence in a lawsuit unless her body was covered, but apart from that I was unable to effect anything.
(McNeill, p. 276)

In Mali, west Africa, female slaves and servants went publicly into the ruler's court completely naked. When Ibn Battuta found a scholar's wife chatting with another man, he complained to the scholar and was put in his place,

> The association of women with men is agreeable to us and a part of good conduct, to which no suspicion attaches. They are not like the women of your country.
> (Dunn, p. 300)

Ibn Battuta left immediately and never returned to the man's home.

---

conversion of, and alliance with, the conquered peoples. A principal goal of conquest, however, remained the creation of a *dar al-Islam*, a rule under which Islam could be practiced freely. This did not mean that the people of the land were forced to become Muslims, only that the Muslims among them must have the freedom to practice their religion and sustain their culture.

Later, when many Muslims lived under non-Muslim governments, the *ulama* declared that any government that permitted freedom of religion to Muslims could be a *dar al-Islam*. The alternative was a *dar al-Harb*, an "abode of war," which had to be opposed because it restricted the practice of Islam.

THE CRUSADES

At opposite ends of the Mediterranean, Muslims and Christians fought each other in war. The crusades (1095–1291) were perhaps more political and economic than religious in motive. After Arab armies captured Jerusalem in 638, they built new, glorious mosques to indicate their own dominance, but they allowed Christians to continue their religious practices without hindrance and permitted Jews to return to Jerusalem officially for the first time since their exile by the Romans in 70 C.E. (see p. 304). Only centuries later, after Muslim Turkish armies won the Battle of Manzikert in 1071 and opened Anatolia to conquest, did the Byzantine emperor, Alexius I, call on Pope Urban II to help fight the Muslims and to recapture Jerusalem and the "Holy Land." The pope seized this opportunity to unite western Europe and its various rulers under his own banner in the name of religion.

FOCUS
Dhimmi Status

Non-Muslims were offered three choices. The first was to convert to Islam. The second was to accept "protected," *dhimmi*, status as worshipers of one God who accepted Muslim rule. All the monotheistic "peoples of the book," were eligible for this status, including Christians, Jews, and Zoroastrians. Later, Islamic governments in India also extended *dhimmi* status to Hindus. The *dhimmi* were often required to pay a special poll tax, but they could follow their own religion and their own personal law regarding marriage, divorce, and inheritance, and they were to be protected by the Muslim government. The third option was to fight against the Muslim state, an option that was chosen least often.

The status of the *dhimmi* was spelled out in "The Pact of Umar," a document ascribed to Umar II (r. 634–644). This document prescribed second-class status for the *dhimmi*. They were not to build new houses of worship nor to reconstruct old ones. They were not to convert anyone to their religion. They were not to wear the same clothing as Muslims, but to wear distinguishing garments. The sounds of their prayers, their calls to prayer, and their funeral processions were to be muted. Their houses were not to be higher than the houses of Muslims. The poll tax, however, was not mentioned in this document. Perhaps designed to encourage non-Muslims to gain first-class citizenship by converting, these rules were nevertheless not crippling to life, and, indeed, they were often not implemented. Travelers throughout the Muslim world noted that Jews and Christians often held some of the highest positions in public and private life and were self-governing in their religious life (see below).

THE CRUSADES

First Crusade (1095–9)	Proclaimed by Pope Urban II, the crusade was motivated by the occupation of Anatolia and Jerusalem by the Seljuk Turks. The crusaders recaptured Jerusalem and established several Latin kingdoms on the Syrian coast.
Second Crusade (1147–9)	Led by Louis VII of France and the Holy Roman Emperor, Conrad III, this was a disaster from the crusaders' point of view.
Third Crusade (1189–92)	Mounted to recapture Jerusalem, which had been taken by Saladin in 1187. Personal rivalry between the leaders, Philip II Augustus of France and Richard I of England, undermined the crusaders' unity.
Fourth Crusade (1202–04)	This crusade against Egypt was diverted, at the instigation of the Venetians, to sack and divide Constantinople, which led to half a century of western rule over Byzantium.
Children's Crusade (1212)	Thousands of children crossed Europe on their way to Palestine. Untold numbers were sold into slavery in Marseilles, France, or died of disease and malnutrition.
Fifth Crusade (1218–21)	King Andrew of Hungary, Cardinal Pelagius, King John of Jerusalem, and King Hugh of Cyprus captured, then lost, Damietta, Egypt.
Sixth Crusade (1228–9)	The Holy Roman Emperor, Frederick II (r. 1212–50), led the crusade that, through negotiation with the sultan of Egypt, recovered Jerusalem. The city was finally lost in 1244.
Seventh Crusade (1249–54) and Eighth (1270–91)	Both led by Louis IX of France (r. 1226–70), who was inspired by religious motives, but both were personal disasters. Louis was later canonized.

Illustration of the Second Crusade (1147–9). Lance-bearing Christian forces face a Muslim army in this scene from the Second Crusade. The fleur-de-lys emblem, here sported on his shield by the French king, Louis VII, was adopted at almost the same time by his opponent, the ruler of Aleppo. (*British Library, London*)

Christian rulers, knights, and merchants were also driven by their own political and military ambitions and by the promise of trade opportunities that would accompany the establishment of a Latin kingdom in the Middle East (Esposito, p. 60).

At first, the European Christian crusaders were successful and brutal. In 1099 they captured Jerusalem, killing all its Muslim residents, men, women, and children. They turned the Dome of the Rock into a church and the adjacent al-Aqsa mosque into an official residence. At the time, Muslim leadership in the region was divided and did not respond. Then Salah al-Din (Saladin) (*c.* 1137–93), who had established a new dynasty in Egypt, recaptured Jerusalem in 1187. But more crusades followed, often revealing very worldly motives. When Richard I, the Lion-Heart (r. 1189–99), captured Acre on the Mediterranean coast in the Third Crusade (1189–92), he also massacred its men, women, and children. By 1291, however, Muslim forces had reconquered Acre and all other crusader outposts. Although four minor crusades followed, none succeeded in capturing and holding any outposts in the Holy Land.

The crusader soldiers themselves were largely mercenaries who sought their own benefit and who attacked many in their path for their own profit. As early as 1096, *en route* overland to Jerusalem on the First Crusade, they paused to slaughter Jews. In 1204, during the Fourth Crusade, Roman Catholic armies, acting against the direct orders of the pope, attacked the city of Zara in Croatia and Constantinople, the capital of the Byzantine Empire, their presumed ally. Instead of uniting Christianity and defeating the Muslims, the crusaders had divided Christianity and were defeated by the Muslims.

CONNECTION: *Europe during the Middle Ages and the Renaissance, pp. 394–407*

A GOLDEN AGE IN SPAIN

At the other end of the Mediterranean, in Spain, Islam flourished, and with it the Christian and Jewish communities of the peninsula. Through a century of immigration, conquest, administration, and intermarriage, Umayyad and Berber invaders brought Islam to a central position in Spain. They also revitalized trade by breaking the monopoly of Byzantine control over the western Mediterranean. They introduced new crops and new irrigation techniques from west Asia (see p. 356). Abd al-Rahman III (912–961) asserted his separation from the Abbasids by declaring himself a caliph rather than just a sultan. A series of rulers expanded the ornate mosque at Cordoba, making it one of the architectural showcases of Islam.

Eastern scholars of law and philosophy immigrated to the flourishing court. Poets developed new styles, based in Arabic but also influenced by local Spanish and Latin styles. Greek philosophical and medical treatises were translated into Latin as well as Arabic, thus opening intellectual communication with the educated classes in Christendom. Although some Christians revolted against Islamic and Arabic inroads, and were killed in battle (850–859), many more adopted Arabic lifestyles.

By 1030, the caliphate in Spain had disintegrated. Various armed struggles broke out between the provinces and the capital, townsmen and rural Berber immigrants, and converts and Arabs. The conflicts did not, however, impede the spread of Islam. As in the eastern Mediterranean, provincial administrations replaced the central caliphate and brought the culture of their courts closer to the general population. Sufis spread their ascetic and devotional teachings.

The vacuum in the central government did, however, provide an opening to various Christian forces to begin the *reconquista*, the reconquest of Spain. In 1085 Alfonso VI (r. 1065–1109) captured Toledo. Two successive Arab/Berber dynasties invading from Morocco, the Almoravids and Almohads, could not stem the Christian advance. By the mid-thirteenth century all of Spain with the exception of Granada was in Christian hands. Granada fell in 1492 to the unified kingdom of Ferdinand and Isabella. Muslim rule in Spain was broken.

During the years of the *reconquista*, culture continued to flourish. The Almohads, for example, patronized Ibn Rushd (known to Christians as Averroes; 1126–98), who linked rationalist thought in Islam with that of earlier Greeks and contemporary Christians. But the Almohads did persecute others, including the family of the Jewish physician, philosopher, and theologian Moses Maimonides (1135–1204), forcing them to flee until they finally found a home in Cairo, where Maimonides became court physician to the sultan Salah al-Din.

Until the mid-thirteenth century, Christian rulers in Spain patronized the rich, hybrid culture. They translated the Bible, the Talmud, and the Quran into Castilian. Arabic texts on astrology and astronomy, and the philosophical works of Muslim thinkers, including al-Kindi, al-Farabi, and Ibn Sina (Avicenna), were translated into Castilian and Latin, as was Maimonides' philosophy. Spain was the entry-way into western Europe for classical writings and their reworking through the prism of Islamic civilization.

By the fourteenth century, however, Christianity became triumphal and intolerant. In 1391, Jews were forced to accept baptism. In 1480 the Roman Catholic Church in Spain established an inquisition to hunt down Jews and Muslims who had not converted. (Later it also attacked Protestants.) In 1492 the Jewish population was expelled from Spain, and in 1501 Muslims had to choose between exile and conversion to Christianity. In 1566 Arabic was banned in Spain, and in 1609 all Muslims were

SPOTLIGHT
The Alhambra

The peculiar charm of this old dreamy palace is its power of calling up vague reveries and picturings of the past, and thus clothing naked realities with the illusions of the memory and the imagination.
(Cited in Grabar, p. 203.)

So wrote American author Washington Irving of the Alhambra in Granada, Spain, as he saw it in the early 1800s. The fourteenth-century Spanish complex of buildings called in Arabic "Qalat al-hamra," the red citadel, had conveyed a lasting vision of illusion and reality intertwined.

With the fall of Seville to the Christian *reconquista* in 1248, Granada remained as the only Islamic kingdom in Spain. Nestled on a spur of the Sierra Nevada mountains in the south, the city flourished thanks to an influx of talented Muslims fleeing the advancing Christian armies, and the enterprise and vigor of its rulers. Two of them, Kings Yusuf I (1333–54) and Muhammad V (1354–9, 1362–91) of the Nasrid dynasty, had most of the buildings of the Alhambra that still stand today built to serve as their home, a city within a city. Their legacy is today the best-preserved palace of medieval Spain, referred to by art historian Oleg Grabar as the "perfect expression of a unique regional tradition" (p. 205).

The Old Royal Palace, the heart of the Alhambra complex, is an ensemble of courtyards flanked by arcades and connected by "secret passageways and small doors [that] led . . . from one marvelous architectural setting to the next"

Figure 1   The Court of the Lions.

(Grabar, p. 114). Among the most elegant of the courts are the Hall of the Ambassadors, where the king's throne may have been placed for public audiences; the Court of the Myrtles, a rectangular court, 120 by 77 feet (36.6 x 23.5 m), centered on a 24 ½ foot (7.15 m) wide pool running almost its full length; and the Court of Lions with its central fountain encircled by a dozen stone lions whose mouths are water spouts (**figure 1**). The geometry of design of the courtyards finds its counterpoint in the richness of ornamentation for which the Alhambra is equally famous, for example in its many "stalactite" domes like the one in the Hall of the Two Sisters (**figure 2**). The adjoining gardens and pools within the walls of the Alhambra (**figure 3**) and in the Generalife gardens about 656 feet (200 m) distant, all meticulously arranged in accord with Islamic traditions of landscaping, complete a regal composition of fantasy and elegance.

In 1492, Granada fell, ending all Islamic rule in Spain, and in 1501 Muslims were forced to convert or to leave. The old era had passed. Patronage for new architectural ventures would henceforth come from Christian rulers and, indeed, in 1526 King Charles V gave orders for the construction of his own royal palace, built to a very different aesthetic, which today stands immediately adjacent to the Old Royal Palace within the walls of the Alhambra. The old order had come to an end.

Figure 2 Stucco decoration in the Hall of the Two Sisters.

Figure 3 Pools and pavilions in the Alhambra gardens.

expelled from Spain. The golden age of religious tolerance and cultural exchange was over.

CONVERSION AND ASSIMILATION: HOW DO WE KNOW?

Only in the last two decades has serious research been done on conversion to Islam, asking exactly how the process worked. Three works stand out. Nehemia Levtzion edited a set of studies on *Conversion to Islam* in 1979 examining the motives of converts. Levtzion argued that "assimilation" was a better term than "conversion" for describing the process of becoming a Muslim. People in conquered areas, especially, were not so much overwhelmed by political conquest as they were impressed with the richness of the culture that Islam brought to them. They found that their lives were enriched by the rituals, philosophy, art, and sense of belonging to a world system that came with joining the *umma*, the Islamic community.

Richard Bulliet's *Conversion to Islam in the Medieval Period: An Essay in Quantitative History* demonstrates that conversion took place at different rates of speed in each of the six societies he examines: Arabia, Egypt, Iraq, Syria, Iran, and Spain. He notes the problems of finding data to understand the process, since "medieval Islam produced no missionaries, bishops, baptismal rites, or other indicators of conversion that could be conveniently recorded by the Muslim chronicler" (p. 4). For data, Bulliet examines the speed of adoption of Muslim names in each of the six societies. He concludes that rapid acceptance of Islam went hand in hand with a breakdown in central political rule. As centralized Islamic rule broke down, paradoxically, Sufis carried the word of Islam more freely and with more backing from local governments.

We also know of the very large-scale assimilation to Islam by the Mongol successors of Genghis Khan and of the followers of Timur the Lame (Tamerlane). These ruling groups were assimilated by Islam because the new civilization they encountered offered them cultural, political, social, economic, and spiritual rewards that were not available in the religions and cultures of their birth. Their biological and cultural descendants helped to establish the great Islamic empires of the fifteenth through the eighteenth centuries: the Ottomans based in Turkey, the Safavids in Iran, and the Mughals in India (see Chapter 15).

Richard Eaton's *The Rise of Islam and the Bengal Frontier: 1204–1760* compares records of land development with records of religious assimilation. Eaton finds that in eastern Bengal (modern Bangladesh) Islam was most successful in frontier areas being brought under cultivation for the first time. In such areas several factors encouraged the assimilation of Islam: first, no world religion had already captured the field; second, a government headed by Muslims encouraged settlers to develop the frontier and favored Muslims in disbursing titles to the land and in tax policies; third, Muslim land developers, sometimes, but not always, very devout in their practices, came to develop and farm the land and in the process introduced the message of Islam to this new region; and, fourth, local peoples who had not been integrated into the Hindu system came to work the land under the direction of Muslims and, following their example, began to assimilate Islam into their own lives. Eaton points out that conversion was not instantaneous, but a process that occurred gradually through two or three generations. Families integrated more and more Islamic ideas and practices into their lives until, finally, they accepted Islam fully.

Finally, the great assimilation that took place outside the heartlands of Islamic conquest, in sub-Saharan Africa and southeast Asia, was carried by traders and later supported by Sufis and *ulama*. In both these huge areas, the trade networks by land and sea were so densely worked by Muslims that indigenous traders began to assimilate Islam into their lives, either from religious conviction or from the promise of trade advantage. They stayed to join in one of the world's richest and most wide-spread civilizations, the *umma* of Islam. By 1500, despite its losses in Spain, Islam dominated much of the eastern hemisphere as a world religion, a polity, a people, and a civilization.

JUDAISM, CHRISTIANITY, AND ISLAM: WHAT DIFFERENCE DOES IT MAKE?

As monotheistic religions, sharing common ancestors, belief in divinely given written scriptures, and common rituals and practices, such as regular prayer and charity; valuing pilgrimage and sharing many common holy places; promising that behavior will receive its proper rewards and punishments in the future, on earth and in an afterlife; balancing and integrating strands of mysticism, legalism, and pious devotion; the three religions of Judaism, Christianity, and Islam would appear to be naturally suited to co-existence and even to mutual reinforcement. And indeed at times, notably in Spain, during much, but not all, of the period from about 750 to about 1250, the three faiths coexisted and gladly learned from one another. But such warm, reciprocally beneficial coexistence has been the exception rather than the rule.

Perhaps two factors can explain the hostility that has often characterized the relationships among these religions. First all three have been proselytizing religions—although Judaism abandoned this practice early in the Christian era—and their very closeness has made them bitterly competitive. Each has had some feeling that it has come the closest to the essential truths of God and the world, and that the others have somehow failed to recognize this. Both Christianity and Islam, for example, accuse Judaism of stubbornly refusing to accept later revelations that modify and update its original truths. Both Judaism and Islam accuse Christianity of a kind of idolatry in claiming that God begat a son who was actually a form of God and who walked the earth in human form. Both Judaism and Christianity argue that God did not give a special, final revelation to Muhammad. In each case these religions have looked at one another and said that, despite elements of deep commonality, there exist also fundamental heresies. Indeed within each of these religions, at various times, splits have turned one group against another amidst cries of heresy and calls to armed opposition. Truth was to be maintained, asserted, and defended through the force of arms. (Religions with less insistence on doctrinal correctness, such as Hinduism and Buddhism, have had less, and less bitter, religious warfare.)

Second, as each religion developed, it sought the support of government. It often sought to be the government. Truth was to be reinforced by power. Basic competition over spiritual and philosophical truths spilled over into competition also for tax monies, office, land, and public acceptance of specific ritual and architectural symbols, and suppression of opposition. When they could, these religions marched through the world armed. The idea that the state and religion should be separated appeared as early as Augustine; but until recently, in the lands where these three religions predominated, the state and religion were usually intimately bound up with one another, and in many places the religion of the leader of the state was expected to be accepted as the religion of his subjects, or at least to be given preferred treatment over others.

Historically, Christianity came to dominate the European lands formerly held by the Roman Empire and, as we shall see, traveled with its European faithful to the New World. Islam dominated North Africa and the Asian lands formerly held by the Persian and Alexandrine empires, and it traveled with armies, saints, and traders to India and southeast Asia (see maps, pp. 345 and 346). Judaism, which lost out to its younger successors both in numbers and in gaining the support of governments, remained everywhere a minority religion, dependent on the tolerance of others. (This identification of different religions with particular parts of the world was typical also of Hinduism, identified with India and, to a much lesser extent, with southeast Asia; and of Buddhism, identified with the Indian subcontinent, east and southeast Asia, and the routes connecting them.)

Nevertheless, amidst the carving up of the world into zones of religious dominance backed by supportive governments, and frequent warfare among religious groups, there were also times of mutually beneficial co-existence, sharing of cultures, and recognition of the commonalities of these religions and of the common humanity of their faithful. In many regions like the Middle East, and in cities along the various trade routes all over the world, members of different religions lived side-by-side, often developing mutual understanding, respect, and trust. And always the voice of the mystic, like that of Jalal al-Din Rumi, called out for recognition of the oneness of God and the unity of God's universe:

> What is to be done, O Moslems? for I do not recognize myself.
> I am neither Christian, nor Jew, nor Gabr [Zoroastrian], nor Moslem.
> I am not of the East, nor of the West, nor of the land, nor of the sea;
> I am not of Nature's mint, nor of the circling heavens.
> I am not of earth, nor of water, nor of air, nor of fire;
> I am not of the empyrian, nor of the dust, nor of existence, nor of entity.
> I am not of India, nor of China, nor of Bulgaria, nor of Saqsin;
> I am not of the kingdom of Iraqain, nor of the country of Khorasan.

I am not of this world, nor of the next, nor of Paradise, nor of Hell;
I am not of Adam, nor of Eve, nor of Eden and [the angel] Rizwan.
My place is the Placeless, my trace is the Traceless;

'Tis neither body nor soul, for I belong to the soul of the Beloved.
I have put duality away, I have seen that the two worlds are one;
One I seek, One I know, One I see, One I call.

(McNeill and Waldman, p. 242)

BIBLIOGRAPHY

Adas, Michael. *Islamic and European Expansion* (Philadelphia: Temple University Press, 1993).

Ahmed, Leila. *Women and Gender in Islam* (New Haven: Yale University Press, 1992).

Bulliet, Richard W. *Conversion to Islam in the Medieval Period: An Essay in Quantitative History* (Cambridge: Harvard University Press, 1979).

Dunn, Ross E. *The Adventures of Ibn Battuta* (Berkeley: University of California Press, 1986).

Eaton, Richard M. "Islamic History as Global History," in Adas, *op. cit.*, 1–36.

Eaton, Richard M. *The Rise of Islam and the Bengal Frontier, 1204–1760* (Berkeley: University of California Press, 1993).

Embree, Ainslee T., ed. *Sources of Indian Tradition, Volume I: From the Beginning to 1800* (New York: Columbia University Press, 2nd ed., 1988).

Esposito, John. *Islam: The Straight Path* (New York: Oxford University Press, 1991).

Ferdowsi. *The Legend of Seyavash* (London: Penguin Books, 1992).

al-Ghazzali. *The Faith and Practice of al-Ghazali*, trans. W. Montgomery Watt (London: Allen and Unwin, 1953).

Grabar, Oleg. The Alhambra (Cambridge: Harvard University Press, 1978).

Hodgson, Marshall G.S. *Rethinking World History: Essays on Europe, Islam, and World History*, ed. Edmund Burke III (Cambridge: Cambridge University Press, 1993).

——. *The Venture of Islam*, 3 vols. (Chicago: University of Chicago Press, 1974).

Ibn Khaldun. *An Arab Philosophy of History*, ed. Charles Issawi (London: John Murray, 1950).

Ikram, S.M. *Muslim Civilization in India* (New York: Columbia University Press, 1964).

Johns, Jeremy. "Christianity and Islam," in John McManners, ed. *The Oxford Illustrated History of Christianity* (Oxford: Oxford University Press, 1990), 163–95.

Keddie, Nikki R. and Beth Baron, eds. *Women in Middle Eastern History* (New Haven: Yale University Press, 1991).

The Koran trans. N.J. Dawood (London: Penguin Books, 1990).

The Koran Interpreted trans. A.J. Arberry (New York: Macmillan Publishing Co., 1955).

Lapidus, Ira M. *A History of Islamic Societies* (Cambridge: Cambridge University Press, 1988).

Levtzion, Nehemia, ed. *Conversion to Islam* (New York: Holmes and Meier, 1979).

Lewis, Bernard, ed. and trans. *Islam from the Prophet Muhammad to the Capture of Constantinople*, 2 vols. (New York: Oxford University Press, 1987).

Lewis, Bernard. *Islam and the West* (New York: Oxford University Press, 1993).

McNeill, William H. and Marilyn Robinson Waldman, eds. *The Islamic World* (Chicago: University of Chicago Press, 1983).

Morony, Michael. *Iraq after the Muslim Conquest* (Princeton: Princeton University Press, 1984).

Nashat, Guity. "Women in the Middle East, 8000 B.C.–A.D. 1800," in *Restoring Women to History*, eds. Cheryl Johnson-Odim and Margaret Strobel. (Bloomington: Organization of American Historians, 1988).

Robinson, Francis, ed. *The Cambridge Illustrated History of the Islamic World* (Cambridge: Cambridge University Press, 1996)

Seltzer, Robert M. *Jewish People, Jewish Thought* (New York: Macmillan Publishing, 1980).

Time-Life Books. *Time Frame AD 1200–1300: The Mongol Conquests* (Alexandria, VA: Time-Life Books, 1989).

——. *Time Frame AD 1300–1400: The Age of Calamity* (Alexandria, VA, 1989).

Trimingham, John S. *Sufi Orders in Islam* (Oxford: Oxford University Press, 1971).

Times Atlas of World History, ed. Geoffrey Barraclough (London: Times Books, 1979).

Tucker, Judith. "Gender and Islamic History," in Adas, *op. cit.*, pp. 37–74.

Vitray-Meyerovitch, Eva de. *Rumi and Sufism* (Sausalito, CA: Post-Apollo Press, 1987).

Watson, Andrew. *Agricultural Innovation in the Early Islamic World* (Cambridge: Cambridge University Press, 1983).

Map of Venice and the lagoon from the Kitab-I Bahriye ("Book of Seafaring") of Piri Reis, written in 1521. By the early 1500s, seafarers and navigators shared information even across competitive civilizational boundaries. Piri Reis, an Ottoman Turkish Muslim admiral made extensive use of Arab, Portuguese, and Spanish maps and charts as he prepared his own navigational texts. Here he has produced a map of Venice, the greatest of the European, Christian ports on the Mediterranean. On another of his maps, from 1513, America appears on the Atlantic almost exactly as Columbus charted it. Within a few years America appeared also on Chinese maps. *(The al-Sabah Collection, Dar al-Athar al-Islamiyyah, Kuwait)*

World Trade

CHANNELS OF COMMUNICATION: THE EXCHANGE OF COMMODITIES, DISEASES, AND CULTURE

In earlier parts of this book we have touched on economic systems and the importance of trade in regional and world economies. Trade linked the oldest centers of urban civilization—Mesopotamia, the Indus valley, and the Nile valley—as we noted in Part 2. In Part 3 we saw that empires sought to secure the principal transportation routes and that the imperial rulers usually controlled a substantial part of their trade. Finally, in Part 4 we noted that world religions spread along the same routes as trade, and that religions were often carried by the merchants themselves as well as by more formal official representations. Both Buddhism and Islam spread to eastern Asia via the overland silk routes, and to southeast Asia via the shipping lanes of the Indian Ocean. The exchange of commodities went hand in hand with the exchange of ideas.

In this part we will look more closely at the traders, the trade routes, and the importance of trade and economics in world history between 1100 and 1776. This part has two chapters, divided about the year 1500, when a series of voyages by Christopher Columbus, Ferdinand Magellan, and other explorer-traders demonstrated conclusively that the world was a globe; revealed that there were continental land masses in both the western and the eastern hemispheres; and linked these hemispheres in continuous relationships of economic and cultural exchange.

The first chapter of this part describes the patterns and the philosophies of world trade prior to this linkage. It indicates the importance of the pre-1500 networks in the establishment of the later systems.

Marco Polo, from *Romance of Alexander, c.* 1340.

The second chapter examines the changes in world trade patterns and economic philosophies from 1500 to 1776, when the publication of Adam Smith's *Wealth of Nations* signaled the arrival of a new philosophy of world trade and economics, later called capitalism. Smith applauded the work of private businesspeople who were pursuing their own profit, and proclaimed them the chief engine of progressive change in world history. He opposed governmental and religious control of trade, the pattern we shall most frequently encounter before 1500. Smith's word was not final, and the philosophy of capitalism is still debated today, reviled by some, extolled by others, but significant to virtually all debates over the larger questions of economics and to many questions of politics, culture, and religion as well. Debates over the capitalist system versus other forms of economic organization open this chapter and reappear frequently in Parts 7 and 8.

12 ESTABLISHING WORLD TRADE ROUTES

1100—1500 C.E.

"A growing mountain of hard evidence … indicates indubitably that the whole of Eurasia was culturally and technologically interconnected [by about 1500 B.C.E.]"

VICTOR H. MAIR

"Stadtluft macht frei" –"City air makes one free."

GERMAN PROVERB

THE PATTERNS AND PHILOSOPHIES OF EARLY ECONOMIC SYSTEMS

TRADE AND TRADERS: GOALS AND FUNCTIONS

Today long-distance, international trade forms a substantial part of the world's commerce and includes even the most basic products of everyday food and clothing. In earlier times, long-distance trade was only a small fraction of overall trade, mostly supplying luxury goods for the upper classes: silks, gold, spices, and the like (see Spotlight, pp. 386–9). Because these goods were valuable relative to their weight, merchants could carry them over long distances and still sell them for handsome profits. The buyers were mostly wealthy, for only they could afford such luxuries. Some commercial goods, like raw wool and cotton, were also traded over medium distances, a few hundred miles. The transportation costs

were justified as these goods became more valuable after importation when they were manufactured into finished products.

The largest part of the exchange economy was in local transactions—food crops traded for local hand manufactures or raw materials. These goods were necessities but they had little value in relationship to their weight; the cost of transportation was a substantial part of their final price. They were, therefore, traded only over short distances. Often, they were bartered in exchange for other local goods rather than sold for money in more distant markets. This exchange of local goods is a fundamental part of local and regional history, but the study of world history focuses on long-distance exchange and its importance in knitting together distant regions of the world. Trade provides an index of economic vitality. It also stimulates economic growth; people produce goods and provide services only if markets exist for them. (Anyone who has ever looked for a job has experienced this. If jobs exist, they work; if jobs do not exist, they remain unemployed and economically unproductive.)

WORLD TRADE: AN HISTORICAL ANALYSIS

Historians studying world trade seek to understand its purposes, conditions, and regulations. We ask about social as well as economic values. For example: What benefits are achieved by each different system of trade? Which systems benefit which members of society? Which systems harm which members of society? What are the trade-offs in benefits and losses under each system?

Some of the most provocative explorations of the history of trade originated in public policy debates in the United States and Europe following the Great Depression. That economic collapse of the 1930s, discussed in Chapter 18, challenged the advocates of market-based, free-trade economies. Traders in a **free market economy** seek personal

MEDIEVAL WORLD TRADE

DATE C.E.	POLITICAL/ SOCIAL EVENTS	TRADE DEVELOPMENTS	EXPLORATION
1050	• Normans under William I invade England (1066) • Seljuk Turks take Baghdad • Franks invade Anatolia and Syria and found Crusader states • Almoravids destroy Kingdom of Ghana (1067)	• Venice dominates Adriatic; trading ports set up throughout eastern Mediterranean (1000–1100)	
1100		• Age of Great Zimbabwe in southern Africa • Wool trade flourishing between England and Flanders	
1150	• Salah al-Din, sultan of Turkish Syria and Egypt, retakes Jerusalem (1187) • St. Francis of Assisi (1181–1226) • St. Dominic (1170–1221) • St. Clare of Assisi (1194–1253)	• Market fairs in the Champagne region, France • Paper–making spreads from Muslim world	
1200	• Foundation of first Muslim empire in India • Genghis Khan establishes Mongol Empire (1206–1405) • Collapse of Mayan civilization in Central America; rise of Incas in Peru • Rise of Mali, west Africa	• Rise of craft guilds in towns of western Europe • Foundation of Hanseatic League (1241)	
1250	• Osman I founds Ottoman dynasty in Turkey (1290–1326) • Emergence of Empire of Benin, Nigeria • Mongols fail to conquer Japan (1281)	• Increasing Venetian links central Asia and China (1255–95) • Revolt of craftspeople in Flanders	• Marco Polo arrives in China (1275)

MEDIEVAL WORLD TRADE

DATE C.E.	POLITICAL/ SOCIAL EVENTS	TRADE DEVELOPMENTS	EXPLORATION
1300	• Hundred Years War between England and France (1337–1453) • Height of Mali (Mandingo) Empire under Sultan Mansa Musa • Bubonic plague in Europe (1346–1350)	• West Africa provides two-thirds of the gold of the eastern hemisphere	• Ibn Battuta's travels in east Asia and Africa (c. 1330–60)
1350	• Ghettoization of Jews in western Europe • Ashikaga Shoguns dominate Japan (1338–1573) • Ming dynasty in China (1368)	• Revolts of urban workers in Italy and Flanders	
1400	• Ottoman Turks establish foothold in Europe at Gallipoli	• Great Chinese naval expeditions reach east coast of Africa and India under Zheng He • China reconstructs and extends Grand Canal	• Portugal's Prince Henry the Navigator sponsors expeditions to west Africa
1450	• Printing of Gutenberg's Bible (1455) • War of the Roses in England (1453–85) • Turks capture Constantinople (1453) • Jews driven from Spain (1492) • Treaty of Tordesillas (1494)	• Decline of Kilwa and Great Zimbabwe in southeast Africa (c. 1450) • Medici family in Florence: Giovanni, Cosimo, Lorenzo	• Bartholomeu Dias sails round Cape of Good Hope (1488) • Columbus reaches the Americas (1492) • Vasco de Gama reaches the Malabar coast, India (1498)
1500	• Machiavelli, *The Prince* (1513) • Muslims in Spain forced to covert or leave • Zenith of Songhay Empire of the middle Niger region (1492–1529) • Hernán Cortés and Spanish conquistadores defeat Aztecs and seize Mexico (1519–21) • Francisco Pizarro and Spanish conquistadores defeat Incas and seize Peru	• Portugal sets up trading port of Goa, in India (1502); Portuguese ships armed with cannon	• Ferdinand Magellan's voyage round globe (1519–22)

economic profit by buying goods at a lower price and selling them at a higher price. In their quest for economic profit, however, businesspeople also risk economic loss because conditions and prices in the market change constantly. In completely free market economies conditions of trade would not be regulated at all. Prices would vary only in terms of the relationship between the **supply** of goods and the economic **demand** for them, and businesspeople would be free to seek their fortune as they choose. All societies, however, do regulate trade to some degree in order also to serve the non-economic goals of the society. Business may be more or less regulated, but it is never completely unregulated.

The questions asked in the 1930s were: Had the freedom given to private businesspeople been too extensive? Had excessive freedom ultimately devastated the economies of the world in the 1930s? Should governments be given more control over the regulation and planning of national economies? As the debate continued, scholars searched the past for relevant experience.

Karl Polanyi, a historical anthropologist at Columbia University, argued that market economies, private profit seeking, and capitalism were a peculiar and unnatural way of structuring an economy. Market economies had not existed in the distant past. Although they had captured the imagination of many people in Polanyi's own time, they were, in fact, historical oddities. With an interdisciplinary team of colleagues, Polanyi examined the past and found that:

> Prehistory, early history, and . . . the whole history apart from those last centuries, had economies the organization of which differed from anything assumed by the economist. . . . They possessed no system of price-making markets. (p. 241)

> Not before the third century B.C. was the working of a supply-demand-price mechanism in international trade noticeable. (p. 87)

The earlier systems had been different because their goals had been different. In the ancient Mediterranean, at least until the time of Aristotle, not private profit, but "community, self-sufficiency and justice . . . were the frame of reference . . . on all economic matters" (p. 80).

> The human economy . . . is embedded and enmeshed in institutions, economic and noneconomic. The inclusion of the noneconomic is vital. For religion or government may be as important for the structure and functioning of the economy as monetary institutions or the availability of tools and machines. (p. 250)

Polanyi argued that the exchange of goods was not carried out primarily in trade-for-profit, but in reciprocal gift-giving between individuals and in redistribution carried out by government and religious institutions claiming to serve the common good. Exchange for profit had been frowned upon or even forbidden because it requires and engenders unhealthy competitiveness, "an attitude involving a distinctive antagonistic relationship between the partners" (p. 255). Economies were to serve the purposes of establishing social cohesion

and satisfying the basic needs of all members of the society—rather than serving the private interests of a few.

Polanyi and his colleagues backed their argument with a series of accompanying historical sketches of "Marketless Trading in Hammurabi's Time," "Mesopotamian Economic History," and "Ports of Trade in the Eastern Mediterranean," and then added studies of contemporary non-market economies from India and Africa, both north and south of the Sahara. Some recent anthropological studies have supported Polanyi's analyses of early economies. Yale University anthropologist James Scott, for example, has found in many peasant villages a "moral economy," a mandate that everyone within the village be fed before any individual is permitted to sell surplus food outside the village for private profit.

Other scholars differed sharply from this historical analysis, citing different data from different kinds of economic systems. In *Cross-Cultural Trade in World History*, Philip Curtin, Professor of History at Johns Hopkins University, presents considerable evidence of market economies based on private profit throughout the world from earliest times. Curtin agrees with Polanyi that trade is embedded in deeper political, social, religious, and moral structures of society, but he notes that more independent trade for private profit exists as well, with equally deep historic roots. Long-distance trade for private profit has flourished in major port cities around the world for millennia. The merchants who carried this trade were often foreigners, with some independence from local political and social structures. They tended to occupy marginal positions in the host society, but central positions in the international trade networks.

> Trade communities of merchants living among aliens in associated networks are to be found on every continent and back through time to the very beginning of urban life. They are . . . one of the most widespread of all human institutions over a very long run of time. (Curtin, p. 3)

These communities were composed of "stranger merchants . . . cross-cultural brokers, helping and encouraging trade between the host society and people of their own origin who moved along the trade routes" (p. 2). They formed "trade diasporas . . . a whole series of trade settlements in alien towns . . . an interrelated net of commercial communities forming a trade network" (p. 2). These trade diasporas appear in the archaeological record as early as 3500 B.C.E. The visiting merchants who carried the trade were marginal to their host societies rather than embedded within them. They were not entirely unregulated by the hosts, but neither were they totally subordinated. They were expected to take at least a reasonable profit; sometimes they took more. "St. Nicholas was the patron saint of thieves and merchants alike" (Curtin, p. 6). To illustrate his argument, Curtin sketches a series of trade diasporas around the world in a variety of time periods.

TRADE NETWORKS: 1250–1500

The historical sociologist Janet Abu-Lughod advances a similar argument and traces eight interlocking trade circuits connecting the commerce of the eastern hemisphere in the period 1250–1350. Her synthesis, *Before European Hegemony: The World System* A.D. *1250–1350*, analyzes and maps six trade routes based on sea travel, primarily in the Indian Ocean; the thousands of miles of overland silk routes across central Asia; and a comparatively short land and river route within western Europe. In *Europe and the People without History* historical anthropologist Eric Wolf also proposes a similar outline of trade linkages, and includes three regions omitted by Abu-Lughod: west Africa south of the Sahara, connected to the Mediterranean by camel caravan; the valley of Mexico with its ties to the Yucatán; and the Andes Mountains of Latin America, with its links to the Pacific coast.

Abu-Lughod and Wolf, separately, reach several conclusions of fundamental importance:

- **Before 1500:** Asian and African trading systems were already well established by the time Europeans sailed into the Indian Ocean to trade in their own ships in 1498.

- **At 1500:** European traders established a permanent connection between the eastern and western hemispheres for the first time following Columbus' four voyages, 1492–1506.

- **After 1500:** As European traders grew more powerful, they attempted to subordinate pre-existing systems to their own centralized control from European headquarters. European control increased as northwestern Europe industrialized after 1750 (see Chapter 16).

WORLD TRADE PATTERNS, 1100–1500: WHAT DO WE KNOW?

THE AMERICAS

In the Andes Mountains of South America, a major hub of civilization grew up after 600 C.E. (see pp. 105–112). By the time the Incas consolidated their empire in the early fifteenth century, the mountain peoples generated extensive trade, connecting settlements over hundreds of miles north to south and linking together a political nation of some 32 million people. Trade was important up and down the mountain sides. With peaks rising up to 20,000 feet (over 6000 meters), these mountain slopes hosted several different ecological zones, encouraging product differentiation and trade. The valleys below provided sweet potatoes, maize, manioc, squash, beans, chili peppers, peanuts, and cotton. The hills above produced white potatoes, a cereal grain called quinoa, coca, feathers, animal skins, and medicines. The highlands people specialized in manufacture and crafts, including gold working. Trade between the ecological zones was controlled by the state and its semi-divine rulers. Under Inca rulers, from the early 1400s until the Spanish conquest in 1535, many of the best of the 15,000 miles (24,000 kilometers) of roads through the Andes were open only to government officials.

In the Yucatán of Central and North America, the Mayan peoples had flourished from 200 B.C.E. to 900 C.E. (see pp. 100–5). Archaeologists Linda Schele and David Freidel tell us that Mayan traders flourished rather independently, amassing a disproportionate share of wealth. "In a culture which regarded the accumulation of wealth as an aberration, this turn of events created unease and social strife" (p. 97). So ultimately the traders were brought under the control of the hierarchical state, creating a new set of unequal relations dominated by kings rather than merchants.

By the time the Spanish arrived in the 1520s, the Maya had weakened in the Yucatán, and the Aztecs dominated the valley of Mexico. The Spanish conquistadores wrote vivid accounts of the great market place of the Aztec capital, Tenochtitlán. William Prescott's classic *History of the Conquest of Mexico* summarizes:

> On drawing near to the . . . great market, the
> Spaniards were astonished at the throng of people

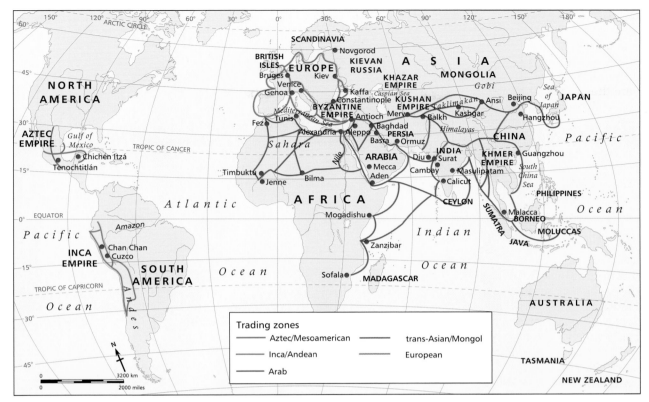

World trade routes Between 1100 and 1500 a relay system of trade by land and sea connected almost all populous regions of Eurasia, as well as north and east Africa. Long-distance traders carried goods along their own segments of these routes, and then turned them over to traders in the next sector. The western hemisphere was still separate, and had two major trade networks of its own.

pressing towards it, and, on entering the place, their surprise was still further heightened by the sight of the multitudes assembled there, and the dimensions of the inclosure, thrice as large as the celebrated square of Salamanca [Spain]. Here were met together traders from all parts, with the products and manufactures peculiar to their countries; the goldsmiths of Azcapozalso; the potters and jewellers of Cholula, the painters of Tezcuco, the stone-cutters of Tenajocan, the hunters of Xilotepec, the fishermen of Cuitlahuac, the fruiterers of the warm countries, the mat and chair-makers of Quauhtitlan, and the florists of Xochimilco—all busily engaged in recommending their respective wares, and in chattering with purchasers. (p. 328)

The market met every fifth day, with perhaps 40,000 to 50,000 merchants swarming in, rowing their canoes across the lake in which Tenochtitlán was built. Prescott compares the market to "the periodical fairs in Europe, not as they exist now, but as they existed in the Middle Ages, when . . . they served as the great central marts for commercial intercourse" (p. 331).

But how independent were these Tenochtitlán merchants? The Spanish described the city's market as being under tight government control. In addition to officers who kept the peace, collected taxes, and checked the accuracy of weights and measures, a court of twelve judges sat to decide cases immediately (p. 331).

A guild of traders, called *pochteca*, carried on long-distance trade, which expanded steadily through the fifteenth century. They led caravans for hundreds of miles, carrying city-crafted obsidian knives, fur blankets, clothes, herbs, and dyes, and brought back such raw materials as jade, seashells, jaguar skins, feathers from forest birds, and, in the greatest volume, cotton from the Gulf coast. They were to marry only within the guild, and, though they were commoners, they could send their sons to temple schools and they had their own courts.

They often gathered both goods and military intelligence for the ruling families. They were protected by royal troops, and sometimes attacks on

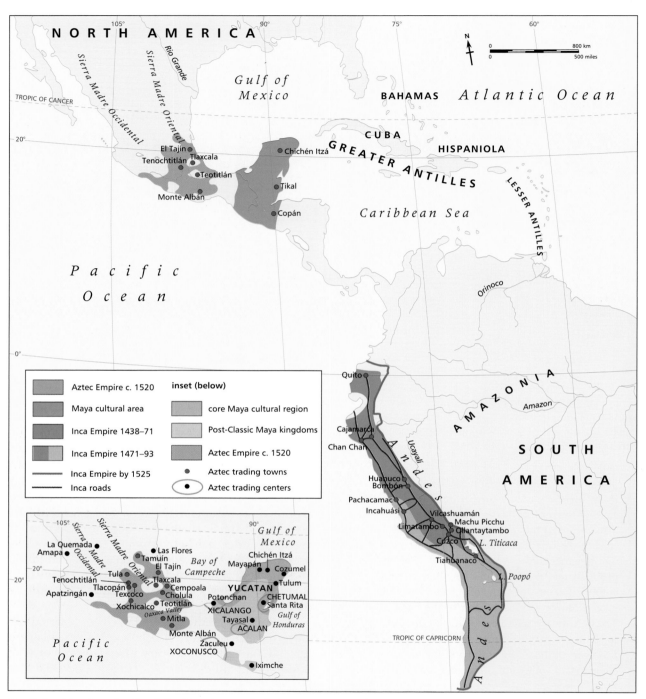

Pre-Columbian America Pre-Columbian America had two great regions of trade and political power. In the north, the Aztec kingdom, centered on Tenochtitlán, dominated. The adjacent Maya of central America were in decline. In South America, about 1500, the Inca dominated the Andes mountain regions, linking them together through an extensive system of roads.

traveling *pochteca* were returned by troops, who used the attacks as a justification for punishing the attackers and confiscating their lands. Curtin notes that the *pochteca* lived in their own wards in the towns, had their own magistrates, and supervised the markets on their own. Their main god, Yiacatecutli, seemed akin to the Toltec god Quetzalcoatl, and this, too, suggests that they were to some degree foreigners living in a trade diaspora. Curtin credits the *pochteca* with a high degree of

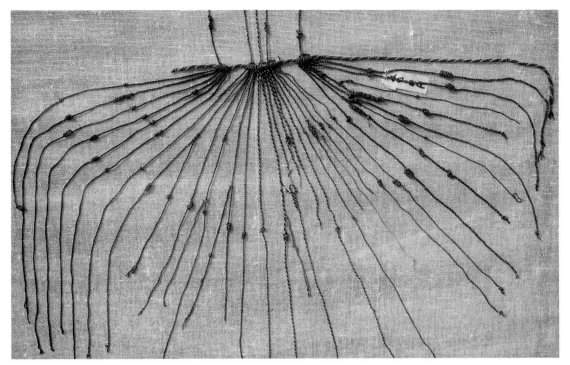

Photograph of a *quipu*. In the Inca empire, which extended from Ecuador to central Chile, trading was facilitated by an extensive road network. This *quipu*, a device of knotted string used to record dates and accounts, would have been a handy aid to the traveling South American businessman of the early 1400s.

independence from the state and temple (Curtin, 85–7).

As the American Indian nations had not invented the wheel, goods were carried by pack animals and humans. Along the South American coast, near the equator, the Incas sailed boats constructed of balsa wood. The Mayans paddled canoes through the river systems of the Yucatán. The two major civilizational hubs functioned independently of one another and both were, of course, virtually completely cut off from Afro-Eurasia. When Europeans arrived in the sixteenth century brandishing new weapons, commanding new military organizations, and transmitting new diseases, the American residents were unprepared for the challenges.

SUB-SAHARAN AFRICA

West Africa

The introduction of the camel in the second to fifth century C.E. opened the possibility of regular trans-Saharan trade. Oases provided the necessary rest and watering points for their caravans, and produced dates, a major commodity of trade. The earliest written records of this trade begin with the arrival of Islamic traders in the eighth century.

For the most part, African political units were local, but three large empires were forged successively around the northern bend in the Niger, near Timbuktu, where the **sahel**, the arid fringe of the desert, meets the vast Sahara itself. These three empires were: Ghana, about 700 to about 1100; Mali, about 1100 to about 1400; and Songhay, about 1300 to about 1600, when the kingdom was destroyed in battle by the Beni Marin tribes of Morocco. These kingdoms kept the trade routes open and secure. In contrast with almost all other governments, which amassed their wealth and power by controlling land and agriculture, these empires drew their power from their control over trade, traders, and trade routes.

Gold, slaves, cloth, ivory, ebony, pepper, and kola nuts (a stimulant) moved north across the Sahara; salt, dates, horses, brass, copper, glassware, beads, leather, textiles, clothing, and foodstuffs moved south. Gold was the central attraction. Up to c. 1350, the gold mines of west Africa "furnished about two-thirds of the gold circulating in the economy of the hemisphere" (Wolf, pp. 38–9). In 1324, when the Muslim emperor of Mali, Mansa Musa

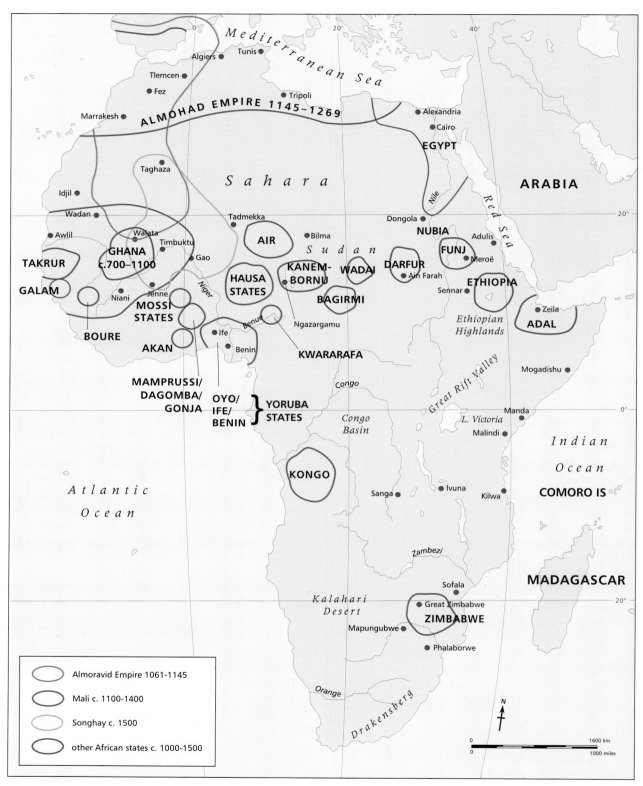

African kingdoms Many states appeared in 1000–1500 in northern and western Africa, their power based on control over long-distance trade—gold, ivory, and slaves moving north; metalware, textiles, and salt carried south. Ghana, Mali, and Songhay are discussed in the text. These states, protected from marauders by the Sahara, could usually maintain their independence.

Mosque at Jenne, Mali, first built fourteenth century C.E. The spectacular mud-brick mosques found in the major towns of the African savanna states, such as Jenne and Timbuktu, point to the acceptance of Islam by the merchant and ruling classes in the thirteenth and fourteenth centuries. The mud, which washes away in the rain, needs continual renewal—hence the built-in "scaffolding" of the structure.

(r. 1307–32), passed through Cairo on his way to Mecca, he dispensed so much gold in gifts to court officials and in purchases in the bazaar that "the value of Cairo's currency was depressed for many years." A European map of 1375 showing a seated Mansa Musa as ruler of Mali is captioned as follows: "So abundant is the gold found in his country that he is the richest and most noble king in all the land" (see also p. 348).

There were many natural break-points for the north–south trade: From the Mediterranean coast to the northern fringe of the desert, trade was borne by pack horse; across the desert, via oases, by camel; across the arid sahel and the grassy **savanna** lands again by pack animal; and finally through the tropical forest, afflicted with the lethal tsetse fly, it was borne by human porters. For the most part, the trade was carried from one market center to the next in short relays by locally dominant trade groups. A few trading communities, however, notably the Soninke and, especially, their Mande-speaking Dyula branch, established trade diasporas which negotiated with the rulers.

Thus, Africa south of the Sahara was not the isolated, backward area of European imagination, but an integral part of a web of relations that connected forest cultivators and miners with savanna and desert traders and with the merchants and rulers of the North African settled belt. This web of relations had a warp of gold. (Wolf, p. 40)

Great Zimbabwe. The biggest and most celebrated of several stone enclosures in east Africa dating from the tenth to fifteenth centuries, Great Zimbabwe provided raw materials for trade at the coastal settlements, especially gold, copper, tin, and iron and was also a trading post for luxury goods—Islamic pottery and cowrie shells were dug up at the site.

East Africa

East Africa, south of the Horn, came into the trade system of the Indian Ocean through the voyages of Arab merchants in the ninth century. The first major port had been Manda, succeeded in the thirteenth century by Kilwa. The ruling Arab dynasty seized control also of the port of Sofala, which lay to the south. Through local African traders they traded with the interior, especially at Great Zimbabwe (Curtin, p. 34).

The gold, ivory, horns, skins, tortoiseshell, and slaves collected from the interior were traded to Arabia and India for spices, pottery, glass beads, and cloth. Under the Mahdali dynasty, trade became a Kilwan monopoly, but both previously and later it was apparently more open. Arab traders carried most of the Indian Ocean commerce, but there were exceptions. In the early 1400s, the Chinese admiral Zheng He, a Muslim, reached Kilwa several times, seeking tribute for the Ming Empire (see p. 393). More frequently, Chinese goods were shipped via India by intermediary Arab merchants.

THE INDIAN OCEAN

Four of Abu-Lughod's routes include Indian Ocean ports. Sea lanes provided alternatives to the overland silk route. They linked eastern, southern, and western Asia and Africa. During the height of its empire, traders from Rome itself plied these waters, and on rare occasions continued all the way to China. They were not, however, ethnically Roman:

> They were descendants of the same people who had been trading to the East before the Roman Empire came into existence: Jews from Egypt and the Fertile Crescent, Greek-speaking Egyptians, and other Levantines from the ecumenical and Hellenized world of Mediterranean commerce. (Curtin, p. 100)

Roman trade left a permanent heritage of diaspora traders, in the form of small religious communities of Jews and Christians, living along the southwest coast of India long after the fall of Rome.

Jewish Traders

During the period of Tang-Abbasid control over the silk route, Jews had again emerged as a preeminent trading community of the diaspora.

> For a brief period centered on the eighth and early ninth centuries, a Jewish trade diaspora became the most important trade group over the whole network of routes linking Europe and China. The Jews who ran this trade were called *Radaniyya* in Arabic . . . [probably from] Persian *rha dan*, meaning "those who know the way." (Curtin, p. 106)

The religious diaspora of the Jews facilitated their trade connections. Charlemagne's ninth-century empire (see p. 329) used them for carrying trade in France. Babylon, astride many of the key trade routes in western Asia, held the most prominent Jewish community in the world at the time, but there were also small Jewish communities in Calicut and Cochin in south India and in Kai-feng, China. When the Portuguese explorer Vasco da Gama reached Calicut in 1498, a local Jewish merchant was able to serve as interpreter. Cairo, one of the world's great trade centers, also sheltered a very significant Jewish community.

How Do We Know?

Information on all Middle Eastern cultures from the ninth through the twelfth centuries has come to historians from the Cairo Genizah (Hebrew for a repository of old papers), studied by Solomon Goitein from the 1950s through the 1970s. Jewish law requires that religious writings not be destroyed; the Genizah was the storage point in Cairo for these documents for three centuries. It also included massive bundles of notes and manuscripts on secular and sacred aspects of life, on society in

Statuette of Semitic trader, Chinese, tenth century. Traders from the Roman Empire traveling the silk routes were likely to be Jews from the Fertile Crescent, Greek-speaking Egyptians, and other Levantines. They and their descendants eventually settled along the trans-Asian routes, which most likely explains the Chinese derivation of this glazed porcelain Jewish (?) peddler, made during Tang dynasty times. (*The Seattle Art Museum*)

general, and on the Jewish community in particular. The centuries-old manuscripts have proven to be a gold mine for historians.

Muslim Traders

With the rise of Islam (see Chapter 11), and especially after the Abbasids shifted their capital to Baghdad, Muslim traders, Arabs and Persians, dominated the routes through the Indian Ocean.

> In the broadest perspective of Afro-Eurasian history, in the period from about 750 A.D. to at least 1500, Islam was the central civilization for the whole of the Old World. . . . it was also the principal agency for contact between the discrete cultures of this period, serving as the carrier that transmitted innovations from one society to another. . . . The Muslim religion was also carried as part of a broad process of culture change—largely by traders, not conquerors. (Curtin, p. 107)

Islam encouraged trade. Muhammad himself had been a trader and caravan driver and he came from a trading town. The *hajj* (pilgrimage), encouraged for every Muslim at least once during his or her lifetime, demanded international travel; trade connections flourished with it. A Muslim trade colony had operated in Sri Lanka from about 700 C.E. Arab traders sailed with the monsoon winds first to India, then on to southeast Asia, and some, even on to the southeast coast of China. Catching the proper seasonal winds in each direction, and using their **lateen**, triangular, sails to maximum effect, sailors could complete a round trip from Mesopotamia to China in less than two years. Carried not by military power but by traders, Islam came to be the dominant religion in Indonesia (the largest Muslim country in the world today), and to attract tens of millions of Chinese adherents. The entire length of the Indian Ocean littoral, from east Africa through India and on to Indonesia, housed a Muslim, largely Arab, trading diaspora. The stories of Sinbad the Sailor, preserved in the tales told by Scheherezade in the *Thousand and One Nights*, reflect the importance of this Muslim trade network.

THE SILK ROUTES AND THE MONGOLS

The great central Asian silk route had declined after the ninth century along with the Abbasid and Tang dynasties which had protected and encouraged it.

Under the Mongol Empire, 1206–1405, the largest land empire ever known, it was reborn. The 2 million Mongols who inhabited the plateau region of central Asia were divided into several warring tribes, each led by a *khan*. The land was poor and the climate harsh. The Mongols shepherded their cattle, sheep, and goats in a circular pattern of migration called **transhumance**: in the brief summers they moved northward; in winter they turned back south. They spent most of their waking hours on horseback and mastered the art of warfare from the stirrups, with bow and arrow as well as sword by their side.

Genghis Khan

Temujin, later Genghis Khan, was born about 1162 into one of the more powerful and more militant Mongol tribes. His father, chief of his tribe, was poisoned by a rival tribe. About three generations before Temujin's birth, one of his ancestors, Kabul Khan, had briefly united the Mongols, and to reunify them became Genghis' own mission. He conquered the surrounding tribes, one by one, and united them at Karakorum, his capital. Although skilled at negotiation, Temujin was infamous for his brutality. Historian Rashid al-Din reports Genghis Khan's declaration:

> Man's greatest good fortune is to chase and defeat his enemy, seize all his possessions, leave his married women weeping and wailing, ride his gelding, and use the bodies of his women as a nightshirt and support, gazing upon and kissing their rosy breasts, sucking their lips which are as sweet as the berries of their breasts. (Cited in Ratchnevsky, p. 153)

Temujin defeated the Tatars and killed all surviving males taller than a cart axle. He defeated the Taichi'ut and boiled alive all their chiefs. In 1206, an assembly of all the chiefs of the steppe regions proclaimed him Genghis Khan ("Universal Ruler"). He organized them for further battle under a pyramid of officers leading units of 100, 1000, and 10,000 mounted warriors, commanded, as they grew older, by his four sons. Promotion within the fighting machine was by merit. Internal feuding among the Mongols ended. A new legal code, based on written and recorded case law, called for high moral standards within the Mongol nation.

Genghis turned east toward China. *En route* he captured the Tangut kingdom of Xixia, and from

Chinese engineers he mastered the weapons of siege warfare: the **mangonel** and **trebuchet** that could catapult great rocks; giant crossbows mounted on stands; and gunpowder that he could launch from longbows in bamboo-tube rockets. In 1211 he pierced the Great Wall of China, and in 1215 he conquered the capital, Zhongdu (modern Beijing), killing thousands. Genghis' officials and successors continued south until they captured all of China, establishing the Mongol dynasty, 1276–1368. They conquered Korea, large parts of southeast Asia as far as Java, and attempted, but failed, to take Japan as well. The planned assault on Japan in 1281 was stopped by *kamikaze*, divine winds, which prevented the Mongol fleet from sailing.

Genghis also turned west, conquering the Kara-Khitai Empire that included the major cities Tashkent and Samarqand. He turned southward toward India, reaching the Indus River and stationing troops in the Punjab, but he was unable to penetrate further. Turning northwest, he proceeded to conquer Khwarizm. In the great cities of Bukhara, Nishapur, Merv, Herat, Balkh, and Gurgan, millions were reported killed, an exaggeration, but an indication of great slaughter. Genghis went on to capture Tabriz and Tbilisi. When he died in 1227 his four sons continued the expansion relentlessly. In the northwest they defeated the Bulgars along the Volga and the Cumans of the southern steppes and then entered Russia. They took Moscow, destroyed Kiev, overran Moravia and Silesia, and set their sights on the conquest of Hungary. In 1241, Genghis' son Ogedei (Ögödei; 1185–1241) died, and during the succession dispute the Mongols withdrew east of Kiev. They never resumed their westward movement. Central and western Europe remained untouched.

In the southwest, under Genghis' grandson Hulegu (*c.* 1217–65), the Mongols captured and destroyed Baghdad, ending the five-century-old Abbasid dynasty by killing the caliph. Meanwhile Mongke, Genghis' grandson and the fourth and last

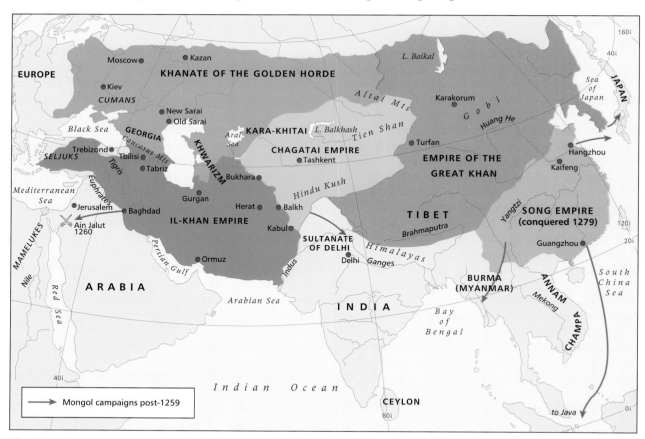

The Mongol successor states After the death of Genghis Khan's grandson Mongke in 1259, the Mongol world devolved into four successor states. Kublai Khan's emerged as the most powerful, but only after a long struggle with Song China. In central Asia, the Chagatai dominated the eastern steppe; the Golden Horde became established in southern Russia; and the Il-Khan in Persia ruled from Kabul to Anatolia.

Genghis Khan, from Rashid al-Din's world history, thirteenth century. Genghis Khan's conquests had as much impact on west Asia as they did on China. This Persian illustration of Genghis pursuing his enemies comes from a history, which some consider to be the first world history, written by Rashid al-Din (1247–1318), a Persian administrator employed by Mongol Il-Khans in Iran. (*Bibliothèque Nationale, Paris*)

successor to his title as "Great Khan," died while campaigning in China and many of the Mongol forces withdrew to attend a general conclave in Karakorum to choose his successor. A small force, however, proceeded to Ain Jalut, in modern day Jordan, and were defeated in battle. The Mongols never pressed further westward. The empire divided permanently into four separate *khanates*, or empires. At their apogee, 1279–1350, the Mongols ruled all of China, almost all of Russia, Iran, Iraq, and central Asia.

Mongol rule was extensive but brief. The Mongols could not govern their empire from horseback, and they were soon absorbed by the peoples they had conquered. They intermarried freely with the Turks who had joined them as allies in conquest. In Russia, Mongols and Turks merged with Slavs and Finns in a new Turkish-speaking ethnic group, the Tartars. In Persia and China they assimilated into local culture, converting to various religions, including Christianity, Buddhism, and Confucianism. In most of the areas inhabited by Muslims, the Mongols and their Turkish allies typically converted to Islam.

After such transformations, the four segments of Genghis' empire went their own separate ways. Slowly they were driven from their conquests. By 1335 the male line of Genghis and his grandson Hulegu died out in the Il-Khan Empire in Persia. The Ming dynasty defeated and evicted the Mongol (or Yuan) rulers in 1368. The Russians pushed out the Golden Horde (named not, as one might think, for their numbers, but for their tents, *Ordu* in Turkish). The Chagatai Khanate was destroyed by Timur the Lame (Tamerlane) after 1369. The last Mongol state in the Crimea was conquered only in the eighteenth century.

Cultural historians credit the Mongols with very little permanent contribution—they were absorbed into other, more settled and sophisticated cultures—but they did establish, for about a century, the "Pax Mongolica," the Mongolian Peace, over a vast region, in which intercontinental trade could flourish across the reopened silk route. Reports from two world travelers, Ibn Battuta (1304–68) of Morocco and Marco Polo (1254–1324) of Venice, give vivid insights into that exotic trade route.

World Travelers: Ibn Battuta and Marco Polo

In Chapter 11 we noted Ibn Battuta's observations on the variety of Islamic practices he encountered during his thirty years and 73,000 miles (117,000 kilometers) of travel (see p. 358). He also commented

SPOTLIGHT
The Ships of Trade

From the late seventh century ships sailed from the Red Sea and Persian Gulf ports all the way to China, returning with silk, porcelain, and jade. Sometimes they traveled part of the way, exchanging their west Asian cargo for Chinese goods at an intermediate port, perhaps in the Malayan archipelago. As trade increased along these routes, the ports grew in size by servicing the ships and crews. They became homes to cosmopolitan business communities that financed and directed the voyages. Al-Masudi, noting the pattern of trans-shipments in his encyclopedia of 916, describes Muslim merchants who had married and settled in the Indian ports.

Regional shipping routes were linked into this oceanic, intercontinental trade, and the Oman–Basra route through the Persian Gulf, connecting Mesopotamia and the Indian Ocean, was one of the most important of them. **Figure 1** depicts a boat that plied this route. The illustration accompanied the twelfth-century *Maqamat*, or tales of

Figure 1 Arab trader, illustration from the *Maqamat* of al-Hariri, twelfth century.

fiction, of al-Hariri and portrays Arab passengers with a crew apparently from India and perhaps Africa.

Europeans bought the silks of China, the spices of south and southeast Asia, and the textiles of India in ports much closer to home, such as Alexandria, where the Arab traders transported them. But travel accounts of more distant civilizations, especially the reports by Marco Polo from his travels across Asia in 1271–95, excited Europe's imagination, as the painting on p. 390 suggests. **Figure 2** is a fanciful depiction of Cambay, the principal port of the northwest coast of India, in an illustration from the *Livre des Merveilles* (*The Book of Wonders*) (1410). Cambay's walls, buildings, and even ships are more European than Indian. The painter had heard wondrous tales, but had not actually seen the port with his own eyes.

Figure 2 Trade in the Gulf of Cambay, India, from the *Livre des Merveilles*, 1410.

With the seven official expeditions of Admiral Zheng He between 1405 and 1433, the Chinese government dispatched foreign diplomatic and trade missions all the way to the Persian Gulf and the east coast of Africa. Inland trade, however, was much more typical. China held one-fifth of the world's population and its internal markets were huge. River traffic at festival time in Kaifeng, the capital of the northern Song dynasty (**figure 3**), show well-developed channels of trade plied by a multitude of Chinese junks. The picture is a section taken from a twelfth-century scroll painting by Zhang Zeduan.

Figure 3 River traffic at Qing Ming festival, Kaifeng, by Zhang Zeduan, Song dynasty scroll. (*National Palace Museum, Taiwan*)

PROFILE
Marco Polo
AND HIS FABULOUS TRAVELS

Almost everything we know about Marco Polo's life (1254–1324) is based on the colorful account he left us of his travels through Asia. Little is known of his childhood years in Venice or his education. Marco's father and uncle, both Venetian merchants, traveled from their home in 1260 on a trade mission as far as Bogara and Sarai, at the northern end of the Caspian Sea. War broke out, and their route back home was blocked. But the route eastward was open, and the brothers finally traveled as far as Beijing, where Ghenghis Khan's grandson, Kublai Khan (1215–94), ruled. The Great Khan invited the men to return with more information on Christianity and a delegation from the pope. The information and delegation never materialized, but in 1271 the two brothers, along with the seventeen-year-old Marco, set out for China again. They arrived in 1275 and remained there for seventeen years. How exactly they occupied themselves during this time is unclear from Marco's account,

but it was not uncommon for foreigners to find employment in the Mongol state. Kublai Khan, it appears, was so enchanted by Marco's tales of foreign lands that he sent him on repeated reconnaissance trips throughout the empire.

The Polos eventually set off for home in about 1292, reaching Venice in 1295. Relatives and friends had apparently thought the men long since dead and the reunion was emotional. Soon after his homecoming, Marco was captured in a battle in the Mediterranean by Genoese sailors and imprisoned. He dictated the tales of his travels to his fellow-prisoner Rusticcello (Rusticiano), a writer of Romances. The language Rusticcello employed was Franco-Italian, a composite language popular in the thirteenth and fourteenth centuries. Europe now had its most complete and consistent account up to that date of the silk route and of the fabulous Chinese empire of Kublai Khan. Marco's *Travels* was soon translated into several European languages, intro-

extensively on conditions of travel and trade. In central Asia Ibn Battuta encountered a military expedition of Oz Beg Khan (d. 1341), the ruler of the khanate of the Golden Horde:

> We saw a vast city on the move with its inhabitants, with mosques and bazaars in it, the smoke of the kitchens rising in the air (for they cook while on the march), and horse-drawn wagons transporting the people. (Dunn, p. 167)

The tents of this camp/city were Mongol **yurts**. Made of wooden poles covered with leather pelt, and with rugs on the floor, the yurts could be disassembled quickly for travel.

Later, Ibn Battuta was granted his request to travel with one of Oz Beg Khan's wives along the trade route as she returned to her father's home in Constantinople to give birth to her child. The princess travelled with 5000 horsemen under military command, 500 of her own troops and servants, 200

slave girls, 20 Greek and Indian pages, 400 wagons, 2000 horses, and about 500 oxen and camels (Dunn, p. 170). They crossed from Islamic Mongol territory to Christian Byzantium.

Marco Polo was a merchant in a family of merchants (see Profile above), and his account of his travels to and in China was thus particularly attuned to patterns of trade. His numerous descriptions of urban markets support Curtin's concept of an urban-centered trade diaspora. For example, consider Marco Polo's description of Tabriz in northwest Persia:

> The people of Tabriz live by trade and industry; for cloth of gold and silk is woven here in great quantity and of great value. The city is so favourably situated that it is a market for merchandise from India and Baghdad, from Mosul and Hormuz, and from many other places; and many Latin merchants come here to buy the merchandise imported from foreign lands. It is also a market for precious stones, which

ducing to Christian Europe a new understanding of the world. In the following extract Marco explains in vivid terms how central Asian routes challenged travelers and their animals:

> For the merchants of these parts, when they travel from one country to another, traverse vast deserts, that is to say dry, barren, sandy regions, producing no grass or fodder suitable for horses, and the wells and sources of fresh water lie so far apart that they must travel by long stages if their beasts are to have anything to drink. (Polo, p. 61)

For seven centuries scholars have hotly debated the authenticity of Marco Polo's account. No original copy of *The Travels* exists and scholars have been faced with some 140 manuscript versions that were copied in various languages and dialects from scribe to scribe before the invention of printing. Recently, Frances Wood, head of the China Department at the British Library, has asked, *Did Marco Polo Go to China?* (1996). Wood notes that Marco did not mention any of the phenomena that should have caught his attention during his reported time in China: Chinese writing, tea, chopsticks, foot binding, the Great Wall. Despite his claims to frequent meetings with the Kublai Khan, Marco Polo is not mentioned in any Chinese records of the time. Wood concludes that Polo's work is actually based on materials gathered from others, that he himself never traveled beyond the Black Sea. As a travel narrative, Wood asserts, the book was a fabrication, but as an account of what was known of China at the time, it was a very rich and very influential source of information. The debate over authenticity of authorship continues.

Marco Polo, title page of first printed edition of *The Travels of Marco Polo*, 1477.

are found here in great abundance. It is a city where good profits are made by traveling merchants. The inhabitants are a mixed lot and good for very little. There are Armenians and Nestorians, Jacobites and Georgians and Persians; and there are also worshippers of Mahomet, who are the natives of the city and are called Tabrizis. (Polo, p. 57)

Central Asian routes challenged travelers and their animals. Despite the Pax Mongolica, merchants still had to be prepared to defend themselves from attack:

> Among the people of these kingdoms there are many who are brutal and bloodthirsty. They are for ever slaughtering one another; and, were it not for fear of the government, that is, the Tartar lordship of the Levant, they would do great mischief to travelling merchants. The government imposes severe penalties upon them and has ordered that along all dangerous routes the inhabitants at the request of the merchants shall supply good and efficient escorts from district to district for their safe conduct on payment of two or three groats for each loaded beast according to the length of the journey. Yet, for all that the government can do, these brigands are not to be deterred from frequent depredations. Unless the merchants are well armed and equipped with bows, they slay and harry them unsparingly. (Polo, p. 61)

Bubonic Plague and the Trade Routes

In addition to commerce and religion, the bubonic plague also traveled the trade routes. William McNeill's masterly *Plagues and Peoples* argues persuasively that "Mongol movements across previously isolating distances in all probability brought the bacillus *Pasteurella pestis* to the rodents of the Eurasian steppe for the first time" (p. 134). The infection apparently entered China in 1331 and decimated its population.

The best estimates show a decrease from 123 million about 1200 (before the Mongol invasions began) to a mere 65 million in 1393 . . . . Even Mongol ferocity cannot account for such a drastic decrease. Disease assuredly played a big part in cutting Chinese numbers in half; and bubonic plague . . . is by all odds the most likely candidate for such a role. (p. 144)

Along the silk routes, after the mid-fourteenth century, the presence and the role of the Mongols declined, probably also a result of plague deaths. The plague reached the Crimea in 1346. There, plague-infested rats boarded ships, disembarking with the disease at all the ports of Europe and the Near East.

In Europe, where the plague was new and people had no natural immunity, one-third of the population died. The ravages of the plague foreshadowed further, even worse, epidemics that would sweep across the continent, as groups of people who had not previously been exposed to one another's diseases began to meet for the first time (see Chapter 14).

CHINA AND THE SOUTH CHINA SEA

Marco Polo reported being overwhelmed when he finally arrived in China in 1275. He described its ruler, Kublai Khan, as "the mightiest man, whether in respect of subjects or of territory or of treasure, who is in the world today or who ever has been, from Adam our first parent down to the present moment" (p. 113). Polo correctly informed the West that China in the late 1200s was the richest, most technologically advanced, and largest politically unified country in the world. Certain elements leading to the creation of wealth had been in place for centuries. In the ninth century, under the Tang, wood block printing had been invented. From that time onward, ideas could spread in China more rapidly than anywhere else. One of the first uses of print was to conserve and spread religious concepts; the oldest printed book extant in the world is a copy of the Buddhist *Diamond Sutra* from 868 (see picture, p. 282). The government also used print to spread information on new farming methods.

The great luxury products of China—silk, porcelain, and tea—continued to attract the merchants of the world as they had since Tang times. Foreign merchants were housed in the suburbs of the capital, each nationality with its own accommodations. Lombards, Germans, and French from Europe were among them. A huge service industry grew up to attend them, Polo noted, in particular, an army of prostitutes:

I assure you that there are fully 20,000 of them, all serving the needs of men for money. They have a captain general, and there are chiefs of hundreds and of thousands responsible to the captain. This is because, whenever ambassadors come to the Great Khan on his business and are maintained at his expense, which is done on a lavish scale, the captain is called upon to provide one of these women every

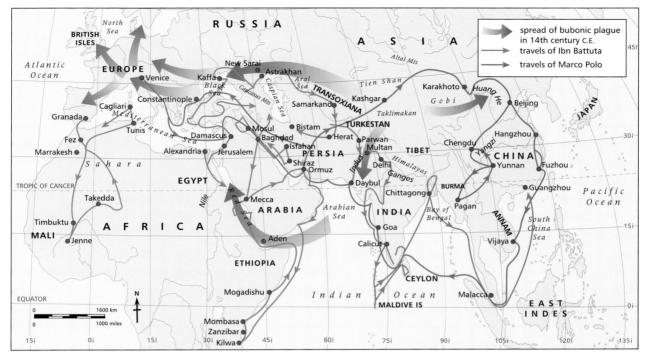

The routes of the plague The central and east Asian stability imposed by Mongol rule—the "Mongol peace"—brought mixed benefits. Trade flourished, and travelers such as Ibn Battuta and Marco Polo were able to write remarkable accounts of the lands they visited. At the same time, however, vectors for other travelers, such as the rats that carried bubonic plague, also opened up. The Black Death, originating in central Asia, was one of a succession of plagues that followed the trade routes by land and sea, decimating parts of Europe and China.

night for the ambassador and one for each of his attendants. They are changed each night and receive no payment; for this is the tax they pay to the Great Khan. (Polo, p. 129)

The international merchants were at the peak of a highly integrated national system of trade and commerce. Market towns sprang up throughout China, enabling virtually every rural family to sell its products for cash and to buy city goods. In turn, the small market towns were linked to larger cities, which provided more specialized products and access to government administrators. At the apex of this national system of urbanization were regional capitals, such as Kai-feng and Hangzhou. Geographer William Skinner's extensive presentation on the geography and functioning of market towns in China demonstrated the significance of this dense network of towns. Here, families could buy and sell, arrange a marriage, determine the latest government rulings, hear about new farming possibilities, learn the dates and the results of academic examinations. "By late traditional times, markets had so proliferated on the Chinese land-

scape and were so distributed that at least one was accessible to virtually every rural household" (Skinner, p. 6).

At the base of the economic system were the rural families, struggling to survive by producing commodities demanded by the traders. Hand manufacture, especially of cotton cloth, often supplemented farm production in rural areas. The producers were integrated into the market system either through direct, personal access or through brokers who supplied raw materials and bought the finished product. Dong Xianliang's "Weaving Song," written during the Ming dynasty, summarizes the industrial organization:

He tends his cotton in the garden in the morning,
In the evening makes his cloth upon the loom.
His wife weaves with ever-moving fingers;
His girls spin with never-ceasing wheels.
It is the humid and unhealthy season.
When they finish the last of the cotton from their garden.
Prices go up and up, if outside merchants come to buy;

So if warp's plentiful a lack of weft brings grief.
They therefore buy raw cotton and spin it night after night.

(Elvin, p. 273)

Women were the chief producers in this supplemental rural industry. They also carried the finished product to market. Conditions both of production and of marketing could be savage. Xu Xianzhong's "Prose Poem on Cotton Cloth" presents the harshness of both aspects:

> Why do you ignore their toil? Why are you touched
> Only by the loveliness that is born from toil?
> . . .
> Shall I tell you how their work exhausts them?
> By hand and treadle they turn the rollers of wood and iron,
> Feeling their fibre in between their fingers;
> The cotton comes out fluffy and the seeds fall away.
> The string of the cotton bow is stretched so taut
> It twangs with a sob from its pillar.
> They draw out slivers, spin them on their wheels

To the accompaniment of a medley of creakings.
Working through the darkness by candlelight,
Forgetful of bed. When energy ebbs, they sing.
The quilts are cold. Unheard, the waterclock flows over.
. . .
When a woman leaves for market
She does not look at her hungry husband.
Afraid her cloth's not good enough,
She adorns her face with cream and powder,
Touches men's shoulders to arouse their lust,
And sells herself with pleasant words.
Money she thinks of as a beast its prey;
Merchants she coaxes as she would her father.
Nor is her burden lifted till one buys.

(Elvin, pp. 273–4)

From Mongol to Ming: Dynastic Transition

Marco Polo reported that the economy did not serve everyone equally well. He told of especially bitter poverty and class division in south China:

> In the province of Manzi almost all the poor and needy sell some of their sons and daughters to the rich and noble, so that they may support themselves on the price paid for them and the children may be better fed in their new homes. (Polo, p. 227)

Polo also understood that the Mongol rulers were resented as foreign colonial masters:

Ink and watercolor print showing silk manufacture, Chinese, early seventeenth century. During the Song dynasty (960–1279), long-distance trade across central Asia dwindled. Maritime trade, with its very much safer and cheaper routes, now offered a viable alternative, and silk, along with porcelain and tea, continued to attract the merchants of the world. Unwinding filaments from silkworm cocoons in order to make yarn was considered women's work, as this Ming dynasty print suggests. (*Victoria & Albert Museum, London*)

All the Cathayans hated the government of the Great Khan, because he set over them Tartar rulers, mostly Saracens, and they could not endure it, since it made them feel that they were no more than slaves.

Moreover the Great Khan had no legal title to rule the province of Cathay, having acquired it by force. (Polo, p. 133)

During the ninety years of Mongol rule, 1279–1368, China's population plummeted from a high of 100 million to just over 50 million. Revolution ensued, and in 1368 the Ming dynasty replaced the Mongols and ruled for almost three centuries, until 1644.

Under the Ming dynasty, the population increased sharply. By 1450 it had reached 100 million again, and by 1580 the population was at least 130 million. Mark Elvin estimates it in that year as "somewhere between 160 and 250 million" (p. 129). Plagues and rebellions again caused the population to fall back to 100 million by 1650, but from that trough it rose consistently into present times.

The population settled new territories as it grew. The origins of the Chinese Empire had been in the Yellow River valley in the north (see Chapter 4). At the time of the Han dynasty, upward of 80 percent of the population of China lived north of the Yangzi valley. Under the late Tang dynasty the population was divided about equally between north and south. Warfare with the Mongols in the north drove the migrants south. At the height of the Mongol dynasty up to 90 percent of the population lived in the south. Economically, the south produced rice, cotton, and tea, three of China's most valuable products, not available in the northern climate. Closer to the southeast Asian and Indian Ocean sea lanes, the south also developed China's principal ports for international commerce. After the Mongols were defeated, however, migration began to reverse. By about 1500, 75 percent lived in the south, and northward movement was continuing.

International Trade and Government Intervention

China's ports, as Marco Polo had described them, hosted traders from around the world. Their Chinese counterparts were both private traders and traders in government service. In the early fifteenth century, the Ming Emperor Yongle commissioned a series of seven spectacular ocean voyages under the Muslim eunuch, Admiral Zheng He. The first voyage set out in 1405 with sixty-two large junks, 100

smaller ships, and 30,000 crew. The largest ships were 450 feet (140 meters) long, displaced 1600 tons, held a crew of about 500, and were the largest ships built anywhere up to that time. They carried silks, porcelains, and pepper. The first expedition sailed as far as Calicut, near the southwest tip of India. In six further missions between 1407 and 1433, Zheng He sailed to ports all along the Indian Ocean littoral, at least twice reaching the east African ports of Mogadishu, Brava, Malindi, and Kilwa. The Emperor Yongle seemed most pleased with a giraffe sent to him by the sultan of Malindi on the fourth voyage, 1416–19.

Why did China halt the voyages? Why did China not dispatch its own missions to Europe, and even to the western hemisphere, rather than only receive voyages from Europeans, beginning with the Portuguese in 1514? Many answers appear possible: The Ming turned their energies inward, toward consolidation and internal development. At first they pushed the Mongols further north from the wall, but an invasion of Mongolia failed in 1449. Thereafter, the Ming limited their military goals, rebuilt the wall, and restricted their forces to more defensible borders.

In 1411 the Ming reconstructed and extended the Grand Canal from Hangzhou in the south to Beijing in the north. The canal was the cheapest, most efficient means of shipping the grain and produce required by the northern capital. The man-made inland waterway also reduced the importance of coastal shipping, enabling the Ming emperors to turn their backs on the seas and ocean. The faction of eunuchs, dedicated court servants like Zheng He, who urged the government to continue its sponsorship of foreign trade, lost out in palace competition to other factions that promoted internal development. International private shipping was also curtailed.

The government limited contacts with foreigners and prohibited private overseas trade by Chinese merchants. The Ming dynasty went further by promulgating a series of acts to curtail overseas private trade. In 1371, coastal residents were forbidden to travel overseas. Then, recognizing that smuggling resulted, the government issued further prohibitions in 1390, 1394, 1397, 1433, 1449, and 1452. The continuing prohibitions reveal that smuggling did continue, but, for the most part, private Chinese sailors were cut off from foreign trade.

The government defined the expeditions of Zheng He as political missions that sought tribute to China from outlying countries. Although products were exchanged on these voyages, officially trade was not their goal. So, while both private and government trade flourished in the interior of China, and while thousands of Chinese emigrated to carry on private businesses throughout southeast Asia, China's official overseas trade virtually stopped. The Zheng He expeditions proved to be spectacular exceptions to generally restrictive policies.

The costs of these decisions to limit China's international trade, both official and private, proved enormous. Chinese society became introverted, and although economic growth continued, it was with no "fundamental breakthrough in technique" (Elvin, p. 95). New "invention was almost entirely absent. ... The dynamic quality of the medieval Chinese economy disappeared. This seems to have happened some time around the middle of the fourteenth century" (p. 203).

Military technology improved but then stagnated. China had invented gunpowder before 1000 C.E., but used it only sporadically. Ming cannon in the early fifteenth century were at least equal to those anywhere in the world, but metal was in short supply, limiting further development. The Ming fought few battles against fortress cities, where cannon were most useful, so they also saw little need to invest further in developing heavy weaponry. No enemies appeared against whom it would have been useful or necessary. In fighting against invasions from the north, the crossbow was of more importance to the infantrymen, who made up China's armies of a million and more soldiers. At first, when China was itself very advanced, these decisions seemed not so consequential. Later, they rendered the country vulnerable. China rested content with its accomplishments and stagnated in what Elvin has called a "high level equilibrium trap" (p. 203).

EUROPE AND THE MEDITERRANEAN, 700–1500

The popularity of Marco Polo's accounts of his travels suggests that western Europeans were paying more attention to international trade by the mid-1200s. The remote western fringes of Eurasia were emerging from the agrarian, localized, **manorial economy** and other-worldly spirit which had marked the Middle Ages, the period from about 700 to about 1350 C.E.

The Middle Ages were named in the fifteenth century when western Europeans were reviving and reintegrating lost Greek and Roman urban culture back into their lives. They saw this new movement as a **Renaissance** or rebirth, and disparaged the previous era from the decline of Greek and Roman "classical" culture until their own time as an in-between time, **medieval**, a middle age, between the greatness that had been and the greatness that they felt was now returning. Scholars today, however, are not so dismissive of this rich and innovative period.

The Early Middle Ages

During medieval times, there had been no political force able to protect trade, build and maintain roads, and provide consistent standards of currency and law. Moreover, with the rise of Islam along its eastern and southern coasts, the Mediterranean had become a zone of armed conflict. Trade in western Europe plummeted and cities declined. Rome's population, more than a million during its days as an imperial capital, dwindled to 50,000 in 700 C.E. Even so it was the largest city in western Europe's new era. Charlemagne (742–814) created an empire centered on his capital in Aix-la-Chapelle (Aachen) in northwest Germany, but the structure did not last (see pp. 329–30). Charlemagne's descendants could not preserve it from internal decay and external attack. Norsemen from the north, Magyars (Hungarians) from the east, and Arabs and Berbers from the south invaded and plundered throughout the ninth century.

In the absence of central government, urban administration, and protected trade routes, two responses emerged. One addressed the need for authority and order across large territories. The other provided a new localized means of production and consumption. Each of these systems of organization, one for government, one for economics, has been called "**feudal**" (having to do with land control) by later historians. Let us examine both, first the governmental, then the economic. Men capable of enforcing law and order by virtue of their military might—their ability to fight as armed horsemen and to gather other armed cavalry under their leadership— ranked themselves by relative military power. They then swore allegiance to one another, those with greater power serving as lords, those with lesser serving as vassals. The mounted horsemen among the vassals were called knights. The ranking was hierarchical, but just as those below owed responsibilities to those above, so those above owed (different) responsibilities to those below. The system thus combined and reinforced legal obligations with personal obligations. At the highest levels, kingdoms might emerge from the feudal relationships. The most powerful lords of France chose Hugh Capet to be their king, and agreed to serve as his vassals in 987. Hugh's descendants occupied the French throne for 800 years, until the French Revolution.

But most people were not lords, vassals, or knights in this military-political system. Most life in Christian western Europe—excluding Muslim Spain—centered on rural manors (see Source below). These relatively self-contained estates,

SOURCE
"Capitulare de Villis"—The Rules of Manor Life

In this list of instructions, Louis the Pious (r. 814–840), son of Charlemagne, outlines the administration of his own estates in Aquitaine. The document dates to about the year 800, and relates to an unusually large and efficiently managed estate, but it provides useful insights into general principles for administering a self-contained rural manor.

1. We wish that our estates which we have instituted to serve our needs discharge their services to us entirely and to no other men.
2. Our people shall be well taken care of and reduced to poverty by no one.
3. Our stewards shall not presume to put our people to their own service, either to force them to work, to cut wood, or to do any other task for them. And they shall accept no gift from them. . . .
4. If any of our people does injury to us either by stealing or by some other offense he shall make good the damage and for the remainder of the legal satisfaction he shall be punished by whipping, with the exception of homicide and arson cases which are punishable by fines. . . .
5. When our stewards ought to see that our work is done—the sowing, plowing, harvesting, cutting of hay, or gathering of grapes—let each one at the proper season and in each and every place organize and oversee what is to be done that it may be done well. . . .

6. We wish our stewards to give a tithe [10 percent] of all our products to the churches on our domains and that the tithe not be given to the churches of another except to those entitled to it by ancient usage. And our churches shall not have clerics other than our own, that is, of our people or our place.
31. They shall set aside each year what they ought to give as food and maintenance to the workers entitled to it and to the women working in the women's quarters and shall give it fully at the right time and make known to us what they have done with it and where they got it.
36. Our woods and forests shall be well taken care of and where there shall be a place for a clearing let it be cleared. Our stewards shall not allow the fields to become woods and where there ought to be woods they shall not allow anyone to cut too much or damage them.
43. For our women's work-shops the stewards shall provide the materials at the right time as it has been established, that is flax, wool, woad, vermilion dye, madder, wool-combs, teasels, soap, grease, vessels and other lesser things which are necessary there.
49. The women's quarters, that is, their houses, heated rooms, and sitting rooms, shall be well ordered and have good fences around them and strong gates that our work may be done well.

(Introduction to Contemporary Civilization in the West, pp. 5–13)

dominated by locally powerful landowners, provided most of their own domestic production and consumption and did very little trading with the outside world. Many of the residents of the manors were **serfs**, people bound to the land by personal status and offering to the lord of the manor their labor and services, or a cash rent, in exchange for the right to work the land, a share in its product, or just administration within the manor, and protection from outside attack. While the system was hierarchical and restrictive, especially for the serfs, it also gave them some degree of control over the land.

The other-worldly Christian ethic that was prevalent at the time frowned on such fundamental business practices as trade for profit, interest on loans, and amassing private wealth. St. Augustine's fifth-century observations carried the day: "Business is in itself an evil, for it turns men from seeking true rest, which is in God" (cited in *Introduction to Contemporary Civilization in the West*, Vol. I, p. 65). By the eighth century, Europe had become a trade backwater of relatively self-sufficient rural manors.

The High Middle Ages

By about the year 1000 signs of economic revival had begun in agriculture and population growth. Lords of the manors began to farm in a three-field system instead of two. That is, each year they left fallow one-third of their land instead of one-half, immediately raising production potential by 33 percent. New harnesses were developed that could yoke horses more efficiently to heavier plows with iron plowshares capable of digging more deeply into the soil and facilitating the expansion of farming into new areas. Up to about 1000, four-fifths of northwestern Europe was covered by dense forests. Peasants then began to clear and cultivate the forests of northeastern France. Germans colonized the Rhineland and Black Forest areas. Scandinavians and East Slavs moved eastward into the great plains of central Europe and even further into the great flat, sprawling steppes of Russia. On the basis of such data as the annual growth rings of trees and pollen counts in bogs, historians now believe that the European climate also changed, becoming warmer and promoting greater agricultural productivity. Population increased and spread. The population

The girding-on of swords, thirteenth-century manuscript. In the feudal system, vassals pledged allegiance to lords in exchange for property and protection: the relationship was invested with religious significance because the ladder of hierarchy from serfs, vassals, lords, and the king was seen as extending to heaven. This manuscript shows the girding-on of swords, part of the formal ritual associated with the making of a knight. Hands clasped above the head was the typical posture of prayer in the Middle Ages. (*British Museum, London*)

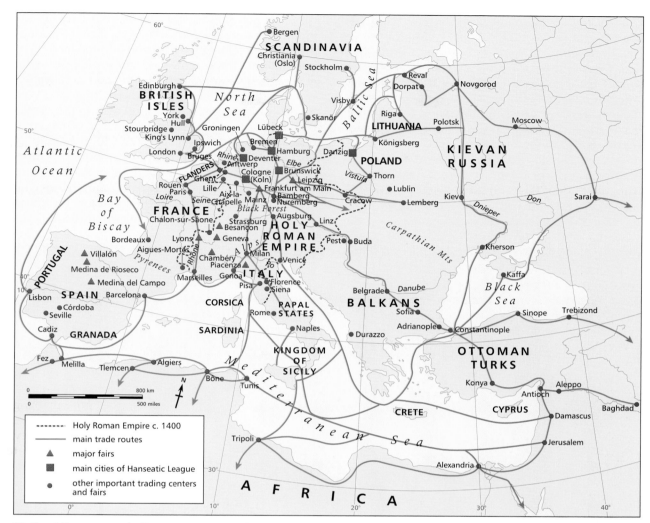

Medieval European trade Four important sets of trade routes emerged by about 1200 in Europe: the ports of the Mediterranean, led by Venice and Genoa; the North Sea and the Baltic, dominated by the Hanseatic League of merchants; a regular system of fairs along the north–south routes between northern Italy and the mouth of the Rhine; and the river systems of Russia, where Scandinavian sailors carried their goods.

of Europe is estimated at 30 million in 1000, 40–45 million in 1150, and 70 million in 1300.

The Rise of an Urban Middle Class

In eastern Europe, Mongol raids limited economic growth. In the thirteenth century the Mongols, moving westward, blocked the Slav advance. In the later fourteenth century, although they withdrew as a conquering power, the nomadic Mongols periodically swooped in to plunder. Their presence inhibited the development of urban areas and trade in Russia's eastern regions. In central Europe, eastern Germany in particular, landed aristocrats blocked the rise of new commercial classes, who

might have built independent cities of trade. The region's economy and government were dominated by a military aristocracy.

In western Europe, on the other hand, cities and an urban, middle-class business community (the **bourgeoisie**—from "burg" or "town"), began to flourish. The restoration of trade, trade routes, and urban market centers, and the increasing importance of businessmen—and some businesswomen, usually widows—marked the later medieval period.

The cities of Italy, preserving some of Rome's urban heritage, and persisting in a measure of Mediterranean trade, had never entirely lost their cohesion and their control over the adjacent countryside. Now, in the cities of northern and coastal Italy—Venice, Genoa, Pisa, Florence, Milan—and along the North Sea coast—Bruges and Ghent—commerce and manufacture combined to propel economic growth. Woolen textile manufacture in Flanders in the north, and cotton and woolen textile production in Florence in the south, began to create industrial classes, comfortable merchants, and thriving markets. Venice, and to a lesser extent Genoa and Pisa, traded across the Mediterranean, bringing to Europe luxury goods from the Middle East and farther Asia.

By 1150 periodic market fairs in the Champagne region provided points for the exchange of Flemish cloth, French wines, and goods from Asia. Henri Pirenne, in his book *Medieval Cities*, hailed the long-distance, traveling merchants who (re)opened these international trade routes as courageous sires of a new age of commerce, wealth, and intellectual cross-fertilization, and the towns they built as homes of innovation and growth. Pirenne notes that these new heroes of commerce often grew from somewhat unsavory roots to positions of distinction through unremitting attention to business matters and, later, through religious devotion.

The new towns contained several classes: the church officials, bishops in the largest of the cities, who had continued through the most difficult times

Aerial view of present-day Delft, west Netherlands. Here, gabled medieval townhouses are seen surrounding the bustling market square in Delft. Since the late 1500s the town has been famous for its pottery and porcelain known as delftware. Dutch products began to compete in European markets with porcelain imports from China.

Painting of 's-Hertogenbosch, Netherlands, 1530. Compare today's photograph of a medieval square on market day (opposite) with this view of a cloth market in another Dutch town painted in 1530. The layout and construction of the stalls are virtually identical.

to maintain churches, cathedrals, monasteries, and convents; artisans and small-scale manufacturers, who were attracted by markets for both labor and finished products; shopkeepers, who traded mostly in locally produced commodities and everyday necessities; and now the adventurous long-distance merchants. By 1200, the largest of the Italian towns had populations of 50,000 to 80,000; in northern Europe, 25,000 to 30,000.

The merchants, both long-distance traders and local guild members, needing both physical and legal protection from attack and looting, began to organize the townspeople to demand charters of independence from regional rulers. They sought codes of law to safeguard them against arbitrary confiscation and taxation; to provide adequate space for markets; to enforce official standards of weights, measures, coinage, currency, and laws; and the construction of protective walls around the cities. To achieve these institutional goals, the merchants and most other citizens swore oaths of allegiance to one another to protect and defend their new urban institutions, by force if necessary. The early modern western European city, the home of the merchant class, took on an entirely new organizational and institutional structure.

Guilds and City-States Confront Rural Aristocrats

As business increased, local traders and manufacturers formed trade organizations called **guilds**, which regulated the quality and quantity of production and trade, prices, wages, and the recruitment, training, and certification of apprentices, journeymen, and masters. The guilds also represented their members in town governments and thus helped to keep industrial and commercial interests at the forefront of the civic agenda. Guild members were mostly males, but widowed heads of households and workshops were also included among the voting members. Most guilds were organized locally, within their home towns, but international traders organized international guilds corresponding to their commercial interests. The Hanseatic League, though lacking the social and religious dimensions of a true guild, was founded in 1241 to represent the interests of leading shippers of the cities of Germany and nearby northern Europe. The League dominated the commerce of their region.

West European cities, organized internally through associations of their guilds and often supported by local clergy, won their political independence from surrounding landed aristocrats. The city-states were strongest where commerce was most firmly established—in north Italian cities, such as Venice, Genoa, Pisa, and Florence, and in Flanders, in Bruges, Ghent, and Antwerp. City-states also asserted political control over surrounding suburbs and the nearby rural areas, which were needed for their food and supplies. They claimed personal liberty from the lord of the surrounding countryside and asserted their own right to govern fiscal and judicial matters. In some parts of Germany rural serfs who managed to escape their manors and survive in a city for a year won their freedom from the land. "*Stadtluft macht frei* (City air makes one free)," they declared.

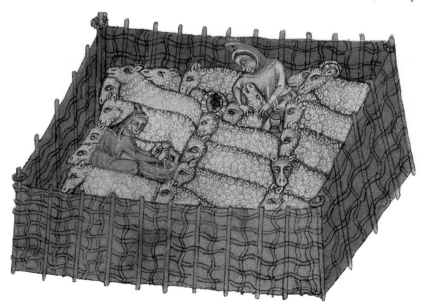

Sheep in pen being milked, Luttrell Psalter, fourteenth century. Woolen-cloth merchants had congregated at Flanders from an early stage, and by the twelfth century the industry there needed English wool to function to capacity. Prior to medieval times overland traders could transport only small and valuable objects over long distances; by the fourteenth century the emergence of sea routes meant that bulk goods, such as wool and grain, could be traded internationally. (*British Library, London*)

In the face of urban cohesion and organization, territorial princes were often forced to relinquish their control. Sometimes these lords were bought off; occasionally they were defeated in open warfare, as the citizens of Bruges, Ghent, and other Flemish cities defeated the king of France, albeit temporarily, at the Battle of Courtrai in 1302. Clergy, who also stood to gain from the independence of towns in which their major churches were located, often mediated between urban and rural interests, usually in favor of the city. The merchants of the city, and the long-distance merchants who traveled through on business, gained freedom to conduct business and earn profits free from princely interference and exactions. By the early 1300s, traders had achieved an independent political status backed by armed force as well as wealth, a status unknown elsewhere in the world.

Economic and Social Conflict Within the City

In two regions of western Europe, north Italy and Flanders, industrialization in the textile industries had proceeded so far by 1300 that latent class antagonisms between employer and employee occasionally broke out in open conflict. Between 200 and 300 workshops in Florence produced a total of 100,000 pieces of woolen cloth each year and provided a livelihood for one-fourth of the city's population.

Other cities of northern Italy, though smaller, had similar industrial patterns. Flanders and the neighboring regions of northern France and Belgium were even more industrialized and felt perhaps the greatest tension between employer and employee. Capitalist traders organized the industry by transmitting the demands for production and supplying the raw materials and equipment to meet it. Below them, the class structure was neither simple nor without the possibility of upward mobility. Guild masters, and the aspiring journeymen and apprentices within the guilds, held the best positions among the manual workers: shearing the sheep; fulling the cloth (that is, shrinking and thickening it by moistening, heating, and pressing it); and dyeing the wool. Weavers, carders, and combers were lower on the pay and social scales, and of these, only the weavers were likely to organize a guild. Below all these, an army of poor people washed, warped, and spun the wool. Female and child laborers, employed at even lower pay and in worse conditions than the men, enabled working families to survive.

Revolts at the end of the thirteenth century broke out in the Flemish cities of Douai, Tournai, Ypres, and Bruges. The leaders were usually craftsmen, and the immediate goal was usually participation in government for members of the craft guilds. The proletariat, the workers outside the guild organizations, could hope only that increased

Italian School, The Oar Makers, eighteenth-century painting of a medieval guild sign. By the thirteenth century, as the advantages of corporate organizations over individual enterprise loomed larger, specific craftsmen's guilds began to appear—in this case, that of the oar makers. Guilds issued regulations that covered everything from protecting the welfare of deceased members' families to ensuring quality of production. (*Museo Correr, Venice*)

wages, shorter hours, and better conditions of work might follow.

In the fourteenth century, increasingly impoverished workers, suffering also from plagues, wars, and bad harvests, confronted increasingly wealthy traders and industrialists. Workers were forbidden to strike and, in some towns, forbidden even to assemble. Nevertheless, a limited class consciousness was growing, especially in Florence, the greatest industrial center of western Europe. Finally, the *Ciompi* (named for the neighborhood of Florence in which they lived), the lowest class of workers, who were not affiliated with guilds, joined by lower level artisans, revolted. They understood the risks: in 1345 ten wool-carders had been hanged for organizing workers. In 1378 the *Ciompi* presented their demands to the officials of Florence. They wanted open access to the guilds, the right to unionize, a reduction of worker fines and punishments, and the right "to participate in the government of the City." They gained some of their goals, but the powerful business leaders of the city ultimately triumphed. By 1382 the major guilds were back in control, and soon a more dictatorial government under the Medici family (see below) was installed. Similar revolts occurred in Flanders, but on a smaller scale, and with no more success.

The Church Revises its Economic Policies

In establishing its independent power, the urban, trading, middle-class community was fighting the two most powerful groups of the time, Church clergy and landed aristocrats. From its earliest times, the Church had taken a dim view of the quest for profit and wealth. St. Augustine, as we noted (see p. 320), perpetuated the disdain. In the High Middle Ages theologians seriously debated whether it was possible for a merchant to attain salvation.

The taking and giving of interest on loans was forbidden to Christians, and for this reason much of the business of moneylending was carried out by Jews, who were so much a part of the merchant classes in early medieval northern Europe that a traditional administrative phrase referred to "Jews and other merchants" (Mundy and Riesenberg, p. 47). Jewish prominence in trade and urban life was, in part, a product of church laws forbidding their ownership of land. By the end of the thirteenth century, Christian rulers were also forcing Jews to live in ghettos, specific areas of the cities to which they were confined each night. Stigmatized four times over as alien by religion, foreign by

ancestry, moneylenders by occupation, and segregated by residence, Jews were nevertheless tolerated as an economically vital trade diaspora until local people mastered the intricacies of business. After that, Jews were often persecuted, sometimes murdered, and repeatedly exiled—from England in 1290, from France in 1394, from Spain in 1492, and from many German cities.

Ironically, the Church had encouraged the rebirth of trade. In Chapter 11 we noted the religious and political dimensions of the crusades. These expeditions, from 1095 to the thirteenth century, were perhaps even more important for their economic influence. In the process of launching the First Crusade in 1095, Pope Urban II not only asserted the military and political importance of the papacy but also promoted the commercial and naval power of the Italian city-states, especially Venice. Fleets from the major commercial cities of Italy boarded commercial cargo along with the crusader soldiers. The expeditions whetted European appetites for the luxury products of Asia, which had been difficult to obtain.

As commerce flourished, the Church built up its urban churches and cathedrals. By the thirteenth century the Church itself had become a great property holder and a borrower and lender. As the Church also sought the patronage of the rising merchant classes, it began to modify some of its earlier denunciations of business and its practices and to turn a blind eye to the charging of interest. The greatest of the medieval Church theologians, St. Thomas Aquinas (1225–74), addressed the issue directly in his *Summa Theologica*.

Aquinas justified commerce: "Buying and selling seem to be established for the common advantage of both parties" (*Contemporary Civilization*, Vol. I, p. 67). He wrote of a "just" price, determined by negotiation between buyer and seller. Neither church nor government needed to regulate prices: "The just price of things is not fixed with mathematical precision, but depends on a kind of estimate, so that a slight addition or subtraction would not seem to destroy the equality of justice" (pp. 67--8). Profit was allowed if its uses were deemed appropriate: "Nothing prevents gain from being directed to some necessary or even virtuous end, and thus trading becomes lawful." Traders were allowed compensation for their labor: "A man may take to trade . . . and seek gain, not as an end, but as payment for his labor" (p. 74). Aquinas elaborated similar interpretations to allow interest on commercial loans.

Renaissance: Intellectual and Cultural Transformation

On the basis of merchant wealth in the cities, a Renaissance, a rebirth, in thought, literature, art, manners, and sensibilities, arose throughout central and western Europe. The Renaissance began in the middle 1300s and continued for about two centuries. Proclaiming that the proper study of man is man, Renaissance **humanism** assigned to God a less overwhelming, less intimidating role in human life and concerns. Asserting the importance of the individual, it challenged the monopoly of the Church over the interpretation of cultural life. In his

Oration on the Dignity of Man, Giovanni Pico della Mirandola (1463–94) places in the mouth of God himself the most succinct statement of this humanistic perspective of the Renaissance:

> I have given you, Adam, neither a predetermined place nor a particular aspect nor any special prerogatives in order that you may take and possess these through your own decision and choice. The limitations on the nature of other creatures are contained within my prescribed laws. You shall determine your own nature without constraint from any barrier, by means of the freedom to whose power I have entrusted you. . . . I have made you

SOURCE

The Realpolitik of Niccolò Machiavelli

Humanism included perspectives on how people actually behaved, as well as on how they ought to behave. In political thought this perspective yielded studies in *realpolitik*, a very down-to-earth, even cynical view of human behavior that argued that ends justify means. Its principal exponent, Niccolò Machiavelli, had held several high-ranking posts in the government of his native Florence before the Medici family came to power in 1512 and dismissed him as a potential enemy of the new administration. Until the end of his life, Machiavelli wrote on the philosophy of government, hoping that his instructions on "good" government would guide some future leader to restore Italy to its former glory.

> From this arises the question whether it is better to be loved more than feared, or feared more than loved. The reply is, that one ought to be both feared and loved, but as it is difficult for the two to go together, it is much safer to be feared than loved . . . For it may be said of men in general that they are ungrateful, voluble dissemblers, anxious to avoid danger, and covetous of gain; as long as you benefit them, they are entirely yours; they offer you their blood, their goods, their life, and their children, as I have before said, when the necessity is

remote; but when it approaches, they revolt . . . Men have less scruple in offending one who makes himself loved than one who makes himself feared; for love is held by a chain of obligation which, men being selfish, is broken whenever it serves their purposes; but fear is maintained by a dread of punishment which never fails. . . .

> A prudent ruler ought not to keep faith when by so doing it would be against his interest, and when the reasons which made him bind himself no longer exist. If men were all good, this precept would not be a good one; but as they are bad, and would not observe their faith with you, so you are not bound to keep faith with them . . . But it is necessary to be able to disguise this character well, and to be a great feigner and dissembler; and men are so simple and so ready to obey present necessities, that one who deceives will always find those who allow themselves to be deceived . . . It is not, therefore, necessary for a prince to have all the above named [virtuous] qualities, but it is very necessary to seem to have them. I would even be bold to say that to possess them and always to observe them is dangerous, but to appear to possess them is useful.

> (Machiavelli, pp. 60–65)

neither heavenly nor earthly, neither mortal nor immortal so that, like a free and sovereign artificer, you might mold and fashion yourself into that form you yourself shall have chosen. (Cited in Wilkie/Hurt, p. 1571)

Masaccio, *Trinity with the Virgin, St. John, and Donors*, 1427. During the Renaissance, people began to rethink their relationship to God and the world around them; at the same time, artists were developing a new means of depicting reality. According to some art history scholars, Masaccio's monumental fresco is the first painting created in correct geometric perspective (the single vanishing point lies at the foot of the cross). (*S. Maria Novella, Florence*)

DATING THE RENAISSANCE: WHAT DIFFERENCE DOES IT MAKE?

We have presented the Renaissance in the context of the rise of trade and the increasingly favorable emphasis placed upon the profit motive in western Europe. In this framework, especially, the 1300s are a good date to introduce it, and this is the date most historians prefer. But the Renaissance marks a shift in religious as well as secular values, and historians of the Church often see this change beginning as early as the mid-eleventh century. (Historians also speak of the Carolingian Renaissance in the age of Charlemagne, but that cultural transformation collapsed along with his empire, while the intellectual shift of 1050 marked a continuous line of development.)

Church historian Carter Lindberg charts some of these early changes. In philosophy, three thinkers in particular suggested that pure faith is not enough to attain salvation. St. Anselm (1033–1109) introduced the concept of *fides quaerens intellectum*, "faith seeking understanding"; Peter Abelard (1079–1142) sought self-knowledge in a way that presaged the later emphasis on individualism, and Peter's physical as well as emotional love for the forbidden Eloise demonstrated the intensity of that quest; St. Bernard of Clairvaux (1090–1153) sought to combine love and spirituality along with faith.

The same era witnessed an intellectual opening to the Arab world especially through links in Spain. Scholars began the systematic translation of Arabic texts into Latin, re-establishing the link with the ancient Roman and Greek literature texts that the Arabs had preserved and developed, and that the European world had lost. The works of Avicenna (Ibn Sina), Averroes (Ibn Rushd), as well as the Jewish philosopher Maimonides helped restore the emphasis on logic and philosophy that Aristotle had taught.

Universities were founded. Most had practical emphases: medical studies at Salerno, Italy; legal studies at Bologna, Italy; theological studies at Paris. Students and professors from Paris seeking more intellectual freedom crossed the English Channel and founded the University of Oxford about 1200, with Cambridge following shortly afterward. By 1300 there were about a dozen universities in western Europe; by 1500, nearly one hundred. The teaching within the universities had to be approved by the Church, and most often centered on theology, but it included grammar, dialectic, rhetoric, arithmetic, music, geometry, and astronomy. And no matter how rigorous the rules, the assembly of dozens of young men in a small area led to challenges to authority and quests for individualism, as demonstrated by the "Goliard Poets," who took their name from the biblical Goliath, a kind of early anti-Christ.

> The writers of the poems rejoiced in the name, for they spoke in behalf of youth and pleasure and were the enemies of sobriety, propriety, and piety. Their output was varied. They wrote parodies of religious literature, irreverent, blasphemous, sometimes obscene – a *Drunkard's Mass*, an *Office of the Ribalds*, a *Glutton's Mass*. Their poetry is filled with mocking allusion to the most sacred solemnities; a Credo in which the poet professes, "I believe in dice… and love the tavern more than Jesus"; a benediction "Fraud be with you." (*Introduction to Contemporary Civilization*, p.105)

Art continued to emphasize religious themes, but it too began to become more earthly, more earthy, and more influenced by business. Masaccio's painting of *Trinity with the Virgin* (1427; see p. 403) demonstrates the evolution of *geometric perspective* in painting, suggesting not only a new artistic technique but also a new relationship of humans to space. (Compare the similar use of perspective in Van Eyck's *Wedding Portrait* (see above) and contrast it with other paintings in this chapter, for example *The Romance of Alexander* (p. 371) and the market scene at 's-Hertogenbosch (p. 398).

By the fifteenth century, intellectual and bourgeois sensibilities had joined together. *The Arnolfini Wedding Portrait*, painted in 1434 in Flanders by Jan van Eyck, depicts in realistic setting and clothing the marriage of a businessman, probably an Italian stationed in Flanders, and his, perhaps already pregnant, wife. Renaissance artists frequently merged their concerns for secular business affairs with their concerns for spiritual life.

Because of its increasing financial success, however, the Church suffered attack from within and without. Orders of priests and of nuns— Franciscans following the teachings of St. Francis of Assisi (1181–1226), Dominicans following St. Dominic (1170–1221), and "Poor Clares" following St. Clare of Assisi (1194–1253)—had challenged the Church to live up to its early ideals of compassion for the poor and simplicity in everyday living. During the Renaissance, however, clergy, landown-

Jan van Eyck, *The Arnolfini Wedding Portrait*, 1434.
Giovanni Arnolfini, a wealthy Italian merchant living in Flanders, commissioned the Flemish artist van Eyck to produce this pictorial record of his marriage. On the far wall, van Eyck has written in Latin "Jan van Eyck was here," much in the way that a notary would sign a legal document. *(National Gallery, London)*

ing warriors, and business entrepreneurs established a hierarchy of three social orders, analogous to similar systems in China and parallel to the caste system of India, and coordinated their efforts to mold the shape of western European society.

The richest fruits of Renaissance creativity matured in Florence (home of the *Ciompi* revolt), where the illustrious Medici family provided lavish patronage. The family's fortune had been built by the merchant-banker Giovanni de' Medici (1360–1429), and enhanced by his son, Cosimo (1389–1464), and grandson, Lorenzo (1449–92). Here creative artists like Michelangelo (1475–1564), painter of the Sistine Chapel ceiling; Leonardo da Vinci (1452–1519), scientific experimenter and painter of the *Mona Lisa*; and Niccolò Machiavelli (1469–1527), author of *The Prince*, which proposed a new, harsh, and hard-nosed philosophy of government (see Source, p. 402), developed and expressed their genius. At the same time, the general population of the city enjoyed high standards of literacy and expressiveness.

Creativity flourished in the practical as well as the fine arts and contributed substantially to the rise of merchant power. Many innovations came from amalgamating local techniques with those encountered in the course of trade, especially with Arab civilization. Improvements in sailing technology included a new design in the ships themselves. In the thirteenth century the caravel of the Mediterranean, with its triangular, or lateen (Latin) sails, used mostly by Arab sailors, was blended with the straight sternpost and stern rudder of northern Europe. The caravel could also be rerigged with a square sail for greater speed in a tail wind. The astrolabe, again an Arab invention, helped determine longitude at sea. The rediscovery in the early fifteenth century of Ptolemy's *Geography*, written in the second century C.E., and preserved in the Arab world, helped to spark interest in proper mapping. (An error in longitude in Ptolemy's map led Columbus to underestimate the size of the globe and think he could reach east Asia by sailing across the Atlantic.)

Cannon, especially when mounted on ships, gave European merchants firepower not available to others. Although the Chinese had invented gunpowder centuries before (see p. 394), the Europeans applied the invention in the fourteenth century to become the masters of gun-making. By the early 1400s they were using cannonballs. The Ottoman Turks employed Christian west Europeans to build and operate the cannon they used to besiege and conquer Constantinople. By the late 1400s European warring powers were competing energetically in an "arms race" to develop the most powerful and effective cannons and guns. Leonardo and others worked on the mathematics of the projectiles. (So did Sir Isaac Newton in the seventeenth century, and his labors led to his invention of the calculus; see Chapter 15.) When Portuguese ships began to sail into Asian waters after 1498, claiming the right to regulate commerce, their guns and cannons enabled them to sink all challengers.

The Chinese had also invented the principle of movable type and the printing press, but, again, European technology surpassed them in implementation. Movable type was better suited to Europe's alphabetic languages than to Chinese ideographs. By 1455, in Mainz, Germany, Johannes Gutenburg (c. 1390–1486) had printed the first

major book set in movable type, the Bible. By the end of the century at least 10 million individual books in some 30,000 different editions had been produced and distributed.

Of specific use to merchants in fourteenth-century Italy, two centuries after the decimal system had been absorbed from India via the Arab world, businesspeople began to develop double-entry bookkeeping. It facilitated accurate recording of transactions and efficient tracking of business profits and losses. In 1494 Luca Pacioli (c. 1445–c. 1514), a Franciscan friar and mathematician, first published the method in systematic form.

Ironies of the Fourteenth Century: Plague and War

The Renaissance in culture and invention seems to have been limited mostly to the upper classes, for in many respects the fourteenth century in western Europe was catastrophic. The area was plunged into famine, plague, and civil, international, and intercontinental warfare, which halted its economic prosperity and population growth for a century. A great famine struck 1315–17 and may have left the population generally so weakened that when bubonic plague reached Europe by way of trading ships in 1348, it killed off a third of Europe's population, reducing it from 70 million in 1300 to only 45 million in 1400. Giovanni Boccaccio (1313–75) captured the horror of the plague in the introduction to his otherwise droll and humanistic classic of the era, *The Decameron*:

> In the year of Our Lord 1348 the deadly plague broke out in the great city of Florence. . . . At the onset of the disease both men and women were afflicted by a sort of swelling in the groin or under the armpits which sometimes attained the size of a common apple or egg. Some of these swellings were larger and some smaller, and all were commonly called boils. From these two starting points the boils began in a little while to spread and appear generally all over the body. Afterwards, the manifestation of the disease changed into black or livid spots on the arms, thighs, and the whole person. . . . Neither the advice of physicians nor the virtue of any medicine seemed to help. . . almost everyone died within three days of the appearance of the signs – some sooner, some later. . . .
>
> Let alone the fact that one man shunned the other and that nobody had any thought for his neighbor;

even relatives visited their folks little or never, and when they did, they communicated from a distance. The calamity had instilled such horror into the hearts of men and women that brother abandoned brother, uncles, sisters and wives left their dear ones to perish and, what is more serious and almost incredible, parents avoided visiting or nursing their very children, as though these were not their own flesh. . . . (xxiii–xxvii).

Paradoxically, the complete dissolution of the norms of everyday life inspired a reassessment of fundamental values and institutions that may have helped carry Renaissance values of individualism and a humanistic perspective to the common people as well as the elites. "Out of sheer necessity, therefore, quite different customs arose among the survivors from the original laws of the townspeople." (p. xxvii).

The Triumph of Death, **French, 1503.** This sixteenth-century work recalls the enormous loss of life caused by the Black Death of 1348. Brought back from east Asia by Genoan merchants, the bubonic plague is estimated to have killed between 20 and 50 percent of Europe's inhabitants. Contemporary medicine was impotent in the face of the disease, whose onset meant certain death. (*Bibliothèque Nationale, Paris*)

The peasants who survived the plague benefited from the labor shortages that followed, gaining higher wages and access to more land, freedom from labor services, and geographical mobility. They began to form a new class of property-owning peasants. With the urban industrial workers and guild members who were similarly confronting their employers, they rioted more frequently and more boldly against kings and nobles who attempted to raise taxes for the incessant warfare of the time.

England and France fought the so-called Hundred Years War, 1337–1453. During this time, France also experienced civil warfare between the followers of the Dukes of Burgundy and Orleans. England saw its barons fight among themselves, Scotland invade, and Wales revolt. When defeat by the French in 1453 pushed the English from almost all the land they had held on the Continent, a civil war, the War of the Roses, broke out at home, 1453–85. Henry VII won out, establishing the Tudor dynasty (1485–1603). The wars at home and abroad created a new sense of national identity in both England and France and helped to strengthen their "new monarchies" in centralizing their administrations (see Chapter 13).

While western Europe was establishing the frameworks of new economic, cultural, and political organizations, in eastern Europe the Byzantine Empire collapsed. Already weakened internally, it could not withstand the advancing Ottoman Turks. The Turks captured Gallipoli in 1356, Adrianople in 1361, Kosovo in 1389, Nicopolis in 1396, and Constantinople itself in 1453. By the mid-sixteenth century, the Ottomans ruled not only the Balkans and Anatolia, but also Hungary, the Crimea, Mesopotamia, Syria, Egypt, and most of northern Africa. They permitted access to the trade routes of the eastern Mediterranean to Muslim traders, but virtually closed them to Christians.

ATLANTIC EXPLORATION

The loss of access to the eastern Mediterranean and its Asian trade pushed western Europeans to explore for alternative routes. Prince Henry the Navigator (1394–1460), a member of Portugal's ruling family, fostered continuous exploration of the west African coast in search of a southern passage around Africa to Asia. Portugal founded small ports and entrepots all along the Atlantic coast of Africa. Portuguese traders carried out extensive trade in slaves and gold, taking some 150,000 slaves from Africa in the half-century 1450–1500. The Portuguese had already captured Ceuta on the Mediterranean coast of Morocco in 1415, giving them (and later the Spanish) a toe-hold in Africa.

In 1488 Bartholomeu Dias (*c.* 1450–1500) rounded the Cape of Good Hope and sailed into the Indian Ocean. Pushing further on that route, with the help of local navigators, in 1498 Vasco da Gama (*c.* 1460–1524) reached India's Malabar coast. On a second voyage in 1502, da Gama captained an armed fleet of twenty-one ships and fought against local Arab sailor-merchants who were backed by a coalition of Egyptians, Turks, and Venetians opposed to the new interloper. Their ships and guns gave the Portuguese the advantage, and they established their Indian Ocean headquarters at Goa on the west coast of India, and a chain of fortified ports as far as Indonesia and China. By 1504, an average of a ship a month sailed from Lisbon to Asia. In the process the Portuguese earned a reputation for violence and arbitrary authority.

Spain, despite its geographical position, had not been among Europe's leading traders. In the late fifteenth century, however, emerging state power and religious conviction joined with Spain's desire to exploit new commercial opportunities. Spain's two major regional kingdoms were united in the 1469 marriage of Ferdinand of Aragon with Isabella of Castile, both devout Catholics. Spanish forces, strengthened by the unification and inspired by the Church, completed the *reconquista* in 1492, driving Muslims out of Granada, their last remaining outpost in Spain, and expelling Jews who refused to convert. In the same year, convinced by the Italian ship captain Christopher Columbus (1451–1506) that a western passage to China and India was possible across the Atlantic, the Spanish crown sponsored his voyages of exploration.

Most professional cartographers believed that the world was a globe, but their calculations had severely underestimated its size, and they had no idea that two continents occupied the opposite hemisphere. Reaching the Americas in 1492, Columbus did not understand that he had not arrived in "The Indies." Ferdinand Magellan (*c.* 1480–1521) more clearly established the general dimensions of the earth's sphere by initiating a three-year circumnavigation of the globe 1519–22 a voyage that altered forever the intellectual, commercial, and demographic horizons of the world. In the process Magellan also established the basis for Spain's claim to the Philippines, later named for King Phillip II of Spain. Magellan himself was killed in the Philippines and did not complete the voyage.

In 1493 a proclamation by the pope charged Spain and Portugal with evangelizing their new discoveries, and by the 1494 Treaty of Tordesillas Rome divided the newly accessible worlds of Asia and the western hemisphere between the Spanish and Portuguese. By persuasion and by force Spanish and Portuguese missionaries converted millions of people all over the world.

Other, more economically advanced European powers did not compete seriously with Spain and Portugal in overseas trade for another century. They were embroiled in their own religious and civil wars and were still integrating their internal economies. By 1600, however, the merchants and rulers of the Netherlands, France, and England were ready for new endeavors. They followed the Spanish and Portuguese and, in many areas, displaced them. They saw the oceans of the world as new arenas of competition in trade, migration, and colonization. They thoroughly reorganized the networks of world trade. The interactions of these trading powers among themselves and with the other great powers of the world through the period 1500–1750 are the principal subject of the next chapter.

BIBLIOGRAPHY

Abu-Lughod, Janet L. *Before European Hegemony: The World System A.D. 1250–1350* (New York: Oxford University Press, 1989).

Adas, Michael, ed. *Islamic and European Expansion* (Philadelphia: Temple University Press, 1993).

Aquinas, St. Thomas. *Summa Theologica* (excerpts) in *Introduction to Contemporary Civilization in the West,* cited below.

Bentley, Jerry H. *Old World Encounters* (New York: Oxford University Press, 1993).

Bloch, Marc. *Feudal Society,* 2 vols. (Chicago: University of Chicago Press, 1961).

Boccaccio, Giovanni. *The Decameron,* trans. Frances Winwar (New York: Modern Library, 1955).

Braudel, Fernand. *Capitalism and Material Life, 1400–1800*, trans. from the French by Miriam Kochan (New York: Harper and Row, 1973).

Chaudhuri, K. N. *Asia Before Europe* (Cambridge: Cambridge University Press, 1990).

—. *Trade and Civilization in the Indian Ocean: An Economic History from the Rise of Islam to 1750* (Cambridge: Cambridge University Press, 1985).

—. *Introduction to Contemporary Civilization in the West*, Vol. I (New York: Columbia University Press, 2nd ed., 1954).

Crosby, Alfred W. *Ecological Imperialism: The Biological Expansion of Europe, 900–1900* (Cambridge: Cambridge University Press, 1986).

Curtin, Philip. *Cross-Cultural Trade in World History* (Cambridge: Cambridge University Press, 1984).

Dunn, Ross. *The Adventures of Ibn Battuta* (Berkeley: University of California Press, 1986).

Elvin, Mark. *The Pattern of the Chinese Past* (Stanford: Stanford University Press, 1973).

Frank, Andre Gunder and Barry K. Gills, eds. *The World System: Five Hundred Years or Five Thousand?* (London: Routledge, 1993).

Ghosh, Amitav. *In an Antique Land* (New York: Knopf, 1993).

Goitein, Shelomo Dov. *A Mediterranean Society: The Jewish Communities of the Arab World as Portrayed in the Documents of the Cairo Genizah*, 6 vols. (Berkeley: University of California Press, 1967–83).

Hohenberg, Paul M. and Lynn Hollen Lees. *The Making of Urban Europe, 1000–1950.* (Cambridge: Harvard University Press, 1985).

Kee, Howard Clark, *et al. Christianity: A Social and Cultural History* (New York: Macmillan, 1991).

Levathes, Louise. *When China Ruled the Seas: The Treasure Fleet of the Dragon Throne, 1405–33* (New York: Oxford University Press, 1996).

Levenson, Jay A. *Circa 1492: Art in the Age of Exploration* (Washington: National Gallery of Art, 1991).

Lindberg, Carter. "The Late Middle Ages and the Reformations of the Sixteenth Century," in Kee, *et al. Christianity*, pp. 257–423.

Machiavelli, Niccolò, trans. by Luigi Ricci. *The Prince and the Discourses* (New York: Modern Library, 1950).

Mair, Victor H. "Mummies of the Tarim Basin," *Archaeology* XLVIII, No. 2 (1995), 28–35.

McNeill, William H. *The Age of Gunpowder Empires, 1450–1800* (Washington: American Historical Association, 1989).

—. *Plagues and Peoples* (Garden City, NY: Anchor Press/Doubleday, 1976).

Mundy, John H. and Peter Riesenberg. *The Medieval Town* (New York: Van Nostrand Reinhold Company, 1958).

Nicholas, David. *The Evolution of the Medieval World* (New York: Longman, 1992).

Pirenne, Henri. *Medieval Cities* (Princeton: Princeton University Press, 1925).

Polanyi, Karl, Conrad M. Arensberg, and Harry W. Pearson, eds. *Trade and Market in the Early Empires* (Chicago: The Free Press, 1957).

Polo, Marco. *The Travels*, trans. from the French by Ronald Latham (London: Penguin Books, 1958).

Prescott, William H. *History of the Conquest of Mexico and History of the Conquest of Peru* (New York: Modern Library, n.d.; 1st ed., *c.* 1844–7).

Ratchnevsky, Paul. *Genghis Khan: His Life and Legacy*, trans. and ed. by Thomas Nivison Haining (Oxford: Blackwell, 1991).

Raychaudhuri, Tapan and Irfan Habib. *The Cambridge Economic History of India.* Vol. I: *c.* 122–*c.* 1750 (Cambridge: Cambridge University Press, 1982).

Reynolds, Susan. *Fiefs and Vassals* (Oxford: Clarendon Press, 1994).

Schele, Linda and David Freidel. *A Forest of Kings: The Untold Story of the Ancient Maya* (New York: William Morrow and Co., 1990).

Scott, James C. *The Moral Economy of the Peasant* (New Haven: Yale University Press, 1976).

Skinner, G. William. "Marketing and Social Structure in Rural China," *Journal of Asian Studies* XXIV, No. 1 (November 1964), 3–43.

Scheherezade: Tales from a Thousand and One Nights. Trans. by A.V Arberry (New York: New American Library, 1955)

The (London) Times Atlas of World History ed. Geoffrey Parker (London: Times Books Ltd., 4th ed., 1993).

Tuchman, Barbara. *A Distant Mirror: The Calamitous Fourteenth Century* (New York: Knopf, 1978).

Wilkie, Brian and James Hurt, eds. *Literature of the Western World*, Vol. I (New York: Macmillan, 1984).

Wills, John E., Jr. "Maritime Asia, 1500–1800: the Interactive Emergence of European Domination," *American Historical Review* XCVIII, No. 1 (February 1993), 83–105.

Wolf, Eric. *Europe and the People without History* (Berkeley: University of California Press, 1982).

Wood, Frances. *Did Marco Polo Go to China?* (Boulder, CO: Westview Press, 1996).

GLOSSARY

Pronunciation guides for selected terms are enclosed in parentheses, with the stressed syllable appearing in capital letters.

Abhidhamma (UB-ih-DUM-eh) One of the three principal divisions of the Buddhist scriptures, or Tripitaka, the others being the **Sutta** and the **Vinaya**. It comprises a logical analysis of the Buddha's teachings, arranged systematically, and is more impersonal and abstract than the Sutta. Its aim is meditational, and an important element involves an examination of states of consciousness.

agora (AG-o-rah) A central feature of ancient Greek town planning. Its chief function, like the Roman forum, was as a town market, but it also became the main social and political meeting place. Together with the acropolis, it normally housed the most important buildings of the town.

anthropology The scientific study of human beings in their social and physical aspects. Physical anthropologists study fossil remains to explain the origins and biological evolution of humans and the distinctive features of different races. Cultural anthropologists are concerned with the evolution of human society and cultures, especially through language. Social anthropologists have typically confined their work to "primitive" societies; they seek to analyze social norms, customs, belief, and ritual.

assimilation The process by which different ethnic groups lose their distinctive cultural identity through contact with the dominant culture of a society, and gradually become absorbed and integrated into it.

balance of power In international relations, a policy that aims to secure peace by preventing any one state or alignment of states from becoming too dominant. Alliances are formed in order to build up a force equal or superior to that of the potential enemy. Such a policy was practiced in the ancient world, for example by the Greek city-states.

bas relief (bah reh-LEEF) In sculpture, relief is a term for any work in which the forms stand out from the background, whether a plane or a curved surface. In bas (or low) relief, the design projects only slightly from the background and the outlines are not undercut.

Bible From the Greek *biblia*, books. The Jewish bible, written in Hebrew, comprises the thirty-nine books of the Old Testament (a Christian designation), the canon of which was probably established by 100 C.E. Regarded as divinely inspired, these scriptures are made up of three parts: the Torah (Law), the first five books—Genesis to Deuteronomy—whose authorship is attributed to Moses; the Prophets; and the Writings (the Psalms, etc.). The Christian Church incorporated these books, together with the Apocrypha (supplementary books written in Greek) and the **New Testament**

writings, into its bible, the form of which was fixed by the end of the fourth century C.E.

bourgeoisie (boor-ZHWA-zee) A French word that originally applied to the inhabitants of walled towns, who occupied a socio-economic position between the rural peasantry and the feudal aristocracy. With the development of industry, it became identified more with employers, as well as with other members of the "middle class," including professionals, artisans, and shopkeepers. (In Marxist theory, the word refers to those who own the tools of production and do not live by the sale of their labor, as opposed to the proletariat.)

caliph (KAY-lif) The spiritual head and temporal ruler of the Muslim community. As successor to the prophet Muhammad, the caliph is invested with absolute civil and religious authority, providing that he rules in conformity with the law of the Quran and the **hadith**.

caste (KAST) An element in a hierarchical social system in which the ranks are strictly defined, usually according to descent, marriage, and occupation. In more rigorous caste systems, such as that of Hinduism in India, mobility from one caste (Sanskrit: *varna*) to another is prohibited, and traditions and ritual dictate rules for social intercourse as well as such matters as education, diet, and occupation.

centuries The smallest units of the Roman army, each composed of some 100 foot-soldiers and commanded by a centurion. A legion was made up of 60 centuries. Centuries also formed political divisions of Roman citizens; they met in assembly to elect the chief magistrates and had some judicial powers.

Christmas The Christian feast celebrating the birth of Jesus Christ. The day of his actual birth is unknown, but the early Church probably chose this date because it coincided with pagan festivals of sun worship associated with the winter solstice. Pagan cults seem to have been the source of some popular customs connected with Christmas.

consul (KON-sul) Under the Roman Republic, one of the two magistrates holding supreme civil and military authority. Nominated by the Senate and elected by citizens in the Comita Centuriata (popular assembly), the consuls held office for one year and each had power of veto over the other. Their power was much restricted after the collapse of the Republic in 27 B.C.E., when the office fell under the control of the emperors.

cuneiform (kyoo-NEE-uh-form) A writing system in use in the ancient Near East from around the end of the fourth millennium to the first century B.C.E. It was used for a number of languages in the area, but the earliest examples, on clay tablets, are in Sumerian. The name derives from the wedge-shaped marks (Latin: *cuneus*, a

wedge) made by pressing the slanted edge of a stylus into soft clay. The signs were abstract versions of the earlier **pictograms**, and represented whole words or the sounds of syllables.

Daoism (Taoism) (DAO-iz-um) A religio-philosophical system of ancient China, which emerged in the sixth century B.C.E. Daoism rejected the activism of Confucianism, the other great Chinese philosophical tradition. It emphasized spontaneity and individual freedom, a *laissez-faire* attitude to life and government, simplicity, and the importance of mystical experience. True happiness could be attained only by surrendering to the Way or principle (Chinese: *dao*) of Nature. The principle texts of Daoism are the *Laozi* or *Classic of the Way and Its Power*, traditionally attributed to the philosopher Laozi, and the *Zhuangzi* of Zhuang Zou.

dar al-Islam (DAHR ahl-is-LAHM) The literal meaning of the Arabic words is "the abode of peace." The term refers to the land of Islam, or the territories in which Islam and its religious laws (**shari'a**) may be freely practiced.

deme (DEEM) A rural district or village in ancient Greece, or its members or inhabitants. The demes were a constituent part of the **polis** but had their own corporations with police powers, and their own cults, officials, and property. Membership of the deme was open only to adult males, and was hereditary; it also guaranteed membership of the polis itself.

dhimmi (dim-MEE) A person who belongs to the class of "protected people" in the Islamic state, who could not be forcibly converted to Islam. They originally comprised the followers of the monotheistic religions cited in the Quran, the "People of the Book" (e.g., Jews and Christians), to whom scriptures had been revealed, and the principle has in some instances been extended to followers of other religions.

diaspora (die-AS-pur-uh) A dispersion of peoples. Most commonly used to refer to the dispersion of Jews among the Gentiles, which began with the Babylonian captivity of the sixth century B.C.E.; the Hebrew term for diaspora is *Galut*, "exile." Because of the special relationship between the Jews and the land of Israel, the term refers not only to their physical dispersion but also has religious, philosophical, and political connotations. The African diaspora refers to the settlement of people of African origin to new locations around the world. "Trade diaspora" has been used to refer to centers of trade in which traders from many different countries live and work.

diffusion The spread of ideas, objects, or traits from one culture to another. Diffusionism is an anthropological theory that cultural similarities among different groups can be explained by diffusion rather than **innovation**, and, in its most radical form, that they derive from a common source.

dominance The imposition of alien government through force, as opposed to **hegemony**.

Easter The principal feast of the Christian calendar celebrating the resurrection of Christ. It is preceded by the penitential season of Lent, which culminates in the solemnities of Holy Week and Good Friday, commemorating Jesus' crucifixion. The date varies, and can fall on any Sunday between March 22 and April 25. The feast was associated by the early Christians with the Jewish Passover, and in some Churches a vigil is held on the night of Holy Saturday.

ecumene (EK-yoo-MEEN) A Greek word referring to the inhabited world and designating a distinct cultural-historical community.

epigraphy (eh-PIG-reh-fee) Inscriptions, usually on stone or metal, or the science of interpreting them.

Eucharist (YOO-kah-rist) From the Greek *eucharistia*, thanksgiving. The central **sacrament** and act of worship of the Christian Church, commemorating the Last Supper of Christ with his disciples, his sacrifice on the cross, and the redemption of mankind, and culminating in Holy Communion, when his Body and Blood in the form of water and wine are conveyed to the believer.

exogamy (adj. exogamous) The practice by which a person is compelled to choose a marital partner from outside his or her own group or clan, the opposite of endogamy, the choice of partner from within the group. Sometimes the outside group from which the partner is to be chosen is specified.

feudal (FEW-dull) Refers to both a social, military, and political system organized on the basis of land tenure and the manorial system of production. Property (the fief) was granted to a tenant (vassal) by a lord in exchange for an oath of allegiance and a promise to fulfill certain obligations, including military service, aid, and advice; in return, the lord offered protection and justice. Originally bestowed by investiture, the fief later became hereditary. Within the system, each person was bound to the others by a web of mutual responsibilities, from the king or emperor down to the **serfs**. Feudalism is particularly associated with medieval Europe, and with China and Japan. (See **manorial economy**.)

free market economy An economic system in which the means of production are largely privately owned and there is little or no government control over the markets, which operate according to **supply and demand**. The primary aim is to maximize profits, which are distributed to private individuals who have invested capital in an enterprise. The system is also known as a free enterprise economy or capitalism.

guild (GILD) A sworn association of people who gather for some common purpose. In the towns of medieval Europe, guilds of craftsmen or merchants were formed in order to protect and further the members' professional interests and for mutual aid. Merchant guilds organized trade in their locality and had important influence on local government. Craft guilds were confined to specific crafts or trades; they set and maintained standards of quality, regulated production and controlled recruitment through the apprenticeship system; they also had important social and religious functions. In India the guilds were associations of businessmen and producers who regulated weights and measures and prices and enforced quality control.

hadith (huh-DETH) Traditional records of the deeds and utterances of the prophet Muhammad, and the basis, after the Quran, for Islamic theology and law. The hadith provide commentaries on the Quran and give guidance for social and religious life and everyday conduct.

hegemony (hih-JEM-o-nee) The predominance of one unit over the others in a group, for example one state in a confederation. It can also apply to the rule of an empire over its subject peoples, when the foreign government is exercised with their substantial consent. Hegemony usually implies exploitation but, more positively, it may connote leadership (see **dominance**).

heliocentric A system in which the sun is assumed to be at the center of the solar system—or of the universe—while Earth and the planets move around it. Ptolemy of Alexandria's geocentric or Earth-centered system dominated scientific thought in the Western world from the second century C.E. until the publication of Copernicus's *De revolutionibus orbium coelestium* in 1543. There was much religious and scientific controversy before his thesis was shown to be essentially correct.

hieroglyphs (HIGH-ur-o-glifs) The characters in a writing system based on the use of **pictograms** or **ideograms**. In ancient Egypt, hieroglyphics were largely used for monumental inscriptions. The symbols depict people, animals, and objects, which represent words, syllables, or sounds.

hijra (HIJ-reh) The "migration" or flight of Muhammad from Mecca, where his life was in danger, to Medina (then called Yathrib) in 622 C.E. The Islamic era (A.H.: After Hijra) is calculated from this date, which coincides with the establishment of the first Islamic state.

historiography The writing of history, or the theory and history of historical writing.

hoplite A heavily armed foot soldier of ancient Greece, whose function was to fight in close formation, usually in ranks of eight men. Hoplites were citizens with sufficient property to equip themselves with full personal armor, which consisted of a helmet with nasal and cheek pieces, a breastplate and greaves of bronze. Each soldier carried a heavy bronze shield, a short iron sword, and a long spear for thrusting.

humanism A term applied to the intellectual movement initiated in Western Europe in the fourteenth century by such men as Petrarch and Boccaccio and deriving from the rediscovery and study of Classical, particularly Latin, literary texts. The humanist program of studies included rhetoric, grammar, history, poetry, and moral philosophy (the humanities); the humanist scholar aimed to emulate Classical literary achievements. The examination of Classical civilization formed the inspiration for the **Renaissance**. Although humanism attached prime importance to human qualities and values, unlike its twentieth-century counterpart it in no way involved the rejection of Christianity.

icon (I-kon) A representation of Christ, the Virgin Mary, or other sacred personage or saint, usually a painted image on wood but also wrought in mosaic, ivory, and other materials. The term is usually applied to the sacred images of Eastern, particularly Byzantine and Orthodox, Christianity, where they are regarded as channels of grace. (*See also* **iconoclast, iconodule**.)

iconoclast (I-kon-o-klast) An image-breaker, or a person who rejects the veneration of **icons**, on the grounds that the practice is idolatrous. Strong disagreements over the cult of images in the Byzantine Empire led to attacks on the images themselves, and the use of icons was forbidden during the Iconoclastic Controversy (726–843 C.E.), when many were destroyed.

iconodule (I-kon-o-duel) A person who venerates **icons**. Iconodules defended the liturgical use of icons during the Iconoclastic Controversy (726–843 C.E.) in the Byzantine Empire. They argued that since God had assumed material form in the person of Jesus Christ, it was legitimate to represent him in visible images; moreover, the faithful could be stimulated to devotion through painted representations of God or the saints. They won their point by a Decree of the Second Council of Nicaea in 787, which was finally brought into practice in 843.

ideogram (ID-ee-o-gram) (alternative: ideograph) A character or figure in a writing system in which the idea of a thing is represented rather than its name. Languages such as Chinese use ideograms, but they cannot easily represent new or foreign words and huge numbers of symbols may be required to convey even basic information.

imam (ih-MAHM) In Islam, a title for a person whose leadership or example is to be followed, with several levels of meaning. In a general sense, it can refer to a leader of prayer in a mosque, or the head of a community or group. Among Shi'a Muslims, the title has special significance as applying to the successors of Muhammad, who were regarded as infallible and exercised absolute authority in both temporal and spiritual spheres (see **caliph**).

Indo-Aryan (in-DOH-AIR-ee-un) A sub-group of the Indo-Iranian branch of the Indo-European group of languages, also called Indic and spoken in India, Sri Lanka, Bangladesh, and Pakistan. The Indo-Aryan languages descend from Sanskrit, the sacred language of Hinduism; they include Hindi, a literary language, the more colloquial Hindustani, and the widely spoken Sindhi, Bengali, Gujarati, Punabi, and Sinhalese.

Indo-European The largest family of languages, believed to be descended from a single unrecorded language spoken more than 5000 years ago in the steppe regions around the Black Sea, which later split into a number of dialects. The languages were carried into Europe and Asia by migrating peoples, who also transmitted their cultural heritage. The family includes the following sub-groups: Anatolian (the earliest recorded language, now extinct), Indo-Iranian, Armenian, Greek, Albanian, Tocharian, Celtic, Italic, Germanic, Baltic, and Slavic.

innovation The explanation that similar cultural traits, techniques, or objects found among different groups of people were invented independently rather than spreading from one group to another, as in **diffusion**.

interregnum An interval between reigns (Latin: "between reigns"). The term may refer to the period of time between the death of a monarch and the accession of his successor, to a suspension of the usual government, or to the period of rule of an usurper.

janapada (juh-nah-pah-dah) A Sanskrit word that occurs in ancient texts with reference to a large political district.

jihad (jee-HAHD) An Arabic word meaning "striving," "effort," or "struggle," established in both the Quran and the **hadith** as an incumbent religious duty. It has been interpreted both as a spiritual battle to overcome evil and as a physical one against unbelievers.

lateen (lah-TEEN) A triangular sail affixed to a long yard or crossbar at an angle of about 45 degrees to the mast, with the free corner secured near the stern. The sail was capable of taking the wind on either side. The rig, which was developed by the Arabs, revolutionized navigation because it enabled vessels to tack into the wind and thus to sail in almost any direction; with a square sail, ships could only sail with the wind behind them.

Legalism A school of Chinese philosophy that came into prominence during the period of the Warring States (481–422 B.C.E.) and had great influence on the policies of the Qin dynasty (221–207 B.C.E.). Legalists took a pessimistic view of human nature and believed that social harmony could only be attained through strong government control and the imposition of strict laws, enforced absolutely. The brutal application of this political theory under the Qin led to the fall of the dynasty, and Legalist philosophy was permanently discredited in Confucian philosophy.

madrasa (mah-DRASS-ah) A traditional Islamic school of higher education, principally of theology and law, literally a "place of study." The madrasa usually comprised a central courtyard surrounded by rooms in which the students resided and with a prayer room or mosque, where instruction took place. Tuition, board, and lodging were free. Studies could last for several years and primarily consisted of memorizing textbooks and lectures.

mahdi (MAH-dee) An Arabic word meaning "the right-guided one." According to Islamic tradition, a messianic leader will appear to restore justice, truth, and religion for a brief period before the Day of Judgment. Some Shi'a Muslims believe that the twelfth **imam** (ninth century C.E.) will reappear as the Mahdi. Several impostors have claimed the title.

mandala (MUN-dull-eh) A symbolic circular diagram of complex geometric design used as an instrument of meditation or in the performance of sacred rites in Hinduism and Buddhism. Mandalas can be drawn, painted, wrought in metal, or traced on the ground. Buddhist examples are usually characterized by a series of concentric circles, representing universal harmony and containing religious figures, with the Buddha in the center.

mangonel (MANG-geh-nell) An upright armed catapult worked by torsion. Mangonels of various types were used in China and the ancient world, as well as by the Mongols and in medieval Europe.

manorial economy An economic system based on the manor, or the lord's landed estate, the most common unit of agrarian organization in medieval Europe. The manor comprised the lord's own farm (the demesne) and the land farmed by peasant tenants or **serfs** who were legally dependent on the lord and owed him or her **feudal** service on the demesne. The manor was not completely self-contained but it aimed more at self-sufficiency than at the market and supported a steady increase in population up to the fourteenth century.

mantra (MUN-tra) A formula of utterances of words and sounds that are believed to possess spiritual power, a practice of both Hinduism and Buddhism. The efficacy of the mantra largely depends on the exacting mental discipline involved in uttering it correctly. Repetition or meditation on a particular mantra can induce a trancelike state, leading to a higher level of spiritual consciousness.

medieval A term coined in fifteenth-century Italy to describe the "middle ages," the period between antiquity and the contemporary Renaissance. It originally had negative connotations, for the Middle Ages were regarded as a period of artistic and cultural decline as compared to the lost glories of ancient Rome and the Renaissance attempts to emulate and surpass those achievements.

monotheism (MON-eh-thee-iz-um) The doctrine of the existence of only one God, or of the oneness of God, as opposed to polytheism, the belief in the existence of many gods, or atheism, the denial of the existence of God. The great monotheistic religions are Judaism, Christianity, and Islam, all of which believe in God as creator and as the source of the highest good.

Monophysites (moh-NOF-ih-sites) The supporters of a doctrine in the early Christian Church that held that the incarnate Christ possessed a single, wholly divine nature. They opposed the orthodox view that Christ had a double nature, one divine and one human, and emphasized his divinity at the expense of his capacity to experience real human suffering. The doctrine survived in the Coptic and some other Eastern Churches.

Neolithic (NEE-o-lith-ick) "New Stone Age"—the last division of the Stone Age, immediately preceding the development of metallurgy and corresponding to the ninth–fifth millennia B.C.E. It was characterized by the increasing domestication of animals and cultivation of crops,

established agricultural communities, and the appearance of such crafts as pottery and weaving. Although tools and weapons were still made of stone, technological improvements enabled these to be ground and polished rather than flaked and chipped.

Neoplatonic (nee-o-PLAH-ton-ick) A philosophical system founded by Plotinus (205–270 C.E.) and influenced by Plato's theory of ideas. It emphasizes the transcendent, impersonal, and indefinable "One" as the ground of all existence and the source of an eternal world of goodness, beauty, and order, of which material existence is but a feeble copy. By cultivating the intellect and rejecting the material world, humans may become mystically united with the One. Neoplatonism, the last school of Greek philosophy, influenced both Christian theology and Islamic philosophy.

New Testament The second part of the Christian bible, written in Greek and containing the writings attributed to the first followers of Jesus. The twenty-seven books fall into four parts: the four Gospels, dealing with life of Christ; the Acts of the Apostles, concerning the early life of the Church; the Epistles (or letters), written mainly by St Paul; and the Book of Revelation. The canon was established by the end of the fourth century C.E.; the title indicates the Christian belief that Christ's life, death, and resurrection fulfilled prophecies in the Hebrew scriptures, the Old Testament.

oppida (OP-ee-dah) Large permanent settlements of the Celtic or Iron Age peoples of northwestern Europe. Fortified and usually on a raised site, they were often densely populated and housed specialist craftsmen, such as smiths and glassmakers. In the Roman world *oppidum* was a term of administrative law for a town to which no territory was juridically attached; it also applied to a provincial community of Roman citizens.

ordo (OR-doe) A military camp of considerable importance among the central Asian steppe peoples.

Paleolithic (PAY-lee-o-lith-ick) "Old Stone Age"—the first division of the Stone Age (the earliest phase in a system devised in the nineteenth century to classify human technological development). The Paleolithic (c. 1.5 million B.C.E.–10,000 B.C.E.) extends to the end of the last Ice Age and is associated with the emergence of humans, the use of rudimentary tools of chipped stone or bone, and the practice of hunting and gathering. Evidence of painting and sculpture survives from the later, or Upper Paleolithic, period.

paterfamilias (pay-ter-fuh-MILL-ee-us) The head of a family or household in Roman law—always a male—and the only member to have full legal rights. The *paterfamilias* had absolute power over his family, which extended to life and death. The family included not only direct descendants of the *paterfamilias* through the male line, unless emancipated by him, but also adopted members and, in certain cases, wives. On his death, each son would become a *paterfamilias* in his own right.

patrician (puh-TRISH-un) A member of the elite class of ancient Roman citizens. In the early days of the Republic, patricians held a monopoly of state and religious offices, but this privileged position was gradually eroded with the admission of other social classes to office (see **plebeian**).

patriarchy (PAY-tree-ar-kee) A social system in which the father or an elderly male has absolute authority over the family group. It is also applied to a society characterized by male-created and male-dominated institutions.

Pax Romana (PAKS roh-MAHN-uh) The "Roman Peace," that is, the state of comparative concord prevailing within the boundaries of the Roman Empire from the reign of Augustus (27 B.C.E.–14 C.E.) to that of Marcus Aurelius (161–180 C.E.), enforced by Roman rule and military control.

Pentecost The Greek name for a Jewish festival that falls on the fiftieth day after Passover. The name was adopted by the Christian Church to commemorate the descent of the Holy Spirit on the Apostles of Christ and the beginning of their preaching mission on the fiftieth day after the resurrection of Christ at **Easter**.

phallocracy A feminist term applied to a society ruled by men, in which women are totally marginalized.

philology The study of languages, or comparative linguistics. Philologists identify common characteristics in languages, study their relationships and trace their origins.

pictogram (alternative: pictograph) A pictorial symbol or sign representing an object or concept. Prehistoric examples have been found all over the world. Because of the difficulty of representing words other than concrete nouns, writing systems using pictograms generally evolved into those using **ideograms**.

plebeian (plih-BEE-un) A citizen of ancient Rome who was not a member of the privileged patrician class. Plebeians were originally excluded from state and religious offices and forbidden to marry patricians, but from the early fifth century B.C.E. they gradually achieved political equality, gaining admission to all Roman offices. From the later Republican period, the term **plebeian** implied low social class.

polis (POE-lis) The city-state of ancient Greece. It comprised not only the town, which was usually walled with a citadel (acropolis) and a market place (**agora**), but also the surrounding countryside. Ideally, the *polis* comprised the citizens, who could reside in either town or country; they participated in the government of the state and its religious affairs, contributed to its defense and economic welfare, and obeyed its laws.

praetor (PREE-tor) In ancient Rome, the name was originally applied to the consul as leader of an army. In 366 B.C.E. a further praetor was elected with special responsibility for the administration of justice in Rome, with the right of military command. Around 242 B.C.E. another praetor was created to deal with lawsuits involving foreigners. Further praetors were subsequently appointed to administer the increasing number of provinces. Under the Empire, the position eventually became an honorary appointment.

pre-history The period of time before written records began, which varied from place to place. In this period the study of human development is dependent on the evidence of material remains, such as stone tools or pottery.

primary source Original evidence for an event or fact, as opposed to reported evidence (*see* **secondary source**).

Puranas (poo-RAH-nuz) A collection of poetic tales in Sanskrit, relating the myths and legends of Hinduism. The Puranas expound such topics as the destruction and creation of the world, the genealogy of the gods and patriarchs, the reigns and times of the heroes, and the history of royal dynasties.

quaestor (KWESS-ter) A junior official in ancient Rome. There were originally two, elected annually, but more were appointed as the empire expanded. Most were financial officials. The minimum age was twenty-five, and on completion of the tenure membership of the Senate was automatically conveyed.

Quran (koo-RAHN) The holy book of Islam, believed to contain the direct and authentic word of God as communicated to his prophet Muhammad in a series of revelations by the angel Gabriel. According to tradition, these were collected in the Quran under the caliph Uthman (d. 656) after Muhammad's death. Written in classical Arabic, the Quran is regarded as infallible and is the principal source of Islamic doctrine and law.

radiocarbon dating A method of estimating the age of organic matter, also known as Carbon-14 dating. Carbon dioxide contains a small proportion of the radioactive isotope carbon-14, which is produced in the upper atmosphere by cosmic rays. It is absorbed by green plants, and passes to animals via the food chain. When the organism dies, the amount of carbon-14 in its tissues steadily decreases, at a known rate. The date of death can thus be estimated by measuring the level of radioactivity. The method is mostly used for dating wood, peat, seeds, hair, textiles, skin, and leather.

realpolitik (ray-AHL-poe-lee-teek) A German term meaning practical politics, that is, a policy determined by expediency rather than by ethical or ideological considerations.

Renaissance (REN-ay-sahnz) Literally "rebirth," a French term applied to the cultural and intellectual movement that spread throughout Europe from the fourteenth century. It was characterized by a new interest in Classical civilization, stimulated by the Italian poet Petrarch, and a response to the challenge of its models, which led to pride in contemporary achievement and renewed vigor in the arts and sciences. The new concept of human dignity found its inspiration in **humanism**.

republic A state that is not ruled by a hereditary leader (a monarchy) but by a person or persons appointed under the constitution. The head of state may be elected and may or may not play a political role.

res publica (RAYS POO-bli-kah) The Latin term for a state in which all the citizens participate in government

sacrament In Christian theology, a rite or ritual that is an outward sign of a spiritual grace conveyed on the believer by Christ through the ministry of the Church. In the Orthodox and Roman Catholic Churches seven sacraments are recognized: baptism, confirmation, penance, the Eucharist, marriage, ordination, and anointing of the sick. The two most important of these, baptism and the **Eucharist**, are the only sacraments recognized by most Protestant Churches.

sahel (sah-HAYL) "Shore"—the northern and southern edges of the Sahara Desert. A semi-arid region of Africa, extending from Senegal eastwards to the Sudan and forming a transitional zone between the Sahara desert to the north and the belt of **savanna** to the south. The area is dry for most of the year, with a short and unreliable rainy season, and is subject to long periods of drought. Low-growing grasses provide pasture for camels, pack oxen, cattle and sheep.

satrapy (SAY-truh-pee) A province or colony in the Achaemenid or Persian Empire ruled by a satrap or governor. Darius I completed the division of the Empire into provinces, and established 20 satrapies with their annual tributes. The term satrapy can also refer to the period of rule of a satrap.

savanna (sah-VAN-ah) The grassland areas of the tropics and sub-tropics adjacent to the equatorial rain forests in each hemisphere and bordered by arid regions of desert. Savannas cover extensive parts of Africa, South America, and northern Australia. The natural vegetation is mainly grass with scattered shrubs and trees, the latter low and often flat-topped. The land is particularly suitable for cattle rearing.

secondary source Reported evidence for an event or fact, as opposed to original evidence (*see* **primary source**).

serf An agricultural worker or peasant bound to the land and legally dependent on the lord, characteristic of the manorial economy and the feudal system. Serfs had their own homes, plots, and livestock but they owed the lord labor, dues, and services. These services could be commuted to rent, but serfs remained chattels of the lord unless they were emancipated by him or her, or escaped. Serfdom declined in western Europe in the late medieval period, but persisted in parts of eastern Europe until the nineteenth century.

shaman (SHAH-men) In the religious beliefs of some Asian and American tribal societies, a person capable of entering into trances and believed to be endowed with supernatural powers, with the ability to cure the sick, find lost or stolen property, predict the future, and protect the community from evil spirits. A shaman may act as judge or ruler, and as a priest a shaman directs communal sacrifices and escorts the souls of the dead to the next world.

shari'a (sha-REE-ah) The "road" or sacred revealed law of Islam, based on the Quran and the traditional teachings of Muhammad. Since Islam does not distinguish between the religious and the secular spheres, Islamic law applies to every aspect of life. It covers such matters as marriage, divorce, inheritance, diet, and civil and criminal law.

sinicization (sigh-ne-sigh-ZAY-shen) The adoption and absorption by foreign peoples of Chinese language, customs and culture.

sophist (SOF-ist) An itinerant professor of higher education in ancient Greece, who gave instruction for a fee. The subjects taught, which included oratory, grammar, ethics, mathematics, and literature, had the practical aim of equipping pupils for successful careers. The sophists were criticized for their ability to argue for any point of view regardless of its truth and for their emphasis on material success. They were prominent in the fifth and early fourth centuries B.C.E.

stela or **stele** (sing.); **stelae** (pl.) A freestanding upright slab, often bearing inscriptions or carved ornamentation. They are usually associated with temples and palaces and are carved with hieroglyphic inscriptions recording the exploits and genealogies of rulers.

Sufi (SOO-fee) In Islam, a member of one of the orders practicing mystical forms of worship that first arose in the eighth and ninth centuries C.E. Sufis interpret the words of Muhammad in a spiritual rather than a literal sense. Their goal is direct personal experience of God, achieved by fervent worship (see **tariqa**).

supply and demand In economics, the relationship between the amount of a commodity that producers are able and willing to sell (supply), and the quantity that consumers can afford and wish to buy (demand). The price fluctuates according to a product's availability and its desirability. Supply and demand thus controls a **free market economy**. In practice it is usually subject to some degree of regulation.

Sutta (SOOT-eh) The second section of the Buddhist scriptures or **Tripitaka**, the others being the **Abhidhamma** and the **Vinaya**. It contains the basic teachings of Buddhism, attributed to the Buddha himself, and expounded in a series of discourses in a lively and engaging style, employing allegories and parables. It also includes birth stories of the Buddha and other material.

syncretism (SING-kri-tiz-ehm) The attempt to combine or harmonize doctrines and practices from different philosophical schools or religious traditions, or the absorption of foreign elements into one particular religion.

syllabary (SIL-eh-ber-ee) A writing system in which each symbol represents the syllable of a word (cf. ideogram). The system appears to have been used for some ancient Near Eastern languages, but Japanese is the only modern-day language to use a syllabary.

TaNaKh (tah-NAKH) A Hebrew term for the books of the Bible that are written in Hebrew. The word is composed of the initial letters of the words Torah (first five books of the Bible, traditionally attributed to Moses), Nevi'im (the books of the Prophets) and the Ketuvim (additional historical, poetic, and philosophic writings). This threefold division of the Bible is commonly found in the Talmud.

tariqa (tah-REE-cah) In Islam a generic term meaning "path," referring to the doctrines and methods of mysticism and esoterism. The word also refers to schools or

brotherhoods of mystics, which were often situated at a mosque or the tomb of a Muslim saint.

teleology (tay-lee-OHL-o-gee) From the Greek word *telos*, "end," the philosophical study of final causes or purposes. A "final cause" is an event in the future for the sake of which an occurrence takes place. Teleology refers especially to any system that interprets nature or the universe as having design or purpose. It has been used to provide evidence for the existence of God.

themes A theme was originally a military unit stationed in one of the provinces of the Byzantine empire, but it later applied to the large military districts that formed buffer zones in the areas most vulnerable to Muslim invasion. By the ninth century the system was extended throughout the empire. Soldiers were given farms in the themes in exchange for military service, but they were later able to commute this for tax, which led to the decline of the system.

thermoluminescence A dating technique used for pottery or other fired material. Electrons produced by radiation will be trapped in the flaws of a crystal lattice, but will be liberated in the form of light when heated. The light emissions occur at a constant rate and can be measured when the substance is reheated, and correlated to the duration of exposure to radiation. The period of time that has elapsed since the crystal was last heated can then be estimated.

transhumance (trans-YOO-menz) A form of pastoralism or nomadism organized around the seasonal migration of livestock, practiced in areas that are too cold or wet for winter grazing. The animals are moved to mountain pastures in warm seasons and to lowland ones in winter, or between lower and upper latitudes, or between wet- and dry-season grazing areas.

trebuchet (TRAY-boo-shay) A military engine for hurling heavy missiles, operated by counterpoise, on the principle of the seesaw. Developed in China, the trebuchet first appeared in Europe in the twelfth century.

tribals The aboriginal peoples of the Indian sub-continent, who are outside the **caste** system and live quite separately from the rest of society, generally in remote places. They are thought to have migrated to India in pre-historic times, probably before the emergence of Hinduism.

tribune (TRIB-yoon) In ancient Rome, a **plebeian** officer elected by the plebeians and charged to protect their lives and properties, with a right of veto against legislative proposals of the Senate. The office was instituted during the fifth century B.C.E. and had great political influence under the Republic, but it lost its independence and most practical functions in the time of Augustus (27 B.C.E.–14 C.E.). Military tribunes were senior officers of the legions, elected by the people.

Tripitaka (try-PIT-eh-keh) The Sanskrit term for the Buddhist scriptures, the Pali Tipitaka or "threefold collection." It comprises the *Vinaya-pitaka*, which concerns the history, regulations, and discipline of Buddhism; the *Sutta-pitaka*, the fundamental teaching of

Buddhism, attributed to the Buddha himself; and the *Abhidhamma-pitaka*, which are metaphysical speculations aimed at dissolving any mental resistance or rigidity that might stand in the way of authentic spiritual insight.

triumvirate (try-UM-vihr-ate) In ancient Rome a board of three men appointed for special administrative duties. An unofficial coalition between Julius Caesar, Pompey, and Crassus was formed in 60 B.C.E. After Caesar's murder in 44 B.C.E., a triumvirate that included his heir Octavian (later Augustus), Mark Antony, and Marcus Lepidus was appointed to maintain public order; it held almost absolute powers and lasted until 36 B.C.E.

ulama (OO-leh-ma) The theologians and legal experts of Islam. The *ulama* form a body of scholars who are competent to decide on religious matters. They include the imams of important mosques, teachers in religious faculties in universities, and judges.

umma (UM-ma) The community of believers in Islam, which transcends ethnic and political boundaries.

Vedas (VAY-duz) Sacred Hindu hymns or verses composed in Sanskrit around 1500–1000 B.C.E. Many Vedas were recited or chanted during rituals; they are largely concerned with the sacrificial worship of gods representing natural and cosmic forces. The foremost collection is the *Rigveda*, followed by the *Samaveda*, *Yajurveda*, and *Atharvaveda*; the *Brahmanas*, *Aranyakas*, and *Upanishads* are later commentaries but are also considered canonical.

Vinaya (VIN-eh-yeh) The first part of the Buddhist scriptures, or **Tripitaka**. It concerns the early history, regulations, and discipline of Buddhism, focusing in particular on rules for monks and nuns and on such practical subjects as ordination, holy days, dress, food, and medicine.

Yurts (YOORTZ) A portable dwelling used by the nomadic people of Central Asia, consisting of a tentlike structure of skin, felt or hand-woven textiles arranged over wooden poles, simply furnished with brightly colored rugs.

ziggurat (ZIG-gu-rat) A temple tower of ancient Mesopotamia, constructed of square or rectangular terraces of diminishing size, usually with a shrine on top built of blue enamel bricks, the color of the sky. They were constructed of mud brick, often with a baked brick covering, and ascended by flights of steps or a spiral ramp. The sloping sides and terraces were sometimes planted with shrubs and trees. There were ziggurats in every important Sumerian, Babylonian, and Assyrian center.

zimbabwes (zim-BAHB-ways) Stone-walled enclosures or buildings built during the African Iron Age in the region of modern Zimbabwe and Mozambique. The structures were the courts of local rulers. They have been associated with foreign trade, integrated farming and animal husbandry, and gold production. The Great Zimbabwe is the ruins of the former capital of the Monomatapa Empire, situated in Zimbabwe and occupied from around the thirteenth to the sixteenth century C.E.

INDEX